# TOMORROW'S WORLD ORDER [TWO]

## A New Chapter
## A New Beginning

Your Future Your Say

By

## David Gomadza

[Founder/President]

Tomorrow's World Order

A David Gomadza Production.

# WELCOME

Greetings!!

I personally welcome you all to this new chapter in mankind's history and to a period of enlightenment in new thinking and different ways never tested before of doing things but nevertheless a journey we must undertake as a people to reach our intended destination. I personally believe humanity has failed. Full stop! Humanity has opted for the cheaper inferior quick ways of doing things yet the most destructive ones relying on outdated ways of going about every aspect of life. Humanity has opted for weapons as a solution to everything. Yes, make cheaper weapons and use these to get the most expensive things unfairly and below market price. I am a businessman as well I understand the rationale behind this approach; make cheaper items and use these to get all the expensive ones. Makes sense. But that makes sense if this is the only option. I understand your underlying rationale, as well as, should I say your methods of dealing with the economy, the financial aspects, the environmental or even the political methods which are outdated and honestly not-fit for the purpose. Mankind has failed to think out of the box. He has opted for the quick, easy methods which are short-sighted therefore just concerned with solving short-term issues. But what if there is a clever even better way of doing things with the only drawback being that it requires bold guts and superior thinking and relies on the foresightedness of the decision-maker? Yes, there is a solution to all global problems. The only method to take humanity to the next level. A perfect method that sees everyone better off. A method that takes humanity to levels of development and wealth never witnessed before. The only way it was intended but also one that requires brave minds and bold guts because this means changing what we have been doing for the past 2000 years. They say hard habits die hard. Your leaders in the past have opted to silence the bold and the brave rather than change their ways. But now they have no option. Time is never on their side anymore. For the past seventy years, we have seen them try all the tactics to eliminate today's problems, but I tell you this; the problems and issues at that time are still the issues now. The current system has crashed. Mankind had a chance after a chance to change and take the right road out of the defensive stages to Networking and Cooperation the way it is intended but there was no overseer or leader bold enough to show them how and which path to follow. Wars were signals to mankind for him to change. Okay, your leaders tried to change soon after the World Wars and opted for peace but after the memories of the war-traumas had vanished so as the need to advance ahead and change for good. A global leader was lacking. One unbiased and not representing any nation, institution or cult. One to put down a platform and laws that will make the transition easy. Soon after the wars in most cases two years after witnessing the traumas of the war, the mind seemed to have forgotten and soon mankind was at it again; killing women and children using weapons and wars to get whatever he needed. Killing millions of the innocent and defenseless to 'control others for peace purposes, to lower prices of expensive resources like oil, etc. But I ask you this. What peace? Whose peace? Do you honestly believe that the innocent women and children who died and are still dying because of wars, sanctions, invasions, etc. don't want peace too? I don't bloody care what justifications they give for all this. To all mankind, peace starts with these. The women and children who are the most precious group of any society but who are sadly viewed as easy targets to be used as baits through sanctions and so on to drive political agendas, etc. I say we must put an end to all this. I understand in the past mankind had no lasting solutions for all global problems. To some degree, this was his downfall, but we are saying we have come up with a solution. There is a way to solve all global problems. Ignorance can never suffice, nor can it ever be relied upon. We have shown the way in this book and as such with immediate effect we have drawn a line and written our laws that everyone must obey. These laws are common; currently known as the Jus Cogens that no one can claim not to know. Everyone knows that it's wrong to kill the innocent, defenseless people of any society yet the most valuable of any society through whatever means; sanctions, invasions, poverty, etc. So, as such, we have banned all things giving your leaders 'rights to murder' these precious people of any society. Things are never going to be the same again. We anticipated resistance and have introduced new ways of dealing with evil. Trust me, there is no way out. Our laws will sink them down. Our system is fair and just. It's universal and I guarantee you today that we already have global appeal. What we stand for is what everyone; the young, old, rich, poor, no matter what background, genetic heritage standing, or sexual orientation wishes for and wants. What we stand for is everyone's dream. We stand for all humanity and will provide solutions to help every nation on earth witness riches and levels of wealth never seen before. Our plans are bold and genuine and will solve all global problems. It's a tough road but I guarantee you wealth never witnessed before, happiness and peace of mind. I am ready. Are you ready to change the world for the better? What's not to like about banning wars through effective war-banning-laws? Banning weapons forever. Banning sanctions. Banning reliance on fossil fuels the main trigger of all wars and needlessly deaths of women and children. After all, it's just a fossil fuel; once it's gone, it's gone what is not to like to start now planning the future through searching of alternate reliable, clean energy sources while saving lives of people who would otherwise end up dead due to invasions meant to beat the oil queues. Above all at the same time fighting climate change. All current vehicles relying on oil and other fossil fuels, to be banned by a certain date. Imagine the military instead of killing, they will be creating. Instead of destroying they will be building. Do you know that it is a crime for our best boys and girls [in soldiers] to die needlessly? Gone are the days when your leaders reduce the government's bill through sacrificing thousands and wiping off thousand names off the soldier-salary-list; sending them out there unequipped well and facing never seen before threats in roadside bombs, etc. without proper informational-intelligence. Everyone must be accountable and should recognize and obey our laws. Life shall be valued and the right to life shall mean that in every sense of the phrase. Trust me after reading this book you will know that I mean business. This is a global movement and you MUST be part of this New World Order. Ladies and gentlemen; join us and be part of Tomorrow's World Order [TWO]. Change is imminent and inevitable. Be on the winning side. It's a win-win situation. But first, you MUST read this book and understand what we stand for and our methods. Let's make today a better tomorrow for everyone even if not for us let it be for our children. Thank You. I am the Founder and President of Tomorrow's World Order. A global movement not biased or linked to any nation nor cult for that matter. A movement to solve all global issues through new laws, new methods and leading the way. We are Sovereign in our own right and have our own currency that will revolutionize life as we know it. An investment for you as well as you can buy our global currency that will act as the New Single Reserve Global Currency also while tackling global issues, a win-win situation. Are you ready?

JOIN US TODAY!

Tomorrow's World Order.

Your Future Your Say. Building a Better Today.

Founder and President

Mr. David Gomadza    Signed 08/07/2019    00447745900178

info@tomorrowsworldorder.com

https://www.tomorrowsworldorder.com

https://www.futuregoldcoin.com

You can donate to our PayPal through this link:

paypal. me/Tomorrowsworldorder.

Your Future Your Say

# DEDICATION

The future belongs to men and women of honor and regimes that uphold the rule of law. There are fundamental laws that are there to safeguard humanity and everyone's freedom and these laws MUST not be broken. Surprisingly, some nations and a few evil people think that it's okay to break these directly or indirectly, but the truth is that it's not. These nations have broken these peremptory laws, but we say we should hold these nations to account. Torture, genocide, crimes against humanity, crimes of aggression, etc. are laws that MUST not be broken yet there are a few countries that break these peremptory norms and laws simply because there are no other powers out there to put an end to this but not anymore. A New World a better today. Things are never going to be the same again. A new chapter in history. This is the million-dollar question. Are you ready and prepared for a completely New World? A new system? A new way of doing things. Change is imminent and inevitable. The system has crashed only a new system is needed and when there is a system crash, we must start over again. Building effective systems that work. Systems that are observed and accepted by everyone. Current systems and institutions are useless they are as good as gone. What a waste. But it is not all hopeless. Tomorrow's World Order is there to lay a new foundation. A new road. A new way of doing things. A new way never seen before dealing with rights violators through our new justice system. TWO is there to implement a new system since the current system has crashed. A system that is effective, is respected, acknowledged and feared by all. A system adhered to by all simply because it is the right path for everyone. To all rights abusers out there, your days are numbered. It will never be the same again. Be prepared for a new system. Surely the current system is now obsolete. Ineffective and honestly useless. Only a new system can solve the current problems. A new overhaul. A complete change.

# ACKNOWLEDGMENT

A big thanks to Tomorrow's World Order.

## TOMORROW'S
## WORLD
## ORDER

## TWO

# DISCLAIMER

The views in this book are for a peaceful world and the methods we advocated center upon the valuing of human life and the provision of a just system that is fair, up to date and one that reflects the wishes of the people through the laws in this book and our courts from the date they come into effect. We stand for peace and everything must be approved by the courts through our justice system and no one MUST take the law into their own hands. Meaningless acts of violence towards innocent people in any form has nothing to do with what we stand for. Every life shall be valued we are strongly against any acts of violence. These acts MUST not be associated with Tomorrow's World Order [TWO]. We are NOT fighting for freedom whatsoever as we are not oppressed. [Therefore, we can't be freedom fighters nor be regarded as terrorists, rebels, lawbreaker, etc. we profusely oppose all these and deny vehemently any association with these groups.] We are a peaceful global leader. Nor does our material have any malicious intent. We are not fighting for anything and MUST not be regarded as such. Nor are we against the current establishment even though we think that the current system is obsolete. We are presenting a New System, and everyone is welcome. We are simply 'a people' who believe that humanity has failed by taking the easy road of making weapons very cheaply and then use the weapons to source and get the most expensive resources. We say affordability is the problem. The current system has crashed and is now obsolete. We are here to establish a new system of doing things. This new system is the only way forward. As global leaders we invite all leaders to be part and parcel of this new system. We would like to work with all world leaders. Once again, we are not against anyone but believe you can all be part of this great movement. Nor are we against religious movements, political powers, monarchies, etc. Anyone can be part of TWO as long as you agree and observe our laws. Every system has a justice system. As such we will vehemently oppose any acts of violence, coups, etc. We are a global peaceful establishment not restricted to any country and our laws are above any country's laws. Our laws have universal jurisdiction meaning all humanity can and MUST be governed by them. All the materials used to advance our arguments and interpretations of world events are available freely online and some can be said to be subjective as some are individual's perceptions of events and the way they interpret the world. But we also gave our stance and reasons to support and justify our conclusions a good example being the effects of sanctions whether they kill or not women and children. You will find out that the countries affected by the sanctions profusely claim that sanctions kill women and children. The West who impose these sanctions argue that sanctions don't kill women and children but just restrict access to certain services etc. We analyzed both and gave our basis and reasons to conclude what we think are real effects of sanctions. There are other issues of actual and perceived risks or reasons. We noted also that something that is just a perceived perception can manifest itself into actual fact. It just depends on circumstances. We looked at the superpowers' roles as role-models and their impact on global peace and justice. We chose these nations simply because they represent most of the countries and we can only get a true picture by assessing these superpowers. All the materials are freely available online. All countries and people if any mentioned here have a bearing on outcomes on a global scale. It will be unjust NOT to mention these when they are the ones impacting the course of world events. Nothing personal and care must be taken when interpreting our findings. Everyone mentioned is because they impact the course of global issues.

No Responsibility or Liability from date of publication whatsoever for any acts of violence or any malicious intent directed to anyone for any reason. We can't be associated with such acts. We stand for a peaceful way to achieve global peace through our justice system and courts. Reading materials in this book does not and will not be regarded as inciting acts of violence. We stand for peace and changing the way we view the world. The expressed views are mine and TWO's as I am the founder of TWO. Materials for peaceful use accordance with principles, laws and rules set out in this book. Signed 09/08/2019 Tomorrow's World Order: David Gomadza [Official date of publication]

# THE PERFECT SYSTEM

A perfect system has a force that exerts pressure but that also has an equal-but-opposing-force that works to maintain the equilibrium over time so that in the end the system can be maintained and sustained for long periods without the system crashing.

Any imbalance over time will inevitably result in the collapse of the system. The extent of the collapse depends on the power and magnitude of the exerting force. The bigger the exerting force and the less or non-existent of the equal-but-opposing-force the more the imbalance and the greater the destruction and the hard it is to fix the system after collapse rendering the system obsolete. That will only pave the way for a new system.

Hence the Rise of Tomorrow's World Order.

A New Beginning. A New Fresh Start.

Ladies and gentlemen, boys and girls welcome to Tomorrow's World Order.

Founder/ President Mr. David Gomadza [Remarks based on Newton's Third Law.]

Signed 08/07/2019

# THE LAW

The law can be a double-edged-sword to those who violates it and a source of hope, comfort and inspiration to those who seek justice and peace.

David Gomadza.

# UNDERLYING PRINCIPLES

Our laws place mandatory obligations and requirements on all global countries on earth or other planets to cooperate and observe our laws in order to put an end to any breaches at all levels. This is because our laws are fundamental to the existence and survival of humanity at large. The laws are critical to the survival of humanity as a whole. Any breach can mean human extinction. There is no derogation whatsoever is permitted. No justifications whatsoever for breaching. No laws, countries or persons can and MUST override our laws. Any breach has express-command for global justice and punishment. These laws have universal jurisdiction meaning that anyone, anywhere who is in that capacity appointed by a recognized official, institutions etc. mainly officials only can and MUST apprehend the violator and initiate the justice process through a proper official system of any country that is the justice system of that country through the courts of such a country [to avoid people taking the law into their own hands] Severe punishment; death, for those taking things into their own hands as a deterrent to abuse. These laws work on the system of IF-THEN. In that, IF the laws are breached and a certain criterion must be satisfied and [can be proved through the official justice system of any country] that breach has occurred THEN such a judgment will be the outcome. There is no ambiguity; to make the system fair and to make everyone know what they are against if they breached our laws. The reason behind this being that any breach can cause and can result in human extinction. We are obliged to safeguard humanity and make sure that such laws won't be breached. Some actions threatening human existence. This means any country whatsoever making WMDs; nukes and stockpiling these etc. Such acts put a risk to humanity's survival. These laws include but are not limited to these;

✓ Making of WMDs, all kinds, bio-engineered, digital, cyber, nuclear weapons for whatever reason. No country has rights to make and stockpile nukes etc. that includes the developed world as well.

✓ Wars. All wars banned from a certain date to be announced.

✓ Weapons manufacturing, production, trading, exchanging, stockpiling, etc. banned. Date to be announced.

✓ Invasions of sovereign nations and any use of force against a sovereign nation for whatever reason banned. A date to be announced where this comes into effect.

✓ Acts of aggression banned. Any acts with intent to incite, stir or cause others to think, act or react so as to start or think or plan for war are banned.

✓ Acts of intimidation or inciting others to fears and panic that might result in acts related to wars or conflicts or cause one to feel insecure so as to start making WMDs to match the threat at hand for example are banned. This might include a grouping of most nations into one powerful war-house or cult that it will be unreasonable NOT to think or start making even more powerful weapons mainly by the weakest as a counteract measure to match the force at hand and give one any chances of survival. Mind you everyone under our laws have rights to life, self-defend themselves and preserve the life of themselves and their citizens. They have the right to act to preserve their people and depending on the size and magnitude of the exerting force they might have a self-defense argument. Initiating and pursuing or perpetuating wars, weapons, and acts of aggression and intimidation, etc. directly or otherwise. Hacking of people [not computers] illegal and banned; with intent to change, modify, alter or stop some functions, kill, control, command, enslave or abuse in whatever way. This include some piracy activities in relation to humans. Issues of false-flagging; false pretenses and giving people a false sense of security pretending to help initially and then alter, change, damage, stop and kill. Severe punishment in form of death. Aim of hacker is to kill in the end. Rights to self-defense as everyone entitled to right to life, quality of life and self-defend. A hacker is as good as an enemy of humanity. So evil that such crimes must receive the ultimate punishment: death. Hacking carries three life sentences in that a hacker is a torturer too, and a torturer is a slave-master too and all three crimes carry maximum sentences. Triple deaths that is three life sentences. Above 300 years [instant death by the assassin approved by our courts] and might extend to future generations as a deterrent. Torture. This is gross violations of human rights. A torturer is an enemy of mankind; the ultimate death penalty. Torture threatens the fabric of international laws as it is synonymous with slavery. In hacking situations there are express-torture violations. In torture there are express slavery connotations because torturers use torture to enslave as well. Two maximum sentences one for torture and the other for implied slavery. All hackers of human beings torture their victims through hidden sophisticated devices. Once hacked obviously that person is tortured too and enslaved secretly. Gross violations of human rights.

✓ Secret or hidden slavery. Genocide. War crimes.

✓ Crimes against humanity. Sanctions aimed at innocent women and children. Destroys innocent lives even though might not carry the death penalty nevertheless are violations of our laws. The list is not exhaustive.

Signed 09/08/2019 Tomorrow's World Order. David Gomadza

# TABLE OF CONTENTS

# CHAPTER ONE

# OVERVIEW

## NATURAL STAGES OF DEVELOPMENT

What is the purpose of life? What are we to do here on earth as humans? What have we done so far as humans and is that all we can do? Have we operated at our expected best over the centuries? If not, why and what are we missing? Is this what is expected of humankind? What can we do as a people to achieve that? What has gone wrong and why?

I personally think that humanity has failed simply because, for the past 2000 years, we have gone in a circle round and round but without achieving anything. We are still stuck in the 'medieval ages.' We have lacked superior thinking over the past 2000 years. Why? One might ask. Fear. That thing called fear has controlled every aspect of mankind. Will you be surprised to find out that over the past 2000 years mankind was and still is in the defensive stages of development? Defensive stages? What is that animal?

Okay, I will explain.

Everything in life has stages of development and happenings. First, let's look at human life. When a baby is born, it goes into different stages of development. I will put these stages into five categories.

### Stage One

In this stage, children start understanding life and learning things about themselves. They perceive life through their senses, feelings, the sight of objects and things around them. In this stage, they have no memory at all so everything they are doing is through senses, seeing and touch. Fear is at the greatest because they don't

1

know what to expect. All their senses are heightened. Their primary goal is defense. Fear of the unknown. In this stage, they are learning about pain and other feelings.

## Stage Two

The child has gathered some information about the surroundings and life itself. The memory bank has developed to such an extent that the baby starts to understand life. The baby as it grows starts to link things and connect things using experiences in the memory bank and current analysis of the environment and life to make informed decisions. In the first stage, and in this stage the baby is egocentric. Egocentrism plays a major role in the life of the child, and all decisions are in line with this notion. The baby thinks about itself. Its protection and well-being.

## Stage Three

Now the child is fully aware that life does not revolve around himself or herself. The child fully understands life and now has developed a huge memory bank to rely upon and use in its judgment. This stage is characterized by a complex analysis of different factors, systems, feelings, etc. to arrive at a decision. The child is less egocentric and more intuitive. This stage is characterized by networking, cooperation with others and the establishment of relationships with friends and the idea to learn from nature and others. The child here is fully aware that there are so many things to life than what is around him. The brain develops much faster as the child is exposed to new and different situations. The brain is bombarded by a lot of new things to learn and analyze. Relationships and networking are at the greatest, as kids spend more time with their friends than at home with parents. Special bonds develop and secret oaths of friendship are made. There is mutual thinking that networking and cooperation are beneficial. There is generally a belief among the kids that networking and cooperation is highly beneficial and a MUST. The child now understands that others are different and might hold different views to theirs. The idea here now is to establish common ground and understand the idea of mutual inclusive and exclusive. The idea is not to disregard the others but to understand each other and establish common ground and agreements.

## Stage Four

The child has developed a huge memory bank and experience. Networking and cooperation have enabled the child to understand the world to a greater extent. This stage of networking and cooperation is reduced to a lesser extent but still a major part of the life of a child. The child now understands that most of the things it had fears about are not things to worry about. The information bank is vast and well developed to such an extent that the child now understands that you are your only enemy. The child now understands that most of its childhood fears are just imaginary in that ghosts and aliens don't exist. Time and resources spent on fear and defense then decline greatly but there are regrets that the child understands that the real enemy is itself. Time and resources are now used to maximum and optimal use with very little wastage. There is a sense of panic and regret. Time and resources once devoted to fear of the unknown and defense are now used to advance the child in other areas.

## Stage Five

The defense is never on the child's mind as he or she grows into adulthood instead the child is fully cooperative and networking with many people. Somehow nature makes egocentric views important once again as the child prepares for adulthood. Fears of a different nature sets in.

## THE CURRENT PROBLEM: STUCK IN DEFENSIVE STAGES

Looking at mankind a clear picture is emerging. Mankind has gone in circles and is still stuck in the first stages of development where defense plays a paramount part. In this stage, everything is centered around defense. Mankind is afraid. Fear is his greatest challenge. He spends $trillion on defense at the expense of other needs. Fear plays a major role in all his decision. The fear causes less networking and cooperation. Fear hinders people from coming together to understand each other. Fear hinders cooperation. Fear makes it hard to trust anyone. Most of the fear was and is still just perceived fear that is and was turned into actual fear by your leaders to justify the huge budgets on defense and the military. Every time someone develops a greater understanding of life and advocate for the world to move away from the defensive economies to more advanced systems, your leaders engage in dirty tricks to instill fear so that defense remains top of everything we do. In some circumstances going to lengths to make sure that defense and fear play a crucial role in whatever we do. Last time it was the aliens and Unidentified Flying Objects [UFOs] of the sixties but recently terrorism has become a major issue, but the goals are still the same as these politicians. We can see a pattern developing. The next stage of development is the networking and cooperation among many leaders, and this has started to happen with sworn enemies coming together to negotiate and even out their differences. In such circumstances there is no need for weapons and huge defense budget, is there? We are all now advanced and knowledgeable to know that there are no aliens or UFOs but just devious tricks by your politicians who are afraid to start something completely new and move away from defensive systems. Would you be surprised that terrorism is now the main concern of all nations? It's not a coincident no. The system is designed and is manipulated that it gives justification for being and stuck in defensive economies. Ask yourself this. If there are no threats from other countries, why would we build weapons and spend huge amounts of money on defense? I have read of countries with the lowest living standards plowing huge amounts of money into defense instead of into food and development programs. The West has played a major role in that area as well. Parading missiles and testing these sending fear among other weaker countries that they end up buying weapons and investing in defense instead of other areas. It's simple, common sense. The developed countries manufacture weapons. They have spent years investing in defense and weapons. Now the world is shifting nevertheless slowly away from defensive economies that means no market for the weapons. How can the developed world make more weapons when wars are a thing of the past? How can they stop also after investing so hugely in defense? They are stuck in a limbo leaving all this behind is like a total waste. We have human rights organizations everywhere now fighting for human rights. A step necessary to move away from defensive economies. The only effective way now is to pass laws that bring accountability to your leader's doorstep making them accountable one-way or the other. We have crimes of aggression now as a law. Over the years a few people have realized that we need to do more to force your leaders to move away from defensive economies to the other stage of development. Nature intended humans to move fast just like in the child development process but sadly after 2000 years, we are stuck in the first stage of a child's development stage. Humanity has left everything to chance to hope that nature will take its role and lead humanity in the right path but that's not happening. A few people have now taken things into their own hands and are now starting to turn ideas into laws. We can't let these politicians make women and kids suffer just for them to have jobs and paychecks. Every time there is a war, women and children die needlessly. Something that can be avoided. A man-made problem that can be avoided surely, we passed that stage when a few can play God at everyone's expense. Who will defend these people who are used as baits just so that these evil people have jobs and titles to feel good about themselves? Surely this is expected in the medieval stages where society was corrupt and the governments there to save a few with certain privileges. Everything was centered around defense and protection of the few perceived more important than others? I am saying mankind has taken the easy way, the road of manipulation and use of dirty tricks to leave us stuck in the defensive economies when we should be networking and cooperating as nature intended. Imagine if all the world's money currently being spent on weapons etc. is diverted to other areas. Do you think we will have the problems we are having today? Defensive systems are the easiest and something we as human beings have experienced over the past 2000 years. You will be shocked to find out that we are living exactly like the early man the only difference is that the threats and our fears have developed as well. Imagine the time mankind had no method of communication. The time sign language was common. Surprisingly we are back to those days. Some few countries are now hacking all their citizens in the name of protection a form of defense rooted in defensive thinking. Now their people can't talk freely and must rely on sign language or an advanced form but nevertheless a sign language to communicate in case someone is listening to their conversation. Now they are like the early man who can't talk. These countries are breaking the Jus Cogens laws by hacking their citizens in the name of protection. These same countries are sponsoring and inciting terrorism to justify their illegal acts. These countries are taking humanity back to the medieval times the only difference being that back then mankind was less advanced to have learned to communicate unlike now when these evil nations are breaking laws hacking everyone even their unsuspecting people. How can you speak when people are listening to your conversations without your secrets being intercepted? These few nations are carrying out blanket surveillance which is illegal. No matter what the justification is, mankind is reliving the middle ages again simply because some countries are breaking the peremptory laws that were placed to safeguard your rights and help mankind move away from defense economies. Considering that these countries are making digital agents that imitate epidemics of the medieval times when mankind was ravaged by diseases with plagues claiming millions. These few nations are now using these digital agents to communicate and as a sign language. The underlying notion here is that they are involved in illegal practices. They are breaking laws contrary to international laws. These same people are hindering the movement from these defensive economies. These nations are making agents and using these to extract money and resources globally. This is a way of creaming the world making humanity think about defense throughout our existence. These nations have relied on cheap ways to gather vast resources and have invested a lot in this kind of weaponry to make the whole world depended on defensive economies. Surely nature intended humanity to follow the path adopted by a child as I have illustrated above. The underlying notion here is that wars and weapons are perceived as the easiest way to get anything your leaders or these nations want. They don't have to pay a fair market price and will still always get what they want. For them, it's a win-win situation but one that is less advanced yet a costly barbaric method.]

I am saying that humanity is not working at its optimal capacity. Our systems are very wasteful and incompetent. Imagine how much is spent on weapons globally. Imagine the vast stockpiles of weapons stocked in bunkers and everywhere. If all that was money in the bank it could have accumulated interest enough to eliminate the problems we are having now. So, what I propose is this. I am going to devise laws that will force humanity to move away from defensive economies. This is for the betterment of mankind. Mankind MUST be guided out of this vicious cycle. 2000 years is a long time and we as a people should have been on another level of development. A stage when we don't think about defense and where defense does not play a major role. Imagine the resources we use for defensive purposes? If that money is channeled somewhere else surely humanity would be in a better position. I am very glad that some very brave few people have fought and won so that a law is passed to help humanity abandon the defensive stage. I am talking about the crimes of aggression, but I must admit this law does not go further as expected. This is a major step towards abandoning defensive economies. Your leaders are now made accountable for acts that exonerates wars. Wars are characteristics of uncivilized societies. Uncivilized in that the people involved are not advanced enough to acquire resources they need, and it could be money. These nations can't afford to pay a fair market price because the commodities sought are scarce and the price easily goes high due to the increase in demand. Imagine a system where money is abundant. Why wage war when another sovereign nation with precious resources e.g. oil in their country decides to nationalize their resources when the other country can easily buy the resources they need at any price? Affordability is the main problem. So, as I have argued above in this case and to your leaders, the best option is to make weapons and use the weapons to get the expensive ones. The money they had they used this to make weapons. Now they must use the weapons to get the resources by force. Surely a deep analysis of this will only point to inefficiency, unfair and a barbaric-medieval way of thinking all because of emphasis on defense other than anything else. This is the problem as your leaders limit other options as being stuck in defensive economies foreshadows other areas and forbids new thinking. In the world I have in mind; something I will advance profusely in this book is the fact that if in the first place we acknowledge that we are superior and smart enough to understand that we are our only enemies then the rest can be changed. Once that is clear only then can we start making the right decisions. If in the first place, we foresaw the need for oil resources we would have saved enough money to buy oil at any price. We could not have spent $trillions on weapons we don't need instead we would have bought oil resources. The other country might have plowed the profits back into oil. That way they could have found cheaper ways of purifying the oil or processing it that in-turn would have made the oil prices lower and affordable in the long run. It is a fact that periods of great human rights campaigns are marked with great acts of violence. The idea behind human rights campaigners is to set mankind in the right direction but your leader's device dirty tricks to instill fear and make defense our priority. So, I think the question that keep popping in your head is this. How then can we move away from defensive economies when you are rightly saying that any attempt is marred by acts of unforeseen violence to instill fear among us?

It's not easy but it can be achieved. I think this is a new topic I am raising here. I am going to profusely advocate that I will put things in place to make sure humanity will move away from defensive economies whether they like it or not. I know changing habits might be difficult and its mankind's greatest strength to stick to what he has known to have worked but also his greatest weakness. Of course, there will be stiff resistance. Most of these people do this because it is beneficial to them. They can bully everyone and get away with it. They can engage in dirty tricks and still get away with it. For most they have recreated the medieval to instill fear and control people justifying their actions on the need to defend themselves and in most cases, they are the greatest threat to humankind. Imagine how many people died in medieval times due to plagues? Millions if history said it right. Someone who will attempt to recreate that is the worst enemy of mankind; hence the term Hostis Humani Generis. It's not thinkable that a reasonable man can recreate something that nearly wiped humanity off the face of the earth. Some people and nations can't understand the grave meaning of such actions simply because no one has told them otherwise. To them, it's a way of life but to most the greatest crime humanity can ever witness. So how then? Okay, I think first I will look at the crimes of aggression.

## Crimes of Aggression.

The idea gives you goosebumps knowing that at last women and children around the world are protected to some extent from unlawful needlessly killing. Some nations kill thousands of women and children in foreign countries like dogs and run around pretending to care. Look at the Iraq war 500 000 women and children died just a few years ago yet no one has been held accountable for this? How can you justify killing such many people? It's shocking and unbelievable that the world can just sweep this under the carpet and let women and kids' murderers walk away and boost for saving people? If these were their own people would they have accepted such a justification? I personally think the crimes of aggression although the idea is appealing does not go deep enough to tackle the issue. A crime should not have time limits. I think it's unfair and absurd that certain crimes are given a time limit, and some are not. I personally think that the crimes of aggression do not do anything at all to correct the past wrongs. A crime should not have a time limit, and this should be for all crimes. The crimes of aggression laws were implemented by institutions erected by the very people at the center of the crime. In that, they adopted and implemented it just to show off and to cover-up. Why the time limit? It's unfair to say okay it can only work or come into force from the day we did not do anything wrong but what about the time you were at the forefront of evil? I will personally advocate that for the system to be fair and to initiate the healing process and the move away from these defensive economies there shall never be a time limit. If the person who commits the crime is alive, he or she is liable and accountable for all his actions on earth. This is the only way people are going to move away from defensive economies and abandon evil acts altogether. I will advocate that any crime committed within the last 70-100 years be dug out and be assessed. The only leniency will be regarding the severity of the crimes. This is the only way humanity will move away from defensive economies. Take the terrorist arguments for example. They argue that whatever they do is in response to atrocities committed in the past or happening now triggered by this defensive approach of running a country. If all crimes for the past hundred years are assessed, and the people tried if they are still alive that will be the only step toward reconciliation, networking, and negotiations some things necessary for humanity to move away from defense economies. The way this law was implemented is wrong. It would have been a cornerstone to solving the world's problems but the fact that its cherry-picked other nation's crimes is not just unfair but a crime against mankind as a whole in itself. To solve the world's problems, we should have a standard test that does not discriminate and favor the culprits and give them immunity. I propose to fight to have this law implemented fairly. The only way that is true and correct. There is a pattern that is emerging in that some nations wait to commit crimes first and after getting what they want, they then quickly establish laws that give them immunity but claim to persecute whoever commits the crime after they have already committed a crime themselves. For the law to stand and be honored the crimes of aggression law should not have a time limit. I know most would say it was not formulated as a law the time they carried out the acts in question but still that can't give some people immunity because everyone knows that killing 500 000 noncombatant women and children is a crime. A law or not killing 500 000 women and children is a crime. Everyone knows this before or after the crimes of aggression became a law. The current system is biased. Simply because all the institutions that are passing these laws were created by the very people we should be hanging. The whole system is biased and corrupt. It's there just to give immunity to the real culprits. These institutions are extended-hands of the people we are saying that are real threats to human existence. So, this is what I will do.

Make sure there are no time limits if the person who committed the crimes is alive any proceedings should be brought against that person if he has committed a crime. Humanity is stuck in the defensive stage because of this. I propose to assess all acts deemed to be crimes and bring everyone concerned to justice simply because they knew that this was a crime when they carried out the acts being a law or not. We have the Jus Cogens notions or laws in some countries that can be used to justify such a stance. These laws are there as deterrents to safeguard humanity. Everyone is aware and no one should use ignorance as an excuse. Considering this the only way a person can escape is only when he or she is dead. Only death shall set you free and, in some cases, you can still be punished after your death. If that person is breathing, he or she must be made accountable. We have seen old former Presidents mainly of African countries dragged by the International Criminal Court to the Hague in their old age so why can't this be universal?

To move away from defensive societies a system crash must happen to justify a complete move and abandoning of the current defensive system, something I advocated in all my books and something I am saying that has already happened. The only problem with the current thinking is to wait until humanity is extinct to believe that the system has crashed. This would be the ideal system crash to force humanity to change but isn't that suicidal as this results in human extinction. Now you see why it is tough to move away from defensive economies. This is the main reason why mankind has been stuck in this stage for more than 2000 years. I explained in other books that a system crash can automatically raise the need for a completely new start. The only way defensive economies can be rendered obsolete is when there is a total collapse of world economies or total wipe-out of humans. This will somehow also be the end of defensive economies if mankind remains feeding this bad habit. Imagine all the weapons we are stockpiling and the new dangerous ones we are making underground, then imagine a system that keeps making these weapons and piling them when there are no wars? Imagine when we all talk and cooperate but still pile weapons. Who is going to buy the weapons? Who are we going to use the weapons on? Imagine also the disgruntled people who are starved as money is used to make weapons. The system will reach a point that a small frictional moment can trigger a global nuclear war that will result in the extinction of mankind. So, a complete change can only come by if there is a system crash, but a crash is something we don't need because letting that happen means the end of humanity something we don't want too. So how can we move away from defensive societies?

**A clean slate.**

A complete start can only be achieved if we as humans we apply laws to all crimes committed by anyone still existing. Those who have died have automatic immunity. The idea is to clean the whole system without causing its collapse. This can only be achieved by applying laws that cover everyone alive today. This is only the start of a clean-up process. The only way to move forward. The only way to stop revengeful acts. The only way to tell the world that we are ready to forgive each other and move forward. The only way humanity will abandon defensive economies. As far as it stands evil can only breed evil. The world will heal faster this way to pave the way for a new beginning, a new people. A New World without weapons. This is the only way we are going to have World War Three. Hold on! No one talked about World War Three.

Yes, I thought I could surprise you. See the problem is that my solutions pave the way to a new start. A new beginning by getting rid of the people who should be killed. But don't forget the reason why they are killing now is that they have people behind them who don't care if 500 000 women and kids die or not. We are all smart enough to know that this is wrong being a law or not. There are peremptory laws in the form of the Jus Cogens which were there to deter and educate mankind and these laws are universal that the claim of ignorance will not succeed. Above all most of these countries would refuse to destroy these weapons and might choose to use them instead. Imagine telling them that you spent $trillion on useless weapons instead of on bars of gold or shares in stock markets. Surely that would make some of them jump on the defensive side and attack instead. Don't forget the idea is to try to move these people from these inferior ways of thinking into superior thinking. I know most brag that the countries they invaded are better off today than before they invaded. Remember the idea is not to judge the before and the after. That is not the theme of this book. The idea is to apportion blame for the killing of innocent women and children. We know you removed a tyrant, but you also killed 500 000 women and children and that automatically label you a tyranny worse than this killer because you are killing people with different genetic heritage to yours with no due care. This evidenced by the fact that in their country one child dies the world country is brought to a standstill. Just because of that a time limit on a Crime of Aggression will not suffice to give anyone immunity. I am saying that this is not just a Crime of Aggression. It is a lack of empathy-motivated attack with no due regard to women and children of other genetic heritage. The fact that they make the noise crying for blood if it's one of theirs and cry for immunity if it's thousands of other genetic heritages is just pathetic. The idea is not to make everything a genetic heritage thing but to put an end to future acts and to reconcile and heal these acts that have a lack of empathy connotations MUST be addressed. I understand also a third argument can be applied to such crimes in that any crimes that have a lack of empathy implications should have at least twenty-five years as the minimum time period that can last before the people are brought to justice. I will challenge any time limits based on the above arguments. My idea is to make it mandatory that no woman or kid will ever die needlessly because of a war. The fourth argument I will advance is the fact that we need to assess the main reasons behind invading and if the ideas are for personal gains and something I will call Society Collapse tactics, then the acts should be brought to the court regardless of when they were committed. The idea applies in cases like the Iraq war where the people involved juiced up dossiers fraudulently and recklessly to get approvals such acts should not be ignored. The fifth aspect will be the material gains from such an illegal war. This is something I will look at in detail later. If the idea behind the war was to extract resources like oil rather than liberating the people, this should be weighed in relation to the number of civilians killed especially women and children. In other words, does it look like they killed women and children just to get oil resources? Considering this I think it should also be established if other methods were available that would be effective without the heavy cost of civilian lives. If other methods are available, then a heavy burden is placed on the people in question. I know most people would say if you were in these people's shoes how would you handle the situation? In short in my world, the military is replaced by assassins. If it means having thousands of assassins on the payroll so be it. There is a saying that one man for himself and God for us all. That is if you believe there is a God and if you don't, then you can say; one man for himself and TWO for us all. So why should 500 000 women and children be killed on behalf of a tyranny? It makes no sense and is not fair. Who will defend and stand for the rights of these women and children? Can't you see that justice was not done here? This is fresh blood and yet the same countries continue to carry on with evil acts. It's true it's human nature if people do nothing then nothing can be achieved. The Crime of Aggression law is just sugar-coating to make everything look alright without substances. What should be done is to turn all military personnel into the highly trained assassins who don't need massive weaponry? Men who will be lethal and men who are trained to target. Saddam in the Iraq case died a hero in that 500 000 women and children perished as well as him. If the world was fair, these people would be hanged too because they are no better than Saddam just another of his versions. So, to answer the above question. I would not worry if all army is retained but it would be ideal for all to be highly trained to target specific subjects. I think if this was so then even Saddam would not have done whatever he was accused of having done. These people do evil acts because they act and operate as a group therefore, they are given automatic immunity to continue carrying out evil acts. Imagine if all army personnel were highly-trained-lethal-assassins who target with a pistol or a rifle only who go about hunting people, we are saying are evil? Do you think we would have these evil people? Imagine knowing that there are thousand trained lethal marksmen to take you down any minute surely no one would think of killing a woman or child ever again. These people kill recklessly women and children because they know that more women and children will die first before anyone can even think of getting to them. Imagine where everyone knows that the mask men will only come for them and no one else. Imagine a world where a man is for himself and God for us all. Imagine a world when trained highly lethal assassins are lurking everywhere in civilian clothes. Surely this is my world and the only way humanity will move away from defensive economies. No point in making huge missiles when the assassin will aim just the tyrant. This will also provide better-paid jobs. This will build trust in the military and army. The men and women will be honored as they used to be. They can't be labeled as women and children killers. This will give our boys high self-esteem and view the military as a career to be proud of. This will free resources to advance these soldiers-turned-assassins as weapons are phased out.

So, it will be passed as a law and made illegal or a crime for anyone to give a military directive or order that will result in the death of a woman or child no matter what the circumstances. Again, no time limits. The idea behind my thinking is that this is a common universal knowledge that it's not just evil but reckless and irresponsible to get women and children to be killed. We have the Jus Cogens laws that say it is bad and wrong and therefore illegal. Everyone knows this. We have people highlighting this during the campaigns to stop the war. We have people demonstrating against the war mainly because wars kill innocent women and children.

If there is a tyrant pay your soldiers or trained assassins and let them loose like wild dogs and hunt this tyrant.

I will make the making of weapons nuclear or otherwise and all missiles illegal and a thing of the past. Sorry but tough luck you might have invested in the development of missiles' technology but it's no longer legal. Its mankind's poor management to waste resources on things we don't need. Others are dying of hunger when we spent $trillions on weapons after all the resources that are used to build the weapons are sourced cheaply from the same countries the missiles are intended to be used.

There shall be a ban on all military vehicles unless for the protection of the President and other members of parliament. Any weapons and vehicles for attacking will be banned and stopped. Only armored cars would be given permits to be manufactured.

The idea is to regard the soldiers as people as well as people with values, rights to life and family life until old age. In that light laws should be drafted to safeguard the life of soldiers throughout their career. It should be a thing of the past that we have thousands of our finest dying very young. Soldier's jobs should be like any other job that safeguard the life of a soldier and put things in place to make sure they have chances of living until old age. Criminal proceedings should be brought where soldiers die young needlessly. I know most would argue that if no soldiers died, the world could not sustain the population. At first glance it seemed true bearing in mind that hundreds of thousands of soldiers die in wars, but do you know how much is spent on weapons, etc. That money can be diverted to be used for enhancing mankind's life. All these technologies can be used to enhance life as we know it today.

There will be a total ban on the making of bio-weapons and their digital counterparts. It shall be a law and illegal to make such weapons. There are no aliens, and no one shall take us back to medieval times. These people are cheap useless bastards who use bio-weapons or digital ones to rob and suppress others. We want a society where everyone works very hard for what they have in life. We don't want a society where bio-agents are used to control, manipulate and oppress others or where people are loaded with bio-digital weapons for being lazy as protection for being lazy. To us, these nations are making illegally prohibited weapons bio-engineered or digital ones for that matter. These are then used as watermarks to seal and protect those who are lazy to work who would rather be injected with this dirty stuff instead of earning a proper living through hard work. Stiff penalties and trust me, a date with the marksmen for nations and people doing this. The idea is to view nations and or people who make bio-weapons to rob others unfairly as Hostis Humani Generis and as such to be treated as such. I will get our best marksmen and unleash them. The world should be a better place for everyone.

# CHAPTER TWO

## THE PURPOSE AND VALUE OF LIFE.

Why are we here on earth? Why were we born? What is that we are expected to do? Expected to accomplish in life? Or maybe I should ask if there is a reason for our existence? Are we just born to repopulate the earth to continue the existence of mankind? What is the value of life? What is your life worth? Or maybe I should ask what would you exchange for your life if any? In other words, what kind of things do people sacrifice their lives for in return? I personally think that humanity is still less educated and knowledgeable about the value of life and our purpose here on earth. If there were stages to the advancement of knowledge about life, let's just say for argument's sake that there are five stages to the knowledge and values placed on life.

### Stage One

This is the stage where nothing is known about the value of life. Mankind in this stage is guided by instincts and pain to realize the need to self-preserve. Mankind in this stage leaves everything to chance simply because he lacks the true knowledge of the value of life and he exists through luck, chance and through learning about the risks that surround him. Instincts induced by fear and pain make him or her take precautionary measures to self-protect. His existence, according to him or her, is purely by coincidence. He just happened to be there and must adapt and live each day as it comes. He is like the-early-man. Learning from mistakes. His knowledge base is empty or just filling up. He is inexperienced and knows only that his role is to populate the earth.

### Stage Two.

In this stage instincts and pain still plays a major role but his knowledge base has increased, and memory now plays a major role in decision making and the value he places on his life. Past encounters with life-threatening forces have helped build his knowledge base. He is much aware that he must self-defend and self-preserve, but he is willing to sacrifice his life for other beliefs he might have. He acknowledges that in life, sometimes he must sacrifice his life for a good cause central to his beliefs. He might be willing to end his life for a great cause. In this stage, there is a common belief that death is not the end but just the beginning. Mankind in this stage believes that honor and the need to be remembered for doing something good play a critical part. We see mankind in this stage fighting for a cause wholeheartedly but also acknowledging that such an act can end with the loss of his life. Here he places more value on the cause he is fighting than to his life in the hope that somehow his death might also help achieve the cause he is fighting. The value of life is somehow not appreciated than the cause someone is fighting for. In other words, mankind is willing to sacrifice his life for some gain or better place after death. There is a strong belief in life after death and religion plays a key role. People in this stage can be said to be uneducated about the value of life and are easily manipulated and tricked. Their beliefs are centered around someone else. Self-esteem about their life is somehow skewed. Life is generally hard, and people would only sacrifice their life for a better one somewhere in heaven or paradise.

**Stage Three.**

In this stage, mankind is well educated to know that life is more important than anything else. Self-preservation plays a greater role in all his or her decisions. Self-esteem is high and mankind is well knowledgeable about life and rarely considers sacrificing his life for anything. Religion plays a low-part in his life. Mankind in this stage believes that there is no afterlife. What is here on earth that is that and aims to live life to the fullest? Everything is planned and centered around self-preservation. Mankind in this stage do everything, to eliminate dangers to life. He carefully plans everything and avoids anything and including jobs that threaten life. In this stage, mankind believes that he exists so he can live longer and more comfortably. Self-esteem is very high. He comes first in whatever he does. His sole existence is to the betterment of mankind and in enhancing life. He believes that there are other people in life who are important than him but is unwilling to sacrifice his life for anyone. He believes that there is a superior being [God] out there but at the same time acknowledges that that superior being created him the same as his image so that mankind can become his own god and not bother him. So, he tries to live his life as a small god but believes that one day when he has done his best here on earth, he will meet this superior being that created him. Mankind in this stage believes that yes there is a superior being but that he cannot sacrifice his life to this superior being until his days are over naturally. Mankind in this stage value life and will never sacrifice their life for anyone even for god let alone any leaders. Self-preservation plays a key role.

## Stage Four.

In this stage, mankind is very knowledgeable about the value of life and everything centers around preserving life to the fullest. Mankind in this stage avoids anything that puts a risk to his own life. Self-defense rather than self-preservation takes center stage. In this stage, mankind is very proactive. He acts and plans to preserve life. He plans everything very carefully avoiding anything that puts a risk to his life. He avoids anything that will threaten his existence. He is on the go, looking for new ways to do things that avoid risks to life. He is always proactive planning ahead, innovating and educating others around him about the need for self-defense. Instead of just focusing on ways to preserve the life he acts in advance to self-defense. In this stage, religion plays a minimal part. Yes, he acknowledges the existence of a superior being but also believes that the superior being [God] created him with his own image and as such he wants him to be his own god. This superior being created mankind so mankind can grow and advance to be like him [God] one day. He believes that God or any superior being who created the earth wanted mankind to end up like him, so he chose the heaven to be his place of residence if you like and created the earth to be mankind's place of residence. This superior being is just and good. He gave himself the heaven as his and created the earth as mankind and to be honest does not want mankind in heaven. Why? When he had put a lot of effort into creating the earth for mankind. Gods in heaven and man on earth. Man must learn and advance to reach his stage. Mankind cannot rely on God. This God does not want to be bothered. He is like a tutor or master or godfather who gets a pupil or a protégé and trains him so that one day he will become like him. In that sense, he is training mankind so that mankind will evolve one day and become a small god. In this light this God wants mankind to grow, advance and evolve to his standard. God or any superior being that is if you don't believe in God has created mankind by his image. He wants mankind to be like him. If only he can master and fully understand what is needed to become God. It is a challenge, but he has faith in mankind that he will learn and discover all the tricks needed to evolve to his standard so that mankind becomes a small god who will end up growing big like the real God and one-day rule earth just like God rules the heavens. This God or superior being is just and to be honest does not need mankind. He created mankind out of boredom so that he can train and set up challenges mankind must tackle and overcome so that mankind evolves and fully becomes aware of what is needed to reach his standard. Fearing that mankind will take the easy road and run to him as a dependent he gave them an option that if mankind fails, he is still welcome to come and stay with him in heaven but honestly this is not part of his plan. It's like a Plan B thing. Okay if you have failed then there is still room for you. Just like a father who is 'driving- or self-motivating' his son. He guides him until he is eighteen. After eighteen he buys his son a piece of land. He expects his son one day to become his own man and end up with his own family. His intention from the word go is to make the son independent of him. To build him through guidance and let him be his own man. I don't think that this father expects his son one day to come back to his own house and say; father I have failed can I move back in? No. Okay, he might say the door is open for you my son but only as a last resort when all has failed you can still come and stay with us. His aim is to build his son so that he can become like him one day, have his own family and roof above his head. This is the same as God. If God or any superior being can create man and earth, it is not because he wants mankind to come one day and stay with him. Just like the scenario above about a father and his son. His aim is to build a man in his own image. A man who will become like him and have his own house. Likewise, God created mankind so he can rule the earth and make the earth his. All this talk about going to heaven if you die is just untrue. To him, it's a sign of failure. If it's an exam, he will simply say you have failed because what he expected was for mankind to prove he can be smarter to solve the puzzle and the riddle and evolve to his status and become gods here on earth. Paradise and heaven are stages that must be reached here on earth and not places in heaven. Okay, these places might literally be in heaven, but God wants mankind to achieve that stage in life where earth becomes like heaven. It is a stage that must be reached. Mankind must crack the code to achieve such a level and it's not something that can be earned by being a suicide bomber nor by dying for a great leader. It is a stage in human development that must be achieved here on earth and not a shortcut to "heaven" by ending one's life. Education in this stage plays a greater role. Today's leaders some understand this but know that too that if the people are aware of this, then there won't be reasons for them to be in power. No one would die for them everyone will do whatever it takes to self-defend and self-preserve. In such a society human rights abuse is minimal as the leaders know no one will self-terminate for them as they would rather take them down. This stage to you all is the stage that is preached in the bible or Quran and a stage that is known in religious circles as paradise. There is a great misconception that these places only exist in heaven. Okay, the idea hints to places in heaven but the truth is that it is a stage in human development that mankind MUST reach one day a theme or idea that is central to this book. Education about the importance of life is crucial if mankind is to move up the development stages. This is a theme that is central to this book I reiterate here. Something I think is not understood and as such I think we are still may be in the stage, two of the development stages of the value of life mentioned above. It will take a lot for mankind to understand that at one stage we ought to be in stage four at least. I think you will all agree with me when I say early man had a slight view of life than us. Likewise, when humanity reaches stage four of the value placed on life surely, they can say people of our generation had different views about life than the ones before. Stage four is a stage mankind here on earth must accomplish one day. It is a stage in the development process that must be reached and not a place in heaven where one must end his life in order to reach. It is a riddle, a puzzle if you like that must be solved to be achieved. Paradise or heaven is known to be a place where people of all genetic heritage come together and cooperate with each other for the harmony and peaceful existence of mankind. It is a stage when mankind doesn't see boundaries and or differences. This is a stage we as humans ought to achieve one day here on earth a theme common to all my books [see Carolinadeivid books]. Mankind is still in the defensive stages of development [Read the Vice President the Electronic transfer]. I argued that for over two thousand years we as humans have remained stuck in the defensive economies when we MUST be in other stages of development where cooperation and networking are paramount. I will look at this idea below when I look at my development stages. When we as human beings have acquired such knowledge that there is more to life than fighting for a good cause then can we only begin to move ahead through the development stages? I believe we all have one shot at life. You only live once. I believe heaven and paradise are stages that MUST be reached here on earth one day. Mankind at some time in the future will move away from the current defensive economies when weapons and wars are used to control the population, get the rather-would-be expensive resources like oil cheaply and provide for the existence of mankind. Just picture all your leaders without the military or talk about defense and wars. They would be like naked models using their hands to cover themselves or hiding everywhere. Imagine a world that does not talk about war or death of women and children, death of soldiers or heated exchange of words between leaders. Today it seems impossible and boring not to do that. Simply because defense in this stage of development we are in is the main "driving force". We are still in the defensive stages of development. Your today's leaders without defense are totally useless. They all rely on defense. Globally we spend $ trillions year after year on defense. Worse nowadays when everyone is starting to realize that we can all live together without wars. Money is channeled to the wrong use when we are no longer in need of weapons. The population is still growing rapidly. Your leaders have used wars to reduce government spending by getting our finest boys and girls die in wars needlessly. Driving the economy through cutting spending as thousand names are wiped off the government bill, state release of insurance money of deceased soldiers to their wives who in-turn spend the money to boost the economy. Reducing the number of people, easing pressure on land and resources by bombing them and making sure that the government act just like God who uses natural disasters to keep population in check. We are still stockpiling thousands of weapons and still creating more and more military wings worldwide just to justify the defensive economies we have adopted and stuck onto when we should be moving to networking and cooperation a stage needed to move toward paradise and "heaven-like" stages. The main problem is that this is the only way mankind has known to do things. The military plays a key role and has played a major part since the early man. But I understand the reason behind the early man's emphasis on defensive stages. A dinosaur, the mammoth or the saber-toothed-cat trust me were fear-inducing menacing creatures that could make a strong man shiver with fear. Not that I have physically seen one, but the images of these animals are terrifying. But since then these creatures have gone extinct and I am like what next why still putting scarce resources on defense? Come the early 1960 with the rise of the rights movements. People now we're starting to understand that we as humans are living below our potential. We were stuck in the defensive economies that were justified by the presence of some menacing creatures but honestly, all these have since gone extinct so why then are we still in this stage? This is the only stage that overrides other laws pertaining to human life and rights. This is the only power stage where your leaders can abuse you and show you power by killing those you are supposed to protect and value etc. without you doing anything. This is the only stage that justifies whatever they do. The only stage that makes them little gods. Your leaders simply because without defense they are nothing and for them to continue abusing your rights they created fictional stories just to justify a huge defense budget at the expense of our rights. They started talking about UFOs and aliens just to keep everyone hooked on defense. They know if they are to let the rights movements take over then there won't be a need for them. No one would die for them. For what? To justify huge defense budgets, more missiles that could reach aliens and UFO's ships above earth were developed. When it was discovered that all this alien thing and UFOs was a hoax, they encouraged assassinations of all rights activists sending fear everywhere to justify defensive economies. It is also in this era that we started seeing the rise of terrorist activities just to justify huge defense budgets. But why defense one might ask? It is the easiest road known to your leaders to do their job. In your mind replace defense [military etc.] with projects that encourage networking like removal of boundaries and joining all countries linking all airports and roads etc. Then picture your leaders. Do they fit as the project managers, the leaders of such nations? Mostly the answer is no. Probably he or she was elected simply because he promised a war with another country or simply, he promised to increase the military spending when there won't be any war. Okay in that case we are just stockpiling weapons when there is no prospect of any war. Look at North Korea and the USA a classic example. A few years back these were sworn enemies now they are cooperating, which is good, but the problem is that we are still making weapons. Are we expecting aliens? Are we expecting UFOs? Maybe the rise again of the dinosaurs, the mammoths or the saber-tooth-cats? Who then is our enemy when we are all becoming friends? I am not saying it's a bad thing I am simply asking if it is not also wise to move away from defensive economies considering the changing political environment. In chapter one I proposed my world. Cut defense. Train our boys to the highest standards as assassins. Increase their wages to levels never seen before as you save on defense cuts. Cut weapons production. Aim to reduce waste. Instead of the rifle approach adopt the shotgun approach. Target. Don't reduce our military personnel but train all as assassins and bodyguards. Money saved on weapons development like missiles is used to increase the wages of our boys and make the military like any other profession that sees them retiring and having a pension. Write up and implement laws that make your leaders accountable if any soldier dies needlessly. Make it illegal to start wars that kill our best boys and girls, women and children. Make these leaders accountable for their actions and target the culprits. Send our best boys as trained lethal assassins to solve global issues. Make it a crime to still manufacture weapons. Remember Tomorrow's World Order will have a global impact and no boundaries. Express-command to put an end to this through our laws and courts as a deterrent. A team of dedicated assassins will always be there to perform the orders of our courts. Any leaders who think they are above the law think again. Instead of getting our best boys die young needlessly we shall protect them with laws. Do you let your best die early or you will keep them alive as possible? Again, like I said education and the need to let everyone know that heaven is here on earth all we need to do is to collectively work together to achieve that. The $trillions we are spending on weapons today will be channeled to the development of highly effective networks that encourage cooperation and interaction as one. I know it will not be easy to make people stop weapons manufacturing and move away from defensive economies but it's a challenge we MUST tackle together to move through the development channels. Why it is difficult now is that there are a lot of double standards. We tell North Korea to stop producing missiles when we are increasing production or diversifying making missile capabilities with long-range. What I can tell you is that this is a mind-game that is meant to justify huge defense budgets. It is human nature that if a small country is sanctioned and ordered to stop producing missiles by a big country that itself continues to make long-range missiles obvious that small country no matter what as a self-defense strategy will keep making missiles for defense. Self-preservation. All this is a mind-control strategy in that the small country would starve its own people and will carry on making weapons and in-turn the big country continues to produce missiles citing dangers of surprise attacks. So how do we solve this issue? Tomorrow's World Order will put up laws that will end the manufacturing of weapons globally no matter how big or powerful your country is. To move away from defensive economies, it will not be easy because this is the cornerstone of your leaders' careers. But TWO will help them by introducing laws that ban wars globally. I will look at the crimes of aggression law that came into effect recently and suggest that this law does not do more simply because it's a law without an implementing and enforcing body therefore useless. How many UN recommendations are not followed, and most are simply advisory and then what? TWO shall aim to address that. Trust me when these leaders know that they can be targeted by assassins surely, they will do their best to self-preserve as well which means complying with international laws. Right now, no one gives a damn simply because hundreds of people are willing to sacrifice their lives defending them even if they are wrong. So, the first thing like I will explain below in later chapters: we need to first change mankind's mindset and build mankind's self-esteem to the highest levels that all men will feel worth to be the leader. That brings me to the fifth stage.

## Stage Five

In this stage, mankind's self-esteem is at the highest every 'man' seems himself as worth a shot at being the leader. Remember my arguments at the beginning that God or whoever you believe to be the creator just like a father-son paradigm I used above his intention is to give mankind everything including his own world so that he becomes his own god and makes the earth his. When this happens then mankind will have solved the puzzle and solved all the riddles. It is a test just like an exam set by a lecturer. All the lecturers' aim is to teach the students so that they become lecturers themselves etc. and NOT so that they keep coming to his or her class year after year, no. The same thinking applies here. God made the earth for mankind going through a lot of an effort to show mankind the way of becoming a god so that one day God would say; 'what a great teacher and God he is'. He might further say that; 'I taught mankind to become God and now he has passed that test and mankind has become like God himself. I will quote a passage from the bible that will help explain my thoughts. This is a verse from Genesis. Even if you don't believe in the bible the father-son or lecturer-pupil paradigm explains the same notion.

Genesis 3v22

22Then the LORD God said, "Behold, the man has become like one of us, knowing good and evil. And now, lest he reach out his hand and take also from the tree of life, and eat, and live forever…"

In this verse, it seems that God is surprised and thrilled at the same time and a bit cautious now that mankind has passed the test. That mankind has solved the puzzle and finally that mankind has acquired knowledge about what is good and what is evil. Mankind now understands the value of life. That mankind now has grasped the need to self-preserve and self-defend. That mankind's self-esteem is at its highest that he would not allow anyone to use him in such a way that conflicts with the need to self-preserve. It's like a man who says I want to live forever but at the same time allow maybe the leaders to use digital communications that are based on viral-mutations to pass commands. Such a person or group of persons have not acquired the knowledge yet of what self-esteem is all about. It can be said that they lack an understanding of the value of life. Such a society is doomed simply because no matter how advanced and intelligent the digital-communications and commands might be they are based on viral-mutations which is a threat to one's life and rights to live forever like God. Admitting to such type of digital communication conflicts with the goals to self-preserve and self-defend simply because the communications are harming you and therefore in conflict with the rights to life and a person's self-esteem. TWO will make it a crime punishable by death. Express-command to put an end to this through our laws and courts as a deterrent. If found guilty to be shot on the spot by an assassin for any leader knowingly or not to manipulate and trick the population that they can secretly communicate through advanced remote operated infrared through advanced gadgets, etc. First of all, they all use radiation forms one-way or the other and anyone who implants devices to communicate this way is no better than a cold-blooded killer and as such should be punished by death simply because such practices are contrary to the values of lives and the need to self-preserve and self-defend. Any communications that use radiation or other remote waves are illegal and there can never be any justification because as I will explain later they conflict with rule number one; the right to life and a high-quality life together with the right to self-preserve or self-defend oneself and preserve and prolong life as possible. TWO shall make it a crime punishable by death at the hands of the assassins to make or manufacturer such devices simply because of the side effects that conflicts with the first rule to life.

Going back to the verse Genesis 3v22.

This stage five is characterized by mankind acquiring great knowledge that he starts to understand his role on earth. God's plan is or was to make mankind discover himself why he is here on earth. I don't think it's simply that we die and go to heaven as portrayed by many. Just know that it is easy to end life than to make one. Someone can wake up and shoots himself or throw himself over the bridge and simply dies. Surely that means death is not the answer but just an easy option out. There must therefore be difficult and challenging activity, that we ought to do to live forever like God. It's like writing a book. Your main actor doesn't just get a gun and shoots himself, no. He must discover something others are overlooking to cross the bridge and rescue something. He must think outside the box. This is the magic phrase here; think outside the box. Everyone looks inside the box for answers, but a few check the outside as well. Genesis 3v22 clearly pointed to what is needed to be able to achieve God's status. It is through acquiring knowledge about what is good and what is evil. God is good and wise and lives forever and here he is telling everyone his secret. Mankind has become like him through the acquisition of knowledge. It is not just knowledge of what is good and evil as this is readily available through the ten commandments and natural instincts but it's a different level of understanding. It's through solving the puzzle of life. Remember the first questions in this chapter? What is life all about? What is the value of life? In stage five mankind has knowledge that God created every man with his image. His main idea is to make mankind like him. So, if God's plan is to make mankind be like him, I can deduce that God's plan is to make us live forever. This is true because God lives forever. His challenge is to make the man think for himself and evolve and realize that he too has and can and MUST live forever. It's not an option, no but a MUST a mandate that we as humans value life and do whatever to live here on earth forever. Fact mankind must live forever, and death is a failure [I don't mean natural death I am referring to the sacrificial death. Joining the army knowing that you are destined to die or killing yourself to save someone else]. God lives forever, he created mankind with his image, therefore, God wants 'man' [referring to both men and women throughout this book] to solve life's challenges and live forever like him on earth. He has heaven to himself and for mankind, he created the earth so that mankind can live here on earth forever. Hurrying to go to heaven to his place is like a squatter invading your house. It's unwelcome but sometimes you just must accommodate simply because there is no other option. God's aim is to see mankind evolve to his standard and live forever. So clearly to value life and have self-esteem is the most important thing to do. Soldiers should demand laws that protect them as a profession just like everyone else to have the right to die old. TWO like I said will write and implement laws to protect the lives of all military personnel in that your leaders only ought to send them to be slaughtered when all other options are exhausted. TWO will solve this by training current soldiers to deadly assassins with huge paychecks with money saved from weapons production. Going back to Genesis 3v22 we can deduce the secret to longevity. It is to take also from the tree of life. This means understanding what God does. God in this verse is afraid for mankind simply because God himself is a spirit and has no feelings and is not made up of flesh like a man what he does is too painful to mankind. God's job is to correct the balance of the ecosystem so that life continues. He uses natural disasters to correct the imbalance. He uses floods, earthquakes, etc. to correct this ecosystem's balance. Now that man has become like himself meaning that some human beings have eaten the forbidden fruits from the tree of life the tree of knowledge. The knowledge of knowing what is good and evil these people have become like gods and as such have reached God's goal for mankind. Now they must do like God but here on earth. They must act like God in other words and correct the earth's ecosystem. Just like what God does they have to kill too to correct this imbalance, and this is God's greatest fear? Mankind since acquiring the status of God has earned himself everlasting life, he can now live forever. Now God can delegate and let mankind do his role here on earth. At last, the student has become a lecturer himself and now his task is to teach other students but that involves punishing new students so that themselves as well become lecturers. God has delegated his tasks but without the necessary gear needed to fully do his job. Mankind is soft, made of flesh and full of feelings and, to be honest for him to do God's job is not an easy task probably not the right thing to do. It's like sending a soldier to war without weapons and as such the blame will still befall whoever sends him simply because he is incapable of carrying such a task without the right equipment. God fears that mankind will self-destruct because being a god of earth involves witnessing gruesome acts. Carrying out murders, killing people in large numbers to maintain ecosystem balance, etc. are not easy tasks.

Just from this verse, I can safely say that the highest self-esteem and preservation of life so that one lives forever are the goals of life. This is a human development stage a human being MUST thrive to achieve and as far as I can say we are still in stage two of the values of life above. After 2000 years we must have moved away from defensive economies simply because aliens and UFOs don't exist and trust me dinosaurs are not going to come back. Everyone around us is our friends and sometime in the future we shall all be networking and cooperating working together as one without seeing boundaries and differences. There shall not be any need for wars. TWO's deadly assassins shall roam the globe all the time taking out rights abusers. The law shall be adhered to by all. Targeting shall be our motto. No child, woman or soldier shall die needlessly. Laws shall protect all and your leaders shall all obey TWO's laws simply because TWO's laws shall be for the good of all mankind so that we move away from defensive economies and realize our potential as a people regardless of genetic heritage, color, creed or social status. The money saved on military weapons shall be used to give everyone a chance in life. Social inequalities shall be targeted, and laws put in place to uplift everyone only competitiveness shall separate the leader from the rest of the group. A better faster thinker with a competitive edge shall become your leader at local levels. We shall foster and reward unselfish ways of thinking. Don't get me wrong I am not advocating for communism, no. This shall be a very advanced way of doing things.

I think it is also fitting here to look at stages in the human development process. Stages I personally think mankind should take to fully realize our potential. I have touched on these in my other book [The Vice President the Electronic Transfer].

# CHAPTER THREE

MORAL DECADENCE EVIL LURKING.

**Issues addressed in this chapter.**

Rights Abusers in the name of the so-called protection and or anti-terrorism.

Make it a thing of the past.

Disguised secret modern-day slavery.

Society Collapse Studies in 1654.

Justifications for defensive economies.

Justifications for wars.

Justification for murdering our boys. I ask you a question?

Do you sacrifice your best, or you will do whatever it takes to preserve them? No more young soldiers dying needlessly. I must put laws to change the way we think today. I know it might be taken in a wrong way but years from now people will understand that the military should be like every profession where you ought to enjoy a pension through laws I will put in place.

Reduce casualties by training them into assassins turning every military personnel into an assassin just to target the rights abusers. There won't be any chance for our targets to retaliate.

One man for himself TWO for us all shall apply here.

Change completely people's thinking. If you are going by the books, you have nothing to fear.

Overview of current institutions and the problems at hand.

Illegal hacking

Evil and cruel ways of claiming illegal possession of assets, etc.

through;

*Watermarks

*Use of digital-viral

* Landmines

Corrupt Financial Institutions.

OK. Let me tell you a story you never heard before. 100 years from now the world had changed drastically from the way we know it today. A New World was born. A New World Order. A new leader was ruling the world. This leader was called David. This leader had done what no man had done before. He had taken humans to another stage of development. A New World, a new system totally different from the way we know it today. He had taken the world away from the defensive economies to the next stage of networking and cooperation the way it should have been. A hundred years before that mankind was stuck in the defensive stage. For 2000 years mankind had only known wars and dirty tactics. $Billions had been spent making weapons and on defense. The population was growing too, and deaths had reduced yet the leaders of that day advanced for defense at the expense of other areas. You can see why their strategies were a time-bomb. At least this was deliberate because that was the only way the leaders of that day could justify huge defense budgets that one day war would break out. That only made others adopt other dirty tactics to equal the huge military budgets of the leaders of the day. Does that include making Weapons of Mass Destruction? One can argue so but now that's not my point of focus. The only unforeseeable threat was from mankind himself. It was only a matter of time before a nuclear world war was initiated or provoked. David had to do something. Surely old habits die hard. Mankind for 2000 years had relied on defensive economies to drive the economy and the political life of the leaders of the day. Defensive economies were the only answer for all. You can say "one size fits all" applies here in that all the components needed to drive the economy included a formula that has defense as the main component. Defense would guarantee that the leaders acted like God balancing the ecosystem. Wars were used to correct the imbalance between population and resources. Wars meant eliminating hundreds of thousands if not millions on earth within a short period to counteract the huge population birth rates. Wars meant reducing the salary bill by thousands within a very short period. This is true. War is a very powerful weapon to tackle government deficit and budget problems. Would you be surprised that huge deficits or budget problems are followed by the declaration of wars? A good example in the USA is the declaration by Donald Rumsfeld that the US government had lost $2 trillion dollars a day before 9/11. In the UK the failure to pay the World War II debt it owed the US was a trigger for wanting to go to war one can argue. Huge balance deficits are indicators that the government is doing badly as it has a huge wage or salary bill with not enough income and to correct this the leaders would often hint on the need to go to war no matter what the reasons, they give you. The underlying truth is to reduce the number of people on their wage bill. Why not kill soldiers reduce their numbers, reduce the wage bills, in-turn offset the deficit? But people over the years have evolved and most understand that war should be a thing for the past. Every time we have advocated for a tactic or path that takes mankind out of the defensive thinking the leaders "instilled fear into the minds of millions" so that defense remained our main priority. Remember the 1960s anti-war rallies and demonstrations and the threats of Unidentified Flying Objects [UFOS] or aliens around that time. People after the 1950s realized that we as humans we were working under our optimal capacity by being stuck for 2000 years in the defensive stage thinking. Every now and then a few foresighted people would rise to advocate and push humanity through the development stages, yet the leaders of the day would do whatever they can to silence these advocators not surprising with the result that most of these people end up dead. Come the 1980s the anti-war campaigns were met with the same skepticism and objection. But now the leaders of the day could not use aliens or UFOS to instill fear among the population. They had to find another way of keeping the people hooked on fear so as for them to justify huge defense budgets. The people now knew that the fear of aliens and UFOS was a hoax championed by these leaders to justify huge budgets. In the late 1980s, these leaders or a few regimes as it will come clear later recruited a people through trickery and torture and blackmail to start what is now known as terrorism. This gives these leaders justifications for huge military budgets as unforeseeable terror is witnessed by many that justify what they call the wars more than daylight robbery going to steal or take by force resources so that they pay their bills to offset the budget deficit. Here you can already see why many still champion defensive economies. An economical method of sourcing scarce yet expensive resources like oil. Make weapons cheaply and then use the weapons to get the most expensive resources. Mainly because they lacked enough money or ideas to increase the money supply. They simply could wage a war to rob someone's resources without anyone complaining about it while killing thousands of women and children. I ask you a question. Imagine if the defense was not an important issue. Imagine a world where we negotiate and cooperate on everything. The money channeled into defense would be used to pay a fair price for scarce oil resources. In such a setting do you think the leaders would channel more into defense or they will save more to pay for scarce but much-needed resources? Imagine a world where to fly their planes they must pay a fair price for jet fuel. Surely in that world, they would rather save the money for jet oil than for weapons. So, having said that you can see that there is a tendency to go bully which is associated with unfair practices. So, now one can argue that the system is unfair. But that's not the point of this chapter. My arguments are that wars were and are still used to correct budget deficits by sacrificing the men and women who give their lives to protect this country. I will tell you a quick story from the bible to support the argument I am going to make. Okay, you might not believe in the bible, but the story is very relevant here. I will quote from Genesis 22v1

This passage is relevant to the sacrifice made by all soldiers and how it is interpreted by the leaders of the day. Abraham feared and respected God at the same time he loved his son Isaac very much. One day this Abraham took his son and went to the mountain. To show his obedience to God, he offered to sacrifice his son not because he did not love him. He loved his son dearly yet to show his obedience he was willing to sacrifice Isaac to God. I ask you to ponder this for a while. Does that mean Abraham valued his son Isaac less dearly that he would sacrifice him to God or that he was so devoted to God that he offered his life to him in the hope that he would in-turn realize how important his son is to him that he would not even think of asking him to sacrifice his son for him? I personally think that Abraham was so devoted to God that much that he believed that God would never ask him to sacrifice his son whom he loved very much for him. I am saying here that Abraham was that much devoted that he never thought or expected God to even think of asking him to do something like that of sacrificing his son for him. I know it's a bit confusing, but Abraham's devotion was total that he would never think or imagine God doubting his faith or obedience. It's that kind of trust that does not require proof of devotion. It's like loving someone that much that you would not expect that person to ask you to do something to prove your love or loyalty in this case. So, I am saying that Abraham was devoted to God that he never thought or imagined God himself thinking about ending his son's life let alone his. In the bible, God acknowledged that Abraham was devoted to him as he did not hesitate that in the end a lamb was provided by God as the sacrifice rather than his son. Having said that, I am arguing also that even though soldiers surrender their lives to die protecting the leader and the country they love the oath of enlisting is a kind of belief and devotion that they would never imagine the leaders in-turn taking their lives cheaply. It's a kind of devotion that has implied connotations that they would not expect to be sacrificed especially as a way of reducing the budget deficit. No matter how it sounds this is the truth. The leaders of the day have embarked on meaningless wars to boost the economy and alleviate the problems of the day at the expense of these soldiers. Surely, I think it's like I die for you so do whatever it takes to make me safe as well. Something totally opposite to what has been happening. Imagine the soldiers being sent to engage in combat without the proper gear, without proper vehicles to cushion them against improvised weapons, etc. So, I tell you this. The leaders of the day acknowledge and believe that just like Abraham the soldiers were willing to give their lives anyway so whatever they do would not make any difference either way they had already given their lives. It seems true if you look at Abraham's situation. It's true Abraham being obedient to God was willing to sacrifice his son for God. So, logic would mean that technically if Abraham was willing to kill his son for God as a sacrifice it follows also that God can simply kill Abraham's son himself without upsetting Abraham or seeing anything wrong with this. But is this true? Is it the same as Abraham killing his son for God as a sacrifice and God taking Abraham's son just because Abraham was willing anyway to kill his son for him? I think it's different. It is true one can argue that the soldier is willing to die for the country and the leader of the day. The question is that is this the same thing when the leader takes that life for himself and the country. Okay, some can argue that it all comes to the same thing. The difference is in the means and not the end as the end is the same. The soldier has given himself for the leader and the country so whatever the leader does is still within the lines of the sacrifice offered by the soldier. Every decision the leader makes is for the country so in that, the leader is exempted from any liability. This is the justification or alibi given to these leaders that they sacrifice the soldiers in a flash. In the New World Order, this is different. The kind of sacrifice is not merely offering to die for leader and country without expecting them to be willing to do the same. Keep in mind the theme of the book is an eye for an eye a soul for a soul. If you are willing to take are you must be willing to give one as well. I have argued throughout the book that people in this stage of development have very high self-esteem that nobody would die for anyone or just sacrifice themselves for nothing. The leaders are in power as a matter of luck as everyone is capable and qualified to be a leader in their own right that everyone's self-esteem is high to be able to see themselves as good as the leader. Chance and luck are very central to the beliefs of the people and they believe that only luck separates the number one from number two. So, looking back at the soldier situation he or she has given his or her life with the hope and expectation that the leader would do whatever it takes to preserve that life in return and not like the current thinking of sacrificing that life cheaply. It's like I die for you and what can you do for me. If I am willing to die for you, will you protect me forever not sacrifice me cheaply? Hence Tomorrow's World Order's new laws. See the chapter of the laws below but in short, no soldier shall be sacrificed cheaply. Any commands for war that results in unnecessary deaths can see the leader be dragged to court or die at the hands of the assassins.

Wars are used to boost the economy. New money is often injected directly or indirectly into the economy. Weapons are manufactured to replace the ones to be used or being used in the war. New business capital for locals as well as jobs and contracts abroad. Above all a new way of covering up the mismanagement of money. This will normally give alibis to any missing money which would have become missing due to the corruption and greediness of the leaders of the day. How is that? Okay, I will explain. Imagine you are the leader and you know very well that politics is a short time game and you damn right know and acknowledge that you will not be in power forever. You have at least four years to plan your future and those of your friends. But you also know that accountability and inspection is part of politics. The question you might be asking yourself is this; how can you make it while you have the chance? I have an idea. Why not come clear first when you know that things are okay and deliver the worst news? Make everyone very angry now when you know that everything is okay and then actually carry out what you have announced in the belief that the people already know and have already reacted to your bad news. Whatever the people's reactions in the future are of no use they can't be expected to react again. Now then actually do what you said happened. It's like if you are the leader then you announce that a $billion dollars are missing when it's not. Then embark on a war where a lot of contractors would be given huge contracts and in the end the $billion would be missing by the time you are out of office leaving a rack for the next leader and making yourself or your friends rich through contacts that makes it easy to siphon money out of the government coffers. To do this first a sense of fear has to be instilled in the people to justify going to war. The only thing left is terrorism after people realized that UFOS and aliens were a hoax. Would you be surprised also that terrorism has grown significantly in recent years? I believe that for every event there is a causal-effect relation and an underlying reason. There is someone always there to benefit from that. Who? This the question everyone serious about combating terrorism must ask? I don't believe people kill each other just because of religion. Someone with a sinister motive is always behind all this.

Having dwelt much on the basic reasoning behind the so-called justification for defensive economies I will continue with my story at the beginning of this chapter of a leader called David. This

David had made an oath to take humanity away from defensive economies to the next stage of development something that was not received lightly simply because this is the only way mankind had known and one that has worked magic for them. Defensive economies meant solutions for all kinds of problems. War leaders are rated as the best and are the most remembered because in most cases something bad had happened first that then went on to trigger the war but first this act instilled fear in humanity that war was the only solution for the people to feel safe and protected again. Pearl Harbor, Hiroshima, 9/11, etc. So, to take humanity to another level this David recruited the best assassins worldwide. Opposition had meant the stagnation of progress that in the end, the consensus was to eliminate all those opposed to this new change. The leaders of the day like their forefathers had embarked on dirty tricks starting and recruiting terrorists themselves secretly through hacking, torture, and blackmail, ordering terrorists' activities globally themselves to justify wars and invasions. The more this David exposed these regimes the more was the opposition. But he knew he had a job to do so in the end he had no option but to eliminate evil. There was a growing trend at that time too where people were starting to realize that the current institutions were not-fit for the purpose. Most were established just after the Second World War and honestly, a lot had happened since then, yet these institutions were not evolving but still practicing secret slavery through hacking and torture. What they did over the years was to find ways of concealing these ill practices when we should be abolition these. They had spent $billions making secret Weapons of Mass Destruction embarking in all kinds of shenanigans to conceal and hide evil. Yet no one said anything but instead victimize the victims to save their jobs and whoever they are protecting. Surely logic would simply point to the fact that something relevant in 1945 cannot be relevant today. Look at how the world has evolved. The only problem is that all are former slaves or one-way or the other were under an evil regime and have been hacked and are blackmailed. So, speaking of freedom to choose is just a mere dream. In the end, people started to realize that some regimes grew out of use of bad practices e.g. hacking and secret slavery. The more people realized that this was and is still being practiced the more the disgruntlement but also the more the hacking, slavery, and the blackmail. A new plan was needed to defeat this evil. Hence, I swear by the assassin slogan. This was the only way to defeat evil. Men and women everywhere fought volunteering to end this evil one-way or the other. It was difficult as retaliation instilled more fear, but a few brave men and women knew we had a job to do. We started gaining favor among former soldiers who were used and abandoned above all who best to be an assassin than a former soldier. Everyone realized that it was one man for himself and TWO for us all. Somehow powerful software developers started offering their services for our cause. Somehow what was used to protect them became a threat to them as we realized that the current regime in order to keep the status quo they had hacked almost everyone making billions of implanted medical devices they used as Weapons of Mass Destruction. Depending on your finances and what you are willing to give as protection money the Intra-muscular Medical Device [IMDs] could be used either to protect you or to destroy you. We realized that we could hack-back. We educated everyone to raise their self-esteem that in the end people started realizing that heaven was a stage here on earth. A stage we as humans will achieve one day as opposed to the current belief that heaven is a place or state of mind in heaven attained after death. We made people realize that life was the most precious thing on earth. We helped people understand that the sacrifice or offer given by soldiers to die for these leaders was a mere symbolic gesture and nevertheless this had great meanings and not literally an offer to die for these leaders but an oath that should be reciprocated with an equal oath to safeguard and to promise the safety of our best boys and girls. It is an offer for one to do even more in that regard it is a request to do whatever it takes to ensure that the soldiers are safe as well and the leaders to be expected to die too to protect these men and women. This applies to everyone and not just soldiers. No women nor children are to die also due to the given command by these leaders. Just like they used GPS synchronization to ambush and get others attacked through hacking we used the same tactics to hack and ambush them as well that in the end, we took out only our targets with zero civilian casualties unlike now where today's leaders would sacrifice 500 000 women and children to takeout one dictator. I ask you who is worse. One who poisons 5000 of his people or one who kills 500 000 women and children of other genetic heritage. To understand this and the point, I am going to make I take you to the animal world. You can google search; animals that kill their own. You will notice that in the animal kingdom it is acceptable for animals to kill their own. Animals for example male lions can kill their cubs for several accepted reasons. Lionesses can do the same as well without any other lions questioning way or interfering with the action. First, the male lion, leader of the herd or the pride of lions can kill for strategic reasons and to preserve the pride. First, the cubs could slow the progress of the lion-pride if moving to another territory. So, as a strategic reason, the leading male or the female lion can make that strategic reason to kill the cubs. If food is scarce as well the leading lion can deliberately kill their own cubs. If the lioness is spending too much time looking after the cubs when food is scarce, or hunting is difficult the lion or lioness can kill some cubs as not to pose a risk to the lioness. Okay sometimes for mating reasons a lion can kill the cubs to relieve the lioness of the maternal duty and make her ready for a new mating period. In some cases, no other animals in the group can challenge such a decision. In other situations, the lioness out of motherly instincts can fight for the cubs but won't stop the killing. I have presented a situation in the animal kingdom where the killing of your own cubs can be regarded as "acceptable." But it's different if it's killing cubs of other animals. Other animals can get angry and attack if say lions are killing cubs of other animals. When you kill something not your own usually, it is killing for no reason and in most cases, it is out of unnecessary cruelty simply because it's not yours and you don't give a fuck. Simple! That is seen as something evil and something not to be tolerated that other animals will come to the rescue and even attack. Simply because this amounts to cruelty as the killer has no emotional attachment to the victims and can't just be asked. So, if animals can distinguish the two acts of killing why we humans tolerate such cruelty? Why bloody on earth can we tolerate people who kill 'a people' to revenge one of their own and let them kill 500 000 out of cruelty simply because they have no emotional attachment to the victims? Obvious it makes little sense. These people are killing 500 000 women and children simply because the tyrant has killed

5000 of his own by chemical gasses. Okay, he is bad or was bad but killing 500 000 should surely turn your stomach no matter the victims are part of your people or not. If animals can risk their lives fighting a lion trying to kill other animals' cubs, why do we keep quiet and pretend that everything is okay? For further points I will explain below I will point for the need to write down laws that take this into account. Killing that involves the death of people not in your genetic heritage group should not be taken lightly. New charges should be brought into play. Where a leader commands a war that results in unnecessary deaths of women and children an assessment of whether lack of empathy-motivated reasons can be the cause of such negligence should be assessed. Such crimes can never have a time limit if the person is still breathing, he or she can be held accountable at any time and such crimes are unforgivable. These are the kind of crimes that will invoke retaliation attacks and as such must be addressed with those involved brought to justice and assassinated in public for there is no other redress of killing 500 000 thousand. The second reason is that the West has become very clever and devious in that it has developed devices in the form of medical devices that are used to enslave others. We all know that some regimes grew rapidly simply because of abuse, torture, and slavery or cheap labor. Stopping this would mean the complete collapse of these regimes so to maintain these regimes they have developed advanced technological devices they are using as slaving instruments hidden so deep into tissue with the local institutions trained to conceal and hide such practices that they are little underground soldiers used to cover up and give these regimes alibis. Do you know that with the study of robots some regimes have developed devices that capture digital emotions and feelings and even imitate feelings, and diseases thus transferring these to the next person if he or she has a similar device too? The first world countries have implanted these devices to all their citizens most at or soon after birth that most don't even know it. Yes, the whole first world is hacked, with recording and GPS functions hence the need to learn secret signing [mirroring] language. That does not stop there. Emotions and feelings can be changed between certain people sharing the same line of transmission. Picture a group of people on a conference call. They all can communicate with each other as they share the same telecommunication line and are linked. So also, there are hierarchies of linking. Presidents can link with other Presidents and generally homeless burgers can't link with others like Presidents. It depends on your status. The higher your status the higher the people who can link with you in terms of social status. Although at first this is regarded as a communication way and channel between people who share certain characteristics or belong to a certain group the system is a cone. It relies on the interpreter being there all the time to translate as the communication is not direct say between two people. It always requires a third-party. Take the telephone for example. To communicate with someone requires a mask that connects and translate the message. You find ambulances loaded with the coordinating equipment to do the receiving and translation. Just like a telephone mask they must be at certain locations for the communication to be received and interpreted. Okay if it was just for communication then that's a different story. But what if I tell you that the same way is used to abuse people and get them ambushed? What if you know that it's a means for raising money and selling a service? Imagine the device capturing your migraine [induced by the device- a software program kit loaded into the device] and transferring that to someone else. Imagine you are shot by a bullet and instantly you transfer the pain to another person. Okay maybe imagine having a boner that escapes you and is received by someone in front of you through the device? A communication way or a sophisticated means of abuse so concealed and sophisticated operated by local institutions. What if the person who receives the digital version does not even want to feel that way? Okay so far, I only talked about what might appear to be the good side. But what if the device is used first to give you pain then you must pay or donate your fortune somewhere for the pain to be removed away from you? What if you realize that the device is shaking you, may be used to make you age faster as it rotates continuously? Then you are blackmailed to do something for the operators in most cases hospitals or delegated institutions like councils in return for them to switch off the rotating concealed device? What if the device is used to torture you or used to stress your genitals continuously non-stop until you buy something or do something? If you don't the devices don't stop? What if the device is used to reap you off? Being tortured so that you use electricity if you don't the device won't stop. The device can be used to make you use electricity in that the more appliances you plug in the less the torture. But what if the local electricity provider gets a contract and buys these weapons from the public health system or hospitals to torture you if you don't use a certain amount of electricity? Until you have used certain levels of electricity the device won't stop? Would you be surprised that certain companies collaborate with the local evil-doctors and buy weapons to use to torture you with managers buying the same gadgets to work you like a robot? Whenever you stop you are tortured literally with electricity passed onto you like with dog collars? If you complain the device is used to make you blind by pulling the iris of the eye to the side or inside the eye socket so that you have an accident through lost vision? Who are the vendors who collaborated with the hospitals so that the device is used to tamper with your body temperature so that you end up buying drinks from their vending machine? The question I ask you is this: Is this not the same as modern-day slavery? But okay I have given you the other dark side of these devices. But what if the device is used first to speed up the aging process by rotating continuously remotely operated and then to stop it someone else must die to remove or as they say it to clean that? Do you know that the first world countries are making digital viruses even though they don't call them that way; they call them digital soldiers. These are like watermarks that need a certain code to be removed. I think you probably know the notion of poison and antidote. If a snake bites you, you will need a certain anti-venomous antidote but specific to that snake. Just like that the West has and is still spending $billions of dollars making "snake poison" in the form of digital codes. So, what is happening is that they are loading local foreigners in the name of the so-called protection with these digital poisons and then ask the locals to do bad things to these foreigners in order to remove the digital poisons. Mainly they say the foreigners have hacked you, so you must bump or hit with a vehicle that person so that he or she stops hacking you. But that can't be the reason for justifying killing 500 000 women and children. Okay, I will tell you why. The truth is that the local leaders of hospitals [public health systems, etc.] develop or are given digital-codes that are programmed to imitate all bad things, and these are used as watermarks. Aging features are induced by certain digital-codes and for the people to stop these codes the digital code they have has to be transferred to someone else. There are no antidotes for some digital-codes or that the people can't get rid of them easily. They need people who they call cleaners. The cleaners can only clean i.e. remove from the locals but since there is no antidote the cleaners can't keep the removed digital-codes without suffering the effects of the code. In short say somehow the local through blackmail or as a punishment for disobeying the rules of the monarchy or whatever end up with the digital code and in most cases simply because they are obedient to the monarchy who is used as a reason for the need for this protection to show loyalty give their lives to the monarchy remember what I said about soldiers above. They are willing to die for the monarchy. So, as such the public health systems and the local councils take advantage of that and use this obedience to abuse the locals. They use these digital-codes as all locals are hacked and have devices tricked as defensive tools needed to protect the monarchy or kids are made to age very faster or used as the devices imitate diseases. So let's say somehow one person [having been set up in the past possibly as a kid to justify hacking and protection] is given a digital code that makes the device rotate faster {bear in mind the device has propellers and operates like a drone} the faster it rotates the faster the wear and tear the faster the aging. There is no way of stopping the device yourself you are told that a cleaner will come to stop the device and the effects, the graying and wrinkles is reversible but what happens is that by the time they realize the damage done by the device it will be too late and the effects therefore irreversible. So, in fact it's too late. The process is irreversible the only hope is that of the cleaner to stop it and stop or slow the aging. When the so-called cleaner finally arrives, the people are very happy at last they know that will stop the aging or whatever is programmed. Note here that the so-called cleaner is someone they consider having committed a crime that they consider resulting in death. In most cases the cleaner is opposite to them. Someone they considered as not listening and disobedient. Someone not loyal to the ideas they all hold, someone they consider to be against their monarchy. Someone who opposes the idea of slavery or death for someone. Someone who cannot do what they have done. So, what they are told is to keep and hold on to this [digital code but in fact digital viruses] which they will give to the cleaner as the punishment for disobeying the monarchy. The cleaner is someone to have committed high treason for example so the person will be hanged and drawn and then quartered in the end. But in modern-day the above punishment is done digitally and highly concealed. The locals are armored with digital weapons or codes that cause all kinds of havoc. When the cleaner [a sinner to be quartered and often given a fifteen-year-old as a wife in the name of the queen if he refuses then he is regarded as dirty and must be set up to protect the monarchy and must be literally quartered.] It's either you accept the fifteen-year-old in the name of the monarchy or if you refuse the hospitals or the public health system will set you up until you are literally quartered ruining your life]. The problem is that nowadays with human rights laws the locals can't kill the foreigner the so-called cleaner but nevertheless a person on death row if you like. It works if the person dies so that the digital code "dies" as well as cleaning all those who were 'holding the codes.' Remember that there are no antidotes for these codes. The death of the cleaner when he is quartered meaning hanged, drawn and his or her body parts sent to all four corners of the earth is the only antidote that will stop the aging.

Globalization has meant increased migration from other parts and inequalities issues have meant the creation of antidote to counteract segregation through the use of these digital-codes. We have people of Arab origins from Pakistan, India, and Syria migrating to the UK with antidotes to neutralize or pass-on these digital-codes if they can't neutralize as a response to these codes. So, the cleaners have become mainly of African or Caribbean origin. So, what has been happening is that the cleaners of African original if they refused to be quartered are put down for quartering. Intimidations and attacks become the norm with the locals led to believe that the foreigner cleaner has hacked them and to be free from hacking one must inflict real harm to this cleaner as he is heading for quartering anywhere. But in recent years change in a hierarchy has meant that some of African origin can now transfer to those of Indian origin. Some of Indian origin have evolved to understand that this is wrong and are able to remove from the cleaners and transfer back to the locals. So, the locals patch the digital-codes onto the cleaners who are supposed to die in order to get rid of such a digital code. But those of Indian origin have abilities to remove the digital-codes from the cleaner mostly from African origin back to the locals. So, the locals are given again the aging codes. So, they now don't like those of Indian origins who might have the same status as them as they can transfer the bad digital-codes to them. Overtime some 'cleaners' of African origin acquire a higher status ending up being able to exchange and take from the locals and give to those of Indian origin. In turn these give-back to the locals. So, everyone in the end won't be happy with such a situation. The locals are happy if it is either them only or them with either of the two, the Africans or Caribbeans or the Indians. Having both is not good for them simply because the bad codes won't go away but are recycled. So, you find people unable to do anything about the situation especially with whistleblowing of any kind of institutionalized segregation instigated to the highest level the locals can't do anything but age fast. That has resulted in the locals setting up the foreigners so that it is easy for them to be hanged, drawn and quartered literally if they refuse to be "quartered". The only way the locals will remove the bad digital-codes like the ones that induce early aging they must set up the foreigners as without these in trouble the bad codes won't go away. So equal rights have created a once-perfect situation for segregation and population control but genocide at an unprecedented scale if you ask me. We see that there is a growing trend. The locals now are unable to remove the digital-codes as the cleaners -those to be hanged for treason, drawn and quartered became scarce. A new way of cleaning these digital-codes was needed. Remember the codes are irremovable. They don't have an antidote. Then it becomes that to remove the codes and to show obedience to the queen one must go to extremes to stop the digital-codes making him age faster. How? The only way is to transfer and murder the person at that time so that the person dies and once he dies the digital-codes dies with him too. As he or she dies the devices stop working too, and the code is embedded in that person's codes. A genius form of protecting the monarchy and their way of life but genocide and or lack of empathy-motivated meaningless killings. Would you be surprised to learn that countries with monarchies see violent deaths of the so-called cleaners or people of low social status? It's not a secret that people of the Caribbean or African origin have faced violent deaths at the hands of the locals. Speaking of institutionalized inequality from the top to the grassroots in broad daylight with the world doing nothing. But still, that does not explain or justify the waging of meaningless wars one might argue.

OK, I will explain why.

In the above example, we saw that the locals can give the bad digital-codes to the so-called cleaners but not to those of Indian origin. The cleaners mainly of Caribbean or African origin can then be attacked that is given these digitals and can give this back to the locals. So, in your view who is the problem here? To the local Caucasian, the Indians are a big problem because of their social standing and or status they have the power to give back to the locals these bad digital-codes. It is true that those of Indian origin are more feared and respected than those of Caribbean and African origin. Those of Indian or Arab origin can attack back the main reason they are regarded as associated with terrorism. The locals now age very fast without doing anything. Before they could stop this by transferring to the cleaners leaving them clean. Those of Indian origins can transfer back to the locals all the unwanted digital-codes. It is those of Indian or Arab origin that are transferring back or passing back to the locals. We have a very aging population that is now dying slowly aging faster than they should have. Surely to the population, a solution was needed and fast. The idea was to protect the monarchy or their way of life by transferring these bad digital-codes that made them age faster to the cleaners. But equal rights and cries for inequality have meant that these bad codes are circulating interchangeable in the society. So how do we stop all this? Surely there is no antidote. If there is a way of removing the digital-codes permanently, then the restoration can start. So now we have leaders waging wars to clean the digital-codes forever. The leaders as a way of preserving their people in the first place had assigned a digital soldier or weapon to use on those who they perceived as threats to the monarchy and or their way of existence. It's like putting watermarks as a way of preserving or protecting their own. That has become a problem as with no antidotes the locals have become like zombies and face death unless something has been done. The politician to gain support have waged wars to kill the cleaners who on their deaths would die with the digital-codes. As a pre-planned situation, the locals have been offered free medical attention not knowing that they were being hacked and tagged. Being reared or groomed like chickens. After some time, unnecessary war is waged. The places they live are through GPS and synchronization the kids and women hacked are killed. When they die the digital-codes die too thereby eliminating the digital-codes forever. But not everyone is groomed to be killed. Some are groomed as time stoppers. The population of these countries is very old and aging. Most cases if it wasn't for these devices most would be bed-ridden. The leaders and all institutions are trained to conceal and hide what I will call secret slavery in that the old aging population can transfer these unwanted digital-codes to the young who are incapacity and left bed-ridden either in sleep or comas. So, if the old person is feeling weak or just plain lazy these feelings or state of mind can be captured digitally and stored and depending on his financial position, he or she can transfer what I call subjugate these digital feelings or state to someone who can carry these for them. So, let's say the aging women did not sleep well. She can subjugate the sleepy feelings and tiredness to someone who will sleep for her. So, the sleepy feelings are transferred or passed to the other person who must sleep the whole day. So, we have a genuine possible reason for waging wars killing women and children after hacking and bugging them so when they die, they die loaded with the digital-codes. In order for the transfer to work the person to receive the transferred feelings has to be confined and has to be in a place where he or she can rest most of the time hence a campaign using trickery to trap and trick young ones in order to send them to prison where they can easily be used as transferring entities where the evil unwanted traits are transferred to them. You can straight away see why the local council would be interested in such activities. They can ask for higher prices or donations in order to make these aging population look ten years younger. There is a market for digital sexual intercourse with unsuspecting people and the local council can benefit in that especially with the way they scare the people. So who owns such technology and who can coordinate the functions remember I said at the beginning of the chapter that a telephone needs a mask in order for two people to communicate such as it is this requires a third person who can use ambulances as a mask to connect two people so that they can exchange the digital traits. To cover up this so that this is accepted the devious hospitals have pretended that this is a communication tool. They say people can communicate digitally and what a load of bullshit. They trick people but in fact, they are abusing kids pretending people can babysit and use these to tell when a baby wants to go to the toilet or not. In fact while passing electricity through your kid's genital stimulating them while young and grooming them so that they will become prostitute who will spread diseases in the form of these digital-codes so that the ambulance can run every second while helping them hack and tag foreigners in the name of protection speaking of gross human rights abuses and modern-day slavery. No wonder why [hospitals] they are linked to abuses of children it's all to do with this that no one challenges them for fear of radiation being passed into them. What they are doing is hacking people at birth without consent or their knowledge then over the years they pretend to teach people sign language [through mirroring] as an advanced way of communicating but what they are in fact doing is hacking people of foreign origin and frying their brains through these devices the Intra-muscular Medical Device [IMDS] which I call Remotely Operated Concealed Implanted Weapons of Mass Destruction. [ROCIWMD] and putting them in institutions. They then through the device synchronize actions of the hacked person and a one whose brain they partly damaged. Imagine or remember when you were with your son you yawn, and he yawns too. You brush your teeth he copies you too and brushes his. Kids imitate everything. So, they are recording every conversation you make and when you use sign language, they just observe the person whose brain they damaged synchronized to the subject. As he is synchronized with the other person even though the whole process is delayed, he would be enacting every move the other person makes. What they do now, is tell everyone your conversation to gain that person's trust. They start acting as a spy telling you or someone close to you all your secrets or the other person's. This starts the grooming and dependency process. The device is like a video sender too in that it records and transmits computer screens and television channels to a computer or television that automatically synchronizes to it. If you are working on a project. They will see everything you are doing on the other screen stealing your ideas and hacking which is a very cheap form of stealing and after that, they pretend they are guiding you as they recreate all that you have been doing some cases changing to set you up. Someone who does this is worse than the devil. This is something only witnessed in medieval times. In modern society, there is no place of people like this. Feel shame towards anyone associated with that. You tell me that after the deaths of all these civil rights people you still engaged in corrupt activities like these. Sometimes you have to say as it is. People died, so that everyone has privacy. You try to lecturer someone when you are no better than the devil. They have violated all international laws by hacking and enslaving people on top of that they invade other people's privacy through trickery and steal and then try to teach people about what is right or wrong even go to extents of using radiation through the device to silence or even kill someone. Put yourself in the victim's shoes surely you will never call yourself what you call yourself. This is not medieval times. It's 2019 devil wake up and smell liberties and human rights. You might think you are smart but sure the world can't say anything probably out of fear, but a new regime is on the horizon. We will summon the whole world to attack all you the way you deserve. In the end, no one shall be on your side.

Hacking is worse than slavery. Hacking is a concealed form of slavery. When was slavery abolished? The very people who pretended to abolish slavery are the very people still doing secret slavery in the name of protection. The very people using this hacking to stir terrorists and to recruit terrorists. What is saddening is that all these countries and institutions know that these evil regimes are behind every attack that happened in the world including the 9/11 attacks but for fear for their kids being killed, they can't fight evil? For every event no matter how, silly it might be there is always someone to gain from it. Look at the Sri Lanka attacks. Okay, one might say it was a revenge attack. But one must read also between the lines that someone must be poised to gain from this for it to make sense

The soldiers later realized that they needed not to die for these short-sighted leaders they realized that the way forward was everything I was preaching after all. If mankind had moved with the time, we could have by now discovered ways to stay young and living longer. Is it against humanity that this evil of today is spending $billions programming software to make everyone age faster and wrinkle than what is natural and use these to blackmail its population? Once the world was educated and after presenting proof beyond doubt that hacking was a real problem and a cause of concern as it was worse than slavery our campaigning was boosted. Those who once opposed our ideas started seeing that the devil was lurking. All calls for change fell on deaf ears that in the end justice prevailed. People realized that this was different from trading a devil with an even worse one as they had been lied to. There was nothing wrong with wanting what's the best life has to offer. Nothing wrong in wanting to be free. Nothing wrong in wanting to be different and oppose evil. I must admit it was a tough road because everything was perfected and polished since the medieval times that it was incorporated in everyday life and was institutionalized. Do you know that the local council would deliberately frame someone so that he ends up hacked speaking of bounties? It is said that during the medieval times the landlords were rewarded with land and more slaves for anyone that it later hanged, drawn and quartered. Do you know that they practiced torture and to conceal such actions they would pretend the foreigner was given the general's daughter when in fact that phrase given the "general's daughter" actually meant being subjected to torture as the torturing machine was the one referred to as the general's daughter?

The cause for concern is the notion of protection.

But why protection in the first place? But I think the question is who are they protecting? To answer this, I will tell you a fictional story.

One President had a quest to rule the earth and in so doing killed hundreds of millions of people that in the end, all the people in his land realized that no one on earth can ever be as bad as this ruler. Although people in his land and surrounding country feared him, he lost respect especially when others committed crimes. When they were about to be tried, they would all complain that it's unfair that they have a devil as the leader, yet they are being tried for petty crimes. Obviously, that was unfair. So, all people would say hey your leader has done evil acts a billion times than what we did, and no one said anything so how could that be fair. In his land, this leader ended up losing any respect that people would curse behind his back and when he is around the people would pretend to honor him. This leader's kids were a "product of abuse" yet he criticized everyone else that the people started distancing themselves. It's like a burger and a homeless person advising you not to be homeless. Or a civil servant advising you to be rich and becoming a million. Or like a blind man leading the way. Or a person with bloody GCSE O levels advising a person with a BSc degree. Or a nurse for old people with dementia advising you to run a business instead of how to wipe someone's ass. You would not listen to that just common sense. A millionaire advises you to be a millionaire. A pilot advises you on how to fly a plane. So, a period followed when everyone rebelled. People started refusing anything they are accused of saying they had a big crook as the leader that alone gave them automatic blanket protection simply because if that leader is enjoying being on top no one would subscribe to anything against him. So, one day his advisers came to him and suggested that what he had to do was to offer protection and make these people commit even worse crimes in the end people would not see how bad he was himself. In other words, make all dirty too so that he resumes commanding respect among his people. So that's how this idea of protection arose. This protection meant setting up innocent people and then blackmailing them and, in the end, that they gave respect to the even worse crook on top. But this is not a form of protection as we know it. If we really want to be honest, this would not be called protection at all. This would be called blackmail. The idea was to taint everyone to lessen the blood on the leader's hands. This protection was a way to gain back respect for the leader by letting people commit crimes so they will not complain about the leader because the leader would let them also get away with murder. It's like a circle of trust with the leader through a process called initiation would give everyone in the group a task that involves making new members have blood on their hands in return for being members. This would guarantee that the new members would not complain outside about the leader's evil acts. This protection is not a form of protection you might be familiar with but a totally different way that amounts to abuse. A deeper look at this will reveal that this protection is not for the new members or other people, no. It is the protection of the evil leader. This automatically established a need to lay down a formula or a plan that would see everyone fall in the guilty-trap so that in the end they would not complain about the leader at the same time cement the relationship and bond the circle together and if all well they would co-exist with the leader having something on them and them having something on the leader.

This setting as you have seen requires a plan to trap everyone into a guilty-trap to protect the leader. But it is difficult to tell people to do something wrong as instincts would kick in and the fear of death would drive one to deny any such a setting. The protectors of the leader drew up plans setting up different traps and among these were plans to separate a man and a wife. After a time of starvation, the man would be unleashed to someone's wife whose husband had been sent away on the leaders' duties. The idea was to trap both on adultery issues where they would then give them protection where they can continue their relationship in secrecy but now through the leader's institutions where they supervise and set up all the meetings so that the other partners would not know. Other plans involved murder where a new member as in initiation would be asked to kill someone in cold blood and in broad daylight where that person would be given protection with his or her crime covered up. These plans soon fell out of favor as people knew about them as they would mean being a slave forever. The leader's men sat down again and thought about their plans. To protect the leader, they had to come up with a devious plan that will trap almost everyone and in return command everyone's loyalty. One of the plans was to misrepresent the facts and get the people hooked and then throw the bombshell. The leader's men started giving people gifts on top of services done on top of their payments. A couple received a car as a gift even though they had refused the leader had insisted that it was a gift but a few months later they were in debt with the leader demanding monthly payments. At the time they accepted the gift the cost to them was nothing simply a gift and at the time they were killed they owed thousands even though they had returned the car. After some time, everyone was now aware of the tricks and people started refusing any gifts as well. The leader one day summoned his men and women. He raised his concerns that his way of life was out of touch with the outside world and his safety depended on how much blood was on the people's hands rather than on his hands. One of the men stood up and told him that they had done everything they can they had no other tricks left. A woman among the group stood up and addressed the leader. He pointed out that the leader's story was like that of the king in the bible. The king when faced with fears of the foreigner's population growing fast someone had suggested tagging and killing children at birth when they are young and then monitor them throughout as they grew and in fact use them tampering every bit of their life so that in the end they would not pose a threat by challenging his authority and power. That automatically meant making all have blood on their hands so that no one would challenge the leadership. In cases where that's hard to do then with the help of the midwives and doctors, they would make sure that everyone is labeled unfit to run for office so that his seat as the leader is guaranteed if that meant driving nails into their heads so be it. That started a phase as institutions and specialists were established to see these plans through. At first, the main threat was from foreigners only, but the number of foreigners was marginal. So, someone thought what if we can go global and everyone who has been through the midwife, meaning tagged on birth and that too meaning neutralized would then be invited here too? Those new generations who had been processed abroad when they arrived in the country, they started noticing that life is totally different here and a few raised concerns. The leader was faced with new concerns. Technically the new generation even though processed by the midwives this was done abroad technically the leader had nothing against them. This ignited new fears that his men and women went to the drawing board again. The same woman who had given advice before stood up and addressed the leader. She raised fears that the new generation was different and a real threat as they knew the leader had a lot of blood on his hands, but she quickly quenched the leader's fears by telling him a story.

"Once upon a time," she began telling a story.

'The Pharaoh had so much blood on his hands and a lot of demons were inside him that he started falling sick. He sent his special men and women everywhere asking why that was happening. He was told that he had been weakened as a new generation of people were sent to monitor previous accusations if they were true. He learned that the supervisors every time they have something on him, he would fall sick. Angered by this the Pharaoh stood up and shouted to kill all the supervisors. Another wise man in the group stood up and told the Pharaoh that that's exactly what they would want so that they can send the military to attack.'

What difference does it make if they are here, I will die anyway? The men stood up and advised that if that happens, they too would be killed and that would not be fair because the leader had promised and guaranteed their safety and that means him taking every step and action to safeguard their lives. Such a move would not only put a risk to everyone but made sure that the covenant or agreement of protection between them would be void. He confessed that the outsiders were offering a lot of money on his head as he was considered bad everywhere abroad. The Pharaoh's men gave the Pharaoh assurances that they would solve the problem. They tried everything to set up the new generation, but they refused all dirty tricks. The Pharaoh then sent his special team to kill the foreigners but every time the men arrived to kill the foreigners and steal their possessions somehow, they would not return. Then more men were sent to check and kill these foreigners but again before they steal and kill, they would all disappear. Then one day the Pharaoh sent the men with other women to check from outside the window what was really happening. One night the men entered the houses of the foreigners to steal the notes and their possessions and when they were about to live the foreigners turned into huge snakes and ate the men. The women who were at the windows outside looking out what was happening saw what had happened, and they ran back to tell the Pharaoh. Instantly he ordered the soldiers to go and kill the foreigners who were turning into snakes every time their possessions were stolen. A temple priest came to the rescue and explained that the snakes were the only answer to the Pharaoh's problems. He needed the snakes alive, but the Pharaoh disputed that and sent the soldiers. The Pharaoh ordered his men again to go and bring the snake. Some foreigners were killed before they turned into snakes but when they died the Pharaoh become very sick. More and more demons started going in and out of the Pharaoh. The priest was summoned again. This time he explained that the snake was needed alive to eat the demons. The soldiers had to bring the snake alive. So, the Pharaoh quickly summoned the soldiers to go and bring the snake without killing it. This time the snake had grown very big as it ate all the soldiers sent to it. Still, with no commands to shoot, all the soldiers perished that the snake grew even bigger. A magician came to the rescue and offered to poison the snake slightly so that he would be able to bring it to the Pharaoh. The magician tricked the snake after poisoning it. The snake fell into a trance as the poison blinded it that it would not see. When he was about to carry the snake to the Pharaoh, the smell of the magician frightened the snake that it instantly fought and opened its blinded eyes. It was about to eat the magician, but the smell was so horrific that the snake ran away squinting to see the way. After that, the snake never trusted anyone and became very violent attacking everyone. The Pharaoh was dying as well that he offered rewards for anyone who would trick the snake to bring it to this Pharaoh, but no one succeeded as the snake ate or just attacked all. Until a woman came and advised a beautiful plan. She asked for rewards when the job has been completed as she was sure this was a brilliant plan that would automatically heal the Pharaoh. She asked questions first. She asked,

"My LORD, you are in this mess in the first place simply because you have killed a lot of people and their demons have remained with you simply because you did what no other man has done. No one can dispute that you are the evilest man who has walked on earth may be second only to Satan." The demons instantly came out of the Pharaoh and circled before disappearing into his body. She continued,

"The snake if brought here will only eat the demons you have now and when that happens you have to keep on feeding it on more demons. As far as I know, that will mean killing even more people than you already have done and the world crying on your blood that could not be good for anyone here."

"What do you suggest?" asked the Pharaoh.

"The snake keeps on growing as it eats all our men which means more and more demons as food in the future and more and more killings on your part. Having said that, I have a brilliant plan."

For days turned into weeks and then months the snake did not see anyone coming to attack it that it felt so hungry and in turn then changed back to a human being. The foreigner who had once turned to a snake one day returned and found his house burgled with all his stuff missing that instincts kicked in and he turned into a huge snake ready to eat when about to strike he noticed footprints of a little boy running out of the house. He had already called for help as he had given his last warning. Now fearing for the life of the boy he went to confront the Pharaoh who had terrorized his life. Still upset he had not noticed that he was still a snake the time he arrived at Pharaoh. The Pharaoh on seeing a huge snake instantly screamed knowing that all the demons inside him would come out to attack the snake hoping the snake to eat all the demons and, in the process, clean him. The woman stood up and clapped hands.

"My plan worked! Now Pharaoh you have what you wanted and as such, I need my reward as promised."

The huge snake on noticing the large number of demons that came out of this Pharaoh which explained how evil he was instantly felt very scared that it turned into a boy who soon got up and ran toward this Pharaoh that the demons that were about to attack 'the snake' flew toward the Pharaoh and noticed a boy that they entered back into the Pharaohs body but this time so scared and fast that they pierced his body.

The woman was still clinging to her reward when the Pharaoh succumbed onto the ground before his men turned into huge snakes themselves before devouring him themselves.

Okay, the above story is fictional, but it points the problem with this kind of protection that it is based on deception and trickery or setting up innocent people and most of all the lowest form that in the end women and children will end up being used and in most cases being killed for nothing being set up by the very people sending them. In that case, what is murder to you? If the people who are supposed to protect these women and kids are the very same people tricking and trapping these women. So, in such a situation how do you solve this issue. Trick as many as you can, offer them a form of protection that will keep them silent hacking them forever against all international laws or start afresh a clean sweep. A new beginning. A New World Order. A clean slate where children are protected the way they deserve. Where women are respected and don't have to fear losing their husbands in the name of protection. Where loved ones grow old together without fear that the need for increased capital gains tax would see their loved ones being killed. Where private lives are respected and where private really means private. It's like you insisting on privacy when you have hacked everyone and listening to everyone's conversations it just doesn't work that way.

I have looked at what I believe is the so-called protection in general and as I understand it. I know someone might argue that some countries offer real protection, especially where there is no death penalty which seems to be true but also in most cases these same countries have corrupt rules and leaders that justifying the death penalty would be impossible. It all still boils down to the same notion that where the leader is so corrupt the death penalty is not justified as everyone would simply argue for the death of that leader first. Look at all countries without the death penalty there are abusive or evil acts often cited as well.

I will look at outdated institutions that can also explain the need for this kind of protection. Some institutions were created during the war or at times of emergency that alone has meant them recreating and acting as if in war times or in times of outbreaks. This is very true that these institutions to remain viable must remain in 'states of emergency' or see their budgets cut. That alone has meant them recreating or setting up situations as in film making just to remain operational and justify huge budgets. But the world is changing. Surely what worked in 1945 can't be expected to be relevant today especially if it didn't change. All the points I will make in this book are all related and should be viewed as a comprehensive problem that requires a comprehensive solution as well.

The pressures of keeping up with the conditions in which these institutions were created mean them breaking all rules to stay on top. This has meant them diversifying into other areas like becoming teaching hospitals as regard to hospitals. This has also meant involved in drug-heroin production, so they have a direct influence on the victims whom they prescribe heroin as a prescription. This has meant hospitals using doctors to act as assassins killing fathers tragically, I have already explained above a tactic called the Society or Colony Collapse Strategy. This is so that they have a direct link to the bereaved female and her kids whom they take over teaching them from an earlier age. It's a cruel form of grooming and fostering where they kill the head of the family so that they take over his family providing jobs for themselves at the expense of the father. This has meant these hospitals involved in grooming children in the name of protection and in the end making them prostitutes through remote nerve interference and tampering through electromagnetic stimulation using sophisticated gadgets. This also has meant using these orphans as bait to trap males who buy these prostitutes in the hope of getting these hacked and tracked as a eugenic measure and a population or immigration control tool. This has led hospitals involved indirectly in grooving and or terrorism. Through hacking these illegally and remotely using drone software to command these to carry out terrorist activities. So, they recreate the war scenes associated with their conceptions after the Second World War. The banks have become involved in bank robberies they have become the new Ocean's Eleven squad using sophisticated gadgets and implanted chips to threaten and steal money. Don't forget they adopted the roles of fostering the orphans after murdering the fathers of the house. Financial Institutions and whether they are fit for purpose

# CHAPTER FOUR

## OUTDATED USELESS INSTITUTIONS AND LAWS THAT ARE OUT OF TOUCH WITH THE CHANGING REALITY.

What is hindering mankind to advance forward through the development process? Could the problem have anything to do with current institutions and outdated laws? To answer this, I point to the fact that we as humans must progress through the development stages. Humanity must move away from the defensive stages to the networking and cooperation ones. The truth is that the current institutions were created, so that humanity gets stuck in the defensive economy stage so talking of progressing through the development stages is a remote notion. A few countries gathered together and decided to get everyone pinned in the defensive stages and therefore created institutions and laws that see that this is the case. Most current institutions were created just after the Second World War to trigger the move away from the defensive stage. Wars were meant to be the trigger and push to move away from the defensive stage. The trauma of witnessing war and the effects of war temporarily provided the platform for mankind to initiate the move away from the defensive economy but the institutions that were created after were meant to see that we remain in the defensive stages. Mankind has been going in circles. At the beginning of the journey, mankind took the correct path away from wars after wasting scarce financial resources on weapons. Wars would give mankind an opportunity of learning from his mistake in the process destroying all the things they did not need; weapons. We have had two world wars but after the wars, people would rally and create institutions that start the cycle again instead of choosing institutions that will take mankind toward the next level of development. Missed opportunity after missed opportunity. Let's look at military organizations and institutions. If we look at the North Atlantic Treaty Organization [NATO] although its aims are to protect its members it is there to make sure defense becomes our priority at the expense of other services and activities. Why is that one might ask? NATO is an organization that is there to expand the military capabilities of certain countries, making sure that defense is part and parcel of every government. I am not saying for the members it's a bad idea no, but I am saying it will become difficult if not impossible for any countries that join to move away from defensive economies. All these countries get hooked into the cult of wars and reconstruction. Fear is the most hindrance to development. Countries get hooked to cults that preach wars and make everyone sacrifice huge budget portions towards military and weapons manufacturing. If the cult is functional, then the idea of moving away from defensive stages is remote or far-fetched. So, in short, some institutions and or organizations were created to keep every country on earth hooked on military and weapons manufacturing. The bigger the cult grows the more it sends fear among other countries that in turn out of fear they secretly make weapons that might be viewed as those outlawed. They in turn increase their military budget as a defensive act thereby augmenting the problem instead of solving it. So, in short, military cults like NATO are there to act as a hindrance to progress. Therefore;

*They are there to spread fear that in turn make every other country turn to weapons for comfort.

*They are there to keep every other member of the cult hooked on defense.

*There are there to see that each member country contributes towards military and weapons manufacture.

All the above guarantees that everyone remains in the defensive stages as there cannot be a move if it exists simply because a move will require the destruction and dismantling of this NATO, unless if it evolves and change. So far NATO is nothing more than a military cult that will keep on growing making sure that for a very long-time defense will still be a major part of any economy something I am saying should not be if we are to evolve.

Institutions such as NATO will see the growth of 'closed cults' that are based on certain characteristics as part of membership. That is opposite to the state in the next stage of development.

Can you imagine NATO without the military component? So, if it exists countries will be obsessed with military and weapons that will see even more increased budgets for defense, but I am arguing that defense should be a thing for the past. We should reduce defense budgets.

Outdated?

Yes. These institutions were created after World War II in the 1940s for consolidating military power ensuring that the members of the cults will never be intimidated militarily. Their idea was to consolidate the power and create a platform for pooling resources and make weapons collectively. That means huge and vast military power and a great pool of resources to make a huge stockpile of weapons.

**Guns. Legalize or not?**

This is a subjective topic with differing views on how best to approach this issue but nevertheless, I think it is clear and true also to say that legalizing guns go hand in hand with the democratic state and a just society. Countries where guns are legalized like the US are more democratic and advanced that issues like police harassment and brutality are minimum as compared to countries where guns are illegal to possess. I can say genetic heritage issues play a bigger part in countries where guns are illegal to possess. Police often take the laws of the country into their own hands and abuse in broad daylight and more often get away with what would naturally be regarded as police harassment and brutality. A gun is a tool, a weapon, and a teacher in itself as well on how to behave. Imagine you are in a position of trust and you abuse someone unknowingly and a gun is pointed at you surely next time you will think twice of repeating the same mistake. It is a different situation also where there are no guns or other weapons, we find police abusing citizens something you would not see, say in the US where gun possession is legal. I say possessions of guns models the behavior of the society and more often removes situations of police harassment and brutality. I think societies that favor gun possessions are better on resource utilization as well. Some poverty today is linked to time and money wasted on those in the authority where they ended up babysitting the whole population simply because they can when homelessness and poverty is an issue. In societies where gun possession is legalized these societies often are more productive as the special time and resources are not wasted on issues that can fall under harassment and brutality. Where guns are illegal often, the police have nothing to do that, they end up doing nanny's jobs instead of being put in the line of fire. When poverty is an issue no matter how rich the top leaders are or how much they feast on state banquets, the lowest man at the bottom detects the lines that must be followed. Countries or societies like these are regarded as unjust and undemocratic and more often corrupt. The level of development of a society goes hand in hand with its views on gun possession. The less the restrictions the more advanced the society is. This is true. Look at countries like the US guns are everywhere and this sends a strong message as well as mess-about-abuse others and be taught a lesson. The law enforcers know this, and they will try to do what is best in the situation for everyone knowing that they can be killed at any time. The fear of death can also model not just the common man or woman but can command dedication and one's worthiness to the job. I am not saying that law enforcers don't get shot out of the blue, but I am saying that silly cases of harassment and brutality are scarce or non-existent. It also produces better law enforcers in that they are vigilant as well and would not waste time on trivial things. Where there is nothing to do, we find law enforcers taking jobs like baby-sitting that would otherwise be done by social workers, etc. These law enforcers also end up using dirty tricks like torturing people secretly then taunt them knowing that less or nothing can be done to them. Surely that would be a different case if gun possession was legalized. So, I am saying that cases of torture are prevalent in countries with restricted gun laws like the UK than the US. Torture and restricted gun laws go hand in hand. The more the chances of revenge attacks the better law enforcers become. The odds of fair play are leveled, and the situation is much fairer that in the end situations are addressed in a more democratic way than in situations where power is one-sided. Everyone needs to protect themselves. I have emphasized in this book that the first rule is the right to life and to defend yourself the rest follows from this. Self-defense is paramount and the gun laws show the status and advancement of the society. To achieve the level of development I am talking about requires freedom to protect oneself as well, and that includes freeing up gun laws so that each person has a right to defend himself or herself. I believe evil can only breed evil. They say guns don't kill people, but people kill people that is very true in that the level of advancement the people are in, the more the understanding and reactions they will have towards gun possession. In a democratic society, guns should and MUST be legalized. Whenever guns are outlawed such societies are often corrupt, undemocratic and very abusive that outlaws of guns help those in authority to create a hostile environment for everyone knowing that nothing can be done to them. There is systematic abuse of human rights and torture is not just common but the norm. Torture is used to command and bully people in broad daylight simply because nothing can be done. If everyone had access to guns surely the picture would be very different. Countries that out-laws guns are undemocratic more often corrupt with only a few rich with the license to own one. Those in power are often corrupt and they damn know that if they were to legalize guns, surely it will be a matter of time before they are gunned down themselves. They are so bad they know legalizing guns will be like signing your own death certificate. So, I know you might be asking yourself; if gun laws can demonstrate how democratic a country is? The answer is that it's true. The more advanced the country the better the understanding that sometimes law enforcers are the greatest threat to self-preservation. Even in countries with strict guns laws, some can manage to break the laws and when that does happen that society often changes for nearly two years after the incident when the event is still fresh in the people's minds and after that, the people tend to go back to their abusive state until another reminder. This is true that after shooting of some of the law enforcers the others tend to change and become more cautious that reduces cases of police harassment and brutality first as they know everyday conflicts one day will result in a tragic loss and human instincts kicks in as they spend time on the more urgent needs. Secondly, they tend to deal with serious crimes as gun crime becomes rampant with copycat's shootings. That produces and models' men and women who are better at their jobs and who are alert knowing that every day they wake up to go to work they might not come back home. Every day is a better day, and, in the end, they become better people. Resources are saved and used where they are needed. If they demand better salaries surely people are better prepared to listen rather than in situations where they waste time on trivial matters just for the sake of overtime. Better be having highly paid personnel who work shorter times but then again, I guess this is the curse of the civil servant. Governments don't pay enough wages to compete with the private sector so more often they have to do overtime to make ends meet. So, does that mean more guns among the people the more democratic a nation is? I think the police would be happy if guns are outlawed but everyone else would rather own one. Firstly, most tend to be babysitters instead of the highest caliber we can get. Bureaucracy and corruption not mentioning police harassment as well. I know this is a topic not often talked about, but this is common. Yes, just like everyone else the police can literally harass you, breach all your rights to privacy and more often put you at risk. Where there are no guns, harassment is high. They might not see that, but harassment can come from law enforcers as well and where there is no risk to them, they can abuse you. It's like a bully when he has too much power, he can abuse fearing nothing but imagine when there is a real danger to his or her life too, then the confrontations become less frequent as well. Usually, there is the showing of respect treating you like a human being and not like an animal. It's just natural instincts and the way things are. The more corrupt the officers are the more they are gun-downed as well in the end that acts like a character modeling tool. In the end, you have better officers as the 'chaffs' or the dirty ones are wiped out. I think every part of life must play fair. Legalize the guns there are so many advantages in the end you have a more democratic society with the officers upholding the rule and not putting things into their own hands and the local people avoiding crime as well knowing that they can also be taken out. You will have the best in the end with all the bad ones wanked out. A reduced salary bill with the option of increasing wages as well as they work hard to do what is right knowing there can be serious consequences.

Fewer complaints of harassment and brutality better public relations. Better officers who value the life of others simply because they know theirs is at risk as well. I think most do what they do, harassing and abusing simply because they have nothing to do. No guns the society is good as dead. Imagine reading a novel like that where you know exactly what is happening the next hundred days. Imagine sitting on your desk with nothing to do you end up stirring people to harass others so that you have something to do. You end up babysitting a fully grown-up man or woman who is in a better position than you. Firstly, because no matter what you do and feel about yourself you are a civil servant. That means a burger on government handouts. The only thing you are still hanging in there is the promise of a good government pension with all those benefits it's so tempting. Please! Who wants a good life when you are all wrinkly? Everything you have is handouts, the uniform, the car, the house for some I mean everything is just handouts. In most cases education is up to GCE O levels no matter we have many burgers and people who are homeless you steal what is supposed to be theirs and what can one learn from you apart from what is torture? The more the law enforcement the more the homelessness and the poverty simply because these provide work for them. It's like a pyramid. The bottom part must be larger than that above it. So, what are you saying? There is a need for a change in perspective. A country is judged by the number of people at the bottom rather than the number of people living lavishly at the top. The more the number at the bottom the more the outcries from everywhere. Look at the UK-UN poverty report. OK no one gives a damn about the poor people simply because they will always be there but that can also dictate the level of development in that this high light imbalances and inequalities and more often corruption and abuse. Neglect and inadequate government policies to deal with such issues or more often the use of hunger and poverty to command the people and as a driver of the immigration policies. The more the poor local people are the more the outcries the more the hostile environment for the foreigners and the more the poor are used as weapons to drive the party's agenda against the foreigners. So, is it a surprise that the last three years have been probably the worse regarding the treatment of foreigners? Serious cases of a hostile environment have been reported with even the High Court cases being noted done. So, humans can be used as weapons, as guns too to fight a cause. So, does my notion as regard-to real guns the same as to 'human guns'? I think it will be fair to say that yes human guns should be part and parcel of the fabric of any party movement, but humans have feelings and rights. If it is a tactic to drive people out, then maybe for a certain period that can be accepted especially in the light that for example Britain is coming out of the EU. What is and MUST not be allowed is a continuous abuse of power that lasts for years in cases like these I think it will be fair to raise lack of empathy-motivated policies that are there to create a slave-master relationship. I think everyone involved should be tried and MUST be brought to justice as accessories to an aggravated lack of empathy-motivated abuse to foreigners for years and not used as tactic weapons to achieve political agendas but used to inflict continuous suffering and degrading treatment. In most cases torture is used and all the people just like the Nazi doctor trials all be brought to justice. Make no mistake these people will tell you that they were doing everything in the interest of the victims this is the same thing the Nazi doctors said. Helping the Jews. This is exactly what Hitler might have said to the Jews. I am helping you: before murdering all. So, read between the lines. These people do not do anything for anyone. They rather take the little you have than help you. It's keeping close to your friends and even closer to your enemies. I think new laws must be written to impose the strictest punishments simply because this is synonymous with slavery. These people have no idea what slavery is and how bad situations like these are. It is through strict punishments that all involve death that people will see the real evil of such acts in the name of doing 'our jobs'. I know I said guns should be legalized but if guns are used on kids and women, then that is a different issue. Shop owners might like the sound of owning a gun for protection just like businessmen and politicians so each case must be looked at on its own merits. I often get people to tell me that sometimes they do bad things to people in order to feel bad later about themselves and then end up helping. This is inferior thinking that lacks the empathy to understand the emotional scars that are imprinted on people's lives due to abuse. You can tell me that you abuse someone for nearly twenty years so that you help that person. Think about the damage you have done in say seventeen years. One could have raised a child and by now the child would have legally become say eighteen and an adult by law. There is no excuse for such treatment and time must be considered and in cases like this any value of the cat of helping is overridden by the scars of abuse and this amounts to abuse only punishable by death. Often this is systemized and institutionalized in that the government apparatus is rotated with new people brought in at every interval to them they have been around for a few years but for the victim, it's decades of abuse. Strict harsh laws to put an end to this through our laws and courts as a deterrent. We want a world where everyone draws a line. A society when people know when to stop. If they can't then they must be stopped. This should be mutual. There are no buts when it comes to cases like these. Be very strict and send shock waves to send a clear message so that everyone understands what is at stake and what their duties are. We don't want institutionalized abuse and where cases can be proven to be real, then the 'I swear by the assassin' to do a great job applies here. No remorse sends a clear message.

Isn't it a contradiction?

I know all along I have been arguing that the level of societal development is measured by its gun laws which seems like a contradiction as you would expect an advanced society without guns at all. In theory yes this is the ideal situation when we are all friends and killing each other so remote than no one bothers about weapons. Yes, we will achieve that. What I have noticed is that all these countries that outlawed guns and the death penalty are no angels at all and in such societies corruption and abuse is prevalent in most cases at the top the only difference is that this is driven and done underground with the countries involved secretly making advanced weapons that are not dictated that are used to torture, punish and kill. So, there are guns but mostly in the hands of the authorities only who operate these illegally to torture and cause suffering before killing that person the same thing that the death penalty does only that the suffering is over months or years instead of a few minutes but killing is killing. I will look at the death penalty below but here I will point out that countries without the death penalty are often worse than those with.

## The Death Penalty.

The death penalty can act as a hindrance to committing a crime. It acts as a deterrent to a crime. That being there is a deterrent to committing a crime punishable by death. It is being there that is a real educator that certain crimes can only result in death. The people make well-informed choices as they know everything. I am not saying that all the killings or crimes that will result in death can be logically explained but I am saying that the people committing these crimes are in a better position as they know this would result in death. In countries, without a death penalty, there are ill-informed moves that can happen simply because the person had no idea about the consequences. People might be tricked as well into slavery or committing a crime, etc. I found out that countries with express death penalties tend to be fair in their dealings with the whole issue than countries without a death penalty. I think there is justice to some extent because everything is transparent. Countries without the death penalty have a secret or hidden death penalty and as you will see later these countries end up tricking, manipulating, blackmailing and abusing the people. It's obvious every country has a death penalty the only difference being that some countries have it as part of the system and as a law whereas others tend to let you do them a favor to be spared or given some years. I think in these countries they have what I will call as protection here. To explain the difference, I will explain the first and obvious death penalty practiced in countries like the US. If someone commits a crime punishable by death, he or she will go through the whole process of trial, etc. until he or she is given a death sentence after the trial and a date probably set. Then he or she will be on death row until the date has been confirmed when she or he will die. It's straight forward. I am not going to discuss whether this is fair or not here maybe later. The second situation is practiced in countries without an expressed death sentence but nevertheless has a 'death sentence'. In countries like the UK if one commits a crime he or she goes through the whole process until he is given a life custodial where he or she will spend the rest of life in prison. But there are other cases which I will refer to as protection. First, I will explain what is called initiation for you to understand this. Initiation is a practice of achieving a certain level in life and entering another level or joining a cult or established body with its own laws. To enter this cult or manhood the person must perform a ceremonial activity that shows he has moved to another level or achieved a certain level in life. Normally if joining a cult, the person is expected to perform a task that will show his or her commitment to the cult and as insurance for example he or she will do something that shows that he is wholly committed to the cause of the cult or group. More often whatever he is asked to do is often illegal in other words he has to surrender himself in exchange for membership of the cult. In normal circumstances, very few people would jeopardize their life forever for joining a cult, etc. It's just plain insane to lose your life forever for something that lasts a few days, weeks, years, etc. So, in most cases, people often refuse because logic always prevails. What often happens now is the fact that people are often tricked with the information withheld not being told every bit until later. A very classic example is the mis-sold Payment Protection Insurance [PPI] issue.

**PPI mis-sold issue and slavery and its relevance here.**

If you want to start a business or raise capital, you can do so by selling shares to shareholders who will buy the shares for a dividend later. Or you can borrow the money and pay back the money with interest rates. No one will just give you the money to use and make more and then return with no interest even your relatives will expect some interests as well. But some centuries ago some wise man realized that raising capital for a business was the most difficult thing to do as everyone will want something in return. So, they realized that the only cheaper way to raise capital was to take and use people without paying them and by force or trickery whatever method was successful. That started the slave trade. Get by trickery or force sell or borrow in return for a price and make a fortune. When you have made a lot, then admit you were wrong only after you have made a lot of gains in terms of profit but never pay compensation to the slaves themselves but to slave owners who contributed. Even to them take back also the compensation by offering them even higher loans that will keep them indebted to you. It worked we had slave masters striving with cheap free labor. When they had made a kill, then abandon the whole thing but only after making a profit. This is as far back in the seventeen centuries. Then come years later we have banks sitting down looking for a cheaper method of raising capital without paying any dividends. They searched everywhere and everyone wanted something back. They then decided to trick and misrepresent the facts in order to raise the money. They started selling what is referred to as PPI. Wait a minute this has roots in the slave trade? I will take you back to the 1840s. According to an article in the New York Times, Newyork life, which was an insurance firm opened firms in lower Manhattan in spring 1845. That year business was very low until the following year 1846 when it started offering slaves protection insurance before that slaves were only valued when alive once dead then they were useless, but the New York Life realized that they could make a score by selling slaves protection insurance. This insurance meant that slave owners would claim as much as three-quarters of the value of the policy if a slave died. To the New York Life, this was a new way of raising more money as the insurance premium that lasted a lifelong of the slaves. Over the years they had managed to secure a huge capital base and with the money either offered loans or invested the money. So what was happening was that in the event of death or when a slave was about to die the New York Life would offer the slave owner more loans or insurances so that in the event of death they won't be able to pay out the insurance and if they did the loan or new insurance would recoup back the paid out insurance payout. That way the funds once theirs remained with them. So, this was a big business model and with the vast base of insurance premiums then invested the money to make more money as the slave premiums were paid throughout the life of the slaves and this could be years and a guaranteed way of raising money.

Come 1847 a one James De Peyster Ogden, now the President of New York Life Insurance denounced the system as evil but only after they had accumulated vast amounts of wealth. Despite his criticism of slavery in 1847 slave insurance accounted for a third of most of the firms including this New York Life Insurance. That was far back in 1847 now just a few decades ago we see banks using the same tactics to raise money to lend out as loans. So, they decided to lie that we needed the insurance policies to cover you if you can't pay due to unemployment or sickness. So, they collected monthly premiums over several years and used the money to lend as loans making more interests on top of that. Once that person who has taken the PPI is out of work then and then can he or she realizes that the PPI is worthless as the banks will simply tell you that the insurance does not cover the monthly premiums. To make things worse, they take months deciding whether the PPI would cover for the monthly repayments by then your unpaid monthly repayments would have soared greatly. When you are about to complain that the PPI was mis-sold you are offered a loan to use to settle the mounting debt. Most of you will be amateurs and you will see this as a solution yes but only short-term until they started taking double payments for the credit card and the loan itself, within a few months you will be in a worse position with now triple the debt. Once you are in debt, the banks will proudly announce that the PPI was mis-sold and as such you are due a refund. You smile and for months you start breathing sighs of relief. You see a lifeline but wait for them. Just after they proudly announce that they are going to refund you the PPI premiums which they publicly apologized for taking these from you they then send you another letter with what they call the offset rule. By this time they will have taken most of the loan they had offered you to keep you quiet so that you can't complain about the PPI and on top of that they would tell you that they will keep the compensation as you are now triple in debt. The time you realize that you have been tricked and abused it will be too late. They had already made deals with the government most of whom themselves former masters of slavery. They have been there, and they have done it nothing you can tell them. You are now technically a slave to debt and the banks will pass you over to the government then you find you are now under another kind of protection more like the death row. Unaware the government has already made deals with doctors and hospitals and in the end, you end up with a remotely operated cyber high-tech device they use to torture you until you die. I will explain this other protection in more detail below. So, you are being a victim you end up on the government's death row being tortured red to become part of the Islamic State of Iraq and Syria [ISIS] or the 9/11 crew. But wait a minute; aren't you a victim in the first place? Let's look again. The banks have tricked you to offer them monthly payments which they have used to loan-out to make more money. The day you lose your job or fall sick that's when you discovered that the banks have tricked you. The PPI can't and will not cover your monthly premiums. So, the banks tricked you, lied about the value of the PPI only to find out that the value was inflated, and the PPI is worth nothing. All alone you were very happy that you had nothing to worry about as you were covered until the day of the truth. You feel tricked, conned and lied to but worse you are now trapped. You are now worse because you will have accepted the loan in the hope to reduce mounting debt. At the same time accepting this loan closes any chances of you receiving compensation for the lies and trickery unless if you acted fast to write the loan off. This could have been through a Debt Relief Order etc. and if you were lucky or educated enough to see the trick, you might still be in a chance of seeing justice. So, what I am saying is that although the example involves just PPI in some countries without the death penalty, the same is happening under the name of protection to put you on death row and make you a slave of the government forever. The question I am going to ask you is this: Is this just? Some countries use this kind of trickery to control the population especially that of foreigners or ethnic minorities so that they can't contest in leadership roles. So technically the government deliberately trick their people into slavery through debt and control them forever and manipulate them to carry out their agendas some of which fall into terrorist activities. So, if I say the death penalty to most it's this legal thing but it can also mean being a slave forever on death row. In situations like this, you are tortured to commit a crime or a terrorist activity as a way of the death penalty that is a way for you to die. They offer you a situation to die that way in style if you like but nevertheless still on death row. I investigated the 9/11 attacks something just did not seem right. Whatever happened was so complicated and benefited only the most powerful people who controlled businesses rather than the terrorists themselves. Even though it's impossible to apply logic to reasons terrorists or murderers, operate I think there was more to it than meets the eye. In some countries, they have what they call protection. Just like the PPI, the governments want people to fight their cause and most people would simply refuse because it's more like committing suicide and against the first rule to self -preserve at any cost. Just like the PPI case above the government must come up with a way of trapping the people so that they end up doing their work against their will more often being tortured to do so. In most cases, these governments are making illegal bio-engineered or digital viruses they then use as on these people making them lab rats. Would you be surprised to find out that five of the five hijackers of Flight 11 had been trapped one-way or the other and possibly tortured into carrying out the 9/11 attacks? So, there is a kind of protection that recruits people to be on death row. In the UK I think this is common simply because there is no death penalty. Those found in breach are offered this kind of protection or tricked into this protection where you are on death row, but you are asked to perform certain roles as an 'end to your life'. To clarify this, I will explain that a long time ago people who were to be killed after being found guilty would be paraded and asked to put on a show before death as they will be taken to a stadium-like where people pay money to witness their death by hanging. They would be asked to perform or act like film stars and show courage to entertain the paying-crowd before being killed. We find this kind of situation too as people after given what is called protection are offered some freedoms while still on death row until a day, they would be asked to carry out an act in which they would die. Ever wondered why in all terrorist attacks there was a pseudo-team rehearing when the actual attack happened? This is the basis in that in all times the people on death row are told to rehearse the events to prepare for the day they would die. Remember these people are not in prison no they are tricked into committing an act which they are told through sophisticated gadgets that they will be killed and are offered options like to carry out the 9/11 attacks as a way-out from torture. The victims are fitted or were fitted at birth with a sophisticated high-tech cyber device that is remotely operated and can be remotely loaded. These people tend to attack through being tricked into crime through misrepresentations and mis-spelling as in PPI causing them to be indebted forever and tortured so bad that in the end, they will choose to obey as a way-out of torture. So, if a country claims not to have a death penalty don't take that for granted instead check or ask what the equivalent to the death penalty is, they have. In most cases, they have this protection. In most cases it's abuse, and people are tricked into debt by the government in that they are automatically placed on death row without them knowing this. In most recent cases the governments and the banks have linked. Banks offer loans without the people even applying for the loans and just a human instinct few would refuse that in the end they are cornered just like with the PPI example above where they hoped the PPI would cover them then the banks play delaying tactics until the debt accumulates through missed payments charges. When the debt has mounted rapidly, the person is bombarded with calls from the bank and threatened until he takes the loan not knowing that is an even bigger mistake. The bank then knowing that the person is hooked into debt then sells the debt to the government. The government has its own players that include the doctors and the hospitals who play a greater role to implant devices on you and all your family as you are now government property or government slaves. You are then given serial numbers and linked to GPS. You are now officially on the government's death row. Through Cyber-attacks you are remotely tortured so that you end up fighting alongside ISIS once you do this the government will have won. Now they have a publicly accepted reason for monitoring you. They will simply say to protect their people and borders against people like you and ISIS and everyone cheers and claps hands. But is that the truth? You went to fight ISIS simply because you are being tortured and only ISIS understands what you are going through. To the government, it's a win-win situation. You end up giving them reasons to monitor you breaching every law on earth and everyone exonerates them, but they are the culprits. They have used tricks to get you indebted to them. They have used torture no matter how concealed the devices can be to force you to act. Torture is breaking all international laws, but they don't care simply because you can't prove it. If you say they are torturing, you then they will simply say call a shrink he is hallucinating unless if you can prove that for sure they have implanted the device then there is no other way. They are that good and you will be fighting against the goads unless if you are very smart and can play their game too. I have seen in other life empires falling simply because of a piece of evidence that is beyond a reasonable doubt that they are evil. The onus is on your part to prove that this is not a mere hallucination but a matter of fact. So, countries without a death penalty have other forms of death penalties and often even more dirty with trickery and blackmailing being the norms. So, this protection is a way of controlling the population so that they don't pose a risk or become a threat. The protection is to class everyone as insane especially of a certain group of people say people of color to restrict the number of people of color people who end up in meaningful roles and above all so that there can never be a person of color say President or Prime Minister. Simply how can there be when they are all classed as insanely crazy or lunatics? So again, what is protection and who are they protecting? This kind of protection is what I call slow genocide yes, it's protection but protection for the leading class. It's protection against dilution of the leading class's genes. It's protection for the leading class against the ethnics who might one day challenge their leadership or contest in the leadership contest. It's protection to keep the status core by slowly eliminating the leadership of the ethnics by branding them as unfit to be citizens by classifying them as crazy. This automatically disqualifies them from a lot of the things that require 'those of sound mind' as a law requirement and that includes prominent jobs in government offices, some leadership roles, in the judiciary, etc. and certain status that will make them remain in the country forever. But is that all? The truth is that everyone born here to a foreign or ethnic parent is illegal hacked to death and as such will become a security threat if or she lives the country because it is a matter of time before someone shouts slavery and put an end to all this. So, in exchange for the limited freedom where those delegated monitors and tell you when you make love or eat abuse you through the high-tech gadget breaking every law on earth keeping you on death row until they kill you. The device is used to make you show signs of aging very fast than what is normal. Generally, on average men die after seventy-five years while women even later maybe eighty years old. Among those with this protection they start aging in their late forties or early fifties when in fact if it's a man he will be halfway through his life. So how come? It's obvious that they are tampering with those on protection. It makes sense simply because those on protection are on death row anywhere so why not make the process faster as well? We see radiation being used literally to burn out all the blackness in all you to leave white and gray hairs everywhere. We see the device being used to make people wrinkling so unnatural you will notice that is something is wrong turning even their own people look like zombies. Is this right and justified? You tell me.

# CHAPTER FIVE

## EVIL REGIMES AND EMPIRES.

To understand the issues discussed in this chapter, I think you need to understand the New World. The New World is totally different from the world we know today. The New World is a stage in mankind's development where humanity has greatly evolved to such an extent that it will be automatic to know what it means to be in this New World. Over the past centuries, nature or a certain force has created a few people among us who are there to guide everyone through the correct path. When everyone was taking shortcuts that will lead to the destruction of humanity a few sacrificed a lot so that we remain on the correct path. First, let's look at the strategy used by most evil regimes to eliminate, assassinate and dominate the world.

### Family Collapse Strategy

To kill the head of house and groom kids in teaching hospitals and police hands. Evil protection.

I was watching one of the wildlife documentaries when I realized that there are some people who still behave like wild animals. In the documentary, a huge buffalo was with other buffaloes grazing in the open fields when one of the buffaloes suddenly stopped and looked around mouth still. After a careful scanning of the whole place, it started chewing the grass in its mouth but eyes looking everywhere. The huge male buffalo suddenly twitched its face and ears and walked forward looking everywhere. Suddenly a face appeared from nowhere and looked agitated before advancing wobbly. The herd of the buffalo suddenly started running away in the other direction, leaving some standing there making noises. Small figures started appearing from everywhere until a pack of maybe ten wild dogs appeared before surrounding the few buffaloes that still stood there. In a matter of minutes, the huge buffalo bull was surrounded and before it knows it the wild dogs were charging one after the other trying to grab anything it can from the bulls behind. The bull charged one wild dog instantaneously the other wild dogs would make a pass attempting to grab the bull's parts or stomach. In a fraction of a second, the bull would turn to protect its backside before charging only to find the other dogs about to rip off its flesh in a fraction of a second. The more the bullfights the more aggressive and coordinated the wild dogs become that the bull would keep on turn charging the wild dog in front before turning to cover its back and attack. The bull suddenly is beaten as tiredness kicks in and it's only a matter of time before the fast-wild dog grabs its undercarriage before ripping everything off. Then one after the other the wild dogs just grabs flesh and rips it off pulling all the insides at lightning speed. The bull suddenly succumbed but still alive and here and there tries to fight off on its knees but it hints that it has lost the fight that gives the wild dogs energy to rip off flash as fast as possible while the flesh is fresh and the blood still hot. This sees even more energy among the wild dogs as they will not relax that they have made a kill, no they do the opposite intensifying the process now that they can rip parts without running away as before when the bull charged. It's not only that the wild dogs are small yet ferociously hungry eating animals that they try to eat as fast as possible pulling insides and running away from each other before returning within seconds. In a matter of few minutes, the stomach of the bull had disappeared surprisingly the bull was still alive down on the ground. In a ferocious ripping off the flesh that sees the bull's end as it finally dies as limbs are ripped off very fast. The ferociousness of the attack makes you at one-point feel sorry for the bull as it was devoured alive but then again once you realized that its survival of the fittest and the way nature intended then you just have to sigh in relief and accept it as nature's way. After that, I was so curious if this is the way all other animals feed in the world. I checked another documentary. I saw the big cats hunting as a pact, but this time it was like a written script from start to finish. The lions hunted with a leader often a female lion initiating the chase while the others follow. There is stealth, precision calculations and then the chase this lasted a few minutes before the prey is caught and suffocated first through a powerful grip in the neck with paws and the lions weight used to pull the animals to earth. The prey was a huge buffalo easy prey for hungry animals. The funny part is something I have never seen before. Once the leading female lion had its teeth embedded into the buffalo's neck, the buffalo succumbed to the ground lying on its back. It was a matter of time before a male lion arrived grabbing the legs as fast as it can prevent the bull from kicking and fighting. Suddenly something strange happened. The male lion instantly released its bite on the bull's thigh leg and reached between the bulls' legs as it lay upside down kicking the legs into the air. Suddenly the lion started licking the bull's private parts with its tongue and instantly the bull stopped fighting. The lion continued using its tongue before ripping the parts off. The bull made a huge cry of agony before the other lions joined in pulling and tearing, and by this time the bull was probably dead.

Then I watched a leopard skillfully attacking a baboon. Stealthily it crawled hiding by the bushes until it was very close before sprinting very fast and the baboon had no chance and within seconds the baboon's neck was in the leopard's neck breathing its last breath. It drags the baboon up the tree and hides the body there only to find something clinging onto the dead body; a baby baboon. Somehow, I expected the leopard to have dessert first but somehow the animal looked bothered and caring that it started caring for the baby baboon picking it up and cuddling it. I know for sure the leopard did not know or see the baby baboon if it did it probably would have spared the mother baboon. After that, the leopard started looking after the baby baboon. These documentaries made me compare animals with humans with the power to know and understand nature. The big difference being that animals when they kill, they kill for food. In very rare cases where animals kill for fun mostly for food or if threatening as a survival instinct. Even animals know that it is wrong to kill mothers with children or fathers rearing children. The leopard is a classic example. It regretted killing the mother baboon that it ends up looking after the baby baboon itself. This is nature's survival of the fittest, but are we better?

## Protection: Family Collapse Strategy

I have finally concluded that some countries and regimes deliberately kill the head of the house so that they take over his roles grooming his kids who they will use to drive their agendas. Everything is institutionalized and very systematic that the whole fabric of government depends on that, creating jobs for everyone concerned at the expense of the head of the house. I have highlighted the Colony Collapse Studies carried out some centuries ago, namely in 1654. The idea was to reduce threats posed by some breadwinners and to a takeover in order to take the role of the head at the same time creating jobs and weapons in the form of kids to drive their agendas. In 1654 a one Christopher Wren discovered that the society will eventually collapse that it will need to be protected if the dominant males are removed and kept away from society. The young males left would not be able to look after the society as they will need someone to look up to. Once those dominant males are removed the other younger males will not be able to sustain the societal functions in that the younger kids will be like orphans with no one to look after. Once these males are removed, the government or regime in power would step in and create facilities like the Guantanamo Bay camps to house the removed males so that experiments would-be done on them being observed on a daily basis to study them the idea being to weaken them in confinements and cause health issues so that in the end they will accept being tagged and have chips implanted in them at first to help say with exercises so they are told that the devices are to help them since they were in confinement for a long time more often for years. The medical devices implanted will be remotely operated at first used to help them maybe walk or deal with the pains of sitting in cages for years. Once the period of successfully lodging a lawsuit is over say six months from the date, the operation was done, then and there are they tortured, and the device used to carry out experiments causing all kinds of problems. The whole system is coordinated and operated in such a way that for the government and evil regime concerned it's a win-win situation. This is the ultimate way of eliminating any opposition weakening the would-be otherwise challengers. Just like they would weaken dangerous viruses in the laboratory by changing the environment until they are weak to cause any harm. Making sure that it's easy to control everyone with the resultant that the society is weakened by any prominent people the likes of Saddam, Castro, Qaddafi, etc. are eliminated and any threats are kept at bay. The caged males like in the Colony Collapse Studies are caged in transparent cages so that people see it as being okay than if the men were hidden in walled cages out of reach. It's a psychological game; a mind-control tool. No one would complain if the so-called prisoners are in the open-see-through cages than if they were enclosed cages out of reach it's just human nature centuries of research coming into play. This gives the government grounds to experiment on people just like Hitler and the Auschwitz camps but now in the name of protection. The prisoners are weakened like the way they weaken viruses in confinements. In the end, they illegally tag and implant devices to torture and decide when they die. In fact, their fate was decided the day they were brought into these cages; they are on death row now. Like I said this is a win-win situation for the government after the dominant males have been 'castrated' they move to those left behind. The government or the regimes concerned have well-established institutions and people to deal with the whole process. The left children just like the brood will have no one to look after as the dominate male their role model is caged. That's when the teaching hospitals and the police come in. These two take over the duty of the alpha male looking after the kids teaching them and grooming them so that they trust them and, in the years, to come to be used as weapons to drive the agenda of these institutions. So as at an early stage, the teaching hospitals and the police will take over as guardians. They will train their secret language using mirroring methods and sirens as commands signals just like the film director will do with the action boards and the louder speaker. At an early age, they are taught secret usual sign language simply because the idea behind the colony society strategy is to cage the dominant male and put him under the institution's supervision on death row until the day he dies. His children are taken over and given the maximum supervision and simply because their father is caged and under surveillance, they automatically are tagged at birth and this means implanted with all kinds of high-tech gadgets like GPS, etc. breaching all known laws to mankind. They are groomed and remotely their private parts played with through electromagnetic stimulus and are taught through this electromagnetic command and if they refuse are remotely tortured until they obey. These children are later used as bait to trick and treat people who they cannot easily tag or put surveillance on. These kids are like slaves. Born into what I will call virtual slavery where remotely commands and punishment are given. Later these kids must do work to certain levels to earn their freedoms in which they will have some freedom without being nagged all the time. In the end, freedom is something that they will earn rather than be offered to them. These kids are groomed sometimes being used as bait and being put to test drugs like heroin through opium cultivation with the fields belonging to the teaching hospitals. How on earth would the teaching hospital own opium fields? It's like hospitals after donor organs owning children whose body parts will be harvested to close the donor organ gap. It's just dead wrong it's like rearing chickens with the hope of selling the meat it's just plain wrong. Speaking of grooming and the breaking of all international laws. Now that the dominant males are removed, caged, and all tagged the offspring are automatically tagged as well and now the whole society or family will fall under the government institutions like the teaching hospitals and the police who will literally groom and abuse the kids through remote electromagnetic commands. The whole society is under the government's supervision thereby creating jobs for the teaching hospitals who will 'run' every day with high-tech gadgets in the ambulances acting as interpreter translating electromagnetic communications. The government has the whole society and individual families under its umbrella hence the term protected person etc. Okay, the first question that comes to mind is this; is all this legit and legal? The whole thing is done in secrecy remotely through undetected electromagnetic stimulus so it's illegal who would allow GPS devices on humans? It's an advanced stage of slavery so sophisticated and hidden that most will doubt it exists. Those who complain are categorized as insane simply because they can't prove it therefore, they must be crazy or something. Jobs are created to be the daddy of the family with the teaching hospitals and police taking over such responsibilities. But aren't they doing such a wonderful job looking after the neglected and poor members of the society? One might ask. After all, that is what their jobs are supposed to be about. I will address this question below but first; we have seen that if you are a political party in power such a setting would solve all your problems. You will have created jobs for everyone the teaching hospitals and the police, etc. The ambulances can have an alibi of running around every day every two minutes as they did the time, the hospitals were established during the Second World War. Mind you I have pointed out that these institutions like the public health were established in times of emergencies during the Second World War. That war as far as I am concerned ended a long time ago, but the hospitals still must create similar situations to justify the huge budgets. This is an issue which I will later point out that instead of evolving and maybe cutting numbers and operations they have increased year after year despite the tremendous improvements in health. After the Second World War, living standards were poor and people often died from diseases and poor living standards. You can't say 70 years later the same issues are still a problem. This is one of the reasons why I personally think institutions like the public health sector are forced to embark on illegal activities to keep the same level of service as when they were formed. I think this is in direct relation to the rise of digital, biological or high-tech cyber viruses so that the case of emergency is maintained all the time, and this justifies the sirens you hear every minute of the day. I think this is the main reason why we have a rise in terrorists as well to maintain that sense of emergency throughout. I think this is creating a huge fuss with the hospital managers that as I will show later, they are directly linked to all the bad things that have happened in the last 70 years. We have seen hospitals now owning and growing opium used to make heroin. How on earth can a hospital own and operate like a drug dealer? We have people on "protection" carrying out the 9/11 attacks how come? That raises one question, are they linked to public health institutions? Are they tortured and if they refuse then prescribed heroin as a cover is this why they end up as terrorists? Who benefits the most if there is a terrorist attack? Trying to find the motive. Obvious this is perfect for hospitals and public health and those who benefit from insurance. Yes, insurance. It's not just about the budget there is a money element to it. Someone will benefit from all this financially.

## Pension Lump sum and Life Insurance.

Some evil regimes have drawn plans through the health sector to slaughter people to release pension lump sums and life insurances. Once that person is dead the teaching hospitals and the police then take over as guardians in the name of protection looking after the kids and using what they call as the protection to sustain the family in that the family will receive handouts. Most often a certain proportion of the lump sum money is not paid but kept back but the family is not told about this. The family after some time when the finances have run out are then offered 'help' being told where and when to go and get help and this is commanded through sirens and electromagnetic commands remotely operated. That's when this evil protection starts. So, I am saying that some of their own money is taken and kept back and is now used to drive these institutions as they themselves cut deals with insurance companies, etc. in exchange for donations or ghost accounts. In short, this is what happens. The father of the house after working for some years and paid enough pension and life insurance is targeted to an extent that he will end up hacked somehow in the name of protection and somehow ends up dead. The institutions like the teaching hospitals steps in and takes over and over the years through "teaching" groom the kids and the kids are used as bait to lure unsuspecting clients who are targeted and are later hacked as well.

## The pressures of keeping up.

I mentioned earlier that institutions like the public health sector were created during and or after the Second World War and as such, they were created in emergency situations and over the years things have changed. Fewer and fewer people are dying due to diseases as health improves. These institutions despite this must maintain the same level of function and the state of emergency more often for them to justify their existence. This has led to the government and or the institutions to recreate periods in history where we had emergencies to justify these institutions. I will look at my justifications of why the hospitals are, or institutions are the ones behind the worst crimes in history and the rise of terrorism and recent outbreaks of diseases.

## The rise of terrorism.

Terrorism recreates situations similar to war times. Terrorism is the modern-day equivalent of war situations. Like I said the public health institutions were created during emergency times i.e. during the war. Over the last seventy years, there were no major wars. I explained why before the establishment of institutions like NATO and the UN the war cycle was roughly after every twenty to twenty-five years with the First World War in 1914 and the Second World War in 1945 and had things not changed we might have had another Third World War around 1965 but we didn't but only ended up with what is called the Cold war of the 1960s. So, as I explained throughout this book wars were there to give mankind a nudge to move to the next level, but mankind decided to break the next gear, choosing to remain at the same speed. If it wasn't for some institutions established after 1945 the Cold war as we know it might and could have resulted in a Third World War. The public health sector became obsolete as tremendous improvements in health called for new strategies in approach to the whole issue. We could have seen cuts and reductions in numbers over the past seventy years but surprisingly we have seen a rise in budgets and functions of the hospitals and other institutions. This could only mean hospitals taking other roles to directly influence how they will perform in order to justify the ever-growing budget. We saw hospitals now involved in firsthand activities that were and should be distanced from them. We have teaching hospitals acting as film directors linked and to some extent involved in terrorist activities, heroin production and as I shall point clearly later in child grooming and prostitution with the aim of illegally hacking and tagging everyone especially foreigners as a population control tool. The teaching hospitals employ a teaching method referred to as the mirroring strategy. It's a sign-based language with people often passing methods of what happened through repeating exactly what happened or mirroring the target when one is acting as a spy. Will this shock you if you discovered that the major terrorist attacks took place when one body or the other was rehearsing or carrying out a drill in case of an attack. Look at the 9/11 attacks the day the attacks happened the fire crews [I think of station thirteen] were rehearsing on what to do if New York was to be attacked. Northern Vigilance was in progress as part of the North American Aerospace Defense Command [NORAD] military action taking place at the same time the 9/11 attacks were carried out. It is not just in the USA look at 7/7 bombings in the UK we have Visor Consultants carrying out simultaneous bombs at the very time the actual attacks happened. Coincidence or conspiracy? There so many reasons to link all these to the teaching public health institutions. The reason being that these hospitals without any state of emergency will become obsolete as they were created in times of emergencies and very poor health. Terrorism creates emergencies that gives hospitals and the public health sector reasons for existence and justification for huge budgets. Hospitals and public health are the only ones who can carry out directly such coordinated attacks without anyone intercepting. They have the technology to do so and the means as well to command secretly and using GPS monitor and plan the attacks. It all starts with hospitals and doctors. The sheer realization that war was a thing of the past meant obsolete of the public health sector as we know it today. So, whoever was responsible or running this public health had to come up with a plan to recreate war situations but without getting caught.

## The recruitment processes.

The first thing is first, the players must have GPS devices implanted somehow. So, the first task is to get these implanted either to all foreigners at birth or everyone in the name of public health records with the devices viewed as personal computer files storages or medical records. Or known as to what I referred to as a form of protection where people are tricked to do something illegal but then offered a way-out on condition that they must carry out such-and-such a task as a price for certain freedoms. I know one of the 9/11 terrorists was tricked into marrying a fourteen-year-old through arranged married and then blackmailed through torture to carry out the attacks. Two of Flight 11 were illegally hacked and abused by the hospitals and suffered depression with reports that they complained of being tortured but that was ignored. So, the first GPS is vital even though illegal but who cares they are on 'death row' anyway. Hospitals and doctors are the only people capable of doing this. Recall the Guantanamo Bay cages? Prisoners caged for years developing health problems and, in the end, given the devices with GPS functions, etc. first as augmenting devices to help easy things out but without being told the full picture only to find out that they have GPS properties as well but can you prove it?

The second point is the need for high-tech-devices that can be used to command and pass signals. We have software developed to send electromagnetic signals that can be used to communicate and pass information. We all been in the science class with frogs' muscles twitching at the pass of static electricity or just salt, etc. These devices could easily be used as drones and remotely operated. The other is a spying recording device that will help whoever is behind this to listen to voices within a certain radius. That will justify the need for sign language in the form of mirroring, etc. There is a breaking of privacy laws where people are implanted with listening devices and microphones, etc. The fourth point is that implanted devices must be torturing devices. This is to command and punish and terminate one in the end to cover their tracks. These people are perceived as having committed a crime and therefore on 'death row'. Since everything is institutionalized, any complaints will be declared as hallucinations unless there is compelling evidence to suggest otherwise. So, torture is prevalent and often people complaining of being tortured but no one ever wins because the whole thing is institutionalized it's either you are hallucinating or out of your mind. Torture is to command and direct and push people to do what they would not otherwise do if not tortured. One thing you must understand is that in most cases these people are said to have suffered a mental breakdown or considered as being crazy, but they carry out attacks so complicated that no one can dictate or anticipate until maybe years after. The highly advanced and sophisticated FBI, CIA, etc. can't solve some cases yet these were carried out by the so-called 'crazy people'? Please! How crazy can that be if the educated in the FBI and CIA can't anticipate such attacks like 9/11? There must be a highly intelligent power then behind all this if the people were crazy otherwise it does not hold water. Only the public health institutions have the technology and the manpower to do all this.

If you know that a NORAD drill was in place to prevent an activity like that, yet they could not anticipate such acts how crazy were these people? Had they suffered a mental breakdown or what and what kind of mental breakdown was that that would brighten their brain not to be stopped hijacking four planes. The truth is that some institutions which are more powerful than the cavemen of Al Qaeda surely are the ones behind this is. The real question is this; Is it the public health itself?

The ambulance acts like the ambulances during a racehorse racing. I once told my friend that everything about horse racing is jinxed. He asked how can that be? I said the horses are chipped and the ambulance you see running beside it is choosing which horse is to win through some sophisticated implanted gadget or diodes that are remotely controlled. He said no way the ambulance is there in case the horse falls and the riders are injured. Okay, maybe but there are two sides of a coin would you agree I asked. Obvious he replied but no jinxing here that I can tell you. He added.

I could not prove it that the ambulances are there for more than if the horse falls or someone else is injured. The ambulances are part of the public health institutions. They must play a new role in society recall that I said the war was their driver and the sole reason for their existence. After the 1960s after the expected war resulted in only a Cold war hospital and the public health had to assume new roles to be viable and justify the huge budgets. They become assassins. Yes, assassins! You read correctly. Selecting which head of the house would die so that they become the breadwinner of the orphaned kids whom they groom. They teach them how to identify which horse is to win say through colors of the horse rider mainly matching either the ambulance colors or the police etc. The ambulance running next to the horses is to pick which one is to win through dirty tricks tampering with the horse's system using remote-controlled gadgets to control energy levels and speed etc. using torture to affect performance so that they generate money for the orphans under its so-called protection. So, the public health has assumed new roles of being the breadwinners after eliminating the father of the house. When the father of the house dies, there is instant pension or insurance lump sums released. So, fortune favors those who have learned and understood the teachings of these institutions. For most, they can't be asked because everything is forced on them having been 'raped by the doctors' in the first place who implanted gadgets in them without their knowledge only to find out when the medical time period to launch a case against them has expired. These doctors are very clever in that they wait for the first six months without you noticing that you have been violated as you will still have legal rights to sue the hospital or doctors concerned. After the time frame has expired, that's when things get bad. You are tortured so for most they don't listen simply because the whole issue is unjust. For the few who listen they do so at their expense. The more you listen the more the electromagnetic commands and the more the wear and tear that your body might react by aging faster than normal. For them, you are like a chicken being groomed for meat. You might be on the donor list without you knowing it with the outward appearances looking horrible but inside your parts being preserved for the next donor. This protection as you will find out later is a big business with the pension and insurance lump sum money as incentives together with the chance of harvesting donor organs in the end. Like I said this protection is another word for death row so they would rather do with you faster. Speed everything up very fast so that you age faster and be harvested or get disposed of quickly. The more you obey the commands the faster the rate of wear and tear. So, the public institutions assassinate your father and groom you and through torture teach you how to revenge or do the same as a ball-rolling effect to someone else. In the end, you become a groomed assassin as well as in the end you must meet your demise how depends on you. Torture will drive you to kill as revenge for the death of your father too. For the public health concerned it's a win-win situation first they will have killed an innocent man in the first place and take over his family and kids grooming them for years. In the end, they will select a target to fulfill their agendas and ask you to revenge the death of your father torturing you if you deny. So, having this in mind the public health has the resources and technology and the motive and means to recruit and direct terrorists to pursue their agendas.

Imagine the scenes of the 9/11 attacks or the 7/7 bombings. Those were scenes of a war zone something the public health service was created for. Scenes like that justifies its existence and everything it stands for.

## Outbreaks of man-made diseases.

After nearly 70 years after the establishment of institutions like public health surely things have changed since the early days. In the 1940s diseases and health standards were very poor giving the health institutions a lot of work and planning to do. Seventy years later things have changed drastically, and the health of the population has improved drastically as well. Now it's pressure for the public health sector to keep with dwindling numbers of people admitted to hospital, etc. Now the public health sector is upgrading to digital form in order to recreate the scenes of the years when diseases were rampant. We now have $billions of precious money used to get everyone implanted with a high-tech medical device and linked to everyone's medical records, etc. The sad part is that people are now making digital and electromagnetic viruses as well as biological ones in order to create work and give the public health something to do. So, the medieval times when we have outbreaks of diseases like the black death are now recreated and viruses in digital or electromagnetic forms are used to create situations of emergency everything now is digital and the only institutions that would benefit from all this are the public health sector.

So far what I have done is look at the lowest level something you might relate to explain why some regimes and government are regarded as evil. It's the same principle applied at local or house level and expanded to society and then national level and lastly at the global level. These regimes have become masters of killing the head of the household for financial gains and as a way of survival and justification for their existence. So, I looked at the family or house level and then at the society level with the Society Collapse Studies. If 9/11 was a plan to cause society to collapse, it could have been a brilliant plan in that it would have achieved just that with the creation of the Guantanamo cages. The imprisonment without any hope of coming out of the suspected terrorists who are imprisoned against all international laws creating jobs for everyone concerned, the public health who will take over to keep an eye on the family the police who will break all international laws breaching all privacy laws putting on a hostile climate and unlawful surveillance so that they have jobs. At the national level, we have countries robbed of their resources and their inhabitants killed with some driven away from their countries. We have bio-engineered viruses being tested on foreigners. So, it's the same model applied at all levels from individual to global levels with some regimes going everywhere gathering resources to make Weapons of Mass Destruction. Evil hacking has become the norm with most people hacked but without even knowing it. This is done through what is known as medical records but in fact, evil hacking where most of the people are spied on without them knowing that. At the national level, we have people like Saddam Hussein targeted and generation after generations attempt to assassinate him a classic example of the National Collapse strategy in that after the breadwinner is disposed of everyone that remains will be so fearful that they will obey the commands of the evil regime. You end up with puppets in place. The nation is expected to pass over some form of protection fee in terms of oil or other resources, etc. At the global level we have the same strategy being employed to different nations with their leaders eliminated and the countries then become part of the evil regime with people chipped and remotely tortured into submission.

First, before I dive into the main topic of evil regimes first what do we really call evil regimes. What are the characteristics of evil regimes? Is there a straightforward definition of what is an evil regime, or it is subjective and as such it is like beauty which depends on whose point of view? Can some good governments be classified as evil regimes in my eyes simply because I distaste everything about them or there are factors that one can use to classify some governments as evil regimes? I will do justice here and explain in detail what can be classed as evil regimes. I think it is hard to distinguish what is an evil regime and such a definition is universally lacking but I will write points on a scale and if a regime has more than one-point and it is a major issue, then that regime can be classified as evil. But is it not easy first to define what is evil in the first place?

Evil according to the Cambridge Dictionary is someone or a

regime, that is <u>morally</u> <u>bad</u>, <u>cruel</u>, or very <u>unpleasant</u>.

All these are subjective as they depend on who is talking. I think all regimes and governments were evil at one point or the other just subjective as it depends on who was affected. To rise to power, people must be killed simply because no one is going to say OK take it. Some people must be murdered to pave way for a new change some morally, bad, cruel and very unpleasant deeds must be carried out. So evil regimes are defined by the time or length of the acts in question. This can also depend on the degree of extent and whether it's carried out by a single person or is institutionalized. The pattern of occurrence also will help pinpoint evil regimes from others. Are the acts in question systematized and organized with the command given from the top? I think as you will find out later a regime to be defined as evil it has to have intentions of murdering a lot of people now or in the future and to qualify as an evil regime the regime has to oppress some of its own people as well. It will not suffice simply to call a regime as an evil one if it perfectly looks after its own people and oppresses the others. It will be difficult to universally define some regimes, as evil. So, in short, evil regimes are regimes that systematically and for a long time carry out morally, bad, cruel and very unpleasant acts not just to certain people but to their own people as well. I think most of the arguments forwarded for attacking countries like Iraq and Syria are that these regimes are evil because they not only oppress others, they are cruel to their own as well. These regimes are evil because they make Weapons of Mass Destruction and at the same time starve their own people. So, I think we have a working definition. Any regime involved in activities that threaten the survival of humanity at the expense of the general welfare of its own people as well. I will go a step further and explain that evil regimes are regimes that pose a threat to the first rule. The right to life and to self-preserve not just to others but also to its own people.

**The right to life and to self-preserve a clear-cut definition of evil regimes**

I am going to propose a thought that will outright classify all current governments as evil regimes. Throughout this book, I have argued that to move to the next stage of development mankind must understand that life is the sole existence of us here on earth and that there is no heaven. Heaven is the life we make here on earth. It is a stage of development that mankind must thrive to achieve where in the end we will have discovered secrets to longevity and defeated death. It is a life mankind must thrive to achieve. The idea being that death is there to cheat us and is an obstacle to achieving the status of gods who live forever. We must be better than the gods and live forever here on earth in flesh and not spirit so in short, the reason for life is to discover keys to longevity where mankind would never die. In this stage, we all will have achieved great that our self-esteem will be at the highest that we will never die for someone else otherwise that would be a failure. So, what follows the first rule the right to life and self-preserve is the right to self-defend. You come first! It doesn't matter you are the President's bodyguard you have the right to self-preserve and self-defend. So, in that light, I will argue that all the current governments can be classified as evil regimes simply because all they are doing is against the first and second rules. The moment any government allocates a budget to make weapons that will one day conflict with the right to life and to self-preserve that regime will have committed a crime so horrific that it will be easy to classify it as an evil regime. The fact that the President asks people to die for him and the country as they take the oath of enlistment will automatically become a breach of fundamental human rights as this command or request automatically conflicts with the right to life and to self-preserve. So, as you will discover in this book, in the New World no one shall be expected to die for someone let alone a country simple because our goal is to live on earth forever. Our self-esteem will be that high that we won't see any reason why we must die for someone else. So, any command that will put the lives of soldiers at risk of death will not only be illegal but a crime that can get any President to be dragged to court. Express-command to put an end to this through our laws and courts as a deterrent. But what you will find out as you read this book is that everything will fit in place and there won't be contradictions like go to war and then ask them to watch themselves and come back alive. War will put a great risk on any soldier's life experienced or not so that command will not only be illegal but a crime. So, I will put laws to outright make any wars or making of weapons illegal globally so that our best boys and girls won't find themselves in a trap of either obey and die or disobey and still die. I am not saying we can do this the next day, but I am writing manuals that will map the road [our roadmap for the future if you like] from the onset and we shall take each step as it comes as long as we know where we are going. So, for now, to TWO, all governments are evil regimes simply because what they are doing now threatens the existence of mankind. Make weapons all the time, increase military budgets when everyone is trying their best to be friendly. First waste of resources and secondly a time-bomb. In the past, as I explained somehow wars were there to offset everything and start again. After wars all the stockpiles of weapons will have been used and all the secret arsenal, they were making will have been tested one way or the other and we will have witnessed the real impact of wars so for some years we dislike everything regarding wars but our future will have been safeguarded as all weapons will have been destroyed. The problem now is that we are still piling weapons and through cults like NATO threaten everyone else and those who feel threatened one day will try to match the mighty NATO and make a secret WMD to level the game that's when things can get out of hand. This is the main reason why the West goes after the oil-rich nations that can pose a threat to their existence. Don't be tricked this has nothing to do with human rights. Look at the USA with the Guantanamo cages. A sophisticated form of slavery and psychologically tried and tested tricks to make everything transparent; transparent prisons, and everything in the open publicized but still a miscarriage of justice. We have countries that torture people in the name of protection and still get away with it. We have countries robbing the poor of their resources in the name of WMD s and themselves making these WMDs it doesn't matter how concealed the WMDs can be and whether operated remotely or not. Every current government right now can be classified as an evil regime they own nukes but prohibits others owning these killing innocent women and children in the process but nevertheless I will try to look at the current situation and define what can be a working definition given the current circumstances.

First, an evil regime can be pinpointed by the degree and

magnitude of the extent of the atrocity in question. Secondly, the duration of occurrences and thirdly if it oppresses its own people as well as evil in this regard must have no boundaries. I will look at a slightly different but same meaning.

**Axis of evil.**

This phrase was coined by George W Bush after the 2001 attacks. According to Bush evil regimes or axis of evil are regimes that pursue projects that bring mass destruction while neglecting their own people. Whether regimes that pursue WMDs but look after their own people can be classified as such is subjective. This is simply because we know for a fact that countries that made the 'Hiroshima Bomb' while checking its own people can never be classified as evil. So, it's not evil making WMDs and looking after your own as well. I will try for the argument's sake and use this definition. It makes sense in that regimes are pinpointed as evil first by their own people who will then send messages abroad of evil acts at home and when that happens then the world starts scrutinizing that.

So evil regimes are;

"regime arming with missiles and Weapons of Mass Destruction, while starving its citizens."

"… aggressively pursues these weapons and exports terror, while an unelected few repress the Iranian people's hope for freedom."

"This is a regime that has already used poison gas to murder thousands of its own citizens, leaving the bodies of mothers huddled over their dead children."

"States like these and their terrorist allies constitute an axis of evil, arming to threaten the peace of the world."

George W Bush

"State of the Union Address (January 29, 2002)". Millercenter. org. Archived from the original on October 11, 2011.

Why very few developed nations will ever the classified as evil regimes is the fact that most are so developed that they will never starve their own people. They are so advanced that they offer their people all the freedoms they need and thirdly they are so advanced that even though they kill it is so hidden and they use so complicated devices that torture etc. that cannot be detected or proved. This is an interesting point. It's not that they don't mistreat their people because they do, but it is so concealed that no one can prove it. They are that advanced that torture is practiced every day in broad daylight by state officials but simply because no one can prove that so no one can complain even if they do, they are simply classed as insane. On top of that, these developed countries are so clever that they offer what they call protection. This is a clever way of defending themselves by branding everyone who accepts this protection as insane so that they won't succeed if they launch a criminal case against the state institutions. Behind their backs, they are all classed as insane with some characteristics of crooked eyes and other body disfigurements. But is it true that the developed countries can't be classified as evil regimes? So, we are saying it's not just making WMDs it's making these WMDs at the expense of your own people that can make any regime be classed as evil. A look at a recent UN report suggested that Britain was among the few developed countries that had neglected its own people with child poverty rampant. The report estimated that by next year 40% of the children will be in poverty. These figures are just for the children what about the homeless and those in unemployment? It is a fact that the Tories have political agendas that use poverty as a tool to command submission and obedience. They tend to use children as well to drive conservative policies that tend to be eugenics in nature favoring the locals at the expense of the foreigners. The children are used as bait to lure the foreigners who might end up being sent back or worse. So, is it fair just to look at the way it treats its people and class a country as an evil regime based on just that? Maybe like I said the poverty is a strategy to be able to control the population. If it falls as a strategy, then I think it will be unfair just to use that to point it as an evil regime. So, we need to establish the second bit, the making of weapons that threatening the peace of the world. The USA is no better. It has high unemployment rates as well although things have changed, I think this kind of poverty is unavoidable and I would like to think that the treatment of its people is fair it's only that you can't please everyone. I think Britain as a developed country is doing less to help its people with money wasted on state institutions rather than providing for the less fortunate with so complicated state benefits schemes designed to make the less educated even worse. Could the USA and Britain have done better? A UN report suggested that it is the leadership's complacency and denial that is an issue here rather than the poverty itself. Britain has the money and resources but it's the lack of knowledge or caring on the part of the leadership. If this is true, then this can make it be classified as an evil regime simple because we are not going to prove that Britain has the resources and capabilities of making WMDs. The fact that some chips can be used through implantation into human tissue to emit radiation from the satellite's points to the fact that most developed countries have WMDs the only factor to be addressed is whether it is neglecting its people as well to fit this profile. I think the handout system is too complicated and demanding from the less fortunate the very people who really need such support. The fact that doctors can easily hack anyone and get away with that is a troubling issue because such acts are endorsed by the leadership and everything is done to cover up such activities and brand everyone as insane. I think the fact that doctors have so much power than the Prime Minister is a worrying concern, but it's not a surprise if you really know what these doctors can do; torture. They have over the years developed high-tech gadgets they used to pass electromagnetic impulses some of which are harmful causing all kinds of diseases and these can qualify as WMDs. The fact that everyone tries to cover up everything is a worrying fact. I think you might be saying it's unfair to single out Britain. I have reasons to look at the two most important countries in the world. Britain was the sole dominator until the late 1990s, but I think up to this day it is still a powerful nation that still controls other nations even though voluntary. The idea is to look at the most powerful countries and highlight why things are happening the way they are. Are these countries obstacles to world peace? Are they putting their personal agendas at our expense? Are these countries a threat to the world's freedoms? I think it's fair as the role models to closely scrutinize them. They say that one-point Britain was the world's biggest regime and such a title does not come cheap. I think to be fair our definition must be broadened to include other factors as well. We all know that this is the title and requisite used to go to Iraq for war and the same argument used to justify the Syrian war, but I ask you if that is enough a classification and justification?

I think to be fair we need to add other factors to be considered. First, I think it's fittingly here to pinpoint that there are certain laws that fall in the Jus Cogens category and these laws are laws that have universal consensus that any derogation from these is not only an offense and not permitted but a breach of the international law and as such there is a collective judgment in that any countries can gather to deliver justice. Torture is one of these things that is outlawed simply because torture is associated with slavery. Think of torture what comes to your mind? Slaves being tortured against their wills whenever they resist. Torture is a degrading treatment that is associated with barbaric treatments of others and as such, any country that offers the so-called protection as a disguise of practicing torture is dead to me. These countries fall under evil regimes simple because where one is tortured then there are no equal rights at all. Torture takes us back to the days of slavery. Do you think they were human rights in slavery days? Any country still secretly practicing torture is also secretly practicing slavery and torturing people in submission. So, for me, torture in any form as a corrective or not automatically qualifies a country to be an evil regime. It's like when eating food just chewing and spitting all the food without swallowing. So, whenever there is torture there must be some form of slavery and make no mistake this is true with evil regimes, dictatorship or associated with monarchies with absolute power. These things go hand in hand, and we have torture cases against countries like North Korea and the UK and even the USA after the 9/11 attacks.

So far, these attributes qualify any country to be classed as an evil regime.

1.    Making of WMDs with intent to disturb the peace of the world by killing masses of people.

2.    Mistreatment of its own people automatically triggers the evil regime mark.

3.    Use of torture; it doesn't matter through concealed devices as implanted gadgets. Torture is the worst form of barbaric treatment associated with the cruelest regimes that existed on earth

100

during the medieval times.

a.     I will add a fourth point that is linked to torture. Modern-day slavery and colonial tactics to steal and take other people's possession using viruses as weapons to weaken the victims. I think this is something not often highlighted but something I think is prevalent. We still have countries using colonial tactics to hack others and steal their resources, etc. I think this is an issue that has wide implications and the recent case being the Chagos case. We have institutions like the UN and other international courts condemning the treatment of the Chagos people and asking Britain to address the situation and call by-gones be by-gones and rewrite history. The world we are living in is changing. There can never be healing and forgiving if we still stick to the old barbaric practices of yesterday. To move to the next stage, we all ought to be in harmony. We out to be on equal terms. Don't get me wrong I am not saying that we all ought to be the same, but we can compromise for the sake of peace we can be whatever. Our first duty as Tomorrow's World Order is to level the playing filled. If you slap someone's left cheek be prepared to offer your right cheek. Until we have leveled the playing field only then will the reconciliation and restoration start. This is simply human nature. I am not saying if they killed you must kill too but I am saying if that what it takes to start the move to the next stage then be it. The USA as well is still involved in colonial activities through the Guantanamo cages. No matter what happened I think it is still modern-day slavery with people being held without any charges brought against them and indefinitely is a breach of fundamental rights. It's something that will not simply go away. I sympathize with the 9/11 victims, but two wrongs don't make a right. It's this fact that we are going back and forth declaring an end to slavery and it's all forms then reverting when something bad happens. They killed the man behind the 9/11 and these cages should have been closed by now. It's blood on our hands too. OK take this into perspective. The terrorists killed 3000 Americans on 9/11. The USA and Britain killed 500 000 women and children during the Iraq war. Who did more damage? When are we going to put an end to this? Do people have to fight slavery again? What would those who already fought this fight and died say if they were here today? I am not saying it's easy, but we can always start somewhere. The time that has elapsed is of much concern here. We must draw a line and say twenty years of Guantanamo Bay Cages is too much especially the fact that Osama Bin Laden is confirmed as dead.

4. I think it will be fair too here to add evil hacking as an attribute of evil regimes. Hacking is a form of a hostage situation in which people are taken or forced to do something against their will without any chances of their demands being considered by the hacker. No matter what reason is given hacking is as evil as slavery. Hacking make it easy to enslave others, to torture others and to use colonial practice in disguise and concealed away from the public and as such I think stiff punishment to hackers of people. Express-command to put an end to this through our laws and courts as a deterrent. Hacking is a form of slavery in that the hacker's aim is to destroy otherwise healthy and well-functioning activities by tampering with some so that in the end there is a system failure. Aims of any hacker is to change, alter, modify, skip, add or destroy through causing a malfunction. A hacker is as evil as a slave trader, a Hostis Humani Generis. Someone considered as the evil, that humanity has a moral obligation to destroy that person for the sake of mankind. He or she is a threat to the existence of mankind and a threat to the world's peace. So, the big question once again is that which countries are prolific hackers? I think most developed countries hack their people in the name of public health and for some it's beneficial to them. But some countries like Britain hack in the name of eugenics to preserve their own and cause malfunctioning in others considered as unfit to have families or with defects of some kind and the hacking causing more problems and giving these regimes justifications for hacking their people. I have read articles somewhere where in the USA's people of color are hacked to be killed in police custody with the hacking device being used to deliver the lethal blows and the police officer giving the doctors alibis; speaking of the Ghost and the Darkness. In the UK I think it's the same situation but the difference being that the hacked are set up through GPS tracking to be ambushed and killed. How many people die in police custody especially people of color?

How many of these are considered as lunatics? You will notice as we go that hacking is done to keep certain groups from holding certain positions. The hacking device acts like a drone with rotating propellers that are used to shake the body and vibrates shaking one's brain so that that person forgets. Above all hacking is used to block certain activities or neurons so that impulses are not sent to the brain and when that happens a person might skip certain activities. Such people can be categorized as hallucinating unless if they can prove that it's due to some evil person tampering with his or her system. Hacking is used to restrict certain activities so that the hacked unless they can prove otherwise will be automatically be denied certain activities like contesting for the President or Prime Minister's role. So, if a regime or government carry out hacking on all its ethnic people can it not be classed as an evil regime? If someone is hacked, there is no talk of equal rights at all. The relationship is that of master and slave. See why I have added these points. [I think going forward we must bring in the E-laws to safeguard everyone despite genetic heritage. Equal opportunities for all. If people fail it must be because there is better competition. We as a global power we strong believe in competition and the best getting the top job on merit etc. We just want the playing field to be fair.] Regimes that does all these is for their benefits in that they get things freely like free labor, or free resources or even free personal pleasures like sex. The main motive of hacking a person in this case is to feel what that person feels and when they make love you feel their feelings as well. Ever heard of cyber-sex. This is the same thing electromagnetic impulses are shared from the hacked to the hacker. When the hacked is thinking about sex for example the hacker gets arousal as well and in most cases these are people in positions of trust like the doctors and the police and imagine when all your kids are hacked at birth and are monitored and stimulated by people in a position of trust in the name of protection who will monitor the monitors? Speaking of abuse by those in authority. Ever heard some monarchies associated with this kind of abuse where old bastards pay high prices to, he connected through hacking to vulnerable people where they act their fantasies and all these supervised by institutions like the hospitals? So, any country that hacks its population or that of the foreigners in the name of population control or eugenics are evil and needs only one thing to be destroyed. In most cases people are illegally hacked without consent or their knowledge and 'sold' to local institutions who abuse them for years creating jobs for these evil regimes. I have dwelt much on Payment protection Plan in the other chapter but here I would like to point out that all this is using colonial tactics to achieve the same results as that achieved during slavery that is obtaining cheap labor or capital where you don't have to pay any dividends. All you must do is trick someone so that he or she can give you what you can call a starting capital. You collect premiums over several years and with these premiums you lend them to others as a loan. When the person finally loses his or her job, then before she or he realizes that the PPI premiums collected were useless and would not cover the insurance repayments delay first until they are so in debt then you offer them a loan that is had to refuse. The loan will be taken back fast as repayments say for the credit card and the loan itself. The time the person realizes he or she has been duped then apologize and offer to compensate the person. But by now without a job and with restrictions on the account he will be on his or her knees and now the debt would have doubled. Then and then you use the offset rule to keep that compensation as well after having recovered most of the loan back. So, it's a win-win situation to the banks. The person will still owe you more money than before and this time unable to pay. Then make deals with the government who will link with other institutions and the persons doctor and get that person hacked if he is not hacked and put him on death row. Torture him until he is so traumatized that whenever you give him any task, he or she will do it even if it means becoming a terrorist. So, as you can see it is a systematized process that involves a lot of institutions and with orders given from the top for whatever their agendas might be. Population control, immigration or simple eugenics. Such practices are forbidden in the New World simple because they are based on trickery, abuse and slavery. The person was not worrying because as far as he or she knew she was covered even though she only found out there was a PPI after they had already taken a chunk of her money. So, looking at this issue I would say there is mistreatment of his or her own people and as such qualifies him or her to be part of the evil regime. You must look at the whole situation to understand the workings of this system and how evil this can be. A look at the debt alone will put one in the wrong direction the main thing those responsible want everyone to believe.

5. I think I can also add other criteria to be considered that of bullying and using weapons to threaten others. Bullies can be easily classed as evil simply because they are only concerned about themselves and more often employ dirty tactics to take whatever they want usually by threats and force. Bullies see no fair play. If they want resources like oil, they simply engage in a war which is often one-sided and topple the leader of that nation and make the country a puppet country that will siphon resources out of the country to the bully's countries. I think nothing wrong in growing big. I think that is everyone's dream if it's a business grow big and keep growing no one will ever complain. Look at Amazon how big the company has grown. Ever heard anyone saying let's split amazon down into smaller firms? But look at companies like Facebook we can hear people as far back as a few weeks ago calling for Facebook to be split up. It all has to do with the impact it has on the general life of the whole world and the influence it has. I would not call for Facebook to be split up let it grow that is the owner's goal. Freedom to everyone including him too. It's a different story when the decisions of a few powerful people can cause the loss of 500 000 lives women and children. You will understand why later when I pass new laws that women and children are to be treated as princesses and princes. Their lives no matter their genetic heritage matters the most. It will be a law that no command shall be given that will result in the death of women and children needlessly without the command giver dying at the hands of the assassins. I will change the world as we know it today and even impose other laws that will look at acts like this if they have a lack of empathy element meaning it's easy for some to kill other genetic heritage and voice concerns when theirs are killed. Where it can be proved that the assault resulted in deaths of the innocent no matter who gave the command President or Prime Minister

they will be dragged to court. Express-command to put an end to this through our laws and courts as a deterrent. If found guilty then the assassins shall have more power than the Presidents and the Prime Ministers of all other. So, you can easily see why bullies will become a threat to all the rules of the New World. I think to understand my point of view think about gangs as we know them through the 1980s movies. Gangs break all laws so that they survive and become even bigger. Gangs are there to rule by fear, intimidation and threats and mostly often not just empty threats but real acts of terror torturing and killing as well as protecting its members so that no one messes-up with them. This is the way they can survive and grow. Those who fear for their lives and their property join gangs for protection and most paying protection money or being asked to take part in evil acts as part of membership payments and showing commitment to the gang. These gangs spent most of their monies making and buying powerful weapons to terrorize the others and get whatever they want at unfair prices. The attitude is to buy cheaper weapons and use these to terrorize others and get the expensive stuff as good as free. To grow the gang must terrorize everyone so that those who are fearful ends up joining in and paying protection money. So, the more the terror the larger the following and the less the equal rights and fair practices. If the gang exist, there will be all kinds of problems with others making goods only to be hijacked or for these to be stolen at gunpoint. The truth is the same with military cults like NATO. The more the cult grows the more the cries for war. Do you think Britain and the USA would have gone to war in Iraq if they didn't have the backing of NATO? Some countries especially the middle eastern countries might have disapproved vehemently if they knew there was no NATO. So, is NATO bad for the future? Why not start your own as well? I am not against NATO. I understand the reasons behind this cult, but I think when it was established it was needed at the time because people lacked the foresight and knowledge we have today. OK just after the war in 1945 NATO was the only way to survive in case of another world war. NATO sealed off any hopes of mankind moving to other stages. NATO made it easy for mankind to do what he knows best; get stuck in defense and that's it. Spend huge amounts on the military and the rest will follow. Yes, a strategy successful even 2000 years ago. This is what mankind has tried and trusted and the only way to boost any President or Prime Minister. Do you know that the most remembered Presidents or Prime Ministers are those associated with wars? Traumatic events bring out mixed feelings in people. War makes mankind realize that there is more to life than just wars and weapons. It's a divine calling to change automatically after a war and dig a small hole and spit in it and never to look back and only look forward. Every war was a chance to go to the next stage and abandon wars totally, but what happened after the Second World War made it impossible for mankind to ever move away from defensive stages. The leaders of the day created institutions like the UN and NATO so that mankind will never ever make weapons to kill each other instead of all that money being spent on research and development to advance other areas. Okay, we are not doing bad one might suggest but I am saying that we are not working at our optimal levels we could be doing better. What can't be done is combine the two stages into one as they are mutually exclusive events? The ideal situation is to abandon one and move to the next one to avoid competing for resources. You can't make weapons and call everyone your friend and link with everyone otherwise it's just plain wrong. Now you see why it made sense and was easy for the past leaders to remain in the defensive economies and with the help of NATO terrorize others frightening them to buy weapons otherwise they would not have had customers for the weapons. If they had abandoned the defensive stage, they would have probably reverted for fear of surprise attacks. Tomorrow's World Order will level the playing field and put laws in place that will see mankind move away from defensive economies without any fear of surprise attacks. We will put new laws to protect everyone by making weapons production illegal and a crime punishable by death. Simply because it conflicts with the first rule the right to life and to self-preserve.

6. I personally think it won't be doing justice if I address evil regimes without looking at the use of landmines. I think it's an evil barbaric way of claiming land by use of landmines. Landmines cost lives

and disable otherwise healthy able-bodied people. Use of landmines I think is the cruelest form of evil. Innocent people are maimed for no reason at all. Thousands worldwide are hurt by landmines. The sad fact is most people or regimes who use landmines have stolen the land in the first place but want to hold on to the land for years even if it means the suffering of the local people. I have no problem with title deeds and the people's rights to possess land and property. What I think is the real issue to address here is the fact that people still cling to land that was illegally obtained during the colonial era. The courts and other institutions have said that this is not correct, yet we still cling to that land and use landmines to maim and kill. Like I have been arguing all along landmines pose a serious threat and conflicts with the first rule. Landmines destroy lives and not just lives but the life of the innocent civilians of which children accounts for more than 80%. I reiterate here that I will pass laws that will see that no child or woman will be killed recklessly without the culprit being dragged to court. Express-command to put an end to this through our laws and courts as a deterrent. In the New World life is valued to the most and everyone works hard and smart to prolong it. The aim of the next stage is to stop and ban weapons production so that resources are channeled into finding ways to cheat and bit death. Production or manufacture of landmines conflicts with the first rule and as such no one should be left to make any weapons in the form of landmines. Reckless and cruel behavior of certain people still making landmines despite figures showing that thousands of children are maimed, killed and orphaned by landmines. It's shocking that we have at least 110 million landmines in the ground. I think it's a time we ask for change seriously. These cruel people plant landmines at $3-$30 per landmine but to remove these landmines cost between $300-1000 per landmine. Do the math this is just not a coincidence. These people are making money doing business at the expense of women and children. I think if someone does not put on a broad pause this will go for centuries with these people making money at our expense, laughing at your years of sorrows. I am not trying to be arrogant, but these people have been killing at will for years. This is a business. The profit to be made in clearing all these mines are so huge that this fuel the need to make and plant more landmines. Imagine land, beautiful land made worthless for decades and people being killed and maimed for decades too. Who on earth would do such a thing? In most cases the land concerned was stolen probably at gunpoint. Where is justice in there? Imagine coming up with a business plan that makes cheaper products and are easier to plant all you need to do is start a war and then plant all these. Once they are all down cease the war and let the landmines do their magic; killing sadly women and children until this has become a global problem then send the others to clear the mines at exorbitant fees and make a kill. But do you know that they are all part of the cult? Yes, all belong to a cult formed after the Second World War. Even though they seem separate and at loggerheads with each other deep down they work as a group with each division with its own functions and responsibilities but at the end of the day working together for the survival of the cult. This is not a coincidence, but a carefully executed business plan to rob in broad daylight and make a kill. After the Second World War countries gathered together to form NATO, the UN etc. to defend their existence at any cost and to expand no matter what. It's a perfect plan. Imagine even now still producing these things despite their horrific effects. You might have seen the killings and maiming, yet no one gives a damn. This brings me to the main issue here. This is not just about banning the manufacturing and planting of these landmines. Surely this must go even deeper than just putting a ban to landmines. Like I have been arguing throughout this book some crimes have a lack of empathy connotations. What I don't understand is why people don't change or stop despite the worldwide condemnation and the deaths of innocent children and women. I think it points to a cruel and corrupt system. A system that needs correcting and the only way to correct this is to introduce compulsory laws that prohibit the killings of innocent kids who are normally not the same genetic heritage as those planting these devices. My argument being that if the kids were the same color as the planters then surely the planters would have taken extra precautionary measures in dealing with these landmines.

## Cyber Electronic Magnetic Attacks.

This is an area that is new and usually misunderstood or unknown as a few very clever countries have developed new weapons that the rest of the world still don't know about gaining a competitive advantage be it in warfare or in general defense or attack purposes. I personally don't object to any technology and in the New World technology plays a crucial role. In fact, technology will help easy our journey forward. I think if technology is advantageous to the whole humanity then there are no causes of concern but to be honesty how many times new technology is used for the betterment of humanity? In most cases, technology is developed to gain a competitive advantage otherwise who on earth would pour $ billions to help everyone? It's human nature to out-smart everything but if it is to kill others to gain a competitive advantage, then we as TWO we are against such a technology simply because it conflicts with the first rules the rights to life and to self-preserve. In recent years some developed countries have manipulated the cyber and the magnetic field to create and develop weapons they are using not just on enemies but on the local ethnic population as a population control technique and to push their eugenic strategies. I know some might argue that it's for defensive purposes etc. but we have a standard litmus test. Any new technology that conflicts with the first rules are banned. Cyber electromagnetic attacks have become so a reality and a new thing that it is used by a few advanced countries to defend themselves against terrorists as they proclaim which is good, but I pose a question to all you. Who is a terrorist? Do all foreigners who object to your oppressive strategies end up being a terrorist to you? I think like what I have been arguing throughout is that humanity or a few evil people what they are doing is to develop new ways of doing the outlawed or morally wrong things. If we say this is wrong under international law what is happening is that people are investing $ billions to find another new way of doing the same thing we have said is wrong. We ruled that any acts of torture and methods used an example like the five techniques of torture, physical sleep deprivation, unnecessary stress through hooding, white noise, depriving basics like food, water, and wall-standing leaving people in a similar position to cause stress are all illegal.

What is happening is that some clever evil countries are looking for new methods using the technology that will still carry these evil acts but now in disguise. I think for you to understand this I will look at these techniques in a great deal and illustrate how technology has been used to still carry out the forbidden techniques. TWO will be proactive rather than the current system that is reactive leaving loopholes that are exploited as clever governments are using technology to replace old methods but still carry out the same forbidden evils. We as futuristic as we can we will ban any future use of technology to carry out outlawed evil practices. The current governments are advancing in the technology to do the same thing we say are wrong but using sophisticated methods in the hope that they will continue to torture until that new method is discovered and outlawed by then they would have done great damage or gained an illegal competitive advantage. I am saying that some governments are just finding new ways, new methods of doing the banned activities waiting for the new method to be banned or outlawed before looking for another new way of doing the same thing. This is what humanity was doing for the past century and a classic example is that over centuries humanity fought and won a war against biological organisms to an extent that all diseases had been brought under control. That means a win for humanity and institutions like the health sector becoming obsolete despite the huge budget. Then humanity then went to create bio-engineered strains even harder to solve than the original ones and rallied everyone to create antidotes and ways to control this all in the name of fulfilling political agendas and for creating jobs and for institutions like the health sector to have jobs. So, it is the same governments that are encouraging the development of new bio-engineered threats through universities and the private sector. Now we have the same governments channeling $billions making what are called digital threats that manipulate the cyber and electromagnetic field to make weapons and digital biological threats that imitate the original biological organism we have defeated. You can see that we have a problem here. These countries have enough resources that even after we outlawed such practices, they are just going to find a new way of recreating the outlawed way.

**The need to be proactive rather than reactive when dealing with evil.**

Tomorrow's World Order is aware of such evil practices where some evil governments are just looking for new ways of doing the same evil, we said is wrong.

Let's look at the five techniques of torture and I will show you that these countries only developed new disguised hidden methods of doing the same thing.

Torture no matter for what reason is banned and illegal globally and no one will succeed in pledging ignorance to that because it's common international knowledge that it is illegal. First, I will look at the traditional methods of torture as I analyze the five techniques of torture namely these are hooding, wall-standing, sleep deprivation, white noise and use of hunger.

## Hooding.

According to Wikipedia is the placing of a hood over the head of a person in order to cause disorientation, sensory deprivation, isolation and causing great fear. To understand this method, you must understand the main purpose of this method of torture. The idea is to close the eyes imitate blinding that a person who had sight and is instantly blinded can become disoriented and very fearful because it's new to him or her. That puts the person in a state of very fearfulness especially knowing that a person who is your enemy is there. It creates a sense of powerless that is so frightening that a person feels very vulnerable and exposed and above all cheated and treated unfairly because say if you are to die this way you will feel the other person acted cowardly. This technique involves placing a hood over the head usually done during the hanging of people. Hooding also hangs on an idea that makes it easy to disguise the identity of the evil interrogator. So that the person being abused cannot recognize and finger the culprit in the future. Hooding relies on the act of restricting breathing as well as creating anxiety in the victim and great fear. So, the old system is to place a hood usually sack or rug over the head of the victim with the aim;

1.    To restrict sight so that a person can't see who is doing what

to him or her.

2.    The second is to restrict breathing by cutting the amount of air intake and restricting the breathing of a person.

3.    To instill fear in the victim to threaten when he or she is hooded increasing anxiety.

After this method was recognized as illegal and banned under international law the culprits simply developed the technology that recreates the same problems in victims, but the method is not in the open but discreet.

The new technologically advanced method of torture known as hooding.

**Technologically advanced hooding.**

The evils simply developed a new method of doing the same forbidden act of torture called hooding. I explained above that hooding restricts vision so the person can't see what is happening. Secondly, the idea is to restrict breathing cutting supply and constricting the windpipes to achieve the same effects as hooding. The third is to instill fear in that the victim does not know where the evil enemy is exactly so he or she might look or turn around listening to the voice-location position. Technology can and is used to do the same even better than the hooding. A device is planted at birth or a chip fired inside the baby in the name of medical records, or national security. This chip is used through cyber electromagnetic interference together with nerve stimulation where a needle electrode or diode is inserted in the buttocks of the child and together with the chip is used to pull the iris of the eye hiding it in the eye-socket so that even if the eye is open, the victim won't see. This is exactly as the hooding effect. This is remotely done with the operator holding a joystick remotely torturing the victim away where he or she can't be seen or identified. The whole system uses the drone technology where the evil culprits usually doctors or the police torture the victim where they can't be identified as the method relies on cyberspace and electromagnetic field. Fear is greatly induced in the person as the person is attacked without knowing who and where the person is. Considering that the whole developed world has been hacked by their own governments at birth in the name of national security Imagine The whole country being hacked and blinded through these chips?

## White noise.

The reason behind white noise is to cause psychological pain in that the person is driven to extremes by the noise that is continuous that overlaps any other voices or sounds. The idea is a continuous non-stop irritating noise that won't stop until the victim is driven mad. This is often used as a supplement to physical torture. The noise of say a white television is continuously played so that the victim can only hear this noise until he or she is disoriented, scared and psychologically in pain. There is no doubt that this is a method of torture that is banned and illegal in international law. After the international world has ruled this method as illegal what happened was simply to find a new but hidden way of doing the same thing.

## Technologically advanced white noise as a torture method.

Technology has been used to develop hidden yet sophisticated methods. Modern-day advancement in technology meant small devices that can be chipped into humans to secretly record what happens around that person and for certain radius ranges. The devices can be used to record all sounds as well even that person's voice that will be manipulated and faked through sophisticated voice manipulation software to fake conversations or sounds that are replayed that the person might hear his or her own voice making that person think that he or she is hallucinating. But the main issue in relation to white noise is a technique that uses the time-space continuum. Physicists believe that time can be manipulated using satellite geographic positioning so that a place in time can be revisited at a specific Geo-location or position so that another person who is transferred in space and time to that specific Geo-location can experience or hear what was said or heard at that time. This is possible because the transmission of an event to the satellites is delayed by say 2 seconds. What happens at a position is registered on the satellites at a delayed rate of 2 seconds and this can be manipulated and used as a method called the delayed time-space mechanism. This enables say voices recorded at a specific Geo-location with specific satellite coordinates to be revisited back so that the person who is at these coordinates can hear what has happened at that specific point as the device replays the recorded sounds at that specific point.

Okay, I think the best way to describe this is to watch what happens when a plane goes down. The investigators can easily look for the black boxes and replay these and use the satellite coordinates and the flight route to recreate the flight plan at specific geographical coordinates as beamed to the satellite. So, we have the satellite coordinates, the exact points and the black boxes that record exactly what happened. So, the investigators can replay the black boxes at specify satellite flight coordinates and know exactly what happened at specific points during the flight plan. So, these sounds recorded by the black boxes can be played and replayed say at that specific point.

The second aspect is based on the idea of encryption. The reason being that secret message needs to be passed without other third parties hearing the message. The art of hypnosis is used here to pass the messages while a person is asleep. Imagine a message that is passed or whispered in the ear of the victim so that only that person hears the message. The message or voice has reduced decibels no one else can hear it only the victim. Now we have the tools. What happens then is that the voices or conversations at a certain point are recorded and faked and replayed so that only that person can hear the voices in most cases his or her own voice so that this drives the person made as the voices are continuously played. This technology exists and is being used nevertheless discreetly by manipulation and tricking governments.

This carries stiff punishment in the New World as it tampers with the right to life as it can drive one to commit suicides as the disorientation can cause long-term damage. These evil acts must never be tolerated and governments doing this killing mainly ethnics, institutionalizing them and depriving a good quality life must be eliminated. This does not only fall under genocide acts but makes one be regarded as Hostis Humani Generis as the intention is not only to get information but to destroy through genocide as well.

## Sleep deprivation.

Originally the traditional method involves stressing the person so much making sure that the person can't sleep asking the person to do acts that make the person so tired and want to sleep and when he or she is about to sleep is then woken up and the process repeated.

The technologically advanced method involves manipulating the nerve system and through the chips manipulate the electromagnetic field through electromagnetic nerve stimulation remotely operated to stress the person. Shaking the nerves responsible for sleep non-stop that the person would want to sleep, and when he is about to sleep, then scare or stress him especially his private parts so that he or she can't sleep. The process being repeated. We are to make it known that TWO will not just put new laws we are going to ban and deal with countries like these as these evil methods have slavery connotations as they rely on abuse. We will go further to bring a lack of empathy-motivated abuse with no due regard to the life of the minorities in the name of national security or terrorism and protection. The New World can't tolerate such evil disguised or not. We shall be very tough and here there shall be an express-command to put an end to this through our laws and courts as a deterrent. Slavery is something that is a thing of the past any forms that resemble that or achieve the same effects are not just illegal or banned but conflicts with the right to life and not just life but also the quality of life.

## Food and water deprivation.

This is used as a government tool to command the population. You will be shocked that this is institutionalized with commands from the top. The political agenda makes it easy to end up with a situation like that of poverty. Say if it's a pyramid what is happening is that we are having irregular pyramids with a heavy top than the bottom. For example providing more nurses or social workers or police in relation to those who need them at the bottom resulting in a situation where the base is small and has to support large numbers above the pyramid with the end result that policies or torture methods are used; sleep deprivation, hooding and hunger to get people out of work through lateness, poor performances, attendances, accidents as eyes are hooded through the chips etc. to expand the base. Ever heard of the saying; too many chiefs and fewer Indians? This applies here and to make things worse the working hours of the above part of the pyramid are extended through overtime or huge budgets that in the end the government mechanism has to find a way of increasing the base of the pyramid through tight social benefits systems that make is obviously harder to get with the people the benefits are meant for excluded as they fail to meet the criteria. In other words, it's a tactical method of offering benefits or social security then put a very strict or tight method that makes it hard to get those benefits. In other words, it's using food and drink as a torture method.

The new technological advanced method of food and drink deprivation involves the manipulation of nerves through electromagnetic nerve stimulation that can be done remotely. This involves using the chip to stress the stomach say just after eating food so that the stomach moves the food before digestion. Or nerve stimulation to stop movement of the bowels. Or the transfer of hungry feelings but in most cases it involves use of the chip and GPS functions to make sure that person loses jobs or can't get help of any form so that he or she can't get food and is being tortured as well when you eat with continuous nerve stimulation to lose that food that next time you will be afraid to eat for fear of torture. This is where the government tries to blind the international community that there is food and they can only take a horse to the river but can't make the horse drink. Secretly they are using the chips to do what a dog collar does to a dog. Imagine what they can do if that can't be proved that for sure hacking has been done. Then imagine what they can get away with. If they complain the people are further abused by everyone who must justify their jobs and the overtime, etc.

My aim is to show you that technology can and is used secretly to carry out the things we banned and issues the international community has ruled as inhuman or degrading treatment. These countries will never stop but will always find another undetected method of doing the same thing that they were accused of and in most cases publicly denied it. So, what do we do in situations like this where certain governments will starve their people to make even discreet devices that will still carryout outdated and illegal things like modern-day slavery, torture and degrading treatment? Where the government gives protection to abusive doctors and encourage the whole institutions to fight for their jobs, meaning further abuse and cover it up. Where we have unjustified huge budgets that can only mean more staff and to make things worse these institutions in large numbers will depend on an even larger pyramid base. If you have more doctors and nurses than the patients what would normally happen? You end up with the hospitals killing fathers so that they take over and raise these kids through teaching hospitals, so they remain viable. We have hospitals owning heroin or poppy fields and implanting chips they used to torture people through remote nerve stimulation or tampering so that the victims are prescribed their heroin. We have governments putting unpractical measures to increase poverty. Not because there is no money, no. The money is there and there are things in place to deal with that but, the processes are so cumbersome that it is as good as that it's not there. Would you be shocked by the UN report that says nearly 40% of children in some developed countries are in poverty? These are developing nation's standards. The government can also easily deny it, but the truth is that something underneath needs exposing if you are serious about tackling the issue. Some use food and hunger as a weapon to start the ball-rolling technique, so you pass the anger as well. This has a lack of empathy connotations especially against foreigners as a political tool to cause hostility and intimidation as the locals will feel neglected and view their problems as being caused by the foreigners who come to settle in their country. This can result in the locals, breaking in to steal not with the intention to steal but to drive the foreigners away, with other institutions supporting that by not reacting to any calls for help, a hostile environment used as an immigration or even eugenic strategy to conserve their genetic heritage. So, care must be taken in dealing with these issues but no matter what there must never be justification for secret torture or the use of advanced cyber technology for purposes of torture.

I think it's beneficial here to point out a recent article referring to this new feature; cyber electromagnetic attacks. Some very developed countries have shifted from weapons as we know them to new never seen before Weapons of Mass Destruction so small that they can be easily chipped into a human body and operated remotely to cause all kinds of torture and they can get away with that simply because as a new technology there are no laws specific for that technology. I think this is the consensus and something I think is wrong.

## International laws that make the Jus Cogens.

There are laws that are universal or certain aspects of the law even if not laws per se but that are viewed as universal and understood by everyone. There are norms that clarifies what is wrong and what is not wrong. I think it is trickery and the abuse of power by some countries for them to kill first in thousands then create laws that exempt them from past killings but punishes others. My concern here is that even when they committed the crime it was internationally believed that such killing was a crime even though there was no specific law that says so. They knew it was a crime. This is true with the Crime of Aggression laws. I think it's not just unfair but biased to create a law that exempts others and punishes others for even lesser crimes. Having this in mind TWO will remove all these time limits to laws. We shall channel a huge chunk to the courts and end all-time limits and remove all forms of immunity so that we can start afresh even if not for us, then for our children who would be happy that we did this as this will be a platform a new foundation for a better future. If that person is alive or even dead in some cases will be answerable for any crime they committed regardless of when.

Considering this we will put a ban on future technology that simply does the same as we have already said is wrong. Our laws will aim to be proactive and punish severely governments that try to be clever by tricking the world that they are doing no wrong when they are manipulating their policies etc. to still do things, we said are inhumane.

## The future of technology vis-à-vis Cyber-attacks

I think the technology used for defense or advancement of

humanity is not just crucial but important to the development of humanity. I think if it is developed to protect individuals and property it doesn't matter who and as such is a good thing. But I ask you a question and you must be fair to yourself and the world. Who on earth develops a new technology spending $billions on the betterment of humanity?

I strongly believe that all advancements in the technology sector are to give the maker or innovator or the intended clients a competitive advantage over others. This is simply human nature believe it or not. I will quote NATO secretary-general praising Britain in developing and using cyber high technology to defend NATO Allies from ISIS. NATO believes that;

"BRITAIN used hi-tech cyber weapons to halt the flow of foreign fighters to ISIS, the head of NATO has revealed."

Can this technology be used to control the population hindering the flow of foreigners not associated with ISIS? If they can use the technology on ISIS can they use the same method on the ethnics and what can stop them? If they can make these cyber weapons that use the electromagnetic field can they also use the same electromagnetic field to make and carry out the torture methods I mentioned above that use the same principles? What can stop them from doing what I have argued above that it's happening? This is not just to Britain but to the whole international community. I pointed to Britain because it is one of the few countries with the USA and the French taking center stage in all previous wars or invasion proposals with the recent being the Syria attacks.

Another point is regarding gangs or evil cults.

### Evil cults or gangs.

What I said above is happening, this is, the new torture methods above all which manipulates or uses cyberspace and the electromagnetic field and the same principles to make weapons NATO declared Britain used to stop foreigners going to ISIS. Can the presence of NATO making countries like Britain develop torture tools regardless of international laws and torturing people simply because they have the support and backing of NATO who can trigger Article 5 if say other countries decide to oppose this? Is Britain using cyber on just ISIS or also on ethnics to stop them living knowingly that NATO will still jump to their defense even if they are torturing them?

Another issue is regarding the use of force not physical force but the proportion of the response to a threat. Imagine getting a nuclear weapon to deal with a cockroach infestation? I want everyone to understand that responsibility is something that should be incorporated in the New World. It's not just about solving problems and it is also about how you solve that problem. I emphasize this point because we don't want a situation like the current situation where one big country makes all kinds of Weapons of Mass Destruction, nuclear weapons, and the new cyber weapons to rule the world or defend itself. It's not just irresponsible to do that in the New World but a no too. You can't claim to defend the world by creating something that can destroy that very same world. Or create a bomb that will cause the extinction of humanity to defend yourself and your gang or cult from the caveman? Okay everyone has the right to life and to self-preserve but endangering the whole world for the sake of the defense of the 'monster' makes no sense and is not just irresponsible but a strong lack of judgment. Who on earth would be a problem to the monster in Britain, the USA, France, and on top of that NATO? And using Cyber-attacks that can endanger innocent people is not just illegal but a lack of proper judgment as to the extent of the effects on surrounding people and the impact. It's like using a nuclear bomb to prevent a war knowing that the effects will kill innocent women and children and the effects last decades to come. This can make a nation be regarded as an enemy of mankind that it would rather destroy humanity to preserve itself. I think the current laws leave loopholes and let evil get away with murder. If we are all humans and history has shown proof beyond doubt that all the killings at massive scales have a lack of empathy clause, why are we not addressing this? One person in developed countries dies killed by a person of color the whole world stands still but when they start an illegal war that kills thousands no one says anything. Is it because it's justified or that the lives of these women and children don't matter much to them? Which seems to be the main reason behind such killings. And as such, I think it would be fair to assess if the culprit would do the same if the people involved are of the same genetic heritage as him or her if yes then it's okay if not then it's a crime. A big no but I explained using animals that it can be okay to kill yours for strategic reasons for example not to slow down the whole group or put the mother in danger if there is no food. But killing other animal's cubs or puppies is hard to comprehend. If animals are this intelligent why we let people murder mercilessly children and women of other genetic heritage and let them get away with such evil?

# CHAPTER SIX

UPHOLDING EVERYONE'S RIGHTS AND WHAT IT MEANS IN THE NEW WORLD.

To hell with rights abusers.

Express-command to put an end to this through our laws and courts as a deterrent.

The fundamental difference between this world and the New World is about upholding the human rights of everyone. The New World is a very advanced state of the current system. In this stage, a lot of things will have changed. People's knowledge and understanding and self-esteem are at their highest. In this stage, upholding human rights becomes a norm something that is obvious, and breaches are very rare and carry maximum punishments usually death by the assassin. It's a highly developed stage that human rights laws are written in everyone's minds and the knowledge is so prevalent that any breach is easily highlighted. The greatest sin at this stage is breaching these human rights with the obvious punishment of death. The current system is so crooked that politicians would rather put emphasis on defense rather than on human rights, for example, innocent women and children might die needlessly if the politicians decide to take military action against a dictator. Look at the Iraq war after 9/11. The human rights of women and children were overridden by the necessity to topple Saddam Hussein. No one even condemned these politicians or try to bring them to account for the death of hundreds of thousands of these innocent victims. Simply because the current system is crooked and needs straightening that's why we now have Tomorrow's World Order. I have written laws in later chapters that will safeguard the human rights of innocent women and children. Their rights will override any other decision proposed by the politicians and leaders of the day. I have introduced new laws and

123

rules that will make it easy in the end to uphold everyone's human rights. I will ban the production of weapons and anything that conflicts with the first rule; the right to life for everyone. Military and defense conflicts with this first rule. Wars are to kill and destroy life and to make things worse. Wars are not discriminatory in that they kill everyone women, children, men, and animals. We don't want situations like this when there is no predictability. I have emphasized the need for global legal assassins throughout the book. The first reason being that assassins target. Target here is the keyword. We don't leave anything to chance. We don't get innocent women and children caught up in the crossfire. There is no need to kill 500 000 in order to remove one evil dictator. I want a world where there is predictability. Where I swear if it's an operation, I can say we are going to takeout twelve evil people only and at the end of the day being what will happen. We must respect life no matter whose life. Respect for life shall be our sole reason for living. The laws I will put in place will remove all obstacles and hindrances to the upholding of everyone's rights. Banning of weapons and their production. Change the functions and purposes of the military making everyone a highly paid assassin with other functions like cyber defending. The military must evolve and adapt to the new system before phasing out all military operations and stopping budget allocation for the military. There will be new laws globally to stop wars and acts that can intimidate others or instill fear so that they end up sticking to defense. Such tactics are not just illegal but would carry the harshest punishments because they will cause others to revert to the defensive stage where everyone is suspicious of others. This is understandable because everyone is afraid of surprise attacks. So, if all kinds of military actions are banned and all weapons production and trading are outlawed, and any dirty tactics banned in the end we have a society that will look ahead for answers. Imagine the global military budgets all being canceled and all the money put on other areas like health, energy and infrastructure and research and development? Surely, we will achieve some form of advancement where it really matters. All the current regimes making viral weapons to be the global leaders will face doom as we will be very strict with these for the sake of humanity. It's our duty to make sure that we protect humanity, and this is the only way forward and if anyone thinks otherwise, then address us. Okay, a few decades ago maybe but open your eyes the world is changing. Education and instincts are kicking in and finally, we start to realize that we are all the same globally. Who would have thought North Korean and the USA can be on speaking terms? So why we keep making nuclear weapons, missiles, powerful attacking planes, etc. Surely, we can create jobs in other ways. I know it's hard abandoning projects where $billions have been injected already. If these areas can't evolve, then we are wasting precious resources. I think it's time someone say something about this. It must start somewhere don't you think. Tomorrow's World Order will make sure that we lay the foundation fast towards that road where all obstacles to upholding human rights are eliminated and or dismantled. I mean everything that makes it easy for human rights to be tumbled on is a threat to everyone's freedoms.

## Problems with the current system.

Developed countries get oil from less developed countries cheaply or by force through wars and they create jobs where the proceeds are channeled towards the military making weapons which they then sell to the developing countries at higher prices. The less developed countries then hold on to the weapons in case the developed countries attack them. Once the developed countries realized that the less developed countries are in a better position to defend themselves, they increase their threat level and in turn goes back to take more resources and make even more advanced weapons. The less-developed nations in turn order an upgrade with more destructive power. The developed countries then increase the less developed countries' threat level. The cycle starts again. What is happening here is the suffocation of other areas and starving these while stockpiling things we don't need in the form of weapons? The developed countries then start talking about even more powerful weapons of mass destruction secretly being made by the less developed countries now so that they can use military force and get the resources even cheaper. All along everything that has been happening is the trampling of all human rights. The women and children all along have been starved when the developed nations bought say oil cheaper than the market value. Preferring to pay less and instead of making something that will benefit the less developed nations they make weapons to get them killed in the future. This is not just a problem in the developing world. There is untold poverty as well in the developed world with people suffering going without food as well while we make the most destructive nukes or planes. The period of ignorance has since passed, and this will never be an excuse. We must start acting like responsible human beings and we must start working at our optimal levels and being as efficient as possible. World War Three is a must so that we get rid of all the stockpiles unless the assassins can avoid all this then we must dump all these weapons somehow.

The problem is not just a military one. We have governments funding the production of lethal viruses be it biological or digital. We have governments encourage research on how to invent the most lethal strains ever. We have irresponsible governments reward institutions and private companies who make the best lethal strains, etc. We have these strains being used on ethnic people. We have governments and institutions making digital high-tech gadgets that they are loading with digital forms of viruses which they remotely load the victims with the results that the digital ones cause similar effects in victims just like the real ones. Yes, some governments spending $billions recreating past epidemics but now with better technology, some can be easily detected. We even have some governments taking us back to medieval times or even far back when mankind has not developed the art of speech. Yes, we have governments hacking everyone loading all their citizens with a GPS tracker and a recorder spying on everyone as a way of running their governments. Breaching all human rights. Above all pretending to be very clever in order to avoid everyone listening to 'private conversations' they are teaching everyone since birth a sign language to avoid others listening as everyone is hacked and has a GPS and a microphone or recording device. This has led some governments to go a step further and develop a language to communicate with each other based on viral-mutations. Yes, they are making viruses and use these to communicate as an advanced method to beat the interception or hacking of conversations like I said as everyone has a recording or talking piece. These governments are deliberately loading all their population with viruses. I don't care what the fancy words they use, implanted medical devices, cyber high-tech gadgets, etc. the bottom line is that they are viruses, or the technology is based on viral-mutations.

## Spying Technology.

It doesn't stop there some governments have gone a step forward and used this technology to spy on everyone. This is how technology works. The victims are chipped at birth without consent and most don't even know it. The implant digitally records everyone's feelings and thoughts. Yes, thoughts as well in that MRI scanning are used to pinpoint what the person is thinking about. Say if you are thinking about driving or buying a car certain area of the brain through MRI will be highlighted on the scan. If you are thinking about making love, certain specific areas will be mapped on the scan. So, the device records these feelings. The system works well when someone who is supposed to be your virtual twin acts as a receiver and a transmitter. The 'twin' then receives your thoughts and feelings and transmits these to a central computer or a person who acts as the decoder. That person who has a gadget as well interprets what are your feelings and thoughts and then the information is passed on to whom ever it concerns. The same technology is used to let out people's secrets as well with a market that those who want to know other's secrets for a competitive advantage would pay a fee for such information. Say you are a businessman and you want to know the dealings the person you are conducting business deals with you simply must pay someone or donate money to a certain charity nominated by the person responsible. Once the fee has been paid you, then receive the secrets of your business competitor. I know some people might say what's wrong with that. In the New World crimes like these are punishable by death, to deter and stop such practicing simply because they tear the fabric of all human rights. The system is possible simply because they breached human rights in the first place. Hacking and implanting of IMDs at birth without consent. Most of the developed people are hacked at birth and this is concealed in the necessity of having medical records or for their protection. The argument being forwarded so far is that the benefits outweigh the risks. These people are hacked as part of the government's protection and defense scheme. So, the need to protect the country outweighs the breaches of individual privacy, etc. But do you know the main reasons for such actions are so that it's easy for them to control and manipulate you? You have no right to privacy at all. For them, it's a way of raising money.

I explained above that for the system to work there must be a receiver and in most cases, this is a person who then decodes and transmits the signals to be mapped and to be scanned using the MRI scanner. So, the receiver and decoder can receive and feel what the victim is feeling. So, if you are aroused the receiver will be aroused as well as soon as he or she receives the signals as he or she decodes the signals. What if that is his or her fetish? That opens doors to abuse not just from the receiver or decoder but from whoever is responsible in that they can offer people with a fetish like that to feel and get connected to you without you knowing. They can feel all your feelings when you are making love to your wife, husband, boyfriend or girlfriend, etc. What if whoever is responsible decides to make say old people whose feelings have ceased functioning feel what it's like to make love but at a price? Who on earth can dictate that this is happening? That raises issues of abuse. So, I ask you again is it fair that your own governments hack everyone at birth in the name of protection. Where is the upholding of human rights? Would you want some deranged person feeling all your feelings when you are making love to your wife or husband? Would you like someone no matter in a position of trust to know what your child is feeling? Throughout his or her life? Are There possibilities that these people after studying you or your child since birth would try to influence who she or he would end up marrying or sleeping with for that matter? Where is freedom in that? Is this not a breach of fundamental human rights to a greater degree? What if the government concerned line up rich men with money and through GPS direct anyone to go and collect money? If the receiver or decoder I mentioned above can feel what you are feeling without you knowing it can he or she not try also to make you feel what he or she is feeling through nerve electromagnetic stimulation? Okay, at a certain stage usually when you have no right to take them to court when all-time frames to raise the issues have expired. They might introduce themselves to you say remotely through electromagnetic impulses. They might get you aroused and or pass static electricity through your genitals. In most cases, I think at first, they try to gain your trust. So, they make your life very hard. Blocking even the simplest things in life. Interfering everywhere in your life behind your back making what is easy to get difficult. Say you went for a job interview you get the job or that the interviewer expressly promised that he will hire you and ask you to wait for a phone call. Then later you find out that the interviewer dumped you instead. So, what they do here is groom you. They block everything you do. You go for a driving test then use the hacking tool to give you a cramp the very moment you are about to do an important maneuver or shake your legs so hard that you stall the vehicle. Even the examiner might wonder what is going on he or she was sure she was going to pass you after witnessing how you drove. Yes, this is what they do. So that in the end you have no option but to submit to their demands. If you refuse all your life, you look like you have and will never achieve anything. So, it is either obey and get everything or deny and never test success. So where are human rights there? Is this not the same as slavery? You have no control whatsoever. They run the show it's either obey or perish. So, the talk of human rights here is simply nonexistent. This is blackmail and a worst form of barbaric treatment only synonymous to slavery the only difference being that if you submit, then you are rewarded. It's a rewarding scheme based on your cooperation and nothing to do with human rights. The question I will ask you is this; is there upholding human rights here? One thing I want you to understand is that this is not on an individual basis, but this is the tip of the iceberg the whole thing is institutionalized. Just another advanced form of slavery or abuse. It's the same system during the slavery days only that now you are rewarded for cooperating. Listen and what you want you will get. Life of everyone is in someone's hands who dictate what everyone else will do. Everyone technically is screwed-up in that he or she must receive input in order to make the next move. The system is that you can't proceed without receiving input. The system makes everyone dependent on that the next move is already predetermined, and you must wait for a signal from someone else. In advanced situations, the information on what to do the next day is passed through dreams. Dreams are you....? Yes, technological advancement has meant sophisticated ways of communication. When I was a kid. I slept one day with a radio-on though volume minimized. I started dreaming. Unconsciously somehow the song was like in my dream and I could see people dancing and singing the song live but in my dream. When I woke up the dream was so vivid that somehow it just didn't seem real, so I checked and listened to the previous night playlist. The song was there on the playlist. When the song in my dream started playing, it was such an unbelievable experience. So, the song triggered the dream I had. So, the song acted as an input to whatever I went on to dream about. Then it hit me. What if some clever people hacked everyone at birth and over the years have developed some high-tech microphones or listening devices that can play songs in your ears while you are sleeping and songs only you can hear and these songs form part of what people dream about? Or tell people what to do the following day as a way of command? I know this is possible simply because growing up we used to record cassettes. I discovered that to record high-quality songs on a cassette you must remove sound that turns the volume down that you can't hear anything, but the songs will be playing. It's like making a gadget that plays songs or sends commands to someone's ears without anyone else hearing the commands but only the recipient. Okay back to my argument, I was saying that there are no human rights upholding as the system makes everyone dependent on those on top who offers commands. Everyone has to wait for an input given through sign language or dreams or commands somehow and those who don't listen or don't receive commands and who are often doing what they think is right in the given situation are referred to as dump simply because they can't interpret and decode the signals and commands given. This is also a trickery way of eroding the people's brains and memories holding everyone to ransom as with time they are left to the interpretation of useless things and codes and messages that they forget what is important in life. They lose the will to fight as they are loaded with useless things and commands that in the end, they are depended on the people involved like the hospital teaching institutions who use that to justify their jobs and the need in the first place. Gross abuse of all human rights with people in a position of trust abusing the victims themselves so that they justify their jobs.

So, in simple terms, these governments violate human rights by hacking everyone at birth and implanting a chip that records and that has GPS functions. In most cases, as I will elaborate below, they control and determine the direction that a child's life will go as the chip or implanted devices are used to control all bodily functions through nerve stimulation through electromagnetic impulses. Now that everyone is hacked, and everyone is listening that necessitates the need for a special sign language so that people can speak in a certain way without third parties understanding what is going on. That triggers the need for teaching hospitals and institutions to teach everyone illegally tagged at birth a certain language they can use so that whoever is listening will not be able to understand it. So, we have jobs created initially based on a breach of human rights. Note my argument here is that the initial start phase is based on illegal hacking and tagging of the child at birth mostly without consent and knowledge that this is happening. To me, that renders whatever follows as void because there has been a breach of human rights in the first place. If it's a contract, this breach nulls it making it void. What follows is not binding and unenforceable instead the victim is entitled to launch a breach of trust and a violation of human rights case and is entitled to sue the government etc. The government points to the need to protect everyone and the country and the hacking is seen as an avoidable reality as everyone must be hacked so the institutions involved in defense can quickly diffuse the threat. You can see clearly why defense is a major issue regarding human rights. The truth is that the main reason one has been hacked is to be able to control and command the population. It is a political tool with the motive to drive jobs rather than anything less. The teaching hospitals then goes on to abuse the victims using torture to command and control. Victims tortured as a behavior-changing stance so that they listen in the future. This is easily done. First, the chips or torturing devices were implanted illegal and no one can take these institutions to court simply because the whole world is hacked. You will be surprised that even the military person and the police are hacked themselves and often loaded with digital or biological weapons themselves. The government knows that all the time frames to bring a successful case against them will have expired by the time the victims notice unusual behavior. To make things worse torture is used in broad daylight simply because no one can prove that they are being tortured and if they do complain then it's automatic creation of jobs as well for them as these people are accused of hallucinations. So, the teaching hospitals go on to torture and abuse the victims. In most cases, they are the Receivers, or Decoders I mentioned above but often delegates or sell or contract out the services to other people who can pay high fees. In the worst cases to people with fetishes who pay a lot of money like celebrities. These people are linked or hooked with people say with a high sex drive induced by the chips, implants or through nerve stimulation by electromagnetic tampering. These celebrities act as receivers and decoders and what happens is that they get aroused as they receive and decodes the signals. Eventually, after some time, they are introduced to the victims who are in most cases young in their late teens or early twenties. These are used to blackmail the celebrities into donating to certain charities or have their fortune and names destroyed before the hospitals set them on fire through radiation and drive the hospital's agenda before death with the abuse concealed or only revealed after the abuser has died.

In most cases the hacking at birth is justified as a form of security to protect the individual or nations of a country but, what is happening is the opposite. The main reason why the hacking is taking place something they don't say is the fact that the government what to be in the driver's seat on deciding who dies and when they die. Imagine a country where improvements in medicine have meant reduced death rates. The population is an aging population and an aging population is a burden to the balance sheet. Pensions and all that stuff related to aging does real damage to the government coffers. Most of these politicians would rather get rid of the aging population as it put a strain on resources. So, these clever politicians decided to hold the bull by the horns and put everyone on death row from the day they were born. This way they control who dies and when and how they die as well. The government has spent $ billions developing digital weapons in the form of viruses and watermarks they use on the population. These acts as a catalyst speeding up the aging process and some causing diseases early and the people being tricked that it's a way of boosting the hospital attendances and praised that they are doing everyone a favor. All they must do is go to the hospitals or doctors who will remove these digital agents. Nothing to worry about. The idea here is to provide a false sense of security until the day they decide they must die. A boost to the hospitals to justify the huge budgets when lifestyle is improving. So, the people are made to age faster than usual setting wrinkles and graying fast than normal usually in the name of protection. I explained above what they are doing for one to accept this kind of protection. They block everything and make your life a living hell so that in the end you accept what they call protection. They will then say X has a house, and he only got the house because he accepted wrinkles as protection or graying early as protection. So, if you want a house then you must accept some grays as well or wrinkles as well. Or they will let the damaged goods- the people who have already been abused fight you. They will simply say it's not fair we lost a leg and a hand so if you want the same you must lose a leg and a hand. In the end either you live or accept this protection and whatever comes with it.

So where is the upholding of human rights there? This is something associated with gangs and thugs and not with people in a position of trust. Since everything is institutionalized providing much-needed job etc. everything is done with commands from the top with severer sufferings of even the local people and most tortured until they start taking drugs with sleepless nights and guess who runs the heroin production farms? The same teaching hospitals are implanting chips and devices to torture the people so that they offer them the so-called 'prescription heroin'. This does not stop there. They use mainly the women as prostitutes grooming them from a young age and offering rewards like enlarged fake breasts after certain tasks and some which involve prostitution or trying to smear people so that they end up being hacked by the hospitals this is usually directed at the foreigners who are not hacked or without chips implanted on them. All the locals are hacked at birth and for most foreigners, there is no evil hacking in their countries of birth so when they visit the advanced countries they are targeted for hacking as a security or population control tool. This means all the local women loaded with watermarks so they can't be touched or the use of very strict institutions like the police who intervenes all the time in private relationships so life with locals is very hard unless when one has been hacked and once hacked a prostitute is given to you. This is not just an individual thing it's a calculated sophisticated way of governing usually augmented by eugenics philosophies that are conservative in that they will try to protect the status quo and therefore avoid dilution of their gene-pool. Okay, you might say from a foreigner's point of view the situation is unjust but for the locals, they don't care protection makes them have what they would not have in the first place. But I argue that no matter what there is no justification whatsoever as this is based on violations of fundamental human rights. I argue that they make life hard even for the locals, torturing them and blocking things and making what would otherwise be easy to obtain very difficult to get so that they justify what they call as protection. If it wasn't for this protection, the living standards, and everything would be easily affordable and easy to get. If that was the case, then who would volunteer to be killed early so that they can have a house or a car? It makes no sense.

I think it's very unfair to put the whole population on death row the day they are born as population control. It's a breach of the fundamental principles of human rights. All these people are on death row being dictated what happens to them and when they would die. So, the current system is flawed. Something that can't be accepted in the New World. No one has a right to do something that interferes with the first rule; the right to life and to self-preserve. The idea in the New World is that of living happily in a youthful state forever. So how can we achieve that if your government has already signed your death certificate the day you were born by implanting a chip or device that emits dangerous radiation doses? They will use the devices your entire life ending up injecting radiation doses deliberately so that the government reduces its pension or wage bill? Open your eyes until you start thinking like a leader yourself you will never notice some things happening around you. Simply because you are concerned about things that surround you and your day-to-day life. Once you lift your head above everyone else, you start to understand things from a different perspective. You start asking questions and when you start getting answers, you will realize that life as it is the worst form and a lot can be done to improve it. We as humans we are operating below our capabilities and if the world was a company, it could have ceased trading centuries ago. Why? You might ask.

Imagine you have a company that takes all resources and makes weapons. Okay, the first years you might find markets as people usually less advanced as you buy your weapons. But as time goes on, there are no wars simply because after the last two major wars you decided to put things in hands to avoid wars but did not see the impact of such moves. Years gone by still making weapons and stockpiling these. Markets become saturated, and no one wants to buy weapons anymore. You employ dirt bullying tactics to make the underdogs buy your weapons after intimidating and antagonizing them. You realize that no one is going to buy you then decided to attack some countries to show who is boss that will trigger purchases of weapons yet still there are other issues like poverty. The lesser governments whenever a leader chooses weapons to their well-being, they would fight to topple him. All resources collected are just being channeled to military and defense. In the end, a world war will break out as other areas suffer, and people would revolt and put you out of business.

Another worrying issue and the main reason behind this hacking at birth is the fact that most of these countries have an aging population with a large percentage of the population made up of the old. Most of these people have huge disposal wallets in that they have worked most of their lives and have saved a lot, but they lack the energy they had in youth. So technically there is a market and potential buyers with a lot of money to spend. So, let's say for argument purposes I want to do business with these people what can I provide them that will let them part away with their money? Can I provide a youthful state to them or some youthful experiences to them? Or can I help them age gracefully? Or in some cases can I turn back the hands of time? What would these people pay to get back some of their youth feelings? Okay, what is happening is what I explained earlier on. There is hacking at the birth of almost everyone and throughout life, the people are spied on with almost everyone having a double or someone who acts as a digital guardian. Someone I mentioned earlier on as the receiver or decoder. That person receives and decodes the feelings of the subject and plans on how to help that person, etc. So, these two are linked and in most cases, these Receivers or Decoders are people in a position of trust. But there is a market as well. Imagine when the old people are used as these Receivers or Decoders. Imagine the old people feeling what a high-testosterone-producing teen goes through as he is growing? Imagine the Receivers or Decoders feeling the same feelings as you with you getting aroused by the slight sight of a woman or hearing a female voice surely, they would pay more just to re-live youths as well. But imagine when the old can transmit what they are feeling and imagine when they are able to exchange and swap such feelings? Imagine an old bed-ridden frail man who has thousands of $ and willing to exchange these for a better life. Imagine when one can be made to sleep all the time through the shaking of nerves responsible for sleep using the chip or device remotely. Imagine when the old man's device can be transferred to the sleeping subject? Imagine the man being given a boost or acting as an invading host subduing the subject that whatever the old man is feeling will be transferred to the sleeping subject. That means requiring a lot of young and able-bodied incapacitate by alcohol, drugs, or confined in spaces so that they can be used as targets. What comes to mind first when you hear this? Slavery! Yes, slavery. People died so that everyone on earth regardless of genetic heritage is a free person and centuries later we are still doing slavery nevertheless more advanced but slavery no matter what form is slavery. So, no matter how that sounds if you are the old person this is something that has barbaric connotations and to be allowed in the New World would not be just plain wrong but a crime to be given the harshest sentence. This stampedes all fundamental human rights and such practices are not just irresponsible but punishable by death.

**What about their arguments that this is done for the protection of the citizens themselves? Does this hold water?**

A first glimpse might suggest that. Most people hacked at birth live normal lives and are in a better position as they are protected by their governments through these devices or chips. The GPS enables them to be located and given maximum protection whenever something happens or is about to happen, they are warned way earlier. These people go on to die in old age so all this talk about infringing on human rights is nonsense. First, they can't kill everyone young and, in most cases, these people have paid a prize themselves but maybe not directly. The government has a system they refer to as give-back to those selected and this goes hand in hand with this hacking and this is referred to as give-back. What's that animal?

I will explain. The idea behind all this is for the government to be able to control the population in the future. If you are the leader it makes sense. You would not want people to die whenever nature dictates them simply because pension and health bills of the aged really does damage to the government balance sheet. If you are the leader you would not want anything to be left to chance, would you? No of course you are meant to be in control, and this is the only way that this is possible. Ever wondered why the health budget grows up year after year when people dying due to diseases have reduced drastically as compared to decades ago. Imagine spying on the whole population of course it takes a lot of money. You will need ambulances that run every second as these acts as the Receivers, the Decoders, and the Transmitters as well. Ever wondered why in developed countries ambulances act like are in a war zone? Ever since these ambulances have taken a different role that of a teaching hospital, agents and as the receivers of the digital signals and the Decoders as well as the Transmitters and the vehicles of torture as they carry the machines and equipment used to achieve this. So, this give-back scheme involves hacking everyone at birth and spying on everyone. Some people in life succeed through efforts of their own and once they have shown that they have potential or have achieved greatly the government then moves in and mostly to tell the whole world that they are the ones behind the person they give that person a watermark of some kind. This is to them proof that they are behind the success of this and that person. They just spy and steal ideas and information as whatever the hacked person does the Receiver, Decoder or Transmitter receives everything on his gadget or monitor. They can tell what television programmers you watched, who phoned you and what websites you browsed. Don't forget the recording piece as well they know all your conversations, so they tap in.

Steal and sell the ideas unless if you have agreed they are behind all your inventions and accepted a watermark in the form of a dodgy eye or something that can't be attributed to nature. They pretend they are behind your success but in fact, they are worse than a hacker in that, in the end, they will be responsible for your death to show others who is the real dad. You might suffer radiation doses to keep you quiet or to scare others who might reveal their secrets.

In case you have no choice and you end up giving in they will pretend to help you. Watching whatever you are doing and quickly run to tell your opponents all your secrets so that without them you will fail until you accept. Once you have accepted, they will protect you but ask you to give back something to their cause. What is their cause? Technically everyone is on death row because the purpose is to decide when you die and with good behavior, you might be spared. If spared you will have to give something of your own or related to you back to them. So, they spared your life but still, you will have to give them something close to you back. In other words, they have removed your name from the death row list but still, you must give something back to the list. Ever wondered why celebrities' sons or daughters or themselves end up dying mysterious deaths mostly related to drugs, suicides, etc.? This is the giving back. They say they have spared your life so give what's yours back. Children, husbands, wives, etc. The success of all of it is down to you. You worked hard but they have a gadget that enables them to spy on you without you knowing. They know exactly what you watched last night, they know exactly how you made love to your wife last night and they even know what time you farted. They have you under control, but you just don't know it. Whatever they did to you, you were a little baby that you don't remember anything. Now you have hit that success and they are taking over simply because you are theirs from day one, the day you were born. Just an infant and these culprits have marked you for death. You proved to be worthy sparing, but you must give something back or face radiation doses. One day you find out that your kid has killed himself or herself of a drug overdose or that has taken his or her life. Or dies or something. To them, you have successfully proven yourself worthy but still, they are going to humiliate you and put you down by killing everything you love.

Or you will die fighting their cause being tortured by them through the gadget or chip implanted in your infancy and radiation doing real damage.

It does not stop there. These people have devised a plan to terrorize you all your life. The devices or chips through nerve stimulation and manipulation will help them generate jobs by causing unforeseen genetic defects and diseases. Through nerve stimulation and electromagnetic interference, they determine when and how people conceive as well. The devices can be used to help people conceive as well or hinder people to conceive or conceive disabled offspring. Remotely they can use the chips or devices to stimulate and increase sperm production by static-electromagnetic stimulation or stressing you to breaking point. On average it takes maybe a good 2-3 days for the body to manufacture healthy sperms, but the device can be used to increase sperm production through the methods mentioned above. I am going to ask you this question. Do you think you will have a good health sperm if the device or chip makes you produce the sperms in a day when the body takes 2-3 days to make the same amount of sperm? These people know this, and they deliberately make the body produce premature sperms and when you conceive you have increased chances of having a child with defects. To them more jobs and better people to fight for their cause but a crime under international law. Why they do it? Simply because you can't prove it and they can't get caught. Who will believe that you are remotely being tortured or constantly shaken but these things do happen? Another reason why they easily get away with this is the fact that like a coin that has two sides the same device is used by most of them to help them. To help people conceive. To help people have better lives. To help people rejuvenate. To these people, everything about this device is good simply because they have never seen the dark side of the devices and when you cry foul play, they think you are hallucinating. To you or someone else who know this evil side of such governments and the only reason they are in power is simply because this can't be proved that this is happening.

Who decides who should be on death row or not? Is population or immigration control above human rights? What can we say is wrong and when can we say that the line has been crossed and if you are all hacked at birth how can you fight this and make it a thing of the past? No matter what the benefits to some are or the justification for this is equivalent to slavery and as such can't be let to see the day. I know it will be hard to fight as the practice is institutionalized with all the people who are supposed to be in a position of trust at the core of this. Express-command to put an end to this through our laws and courts as a deterrent. But I swear the answer is the use of the assassins [through our courts lawfully] to collapse the top bracket giving commands. If no one gives commands at the top, it is unlikely that someone at the bottom will give the command. So, the solution is to aim to collapse the top brace as a last resort. I know there are a lot of people out there themselves victims of the give-back scheme who will fight our cause once we are fully operational. We must collapse the current system, eliminate regimes that treat and see their citizens like dead meat. We will send shock-waves to the system. We are not going to employ the same tactics as these evil regimes of killing innocent people. We shall aim to use the assassin to target whoever we think has much influence on this. I swear by the assassin to carry out a marvelous job while achieving a zero civilian causality that is limiting innocent casualties. It shall be one man for himself and TWO for us all. I will urge everyone to see and realize that these people give you a false sense of security. The protection they give is designed to give you a sense of protection, so you trust them. Okay, the first time they might be helping you but it's all grooming so that they have you under control. Like I said, from your day of birth you are on death row and assigned someone to monitor and spy on you rather than protect you. Over the years you tend to trust them until the day when you least expected that they send one of their own to finish you off or torture you to death.

Okay, today you might have heard things you might never have imagined. Is it all true or not is not the point? My point and main arguments are that whatever their reasons this is a fundamental breach of human rights and against all international laws and as such a crime in the New World punishable by death. Whatever is going to happen is directly linked to that first incident at birth. It's like a doctor raping you by implanting these devices without consent and then the government tries to take over and make everything legal? Accessories and accomplices to a crime in the New World punishable by death at the hands of the assassin. If gangs and gangsters can be killed for doing the same what gives the government, the right to institutionalize the same evil crimes? The government encourages the doctors and the doctors to do it in broad daylight simply because they have the government's backing and the whole institutions will try to sweep everything under the carpet until all court lifelines are extinct.

Okay, what can be done to eliminate such evil acts as being institutionalized-organized by the current governments and how do we safeguard everyone's rights from the first day of birth?

I think before addressing this question I want you to understand the meaning and purpose of hacking.

All that I have mentioned above, and everything is done by government institutions and other parts of the government all fall under the term hacking. I don't care what fancy name they might give it; it is hacking.

Hacking according to the Cambridge Dictionary is;
the <u>activity</u> of <u>illegally</u> using
a <u>computer</u> to <u>access</u> <u>information</u> <u>stored</u> on
another <u>computer</u> <u>system</u> or to <u>spread</u> a <u>computer</u> <u>virus</u>.

This hacking refers to computers but equally applies to humans as well. It is an illegal act or activity performed by those in power or in a position of trust to enable the government free easy access to people and their information of their activities etc. or to spread diseases in order to control, change, modify, manipulate or kill as a governing tool. The definition is fitting here. The aim of any hacker is to change something that works well so that it is easy to determine when it crashes, or collapse, or falls ill or dies. The idea is for the government to be able to spread viruses that cause all kinds of problems, wrinkles, graying, diseases, disabilities, crashes, suicides, and deaths so that they are in control and mostly there is always a financial element. In this case first, create jobs to justify huge health budgets and to reduce the pensions and health bill. This is true in developed countries where better living standards meant people living longer and the strain on the government coffers. A hacker is as bad as torture and as good as a Hostis Humani Generis an enemy of mankind. Simply because the motive is to cause the malfunctioning of an otherwise healthy system or individual. They hack to stop some functions or change the way the body operates with certain functions changed or reversed. The idea is to change and later or cause malfunctioning. When someone is hacked the talk of human rights is nonexistent. A hacked person is a slave. He or she has no rights or say to what goes on inside him or her. A hacked person is in a hostage situation where he is being held to ransom without consent and we know when one is hacked or in a hostage situation, only external help will be able to free that person. So, the whole country is under a hostage situation and only external help will free the inhabitants of such a country. These people need freeing. TWO will do whatever it takes to make sure that governments will never again hold their citizens to ransom as hostages. The New World is made up of free people in the true sense of the word. You can't say you are free when someone else not only plays with your private parts remotely but delegates such activities to whoever can pay for such joy. Imagine something like this happening to your leader or your Prime Minister or President trapped into the system, being made to wrinkle so bad that you can tell that it's artificial and some being made to do wrong things. If it means destroying the current health system that is so outdated and corrupt, then so be it. I understand that these institutions were created during war times and as such must recreate such scenes to remain viable, but I tell you this that the world is changing. Evolve or perish. No point making biological, now digital viruses in order to recreate fourteenth-century scenes of a pandemic so your budget can't be cut. I am not saying it is every government doing this but trust me when I say there is still evil lurking out there. Some people have not changed at all and this is the only way they know and as such would make everyone else fall with them. History through Hitler has taught us what to do if someone tries to take the law into their own hands. We have a moral obligation and duty to act and now the system has collapsed as there is no effective leader or world power that is not tainted with the blood of innocent women and children or biased to address the world's problems. They all have fallen into the trap of joining gangs and evil cults to terrorize everyone else and rob by force the poor's resources. They failed to think. They have relied on weapons as answers to everything. Affordability is the problem so focus on ways to increase the money supply in order to buy at market prices instead of making weapons cheaper and use these to rob and kill to force increased supply and lower prices in the process of killing our precious women and children. I am personally saddened by mankind who has failed to have superior thinking and solve global problems hence the rise of TWO.

## Evil cults as the catalyst for abuse.

There are evil cults that make it easy for a few to ruin the whole egg basket. After the war institutions like the International Criminal Court, The International Court of Justice, The UN, NATO, etc. have only made it easy for the real culprits to apply their philosophies in order to control their destination. At the beginning of the chapter, I have argued that a few evil countries use and apply an idea developed in 1654 referred to as the Colony Collapse Strategy or Plan. The principle behind this is to use this plan to eliminate all potential enemies and render everyone incapable of launching an attach therefore becoming a threat that would destabilize the main body or pose a threat to its survival. The idea is to target the alpha males of any given society to weaken the whole society that after removing these male alphas the society will collapse and eventually fall under those who have implemented the plan. After the Second World War, a few countries gathered and wrote a plan never to be defeated or face what they witnessed in the Second World War again. The plan was to put institutions like the International Criminal Court, NATO, to target and eliminate all alpha males who posed a threat to the survival of the cult. The plan was the Society Collapse Strategy Plan. The leaders would be targeted and even helped to commit crimes through free supplies of weapons and then later be brought to the International Criminal Court to be tried and imprisoned forever leaving the cult to put a puppet who then carries their agendas before the cycle is repeated This was the plan for low-level threats that is leaders who pose less direct threats to the cults but those perceived as high-level threats especially leaders of countries with oil or other minerals who have the potential to buy or make WMDs these were to be dealt with differently namely through military action. You can see that the same method has been applied since the end of the Second World War to eliminate all potential threats. Most of these people voiced concerns against the cults or the West and as such were targeted. Institutions like the UN, the International Criminal Court [ICC] or the International Court of Justice [ICJ] are there to see to it that the cults will keep growing and any threats are dealt with in all kinds of manners with the less low-level threats dragged to the courts and those perceived as high-level threats silenced through military action. The ICC was established after the world war to help reduce or eliminate threats or forming of other cults that would otherwise pose a threat. Ever since their establishment, they have been biased in their dealings targeting the low-level threats from Africa and direct military action targeting the high-level threats from mainly the Persian Gulf. Countries rich in oil who can influence the survival of the cults. NATO on the other hand has acted like a bully through threats and intimidation carrying out war rehearsals and this causes fear and anxiety among the weaker countries who in turn end up buying weapons out of fear of being attacked.

## What is the future of institutions like the ICJ or the UN, NATO or the ICCJ?

To understand their role and implications, one must understand why they were created and whether they have evolved for the past 70 years. First, let's look at the ICC.

## The ICC.

Even though it started functioning in July 2002, the same day the Rome Statute came into effect its origins date to the time after the First and Second World Wars. The Allies sat down and drafted a plan to establish a court that will try to persecute the opposition axis leaders who were accused of acts of terrorism. In short, the court was established to eliminate the opposition leaders accused of terrorism. The inception of the court has nothing to do with human rights as what people often associate it with. The court was established by the Allies after witnessing the impacts of war and to prevent such things happening again and to guarantee themselves victory in case of future wars all axis enemies were to be eliminated in what you can call a 'Clean as you go plan'. War was not predictable and as they witnessed after the two world wars anyone can win a war. The trauma and the severe casualties made the axis draft plans to establish this court not to uphold human rights but to be honest to quash any enemies through courts first and try to avoid future wars. I spoke of the notion of the Society or Colony Collapse Strategy that its aims were to quash the enemies and not wait for them to start a war simply because anyone can win a war and even if you win, you might suffer tremendous causalities too.

The theme in this book is the making of weapons; collecting scarce resources worldwide and starving other areas and using dirty intimidation tactics to make poor nations use the little money they must buy weapons. But I ask you this; what does that have to do with genocide, war crimes, crimes against humanity and crimes of aggression? One might ask. The West have a highly developed system that collects resources all over the world at a low price in order to make weapons which they sell back to the poor countries knowing that the people having been starved of basic rights like access to food and water one day will up-rise, fight or simply start a war that in turn demands a supply of weapons. Everything is connected. All resources and money are plowed back to weapons and the military starving other areas thereby creating a vicious circle that will constantly require weapons. Starved people will fight as a hungry man is an angry man. This justifies the making of weapons and there is always a demand. When they do this, the leaders who will have bought weapons from them would end up using the weapons. Once they did this is genocide, war crimes, crimes against humanity and acts of aggression and that can only mean one thing jobs created for the ICC who will try to jail the leaders who bought the weapons from these developed nations for fear of being attacked. Once that happens, the leader is sent to trial. A sophisticated Colony or Society Collapse plan. A market for gun production by the West and a way of eliminating its opposition and any future threats to avoid any future wars. The ICC, the United Nations Security Council, NATO, you name it were all created by the Allies, the West the very people buying resources at below market value and in return sell guns to these leaders in the first place. I argued throughout this book that the West has a clever way of creating a problem, magnifying the problem and then propose solutions at very high prices creating jobs for everyone concerned. Like I said the ICC was a product of the Allies after the First and Second World Wars. All the judges were put in place to avoid accusations of bias towards people of color but in fact the whole system is based on the Colony or Society Collapse Strategy in which the leaders are targeted for elimination as a way to neutralize future threats and maintain the status quo of the cults like the NATO the United Nations Security Council [UNSC] etc.

I argued throughout the book that the West has a strategy of creating a problem, then magnifying the problem before proposing solutions at a higher cost price. Creating jobs and causing the collapse of the society or leaders concerned. A classic example here is the making and implanting of landmines at very cheap prices of $3-10 and then proposing the removal of these by one of its subsidiary branches at exorbitant prices between $300- 1000 per landmine. This is the same strategy they are using here. They sponsor most of these leaders in the first place when they are rising to power offering guns in exchange for resources, etc. through the fears instilled by other institutions like NATO whose power makes these nations ignore their people and instead spend the little they have on weapons. Surely something got to give one way or the other and one day the people would revolt and when that happens the leaders end up killing their people. Once that happens, the ICC or UNSC then finger these leaders for trials. OK to normal people these are crimes of aggression, genocides and war crimes, etc. But do you know this is a strategy to eliminate opposition leaders by the Allies devised after the First and Second World Wars disguised as a human rights intervention? Do you know also that this court can only prosecute crimes committed after 2002? When the West had finished its crimes which they swept under the carpet. I ask you a question since the day you were born did you not know that killing people in large numbers is a crime? We know through documented cases that the West killed a lot of people in the tune of millions. We have information and evidence to prove that they were worse killing up to 150 million people and yet because all these happened before 2002 therefore, they are not crimes worth looking at. My question is that did they not know that killing all these people were crimes that could get them put on trial? Look at the list of the forty-four people the ICC claims to have brought to justice.

Colony or Society Collapse Victims?

2.1 Bahr Abu Garda

2.2 Mohammed Ali

2.3 Abdallah Banda

2.4 Omar Al-Fashir

2.5 Jean-Pierre Bemba

2.6 Charles Blé Goudé

2.7 Muammar Gaddafi

2.8 Saif al-Islam Gaddafi

2.9 Laurent Gbagbo

2.10 Simone Gbagbo

2.11 Ahmed Haroun

2.12 Abdel Rahim Hussein

2.13 Saleh Jerbo

2.14 Germain Katanga

2.15 Uhuru Kenyatta

2.16 Tohami Khaled

2.17 Joseph Kony

2.18 Henry Kosgey

2.19 Ali Kushayb

2.20 Thomas Lubanga Dyilo

2.21 Raska Lukwiya

2.22 Ahmad Al-Mahdi

2.23 Callixte Mbarushimana

2.24 Sylvestre Mudacumura

2.25 Francis Muthaura

2.26 Mathieu Ngudjolo Chui

2.27 Bosco Ntaganda

2.28 Okot Odhiambo

2.29 Dominic Ongwen

2.30 Vincent Otti

2.31 William Ruto

2.32 Joshua Sang

2.33 Abdullah Senussi

2.34 Mahmoud al-Werfalli

A Colony or Society Collapse Strategy in which the threat usually the alpha male is eliminated in public and the locals too given the chance to kill him or voice concerned for his death, so it looks like a human rights case. The ICC was established or drafted by the Allies as a way of bringing the axis leaders to trial so as a 'never again' approach of avoiding future wars simply because during war even those who end s up winning will suffer heavy casualties too. This was a sure way of guaranteeing that deadly wars would be a never again thing. I think it's a fair comment to say the West is all white. Don't get me wrong I am not playing the genetic-heritage-card here, but you must understand the rationale behind all this. These institutions are vehicles of abuse and part and parcel of the strategy to eliminate the Allies' enemies to avoid deadly wars in the future and make these leaders incapable of forming their own cults that would pose a serious threat. Now we have NATO members as;

In the order of joining NATO:

1949–Belgium, Canada, Denmark, France, Iceland, Italy, Luxembourg, Netherlands, Norway, Portugal, United Kingdom, United States.

target Africans and in this book I strongly believe that they are part of the Society Collapse Strategy to take out opposition and potential threats. To contain a threat very early if you like. But whose threats? Here. The African Union supports my arguments as they also believe that the ICC is biased towards Africans and people of color advocating for boycotting. Read the article below.

https://www.washingtonpost.com/news/monkey-cage/wp/2017/03/06/is-the-international-criminal-court-biased-against-africans-kenyan-victims-dont-think-so/?noredirect=on

But I call for caution in reading this stuff about Nigerians I'm just generalizing on this issue so you understand why some Africans would make a judgment as soon as they know they might be a Nigerian as the leader or judge. This is based on a legal concept referred to as legal precedents. If a government organization employees Nigerian's as leaders and then a court later establishes that the government organization was flawed in its dealings one can quickly look at another case that has similar issues at hand and with a Nigerian as the leader or judge and make a quick rough comment based on the past legal precedence. This topic is subjective, and readers are edged to exercise extreme caution it's not a blame game but through legal precedence, if you like.

So, what is the future of the ICC in the New World? I think it's straight forwarded these institutions were created to help the Allies eliminate any opposition. They are killing machines if you like. But not just killing machines but eliminators of any potential threats within the Arab and African space. They are the implementers of the Society or Colony Collapse Strategy meant to weaken the society concerned by targeting the breadwinners so that the society will collapse, eventually.

So, the ICC, etc. are they good or not? Find out in later chapters.

# CHAPTER SEVEN

THE NEW WORLD. HEAVEN ON EARTH. WHAT DOES THAT REALLY MEAN?

First, I think it's wise here to try to clarify what the New World is all about and clear any misconceptions or misunderstandings of what really the New World is. Yes, I sometimes get people referring to the New World as the end of days-era like the one in the Bible. This is totally different and must not be confused here. The idea of the New World, as I have argued throughout the book, is a stage in human development not an end of the world, period. It's an advanced stage of human development where we have achieved most of the things we are currently aiming to achieve right now. Picture yourself planning a journey to a destination. Okay, the destination can be the final goal of the journey but not an end but a means to an end of the journey if that makes sense to you. It is a stage where humans have achieved everything, they aimed for thousands of ages ago. I know most people when they think about life; they think life as a knockout game, for example, the champions league where humans, generation after generation enter the tournament to try to do their best to win the trophy; to achieve longevity and live here on earth as if in heaven. It's like the knockout stages where each generation has to enter the tournament and see what they can do in a hundred years if they fail they are all knocked out as they die and a new generation enters the tournament and try to be the one to find answers and solve the puzzle so that they can find solutions to death, aging, diseases, and increase the whole population's self-esteem. Instead, life should be viewed as a do or die journey where we as humans the most superiors of all animals are expected to throw everything, they have for hundred years and try to cheat death, cheat aging, cheat low-self-esteem, etc. all the things that are making us perish.

154

Recall the arguments that life is a test for us to solve all the puzzles created by God, or the creator and find all the answers that we can earn wisdom to find cures, to stop aging or reversing aging completely and attain a status that matches that of the gods who created us or match whatever you believe created humans. We shall one day reach a stage when we have gained enough wisdom to know all the answers to all our problems. A stage where we won't see divisions and differences. A stage when we are not concerned about materials things like knowing if we have title deeds for everything or not. Not that title deeds are bad; no but they show we are still far away from fulfilling what we are meant to do here on earth. To understand things, I will point to certain situations you are probably familiar with. Imagine for the first time you have saved say $10 000, and the money is sitting in your account. Imagine your girlfriend or boyfriend suddenly appearing from nowhere and suggest you go on vacation. You want but a sports car you saw in town caught your eyes too. You don't have enough to do both it is either-or. Then years later you have a $million and you don't even care you leave her or him with all your bank cards. Then imagine now you have a $100 million. The moment she or he appears, you transfer $10 million to her or his account. So, the more settled you are, the fewer worries about what I can refer to as the basic needs you have. Over the years, when we have developed highly, issues of focusing on material things will have evaporated. Imagine if the whole world was not wasting money on any weapons or the military and all that money plowed into transport, housing, infrastructure, research and development and into other new projects. We can advance forward faster and surely; we would not worry about boundaries or who comes to our country simply because we have advanced highly that worrying about immigration would be a trivial thing. In the end, the ideal stage is where humans are so sophisticated and interact like a family. Yes, with rules and rights and probably grounding and all that but without the kinds of boundaries we have today. All talks of building walls will be a thing of the past. Look back for every decision that is made today history has an answer already. Look at the Berlin Wall. So, if I can look at America today it's like the Berlin Wall era with calls to separate one country from the other and calls to 'protect our borders'. We also know what happened to the Berlin Wall. We are just going in stages throughout the last 2000 years, but here is an opportunity for you to take a different road. I will show you where we want to go and how we are going to go there. So, the New World is not the end of the days thing where people talk about death and destruction. OK, we might experience that depending on the amount of ignorance and resistance still within today's leaders, but the New World is imminent and inevitable. It's a stage we will reach one day. An era when mankind has used resources wisely into things that matter the most and the world will be at optimum levels making sure our goals and targets are to make everyone on earth become like a god. Again, this is not talking about socialism, where all resources will be put together for the good of all. Although in certain areas we will put things in the place like laws, rule, etc. to make sure that certain activities will be banned, and the resources used to advance mankind so that one day we will be so advanced that we won't worry about little things.

## What is this New World?

The New World is heaven on earth. I have dealt with this idea in an earlier chapter, but here I will take the idea to another level. This is not to be confused with the bible 'idea' of heaven, where afterlife souls are expected to go to heaven. My arguments throughout are that the New World is heaven and the major difference here being that this 'heaven' is a stage of development where mankind has achieved a level of advancement that earth becomes so sophisticated that it resembles the conditions talked about the bible heaven. The major difference between the bible or Koran's heaven and paradise is the fact that mankind does not have to die. In the bible-heaven humans must die first in order to enter heaven. This is the current situation where death can take us to heaven. Death is the vehicle to heaven. We have seen the rise of suicide bombers and people killing themselves because this is the only way to go to heaven. I argued throughout this book that this is a misconception. OK maybe for now it is correct to say that simply because we are not working at optimal capacity to solve a lot of the problems we have.     If we work towards eliminating death, then if we don't die then we can't go to heaven as death takes people to heaven. So, if we cheat death then heaven will be here on earth or we will work very hard to make sure that we make earth as good as heaven, so we won't lose anything by eliminating death. Now people die simply because we are not investing as we should in research and development and to make things worse, we are spending $billion making things that kill humans. Some governments are spending $billions making all kinds of viruses, biological, digital and cyber to try to recreate the worst parts of history as a weapon to command its people and control the world. I think it's just simply plain wrong to try to recreate the scenes of medieval times during the black death. It is a crime that in the New World is punishable by death by the assassin. What I am saying is that if we stop all activities that conflict with the first rule the right to life and to self-preserve, we will be taking a bold step toward achieving the New World. Things like weapons manufacturing, defense, making of viruses and using these as weapons or as watermarks to claim rights to property or even people all conflicts with the right to life and to self-preservation. All these activities will be banned through laws that will be into effect as soon as possible. The stage I am talking about is a stage where we will have found all answers to death and especially aging. Mankind will live longer than now without aging. You will be shocked that some governments in the name of protection are deliberately making their people wrinkling and age very fast as a protection so they can have jobs and achieve party agendas, a crime in the New World only punishable by death by the assassin. This is a violation of all international laws pertaining to human rights. People like these are worse than evil tyrants like Hitler and worse than the devil himself. This is the greatest sin as this not only conflict with the first rules but hinders any form of progress through the development stages and probably one of the sins that any government can do. It is fitting here to call governments or leaders involved as Hostis Humani Generis; enemies of mankind.

## OK, what is the New World?

The New World is a single unit with all different parts which are so diversified all working together as one with a single aim to maintain and develop the New World further until the benefits of the unit out weights any other situation. Picture the New World as a single-family unit all working together for the better of the family. The unit is so connected and networks in order to further its development. Everyone works together for the benefit of the family. There is fighting, quarreling and all kinds of fighting but all for the benefit of the family. Everything is done in a positive way to stir competition with all good intentions. At the end of the day, everyone works to enhance the family. I have given you the analog of the family unit because this describes correctly the New World. The family is the closest thing to the New World in that a family unit is the best unit close to heaven. In a family, you don't see differences you are all connected to each other somehow. Even if you fight, it is for the best of the family. All rules and laws are for the best of everyone. You don't build a wall to separate your room from that of your sibling. You don't invest a fortune in weapons with the aim of using them on your family. You don't make viruses to use on your family. You save for yourself but occasional to help your family too if they are struggling. If you have any extra money surely, you won't buy guns in case, you have a fight with your siblings. Everything you don't do regarding your family are things that will be banned through laws. The family is a classic example, a model of the New World. A world where you don't see boundaries. You all live under one roof. You don't need a permit to go to your siblings' room. You don't need title deeds for the sitting room couch. If for argument's sake, say you win the lottery, you don't spend the money buying or making guns you will use on your siblings, but you might buy them a car, etc. Here I often have people cry; socialism. This is not socialism. No one is saying you should not work for your own betterment no. In fact, the family is the best unit that encourages competition and effective use of resources and encourages expansion all in the right direction.

**The family is a perfect model of the New World.**

Families work for the good of the unit and are the most sophisticated forms of interaction. Ideally, if the world can live like a family unit, then it will have achieved the New World. It's easy for a family to achieve this status and work at optimal or above levels because all people in the family share more common attributes and are bonded together through the parents the mother and father. So, it's easy to see why this is difficult when people are not related. As the family grows and the siblings grow, they are at one-point going to leave the family to start their own in society. So, the family after having have started well will reach a certain stage when the siblings have grown too to start their own families. The family then collapses in that in the end it will get back to the original forms where the parents are left alone.

## The Society Level.

The family expands and the siblings move out into the society and here the people are all different without any common attributes that bring them together. They are all not related either by blood or DNA. That's where all our problems start. We have people working to sabotage others to gain an advantage in society. Everyone works to better themselves at the expense of society. We have all kinds of problems. These people are not related and fight with aims to kill each other to eliminate competition completely. The big question is how can we make a society function as a family with all the different people fighting for resources, etc.?

## The National Level.

Even worse is the national level. We have so much diversity with people not related and all from different backgrounds living and working together but one for him or herself. The relationships are complex, and people's tastes and views differ greatly, and it is difficult to allocate resources as it is hard to find things people like. The leaders have a dilemma and end up doing what the majority like rather than what each wants. In a family it is easy to please everyone as the head of the house can say, buy a present for each family member as they like them. At the national level that is a different situation. The big challenge is to harmonize everyone to work together.

## The Global Level.

The problems become even worse at the global level.

How can you bring the whole world together to work together as a family eliminating divisions and all obstacles? The world is not connected by anything and as such it will be difficult to see everyone working together to achieve common goals. Instead, people would rather kill each other as a survival tactic.

## The New World.

So, I am saying the New World will operate like a family even though the people are not bound by blood or DNA. The challenge is to bring everyone together and keep them living as a family even though they are not related in any way. Sounds easy but for the past 2000 years all mankind did was wage wars on each other killing women and children. Spending precious resources on weapons which only fuel divisions and selfish fighting. So why was it difficult and what has changed?

Wars were calls for help to change totally abandoning the defense stages and all its attributes like emphasis on weapons and huge spending on the military. The idea was after the two world wars for the people to dig small holes and spit in them acknowledging that wars were evil and something that should be a thing for the past. Wars were wake-up calls to stop allocating any money for the military. The idea was to recognize that everyone is like a family and as such there was no need for making weapons. If you win the lottery would you buy guns to use on your family or you would buy them presents? The problem was that no one had foreseen the problems nor took steps to facilitate the smooth transition from the defensive stages to networking and cooperation. This is something I am going to do.

## Put new laws to eliminate the fear of surprise attacks.

Laws to outlaw weapons production with immediate effect. Make it illegal to allocate budgets with the aim of inciting wars and cause others unnecessary worries in fear of being attacked. The military will be a thing of the past. I argued throughout this book that these stages conflict and cannot be combined. The main reason why it was a big issue and in the end after the two world wars choose to remain in the defensive stages instead of abandoning this altogether. This time it will be easy because before the Third World War new laws will be in place to ban everything that hinders the move to a new stage of development. When everyone in the whole world has stopped making weapons and abandoned the defense or evolved with the current military with new tasks that don't conflict with the first rules.

## How can we make everyone become part of a 'family'?

We have seen that a family easily works together and often works at optimal levels simply because everyone concerned is related to each other. They are all bound by blood and DNA or genes. In theory, if the whole world was related then heaven would easily be attained. The whole world would have worked together in harmony. There was surely no need to spend $trillions on weapons. All that money could have been used to target aging and death. Mankind could have developed sophisticated systems by now that we would not talk about building border-walls. We would be on the internet offering our houses to be booked by others when we are not using them. We would be traveling globally easily as everyone would by now have their own airplanes so fast and sophisticated that traveling around the globe would be in minutes. Imagine the whole world as a family with everyone linked and related to each other. Imagine what could not have been done and what would have been achieved.

## Yes, the secret is to make the whole world a family unit.

Now you can easily understand the New World and the idea of heaven. This is a family that will exist forever without siblings moving out. This is a family that will never fight if they do it's for the benefit of the family. There is still competition but, in the end, all that everyone is doing is work together. If the family unit grows with new siblings being born the parents are never going to make digital viruses to control or kill the siblings like what is happening today in developed countries. Instead the father or head of the house is going to look for a bigger better house. If there is no food in the house, the head of the house is not going to buy poison to kill some siblings like what is happening today. The head will not build walls to separate the siblings instead he is going to build a common area were all siblings can gather together networking and cooperating. It's easy because the head is not wasting money on weapons making weapons that are not needed. Every cent is put to good use by developing the family. New houses for the siblings, new computers, new cars, etc. In the end the family blossoms and becomes even more productive. The family will fight to promote good health so they live longer as much as they can. In the end, they work together and their life on earth will be like the so-called 'heaven life'. This is the New World. A world that uses resources effectively eliminates all negative activities that conflict with the first rule. Imagine never making weapons or missiles or biological or cyber weapons? Imagine all the money on military and defense being channeled into health or education or technology? Surely by now, we would have developed sophisticated planes. Connected globally. Eliminated all boundaries and introduced other forms of security that we would not worry about locking our houses when we are not there. We could easily offer someone traveling to our country to use the house for certain hours when we are not there. We will be doing everything to make sure we use resources effectively. Health and living standards would have improved tremendously as fewer people would be dying. Population pressure on earth would have made others look for other forms of accommodation or in other planets. Some people would be literally living in the sky. We would have developed ways to live in the sky or to build skyscrapers that would go all the way up. This is the New World, the heaven in the bible the only difference being that we don't have to die first to reach this heaven. So, all money on military and defense to be channeled to other areas. I am going to ban defense and the military will evolve and soldiers etc. will be trained as assassins and paid highly. Express-command to put an end to this through our laws and courts as a deterrent. Anything to make anything that conflicts with the first rule is not only a criminal offense but punishable by death [through our laws and courts]. We are going to be very bold. Eliminating all people's fears. The current culture of intimidation and threats will be a thing for the past as new laws will be in place to not only ban dirty tactics that keep people hooked on weapons and defense for fear of surprise attacks. Express-command to put an end to this through our laws and courts as a deterrent. Such tactics are barbaric and used by low lives who have nothing to offer and to keep their jobs would rather intimidate everyone, so they hang onto an obsolete culture and institutions. This New World is not for people like this. Trust me some people are evil to the bone to cleanse them means to drag all to court and give death sentences. Some people have for centuries used these dirty tactics and made their living doing that. This is not just the only way they know how but a method they invented to get things easily and cheaply. They would rather die defending these evil practices and we say so be it. I swear by the assassin to do a wonderful job. What we are claiming is transparent and for the good of everyone. Where everyone has rights and the system fair. No one shall die for anyone. Everyone shall have the highest self-esteem that they will see no point to die for someone else. Everyone will want to live forever because life will be good. No one will torture anyone so that they kill someone on their way-out with the given hope that they will go to heaven where life is easy. People will have been taught and educated that heaven is a stage of human development that will be achieved here on earth. Somehow, we will be able not only to reverse aging but to eliminate aging completely. Imagine living for centuries in your youthful state?

I had someone suggested that it was willful thinking. That is what they said when someone said one-day mankind would fly but somehow mankind managed to make planes. That is what they said when someone said mankind would make space stations but somehow people live in space. I believe everything is achievable. The only problem is resource management and affordability. We are using precious resources on useless things; like weapons when the whole world is becoming friends or if you like families. A new leader in me has arisen to put laws and rules that will see mankind abandon being afraid and take the next step into the development process. It's never going to be the same again. A new hybrid is rising that will not tolerate nonsense a topic to be discussed later in Chapter: Justice and Reconciliation. It requires a bold strategy to achieve what I am advancing. All these people reversing previous achievements and taking short cuts of making deadly-agents which they use not just on foreigners but on their own people as watermarks so that no one touches them. An inferior irresponsible cruel form of running a country or conserving their people though Eugenics all this would be a thing of the past. We shall publicly challenge and eliminate these. They are Hostis Humani Generis. An enemy of mankind and as such as good as dead.

## So how can we make everyone in the world feel and act as if they are related and part of the 'family'?

They say that blood is thicker than water and there is some truth in that. It's easy for people to accept their differences and work together if they are related by blood. Whatever they do is for the good of the family unit. But what about in the real world where people are not related? How do we begin to make them somehow become related? I put the question to one of my colleagues and his answer was somehow interesting. His answer was in research and development and genes manipulation. He suggested that it's not the blood that binds people together but some undiscovered genes that can be replicated and as such be used to make all people feel related somehow. Good answer, I replied, but that system is easily manipulated and abused nevertheless still a good reply. I think all the major problems we have today are a result of this kind of playing God. Those in power and position of trust have gone on to use this research and experiments to their advantage of taking people for granted. Before dismissing the idea, I think a lot of research and development must be done. The second solution would be to make digital chips that carry some form of code after studying families. The chips are then implanted, and these chips would act as the same family's genes or blood that connects the whole world together so that the world acts as a family with the chips providing what blood and the same genes provide. This would be ideal but then again, this conflicts with the first rule above all these would easily be abused to manipulate others and use radiation that is harmful to life so conflicts with the first rule.

# CHAPTER EIGHT

CAN YOU MIX THE OLD WINE WITH THE NEW WINE? WHAT
IT REAL MEANS TO START AFRESH FOR A NEW WORLD.

The need for a clean shave.

A new beginning.

No excuses.

A new people.

A new way of doing things.

A new way of thinking.

At the beginning of this book, I discussed the only way we can
move from an obsolete system to a new one. It's something that
cannot happen as a transition. A transition involves merging and
interchanging, which means that some old components of the
system must be passed over. But the question I posed at the
beginning of this chapter is whether new wine can be mixed with
the old wine. Or new wine put into old wine containers? Just can't
work. The change I am talking about in this book is a total change.
This change arises because the old system is outdated and
therefore out of touch with reality. The system, in other words, is
obsolete. Only a new system would render the current system
obsolete. But how can we change from an old system to a
completely new system without taking over parts of the old
system? Only the crash of the current system would invoke the
need for a completely new system. Something that will cause a
crash of the current system would pave way for a completely new
system. I am saying the current system must crash to pave way for
the new system a New World Order. So, to answer the question at
the beginning of this chapter, whether we can mix new wine and
the old wine, the answer is no. The old system is of no use to the

New World. We have all the problems we have simply because of the old system. To start a new, we need a complete going back to the drawing board. A fresh start from stretch. The old system must crash. I am proposing that the current system must crash or has already crashed for the new system to be implemented without any problems. Imagine rebuilding after a great tsunami that killed everyone. Imagine rebuilding after a huge storm? Imagine rebuilding after a huge volcanic eruption? I think one of you might say stop there. If it is this easy how come no one has ever proposed to do this? Some have tried but, in most cases, their chosen methods involve mixing the new wine and the old wine. The new wine would simply corrupt the old fermented wine and in the end, the new wine would turn into the old wine so that in the end we end up with the situation at the beginning. The old wine is already fermented and strong that it will overshadow the new wine. What we want is for the new wine to take over and be the dominant power or force but as long as the old wine is there this will take time to achieve. So far, the people would go for the tested and trusted and already fermented wine. If to ask people which wine, you would prefer the new or old wine of course everyone would go for the old wine simply because it's fermented and matured enough to taste good. But is good the same thing as being the right thing? It can be good but still not the right system or fit for purpose. OK, the old wine might be best, but we will still end up in the same situation as at the beginning with the same problems. Surely this is what we don't want simply because this is just for the great taste that won't last long after the wine has escaped our body, we feel empty again as at the beginning. As with the new wine, one would argue that even though it's not mature enough and or doesn't taste really great the way it is made and the ingredients are for everyone's liking simply because unlike the old wine that is meant for a few privileged the new wine is universal and the only way forward. OK, I have established the rationale behind the new wine. It up-to-date with the taste of the people and it lays the New World principles of upholding the rule of the law, diversity, equality and empowers high self-esteemed people. A people who work not harder but smarter for everything they have. This eradicates lazy people who would rather choose to be loaded with digital viruses in the name of protection rather than work harder and smarter. As in earlier chapters humans are meant to develop and evolve to stages where life on earth would be comparable to the state of mind known now as the heaven or paradise. I have personally argued that this" heaven or paradise" is a phase in human development that will be experienced here on earth. The current belief that people must die to go to heaven is a misconception. We as humans must fight these wasteful leaders spending resources on weapons that will kill all humans instead of on advancing through the development process. It is our responsibility to show the way and pave the way for the journey to heaven but here on earth. All this talk that if you die, you will go to heaven is a misconception. The idea is not to fight to die so that you go to heaven. The idea is to fight these evils so that we make life on earth the same as life in heaven.

**God's Dilemma.**

I explained also at the beginning of this book that God out of boredom created man. First, he didn't need mankind at all. But as I will explain later, there are three attributes of God that made him create man. I am saying God simply because he is omniscience, omnipotent and omnipresent he created man in His own image so that man will become like him one day. He created man with his image. God created a small god in the man so that mankind will grow, evolve and develop into him. God new man must evolve and think fast and advance so that one day man would become God himself a theme I have advanced at the beginning of this chapter supported by Genesis 3V 22

22Then the LORD God said, "Behold, the man has become like one of us, knowing good and evil. And now, lest he reach out his hand and take also from the tree of life, and eat, and live forever..."

Man will one day become like God after evolving to know what is good and evil. This is the stage that makes man become God knowing what is good and what is evil. After acquiring this knowledge man must evolve into another stage. This stage involves killing and metaphorically eating the fruits of life to live forever. In short, if we what, to be honest, it is true that mankind can live here on earth as God does in heaven if mankind evolves to such a degree of knowing what is good and what is evil. Furthermore, man must eat the fruit of the tree of life in order to live forever here on earth. So, this makes sense, and it goes hand in hand with what I am saying that man one day will evolve to live like God. I have advanced these ideas from my other book [The Vice President the Electronic Transfer published 17/01/2019].

So, evolution is part and parcel of humanity. We need to conquer our fears in order to move to the next development stage. Over the past centuries, fear has made us stick to what we know best but at the same time hindering progress. Your devious and manipulating leaders have themselves embarked on dirty tricks to instill fear into your hearts so that you put defense as your priorities a strategy that satisfies their political agenda at the expense of humanity's development.

Above I have argued that the system must fail. The system must crash. I know some people have tried everything they could to take us to the next stage but have failed. Why have they failed and what makes you special that you will take humanity to the next stage of development? Fact, yes it seems some have foreseen this, but I think they ignored the question at the beginning of this chapter. Can you mix the new wine with the old wine? I think they mixed the new wine with the old wine. I think they tried to adopt the new wine into the old wine and hope for a smooth transition. There are very few cases in life when a new system takes over a current system as a handover. Why? Simply because often two systems are not compatible and if they are, then it's not referred to as a new system rather than as an upgrade. A new system will totally replace an old system and if this happens, then there is a system change rather than just an upgrade. The old system to reiterate must crash. Once it has crashed, then and then the new system can take over. There can never be a smooth transition in that case if it happens then it is not a complete change but just an upgrade or alteration of the current to accommodate the new system, but this is not what I want to happen. What is needed is for a complete change of the current system? OK, I have given you the background justification for a new way of doing things but how do we go about achieving that?

First to answer that I must address the problems associated with change. Change is something that can't happen overnight simply because you can't change people's habits overnight. Therefore, for over 2000 years we are still in the defensive stages. It's not easy as advanced in the earlier chapters. Defense is the hinge-pin of all politicians. Defense drives the economy, and it's easy to meet all the manifesto's goals. Defense oriented politicians are the most popular and most remembered. Is it a surprise to you that threats to defense are followed by wars? Can it also be said that to invoke a war you just need to threaten the people's defenses and you have a war? This is the politician's greatest trick.

In the past, the methods adopted only created a vicious cycle in that the method adopted ended up causing people being stuck into the defensive stage. The 'perfect method' often chosen to drive humanity out of the defensive stages was waging wars. Mankind has used wars to try to make humanity move up to the next development stage but to no avail. Wars in theory create a situation that will make it easy for humanity to move away from the defensive stages, but surprising wars fuel the need for defensive strategies. Wars seemed ideal as wars often killed more people living a few who if things were perfect would now move to other stages but wars only fueled the people's fears. After witnessing the effects of war, the remaining population would invest and priorities defense in case they are attacked again. It's just a natural human instinct. Witness a traumatic event then it's natural for your fears to increase. After wars for a short while people move away from the defensive stages and start networking trying to avoid further wars in the future after witnessing the effects of wars. After a period of two years a time that fears are still vivid in the people's minds then people revert again to the defensive stages. Look at the period after the Second World War. A lot of networking among all countries and people happened at their peak with the establishment of international bodies. Two years after the war people had forgotten already and back to the situations that created the world war in the first place. Nature or nurture has played a major role in trying to push humanity out of the defensive stages of development. Look at World War I, this was the first opportunity to kick-start the move away from the defensive stages to the next stages of networking and cooperation. Like I said above two years after the war the people have forgotten already. Through a few people with foresight, humanity was directed through the right path; use wars to destroy all the things we don't need and see the effects of war so that in the future you come together thereby going into the next stage of development. It's another clever way of teaching these politicians how to use scarce resources effectively and on something else other than weapons as you will end up killing each other. So, wars created perfect situations of making people realize that wars were not good, that making weapons was a dumb thing and that people must cooperate all the time and negotiate. But wars had downsides as well as the traumatic experiences instilled fears into people so much that they ended up prioritizing defense. The actual opposite of what was intended. Initially, the idea behind wars was to fight and make-up to prevent another fracas but the effects of the war were so traumatic to cause mistrust and not trusting. This phenomenon is best explained by the Cold war. Fears and mistrust become a big thing after World War I. That in turn fueled the need to make more destructive weapons. We have many nations secretly making Weapons of Mass Destruction out of fear of surprise attacks. So, we see how the chosen methods instead of solving the problem caused people to prioritize defense. So, wars have in the past fueled fears and made people prioritize defense. A vicious circle would you agree. This has created what I will call a vicious circle in that wars made people go around and around ending up in the same situation. That fueled huge defense budgets as well which in turn made defense a priority and over time the huge stocks of weapons had to be destroyed and that meant wars too. After wars, the people are more afraid after the experiences that defense becomes a priority. Clearly, you can see that people underestimated the traumatic effects of witnessing a war. They hoped wars would automatically make people realize how bad they are and simply move to the networking stages. It can be said that to some extent the two major world wars have played a major role and pushed humanity to the next stage of networking and cooperation, but this was for a short period as certain countries forced everyone back to the old stage. I know you are wondering why it's that difficult since everyone loves an upgrade be it a new phone, a car, a house, etc. Recall at the beginning in chapter I explained that this is the New World; a heaven on earth where everyone has rights under the law. A New World where women and children's lives are valued greatly that the leaders can die at the hands of the assassin if they abuse this right. A world where making the oath to die for the leader and country is valued so much that it becomes a criminal act for our best boys and girls to die needlessly in combat. A world where there is networking and negotiation. If for argument's sake let us say that country A needs oil, it must negotiate peacefully to have that oil and pay a fair price. You can start to see the problem. The current system and institutions are based on the bully-victim, slave -master or thieve-victim notions. Look at every current incident. Look at all recent wars. They are all the bully-victim prototype. In 1956 Eisenhower the then US President declared that he would only go to war if any nation nationalized its oil resources because oil depletes a nation's financial resources.

Nationalizing the canal "was not the same as nationalizing oil wells... [which] exhaust a nation's resources."

We can see clearly that whatever follows is just a justification, but the main reason is that a bully would not want to pay a proper price but instead would rather take by force. No matter how wrong it sounds that is the reality. We have seen countries stirring up events so that they justify going to war to steal resources. I have also mentioned above that we have seen a new form of threat now known as terrorism just to keep in the fear so that defense becomes our priority. We have seen shocking events like the 9/11 attacks which I think are related to the issues discussed here; to keep people afraid forever so that defense remains our priority. You can easily see why it will be difficult for people to move away and why the politicians would want everyone hooked on fear. This is a cheaper method of running the country and getting what you want. Imagine if the world was a fair place as in the New World Order and everyone pay the market price of a commodity do you think people would spend more money on weapons if the oil was dear? The truth is it is cheaper to spend more on weapons and use the weapons to take by force. This is the truth and the main reason behind huge defense budgets. I ask you what the difference between these politicians is and say with bank robbers. Have you imagined why robbing banks is a major problem? Simply if the politician can do the same and get away with that why can't they? It's the same thing. A camouflaged gang of oil robbers sent abroad to steal at gunpoint the same as a gang in balaclavas stealing at gunpoint. Someone might say these guys in camouflage were authorized but one can also argue that the guys in balaclavas were authorized too by the gang leader. Who has a right to take other's resources? Who says nationalization of oil is a sin and to who?

Having said that, it is clear why humanity has been stuck in the defense stages of development simply because it is a cost-effective way of doing things. All you need to do is to make the biggest weapon and all you want you can get. So, the current system is corrupt. The current system is based on who has the biggest weapon. It's based on who is the biggest bully. Worse of all it's based on which evil cult you belong to? We have seen the fueling of evil military cults fueling this movement making sure that mankind will remain in the defensive stages. It has become synonymous with obey or die. You can see for yourself that there can't be honoring rights whatsoever. These cults are not open to everyone you must have certain characteristics and attributes to qualify. Okay, maybe that matters less but are they upholders of the rule of the law? In a nutshell that is just a dream as with power comes great bullying too. We have countries torturing people in broad daylight and getting away with it simply because they belong to these evil cults. You can see also that a move away from these defensive strategies would render all these cults obsolete and so we have these cults hanging to the rails with both hands threatening and all the like. A New World is a world of advanced people, high self-esteemed people and people who want the better out of everyone. This is against the current situation. The current situation is about protecting your own at whatever expense and to use any force necessary if we have the necessary weapons. These cults have gone all over the world stealing resources or getting them at unfair prices to build weapons. Who needs weapons? At the beginning of this chapter, I mentioned that it is not possible to mix the new and the old wine simply because the two are not compatible. The old system without weapons it's instantly rendered obsolete. These institutions were created with weapons at the center of everything they do. No weapons and they stop to exist. A move to the next stage of development renders them obsolete. I take you back to the above arguments that God created man and hoped that he would teach him so that one day he knows what is good and bad and, in the end, become 'God' himself. So, from the beginning, God has a plan for mankind. He created man to test his intelligence if he can evolve and progress through all the development stages without any difficulties. It's like testing a raccoon. Setting up challenges for it to complete in order to move to the next stages. A raccoon will do whatever it takes for a meal. It can perform great tasks to achieve their goal and get a meal. Ever watched these videos of Racoons multitasking to get a meal? This is what humanity was doing all these past 2000 years. I ask a question. Do you think this is what humanity is destined to do? Fight for food and quarrel for positions to be on heaven's list? I know this is what most people think. This is what your leaders for the past 2000 years have been doing. Fight for resources and make sure you are on heaven's list. Really? I think mankind is wasteful. Lacks foresight and the ability to understand what is really needed to do to progress to the next stage. Imagine a raccoon fighting hard to think ways of getting food when it should be thinking of a way to free itself from captivity. I don't care how smart it might be if it can't free itself then whatever it does is meaningless. The first rule is critical here. Right to life. If you are under someone else, then you are good as dead. The raccoon okay it might be clever it gets food in the end, but do you think God created man with his image so that the sole purpose of mankind is to look for food while as slaves for God? No. God created man in His own image so that man becomes like himself. To answer this, we must analyze in detail who is God, what he has done and how he lives on earth. I know some people might not believe in God but whatever you believe my arguments still apply. If another force, nature, etc. created mankind then that force had the same intention as God.

I will explain what I think happened first before analyzing God.

God after creating the world realized that he could create a man who will become like him. But as we know God is a spirit and as such lives in heaven. He manages to live in heaven because he is a spirit. He blew this spirit into mankind but created man with his image and covered his body with flesh that suits earth. He set a challenge to teach man so that one day man will become God on earth and in the end as he evolves will live just like God does in heaven but here on earth. Man must advance and evolve so that one day he would not die but live on earth forever. Clearly, the task at hand here whether you believe in the bible or not is to do whatever it takes that we dominate the earth and live on earth forever. I argued in the first chapters that the fact that we must die to go to heaven is wrong. Okay maybe that is what is happening now, but the idea is to evolve and advance so much that we will find ways of stopping aging and death so that we live in human bodies here on earth forever. It's a challenge that mankind must endure and conquer to become God himself but on earth. Okay if you have chosen the short coward way you can die and go to heaven. God would still accept you there but honestly, that is not his plan. Mankind is lacking foresight to realize that we must find ways to advance. It's a shame some regimes are making digital viruses and lace everyone in their country as a protection strategy a recipe for disaster if you ask me. People are being loaded with these digital viruses as weapons to safeguard their leaders and their way of life with serious mutations effects that we have what might be called a zombie land. I personally think God if he existed would send a huge storm that will kill all and preserve a few unpolluted ones. I can easily see why God would recreate a Noah. Or why God would send the angels of death to kill everyone as in Revelations. It makes sense. These leaders are doing great harm to their own people in the name of protection breaking all international laws. So, God's plan was to make mankind be God on earth just like he is God of heaven man will become 'God' on earth. In the end, we will have two paradises for the spirit in heaven for those who died before mankind gained foresight and wisdom and heaven on earth when no man dies but all live forever. This analysis is important as I will explain the New World and how it is different from the current world. We have our goal to change from the current situation to the New World. We now know what the New World is like. We also know what is stopping humanity from advancing. We know the methods that were used before and their shortfalls.

I explained the need for a system crash before a new system is adopted. The current system must crash first to pave the way for a new system. The magic word here is a crash. I believe the system crashed years ago but how do we proceed from here? This is the magic question.

# CHAPTER NINE

WAR?

Not even a smoldering stump left.

One man for himself TWO for us all.

Takeout all at once.

War. What is it good for?

Ever wondered why mankind kill each other for? Is it to do with natural instincts to relieve pressure on resources or is it simply out of inferior thinking? It can be said that natural survival instincts cause mankind to kill each other. If it were animals, then one would say that it is simply nature, mostly for food. But for mankind, what are the real reasons to kill each other? It can't be for food surely as in the animal kingdom. There it's self-explanatory; anyone other than your kind is either food or an enemy. But if you all can talk and understand each other, why kill each other? But one might argue that this goes way back to the beginning of creation. Killings becomes part and parcel of mankind. Honestly, if you believe in the creator, then one would argue that it is part of creation to give mankind instincts to kill for the sole purpose of survival. Either kill or be killed. But is the killing as we are witnessing nowadays the intended plan of the creator? I know during the beginning days God or the creator made killing part and parcels of the whole system. The ecosystem cannot maintain the balance on its own therefore mankind has to keep everything balanced by eliminating others usually what they called the weak simply because these put a drain on resources for nothing without much benefit. It's more like survival of the fittest evolution in creating people who have a will to live and fight forever possible the only way mankind must survive. Recall in earlier chapters I pointed out that the creator God or who you think created mankind new mankind in the end must become like him

176

and manage earth just like what the creator does in heaven. God is like a master teaching mankind his student to become like him one day. But to be God or the creator is no easy task. Mankind must go through a series of tests and challenges and overcome all to be God one day. It does not stop there as mankind has to evolve and develop through all the stages and start thinking smarter rather than harder as what is happening now. The first chapters clearly laid out what I think is the development process the way we as humans must take to progress to the next level and one day think and act like God that is a superior being. Everything that is on earth is for our benefit to use and move to the next level. Likewise, there are also things on earth that are there as challenges to progress. Death itself is a test. A challenge to mankind. The difference between the creator and humans is that the creator does not die. Death is the only factor that distinguishes mankind and the creator. All humans no matter how powerful and rich you are death will come knocking as well. God knew for mankind to be like him he must go the extra mile and acquire superior knowledge that will see him overcome this challenge and live forever. I pointed out that even though you might not believe in God and all this creator stuff; it is more like general knowledge that can be applied to everyday life. If you are a teacher and you find a protégé obviously you will want your protégé to become like you one day and with this, in mind, God or the creator set up challenges that mankind has to overcome one day and one of the challenges is that of cheating death. Eliminating death and extending life to live forever. This is supported by Genesis 22v1. That God or the creator setup obstacles so that man cannot live forever unless he eats fruits of the tree of life. This is not literally eating fruits, but it's acquiring knowledge that distinguishes you from everyone else that you will understand that death itself is a failure. Everything on earth that causes death can be overcome once one has gained that enlightenment. They say the biggest killer of mankind is wear and tear in old age that everything stops functioning but that wear, and tear is a challenge. Let's pause for a while and ponder. Take the mechanical pulley system designed by man; the more it is used the more the worn parts and the less the lifespan. One day parts will simply fall. But a wise engineer will look after the pulley system maintaining it over the years.

There is no engineer in his sound mind who would put grit inside the pulleys system simply because it will wear and tear very fast before you know it will simply be out of use. Is it wonder why a tortoise would live up to 200 years or more? It is not rocket science; wear and the tear simply do more damage and reduce the lifespan of tissue. This knowledge must be acquired mankind has to figure out a way of overcoming all the obstacles. Whether you believe in God or not, it is common sense that the sole purpose of life is to survive. Okay, mankind no matter what has natural instincts to survive. Some people have to die as part of nature to maintain the ecological balance but over some years it seems an evil force possessed mankind that the whole world started killing each other after some years that turns to be forgotten until a time when things turn ugly again. Mankind would group and start killing each other again.

## War what is it good for?

I know most people would jump to the conclusion that this is part of nature's clever plan to balance the ecosystem. As more and more people are born fewer and fewer people die especially when we spend a lot of money on the weapons and defense that makes it a time-bomb that war would be inevitable, I mean world war. It's perfect logic that the more weapons we make the more we will need to justify such wastage of scarce resources that can only mean dirty tricks and all the sort and that alone will trigger a major world war. I know it might be remote, but everyone is watching everyone else and the watchers are being watched as well. They might pretend that their acts are Bonafide when we all know that they are evil to the bone and what can that only mean; future wars. But again, is this war just a war to balance nature? I think over the past 2000 years mankind has been missing these great chances, these great calls for help to move to the next level of development and in the end, mankind has failed to take the right turn going back round the way he came. It's an opportunity being presented to him to challenge the norm and take a different route. We have gone in circles over the centuries. Wars have created a situation for us to take another route so that we don't end up on the same route as before. I don't believe these wars were just wars to easy up pressure on population and resources as some might argue? These wars were opportunities to push us out of defensive stages to another level of development. How often do you see the whole world taking sides to fight each other? I know it's a fact that we are the architects of our downfall as we keep on making weapons and spending huge budgets on the military at the expense of other areas. This will only end up in a world war. The two world wars we had; namely World War I and II were not coincidences, no. These were outcries for help. Change or perish. Take a different route and one day become like gods. I know people might think I am taking them back to socialism. Is this socialism? But before I answer you let me finish on these world wars. A force in the world created sparks that would trigger a move away from defensive economies. These world wars were meant to traumatize mankind thereby temporarily making him insane or incapable of resistance so that the trauma of wars would push him to abandon making weapons and thinking about defense. In other worlds imagine witnessing a traumatic event so shocking that in logic terms you might be referred to as temporarily impaired in that whatever decision you make will be to a greater extent be influenced and guided by the traumatic events. In such cases, if given the same condition anyone put through this trauma but without experiencing this trauma would not make the same decision. Let's say someone witnessed someone being hit by a car while walking on the pavement and soon afterward calls for a taxi to finish his journey. If that person had not witnessed the traumatic accident that person would have continued his journey on the pavement and on foot. In this case, the traumatic events enhanced the fears this man general has about the dangers of cars as we cross the road. This event is the trigger of the actions that followed soon after witnessing that event. Had this person not witnessed this event he would not have made such a decision? There are so many events that can be said to have a contributory effect in that the event acted as a trigger to whatever that person went on to do ceteris paribus. I can look at the 9/11 attacks in the USA and I can say with much conviction that what later followed was influenced by this traumatic event. We saw a lot of people buying their own homes fearful of towers and mistrusting renting property that in turn resulted in a lot of people who would not have taken out loans and mortgages to buy houses doing so. This later trigger the housing market crash as the people who could not afford in the first place just because of the trauma of witnessing the 9/11 attacks made unsound judgment out of fear and spend their savings getting homes they cannot afford in the first place. Had they not witnessed this event they would have kept their savings in their savings accounts and not opted to buy homes? Defense instantly becomes the sole determinant factor triggering the sudden rise in people taking mortgages and loans at the same time using their savings as deposit opting to own their homes away from the tall city buildings. When savings are gone all given to the banks, then there is reduced disposable income that in turn will trigger low purchasing power and less sales and profits of companies. This will trigger job loses that in turn will trigger repossessions and the people all now stripped off their savings are even more exposed. Now their savings have been taken by the banks and their homes repossessed and the traumas of the 9/11 events are still engraved in their minds that will send shock-waves that can result in a system crash. You can clearly see that every part is linked to the first trigger of the traumatic event. If it wasn't for this event, the people would not need to be afraid of anything. They would have continued piling their savings. They would not have taken mortgages they cannot afford. They would have kept their jobs. One can vehemently argue that it is this traumatic event that caused the following decisions. If it wasn't for this event, the people would not have taken the decisions, they took. But all this has nothing to do with the economy or does it? To answer this, I ask you a question. Who benefited from whatever happened after? To answer this, I will tell you in more detail the impacts of what happened.

9/11 attacks were meant to trigger fear, so that defense becomes our priority. Okay, you have been told that the idea behind the attacks was to instill fear by the terrorists. But hey this is a misconception. Fear that is meant to be induced by the terrorist would have little effect on your immediate and afterlife. Okay, you might not travel for a while, but life does not stop. It's human instincts that people continued traveling the only difference being that they started taking precautions avoiding some airlines or airports, but this fear was only 'imaginary'. No doubt that the acts were to instill fear but fear to do what or to trigger what? This fear was to traumatize the American people, so defense becomes the priority. So, you prioritize defense and temporarily make irrational decisions about buying homes which you can't afford. So in short the event is meant to trigger temporary insanity so that you make irrational decisions and buy things you don't need something that can be said as panic buying using the savings you have, actually stripping away your buffer the one you have before they make you lose everything. That time it will be a long time mainly two years after the traumatic event that at the point the fear due to nature will have disappeared as our minds would have forgotten that event from our immediate mind. In these situations, you hear people cursing themselves as if awoken from a trance. Okay, one might say it is their fault because no one held a gun to their head and say buy the house, no. So, everything bad is attributed to them in the end that they lose everything, the savings, and the house and now they are exposed even worse but at the same time, they have forgotten the traumatic eclipse that had clouded their judgments. They can't blame the trauma simply because two years had elapsed and everyone 'can't feel it' like the days and months after its occurrence even though it is still vivid in their minds. I am arguing that this is the work of a sophisticated highly educated and manipulating devil who has detailed knowledge of all this who plans relentlessly to manipulate and steal the people's savings, putting them out of work and leaving them with nothing. It's not a coincidence, no. I ask the question of how terrorists benefit from all this? This is the work of someone who wants to rob every one of their savings plus their incomes after that as they will spend more of their income on repaying the loans. Okay, I will put this in other words. 9/11 was a trigger to 'take back the money from the people leaving the people in such a state that the economy would crash. Does this rhyme like a song? The trigger here is the crash.

"But wait a minute. Isn't it the main purpose of that traumatic event?" one might ask.

Yes, this is the work of a very clever highly educated manipulating devil. 9/11 was meant first to crash the people; to put everyone who has witnessed the event in temporarily insanity state that they 'crash' to make irrational decisions and buy. This is the keyword. So, the event is not an event but a trigger of the decision to buy. Without this then the purpose of the event is not fulfilled. The traumatic event renders everyone who witnesses it incapable of making sound rational decisions. Fear incapacitates them that they only think about finding the strongest form of a place to live having seen the tallest buildings crumble to earth with such swiftness the only option temporarily considered as secure is the homes. I remembered in the science labs at school where you elevate the temperature of a lab rat through a diode chip fired into the lab rat so that the rat becomes thirsty and if thirsty body temperature is elevated, then it becomes hyperactive and if you don't give it the milk or water, it becomes relentless and finds a way to get out. If it wasn't for the chip diode fired into its body, the rat would not need something to quench its thirst. Or a perfect example is what these takeaway companies used to do before the salt ban. They used to deliberately increase salt levels of all their foods so that the customers naturally end up buying drinks not because they needed to but simply because the salted food would increase the need to drink soft drinks after. So, is this not what they call manipulating tricks? To answer you maybe I should ask who benefited from all this? But then again, I think it's best to say the effect of such a move. Okay, the effect of all the fear and panic buying and the housing market crash, financial collapse, etc. was to take away money from the people, yes that's right was to take money away from the consumers to whoever benefited in the end. What?

Yes. The effect is what I call rolling-back and taking whatever the people had back to the master planner. It's like giving people then take back what you have given them together with what was theirs; in this case their savings. It's like stealing. Giving them a magnet that will take all that they have when you take the magnet back. What?

Yes, it's traumatizing you first then give you something so that when I take whatever I give you will lose whatever you have before the gift in other words a sophisticated robbery? The idea behind the plan was the targeting of the people's savings taking everything they had saved and whatever they will work for after the gift and then take everything back and making people lose their jobs in the process so that in the end, they are worse off. Who on earth would do such a thing?

Terrorists? Please!!

Terrorists are people who live in caves. These people worry about putting food on the table let alone devising such a plan. It just doesn't fit the picture. Terrorist's aim is to kill and maim and even if they plan to rob your savings how will they get the money? Whoever is behind this is connected to people who would benefit from all this? Okay, I argued that the idea was to take money from the people, what they have saved and whatever they will work after that. The effect is like that of rolling-back. In the monetary world, we have the banks, the financial and investment institutions and then the government and on the other hand, we have the consumers most of whom work very hard saving for the future. In theory, money moves from the central entities the government, banks, financial institutions, etc. to the consumers as they work very hard and are reward or they borrow money as loans and repays these with interest. So money in theory can move from the central entities to the consumers and it can also roll-back from the consumers but only in very small amounts simply because the consumers are clever enough to understand that they have to keep much of their money in savings accounts away from the central guys who might want it back to their coffers. In reality, huge amounts of money flow to the consumers from the central entities and very little amounts trickle back as interests, bills, repayments, etc. The consumers have been very clever to put safeguards so that the money does not flow back to the central entities. Over the years the consumers have come on top with clever planning to avoid the rolling-back of the money. So, the central entities need a very clever plan to outwit the consumers who stick to their monies like magnets never letting it go. So logically the consumers are of very sound-minded very clever at their own game I think you can agree. The central entities to outwit them they must put them in a position of temporary insanity so that they don't keep their money so tight. In that state, they can easily do things they would not normally do. But you are talking of torture. This is the only method that can render someone temporarily insane. This is a fact as even the FBI and CIA are known in the past to carry out torture practices, that often left a full-grown man with a brain of a toddler. So only torture can achieve their goal. Recall the rat lab in the science class with a chip diode shot into its body and the diode remotely heated up that in turn put the rat in hyperactive mode. All that is simply an act of torture. But in real-life unless secret weapons or instruments are used possibly stuffed deep in the muscles to torture the whole nation would be impractical and the consequences would be detrimental. But trust me another method can achieve the same results. The event must be broadcast live. Why? So that it is witnessed by many to have any traumatic effect. Ever wondered why we had camera crews waiting to film 'perceived 9/11' when the event occurred. The event to take any effect must be broadcast and seen by many. The horrific screams of people and the desperation must be live, so people feel the fear as people hopelessly meet death with everyone sitting unable to do anything. The idea here is to strip all those who witness the event in any form of hope. That makes the event so horrific that people would wish to dig holes into the earth and hide into them. Ever listened to the 9/11 calls when everyone is told to remain and sit still and wait for the rescuers until the final moment when they realize that it's a death trap. This put's the people in a serious traumatic position that some 'temporarily crash'. This is the main idea. Crash. Once that state is achieved the event remains so vivid in the people's minds for at least two years. I said that the effect is that of rolling-back the money from the consumers but what money needs to roll back?

On 10 September $2,3 trillion dollars was missing from the government coffers. What depletes the government's resources more? Wages and salaries. The more people who are employed the more the government must pay more wages, etc. But I am not saying the government was behind this, no. Read carefully. Someone a financial institution or even a foreign government can be behind such a calculated move and just set up the government. This makes sense because I argued that the effect is that of rolling-back the money from the consumers back to the central entities. This would have taken all the people savings and income after that roll-back to the central entities. Is it wonder also that just after the attack huge housing initiatives were adopted to spearhead a housing boom? I am not saying this government policy was a calculated plan, but the government might have simply needed to address the people's fears. It does not make sense though why housing when the towers were the ones destroyed. This method is what I call a third type of error. The only perfect situation this would have worked was when it was the people's homes destroyed in the first place so that the government would provide cheaper houses. This would make sense as the home insurance payouts would be used as deposits for the homes issued by the government. Ever read about the great fire of 1666 Britain? So clearly from the onset, the method is set to fail. Imminent disaster. Such a traumatic event can only leave the people even more fearful and untrusting that they would only feel comfortable in their homes and not rented high rise accommodation. This as I shall point out is a third type error in that the government proposed solutions to wrong problems. First, the destroyed homes were not residential but some city office high-rise flats. This solution would have been the best had the planes destroyed people's homes. This would have meant increased insurance payouts to cover and replace damaged and destroyed houses. So, the insurance money given by the central entities would have been used for deposits instead of the people's savings. Okay, that is the monetary aspect of this event was this all? Unless it was deliberately to steal the people's, savings and initiate a roll-back.

Fear and traumatic events of such magnitude would leave the people very vulnerable and scared that defense at any cost would then become their priority. This means even if before the event they were opposing e.g. any military action to be taken, now they would fully support revenge just as a natural human instinct they say nothing sweeter than revenge. A taste of your own medicine. Sometimes you are your best interpreter. Who best to tell you than yourself? So, one can argue also that this event made it possible to turn the hearts of the people in favor of military action than before the event. This is true two years after the event as the event is still in people's minds. Support for retaliation and any defensive action is at the highest within the first two years than after as the traumatic imprints of the event are slowly erased to a mere recall of what happened that day rather than a stomach-turning event. No wonder sometimes we have horrible events every two years. Look at the USA 2001 we had the 9/11 attacks. In 2003 there was the space shuttle disaster and the Iraq war. 2005 Hurricane Katrina, 2007-8 Global financial crises. 2009 Global financial collapse. But what has all this to do with the wars?

Such events often trigger wars between countries because such a loss of life is very traumatic that countries might group to retaliate as with the Iraq war. Yes, this is the way mankind has been perfecting over the years to maintain the ecological balance.

Why the defense stage? To grow and prosper there must be an imbalance. It's simple it must be easy to find resources and it must be dear to buy things. In a society that is fair then the price is set by the markets and other conditions. More often it is dear as well to buy and could be less profitable to sell. This is because a fair price of goods and resources is set by markets, so everyone pays a fair price. But when you pay a fair price, it means it's expensive if you are buying and if you decide to sell, you won't make a lot as the price is fair even to buy generally low returns. But when there is a huge imbalance and the prices are set by whoever has power, then it is easy to make huge profits as you can buy very cheap and sell at high prices. The defensive stage creates a situation where it is easy to get things if you can use some influence or worse force. That's where weapons come in. The whole idea behind sticking in the defensive is that you get things cheaper. You can bully some people to get what you want. The defensive stage creates a bully-victim situation which facilitates the growth of the bully even to the enormous size. This is simply because the bully does not pay a fair price instead, he uses military force to get what he wants. Ever wondered why NATO etc. were really established? These institutions were created to sustain the bully-victim situation. After the war fuel rocketed sky high as demand increased as countries rebuild at the same time countries with oil supplies nationalized or come together too to act as oil cults in order to control supply. They knew oil prices will exponentially grow over time that it will be hard to buy this commodity at a high price. In response to the oil cults, the West established the weapons cult in NATO. Their only solution was to take by force if need be. No wonder now military cults were ever-growing receiving huge budgets and stockpiling weapons. We can see how world wars are inevitable simply because what is happening is that developed countries and military cults are getting resources all over the world and buying these at a fraction of their real worth and using these to make weapons and then in return use the weapons to take whatever is left and the money obtained is then plowed back into making more weapons starving other areas. If you recall earlier on, I talked about a process I referred to as rolling-back. This instance I am going to talk about a process I will call creaming-out. For an empire to grow fast and very big it can only do so if there is some form of inequality or bully-victim situation. The bully must get resources at low prices in this situation whatever is made by the bully is sent back to be sold at higher prices. But imagine when the bully is getting resources using threats and or force or buying very low through manipulation but whatever is taken is plowed into weapons manufacture. The weapons are then used to further take money from the victims unfairly and in most cases, through threats and intimidation the victim ends up buying the weapons at a high price creaming whatever is left. The process goes on and on but this time the victim is gaining weapons and now the more he starts seeing the bully-victim situation. Now the victim is slowly growing into a bully too. Now we have a bully to bully the situation a recipe for war. The more weapons he gets the more the anger and the danger. The bully, if he does not do anything, will be matched by the victim and it will be only a matter of time before a war breaks out. After the first two world wars, people realized that if nothing is done, these major world wars would be a common thing, and something was needed to ensure the forever existence of the bully-victim situation. Hence the creation of military cults like NATO. This guaranteed the bully-victim situation hence the imbalances, threats, and wars against often the victims whose resources are stolen or taken cheaply in exchange for weapons and support in terms of military training and personnel another form of bullying as a puppet is placed to replace the "evil" leader. Who does great harm someone who kills and oppresses his people over decades but hands out food to some or a force that kills 500 000 women and children in few years than the tyrant they toppled? That is a bullying tactic that silence any form of opposition from other countries in fear that they might end up experiencing the same fate. Everything is well planned and carried out according to the plan. They are very clever and very devious and manipulating. They are all members of a cult and what happens is that the major force proposes a plan to rob and take at force. They then decide others intervene as opposing but they make sure that the majority is in favor of the plan of the major force. In the end, the plan goes ahead but to all, it will appear as if the world is functioning with the observer and checkers and opposers who defends the weak and try to uphold the law but, it's just deception. The bully has grown to such enormous size that talking of freedom and fairness is remote. Nothing wrong in growing to huge sizes but we know what happens whenever there is a bully. There is no talk of human rights or upholding international laws. We have countries abusing all laws on earth, torturing people in broad daylight, practicing modern-day slavery something purportedly to have been abolition years ago but just driven underground now being carried out through sophisticated devices remotely operated like drones. So, what the cults and institutions are doing is refraining and keeping the victim at bay so that they can't form any military attacks. The cult grows huge and huge making even more weapons selling these and stockpiling some. The more power the cult has dominance over time and the less likelihood of major wars. In the past we have had world war one in 1914 to 1918 followed by World War II from 1939 to 1945. A closer look no matter what the reasons are, we can see that it took only twenty-five years to start the war cycle again. Then just after eight years, we had a Cold War that could have resulted in a Third World War. Come the 1960s just twenty-one years after the Second World War we have the possibility of another major world war with the threat of nuclear threats around the world. The reasons why these happen is not important in this chapter. Emphasis is to be placed on what I will call a war cycle. It seems at least every twenty to thirty years the war cycle repeats itself. I will look at the war cycle and its significance.

The War Cycle.

Like I have pointed out above nature has a secret system embedded in its DNA that is if it has one that stipulates and coordinates when we might have a world war. I have pointed out that every 20-30 years nature creates situations when mankind has to destroy all the weapons stockpile in the hope that mankind will see their mistakes and feel the pain of wars so that they can say 'that's it' we have seen enough we don't want any more wars. It's a clever system to help mankind to move through the development stages. We have spent centuries in this stage from the early man-days. But those days it made a real sense. Defense was a priority or perish. Nature and everyone knew this. Those days it was defense first or perish. To explain the issues in this book, I used scenarios of the creator what I call, God's plan. I argued that God or whoever you believe created mankind out of boredom set himself or herself a challenge; To create a being that will pass all the stages he has set so that one day the creature in man will evolve to the highest level of development like God himself. Here I am emphasizing that out of boredom God, or the creator created mankind to see if mankind can become like him and be a God here on earth. Something I have referred to as; God's Dilemma. Same as man's quest to create robots that can become like man himself; Man's Dilemma. God or the creator does not need any creature mankind etc. to exist. God is omnipotent, omniscience and omnipresence and as such is the ultimate in terms of evolution and development while on the other end mankind is the low-level evolving creature same as animals but unlike animals with a potential to solve puzzles and evolve in the process to acquire such knowledge that he will become just like God; and live for forever. So, there are obstacles we must overcome and puzzles we must solve to evolve to other stages. Nature itself is designed by God to sort of guide mankind in which direction to take. Why I say this will come clear later. My arguments are that God drew a plan already and through the books bible etc. has given mankind hints on how to evolve. All mankind must do is to think and listen to all the tell-tell signs and progress to the next stage. Just like any puzzle, some stages provide perfect situations that I can call temptations, but these are to hold people in that stage stalling development or progress. It takes a great brain to notice that these are only stalling tactics just to slow progress and make you waste resources at the expense of other sectors. So I am saying that mankind instead of working around the issue has instead pretended to be clever and formed 'cults' to keep us in the defensive stage instead of thinking ahead and smarter and call wars a day and a thing of the past and progress to another stage of development. Why I am against sticking in the defensive stages is the fact that it wastes resources at the expense of other sectors. Your leaders are trying to juggle everything at the same time and instead of devoting resources where they are needed, they waste a lot on the military. God or the creator in my fictional analog created a plan where it is superior thinking to distinguish the important from the not so important and to choose the correct path. The idea throughout my book is the fact that a system crash is inevitable and a requirement. This can make sure we leave the current old system behind and go for a new system. A system crash can only pave the way for a move to a new stage. Why I am saying that there must be a complete crash and then a move is that like I pointed out above war and defense should be things of the past. In this analog, you cannot combine or transits to another stage carrying the two aspects simply because in my scenario the two are not mutually inclusive nor complementary. It's either you drop defense and move to a new stage or stick in the defensive stage. The reason is that fear and threats whether perceived or imaginary cannot be quantified and as such defense and fear will only have exponential capabilities in that they are hungry for resources and cannot be tamed. How can you measure the threat posed by the opponent? Such attributes make defense a huge consumer of scarce resources and an ever-hungry animal in that as threat level changes we will keep making new and advanced weapons as technology changes wasting resources that could be used for something else. So defensive stages are popular as they consume a lot of resources and are challenging and very important to any success. This makes finding resources at any cost an important part of any government, cult or leader. The fact that defense also arms the bullies makes it easy for the bullies to use the weapons to fetch more resources to make even powerful weapons. Any system that is sustainable is a system that takes and contributes among all its parts. We have people buying resources to build goods and then the goods are sent and sold back to the people who in turn use the resources to make more money and resources. The resources are sold again and bought to make goods that are to be sent back to be used to make more goods. You can see that it is a cycle with everyone benefiting and resources and goods plowed back and exchanged so that the system is complete in that every part somehow relies on the other part to exist and function. But in defensive stages, this cycle is missing or ill-defined in that in the end war is inevitable. You can see that such a system is poised to fail and will only result in a war. War throughout this book as I will explain should not be viewed as a bad evil, act by mankind, no but as a call for help to change. The system as I explained has obstacles, bottlenecks, and puzzles together with temptations that will only stale development and make you waste resources. It takes a clever brain to notice all these and make the right decision. So, is an outcry for help the first proof that the system is not fair? Unless you change, then expect war. So, war is a trigger point. A highlighter that shows you malfunctioning in the system. In defensive systems or stages, the system is unsustainable in that it is meant to crash simply because it is unbalanced and unfair. I explained that the system needs an exchange of resources that facilitate the development and progress of those involved. The perfect system has inputs, processes, outputs, and feedback. In defensive stages the system is bound to collapse simply because resources taken are not matched by a share portion of goods or resources that some parts are stuffed continuously that in the end they are bound to fight back and crash the whole thing. This is the way nature intended things. But after the Second World War a few 'clever' or just plain arrogant leaders gathered together and tried to out-smart God or the creator and the system by removing a fuse and put a wire so that the system will never collapse or crash. But hang-on, wait a minute the idea behind a fuse is to protect any surge of unwanted power and prevent human destruction. These people have created a crime simply by creating these institutions and cults. See my point. The institutions created after the world war are there just to act to safeguard and perpetuate injustice and imbalance by removing the natural shock-wave into the system that will result in wars that will crash the system and corrects the unfairness. So, you can see my point that these institutions and cults are like wires replacing fuses. So, in fact the cults and institutions created after the world wars are there to keep us in the defensive stages forever or if they exist. If it is a safety test on a building, the building will fail the safety test because the fuses have been removed and replaced with wires in NATO, ICC, UN UNSEC, etc. It is a health hazard bound to explode. The warning system and the fuse system has been disabled. I pointed out that God is clever and therefore to test the cleverness of mankind he created he also created booby traps with a lot of temptations that will make mankind seat comfortable losing time and opportunities wasting resources in this stage. If this was a Survival-of-the-fittest or Rat-race competition, mankind will have lost already. Mankind might feel as intelligent as ever by creating these institutions and cults to keep us hooked on military and defense using the scarce resources on weapons which he stockpiles. This is going to result in total human wipe-out in that the fuses have been replaced by a wire so that in the event of a power surge there won't be a fuse that will blow to stop and contain the power surge to avoid human extinction. I pointed out that in the early year's survival depended on your defense. I explained the menacing dinosaurs, mammoths and saber-tooth cats. surely without proper defensive weapons and systems mankind could have been wiped out. So, defense was important to survive. But the dinosaurs and all that have since long gone. It is God's or the creator's plan that in the early stages yes defense should be the sole existence of any government, institution or cult but as we evolve, we must put emphasis on other things in order to progress. I pointed in an earlier chapter that over the years simply because defense is the only stage mankind knows the best we have got stuck in this stage like forever to such points that even after the few foresighted argued for a move to the next stage of development your leaders went on to fake evil creatures like the UFOs and aliens to spread fear so that we remain in the defensive stage. This is the easiest stage mankind has mastered throughout history. We have heard stories of great battles and wars. After every war mankind has built even more destructive weapons and waited for the next war hoping that this time, he will win without losses, but my question is this; Was this the sole purpose of the war? Wars happen for a reason. I know most would jump to point out that the assassination of Ferdinand triggered the First World War and Hitler's greediness when he discovered how beautiful the Polish women were that he decided to conquer Poland and decided to make them his were triggers of the Second World War. Or some might argue that it was the persecution of the

Jews that triggered the war but do you know that all these developed countries especially Britain and Germany were advocates and some are still advocates of eugenics movements that incorporates and encourages all what happened to the Jews the concentration camps and all that? In this book I will use the idea of a perfect system I presented earlier on. The perfect system has inputs, processes, outputs, and feedback. In the early years before the first and Second World War ships roamed the earth collecting resources for making and expanding industries and making weapons, ships, etc. The weapons would then be sold back at huge prices facilitating and augmenting this process so that the bullies grew even bigger making even more weapons and goods and reselling them back. It was a perfect system. The only problem is that the Jews did not subscribe to such systems themselves having been taught by stories in the bible knew that the system was flawed and could only benefit the bullies. The main reason behind the extermination of the Jews was that the Jews were clever and never parted with their money. They created a bottleneck in the system in that the bullies made weapons that there was no market for and in turn could not get more resources to make more weapons and goods for expansion. Simply because the Jews those days when it comes to money were regarded as tight as can be. The Jews were very business-minded and would rather stuff their money away somewhere under beds and not in banks. This stalled the whole process. This is their only evil deed. Keeping to themselves what they considered as theirs. Hitler knew that this would stale the system and possibly crash the whole system and stale development. As such he rather would crash the Jews than let them crash the system. Damage was already done, and a new system was needed, and this came as an opportunity to them to in the process study the human body to understand it and develop medicine, etc. My point is that the imbalanced system if unchecked is poised to fail and crash resulting in a war. So, war is not a mere war but a highlighter of a problem that the system needs to be changed or corrected. We as humans we have feelings and flesh designed to suffer great trauma that will temporarily weaken mankind in that after the trauma fear and pain will make mankind take a different route and change. So, the idea of war is not simply to punish but to cause mankind to move to the next stage. This is different from torture in that torture is a crime, wrongdoing that will not encourage change but make whoever is tortured to remain in the same stage in the hope that torture will stop. It makes sense that this kind of pain is different from traumas of war that can awaken people if you like rather than dampen then simple because once torture is used and if you react, then torture becomes a form of communication and a form of forever-abuse. This is the main reason torture or any form that resembles torture is internationally outlawed. But you might ask why torture is prevalent in Britain and USA etc. Simply because these countries know that they have put institutions and cults that first make them big bullies that no one will challenge them. Look at all the wars these two are at the forefront defending illegal practiced outdated laws and views. Using weapons to rob oil and kill 500 000 women and children in a few years more than killed by the person who they are toppling. They have the backing of their institutions, UN, NATO, etc. in which they are all members. They have grown to such an extent that if it wasn't for these institutions a World War Three could have already occurred and mankind could be at another stage of development. Imagine a world without the UN or NATO? Do you think they could have invaded Iraq? All the UN resolutions and voting it's just to make you think that the world is fair and there are caring people who want justice but no matter how hard and sad the picture is the world is not fair. If this were a company, it could have been broken or split into smaller companies. The institutions and cults as I pointed and will continue to do so were created by the same people, we are saying that they are abusing everyone putting themselves first at the expense of everyone else. We have now what we call a bully-victim situation that they don't even listen to themselves. Everything starts to look like a drama episode. To make things worse these institutions, cults, and empires grew simply because of this bully-victim situation. To remain operational and in existence, they must continue doing the same bullying and getting their way. They were built out of illegally practices like forced slave labor, torture and forced collection of resources to pay their debts whenever they run out of money. If they were individuals, they all could be behind bars. But they are clever and choose to out-smart God's plan for humanity. Okay, it seems they are doing well shielding smaller countries stealing behind the poor country and even starve that poor country they claimed to be protecting with sanctions, etc. So, you can see the picture that is emerging. They are all linked. In the early part of this chapter I introduced notions of rolling-back or creaming as an effective tool to take after pretending to give just to blind the people. The institutions are meant to act as if they are there to defend the defenseless victims but in fact the whole process is linked in that one part is meant to take from you the other pretends to correct the situation but before you know it, there is another part that will take even with the little you had. So, we have one part buying but at unfair prices then the other part through development packages, etc. try to correct the first wrong and then another part that will through sanctions, etc. roll-back everything. They are all cults with different functions, for example, one emphasizes defense, the other immigration, the other finance, etc. but in the end the decisions are collectively made. Nothing wrong in grouping and expanding but the reason why monopoly is a crime throughout history is the fact that it stifles competition and encourages the bully-victim situation and gross abuses simply because no one has the capacity to challenge them. Ever watched the Ghost and the Darkness? Then you will know what I mean. There is no justice or upholding of the rule of law. Torture is practiced in broad daylight and no one the whole world even takes notice. If the system was fair, surely this could have stopped a long time ago. I give you a good example.

In 1654 in England, a scientist, surveyor, physicist, anatomist, etc. decided to study everything he can through experiments and observations. In that year he designed a container to carry out experiments and observations called the Colony Collapse Studies. He designed a container for the bees with see-through glass where he could see and observe the trapped bees. His studies focused on what would happen to the colony if the active hard-working bees are taken and removed from the colony and kept in these see-through containers. He noted that the bees simply because of the tallness of the containers never stayed or laid honey in the upper levels. The bees were unable to escape through the top and in case of a fire they all happened to die if they were at the top. He noted that once the working bees had been removed, the colony will collapse even though other young male bees were still in the colony. He observed that the young male bees even though they had the ability to look for food if the dominant male bee was absent, they would not bring food for the whole colony and in the end, the colony starves to death. The younger bees only followed what the dominant male bee does as they grow. He noted too that the brood that is unhatched bees would remain as larvae as no one will look after them once the dominant male worker bee is removed. The designed blueprints of his containers which had three stores ended up being the background blueprints of the twin World Trade Center Towers. Can you imagine? It does not stop there the containers were the basis of the Guantanamo Bay cages. Read between the lines this is in 1654 when this 'great scientist' designed a container for the bees with see-through glasses and we see his blueprints being used to build the Twin Towers, Guantanamo Bay and all his experiments given a real-life test. What else would you expect? Have you seen the Twin Towers burning with smoke coming out of the top windows and people clinging to top floor windows trapped waiting to die? The same thing he observed with the bees that the top levels were death traps. The design of the Twin Towers with ribbed glass see-through columns all were from this Christopher's Wren container blueprints. The Guantanamo Bay resembles still the smaller version of these containers. I noted above that Christopher Wren's aim was to understand the Colony or Society Collapse Studies, would you be surprised that we have the Arabs taken from their society and cages in these see-through cages for observations and experiments to see if they are a threat or not? This Christopher Wren did his experiments in 1654 the same year slavery was introduced in the North Virginia in the USA. We see just a few years back his ideas applied in real-life with what I call the Society Collapse Studies. We have Arabs caged with no rights and chances of coming out just like what this Wren did with the bees and introducing smoke to see what the bees would do. Have you seen the planes hitting the towers watching people jumping outside the buildings or stuck inside the buildings? Please! Where are human rights there? The other idea behind Christopher Wren's studies is the fact that he wanted honey to replace sugar and be able to control supply and demand. At that time sugar was expensive as it had to be shipped from countries like Trinidad where there were slave plantations. In the twentieth century we see the same principles used to illegally tag the Arabs; caging them for years so that in the end they require medical assistance and then getting tagged and through chips remotely controlled therefore control the 'terrorists' population'. It does not stop there, during the year this Christopher Wren was busy experimenting and all that stuff in the other corner of the world in America laws were being passed that meant children of slaves were automatically slaves as well even though their new fathers might be white and free. Mothers and caged father's status determined where their children would be free or slaves and not the new father. In 2001 after the 9/11 attacks we see all Arabs rounded up and caged for observations. Anyone caged is a threat and therefore his children must be tagged as well and monitored and eventually caged and killed as well. The years in cages means health issues that give rise to the need of some sophisticated technologically advanced small implants that are Weapons of Mass of Destruction used to pass radiation, age the population faster and torture secretly at unprecedented levels; 'white sugar' if you ask me. Anyone who complains is a lunatic. The device is designed to shake your brain and muscles until in the end, it destroys you. Have you ever heard of genocide? Killing an ethnic minority in order to control them and justify wars and human testing. Open your eyes this is 2019 yet we have practices formulated in 1654 still in place and the open containers with glass as in Wren's designs, or see-through rib-caged columns and buttresses as in the Twin Towers and the open-see-through fences are all psychological trickery to make you think that everything is okay and fair. This Wren carried out experiments observing the perception of people if something is done in the open as compared to something done in the closed doors. People tend not to worry too much about people placed in open cages than those put in closed cages. A good example is the fact that the USA even though not on its soil runs and maintains the Guantanamo Bay cages even after the death of Osama Bin Laden, torturing and abusing the human rights of the victims in the name of the terrorism. North Korea used the closed system but all carrying-out loud foul play, but it is the same technique. We have worldwide outcries about North Korea while everyone ignores the Guantanamo Bay cages. So far Britain has gone a step further and developed advanced technological WMD used secretly to torture that if it wasn't for technological advancement and appeals worldwide, no one could have believed that Britain is still torturing people. Mind you this is the twenty-one century. It is common knowledge that torture has no justification whatsoever as it falls in what is referred to as the Jus Cogens norms where no derogation is permitted. I know you are thinking; Hey if that's true why no one ever complains about all this? Why the so-called " superpower" the US is not even fighting Britain or other countries like North Korea etc.? Simply because they have dirt on their hands too. Why is that? One might ask.

### The Root of The Problem.

The USA was founded out of the struggle to free it from Britain. Even after freedom the USA and Britain connection are forever manifested in many aspects of life; with the same language and strong ancestral links. Do you know that the blueprint of London 1666 is the same as today's New York City? Britain is one of the few countries that documented all its history into books, etc. A good thing and it's downfall too? We have seen very documented cases again and again reapplied to real-life recent cases in the USA. Christopher Wren's experiments are a good example. I will explain in more detail the idea of Master-protégé that later turned to bully-victim. Britain as the advanced once superpower was like a master to the once colonized USA teaching it after independence the ways of life. Whatever the USA has problems with Britain always has documented antidote to the problems heavily documented somewhere. The idea behind this assumption is that history tends to repeat itself and whatever the problems at hand they will always have a solution. In the end, you will find out that these two countries are like twins. Wherever you go, I will go too. Whatever you do, I will do that too. So, what if the solution prescribed is not the correct one? The idea here is that okay the USA is a sovereign country but most of its laws etc. are taken from the British system but what might happen to Britain even though similar might not need the same solution as other factors might come into play. I can give a quick example. In 1666 a huge fire destroyed the whole city with the people losing their houses but even though there was a delay the insurance companies paid out the insurance for the destroyed houses. The people got insurance money and used this to rebuild their homes. This same Christopher Wren now a surveyor helped to rebuild the city and advising people to sell their rights to land and houses to pave way for the development of the city but with stiff rejections as the people refused to sell their land. In 2001 we have a similar situation and the difference is that the Twin Towers were destroyed instead of the people's houses, but the proposed solutions seemed to be the same and would you be surprised to find out that we ended up with the 2008 financial crisis? The 9/11 2001 attacks triggered the collapse of the world markets. I point you to the principle I developed throughout the book that a crash will mean a change in direction. 9/11 planes targeted the fabric of the financially strong point and database with the inevitable collapse of the world markets simply because a shock-wave in the system is likely to affect the whole system globally. The World Trade Center as their names depicts were the center of world trade with most financial institutions and governments situated there. Most of the investment banks, companies, etc. were situated in the Twin Towers. Most had offices in the towers but on different floors, that means all their back-up files, etc. in one building or one of the three towers that got destroyed that day that is including building number 7. This in turn as we have seen that a lot of investment companies in the destroyed buildings after the attacks were later accused of unfair practices, corruption, mis-selling and fraud, etc. I explained in detail that the attacks were meant to instill fear so that defense becomes our priority. So that we say yes to war. So that no one challenges the huge defense budgets. So that defense is the key driver of the economy. But still, that can't be the root of the problem. One might argue. The idea behind twins is that they cover for each other. It's in their genes. In some cases, the other tricks the other to get him hooked too so that he fully cooperates and supports the other. So, what they do is make the innocent one dirty so that he won't complain but to either ignore or support whatever the other will embark on doing. It's a case of you too so in the end they have a shared goal. After the 9/11 attacks, America was furious attacking mountains in Afghanistan but soon the tone changed to include Iraq. But why Iraq if all information pointed to

Al Qaeda in Afghanistan so the world refused and carried out huge protests throughout the world. Okay, one can say with sure that America did not want to go to war straight away without the UN approval despite losing 3000 people. But one can also say it's a psychological mind game as they are all one with the UN etc. created by these countries to give them backing and make a wrong a justified act. The 9/11 attacks alone were not enough to convince the world that attacking Iraq was unacceptable. Then America suffered another casualty with the Airspace Challenger disaster of 2003. After that Britain then cooked the Iraq dossier to justify a war and without proof convinced the US and the world that Saddam had Weapons of Mass Destruction. The USA then embarked in a war that killed 500 000 in a few years when it took Saddam Hussein decades 25 years to be precise to kill half the number i.e. 250 000. It only emerged after the war that Britain had hooked the USA through the inaccurate dossier and dragged the USA to go to war. I think if it wasn't for the dossier the USA might have not embarked on a war or might have waited for the UN's approval. It is worth pointing here too that the day after Saddam's death Britain announced the decision to pay back the US a war debt it had failed to pay over the years. One can say too that the USA might have gone to war with Britain on its side simply because it had a vested interest as Britain owed it war debt money which it was to get after the war. After the war inquiries revealed that the British government had cooked up the Iraq dossier and dragged the USA to go with it to war. One can only infer that Britain must have misrepresented the facts knowingly to trick the USA into going to war with it. The USA now has no option with 500 000 women and children dead, if it is to act against Britain then the world would say both guilty 500 000 already dead so now it stands with Britain. Together stronger any opposing means it is the end as well now it is forced to support Britain and justifies and defends the war. Their bond is now forever strong a true friendship but to the world, this is another bully-victim relation. The country that benefited from all this is Britain. It paid its debt. Ensured future oil supplies and strengthen its relationship with America and covered its back hiding its dirty under the carpet. After the Iraq invasion, even more people died from insurgents and the country is worse off one might argue. I look at Britain and America as the two prominent world players who live by example as these two intervene in people's affairs the most. You can see the root of the problems. They are both in the wrong simply because one dirtied the other and now, they are mutually a pack so it is common sense America can't condemn Britain's atrocities simply because Britain is simply going to laugh and simply say look who's talking. You see why the US stopped provoking North Korea with human rights and Weapons of Mass Destruction? The USA has been weakened. The Guantanamo cages are proving that the world is not straight and just. Society/Collapse studies at its best devised in 1654 by this Christopher Wren who is British now adopted by the USA somehow or again the USA tricked into trying things they don't know the implications. Modern-day slavery and no one even point a finger they all say look at 9/11 but as I pointed out 9/11 was planned within either the government or imported from one of the foreign governments who are part and parcels of the cults and institutions. So surely it will be insane for the USA to say to North Korea you are torturing people in closed doors when they are doing the same thing in the open in front of everyone in the open through the Guantanamo Bay Cages. Again, the USA once a defender of the weak now weakened even worse. You see, the problem at hand. The so-called superpowers are worse now than the people they are condemning, and, in the end, they are going to see who does it better instead of who will stop it, automatically, so the world's justice system has literally collapsed after 2001 hence the rise of TWO. I have pointed out that whoever is and was behind 9/11 posed to benefit enormously from this act and the collapse of the financial markets illustrates the rolling-back of finances from the consumer to the central entities. At the beginning on 10 September 2001 we have $2,3 trillion missing from the government and in the end, we have the consumers and some banks begging the central for handouts. The effect of all this was to export all the countries bundled mortgage deals reduced in value by the collapse to be bought abroad at a fraction of their real values later to be sold at high prices. That explains why banks nearly crashed. All the money was rolled out of the country by some genius. The USA just like Britain have blood on their hands; 500 000 women and children killed in Iraq due to cooked Iraq dossier. The Guantanamo cages with their implications for colony collapse, modern-day slavery, illegal hacking and tagging, torture, abuse of human rights, caging people like animals violating all international laws and to make things worse indefinitely without any chance of coming out so in cases like this the talk of justice is remote and clearly unfounded. The global justice system has collapsed. The same countries crying that Iraq, Syria, etc. have Weapons of Mass Destruction are embarking on wars to collect resources globally by force to make Weapons of Mass Destruction WMDs in the form of advanced technologically advanced torture chips, etc. It does not stop there how do you expect a fair world built on human rights when the foundations in place were built on abuse. They were established on abuse through illegal practices like slavery, torture and barbaric practices. The USA should know better after having been a colonial entity of the British government. When someone shouts-abuse, then he must be taken seriously because there are precedents already. In 1776 the USA after fighting Britain gained its independence and the relationship now is that of trickery, hacking and misrepresentation for the other not to condemn its evil practices. Even though the US adopted the more democratic system still siding with Britain overshadows everything. Britain as a superpower and with all the countries it colonized has more responsibility to reform and show the world that it has changed and serious about democracy. It is a country that murdered 150 million people as its empire fed on slavery and torture grew and this is documented. Surely to be taken seriously it must modernize and conform with reality. They tortured people in secrecy if it does not come out, they will still pretend everything is okay. Hitler created concentration camps and offered to help the Jews before gassing everyone dead. Hitler experimented on humans tagging and hacking illegally to experiment and test drugs without consent denying basic rights like access to family and loved ones using all dirty tricks. In the holocaust they drove the Jews away simply because they saved their monies and did not spend and as such were the root of evil before Hitler offered to help them by gasses and killing them. The Japanese's slaughtering the Chinese, Belgium's slaughtering of the Congolese people, The British Empire is no different concentration camps against the Boers of South Africa, the USSR on enemies of socialism. In all gas plays a huge role in everything. Ethnic people pollute everything and are bad, but the truth is they are making digital weapons and testing these on ethnics all these just like Hitler in broad daylight and no one even points a finger. Here comes the unfit for the purpose of all institutions like the UN, NATO, etc. These claim to stand for the human rights of everyone, yet they only cater to their members who must be white, of North European and there to protect them believes automatically one can say it's biased simply with the way it was founded. The British are even behind the holocaust. This Christopher Wren is the man who started what was witnessed during the holocaust. Mind you Hitler experimented in the 1940s, but this guy wrote manuals in 1654 on how to do it. The USA have their own version of the concentration camps in the Guantanamo Bay Cages. See every one of them is tainted. Hitler was a prolific reader, and he even went on to write his book. He had links with the British king who once visited him so one can only infer that he was exposed to this ideology. It's true also that he called for the withdrew of the attack on Britain out of respect for Britain and went on to suggest that the British shared similar views as Nazi Germany. There is even more evidence that Britain carried out the same techniques used by Hitler creating concentration camps fighting the Boers of South Africa. Using food to starve and command the Indians. Even today the UN report pointed out that the Tories use food and other austerity measures to control the population and command these. Their name conservatives speak for itself. I will put it straight they are not for the dilution of their autonomy. They are by nature skeptical of foreigners. They might as a policy of appeasement pretend; they don't bother but there are for the preservation of their way of life. Why the British Empire collapsed in 1997? Simply because it grew through slavery, secret intimidation, torture and the rule by a rod. They are best known for their five torture techniques which are evident even today. Imagine more than 40% of children living in poverty in 2019 in a developed world? There is surely more to it than just poor planning or austerity measures. Food is a weapon to command so that people do what you want whether it's right or not. 40% is a figure that is associated or should be associated with third world countries and to see this attributed to a developed world it's shocking. One can say that children are being used as weapons. They did the same with the Indians taking away food so that the people submit. Children are a powerful force to drive out ethnic or end up hooked on their opium fields being tortured to drive agenda by the public health system possible illegally tagged on birth without consent from the parents. The death scandals associated with elder people like the Shipman case might have closed doors to adult killings and a new door maybe is opening. The leader must be told that if they don't change the world has a duty to come together and carry out justice. They are professionals as they were at the forefront of toppling Hitler, so they know better and have experience but it's a shame when it comes to human rights reforms they are at the forefront of hindering progress. Look at the crimes of aggression stance; they were the forefront fighting against this new law a contradiction of what is expected of the country that fought hard to topple Hitler or was it a Germany overtake? I pointed out that the British Prime Minister has roots as being just a translator of the Germans. They might simply have reformed and ousted their counterparts as in Hitler and took a new form but nevertheless still doing the same things. Look at the Chagos case a clear indication that a new superpower is needed to restore confidence in the global justice system. I have pointed out that all the so-called superpowers and advocates of human rights all have hands tainted with blood of women and kids. America chooses to stand by its ally to the end so it shall fall with its friend too. You can't put a thief to catch a thief. A new superpower is the only answer to the current world problems. These two powers have become obsolete, out of touch with reality. Look at the USA's dealings of the 9/11 suspects almost 17 years and still some locked up with no hope of release and to be honest forgotten and experimented on. In a fair justice system, no one shall be held like that without charges brought against him. International laws forbid all this. Don't get me wrong I sympathize with the victims and the people of America and over the years has concluded that okay Bin Laden was behind the attacks, but do you also know that his father owned a construction company? I looked at all the Al Qaeda attacks and surprisingly most of the attacks only destroyed prestigious buildings and most linked to the USA, embassies, ships, buildings, etc. The first question that came to mind was; Were the World Trade Center Buildings ever considered for demolition? You will be shocked. I can say they were written off or depreciated by a huge percentage and they were inefficient and the Newyork port authority leased them because they cost more to demolition than to maintain. The deeper you go into the problems at hand the more you start to question everything. Just like all these institutions and cults, the time the towers were built asbestos was legal and good material but taste, rules, and laws over time change. Asbestos became a problem and had to be removed. The city authorities knew it would cost them a fortune in $millions if not $billions to remove. Demolition the normal way was a slow and expensive process and so to remove liability leased the towers to someone else. I explained that Christopher Wren experimented on a lot of things in the 1600s and one of this involved testing gunpowder as a demolition weapon. He carried out two experiments with different amounts of gunpowder. At first the explosion was not even, so he increased the gunpowder and on the second attempt he managed to lift 3000 kg of rubble into the air. Some centuries later we see the same experiment with the use and manipulation of gravity and use of another form of gunpowder called thermite a mixture of aluminum and oxide and the use of space shuttle thrust theory to crash the towers with the resultant that 3000 people died. Don't forget I explained that the same blueprint for London 1666 drawn by this Christopher Wren was the same as those used to construct Newyork a twin's sister city the same area where the Twin Towers stood. It becomes clear that the 9/11 attacks were a cold calculated plan to murder people in cold blood as a sign of power and to collapse the entire world and cream all the money and mortgages collapsing all banks, etc. Whoever was behind 9/11 knew that the people were all destined to die. Just like a container designed by the same Christopher Wren smoke was introduced in the containers to kill the worker bees with intent in order to study what happens to the rest of the society in Society Collapse Studies. The idea was to see if one can boost the economy through insurance payouts and cut the government wage bill. The towers housed government agencies, etc. One can also say that the destruction was to delete all financial records so that it will be easy to steal in order to collapse the economy and this is true as investment companies in these towers committed fraud simply because they could as all records were destroyed. If the role models are the ones robbing us, then the whole system is dysfunctional and just waiting for the new superpower to eliminate evil and take over just like what the British did to Hitler. This is also true; the world knew that Hitler was involved in eugenics policies years before they decided to invade simply because they were also practicing these eugenic policies. Britain even today they have these eugenic movements carried out by the public health system loading people described as bad with digital agents with women having their wombs tied forced into opium fields owned by the public health system. Recall the rolling-back notion. Since when did a hospital or government institution own opium that is heroin fields. What distinguishes them from drug dealers? It's like having a huge shortage of organs and then let the public health system be responsible for the 'to be donors' who will end up being victims. The world does not operate this way. Look at yourselves first before pointing fingers. It's just the same as genetically engineering of viruses and digital agents are owned and carried out by the public health system. The same as torture tools are given to the public health system so that they implant these during hospital operations so that they can torture people, who in turn have to buy their opium to ease the pain before being killed by the implanted medical devices so that their organs are removed and in the end the organ waiting list is reduced. It's the same as grooming or rearing chickens. These practices were witnessed in medieval times. Has Britain moved with the time? Has Britain abolished slavery? Has Britain stopped torture? America is in no better position. Terrorists killed 3000, and they went to kill 500 000 women and children. Who is going to kill 83 million British and American people to equalize the situation? So, the cults like NATO and institutions like the UN are there to suppress retaliation through fear and intimidation. So, the cults are there to stop the cycle of war. OK I think right now you might be asking what the problem is with stopping wars.

The Cycle of War.

A recap of the cycle of war. I pointed out that nature has included wars to help humanity jump to the next stage. This is like a safety system. Imagine what will happen if the world keeps on producing weapons and increasing military budgets year after year? The

206

world's cults are growing thereby creating one huge bully with little powerless opposition and the fact that these cults were established to stop future wars but while still increasing weapons manufacture and the military budget is a cause for concerns. The cults stop the war and remove competition, in the end, the world is going to keep making weapons that we don't need at the expense of other sectors. If this is a business, you would not keep on producing products where there is no market for them. Another scenario is the fact that the cults will grow to such an extent that any opposition countries or other cults will have to make even more powerful weapons to stand a chance of winning. That can only mean one thing; nuclear weapons and the Weapons of Mass Destruction. Ever wondered why in the last decades the major cults have been so afraid of countries like Iraq fearing that they are making Weapons of Mass Destruction. This is the major reason because they have become so big that to be fair and to stand a chance of winning any confrontations the small countries must make weapons that are very powerful; yes, nuclear weapons. I think now you can see the fears that were being expressed by the USA and Britain before the Iraq invasion. It's just a survival instinct. There is only one result in the end total annihilation of mankind as the weaker will have no option but to find mass murder weapons. The war that will result will if unchecked result in the extinction of humanity. We have lived up to these centuries simply because wars relieved the pressure before the burst. Wars made it easy for mankind to destroy want he does not need; weapons. Wars gave mankind another chance to realize what is important in life and start again. Wars gave mankind insight into what to invest in other than the military. Wars were supposed to make mankind realize how reckless he is wasting resources on weapons. After wars people come together and cooperate and form cults and institutions to prevent future wars. Look at all these institutions they were formed soon after the Second World War. The idea to stop killing each other and to move to the next stage of development. The next stage of development is the situation just after the war, especially after the Second World War. Mankind has been given opportunity after opportunity to move away from the defensive stage but somehow mankind has created cults and institutions that will make it impossible to move from the defensive stage.

## So why has mankind failed to move away from defensive stages?

To move away from defensive stages mankind must have the foresight and the ability to take another direction. It's not easy as it requires a total commitment from mankind. But if you are saying that the situation after the Second World War is a step toward the next stage so how come mankind is still in the defensive stage? I explain that war is not just a war. It's a misconception that war's sole purpose is to correct ecological balance and see who has the big guns. But I think there are more answers than just this. I explained above that wars are to traumatize mankind so that he moves to the next stage. So, war is to benefit those left or those in leadership and decision making. It's not the suffering itself that was to change decision making simply because if you were the victim then the fear of such a traumatic event would make you build walls to overcome that event but without changing anything. To the leadership and decision-makers, it's a different story. The victims normally instead build bunkers to hide in. So, to the victims' wars changes nothing but just bring traumatic sufferings. To the decision-maker, it's insight and a push to do something about this. To join hands with your enemies to avoid such sufferings in the future. Mankind instead of abandoning weapons altogether went on to form powerful military cults that would make it easy to win the battle in the future. So, what should have mankind done?

## The Way It Should Have Been or Should Be.

Wars are and were chances created by nature so that mankind witnesses' traumatic events that temporarily rendered him temporarily insane so that he cannot fear of future attacks and abandon all together making weapons in the future. The idea is to push mankind to the next level. This is not just a war between countries. I am talking about world wars. These can trigger the need to act. The idea was to sit down and sign treaties to avoid wars in the future altogether. To start afresh and take a new route. Isn't that what happened? I remember treaties being signed etc. one might argue.

True treaties were signed but only to come together and become stronger that is to keep on making weapons even at greater volumes and to form cults and win any future wars? To win? Misconception and lack of foresight. What should have happened was to sign peaceful treaties never to make weapons again? Like we have done. To ban wars forever. Like we have done. Is it a surprise that there is no direct law that bans wars? To avoid wars in the future completely. So, what happened was to create institutions like the UN and NATO institutions that will 'pretend they are the voice of the voiceless' but in real fact, their sole purpose is to safeguard the interest of the creators. These institutions were created and are funded by the very same people we are saying are breaking international laws. The instructions either they are biased or powerless that they are just there for display to play with our minds thinking that the world is just and fair. They are like the mannequins in shop windows so that the owners can display their best 'acts' so that people can see from outside the window and say the whole is just. But is the world just? I mean with all these institutions and cults? I am saying the institutions were created to stop war at all but without any change. The idea in this book is for a world that does not make weapons at all. Countries might have the military, but their use and strategies are totally different. The military budget must be smaller just for protection purposes.

### The Ideal World.

World Wars are there to let mankind see and feel firsthand the impact of wars and instinctively make mankind move away from the defensive stage. What happened is that after the Second World War mankind simply fortified the current situation instead of abandoning it. So, after the Second World War since this was a world war all countries had a chance to sit down and sign treaties Never to make weapons that destroy mankind. They were supposed to write treaties and sign these to prevent situations of bully-victim augmented by weapons manufacturing. After the war, there was supposed to be a shift from defensive to networking and cooperation. So why has mankind remained in the defensive stages?

## The Obstacles.

Mankind lacked the foresight of seeing what was needed just after the first and the Second World War. Mankind was expected to sit down and agreeing worldwide that wars were bad and evil in themselves and that no humans will die from weapons in such numbers ever again. The whole world was to agree not to make weapons. Laws were to be written down and things put in place imposing stiffer penalties to those who break them. Ban wars globally but nothing of that sort ever took place instead they joined cults to be stronger not to stop wars but to be prepared and ready to win the next one. Skewed minds if you ask me.

## The fear of surprise attacks.

So, this made the above idea impracticable because you can't abandon weapons manufacturing when others are still making them and clinging to some. It will be plain unwise because you are just going to be attacked and robbed or even worse. But like I will do. I will make it a law globally that weapons manufacturing will become illegal. No one should be forced to make weapons simply because others are making. If weapons-making is outlawed globally then and then will we be able to move away from the defensive stages? This has been something mankind was not doing after every world war. Any serious decision is and must be based on this outlawing of weapons and wars. Look at countries like Iraq, North Korea and recently Iran. They are forced to make weapons even nuclear weapons simply because it's a reasonable thing to do. Look at the opposition they are facing or will fight; they are all cults consisting of over 20 countries. The sheer size and power would kick-start instincts to match that power with destructive weapons to level the game up. The cults like NATO have grown to enormous sizes that now what they will do is target any 'threats to them' and eliminate at will. Look at Iraq as a very good example. If Saddam had not nationalized oil, none of this could have happened. Look at Iran they are now under constant threats from the USA and its Allies NATO etc. the bullies simply because it nationalized oil reserves. Look what happened during the Iraq war protests. The UN and other countries all part of these cults just to trick people voted against the war but had no power to stop Britain and America from invading. I will discuss useless institutions later, but you can see the problem at hand. So, as I was saying the world after the Third World War will have to come together. First, I will write and put laws that will make it easy to move away from defensive stages by making it illegal globally to waste money on weapons. I will make laws to reduce spending on the military. I will put laws that will eliminate fear that make us think about weapons. Surely if everyone has no weapons, then what is the point of making some. I know it's a fact that even some poor countries are allocating huge budgets on military and defense at the expense of other sectors simply because the cults are growing and as the bully grows bigger so as often the threats and not just empty threats. It was difficult because a complete change is needed. What mankind did was to incorporate the two the defensive stage and the networking and cooperation and this is the situation today but a recipe for disaster. The two are not mutually inclusive. You must abandon one. Obviously, the defensive stage is a resource-hungry stage no point to do both at the same time. Choose to move ahead to networking and cooperation or stay in the defensive stage but not both. I am going to explain why this does not work. After the Second World War countries came together and formed cults to make even more destructive weapons. This is contrary to what is needed in order to move to the next stage. It's contradictory. You can't say I don't want any more wars and fighting and then go on to join a warmonger cult like NATO and make weapons. This is what was the main problem. Countries after the Second World War agreed to be peaceful but also created institutions that help produce more weapons and laws that defend all this. So, you can't say I will be your friend then go on to make weapons to use on the very person you are saying we can be friends. Even if that person trusts you what would we think on his part? Who are you making the weapons for? A few people saw the problem with this. It's a psychological mind-game by the big cults so they can forever bully the powerless and get them hooked on weapons like opium. A way to find markets for the weapons and cream away money leaving the powerless in poverty. Even though peace agreements are in place, the fact that these countries and cults keep on making weapons will automatically make the weaker countries worry about defense in fear of surprise attacks.

In turn, they then buy the weapons creating a market. The big cults now have a market and to keep producing the weapons all they must do is make a threat and attack against all international opinions to show power and send even more fear so that the weaker sacrifice other areas buying weapons and other forms of defense. The more people become smarter they start seeing the effects of such a setting making it hard for the cult to make money from the weapons. So, in turn, and as a growth strategy the cult will target the powerless countries first with those, they have a vested interest in. One after the other the powerless countries are literally colonized in broad daylight in the name of giving the locals human rights. But whose human rights? What about the human rights of the women and children they kill through sanctions and invasions or missile attacks? Before you know it, the cult has grown very big and has attacked almost all the countries that can be a problem in the future. All the countries are now part of the cult who indirectly runs these countries through its appointed people and puppets. Can you see what is happening? Now we have the most powerful countries one or two now e.g. Britain and the USA backed by the military cult NATO that provides backup attacks and the negotiating institutions like the UN that are there to negotiate to end wars. But do they really end wars? In the end, all the smaller or weaker countries end up part of this cult invaded and torn apart now run by puppets and the others sought after one after the other. Look at Iraq, then who followed? Iran and recently attacks on Syria.

Signing peaceful treaties without abandoning weapons and institutions and cults that advocate weapons is an empty contradictory act. So, what should have happened was the passing of laws globally to ban weapons and to stop wars. So, the two stages are not mutually inclusive nor complimentary, no. This is a case of either or if you want results. So, after World War Three I am going to put laws that help abandon weapons and emphasis on defense. It is true that we are our worst enemies. It does not stop here. Ban cults that promote wars and weapons-making it easy to develop a bully-victim structure. Unless if they change cults like NATO and institutions like the UN, UNSEC or ICC are a thing of the past. Even if they change, I think they only encourage segregation, discriminatory acts, and robbery as they were created to serve those who created them and nothing more. I am saying that their Founding Acts have clauses that forbid them challenging the founder member states meaning they are useless to combat today's global challenges. They will do whatever they can to cover up for the gross breaking of international laws. A recent claim by the NATO leader is a good example. Even though they have now admitted that member states like Britain used Cyber-attacks to combat ISIS' growth. To many people this sounds normal but if you know the truth the advanced weapons used are sophisticated advanced Weapons of Mass Destruction using radiation and electromagnetic effects to attack not just ISIS but foreign ethnic minorities as well. There is no doubt that its torture. If they can do that to ISIS what stops them doing the same to local ethnic people. Silence does not mean that things are okay. There is a strong atmosphere of intimidation and attacks.

NATO:

'BRITAIN used hi-tech cyber weapons to halt the flow of foreign fighters to ISIS, the head of NATO has revealed.'

What are these 'hi-tech cyber weapons'? Do you mean Weapons of Mass Destruction? They are making small very sophisticated weapons that emit radiation and other harmful factors to kill masses. The sad fact is that it's the same people going globally killing innocent leaders accusing them of having and making WMDs. It's a pity the world cannot see what is going on. These countries with their supporting cults and institutions are carrying out a strategy developed in 1654 by one Christopher Wren. This scientist formulated and studied what he called the Colony Collapse Studies. I looked at the topic in earlier chapters but in short, this is a study to see the impact of removing the hard-working breadwinners of the Colony or Society and see what happens to the Colony or Society.

This scientist through his studies realized that the colonies are easy to control if you remove the leaders or breadwinners. Once removed the colony is left to collapse simply because the people, they remove are the role models and when they die the spirit and will to fight dies as well. This is because these people were very brave and role models but the way they die mostly in captivity sends fears everywhere that most people give up hope.

## Colony or Society Collapse Studies.

This Christopher Wren a British scientist realized that;

>If the leaders are removed and paraded before death that this will weaken the ability of the colony to sustain itself and fight that will result in its collapse.

This is a method that is being used by these superpowers knowingly or not. Christopher Wren realized that the brood of the colony with missing workers would die all they needed doing was to remove the role model bees, the workers.

>His other aim was to substitute expensive sugar with honey and be able to control the colony and the supply of honey.

First, to fully understand, let's look at the threats to the superpowers, cults, and institutions.

The major threats are from countries and leaders who can never be part of these cults. Simply because first, they will never qualify to join. These cults like NATO; the North Atlantic Treaty Organization means countries out of the Atlantic will never qualify simply because of geographical position, therefore, these countries are threats. Secondly, countries with oil are threats not because they have oil but because oil can be used to weaken the strength of these cults. Nationalizing oil is a factor that has led to the death of leaders like Saddam. It's not because he was oppressing his people no. We have even worse countries, but they have nothing to offer. This was laid down during the 1950-60s in the Suez Canal saga. The then US President Eisenhower declared that nationalization of the Suez Canal was a trivial issue that would not justify a war but that if it were the nationalization of the oil reserves, then it would be a different story.

Nationalizing the canal, 'was not the same as nationalizing oil wells....'

So, the nationalization of oil wells would one day see a country attacked simply because of this.

So, in short, the superpowers are putting in practice the Colony or Society Collapse Theory. Targeting and eliminating the colony's leaders knowing that killing these would render the whole colony unable to defend itself and under the control of the superpower. This is the same during the colonization period. During colonization, the evil regime would do the same. Invade and attack then capture the leader and parade him before giving him to the local authority to kill so it looks okay. During the colonization period, the main aim was to create a colony although independent but still under the authority of the superpower. There is usually an out-flux of resources from the colonized country to the empire. To fully control the countries whose leaders are killed the superpower then goes in and illegally tags all males potential of uprising implanting the so-called hit-tech anti-cyber devices but simply Weapons of Mass Destruction with GPS and video sending properties that ensure surveillance against all international laws. The superpowers have the backing of the cult and use this to send fear and reduce the chances of an uprising. In the end the locals are under surveillance being set up or ambushed as GPS is used to track them or tortured with no-way-out forced to go and fight for organizations like ISIS and this in turn to them justifies such Draconian practices and in perpetuity the colony is suppressed and colonization in modern-day is achieved once again the only difference is the degree of treatment. This time it's better than before in that the victims are offered incentives for not uprising like being offered jobs, housing discounts, etc. but after being loaded with watermarks which are in most cases viruses whether digital or generic as signs that they belong to the cult or that they are an entity of the superpower. So, we can see how colonization and slavery is still a major problem. The superpower keeps on growing as it kills the leaders and establish that country as an independent entity but nevertheless still answerable to the superpower. The people through watermarks achieved by implanted 'hi-tech anti-cyber devices' which are loaded with digital viruses with the person given an antidote as a way of keeping quiet in that if you report them, then the antidote will be removed. So, it's the same as the practice during slavery with the slaves marked like cattle with stamps showing that they belonged to a certain master. Okay, we are in the twenty-one-century things have improved these 'slaves now have rights to a job arranged for them, a house or even a wife or husband in return for their silence.

But slavery is still an evil act and a person doing that as such a Hostis Humani Generis.

The problems of the current system are that it only serves to create a bully-victim situation as the superpower with its cults and institutions put laws that facilitate its growth at the expense of other freedoms that enemies are systematically and targeted eliminated one after the other. Every new President must take one enemy as initiation of the cult. It seems a list is already drawn up only to be fulfilled as the Presidents take their place in office. Whatever is happening has nothing to do with the presence of fears of WMDs. The fact is that the superpower with the backing of the cults and institutions is going around the world killing leaders of societies that have the potential to pose a threat to the survival of the cult. They are going around the world taking resources so that they themselves make Weapons of Mass Destruction often 'hi-tech cyber' devices but WMDs as they use radiation and are small as chips and can be implanted and operated remotely torturing and killing often foreign ethnics. Yes, this is a daylight genocide. Going worldwide stealing resources using the weapons and killing with no sign of remorse. When they kill, they kill in thousands mostly women and children. That gives causes of concern. Have you watched the riots and protests that happen in developed countries if one or a few kids are killed? This sends shock-waves into the fabric of the society but when 500 000 including women and children are killed, no one even cares. First, I pointed out that some countries just because of their geographical position will never be part of the cults like NATO. But this alone can't be a reason for not showing fear to kill so many people. If we look at the genetic heritage profile although not the intended points, we can see that the factors make it easy for these superpowers to show no regard for the life of women and children if they are not like them. First, don't dismiss the point I will elaborate on. I have raised this point already although looking at different aspects. To reiterate.

In the animal kingdom, it is normal and acceptable that animals can kill their offspring and females for different reasons including strategic and safety reasons. A lion can kill its young ones without much objection from the other members but it's a different issue if it kills someone's puppy or calf. You will find out that other animals might attack to prevent that from happening. So does the same apply to humans? Should weight be given to people who offer reckless commands that result in thousand especially children and women of the other backgrounds? Should different backgrounds or a lack of empathy solve the problems we have today? I am going to mention a lack of empathy NOT the way you understand it. I am not saying they are evil just because of this not and if that's why they are killing as part of the Colony or Society Collapse Studies, but I am saying that they are lacking the kind of care that is needed if the victims were of the same background as them? Read carefully I am not using differences just for the sake of it but I am saying they lack fear to kill or torture simply because these people are foreigners and ethnics and as such don't matter much whatever happens to them because they don't relate to them? They don't empathize with them. I think there is an element of truth. The Colony Collapse Studies developed by the British scientist Christopher Wren applies here. What has been happening in the carrying out of the Colony Collapse Strategy on ethnic countries? It's simple. Takeout the corner pillar and the rest will fall. The oldest trick in the bible. Jesus had twelve disciples. The then king fearing that his empire will be challenged one day, and his authority questioned embarked on a plan and quest to kill the leader in Jesus Christ and turn his people against him. We have seen the same strategy adopted in the Saddam Hussein saga. Don't forget Britain and the USA the two superpowers are part of NATO. For these to last forever they must takeout systematically and continuously the leaders of the opposition to move-in and put surveillance on future challengers. So those who don't qualify are often people of color who will never be part of this cult. Whose fault? You tell me. During the Iraq war, the two superpowers went ahead with the war despite the UN condemning the plans to invade. First that sets out some problems I will address later that these institutions are useless and need to cease to exist simply because they will target the foreigners as they carry out Colony or Society Collapse target as a self-preservation tool. It's not because they are not doing the same; torturing foreigners in broad daylight and killing at will. They are doing worse making WMDs the only difference being that the weapons they are making are concealed and small like chips that are operated remotely like drones with GPS and untraceable so it's easy to get away with murder. The fact is that they are the worst culprits making digital viruses and using electromagnetic and radiation attacks. Now we have seen they have jumped onto the next target on the list; Iran. North Korea escaped by a needle hole. So, what I am saying is that this is going to be the picture of the future. Yes, but my point is to look at what is really hindering humanity from moving to the next stage of development. I mentioned earlier that these institutions like the UN and NATO were created to stop tampering with the growth of the big bully superpower, but I am also saying that the growth to such an extent is a problem as weapons and defense will always be a priority for them.

Express-command to put an end to this through our laws and courts as a deterrent. I think laws need to be put in place to shock and kill [through our courts] and here the I swear by the assassin policy should apply. New laws to save and protect women and children of ethnic backgrounds. So far, the people eliminated by these cults, institutions, and superpowers are people of color. I know you are going to say that most robbers and abusers are people of color so it's a true picture. The fact they justified the war is the fact that Saddam had and was making WMDs. This is the only logical point they could make that justified the war. Why simply because WMDs can cause human extinction. You can why they use the presence of WMDs. It's a win-win situation. It justifies invasion that they face little opposition because it's every human being's responsibility to ensure that humanity won't get extinct. Now we have official NATO confirmation that countries like Britain have WMDs even though they call them hi-tech anti-cyber-attacks. These are WMDs in that they can wipe-out the entire population. Weapons that use radiation and electromagnetic attacks. Secondly, that does not stop there we have ground two that they used the WMDs against foreigners to 'stop them joining ISIS.' So, it's not just possession here it's using these WMDs on ethnic minorities. So, we have good grounds for calling international laws to be applied here, but it's no use we have a bully and cults that will protect each other. So, you wonder where is the justice there? The people they are accusing are people who have no technological advancement or capabilities to make WMDs.

The ideal world therefore will be a peaceful moment in the history of mankind. Laws will be in place to stop weapons manufacture all together globally. There will be laws to safeguard the lives of women and children of different backgrounds to the accused. If the accused is of a background different from the victims, I think it would be fair to look at this as well. Since World War II what these superpowers have been doing is put into practice, the Society or Colony Collapse studies eliminating all leaders of the 'competition' in the name of WMDs when in fact it's them making the WMDs. Before the Second World War, the wars kind of acted as fuses blowing up when the surge was too large and helping start again or jump to the next stage at least those days global wars were inevitable as many countries only gathered as individuals to fight the other individual groups. NATO, UN, EU, etc. made that impossible by creating a bully who is feared and bullies everyone. No one dares fight it so now the chance of a world war has been removed yet we keep making weapons. The fight is imbalanced, and the less powerful countries one day will resort to use of WMDs as well to level the playing fields something I think it is reasonable in that a sound mind faced with such a threat in NATO, the USA, UK, France, Germany, etc. has to look for the most powerful weapons like nukes to match the threat level.

The cults and institutions as presenting a real risk of a deadly global war that will cause human extinction or results in genetic deformities for future generations. In other words, these cults are obstacles to progress. To advance to the next stage is to abandon the current system, putting laws that reduce the fear of being attacked by banning all kinds of weapons and severe penalties of express-command to put an end to this through our laws and courts as a deterrent. All kinds of weapons especially those used for torture and hacking are played down that is, softened and regarded just as hi-tech cyber weapons but nevertheless WMDs. The current system is biased and as such must be changed.

Now I have explained the problems at hand now I advocate for World War Three. War in this way is a good thing as all weapons are destroyed and mankind is given a second or third chance to move forward. When Hitler killed the Jews, the world came together to save the Jews. It's just human nature for people to step forward and act accordingly. But when the same thing is happening nevertheless how secretive and concealed, it is the same fate that must face the culprit. I think when people saying slavery is bad, and that torture is forbidden people often give excuses to justify such denounced practiced. People lack the fear and understanding that these methods are outlawed and as such, there is no justification whatsoever. No matter how you think your reason is justified there is no justification whatsoever. Countries with monarchies are the most culprits as torture is done in broad daylight 'to protect the monarch.' There is no sense of fear as often which is true these countries have never been invaded and or oppressed so they don't understand what it means to be free for the victims. Secondly, the monarchies have immunity so whatever they do they are protected. Thirdly these countries will never change they keep and maintain what was years ago. Their laws as old as 400 years but what was right 400 years ago is it right today? If it's a superpower like the USA, they break all laws first and oppress in broad daylight look at the Guantanamo cages. That shows that the institutions and the current justice system does not work or is obsolete. We have people caged for life without any chance of getting out and not charged with anything and as I pointed out part of a Society or Colony Studies. To dominate in every way in the end forcing these people to have these 'hi-tech cyber devices' as part of monitoring against all international laws. These institutions are outdated and don't function as required. So, the superpower often shows the power by breaking all rules at the domestic level and when challenged then puts in new laws to justify its actions. So, the current system is obsoleted by the presence of a bully. There is anarchy now that laws are changed and implemented overnight to justify whatever is the act of the day. A crisis point has already been passed. The major problem is that the possibility of leveling off through world wars has been removed by the presence of cults like NATO. The only way now will become obey or perish. We are back to advanced stages of slavery where the slaves now have rights and are rewarded according, to the level of cooperation but still, the system is not fair. The other problem is that people over the centuries have died so that we have what we have today. What is happening these days is what was the situation years ago? We keep going in circles but round and round what is changing is in the kinds and severity of the problems otherwise the cycle is the same. There was slavery and through laws and wars, slavery was abolished. Over time an empire or superpower with the help of its cults then grows to enormous sizes that all other institutions are rendered useless because whatever they say or do will not have any effect on the regime or superpower. That means they have gone obsolete. We have a monopoly situation that the already written laws are changed and replaced instantaneously as soon as the regime or superpower is challenged. The institutions make judgments that are not followed simply because the superpower cannot recognize them or their importance. This is true in that the institutions are funded by the regime or superpower and most of the people running these institutions are appointed by the regime or superpower. Read the black Sunday among others. A crash of some sort would normally bring things to normal. The cycle then starts again with new laws to stop this from happening and establishing institutions people listen to until we have a monopoly situation again. The regime or superpower would have grown big enough to challenge the law and become the law itself. This is the case right now with the Ghost and the Darkness mauling people for fun just because they can. The only problem here now is that the change-gear has been jammed so the car can only drive in cruise speed. The thing that used to reset everything was world wars but NATO, UN, etc. have removed that now we have one big bully and small countries that don't dare total annihilation. Torture and other illegal practicing like robbing using guns and killing of women and children becomes a norm and everyday life. The bully will just move from one opponent to the other crossing the lists and only shouting that who is the next one.

Iraq!

Shouts one and

Crossed or Done With!

replies the other.

Iran!

Shouts one…

Next on the list shouts the other.

Syria!

Shouts one.

Already bombed. or looks like already bombed…

They laugh and went on to the next on the list.

Saudi Arabia!

Next and so on.

We now have bank robbers stealing at gunpoint only difference is that they don't even wear the mask to hide. They are doing this for the common good; to protect their existence and remove the possibility of any future attacks. robbing is the sole funder of the development of Weapons of Mass Destruction. But still, the bully would invade and lay waste women and children in the name of WMDs but itself making very sophisticated WMDs. Now you see where I am going with this. There is a problem in fact this problem has been there for some time now, but we are starting to see it now. We have a bully or bullies who grouped themselves into cults. They don't listen to international laws now. The change of wars has been removed so a new method to deal with this bully is needed.

These institutions and cults have grown using the Society or Colony Collapse tactics targeting only the leader and killing women and children just to send a powerful message that we don't give a damn now to reverse this imbalance we can also apply the same tactics and principles and target just the leaders and because we really mean change we have written laws to protect women and children. As such no women or children shall die due to any form of weapon used on them. There is nothing like collateral damage when it comes to the lives of women and children. We shall spill blood when even one life of a woman or child is taken without due regard. We shall assess if the killings can be said to be lacking empathy or not. Animals forbid the killing of other species' children so why do we humans allow the same thing. If considered as lacking empathy we shall do whatever we can to obsolete that cult, institution or government. There shall never be cycles again. If a leader commands and gives orders indirectly or implied that results in the death of women and kids, there shall be an express-command to put an end to this through our laws and courts as a deterrent. We have been going in circles for a long time. Do you know that during the medieval times the black death and bubonic plague nearly wiped out humanity? But don't be shocked these things happen in circles. Now in the twenty-one century, we have countries robbing all banks in the world in broad daylight to make Weapons of Mass Destruction. Weapons to recreate in digital form or genetically modified viruses that nearly wiped out humanity. Yes, imagine a human being spending $billions on advanced hi-tech weapons to recreate the black death. Imagine someone making genetically modified viruses to recreate the bubonic plague. Imagine someone making these weapons to mark people with watermarks and recreate slavery. Arrogance? It can only prove that the system has crashed, and we have a bully, a monopoly and the other institutions have automatically been rendered useless simply because they are there for 'appearances only' they have no power to make any decisions that are listened to. They are challenged all the time and concede to changing the rules to suit the superpower. Ladies and gentlemen only the reverse Society or Colony Collapse is the answer.

Most of all fear not for we shall take the leader out and all those who hide behind hi-tech-devices to carry out torture and inhumane degrading treatment and calculated genocides around the globe. I swear by the assassin you shall reap what you sow change is coming and is inevitable. That day you shall dig holes so that you hide for evil shall only breed evil. We know you have closed all loopholes by establishing evil cults who will defend you no matter what. We are part of the equalizers whatever you do you shall experience the same. Whatever you do in closed doors we shall expose it in public. Technological advancement has meant we know what you know too. We listen to what you listen to. You can hack every foreigner and use these as spies, and we shall listen to whatever you are listening to and recreate the situation with disastrous consequences for we shall magnify everything. For now, you rejoice but tomorrow you shall weep. In life to understand so that you change and become better people it's ideal you feel the same as others have felt. If you never cried how can you understand someone who cries every day? It's just nature you can't understand such things unless you have gone on the same road or even worse. It's best if you yourself can be your own interpreter or translator. We believe equalizing is the solution. But we don't target women and children. Our motto shall be I swear by the assassin. Many people will be happy to fight our cause. It's a just cause. We are simply saying obey the law, uphold human rights and live. The best thing is that we say one man for himself TWO for us all as our aim is to get the change, we want we shall make sure the decision-makers shall obey what is universally regarded as just. I know with time we shall catch up too on the technology if the predictions are real and we know you all have chips and diodes we shall equalize the situation and load all you with digital agents. Make no mistake some of you rely on today will turn against you tomorrow. I think it's a crime against all humanity to recreate the worst period in human history, so you have a competitive advantage over everyone else, robbing everyone, killing in the name of terrorists and hacking everyone to become terrorists themselves under torture and duress. The law shall set them free and I swear the assassin shall come knocking you better not have a GPS up your butt every time we bump into you we collect information and send it worldwide get all your habits too and if you are lucky, get you your own watermark that will turn everything you have and cherish into obsoletion. I think it will be great to recreate ghost towns and zombies everywhere. I just can't get things done fast around here!! We are working very hard too. It's nothing personal they say revenge is the best medicine. It soothes and offers instant grounds of reconciliation and a new beginning. To move forward everyone shall have no drudges with others otherwise these are the reasons to look for weapons. Once we have leveled the playing field, then and only then shall reconciliation and reconstruction begin. Bear with us we have a lot of work to do we will keep on updating you as we advance. A New World a new beginning. It will be hard to walk to someone you have tortured and say forgive me and they just forgive you. It's just not human nature. So, it will be fair for you to be tortured as well. Some torture others simply because they don't know what torture is or not and have never experienced it. One day we will give everyone an opportunity to translate to themselves and only then can we move to the reconciliation, networking and cooperation stage.

If you look at history, I always give the Romanov saga as a classic example. The Jews were persecuted just because they never parted with their money and were obstacles to the system of the day. The Tsar then mistreated, murdered and tortured his people and only for Jewish assassination to assassinate them. Their blood washed away the sins of others so that there is reconciliation. We have Hitler ganged upon and it's a sad thing that some leading liberators at the time are now at the forefront of repeating what Hitler did it does matter whether it is done using advanced hidden high-tech devices evil is evil and the same fate shall apply if it means World War Three so be it. The Jews were persecuted, and people run to the rescue. Today the people of color are facing the same fate people MUST run to the rescue too. No one is greater than the law. No one is afraid of everyone or respects the law. The system has crashed.

# CHAPTER TEN

## JUSTICE THROUGH THE COURTS AND RECONCILIATION TO SOOTHE EMOTIONAL SCARS OF PAST EVIL REGIMES.

*A new beginning can only start if there is a form of balance.

*Evil with evil. Kindness with kindness. No one is immune.

*I think it's fair to address a question I often find being asked;

*Express-command to put an end to this through our laws and courts as a deterrent.

### Freedom Fighter, New Visionary, New World Leader or Terrorist?

First, what is a freedom fighter, a new visionary, a New World leader, and a terrorist? I think the point to note here is the fact that this is a subjective subject, and it all depends on who is talking and from what point of view. I think the current system is oppressive but I can't call myself a freedom fighter because I am not fighting for any freedom rather I think myself as a new visionary a powerful tomorrow's world leader someone who wants to lead the way but here and there look back to see who is following and decide if I have to drag you if your pace is slow? I think ignorance is a real reality, and most people do what they do simply because this is the only way they know. All past generations have lived this way and were successful so why change if things are working properly. The saying that says; don't fix it if it's not broke apply here but I think if you show people another way and convince them that this is the right path and this is how I think it's the right path some people might and will change their ideas about the current situation. I highlighted from the beginning that we are still in this defensive stage of human development simply because this is a tried and trusted way of doing things. It is the most successful way of running a country. Do you know the most remembered Presidents or Prime Ministers are war leaders? Yes, it's human nature that sometimes we are brought alive after seeing or experiencing traumatic events so wars kick-start or rejuvenate people's lives. I think we have been led to believe that life is tough and to survive some of you must die it's like a survival of the fittest thing. It seems it is in our DNA to kill others, so we survive in relation to resources, etc. but did you ever think that no one must die but we must get rid of some activities to free up resources for other pressing issues? I know centuries ago war and the military and defense were very vital to the survival of any country and its inhabitants. Defense was paramount as we had all kinds of threats from dinosaurs to other barbaric people. Yes, without a strong defense surely you would not stand a chance. But this is 2000 years ago. The only threat as far as I am concerned is from mankind himself. The more we became advanced, we became more knowledgeable as well, and we tend to understand things better. Every time we had a major war was a critical chance to move away from the defensive stages to the next level. Every world war must be viewed as a crash of the system. Recall from earlier chapters I explained that if a system is not fit for the purpose and it's not working that system will inevitably crash to pave way for a new system. So, whenever we had a world war that was a critical point in time because it means that the system had crashed, and a new system was a must. It's the same with the computer system if a system crashes usually a new system is needed there is no point trying to fix it simply because once it has crashed it means something is wrong and this might happen again. A wise man would not try to fix or mend the system but would understand that the system is unworkable and must be replaced. Having this in mind, I think to understand this look at it this way. View the whole system as an airplane. Imagine it's a cargo plane and somehow something goes wrong and the plane crashes to the groundbreaking into smaller pieces millions of them. Would you take all the smaller pieces and reassemble them and fix back the plane? What would be the chances that it will crash again? It's the same principle some things are not amenable once it crashes no matter how you can fix it that's not the point once it's down it's rendered obsolete. Fixing would only increase the chances of the cargo plane crashing again. Once broken and will never be the same again. So, having this in mind once the First World War broke out in 1914 it was time to completely change the whole system abandon war, abandon making weapons, work hard to establish links and relationships so that tomorrow you negotiate and try to find solutions. The best period for negotiations is and was after the world wars. This is true we saw people forming partnerships and groups and negotiating deals but because there was no one with a vision to solve the issue once and for all and lay a clear foundation that will make wars a thing of the past. That catalyst, that visionary was missing and as people make deals, there was no one to put down plans and laws that will make wars a thing of the past. So, whatever the people negotiated was simply in vain as suspicion and the fear of surprise attacks made countries group together forming cults. It's a fact that wars have no winners simply because everyone suffers horrendous causalities with millions of 'boys' and girls' [soldiers] dying. So, what happened after the First World War was that people gathered together to fix the system rather than to replace it with another system that avoided wars. So, fixing only made the countries group together to avoid heavy losses in case the war broke again. This was not the answer. It is human nature that experiencing such traumatic war events was meant to send fear and trauma so traumatic that people would throw away anything to do with wars away; weapons the military and seek links and connections. But they only fixed the system and even made more destructive weapons. Nature somehow sensed that mankind had not learned a lesson. If I was father-nature, I would be saying I told you, you are wasting time and resources. War! What is it good for? See the destructive effect of wars. So why not change completely? Abandon wars and start listening to each other. All this money you are wasting on wars surely could be used somewhere as. Why not build personal planes and travel around the globe? You don't need weapons. Dinosaurs are extinct. There are no aliens and your only enemies are yourselves. So wise up!

Just after 22-25 years, another war broke out the Second World War. Another system crash in less than 25 years. They fixed the system instead of putting a complete new one. Yes, they simply fixed that cargo plane with the same materials what else did you expect? They saw this coming. This is another call for help. It's a critical time change quickly, but that fell on deaf ears. Another traumatic war broke out. Millions lost and now this time the people acknowledged that they had made a mistake the first time after the First World War. Yes, they had fixed the system instead of completely changing it. Something crashes simply because it's not fit for the purpose. Again, the same mistake. Instead of a complete change, another system fixes, but now with added support that it will never break again but at the same time never be fit for purpose. Okay, the first picture might seem like a perfect solution. This was their solution. Group into even bigger cults to avoid the impact. Now be proactive don't let these enemies group as well. After the First World War what happened is that the Allies grouped into military cults without being concerned about what the enemy was doing. They chose what I would call a defensive approach.

## Defensive approach taken after the First World War by the Allies.

A defensive approach does not consider or consider the enemy's strength and weakness in that you are only concerned about protecting yourself. The Allies [UK, USA, France, Belgium, etc.] took approaches to fortify themselves to avoid severe casualties. Strength in numbers. They did not worry about what the axis [Germany, Japan, etc.] would do. They increased their budget spending and built more powerful weapons hoping that will put the enemies at bay and in the event of a war they would stand a better chance of winning. Just after twenty-five years, this proved as an inadequate approach as the Second World War broke out with even severe casualties. They realized that no one wins a war and war is not discriminatory it impacts everyone. A new approach was needed.

## The Attack Strategy.

The Second World War was even worse than the First World War. The Allied realized that being just defensive was not enough they had to put things in place. No one was there to act as a visionary and mediator a negotiator leader to lay the new road. They knew fixing and mending the system was not the answer, but they did not know which road to take. So, they stuck to what they know best and put things in place that will make it hard for a Third World War to break out. Still not the correct solution. The system had crashed twice in less than thirty years. Surely something was not working. So, they fixed the system and put things in place to hold the system in case it crashed again. Taking our example of the cargo plane what they did was fixing things like foams underneath the plane and parachutes to hold the plane in the air even if it stops working in the air so that even if it crashes, the impact will be a minimum. But is this a solution? It's like a mechanic when the gearbox breaks take wires and hold the gearbox together and continue to drive. Yes, the car might still drive but it's only a matter of time when things will go wrong with serious consequences. This time the Allies adopted what I referred to as the Colony or Society or Enemies Collapse Strategy.

## Society, Enemy or Colony Collapse Strategy.

The Allies realized that attack is the best form of defense. The last method of being defensive yielded even more pain. The best form was never to make their enemies be able to group. They realized that they let their enemies also come together and mobilize. This time they targeted any potential enemies who might start a war. They adopted the Enemy Collapse Strategy. This strategy targets the male alpha who is a leader and a role model. Someone the young fighters would die for. The strategy is to eliminate this leader in public using extreme force sending shock-waves so that no one will think of mobilizing support against the Allies. Once eliminated the Allies then would choose a puppet who would comply with the Allies demands. A list is compiled for the next 25 years showing who and when to eliminate that potential threat. The potential threats are ranked in order of the threat they pose. If the threat is a low-level a court that was to be established would deal with him and if the threat level was considered high military force would be used. So, we can see a pattern appearing here. Oil-rich countries mainly in the Persian Gulf have the potential to buy WMDs or nuclear weapons and so are a higher-level threat and for these only immediate military forces must be used. The idea is not to go to war with the whole country but to target the tyranny but in the process send shock-waves that no one would think of assembling support against the Allies. Whoever is left is rendered useless to launch any attack. Just like in the Colony Collapse Studies. The young males who are left will have no role model in the alpha-male-bee to look up to are afraid that they ignore their duties to take over as the new leaders. The colony suffers as no one will take leading responsibilities to look after the colony. The young ones have no one to feed them poverty and starvation weakens the people that in the end, the colony collapses.

## Their strategic methods.

So how to carry these strategies? Establishment of the ICC to target the low-level potential threats mainly from Africa. NATO to act as a deterrent to any other countries forming into cults like NATO itself. Even after calls for the Asian countries to establish their own equivalent of NATO, they have refused simply because they know they would be attacked and can't match NATO. But if NATO would go around exercising military attacks, then it would be seen in a bad way around the world. So, the two most powerful countries the 'Ghost and the Darkness' in the USA and the UK would militarize around the enemy the potential threats with a 25years list compiled targeting potential threats.

You see what happened is a third type error prescribing a solution to the wrong problem or prescribing a wrong solution to the problem with the result that that does not solve the problem. World Wars were a critical point that highlighted the need to change. Think of this like a fire alarm. If the building is on fire and is going to collapse and the fire alarm sounds, you run out to safety, right? What happened when the first fire alarm sounded no one ran out of the building but they fought the fire putting pillars so that the building doesn't collapse? They put even more fire alarms to warn them much earlier so that they have better chances of fighting the fire. This was the First World War. Years later another fire broke out and the building was going to collapse as well, and the fire alarms sounded. Again no one ran out of the building instead they fought the fire very hard putting more pillars so that the building won't collapse. They contained the fire, but this time removed all fire alarms so that no alarms would sound again but instead nominated institutions to deal with whoever was causing the fire. They ranked the threats and delegated people, institutions, and countries to deal with the fire starters. The ICC to monitor low-level leaders while the Ghost and the Darkness monitoring high-level threats. This must be reviewed every 25 years. So, what I am saying here is that this is the wrong solution. Surely when the fire starts, and the building is going to collapse you don't use pillars and fight the fire and remain inside. Common sense you would run out. Get the building destroyed completely and build another one. This is human nature. This is the way it should be. You have peace of mind. Stress levels at a minimum you are not going to worry that the building might collapse again. Above all, you build a new building that is even better and fit for the purpose. Imagine the building was built 25 years ago. The materials might be old and weak. You might have used out-of-date materials or paints. There could be now environmental good paints that are not harmful to humans. Trust me the building you make now will represent you and the current atmosphere than continue in a building built 25 years ago maybe for a different purpose by different people. I am saying we are still in the building that collapsed not just twice in 1914 and 1945 but three-times and in the 1960s. Yes, the building collapsed three-times. In 1960 we had the Cold war. But I told you what happened after the Second World War. To prevent this from ending up into another World War Three they removed the fire alarms completely. So, it was not so loud than the first two world war alarms and a few people knew about this the sirens were silent hence the Cold war. But it does not mean that the system did not collapse. This time they had put firefighters inside the building to tackle small fires quickly before they became a problem. We have the ICC inside the building that collapsed three-times tricking and trapping low-level threats in African leaders and some Asian leaders. On the other side, we have NATO doing nothing but simply expanding its wings and showing off its potential destructive power as it simply sounds warnings constantly to deter any, enemies. In the center of the building, we have the Ghost and the Darkness mauling any potential threats working on the list they were given 25 years ago. It has been another twenty-plus years, and now the NATO, ICC and the Ghost and the Darkness inside the building have made it less visible to outsiders that the building collapsed. These three are there to support the three-times collapsed building. The structural damage is massive, but they would rather leave it that way. A few people knew this third collapse I told you why they disabled all the fire alarms, so the third collapse is called the Cold war.

Yes, the building collapsed three-times, 1914, 1945 and between 1960-1970s. But it's not just that. The potential threats have realized that the Colony Collapse Strategy is in effect, so they have devised new methods of revenge attacks. The rise of terrorism. They have realized that the Allies are never going to run out of the building but would rather hang in there. So, they devised plans to go in there as well and blow the building up to cause it to collapse. We have terrorist attacks, but the Allies are adamant that this system is fit for the purpose simply because they built the system and it only benefits them at the expense of everyone else. It is like a gangster or a bully now. Going around flashing guns and even using these to take resources when the poor nationalize their resources. They often send the Ghost and the Darkness the front line to do their dirty work.

The Allies removed fire alarms so that they will never leave the building. Why leave when they are winning when they want, they just use military force to invade a sovereign state. NATO is there backing them deterring any potential threats. We have a bully and or a gangster and he is raking havoc everywhere. 500 000 women and children dead within twelve years and it took Saddam twenty-five years to kill half; 250 000. Who is the real tyrant here? But this is not the issue of the day.

**The real issue of the day.**

It's not about the gangster in the hood or the bully no. A visionary would see the potential impact of the current system. We are still spending a lot of money on the weapons and the military but the ICC and the Ghost and the Darkness are working very hard to eliminate the potential threats. Who will be your enemies? Who will you go to war with? Despite the growth of NATO in recent years still, the Allies are eliminating any potential competitors. In the past, we had two world wars because no one targeted the opponents. It was a fair playing ground. Now they are eliminating all the potential competitors while still making even more destructive weapons. Even the Allies realized that the play aren't fair and now are afraid that the current opponents would end up making secret nuclear weapons that are even more destructive to match the Allies, NATO, ICC, the Ghost and the Darkness' power. Yes, any reasonable man faced with such a mighty destructive power would only look for ways to increase his own impact in case of attacks and the only answer is to go nuclear. This is the greatest problem. This is the problem the Allies are afraid of because both sides will use whatever they can with the smaller enemies with nothing to lose. This is a critical issue. Dangers of human extinction.

## Cries for fear of production of nuclear weapons or WMDs.

It's not surprising that the Allies were on the forefront crying foul play fearing that the opponents were making WMDs. It's logic that if someone is squashed like they have done to the Africans and the Persian Gulf countries, in the end, they will have nothing to lose but to try to out-smart the Allies by making even more powerful weapons. We have seen the Bush government using this argument to wage wars around the world. They even know that the system isn't fair and is one-sided and what a bully can only do, or a gangster is to get whatever they want using force. The scary question is this; does that include eliminating certain countries or even continents using even more powerful weapons? Could this have led to the uncontrolled use of biological and recently digital or high-tech cyber weapons to eliminate certain people off the face of the earth? Who will stop them the more they grow and the more they eliminate people on the 25-year-old list? Who will level the playing field? There are rumors that they are crying foul-play with regarding the production of WMD, but they are making these WMDs. These are in the form of small high-tech-devices that are implanted or chipped into the body. These devices are remotely loaded with digital viruses and cyber electromagnetic weapons to test and eliminate the less developed countries. Who will stop them?

My personal issues are not fear-founded as a visionary I don't care whether NATO grows even bigger or not my concerns are with being stuck in the defensive stages of development where wastage is at maximum and progress minimal. Where the underlying principle is that of making weapons cheaper and then use these weapons to get all expensive resources like oil etc. Okay if there is no other option it can be expected. But we are saying we have solutions. But first, let me explain more. In the defensive stages, fear makes mankind get stuck in there with little progress as mankind invests heavily in weapons and the military. Imagine all that money being spent elsewhere in research and development to live forever, to fight aging, to connect the world, to look for other planets where humans can relocate to make robots to work for us, etc. My concerns are that humans have removed the fire alarms in the form of wars but continue to make weapons and creating a bully or gangster while eliminating enemies one by one year by year. My main concern is that they still invest heavily in the military. Who is your enemy? I know the first word that comes to mind is Russia. Russia? So more than twenty NATO countries are investing heavily in the military to fight Russia? I know the military solves every President or Prime Minister's political problems. The military provides easy reasons to achieve political agendas. Huge military budgets mean plenty of jobs everywhere, weapons, satellite, aircraft, infrastructure, personnel, etc. But we can do better as a people. The more we form partnerships globally with North Korea and the USA once sworn enemies negotiating the more the chances of moving away from defensive stages. I think we need to evolve as well. Reduce the budgets, ban wars and weapons production globally, evolve find other activities like research into space crafts, passenger-planes operates like missiles, etc. to send people to other planets, etc. even into research and development to increase life instead of taking life.

The defense stage is the greatest impediment to the New World. All the problems hindering progress are because of this stage. Like I said earlier on these two stages are not complementary it's an either-or situation. Defensive stages encourage everything that conflicts with the first rule; the right to life and the right to self-preserve. This stage is a resource-hungry stage that will only mean starving other areas. It's impossible to choose defense and networking and cooperation at the same time. You can say everyone is my friend and carry on making weapons. Who you are going to use the weapons on? You can't say everyone has rights to life and nothing will override that rule and declare a war that is poised to kill thousands of innocent women and children something against the right to a life of everyone. So, it's an either-or. Hence the current problems.

Defensive stages encourage the making of weapons to end life in the form of guns, missiles, grenades, etc. and recently the rise of biological, digital and electromagnetic weapons in the form of viruses. Defensive stages encourage governments to starve other areas. We have poverty in developed countries like the UK and the USA. This is shocking but understandable as a misuse of resources and regardless of human life. A misunderstanding of the first rule that everyone has a right to life and to self-preserve. Starving someone threatens that person's right to life as food is needed to sustain life. So, you can see why this is not just a gross violation of human rights but a crime in the New World that can result in a leader losing his or her own life. Value other people's lives and have yours valued too. Disregard the lives of women and children and face the assassin. It makes sense if you follow the new rules and acknowledge the first rule everything will fit into place. Value the lives of children and women and everyone else then you would not build massive weaponry instead you would make sure that these people have everything that they need to live forever. That forbids misuse and unnecessary wastage. You would not make weapons that would threaten the lives of kids. I know now no one cares if the kids are not the same background or genetic heritage. Therefore, I have introduced laws that look at a lack of empathy connotations in relation to the needless loss of human life. I explained in other chapters that in the animal kingdom it is acceptable for animals to kill their own for strategic reasons for example if the presence of a young one threatens the survival of the whole group. This is because food might be scarce, and this puts the mother in danger as it might have to travel far where there is danger looking for food. But for another animal to kill another's curb that does not belong to itself is another issue. If animals are clever to recognize this why do, we let some people kill thousands of other genetic heritage's kids when one of their dies the whole world stands still?

As a visionary and the leader of the New World, I think my concerns are that the more weapons we make the more we are shooting ourselves in the head. The bigger the bully becomes the greater the chances of nuclear self-destruction events. The weaker will one day find ways of matching this ever-growing bully or gangster group that one day they will use WMDs for real as they will have nothing to lose. The second reason is that it's unwise and irresponsible to remove fire alarms and fight the fire in an old building that has collapsed more than three-times. Why not be clever? Run out of the building when the fire starts but first reinstall the fire alarms. Remove this ICC and NATO and level the playing field again. Play like boy's fair and square encourage competition let be there another World War 3 or 4 whatever once you have quenched your ego then can I lead you to the next stage. I know boys being boys' weapons are your best friends. Big guns better! What I am objected to is just having big guns just for displaying. That's bullshit. We need all the scarce resources we can get. If you have no guts to use the weapons why do you make the weapons in the first place? Have guts and balls of gold and level the playing field. Let's see who the big boy is. Let's destroy all these weapons we surely don't need these. Why make things you will dump in the end when kids are suffering for a meal? Make things you can use or don't make at all.

Or if you are a chicken, then forget about fighting and all that. Throw away all these weapons admit you have wasted your resources but draw a line and never waste these scarce resources again. Change. Dig a small hole and spit in it. Say never again will I waste resources when kids are dying of hunger. I will show you a new way. But first I want you to quench your fighting thirst. So, I will invoke the third real-world war. I will give you a chance to play the boy's games. Kill each other. Test your weapons. Celebrate victories for this shall be the last time you will ever experience war again. After this, I will change everything for good, I mean forever.

Enjoy this last war for I have written new laws already. Wars are going to be a thing for the past. The military shall evolve into the highly trained and highly paid assassins. There shall never be any weapons manufacturing. The military budget will be cut or reduced depending on the amount of evolution. I shall declare the end of the defensive stages. No enemies anywhere unless we have new threats from other planets. We are going to work together, competing and investing heavily in research and development. We shall work at our optimal capacity using resources wisely. The self-esteem of the world's people shall be at the highest levels that no one will think of killing themselves or dying instead all will try to find solutions so that they can live forever simply because life will be that good that everyone will long for more. The defensive stages will be a thing of the past with its depressing attitudes. In the New World, everyone will have the basic life with no beggars, etc. Unless institutions like NATO evolve greatly, I don't see their future in the New World simply because they were created with wars and defense in mind. It's because of these institutions that we have been stuck in this stage for the past seventy years. I explained why. It's like removing a fuse and replace it with a strong wire and the end is going to be very bad. The whole thing can explode killing everyone. This is a poor inferior way of solving problems. I suggest building a brand-new modern building with everyone chipping in their desires, plans, and visions. All this issue of staying in the not-fit for purpose old building, removing fire alarms and putting in the ICC and NATO to prevent the inevitable is not only silly but a criminal offense. If it's an electrician doing this, he would not only lose his job but will have criminal charges brought against him. This is dangerous and likewise, the current system is like a time-bomb waiting for the slightest trigger not just to kill the enemies but everyone else so it's suicidal. We have a moral duty and obligation to protect humanity even if it means protecting it from yourselves. There are international laws that fall in what is called the Jus Cogens laws and these laws are universal in that everyone knows these laws and there is no excuse whatsoever. Ignorance is not an excuse. Breaching of these laws can and will make one be regarded as Hostis Humani Generis; an enemy of mankind in that such a person or cult poses a real threat not just to others but to themselves as well so as such everyone else has Responsibility to Protect everyone else from such a person or group of people. If it's a cult such as NATO provoking others committing crimes of aggression, the whole world can gather together and serve justice. No one is immune. Having said that, I think it's fair to move to the main theme of this chapter. Justice and reconciliation.

But first I think it's fitting to address the issue of a terrorist or not.

I know I have been very harsh throughout this book and some might start to wonder whether there are chances people might regard this as terrorist material.

What is a terrorist?

"a person who uses unlawful violence and intimidation, especially against civilians, in the pursuit of political aims."

Google Dictionary.

'someone who uses **violent action**, or **threats** of **violent action**, for **political purposes**.'

Cambridge Dictionary.

"Domestic terrorism: Perpetrated by individuals and/or groups inspired by or associated with primarily US-based movements that espouse extremist ideologies of a political, religious, social, racial, or environmental nature."

FBI website.

The first definition clearly states that a terrorist uses unlawful violence and intimidation, especially against civilians. This is true of terrorists they target civilians in what is called ball-rolling. They let the civilians interpret or translate their messages. They are indirect complainers if you like. Terrorists most will never target the politicians concerned but rather would let civilians plead their cause. They go behind someone else; - the civilian. In the New World, I explained that civilians are the most valuable of all in that new laws protect them at the expense of the politicians, etc. This means that I am different from these terrorists who target innocent people. Terrorism conflicts with the first rule. The right to life and the right to self-preserve and terrorists are illegal too in the New World. We as the New World will never target civilians no matter what. We don't do ball-rolling. Terrorists are freedom fighters, and most grieve and advance certain issues they want addressed by the politicians of the day through civilians. Terrorists' agenda does not involve changing the current system rather they fight for certain freedoms or rights or access to certain areas. Unless their demands are met, they will keep on killing innocent people. This has nothing to do with advocating for change for a new direction etc., no. Terrorists might have cells everywhere, but they fight in certain areas at a time. Their demands are usually trivial and specific to certain areas. They often have specific demands with certain countries e.g. the USA and certain individual groups like Christians etc. there are of a local nature. This isn't us for we represent the whole globe. Our issues are not tied to a certain country or region or continent, no we are global. The issues we advance are on behalf of all mankind regardless of genetic heritage, social standing, religion, creed, etc. we are a global movement. Our issues have a global impact and we don't address specific countries we address the whole globe and the key players like NATO, the UN, ICC or the EU, UK, USA, etc. Want we are calling for is for the betterment of mankind regardless of geographic area or religion, or color, etc. We represent humanity and it is our Responsibility to Protect humanity from a few irresponsible people who want to take things into their hands and bring all humanity to extinction. I ask you a question; when you call for a cab going home after drinking just a glass of wine at dinner then you realize that the cab driver is so intoxicated that he doesn't even know what he is doing would you just sit in that cab and hope for the best? Or either you shout and ask to get out simply because the driver is putting your life in danger. So, if this is the case how would our movement be compared to terrorism? Terrorists kill to revenge their own losses. They don't kill to push agendas, and, in most cases, they are reactive in that they have grieved first and then take revenge action to send a clear message. We are not revenging anyone for the sake of revenging there is a big difference. What we will do is level the playing field. See us as the equalizers. We are not revengeful as the terrorists do rather, we let you decide if your acts have been just. If you cry foul, then you are guilty because all we did is recreated your own acts and so since you started the ball-rolling you face the consequences first. It's fair and square. Sometimes people make decisions and don't even know the impact of their actions so our duty for the sake of peace is to recreate past evils and see how you react and judge our next move based on that. To move forward to the next stage of development requires a neutral position from all people involved. This is very important. I illustrated that it was hard after the two world wars for the people to trust each other that there will never be war again without anything tangible. Imagine if you have lost a million soldiers then after the war someone says let's make peace from now on let's shake hands on it. You then find out that only you suffered a million loss, and they lost only a hundred men would you take their word for it and forget a million of your men that perished at the hands of the person you just shook hands with? Imagine the families of those who died coming to you and ask you if it really was peacetime dreading further loses. Surely it will be hard to trust your enemy especially if they have lied or tricked you before. You will be cautious. Our duty is to come and level the playing field. Offer everyone a neutral position put laws and follow these to make sure that no one reverts. Assess situations to make sure say in the above case the other man lost a million men through a genuine mistake then we can assess for any deception etc. and level the playing field so that deals that are to be made tomorrow will be binding and trusted by all. When I say no more wars, no more weapons manufacturing, selling or exchange or any use then no one will ever use these again. We don't want situations where people would secretly make weapons to ambush the people who have done great damage in the past. When war is over, then it's over because no one will be allowed to put huge defense budgets all this money will be channeled into other areas?

## What are our aims and objectives?

Our intentions are bona-fide. We are not a bunch of some inferior-thinking or grieved lunatics bound for revenge. Whatever we do today has great implications for the day after tomorrow where it really counts. It will be hard but with all the things we are putting in place, we will achieve our goals. Our aims are for the benefit of all mankind. I think it's irresponsible and an unforgivable crime to make massive highly destructive weapons to kill the starved women and children to get rid of them or reduce their numbers that way. We can't tolerate that anymore or let anyone do such an inhuman degrading treatment. It's time someone stands up and shows you the way. So here I am. Our plans are perfect plans for everyone. Imagine in 2017 global spend on military was $1.7 trillion according to the arms watchdog. If it was ten years ago, no one would care because the world was volatile. Nations were against each other. No one knew if we were ever going to come to talking terms. So, defense was justified. Ten years down the line surely a lot has changed, and it's time we also realize that the military has become obsolete. Our own threats are our own selves. We would like to build a better world. A world where people would wish to live forever not like today where suicide rates have shot to the roof. All this money can do good in other areas. We can eradicate poverty and all kinds of problems and give humanity a basic life. I know some might be saying here go the socialist again. There is nothing socialism about our aims and objectives. If there is an element of socialism, then it's a by-product of the outcome and not our direct intention. We are not saying give away all your wealth to the poor, no. We are saying let's use the resources effectively and where they are needed the most. All these fancy weapons and the like are just big boys' toys. Let the big boy grow to a man, a family man and realize that the whole world is your family. Stir competition in research and development. Let the military evolve let them lead the way to show us how we can live forever for a change. The past 2000 years these guys have been showing us how to kill. I think by now we know how they really can kill but this is just one side of the coin. I stand here in front of you and say I want to see the other side of the coin. Show me how you can extend life. Show me how you can close wounds your dagger has made. Show me how you can close the hole your bullet left on the forehead of another. Show me how you can raise the 500 000 women and kids who have died. Show me how you can make even better roads than the ones you blew up. Show me how you can build missiles that can pick up the people you killed. In other words, can your missiles that sunk the people in the ground also make them fly to another place? Show me how your mother of all bombs can recreate new people through birth or whatever. Can you swear not to kill innocent women and children? It's time we see the reverse of everything you do. If you have been killing can you make or create life? Show us something we don't know. Evolve or face closure. I am not saying that the military is now a thing of the past. I am saying evolve and exist remain killing then conflict with our new laws and rules and face the consequences. Our message is that strive for advanced technological advancement never witnessed before at fast rates than now. More resources towards things that really matter. I know we will have problems having people listening to us simply because for some they have everything to lose because killing innocent women and children is what they know best something we will vehemently defeat.

We will encourage competition between everyone; businesses, local governments, institutions, individuals, etc. We will reward talent and smart-hard-working and those investing in things that matter get extra funding for money we will set aside. We need personal fast planes. Establish global networks. We will create one global identity one global passport for everyone which you can use worldwide. No boundaries no restrictions in the New World. We will create effective transport networks global in partnerships with other countries, but Tomorrow's World Order will oversee the project and create and allocating funds so that progress is a fact and there is someone to make sure that everything goes according to plans. We as Tomorrow's World Order are not confined to a certain country. We will establish offices in every country and the whole globe shall be one like a single-family. I argued at the beginning of this chapter that a family is the nearest we can have to the New World nevertheless on a small scale. The family has all the characteristics of the New World. They work together for the betterment of the family unit. There is stiff competition don't get me wrong there are fights too but not just empty cowardice fights these are fruitful fights that bring results and only add to the value of the family. Competition in the family is the same competition we will want to see. Everyone working their own way trying hard any way they could to be the best the bright sibling, etc. I explained the obstacles we have in real-life in trying to recreate the family unit on a nation or global scale. I had an idea earlier own getting everyone chipped and connected through that chip as a digital nerve or whatever you want to call it so that that nerve acts the same way as the family blood. If people know they have the same blood, they work together for the betterment of everyone. Family blood removes jealous, evil thinking and all negative feelings. We would not even contemplate spending dosh on weapons. So maybe I should patent this idea to get a chip that will be implanted and act as blood or family DNA. I know you might be saying you start sounding like today's leaders. Trust me, they are not like me. Their intentions are short-term just for their career 4 to 8 years that's it whatever happens while my dreams will last through future generations. I am not changing countries etc. no. The only way I will see these changes is to incorporate my vision into their long-term plans. This is a global movement rather than a political party. My plans are for everyone regardless of color, genetic heritage, creed, social standing, gender, etc.

Trust me there are no terrorists who will come up with similar plans to better humanity. We have potential as 'a people', and it is a sad fact that we would rather waste precious resources on fanciful boys' toys than with things that matter. We can do better that is a fact. We have potential and we can do much better as 'a people', but we need to work together and not be afraid of change. We should be very dynamic to be flexible. In my dream, the globe is like just that big family house you grew up in. Picture that and you have all the answers. Imagine going to your brother's room anytime and getting kicked out for entering without knocking. Remember going back to his room only to be screamed at when you find his girlfriend there with him. No matter how many times you have just entered uninvited he will never close the door forever. It's a matter of going there at the right time. Imagine all gathering in the sitting lounge talking until the next morning making plans etc. Imagine your brother coming home unannounced with his car raving outside waking up everyone? Imagine sometimes contributing to a barbecue outside. Imagine all painting the house or doing gardening or all buying new furniture for the house? This is not socialism because it's still one man for himself TWO for us all. There is still competition and individuality. Each sibling can save his or her money building his or her own family on the side. So, all this talk of socialism. We can do better. We are wasting resources and can work at above optimal. I will create the conditions and new laws so that it is a smooth move to another stage. So, let's work together. If you are all prepared to change so be it but if not, then I am afraid to say we can't revert to the old ways. I can't seem to stress this enough. We are not going to let you take us down with you. If you can't stop, we will stop you.

So, a Visionary; a New World Order leader or a Terrorist you decide. I know these people might want to include me on their Colony Collapse Strategy list and try to link this to terrorism, but I vehemently deny any linking to these low-lives people who kill women and children. I am a visionary and women and children will never be on the table unless you violated our rules especially the first rule the right to life. If you can't be afraid for the life of your own family, then you and they are of no good to us. If you don't value your own, then of what value are they to us? There is nothing terroristic for wanting what is best for all mankind. We can do better together. This is not one of Jesus' messages of peace and love your neighbor, etc. This is a real challenge to all mankind to change and take a new road. I have a vision and can take you there. Aren't you tired of killing each other? Aren't you tired of routine lifestyles? Aren't you upset with these people aging you deliberately faster? Aren't you angry at these people loading you with all kinds of watermarks claiming to protect you against greedy foreigners who would want to tear your soft parts? Mind you these people treat you like cattle on a farm being burnt on the butt with that iron steel giving them a mark so that everyone knows who they belong to and never to mess up with them. Okay, you might be safe but hey you are not free because that mark classifies you just as a property of someone else, I don't care a teaching hospital nor the President nor Prime Minister for that matter. Where can we draw a line on what is acceptable and what is not?

So clearly not a terrorist. We will never target civilians deliberately or indirectly and we will never do anything that put civilians in danger and likewise we will never expect to see or experience cases where our enemies will try to use civilians to bargain with us. We have very strict rules regarding this. This is the only time we will consider your family as well. Remember we are the equalizers as well. We let you fight our case. We will simply recreate what are our grievances and once you shout foul play, then we have a case against you. It's a fair system nevertheless rarely used but one that is just for you will decide for yourself. So once again surely terrorists? I don't think so.

Terrorists are freedom fighters and we are no freedom fighters for we are not oppressed. We are into this together. We are in the same boat with you only that we think that you are intoxicated with ignorance and far-fetched from the changing reality, and you will rock the boat. So, all we are asking is for you to step down and let us be the driver. We know a better road all the to the ocean waters. I know the first thing that comes to mind is the word bullshit just because you don't want to change. No bullshitting we have studied these ocean waters and although it's not obvious, we have discovered a way through these waved-waters of the oceans to paradise. Sounds good! So, jump in let us lead you all the way. Even considering the worst-case scenario, if we are terrorists so as you because we are in this together only that we think you are a screwdriver and you might screw everything up.

**Now I can address the real theme of this chapter; Justice, and reconciliation.**

Express-command to put an end to this through our laws and courts as a deterrent.

We are not bloodthirsty terrorists bound for revenge aiming to kill innocent civilians; no. Nor are we mad lunatics ready to shed blood for nothing or for political gains, no. Neither are we power-hungry mad-dogs ready to kill everything in our way, no. We are going to put new laws that everyone no matter how powerful must observe and obey. Express-command to put an end to this through our laws and courts as a deterrent. These rules are universal norms you already know but which we have put into laws, so they are followed by everyone. These laws are to safeguard a smooth transition to the next stage of development. These laws are the cornerstone of the progress we are going to make. So, as such we expect everyone to abide by them., They are common-sense laws that protect everyone especially the vulnerable women and children. It starts with these if we are to achieve the level of development synonymous with the New World. We must solve the obvious but often neglected issues. Your leaders have chosen fancy more destructive weapons instead of the welfare of these hoping that these weak people will revolt and then test the weapons on them. Killing two birds with one stone. The chance to 'eliminate the nuisance of the world' and a chance to test how destructive that missile is. This kind of thinking is a thing of the past. We have a New World Order now and it shall never be the same again. We shall put laws that removes everything that is causing bottlenecks. We will remove and tackle everything causing fears and anxiety making people still want to hang on to their weapons. We will find ways of dealing with bullies and gangsters terrorizing small countries forcing them to buy their weapons. This shall be a thing of the past. No one should be pressured into doing something they don't want to let alone tricked or forced into buying weapons. We will look at all areas of life from general health to dealings with state officials. Those dodgy doctors abusing their patients implanting WMD devices with the hope that they will never get caught beware we have advanced technology too that can detect these beyond doubt and we shall be strict simply because these people are in a position of trust and it's a worse crime beyond comprehension if someone in a position of trust gets found out abusing people they are supposed to protect. I think it's worse because to trust the system it starts with these. If they can't be trusted, then these as they reflect the image of their leader the one in charge, we shall assume the whole system is corrupt too. Make no mistake here because we shall assume that the person in a position of trust was following a command from the top. A command which he or she can't reject. As such that they carried this act as an order which he or she can't refuse to act on and as such this has implications on how we will view the leaders in question. Very strict measures to combat this simply because a bad egg spoil all. Express-command to put an end to this through our laws and courts as a deterrent. Usually, these people will try to translate what is happening in the institutions of governments concerned unless if the crime is for personal gains. Issues of illegal hacking with the whole institutions and government trying to cover up the doctor's abuse by further abusing the victim shall be dealt with in the strictest sense. We shall aim to just to put an end to this through our laws and courts as a deterrent where it can be proved that the doctor abused the victim. You must understand that such acts go beyond just being a mere crime as they are threatening the fabric on which the New World is built on. The New World hinges on trust and honor and respect for individual liberties and rights. In the New World, no laws will override the first laws that deal with individuals. Unlike nowadays where a military intervention can override the risks to civilians. In the New World, the person or individual comes first. You have the right to life and to self-preserve at any other cost. A President or Prime Minister can be stopped through our laws and courts as a deterrent if he or she gives a command that gets civilians killed. No command shall be given that conflicts with the first rules. Once that has been established you will see that everything else easily falls into place. You can't make weapons if they result in the death of civilians or even your own or the opponent's soldiers simply because these laws are universal. Killing enemy soldiers will end up in you being killed too simply because you will have violated the first rule. Your enemies' soldiers or civilians are people as well governed by the same rules so in that case, it means no wars. No weapons use, manufacturing or selling whatsoever. That way the military shall spearhead research and development into saving life rather than killing life. Into prolonging life rather than shortening life into sending people to space, to other countries, etc. rather than sending people into the ground. The same goes for these governments practicing secret eugenics and slavery. You can never hack or implant a chip or a device that will conflict with the first rule the right to life and to self-preserve. Here it is not just the right to life but the right to a good healthy lifestyle that is meant to be forever depending on how fast these guys are going to come up with solutions. It's a right to a happy life free from any remote stimulation against your will or abuse through cyber genital arousal any such abusers in a position of trust will be dragged to court simply because these people for fuck's sake are in a position of trust. Express-command to put an end to this through our laws and courts as a deterrent. Loading all your people with watermarks and holding them to ransom is a thing of the past. Life should be respected; the body must be treated as holy and as such shall no digital or bio-genetic stuff be loaded into it. I don't care if it's for their protection or not or for the preservation of a people such practices are outdated. People are not like animals' cattle for example to be treated as property given watermarks that must be removed if the right price or person comes along. What is the difference between this and slavery? People put on a stand and with potential buyers examining them with a view to purchasing them. This is barbaric; beware of the great risk of getting dragged to court. Express-command to put an end to this through our laws and courts as a deterrent. This thinking is dead wrong and outdated. A body to live long should not be intoxicated with watermarks or devices that emit radiation but should remain pure forever. Loading your own with watermarks isn't going to prolong that life: fact but reduce it and as such in direct conflict with the first rule. A mass murderer in the New World and only death fitting for that person if found guilty through the courts.

Look around you ask yourself all the issues I have addressed so far in this chapter. Try to locate and point to what I have mentioned above see if you can relate all this information to someone you know. Check for human watermarks. Check for abuse by those in a position of trust pretending to help but torture someone behind everyone's back. Look for people putting emphasis on material things like missiles while children die in millions of hungers, worldwide. Look for evil people who would test weapons and viruses on others in most cases not the same genetic heritage as them. Look for evil hacking and those who would have a salary at your expense. Look for those who would rather make everyone homeless and out of work so that they have people to coach. Look for those loading innocent women and kids with digital or cyber viruses so that they run around the whole day making noises. Look for all kinds of things we can easily change if we had the time and money. Now picture my boys camouflaged among you but only you can see them for now you have the wisdom to understand that we can be better as a people. We can do well, and we don't have to kill others to achieve great we just need to be bold and say hey big boy we have seen your toys all these centuries we are fed up. Put that away we have grown up now see my son is running in the fields and I hate to see that thing exploding near him. Look around you can you see my boys with deadly rifles waiting for your command. If you have seen what I talked about in this book, give the command. I delegated the very moment you start seeing what is in this book. Close your eyes and now can you see the New World. It's by necessity. This is the only way mankind will understand we mean business. We gave everyone a chance to see and share our vision and above all join us. Our cause is for all mankind. Tomorrow you will thank us and so as your children and their children. We can't afford to waste any more time and precious resources. Time to act is now.

I can still see justice through our courts simply because some people will never change, and we have no option. Some people would rather defend what they know best simply because this is the only way they know, and it has been successful for centuries and has been passed down from past generations and it works. Okay, it works but can it work in the New World? Can you swear that you shall never conflict with the first rule and spill blood of the innocent? If so then nothing to worry about but I guarantee you that there is a 99,9% chance that it will conflict with our dream of the New World and as such incompatible.

### I swear by the assassin.

Express-command to put an end to this through our laws and courts as a deterrent. Every decision must be approved by the courts. We are open to arrive at such a decision guaranteed by our laws which are formerly the Jus Cogens where no derogation is permitted. Laws with universal jurisdiction as a global power; that anyone in any jurisdiction can and must exercise mandatory obligations to bring violators to justice through our laws and courts. Every system has a law and order component. If found guilty to delegate to the assassin. Our laws are universal laws that no one in their right mind will be expected to break these laws but if they do there is also express judgment that swiftly anyone can through the courts and our laws seek for justice and the method of executing the decision of the courts can be through the assassin.

The main reason and how these are different from the current system is that we operate an IF-THEN system. This is so we remove ambiguity and bias. The law must be straight forward going forward. If you hack and torture others obvious your fate is at the hands of the assassin although we can formalize this through the courts. So, the judgment is express. In that IF you hack others obviously means you will torture others also, THEN you ought to be shoot but our courts need to confirm this. So, going to court is just to formalize everything to avoid others taking the law into their own hands.

We have a huge mountain to climb simply because we are fighting a long-established well-equipped system that don't want to change, but we shall swear by the assassin to deliver a clean shot [again only as a final judgment after the courts] and we shall stand by him that no ounce of blood of any civilians shall soak the dust on the ground nor quench the ground. Everyone has felt the pain people are going through. If you are for change, we are on your side. Most of these issues are institutionalized and as such commands come from the top so we shall aim to change the rogue top brace. It will be one man for himself and TWO for us all. Express-command to put an end to this through our laws and courts as a deterrent.

# CHAPTER ELEVEN

## LAYING THE FOUNDATIONS.

I will reiterate here that for a new system to be put in place, the current system must crash and collapse. Only then is a new system justified? A system crash is an indicator that something is wrong. How and why they crash is another issue but of interest here is the fact that at certain times the system can be induced to crash and collapse. To smoothly implement our strategy, the current system must collapse to pave the way for a new system. Anyone who subscribes to our system is on our side but for the few who think they are above the law; our new laws then think again. Our aim is to implement this system as smoothly as possible and where we have opposition and we are sure that the opposition is just a 'stalling nuisance or tactic' to delay the inevitable we shall get a court order through our justice system and courts to remove any bottlenecks and obstacles. Our work is for the good of all mankind. We are not proposing to rob people or introduce a system that destroys people's hard-earned wealthy, no. We are going to add value to you as a person, and the rest will follow. It starts with you. The current system places importance on material things, hoping that material things will enhance the life one has and somehow increase your value. Honestly, that line of thought has failed as for the past seventy years that has failed to see any real changes. The problems then are still the problems now. Our approach is to say no to that. It starts with you. All laws start with you and the rest follow. You have the right to life and to self-preserve as the priority laws. Whatever follows must and should not conflict with that rule and no other law can override that. So, all current leaders must abide by our laws and follow these. Tomorrow's World Order is above all leaders and governments as we are the overseers of humanity and as such, we have absolute power to put new laws and to make sure that the new laws are adhered to. Our laws are for the good of everyone. We will give current governments time and chances to replace their laws with our laws.

## Laws that have Universal Jurisdiction.

Our laws have global jurisdiction that means that the laws raise issues too serious to be interfered with by local country laws. All countries must incorporate these laws into their systems as the main laws that can't be overridden. These laws fall under what is referred to as the Jus Cogens norms in that they can't be broken and that there is no derogation permitted. These laws are binding on every state and individual. As such, there is no breach indirectly or directly allowed in case some few leaders think they are above our laws. So, it is in your best interest to cooperate and be part of something great. Wealth never achieved before taking humanity to another level of development. Our request is simple. Look at our laws and let these be your main laws. These laws must be implemented at the same time globally, so we all start afresh together which means sticking to the time frames. I know some will argue that Presidents and Prime Ministers have more power than say Tomorrow's World Order this is not the case. Previously this could have been possible simply because of defense. Defense is cited many times as the main reasons for infringing on human rights, for example, a President or Prime Minister is said to have Unchecked Executive Powers for defensive purposes. This means the President or Prime Minister can deliberately choose to break our new laws for defensive reasons. Defense gives the leaders unprecedented powers that in most cases they end up abusing their position and taking the law into their own hands but later regret it after office when courts cry for their heads. In the New World, the defense is not an issue anymore so there are no justifications for Unchecked President Powers. It is true that all excessive executive powers granted to any President are associated with wars and defense. In the New World wars and defense are going to be banned. That leaves the President to put our laws first which puts a person as the sole existence of any government or President in that the right to life must be a priority and it doesn't matter whose life. This could be the right to a life of the enemies and the new laws state that the President will and must observe the rights of these enemies' people. Wars and defense put the leaders in such a position wherein the end they prioritize material things over human rights. A classic example is what happened after 9/11 where the President used his unchecked powers to imprison people in Guantanamo cages without any rights. I think in cases like 9/11 in the future, Tomorrow's World Order will be responsible for dealing with such issues. We are unbiased and we represent humanity at large rather than national interests. The idea in the New World is to put a system that is fair globally and let TWO deal with issues like terrorism even if they occur in a specific country. TWO represent the whole globe and we would not want state Presidents involved in defense rather than running their countries to achieve our global laws.

It's more like contracting out security issues to us with collective powers and resources to deal with such issues fairly because what is happening at the moment is the President's executive powers give him too much power that in the end he will choose which laws to follow and which once to put aside in the name of national security. This creates ambiguity in the law in that the President will cherry-pick some laws or quash some which can limit his powers, and this can give him extra powers to give a command that will conflict with the first rule. To protect a nation in time of national security can mean overriding the first rule that is killing some which he might argue as collateral damage to protect the rest. During the 9/11 situation a plane was shot down or 'fall' carrying passengers who were US citizens., In the New World he cannot order the shooting down of the plane simply because the right to the life of the passengers will be violated and as such the President will be answerable for the deaths of the passengers as well even though that would save other people. This is one of the reasons why TWO will be able to deal with threats like this and relieving the Presidents from such complicated decisions that will see them being arrested after the end of their term in office. The fact that Presidents and Prime Ministers are pursued after their term in office has ended only points to the need for a new system. The current system is flawed. These Presidents or Prime Ministers are breaking international laws and are only free because of immunity given when in office. We don't want a situation like this. In the New World, there is no room to carry out a crime knowingly with the belief that you have immunity. In the meantime, defense makes these people get away with murder. Once the defense is not anyone's priority when I pass new laws banning wars and all acts of aggression, then life will be easy, and decisions will be easy to make too. Everything will be clear it's either you follow the law or not. If there is a law that says don't kill children and women, no matter what you can't kill children knowing that you will simply say I am the President. That creates confusion and in the New World, everyone has high self-esteem and will be capable of being a President simply because all will have achieved a high-level in the society that a few merits will separate one from the other. Being a President will not give you immunity to kill while in office and get away with it. Those you are killing will have a status the same as you that of a President and only by lucky or merit that you became a President. Women and children will have the same status as a President or even greater as all the laws will center around them. Killing even one can and will cost the President's life. So, to be a President in the New World caries much responsibility and weight that respecting life will mean respecting life and most Presidents or Prime Ministers if they really know what is in store for them will opt out of exercising executive powers because any move can and will cost them their lives. This is also to make sure that no one is above our laws and this will make it easy to apply the law globally and uniformly with ease. We will apply our laws to deal with any security issues. I think also the fact that certain countries have more attacks than others can show that these countries take things into their own hands and without a broader view of the world they like to play the world superpower available to everyone's rescue but miscalculating local issues. This leaves them open to attacks directly. In the New World, TWO will take over as we represent the whole globe. Leaving states to concentrate on their internal affairs. The US has intervened globally, and their foreign policy must just be the reason why they also get attacked. Can you say with sure that their foreign policy represents the wills of everyone concerned? People have different preferences according to religion and culture. I think TWO is in a better position to deal with global issues we are not biased, and we don't represent any country. We can tailor our solutions according to local needs using our laws that have universal jurisdiction to make the world a better and fairer place addressing any grievances.

TWO is there to clarify the law and make it easy for the Presidents or Prime Ministers to decide what to do too. The idea behind this is that as a matter of fact all current Presidents or Prime Ministers relay on defense for a successful career. The whole system relies on defense and the military. If we takeout defense from the equation this will create problems for the current Presidents or Prime Ministers. In the long run, a defenseless world will remove all current issues of human rights abuses. First, we will be guiding the leaders on what is important to them and to their nations. Remove the defense and they are left to choose other areas. Writing down laws that show them what to prioritize is a great help for the whole globe in making effective decisions. We don't want a world where leaders are later dragged to the courts for the lack of empathy regarding children, neglect and starving their own people. The leaders will know who comes first and once that person is served then other things follow as well. So, children and women come first then if you are about to allocate money to other areas you must see if that conflicts with the first rule if it does then it's not a good priority. Say you want to invest in a satellite that will be used to spy on your people. You check if this conflicts with the first rule. You ask yourself does the satellite emits harmful substance that can conflict with the first rule? If it does maybe in the form of radiation, then it means it's a bad decision unless you can be sure that this won't affect the children and women. Then you can look if spying can interfere with the first rule. Do you actual pose a risk? How are you going to be spying on them? Do you have to use electromagnetic waves? Will these be tampered with and abused as this is done remotely and can't be proved? Etc.

Removing defense leaves a world that is just and fair and where human rights can be adhered to. It's not eliminating defense altogether it's contracting out, so that TWO is left to do this job.

I know one might be thinking that we are duplicating organizations like the United Nations. We are not the United Nations and we are different from the UN as I will illustrate in later chapters. The UN is rooted in the current system that we are saying that it is now obsolete. The UN is based on laws established after the Second World War laws to keep every one of you hooked on weapons and wars. It is based on biased ideas and is there to protect those who created it the same countries etc. causing global issues to gain at the expense of everyone else. It has been more than seventy years and we believe that these laws are obsolete or don't reflect the New World. What makes us different from the UN?

First to recall I argued that after the First World War a League of Nations was created to maintain world peace and prevent future wars through collective security but the major drawback is that it was biased in the first place as it was to help the Allies win any future wars all this talk about preventing future wars is just imaginary. It was to prevent not to stop wars. No laws whatsoever to effectively ban wars like we are doing. It aims from the word go where to provide a platform to reduce the effects of competition in the form of the axis. It had no military wing to enforce its commands, yet it claims to prevent wars, how? To reiterate, it made no laws to prevent wars. If you are serious about preventing wars, you don't wait for wars to happen in the hope of bringing everyone to the negotiating table. To make things worse, they were biased as they relied on Allies forces to help them enforce their proposals. Then it's nothing to do with world peace but protecting the interests of the Allies; - Britain, the USA, France, Italy, and Japan. No wonder the Second World War broke out the axis noted this that the League of Nations was there to support the interest of the Allies.

If you are serious about preventing wars, you don't go with the current system hoping that wars won't break out. You do like we are doing. Put laws to stop anything to do with war and remove everyone's fears that make them hang on to weapons. Deal with bullies intimidating others and ban spending on defense and this should be globally and at the same time so that no one is left hanging to weapons when some have put theirs down. The system should be fair to all otherwise it will only make say the opponents suspicious or even more aggressive. This league ends up creating a lot of current institutions like the World Health Organization. The ICJ, etc. The original four countries that comprised the League Council were Britain, France, Italy, and Japan. This league went on to become or 'was replaced by the United Nations' after the Second World War. The League of Nations failed to prevent any future wars simply as I will explain later it was not meant to prevent wars but to protect the interest of those who established it. The Second World War occurred when it was in existence so no fit for the purpose. Come the Second World War and after the war, this league was replaced by the UN which took some already established bodies and institutions. The UN had the same functions as the League of Nations [LN] it was like a better version of the LN. So obviously you can tell that it was bound to fail just like the LN. Just like the LN, it was tasked to prevent future wars but with the Iraq war happening in 2003 it is as bad as the LN and therefore unfit for the purpose.

"Its objectives include maintaining international peace and security, protecting human rights, delivering humanitarian aid, promoting sustainable development, and upholding international law. The UN is the largest, most familiar, most internationally represented and most powerful intergovernmental organization in the world. At its founding, the UN had 51 member states; there are now 193."

Wikipedia.

We have the UN and this decade is possibly the worst decade in terms of human rights violations. We have had wars started by the founding members of the UN namely Britain and the USA against Iraq, Syria, Afghanistan, etc. on its watch. We have had human rights violations perpetrated by its founding members with torture in Iraq and at Guantanamo Bay on its watch. Speaking of international upholding of the rule of law there is little the UN can do apart from being reactive.

The UN just like the LN before it is reactive unlike TWO. We are proactive and we will put things in place that will prevent all the problems we have today rather than wait for the torture to happen and investigate. Okay, I am not denying that it might have some successes in other areas since its conception no, but this was formed in 1945 some seventy years ago and was meant to stop wars and arms dealing but without making laws to ban wars globally. To make things worse, whatever they say or decide has no effect at all on anyone. In other words, no one listens. They are there to make recommendations which no one can follow so what is the point. It seems they all simply say; who listen to this anywhere and continue with abusive acts. Mind you this was created and is funded by the very people who we are saying that they are using all these institutions to keep on breaking international laws knowing that nothing can be done to them. The UN is easily overruled by the founding nations, namely Britain, France, Japan, Italy, and the US. They have no military or anything whatsoever to enforce their decisions. In short as good as if they don't exist. If we look at the events leading to its formation, you can see exactly the main reasons behind the UN and why people say it's ineffective in solving today's global peace. After the First World War, the Allies met with Germany and the Austria-Hungary pact to negotiate peace, but Britain and France were not interested in peace as they wanted revenge. I think to understand what I'm going to propose, something I have already covered under Society or Colony Collapse Strategy you must understand the events leading to the Iraq war and the position of the UN. You can easily see that the UN has no power at all simply because it is a vehicle for fulfilling this Colony Collapse Strategy. It cannot challenge the creators and its funders all it has to say is that the war was not in its name. So, what is their purpose then if they can't prevent their founders going to war when they clearly say it's an illegal war.

On September 16, 2004, <u>Secretary-General of the United Nations</u> <u>Kofi Annan</u>, speaking on the invasion, said, "I have indicated it was not in conformity with the <u>UN Charter</u>. From our point of view, from the Charter point of view, it was <u>illegal</u>."

I pointed out earlier that the Allies after the world wars came up with a solution to prevent heavy losses in case of future wars and to prevent any future wars. They established the LN which was replaced by the UN to help suppress opponents rather than maintain peace and security. Yes, you heard me loud and clear the UN is a killing machine to weaken first and take out all opponents of the founding member countries. They are there to weaken the enemies through mainly sanctions before the founding members launch military attacks. I have pointed earlier that the Allies adopted the Colony Collapse Strategy as a way of reducing the impact and effectiveness of their opponents so that victory is guaranteed without major losses in case the war broke out. This strategy takes out leading male opponents to send shock-waves and fear so that no serious enemies' opposition is left to pose a threat in case they decide to group and start a war. This is the reason why they don't care if sanctions kill women and children or not the idea being that it is a strategy that will ball-roll anger to the rebels in that country as women and children die. These rebels will then fight what they see as a 'useless government that saves its skin at the expense of women and children. But what happens is that the government after being humiliated and proved not to care enough to prevent the deaths and suffering of women and children through sanctions will use extreme force mainly through the use of illegally banned weapons like chemical gasses against the rebels. Ball-rolling their anger as well as they cannot attack the sanctions-imposers as they know why the sanctions have been put in the first place; to provoke them and justify the invasion if they retaliate. The main goal of the sanctions; to give the invaders reasons to invade and attack on humanitarian grounds. Just like the terrorists, sanctions kill women and children and use these as baits. Something that will see the assassin take aim and takeout these evil clever calculating bastards in the New World. The UN through the ICC was to deal with the low-level threats posed by the African leaders and some middle eastern nations while the high threats of the Persian Gulf were to be dealt with a military force instituted by the two superpowers of the day Britain and the USA. The LN did not prevent any wars as envisaged with the resultant Second World War. The Allies had to drop the defensive approach of fortifying themselves regardless of what the enemy was doing. After the Second World War, they adopted an attack approach and through the ICC, UNSEC and the UN to monitor, record and report serious threats under the disguise of human rights abuses. Like I said the two superpowers were to deal with the higher threats of the Persian Gulf who have oil which they can use to exchange for or use the proceeds to make or buy nuclear weapons. So, in a nutshell, all this talk of peacekeeping is to blind the world. Do you think if they were to keep peace and prevent the war, they would have let Iraq be invaded? They might not have done anything as they are powerless, but they might have rallied heavy support against the war, at least delay the invasion and give women and children time to escape to other countries but they let it happen. I will address the real crime of these institutions the UN, ICC, UNSEC, etc. in later chapters; namely the crime of giving women and children a false sense of security stealing valuable time from them. Time they might have used to escape the invasion and wars. A greater crime in our eyes greater than that of the murderers. Impersonating a real war-stopper and negligently causing the deaths of these innocent people. We are going to add more charges of a lack of empathy with the victims simply because they don't relate to them therefore uncaring. On top of that these institutions prevent others from helping they trick potential helpers just like rugby players do obstructing the opponents so that their striker can score an easy and perfect try-score. All potential stoppers of the war will not react as much as they would have done if there were no UN, UNSEC, ICC, etc. Other countries like China, Russia, etc. might have objected more vehemently if there was no UN, UNSEC, ICC, etc. but their presence gives everyone delayed-reactions in that they can assume the UNSEC, UN or ICC to do everything in their power to not just declare that the war is illegal but also to do something about it even if simply means delaying the invasion giving women and children critical time to escape. But to everyone's surprise, they did not do anything despite global rallies. Therefore, their presence puts risks to lives negligently, and it's a great deception to talk about preventing wars when you have no mechanism of doing that. The greatest crime of the century and the UN, UNSEC, etc. must pay for every child and woman's death through sanctions and wars since their inceptions. Drag all to court and make compensation claims collapse these institutions.

I mentioned again the main reasons for invading Iraq had nothing to do with Weapons of Mass Destruction. After the First World War which broke out in 1914, the Allies realized that after every 20-26 years it is likely that wars can happen and they took measures to prevent the Second World War by forming institutions that will put 'blocks' to prevent enemies mobilizing. But the main reason they invaded was highlighted during the Suez Canal in 1956. At that time the then-President Dwight Eisenhower stated that;

Nationalizing the canal "was not the same as nationalizing oil wells… [which] exhaust a nation's resources."

This was after Nasser the Egyptian President had nationalized the canal. Britain and France invaded to take back control of the canal. The US President then refused to join the invasion citing that the canal was a trivial issue just like a public utility and as such not worth fighting for. He only agreed to fight if any nation had nationalized its oil reserves because oil does real damage to the country's balance sheet. So, no matter what they say, WMDs or not this is the main rationale behind the wars; to get the oil. They can't just go and say we are going to get the oil, otherwise they would be criticized but if they said Saddam has WMDs, then they face less opposition. Again, I reiterate here that the attitude of today's leaders and all past leaders is that of making cheaper weapons and use these to get things they can't afford through wars. Keep this in mind you will see that this is the cause of all global problems as I stated in later chapters. The main difference in our approach. Our strength is that we tackled financial affordability as the critical single factor to address. Read also my book or our Whitepaper; The New Single Reserve Global Currency in all bookstores. Tackle affordability and you solve all global issues. Your leaders make weapons because they can't afford to pay market prices. They must use wars to lower oil prices and availability. If every nation has enough money to buy oil at whatever the market sets the price, then what is the point of making weapons? To address global issues, address the purchasing power of all nations. The only true source of new money is through printing new money. The hinge-pin of our method but it's not a simple process because hyperinflation plays a greater role to reduce the nation's wealth to nothing hence our perfect method. See later chapters.

The UN knew that oil is the main reason for all invasions but what can they do when they are funded by the proceeds of these oil resources directly or indirectly. If a nation saves money on oil purchases money that would have otherwise paid for oil the UN might gain as well as it relies on contributions from the USA and the UK etc. So how can they be fighting the breadwinner?

# CHAPTER TWELVE

EDUCATION TO BOOST INDIVIDUAL SELF-ESTEEM THEN
EVERYTHING FOLLOWS.

*A new beginning. Appoint new fresh thinking leaders.

*Establish and implement new laws. A one world.

The New World is a stage where people are advanced in that they
have enough knowledge and self-esteem to fight for what they
want on their own. At this stage, they are aware of most of the
tricks being played on them right now in the name of protection,
etc. where they are held to ransom and where viruses are loaded
on them in the name of protection or in the name if eugenics or
population control. In the New World, these people are well
educated and knowledgeable that they would rather sue whoever
is doing this to them than to receive handouts so that some evil
people can have a job. What is happening now will never happen
in the New World without someone dragged to court. In the New
World, high self-esteem will drive people mad when they discover
that the governments or institutions are using digital remotely
operated weapons to age them faster. They will never agree to be
guinea pigs to be experimented on like what is happening now.
Current governments make all kinds of stuff, bio-engineered or
digital and recently cyber agents and test these on people as
watermarks, etc. deliberately reducing the life span and quality of
life all which conflicts with our first laws. People will never be
tricked that they are given a dodgy face to protect someone else or
as a way of communicating or teaching someone something.
People will be clever enough to realize that all this is illegal and
all they must do is take all these culprits to court or take the law
into their own hands simply because whatever they are loaded
with will never be reversible, a death sentence and currently on
death row. It's inhuman and an act that makes one be recognized

as Hostis Humani Generis. People in the New World have courage and are willing to work hard and smarter and all these issues where people are lazy and must be given the so-called protection literally loaded with viruses for being lazy in return for handouts is a thing of the past. These governments who pretend to help their citizens in the name of protection while testing viruses on them are not only breaking the law. Express-command to put an end to this through our laws and courts as a deterrent. Risk of death by the assassin if found guilty by the courts in the New World. We can't let governments make viruses on our watch and test these on their people in the name of protection. Express-command to put an end to this through our laws and courts as a deterrent. Any watermarks in the form of viruses be it digital or biological can't be tolerated in the New World. Most of these governments are exploiting loopholes in the law. They wait until all lifelines to take the issue to court are exhausted or expired, and after that, no one can do anything. The whole institutions and governments then further abuse the victims using these as baits. This is barbaric and we shall be tough with these evils simply because all this protection conflicts with the first rule the right to a healthy peaceful life and the right to self-preserve. Above all, it creates a zombie world with people lacking creativity and innovativeness. In short, it creates dependencies on the main aim of these governments so they hear a lot of thank you and feel better about themselves when in fact people without them can be better people who are very creative who can work to find lasting solutions. How on earth can one have a right to life when he or she is choking with watermarks? It's very unwise on the part of the victims to allow these teaching hospitals and the doctors treat them like guinea pigs and using them as bait. In the New World people will have advanced knowledge and would be very smart through intensive education not academic but life knowledge through our laws etc. to know that this is wrong. If someone is reducing your life span making everything go faster would you not be angry? I think most people if they were free, would fight, but this is prevalent in countries with dictatorships, monarchies, etc. where people are expected to do whatever for protecting the dictator or monarchy. I am not saying monarchies are bad, but they are not aware that leaders or certain institutions like teaching hospitals and doctors abuse people in their name.

They tag all the population putting them on 'death row' since the day they are born just to justify protecting the monarchs. This is also true in dictatorship settings as well so it's not monarchies only. Surprisingly monarchies themselves don't know that their name or institution is used behind their backs to break all rules. So, I don't blame them, and we support monarchies and will protect monarchies. The issue is not with the monarchies but governments and institutions who trick their people.

Most of these people are hacked at birth and most don't even know they are hacked until it's too late. Regimes that practice this kind of protection of making viruses and loading their people as watermarks to protect their people as in eugenics and the monarchy must be dragged to court. Express-command to put an end to this through our laws and courts as a deterrent. The New World is not about making excuses about dictatorships, eugenics, population control, the monarchy or national security at the expense of individual rights. No one has privileges and if it's true that all these people are suffering because of the dictator, eugenics, political party or the monarchy then whoever is doing this is not good. People should have high self-esteem. Express-command to put an end to this through our laws and courts as a deterrent. These people are reducing the life of their people and that of foreigners as well.

**New Laws in relation to the above issue.**

No government or country shall abuse its own people by making viruses and loading their people as watermarks to protect important people or vulnerable people or in the name of eugenics, nor security nor population control. Making of any kind of watermarks-based viruses be it digital or cyber are illegal and continuing to do this when outlawed will result in the leaders being dragged to court. Express-command to put an end to this through our laws and courts as a deterrent. Viruses and watermarks reduce lifespan and the quality of life and treating people like cattle being stamped before a sale will never be tolerated. All kinds of protection are outlawed simply because they are prone to abuse and rely on a principle of scratch my back, I'll scratch yours something that can't be associated with any governments nor institutions and people in a position of trust for that matter simply because most of the people involved are children and the vulnerable women. It is true to say that these governments deliberately starve their people reducing circulating income, making the benefit system very strict, deliberately so that people will 'scratch' their backs e.g. children used to trap all untagged foreigners or used as prostitutes so as to trap the untagged so as to bring them in the 'system'. I remind you that the use of hunger or poverty is a form of torture as in the five techniques of torture and therefore an international crime. This increases cases of child prostitutes as the children are used as bait putting innocent kids in danger if that means closing all these useless teaching hospitals and other government institutions so be it. Very stiff punishments simply because these people are in a position of trust. Express-command to put an end to this through our laws and courts as a deterrent applies here.

**Banning all time limits to bring a case to court especially where there is abuse by those in a position of trust or in power.**

There shall never be time limits to take a case to the court that involves abuse by people in a position of trust like doctors, government institutions or teaching hospitals. All cases can be brought to court at any given time by the victim or his or her representatives and it shall be free the institutions, governments, hospitals, etc. accused must pay for all court fees. The current system encourages abuse after abuse by doctors and hospitals. To make things worse, the other government institutions then try to further abuse to silence the victim. The victim has no way of complaining. The hospitals won't look at the case after a certain time people even if you have compelling evidence. The High Court is very expensive mind you most of the victims have no source of income they are targeted with all governments making sure they only get amounts they set influencing managers, other income sources, etc. as all are illegally tagged. The abuse by the doctors involves the implantation of GPS and devices they operate remotely. The first six months when the victim has a lifeline to take the hospital to court the institutions work very hard to make sure that the person will never save enough money to take them to the High Court. The High Court fees start at $600. Commands are from the top and everyone will frame and do all the dirty tricks to make sure you can't bring a successful case to the court. The whole governments are corrupt, abusive and trickery. Tricking their people into modern-day slavery. All this gives jobs to teaching hospitals and other institutions at the expense of innocent victims who are tortured using the implants that they will end up on drugs giving all the institutions alibis and jobs. This can't be tolerated these people are worse than the pirates and the slave trader before them. It can't be tolerated. The laws must be changed. The whole system encourages abuse by people in power.

A hacker shall be treated as a pirate or slave trader. Governments hacking all their people are breaking the law. How on earth can a government load its people with radiation-emitting devices with GPS functions and operated remotely? Its genocide and can't be tolerated. No governments shall be permitted to implant deliberately or indirectly secretly or otherwise for any reason. There shall never be any justification for such abuse. National security, dictatorship, eugenics, protection of the monarchy, immigration or other reasons must never override the right to life so these excuses will never exempt anyone from being punished for that. The teaching evil hospitals etc. a thing of the past as they are illegally operated because they are like assassins and drug lords taking everything in their own hands. How can those looking for organs also be responsible for the 'potential-donors' or own heroin fields to be prescribed to potential victims and above all be allowed to illegally implant torture medical devices? Speaking of grooming and cultivating for a benefit or profit. The so-called personal motive. Life must be respected. They encourage assassinations of the head of the house in order to recruit people they will teach. Their main motives are to use these orphans as bait so that they trap more people who they tag. The hospitals through the ambulances must help and trick everyone getting tagged and implanted with a GPS. Using these orphans as bait involves them being prostitutes and after using these orphans, they dispose of them by torturing them through the device implanted at birth, or loaded with watermarks so they are hooked on drugs and in the end are given prescription heroin from the hospital-owned fields. There is a need to overhaul or get rid of the current health system reduce ambulances, sack most of these and with the money to fight poverty. Ever heard the saying that too many chiefs with a few Indians? Applies here. Too much wastage. There must be a noise reduction law to ban sirens as sirens are abused and used to intimidate and frighten people. This is done to 'open them' trying to trick them or weaken their system so that they are easily attacked. In the digital world, this makes sense. A lot to learn here. Bear in mind these institutions were created in war times and they in vainly recreate war scenes to remain viable. This reduces the quality of life of the locals driving the locals crazy.

# CHAPTER THIRTEEN

THERE IS HOPE AFTER ALL.

*A New World.

*A new beginning.

*But there is a lot to be done.

*What have we achieved and what year is it?

Our plan is to achieve most of our goals by a certain date. New laws will make this a smooth process. Our aims are to solve all of today's global issues with little effort.

## Democracy.

Global democracy by a certain date. I think the new laws and banning of wars and weapons together with evolving the military will solve most of the problems dealing with democracy. This must be globally developed or developing countries there are no excuses. All loopholes to be closed and violators to be punished with swift justice.

## Decolonization by a certain date.

I think when the new laws take effect as self-esteem of everyone increases and people start realizing that there is more to life than worshipping others then and there will people reject any form of colonization. I think it will be irresponsible for former colonial powers to hang on to countries and land obtained by force during the colonial period. New laws to make it illegal to keep land and countries obtained by force and unfairly. It's like stealing; to avoid any criminal proceedings former colonial powers will be given a time period, to return land deemed by all to have been taken unfairly or can sell it back at a fair price to recover some costs. Open to negotiations.

New laws to force former colonial powers to be responsible for the removal of watermarks and any form of claiming possession e.g. through the use of landmines, etc. The colonial powers must be given a timeline to remove all landmines at their own cost before handing over land or countries back to the rightful owners. Compensation for damage caused using landmines and any deaths due to landmines etc. will result in criminal charges brought against the former colonial powers effective from the day the landmines were planted. The number of deaths if more than a certain number more charges will be brought on top of that if it can be proven that planting of these landmines was without empathy for the people affected therefore a lack of empathy laws to be used. I raised the issue earlier on that some people do what they do simply because those whoever dies are not related to them by 'background' and as such we will assess if it is just or not. The use of cruel tools to claim possession will cost anyone their lives. We look at a notion often argued that evil can only breed evil. It's true to say, for example, that kids are influenced by their parents and, in most cases, will do and follow the same principles of their parents. In most cases, it is difficult to divert from the principles of their parents and will continue the same legacy.

**Use of secret slavery and viral be it digital or not to control the people.**

A point related to the above point to see global decolonization is the fact that some countries might want to cling to former colonies through secret slavery where people are forced indirectly to obey some acts against their will for fear of being further abused. Very stiff punishment regarding anything to do with secret slavery or any unfair practices that have slavery or other forms of human degradation. There are no justifications whatsoever. I know in some countries they abuse people amounting to degrading treatment as part of initiation or protection. Be warned these rituals originated from a time when no one had human rights so listen to me and stop! It will cost you your life. Ask yourself when the rituals or protection of this nature first came into effect if more than a half a century ago stop automatically you are breaking the law. Change or we will change you. Time and duration must be considered as well. A ritual that can be done a few times might be okay as the same ritual done over decades becomes gross abuse. So be careful to check time limits. Some acts leave permanent emotional and physical scars over a long period. Be warned because what might seem harmless over time can amount to a serious crime. To be on the right side of the law sit down and assess all the practices that might have issues with the new laws and ask yourself when these laws or rituals were created and assess if there were any human rights? How were the human rights issues at that time and check if they observe the first rules or laws; the rights to life and to self-preserve and to a great quality of life? If not, then you are breaking our laws to change immediately. These practices in most cases were formulated to weaken people so that they are abused or perform certain favors. You might not know that, or things might have changed but understand the underlying principles. All these rituals are meant to destroy a person's self-esteem and we can't tolerate that because like I have said our goal is to boost self-esteem to the highest levels ever or even to break the barrier. So be warned. Most practices are to weaken so that the victim will obey say sexual favors etc. It's like calling a person derogating names to reduce them so that one can get them when they are 'cheap' or load them with watermarks so that no one else will touch them therefore lowering their value by eliminating competition. This happening to humans in the New World? Hell no, no, no watch it. Express-command to put an end to this through our laws and courts as a deterrent.

## Food and basic rights.

You will be shocked that some governments even developed ones are using food and essentials like water as a weapon to control their population. Food is used as a tool to command people. We will fight for the provision of basic rights globally first. Our strategy will make it illegal to override the first laws in favor of policies that make them starve their people. Above all, starving and intimidating your people is a form of torture and damn right torture is banned by international laws.

### Climate.

I think most of our policies might be indirect but will have a huge impact on climate. Banning of weapons, wars, changing how the military work, banning of all fossil fuel consuming vehicles, machinery, and buildings, etc. will help tackle climate change. Replacement of fossil fuels with cleaner ones, electricity solar, etc. Replacing all-metal vehicles with other ones made of recyclable material toughened fiber, etc. Research and development of better sources of energy. I think all these summits on climate change are a joke. You say zero-carbon reduction by 2020 and don't ban but increase fossil fuel consumption as oil-related vehicle production continues to increase etc. That's pathetic.

### Useless institutions.

I think most of the institutions today are useless and are there only for cosmetics reasons i.e. to make the world look better and not actually be better and for other reasons which I will discuss at the end of the book. They are there to make it look like they are doing something, but the truth is that there are there just to create jobs compete with the world's poorest for resources. The world is in a state it is simply because you are there you bastard's competition with the poor. If you were not there, then we would not have all these problems. This is a troubling truth. Most encourage poverty to justify their presence. We are going around this and ban some of these institutions. I think for most of these people who talk about human rights they don't even know what it means. There are so many human rights organizations in the world, and we have so many issues still problems, yet these institutions have been there for decades. I will make new laws that evaluate the effectiveness of these institutions and close some that might be causing some problems we have.

### Increased risk posed by the presence of certain institutions.

The reason why I am against useless institutions is the fact that they put lives at risk. People when they see the number of institutions and organizations that claim to offer help, they can get the belief that there is help there when most are just paper pushers with no ways of helping at all. I think most are for 'cosmetics purposes' only put there by the very people we are saying are breaking our laws and other international laws to keep people quiet.

## A job creation strategy at the expense of innocent victims.

I argued above that it is a common strategy of some developed countries to create lucrative jobs at the expense of the poor. It can be argued that developed countries for example might create a problem through say invading a country and planting landmines so to render the land useless. After some time when the landmines have done some real damage through deaths and maiming then the land is devalued. Once that happens, they then send their multi-national companies or other branches like the Red Cross to remove the landmines at exorbitant prices thereby creating jobs and lucrative markets landmines can be removed at 1000 times the cost of planting. I will reiterate here that laws to assess for a lack of empathy aggravated decisions will be done and if it can be proven that the decisions if maliciously given without due regard to life. Our aim is to be fair and to deal with evil according to law.

## Lack of empathy connotations in all cases.

It will be a law that crimes that are considered as cruel are to be assessed if they can be said to have lacked the empathy element. I think this is a great step towards equality, reconciliation and rebuilding the world. This will act as a deterrent to future crimes and will make people think again before committing crimes. Again, if a person is breathing by any means through a machine or not has to be held accountable for any crimes committed since the day that person was born.

## The age to be tried for crimes.

I think I personally learned this the hard way. Imagine a kid making a silly mistake that ended up costing his life at 17 years old. I think this is a debated subject, but it might be wise to increase the age of responsibility. Open for debate.

## Global Health.

A very sensitive area but one that we have sure plans. Our current system has gone bonkers. It's humanity's inferiority to do what is going on globally with the health sector. I personally think it's time we take a turn for good. The current system is against all our laws and not only conflicts with our first rule but contradicts our laws so we can't work with this obsolete system. Full stop. There is no negotiation at all. Crash the whole thing to the ground with immediate effect and replace most. The current people if not lazy then they are very complacent and if I have my way drag all to court. How on earth can you recreate the worst time in mankind's history? How on earth can an institution trusted with the health of everyone be making and using viruses be it biological, digital or cyber ones just to create jobs by recreating the worst epidemics and the war conditions to justify existence? I mentioned above that the current health system globally is obsolete and must be replaced with immediate effect. The health system was created during the war or soon after and as such they try to recreate those conditions so that they are viable and justifies the huge budgets. Can someone tell me that life expectancy and the health of global nations is the same as seventy years ago? Not the same obvious so would you not expect the health sector to change? I know this for a fact that the health sector especially the hospitals have diversified taking other roles which were currently not for them.

1. The hospitals in other countries now compete with killing agencies like the CIA. In some countries have become the vehicles of the death penalty themselves caring out the executions taking things into their own hands. The sad side is that these hospitals or the health sector target fathers who they regard as weak who they 'assassinate' as most are illegally chipped at birth and they can't complain because all court lifelines had expired by the time they discover that they have a needle electrode up their ass by then it will be too late already marked for death at birth. Why one might ask? So that these institutions look after the orphans through teaching hospitals who run day by day robbing banks to reward orphans who obey and listen but punish those who refuse. That brings me to the use of torture.

2. They practice torture.

You will be shocked to know that our public health competes with gangsters for heroin customers and they even have their own heroin fields. To make things worse, they implant chips that are remotely operated to all children at birth which they later remotely operate torturing the orphans as behavioral change therapy. Just imagine how bad it can be if no one knows and believes that these kids are being chipped at birth and imagine the kind of torture when no one can prove that they are chipped? Do you also know that the same hospitals prescribe heroin? I am 100 percent against everything our public health system stands for. They are going for short cuts kill rather than create.

3. They are involved in child grooming.

The orphans of dead fathers are looked after by the hospitals who take over as guardians providing for the orphans teaching them to bet on say horse racing where they have the control as horses can be chipped to control energy levels. In return, they link through the chips to potential buyers' or people who might take them as wives, or they might end up as prostitutes being tortured and told to go and meet someone the hospitals might want to get tagged. So, in fact, it's the hospitals that are training prostitutes to use as bait. We know agencies like the CIA used the same techniques to get to some people including politicians, etc. If they refuse these kids are tortured until they are taking their heroin as a prescription. In the end, they are disposed of to keep the whole issue a secret.

4. The public health sectors have become the worst hackers. You will be shocked that the hospitals use James Bond gadgets to spy on everyone globally. To make things worse, they breach trademarks or patents rights by stealing the person's designs and falsely claim to be behind that person's success but what they are doing is using a video or screen sender linked to a chip implanted at birth to spy on everyone and then follow those who might be working on something. What they do is use the screen sender to monitor whatever you do, what you watch or who you call on your phone. Behind your back then stab you in the back blocking your meetings or clients until you accept that they are helping and in this case, they damage something on your body, eye or make you age faster as a mark that you belong to their 'cult' or whatever. Gross breach of human rights. A hacker is as bad as a slave trader

Hostis Humani Generis and as such an enemy of what we stand for.

5.  Hacking and implanting chips at birth etc. all is against what we stand for. There are no justifications whatsoever simply because all these gadgets, chips, etc. are operated remotely and have GPS functions that mean they use radiation and other dangerous waves. All this is against the first rule and all reduce quality of life amounting to gross abuse. Imagine someone in a position of trust with a joystick in the hand stimulating the genitals of your wife or child for that matter? Gross abuse. Express-command to put an end to this through our laws and courts as a deterrent is appropriate here because it's either kill or be killed in the end because the goal of a hacker is to change, modify, damage and in the end cause malfunction of an otherwise healthy system or body. Against the first rule; the right to life. How can you have a life when it's in someone's hands and in most cases someone who despises you? Express-command to put an end to this through our laws and courts as a deterrent. Track and trace; new roles of our military or organizations like NATO as an 'evolving task'.

6.  Our public health is involved in eugenic thinking. Okay, I am not against the development of perfect genes but if you are the ones causing the bad ones in the first place, then it becomes a different issue. The chips implanted to all people in developed countries can be remotely operated and be augmented by further needle electrodes or diodes to stimulate nerves in electromagnetic stimulation and tampering to or obstruct many bodily functions like egg production. They are deliberately causing genetic defects to create more jobs and justify chipping kids at birth but remember the chicken or egg scenario here. What came first? Is it the egg or the chicken? If they can influence egg production and if it takes say for argument's sake four days naturally and if they make your body produce an egg in two days are there chances that the egg might not be ready or deformed or lack something that if fertilized might lead to disability? Take me seriously here. What makes then expects to look at the number of disabilities especially the obvious ethnic population that is obviously chipped at birth as population control in certain countries? I know there are arguments that people like Asians they marry their cousins so say if people with

the same genes if they met, they might have a baby thereby increasing the chances of genetic defects. Okay, but could it be the fact that the chipping on population control could be the main problem here. Over history, people married a close relative from the Roman empire why we didn't have so high cases of disabilities than recently. Not documented? Not good enough reason. Something is going on. Is this another chicken and egg thing?

7. I think we need new laws around this. We need a clear and transparent system where everyone illegally chipped at birth must be told and give consent and chose to be clean of all chips. There must be investments in the technology that overcomes these issues. There must be machines everywhere that can check if people have been violated by being chipped without consent and are used as bait or abused or their systems tampered with.

8. Very stiff penalties resulting in death simply because radiation is no friend to humans. It's irresponsible for the governments concerned and the leaders if they can't justify these acts must be dragged to court. Express-command to put an end to this through our laws and courts as a deterrent. They are no better than a mass murderer, a person who commits genocide, etc.

9. Laws to ban such practices unless if the person is advised of the risks and agrees. This is no different from slavery and as far as I know, slavery was abolished many years ago. In most cases, this is for population control where the government chooses who to kill and choose when they die.

10. This is true in countries without the death penalty that everyone is put on 'death row' on birth by being secretly chipped and that chip is used to control the life of that person and how he or she will die. Simply because people now live longer, and the government knows the population is old and will do real damage to the balance sheet.

11. Stiff laws to outlaw and ban such practices even criminals do not deserve to be treated this way because you have committed a crime equivalent to murder the day you chipped that kid or person. It will be possible to bring charges against these doctors on self-defense ground in worst case scenarios, but everything must be through the courts. You can justify this on grounds that they are trying to

kill you attempted murder from the day they implanted that chip.

12. It will be a law to kill in self-defense if the person has done an act that violated the first rule; the right to life and to self-preserve so a person can defend himself or herself. Remember this is because that the chips are planted to act as killing weapons through the use of radiation emitted secretly by these chips. So, the doctors are murderers as well who must face the law too.

13. More serious issues regarding the making of digital, cyber or biological weapons for the hospitals to remain viable. You must go to your doctors for digital weapons that might be used on you to drive attendances? To create and use these weapons as they lower quality of life in the long run.

14. Ban all companies making this kind of stuff. Close all universities' departments involved in producing all these stuffs. Express-command to put an end to this through our laws and courts as a deterrent. Drag to court all leaders approving such practices simply because the acts conflict with the first rule they are like murderers.

15. Involvement in terrorist acts. The command givers and drivers behind this using siren to direct just like a film director. Listen to sirens they coincide with critical points of attacks etc. can't be a coincident. I discussed this in earlier and later chapters.

16. Yes, you will be shocked that through what the hospitals call protection they are recruiting and training all terrorists we know today from 9/11 hijackers, etc. all chipped with gadgets that are controlled by only people in a position of trust. Yes, the chipping is used to torture pulling eye iris causing great pain and stressing life until the person finds a way-out through revenge. The targets have themselves been put through a grieving stage or tricked into committing a crime then blackmailed to revenge by killing innocent people. Again, care to be taken here ask yourself what came first the chicken or egg because they might argue that they chipped the person because they suspected him or her as a terrorist but maybe they made him or her a terrorist. It's hard to believe that a person who is chipped like most of the 9/11 attackers can escape the radar of those who have access to these chips. Do you know the teaching hospitals train people to be prepared for say terrorist

attacks and what are the chances that on 9/11 we had a group of firefighters rehearsing when the 9/11 attacks occurred to check the firefighters who filmed the first plane hitting the Tower? Check also in UK the 7/7 attacks happened when a group of people were rehearsing as well see the film Loose Change for details.

17. I think the whole system has tarnished once was a respected profession to the lowest of lows. These people are supposed to be trustworthy and honest. Imagine them hacking your items and pretend to be clever and teach you how to run a business when their profession is about wiping the elder's buttocks. It's pathetic. It's bad judgment they are not qualified as managers to run a business. If you want business ideas, you don't go to teaching hospitals but to managers, universities, etc. Most of the problems we have today are a direct result of this abuse of trust and power. They are not afraid simply because literally, they have a joystick in their hands to control everyone remotely like operating a drone. Imagine the bad aspects of technology? But we shall put new laws and swear by the assassin that he or she will do a great job to clean this mess.

18. Huge investment in the technology with the military who are used to kill now forced to look for answers as well. Tracking and tracing all kinds of shenanigans.

19. Cyber-attacks by the hospitals as they have access to billions of medical records through these chips. A new threat and a risk to humanity a cyber nuclear electromagnetic attack or bomb can be used to wipe-out everyone with a chip that is all people born after a certain time having their devices switched off some even blinded as the chips can hide the iris in the eye-socket preventing vision. A cyber electromagnetic bomb or attack is a new global challenge. What is happening with humanity is that when we win over certain threats like biological bacteria and viruses, then these people create digital versions taking us back to the beginning? Now we have the same threats but different versions. We start all over again, wasting time and resources when we should be looking for other things to enhance human life.

Very stiff punishment to these people who would create deadly threats to mankind. To hell with them. Stop funding anyone developing digital threats or other new forms harmful to humans. Open your eyes and see that we are going in circles. In truth, we are still in the medieval period when the black death was killing people only that we have substituted the real pathogens with digital ones, and we are trying to recreate those scenes, so our public health has something to shout about. That's not just evil but makes these people Hostis Humani Generis people fit to be attacked by all nations without any mercy.

**Hostis Humani Generis.**

Express-command to put an end to this through our laws and courts as a deterrent.

Tomorrow's World Order will have express authority to finger a country to be ganged-up-on by the whole world if they pose a real threat to everyone's future. I will have the power after investigating any nation to get it attacked without need to bring the matter to the court simply because a person or country that practices evil at such levels will have people in the courts as well to manipulate and stall progress buying time may be to destroy the whole humanity. We can't take chances we just need to convince other nations that this is happening and if a certain number concurred, then there is no need to consult that country but to act swiftly. Look what happened to Hitler. No one decided to take him to court because people were afraid that he might kill more before he is stopped and as such, we will do the same. Some chips like I said can threaten the survival of all humanity. Some countries chip everyone in the name of protection to safeguard their way of life. But say in case of an electromagnetic bomb that explodes all chips we might have total wipe-out and human extinction and as such, I think if it can't be proved otherwise, I think that can automatically make a country or their leaders qualify to be Hostis Humani Generis. Such acts of chipping everyone can result in human extinction who knows what technology brings tomorrow and the fact that this is done secretly raises grave concerns. Here it's not just laws that need to be enforced I think that can justify isolation of that country on the grounds that it poses a threat to all mankind and as such, all its people who are chipped might be prevented going abroad until investigations prove that these chips are not harmful to others. As the chips can be cyber electromagnetic bombs. A point in relation to the above is the fact that such chips are used as weapons to mobilize anyone who might come near them. This is true as the chips are used to trigger a defensive mechanism that immobilizes others by blinding them as the chips can be used to pull the iris of the eye and hide it in the eye-socket rendering others prone to attacks putting life in danger and as such can be said to conflict with the first rule. Think of a car immobilizer that instantly stops the car. Okay if for safety reasons this can render say an attacker immobilized as he or she is blinded by the chip but what if the chips are used to rob people or trap the whole world all getting blinded so that you are forced to sign your life away in exchange of your sight? If you refuse, then you are killed or forced into slavery or prostitution or to become even a terrorist? Who knows the real intention?

## Equality.

I have no doubts that once the laws are into effect, we won't have problems with equality. We are working very hard to change current laws that make it easy to break some issues that matter to us. The wars, military, and weapons were a major issue conflicting with all other issues we have today, but all these are gone or will be banned so I think once everyone's self-esteem has reached higher levels, we will automatically treat others, respectively. I think it's a fair statement that the abused are the people who abuse too. The idea of ball-rolling applies here. They are abused so that they abuse others. Those shown love at earlier ages are more likely to show others love and respect. This goes beyond just talking about equality we must look at this issue in broader terms. Addressing other areas as well but I am not worried about this. It's something that comes naturally once we have achieved and solved other issues. We will see.

## International law and justice.

I think our laws represent international law and we will work very hard to make sure there is justice in this world. We are not creating laws that people don't know about or never heard about. We looked at the common problems and then assessed why we have these problems. We also checked if we have international laws that support these issues. The truth is all our laws are there in international law, but we are rearranging and prioritizing certain fundamental principles, making things that are believed to be the norms now; right to life and self-preservation as priority laws and paramount ones that must be observed first and never overridden. Currently, there are other laws that can easily override these laws and people easily find justifications and get away with that. So, what we have done is to remove these other laws or areas that give people in power reasons to override these laws; the major one is the military, wars and security reasons. We have protected all future and current leaders from persecution when their term in office has ended by removing the need to commit crimes in the name of self-defense. When your term in office has expired, you won't need to be blackmailed by these teaching hospitals into signing your life away or the life of a close relative no. You can enjoy being a great leader and be remembered as such.

## Migration.

Our aim is to create one globe with no walls or boundaries where there is one dominant currency that works side by side with a country's own currency to boost wealth and growth to encourage free movement. I think the differences would be the amount of the fee's countries would like to charge for entry as we would like to make sure that there is some country autonomy left. The only restrictions might be due to the fees payable as we would like to encourage competition as well. I think this is another area open to discussions as it might be good if decided by each country if they know this is the networking and connection era enough of building walls.

## Peace and security.

Banning weapons globally and wars are great strides towards achieving global peace. I think it is highly correct that we have been talking about global peace for decades and yet we achieved none. So, as Tomorrow's World Order we have come up with laws that will be observed globally to change the way we do business. The current system crashed years ago, and we just mended it and we are hanging by a thread or was hanging by a thread until now. I think either the whole world wants to create jobs and talk about global peace and security just to push for more salaries or they don't understand what is needed to achieve global peace and security. I think the world is playing games talking but doing little. I know this other woman said to me that if you solve all the problems, then what are we going to do and how are we going to create jobs or not have anything to talk about. In short, she was saying that things are the way they are because this is the way that works. Newspapers have stories to tell. Every time a picture of a poverty-stricken kid is flashed on the front page the papers sell like hotcakes. United Nations Children Funds [UNICEF] has something to look forward to. The government has something to argue about. Your politicians have reasons to push and campaign for. Globally the world goes around. But if there is no poverty or kid starving, there is no business for the newspaper, the politician, UNICEF, etc. are all deprived. Then again, I said what if we can hear what that child wants for a change? You have been doing this for decades if it's a novel okay at first it was the best novel, but you have read this novel too many times that now you think you are wasting time. Why not this UNICEF or the newspaper or the politician evolve and start looking for ways to reduce aging? Or to create humans. Surely, we have pressing issues at hand, yet we obsess with things we can easily change without feeling any impact. I think the whole world must evolve and everyone must do what they have never done before because change is coming, we will ban all useless activities and monitor these institutions and recommend other areas that need looking at. It's not a dictatorship but as I have argued we must use all resources wisely and work at optimal capacity. Read this together with 'Useless Institutions' in later chapters.

## Population.

I think this is an interesting topic because it raises a lot of questions and this makes Tomorrow's World Order differ from all current institutions like the government and its hospitals and the killing squad and even the New World Order. All these people are advocating for the control of population through a lot of strategies like chipping to be in direct control of deciding how many dies this year and how fast they can age this year to playing God as to go to extreme cases of say vaccinating everyone with viruses that become deadly after say 20 years when the kids immunized will have grown for all to die as a population control. Everyone else is playing God to kill through any means. People are investing $billions in making chips to illegal implants at birth every newborn. To a scientist as technology developers making devices that are easily hidden that can emit harmful radiation or be switched off or exploded like bombs killing everyone. Everyone has lost the plot. The reasons given are that the population is growing at alarming rates and very few are dying. So, we must do something before it's too late. Yet despite all these alarms we still make weapons. To make things worse, we are becoming friends. Wake up!! It's contradictory. Make weapons and create enemies this was a strategy used for past centuries and it works because in the end you will be given a chance to check who has the big guns and who can do real damage. I explained throughout that the Allies decided to play it rough and write a list every 20-25 years with potential enemies to wipe-out using the two superpowers Britain and the USA through CIA etc. and to wipe-out the low-level culprits mainly from Africa and other middle eastern countries using the ICC a strategy I have referred to as a Colony Collapse Strategy. At the same time using NATO as the big bodyguard who doesn't talk but just stands behind the leader of the gang with folded hands to send a clear message that; mishandles the situation with the boss and be beefed. Ever watched the 1980s gangster or mafia movies? The weapons market is saturated and at last, people have realized that it's better to make friends than being intimidated and threatened all the time. It's a bargaining era. So, who are your enemies? Who are you still making weapons for? Aliens? Ha-ha, I have heard that trick before. We removed all the alarms that would warn the system of the need to eliminate weapons through world wars to avoid piling. Now humans are going to keep making weapons until one day when friction results in a massive global war that causes human extinction. As recently as 2017 gone we have increased military funding to $1.7 trillion. Where are your enemies? A little friction will cause a Third World War which can result in severe casualties. Wars to be honest they have no winners, if you face heavy casualties as well there is no winning unless your plans like most of these politicians are to reduce the budget bill. Just imagine in one of the wars 60 000 soldiers died in a day. Imagine 60 000 people off your monthly salary bill and maybe two million soldiers off your balance sheet by the time the war ends. Huge savings sad but a fact.

Our new laws will make the military like any other profession where our best have greater chances of enjoying their pension. We will make the military evolve by finding other things to do. This time to enhance life or even to create one with time. I think we have been looking at this the wrong way, otherwise, we could have had answers by now as it has been decades now. Unless like that lady the reason is to run around the whole day playing crocodile-smile and then go home and relax hoping for another running around day at work and a fat salary at the end of the month. Why not? Who cares? They come and go. Someone might suggest. I think we can change for the better and create stress-free jobs that reduce aging rates and make people feel good about themselves doing something beneficial rather than pretending. That takes me to the next point.

## A comprehensive approach.

I personally think that mankind has chosen what he calls the easy approach. Stall and waste time pretend, go with the flow, running around the whole day and then pretend everything is okay after stressing about the issue. Most would prefer to make a loud noise to look as if they are doing great; working hard. What you don't realize is that all the time you are running around pretending to work and solving the issues so that you keep your job etc. maybe you are doing real damage to your personal health. Stress levels reduces life span, makes one age very fast, you wrinkly faster, your sex life might not be great, your relationships might not be so good because your partner might not tell if you are pretending or not because you have perfected the art so good, but deep down you might be reducing your own quality of life. I have worked for a company where the boss would let you decide what to do in terms of your approach to work. Work to deadlines, smarter and faster and lose on overtime or whine and delay orders and accumulate a lot of overtime to match the boss's salary. I chose for the deadline, fewer hours and less salary as there is no overtime. My friend went with the crying game, overstretching game and delaying tactic to accumulate over time. Okay initially he had more money, but he had to work very long hours, missing on social life and stressful all the time although it was in pretense with time, he ended up bitching about everything else because it made him money. In the long run, I had a promotion and my salary raised and got more for the same fewer hours and I had a great life, felt good, looked great as well and felt valued by the company. This is the kind of approach we will encourage in the future.

Life is not about money although we need money to live. In the end, humans will not work somehow, we will spend time talking and debating life issues while still earning very high. This is the task for everyone today. Find a way we can never go to work again but spend time learning about life or enjoying life or creating life or visiting other planets ourselves. In the coming years maybe, robots will do work for us. Or we are all going to be putting money in investment funds or something new that can create more money for us. So, let's start thinking about the future as work-less. So, it all adds up. This is one other reason why I think that the current public health system is dodgy. In the scenario above of the whining guy what he doesn't know is that these companies make deals with hospitals to buy digital weapons. This is what these people don't know. For everything you do the manager who as I said is loaded with all kinds of digital junk by the hospital will load you each time you do something that even the manager would not do. These digital weapons range from wrinkle making agents to butt-poking-agents. I told you that almost everyone in developed countries is chipped at birth. The guy in the scenario above might start to notice that he will be wrinkling faster than normal and since he has given the manager an alibi of stressing over everything, the manager can load him with an agent that acts as a catalyst and speed up the process. In most cases, these managers calculate the value of work done and then estimate the time it can take to do that order. If you exceed that time by a wider marginal, then you are technically stealing from the company. The more you work there the greater the junk stuff loaded into you. Okay ideally in other countries you can easily go to doctors some can easily remove these in return for boosting attendance rates but in some countries, you will slowly be bought by the hospital there and be put on 'death row' because they are like watermarks. You exceeded the time it reasonably take, so the manager decided you stole the money because the value of work does not match the value put into the company and in most cases for a company to reduce costs and make a profit you must meet deadlines and send perfect orders otherwise errors all the time will cost the buyer or customer in terms of delay in the long run the company can go out of business. So, these managers sell you to the hospital. They load you with stuff only the hospital can remove. You look at your friends and yourself you see real changes. So, okay you might have got a lot of money unjustly but it's like exchanging with your life because the manager does not want lazy people you are a cost to a company you are better dead not just sacked because you will do the same to the next manager. Your quality of life will be poor in the long run filled with regrets and these managers won't tell you they are also being blackmailed by the teaching hospitals. So, you think you are clever?

Okay, so a comprehensive approach will educate people to choose what is right. Our goals will help everyone decide what is best for you as the world we live in is full of evil people it might take time to get rid of all evil so be educated and assess what is right for you. Life or money? It is these small things that add up in the end. Remember our goals; first, it's the right to life and to self-preserve and it's not just life but the best quality life. We will work hard to ban such situations where managers are loaded by the hospital with all kinds of gear.

**Very stiff punishment because all these affect the quality and right to life.**

**Governments.**

We are not trying to change the governments but we aim to make being President or Prime Minister the best thing to do with everyone aspiring to be one as our laws and policies will guide you with best guiding notes and remove all the unnecessary clutter and cumbersome decision-making process. Remove any risks associated with the Presidency or Prime Ministerial roles. Make the law clearer and remove any ambiguity and the need to press nuclear buttons and leave it to us with no affiliation to parties or need not the votes of the people. I think we will at some point when things get clearer act as overseers and enforcers. I can tell you that institutions like the UN etc. are therefore cosmetics and as killing machines to eliminate opponents on the 20-year lists to perpetuate the Allies dominance of power and to rule out global wars without stopping illegal invasions and maintain the status quo where innocent women and children die needlessly. Nothing to do with solving the issues they claim to solve. Mind you they have been in existence for seventy years the average lifespan of an adult in other countries, yet problems are becoming worse hence the rise of Tomorrow's World Order. I say all you old forks [the UN, NATO, ICC, etc. now seventy old pensioners [no offense to pensioners in general] get your pensions [assuming they are old people now old and obsolete] and get out of my way I have a job to do your time is over! The UN was to stop the war, yet its core founders are at the forefront of wars. the war in Iraq where the UN failed to stop the invasion and recent attacks of Syria by the UK, USA, and France still the UN did not prevent it, but we will change the way things are done. Mark my words. Tomorrow's World Order as a global leader does not obsess on who is running the individual countries if you observe our laws and all international laws. We are champions of good governance everywhere.

### Internet and government censorship.

Someone asked me about government control. He said look at you. You are doing the same as the current system dictating; don't do this and don't do that. I said it's not the same. Who on earth right now do not know that it's wrong to kill women and children for whatever reason? Who on earth does not know that life is more important than anything else and as such must be prioritized? Who on earth does not know that weapons destroy lives and it's a waste of resources channeling $1,7 trillion on the military? My main point is that all these countries are just bitching about bloody cowards grouping into massive cults and assassinating opponents cowardly. World War Three would be better. Destruction of the things we don't need. The perfect way to give these boys to tests their toys, safe reduction of populations without threats of human extinction, reduction of balance sheet bills, the chance to see firsthand the traumatic effects of war that can trigger abandoning the military altogether and form networks and connect with each other to reach peaceful agreements. The benefits are endless. Now we are stuck in this stage with no world wars for 74 years when we were supposed to have a world war every 20 to 25 years. It's like driving a car stuck in first gear. Nature made it easy for us before. Every 20 to 25 years you have a war. If it wasn't for the Allies who decided to attack and takeout potential warmongers, we could have hard a major war in the 1960s thanks to these cowards we have just a Cold war. In the 1980s it was a one-sided war after targeting Iraq but with no success. In 2001 the 9/11 triggered another one-sided war ending with the war in 2003 that toppled Saddam Hussein. Another mother of all wars was destined or is still destined in end 2019 or 2020. The 2020 war might just be a gang attack with all world nations attacking a very evil nation with everyone turning against it out of the blue. Remember what happened to Hitler? I don't advocate for wars but no point putting laws while you haven't quenched your thirst for war. I know it sounds contradictory but why make things you don't use? Better stop at all and channel the funds somewhere. Who are your enemies? This is the million-dollar question?

**Nuclear Weapons.**

Our stance is unmistakable we agree with current laws, but we think there is a lot of bias and deception on all parts. I think all countries must abide by international and our new laws banning nuclear weapons. I think all countries now admit to carrying out nuclear weapons as a bargaining tool to make deals to remove sanctions etc. Something I will look at next under sanctions. All countries, especially the Middle East must take us seriously when it comes to nuclear weapons and stop any production or plans to do so. I know the current system isn't fair as we like it to be in that it encourages the use of nuclear as the situation is one-sided and imbalanced that one is left with no choice that it's better to die trying for them. This goes to all nations Iran, Syria, even the developed nations themselves. I think it is fair to leave a chapter to discuss this in more detail as this is such a sensitive issue often raised as a reason for opting for war and above all the developed nations own nuclear weapons but prohibits others from doing the same.

## Sanctions.

I think sanctions are evil simply because they punish women and children. I know these people have been getting away with murder causing the deaths of thousands of women and children through sanctions which are ineffective just as a bargaining tool used by a bully and or a coward. Sanctions to be banned with immediate effect it's an evil and barbaric way that encourages wrongdoings as people would use the threats as a bargaining tool to ask for better deals. I think the world when it finally realizes what is in store for them, they will dig holes and spit in them. We have been studying how these people, decade after decade they cause the deaths of thousands of innocent women and children simply because they are of a different background to them and would not be bothered and when one child dies in their country, they slaughter people in revenge. I want to make this clear that the new laws will close all loopholes and actual bring more laws that make it harder to escape justice as we introduce a lack of empathy laws to crash these leaders the way they are destroying the innocent, defenseless yet the most valuable people of any society or country on our watch. Killing of anyone through evil punishing sanctions if assessed to have a lack of empathy with the victims will make some people regret being born because new laws will go a step further to deter. We believe that to start afresh and to reconcile each other and for us to bridge the world together we must be on an equal footing are you with me? Remember those fights when you were kids meant to make you stronger. Imagine even after the fight has been officially been stopped and over when you are asked to shake hands and you still feel you owe that other person a punch. Just one more punch to even the game out and you through a jab just one punch with all your energy and the other person staggers backward and touches his cheek and concurs that the punch was overdue but should be the last? It's like that and after that, you become very good friends. Why? You are on equal terms after that and you easily forgive each other. It is like that. We are not revengeful, but we can do whatever it takes to make sure reconciliation and working together will be fast and painful even if it's not for us but for future generations. So, new laws to ban all sanctions. A criminal offense with extra lack of empathy aggravated killings of innocent women and children through sanctions can and will catch up with you one day better not abuse kids and women of others because we shall be swift to judge and call for justice. Make no mistake, be warned for you have become like terrorists yourselves killing women and children to get what you want using the same tactic used by terrorists therefore in Tomorrow's World Order guilty too as terrorists to these women and children forcing TWO not to have any other option but to wear the shoes of the innocent victims and label you as a terrorist as well. Life for life in this case applies. This is because sanctions just like terrorists' activities depend on the notion of ball-rolling. Sanctions are meant to kill women and children or to put it in other words to test the caring aspect of empathy towards the own people of the accused government. To test if they can stop whatever the wrongdoing to save the lives of innocent women and children or continue at the expense of these people. Using these people as baits. In most cases, these governments know it's a test for them. Change quickly to save lives and risk being attacked as this means automatic stopping of what you are doing and an admission of guilty hence the risk of instant attacks. So, the governments will let women and children die as a hard stance. This will anger local opposition who will become rebels who will uprise denouncing the 'coward and weak government' who let their women and kids be killed without doing anything to stop it. So, the rebels will threaten to topple the government ball-rolling the anger. This government to feel good about themselves will ball-roll their anger at these rebels using maximum force to find comfort for the women and children's deaths. Meaning the use of prohibited agents like the poisonous gas to deter further uprising thereby committing an international crime. The main aim of the sanctions to justify an invasion on humanitarian grounds or the Responsibility to Protect.

One man's freedom fighter is another man's terrorist.

I think after careful considerations I find it easy to see why maybe we had more terrorist attacks in recent years. These institutions who are thought to be 'perfect ones who do nothing wrong' have been using the same tactics as the very people they are calling terrorists. I have looked at grievances on both sides and was astonished but saddened as well to find out that they are targeting women and children to bargain and get their demands met. Sanctions kill women and children.

"As many as 576,000 Iraqi children may have died since the end of the Persian Gulf war because of economic sanctions imposed by the Security Council, according to two scientists who surveyed the country for the Food and Agriculture Organization."

**The New York Times titled: Iraq Sanctions Kill Children, UN Reports**

By BARBARA CROSSETTE DEC. 1, 1995

A recent report in the Independent of 26 April 2019 States that;

'As many as 40,000 people may have died in Venezuela as a result of US sanctions that made it harder for ordinary citizens to access food, medicine, and medical equipment.' A new report has claimed.

The report, published by the Center for Economic and Policy Research (CEPR) a progressive, Washington DC-based think tank, says those deaths took place following the imposition of sanctions in the summer of 2017. It said the situation has probably worsened since the imposition earlier this year, of tougher sanctions targeting Venezuela's vital oil industry, as part of the Trump administration's effort to oust President Nicolas Maduro.

"The sanctions are depriving Venezuelans of lifesaving medicines, medical equipment, food, and other essential imports," says the report, co-authored by Jeffrey Sachs, an award-winning economist based at Columbia University, and Mark Weisbrot. "This is illegal under US and international law, and treaties that the US has signed. Congress should move to stop it."

I know it is subjective whether sanctions kill children or not but overall if they did not kill so how are they supposed to work? Sweet talk the leaders to an agreement? I don't think so. I think sanctions are meant to kill and force the leaders to cooperate to avoid further deaths. Any economic hardships will first affect kids, lack of supplies, medicine, food, and other basic services. I think we can have strong grounds to persecute sanctions mongers on grounds of a lack of empathy aggravated needlessly killings of innocent children on grounds in that no due regard was given to the lives of the children in imposing the sanctions as we will argue it can be justified that sanction's aim here is to force the leaders concerned to come to the bargaining table after the deaths have started and not before the deaths. We will also look at the length of the sanctions for example if a year without medicine and access to food we can assess if it can be said to be reasonably justified that kids can go for such a long time without medicines and food. But I think it will be safe for most of those leaders to start thinking about their future when it comes to sanctions. We are going to revolutionize the way the law is interpreted and to whom. It can be okay to all global countries to act like those who plant landmines and kill children and maim some and only to react when it becomes a global issue and simply apologize and go to their big mansions and forget it ever happened before sending their other agencies to clean at exorbitant prices making huge profits. I strongly advise you all to think again. Gone are the days when you do whatever you want and hope for a peaceful after-office term life. We believe cases where it can be proved that the act was carried out with undue regard to kids and women lacking that element of empathy surely because they were of a different background there will never be time limits to when a case can be brought against you. I want a world where what can't be done to your kids can't be done to mine too. TWO will put resources in these areas to open as old as 70-year-old cases and if that means having 24-hour courts so be it. I think this is another gray area especially to the issue of whether sanctions cause the deaths of children or not and as such I think this topic deserves its own chapter.

## Internet.

The idea is to connect the globe, and this means a fast and effective internet system globally. I think every city should have free access. I think every city must view this as a basic mandatory and a service and a task they are all obliged to fulfill especially in developed countries first.

## Colony Collapse Strategy Analysis.

Nations in which the CIA has assassinated or attempted to assassinate a movement leader

2011   Pakistan        Osama Bin Laden. According to the US government's official

2003   Iraq    Saddam Hussein and his two sons. Two murders and a semi-judicial execution.

2002   Afghanistan   Gulbuddin Hekmatyar, Islamic leader, and warlord

1993   Somalia       Mohamed Farah Aideed, prominent clan leader. Failed attempt but he died later.

1991   Iraq    Saddam Hussein, leader. Attempt to kill him?

1985   Lebanon        Sheikh Mohammed Hussein Fadlallah, Shiite leader (80 people killed in the attempt)

1984   Nicaragua     the nine comandantes of the Sandinista National Directorate

1983   Nicaragua    Miguel d'Escoto, Foreign Minister

1983   Morocco        Gen. Ahmed Dlimi, Army commander

1982   Iran   Ayatollah Khomeini, leader

1986   Libya   Muammar Qaddafi, leader, several plots and attempts upon his life

1976   Jamaica       Michael Manley, Prime Minister

1976    Chile    exiled Chilean Foreign Minister Orlando Letelier is blown up in Washington DC, part of Operation Condor with at least tacit US support

1975    Zaire    Mobutu Sese Seko, President.

1972    Panamá    General Manuel Noriega, Chief of Intelligence. Captured alive and been imprisoned ever since.

1981    Panamá    General Omar Torrijos, leader

1970    Chile    Gen. Rene Schneider, Commander-in-Chief of Army.

1970    Chile    Salvador Allende, President unsuccessful US supported coup "Project FUBELT"

1967    Bolivia Che Guevara, revolutionary leader. CIA-organized military operation ends in capture and execution by the Bolivian Army.

1956    France Charles de Gaulle, President

1965    Dominican Republic    Francisco Caamaño, opposition leader

1965    Zaire    President overthrown and replaced by Mobutu, see entry for 1961, deposing of Patrice Lumumba.

1960s    Cuba    Raúl Castro, a high official in the government

1970s    Cuba    Fidel Castro, President, many attempts on his life including poisoned cigars.

1963    US    Assassination of JFK, President. Originally hawkish, JFK's moves towards peace alarmed the MICC

1963    South Vietnam Ngo Dinh Diem, President. Successful attempt to replace one puppet leader with another.

1963    Iraq    The CIA supports the Ba'athists, including Saddam Hussein, in a coup in Iraq against the Qassim government]

1961    Dominican Republic    Gen. Rafael Trujillo, dictator since 1930 shot dead in 1961

1961    Zaire    In June 1960, Patrice Lumumba became the Congo's first Prime Minister after independence from Belgium. Calls for the nation's economic liberation and is branded a communist. Eleven days later, the mineral-rich Katanga province, owned by Belgium and prominent Eisenhower administration officials, secedes. Lumumba dismissed in September at the instigation of the United States, and in Jan 1961 assassinated at the request of Dwight Eisenhower. Several years of civil conflict and chaos end in the CIA backed deposing of President Joseph Kasavubu and the 1965 accession to power of the CIA linked Mobutu Sese Seko. Mobutu ruled and robbed the country for more than 30 years (a "kleptocracy") while the Zairian people lived in abject poverty.

1961   Haiti   François "Papa Doc" Duvalier, leader

1950s - 1970s Costa Rica      José Figueres, President, two attempts on his life [9]

1960   Iraq     Brig. Gen. Abdul Karim Kassem, leader

1959   Cambodia      Norodom Sihanouk, leader. And again in 1963. And again in 1969.

1957   Egypt Gamal Abdul Nasser, President

1955   India   Jawaharlal Nehru, Prime Minister

1951   Iran     Mohammed Mossadegh, Prime Minister

1951   North Korea   Kim Il Sung, Premier

1950s (mid) Philippines     Claro M. Recto, opposition leader

1950s, 1962   Indonesia     Sukarno, President

1950s   China   Prime Minister Chou En-lai, several attempts on his life

1950s   Germany      CIA/Neo-Nazi hit list of more than 200 political figures in West Germany to be "put out of the way" in the event of a Soviet invasion

1949   Korea Kim Koo, opposition leader

[Wikipedia].

The ICC is working tirelessly to takeout African leaders on the other hand.

Abdel Rahim Hussein

Saleh Jerbo

Germain Katanga

Uhuru Kenyatta

Tohami Khaled

Joseph Kony

Henry Kosgey

Ali Kushayb

Thomas Lubanga Dyilo

Raska Lukwiya

Ahmad al-Mahdi

Callixte Mbarushimana

Sylvestre Mudacumura

Francis Muthaura

Mathieu Ngudjolo Chui

Bosco Ntaganda

Okot Odhiambo

Dominic Ongwen

Vincent Otti

William Ruto

Joshua Sang

Abdullah Senussi

Mahmoud al-Werfalli

[Wikipedia].

I pointed out that they adopted an attack strategy after the LN failed to stop the Second World War. This involved what I referred to as the Colony Collapse Strategy of taking out all prominent leaders that can become future threats as to cause a war with the USA and the UK using military force or the CIA to target high-level threats with money from oil to launch a real fight and the ICC rattling the weaker low-level threats mainly from Africa. All one big cult members in NATO. The playing field is not level and heavily biased. I think all these can be murder charges of a genocide-nature rather than eliminating enemies. I have stressed the need to assess if the killings might be said to have a lack of empathy or have other connotations. Unless they can prove that only Asians from the Middle East and Africans are culprits then we have serious issues. Any crimes or approved assassinations like the list above will be assessed by Tomorrow's World Order to assess if there are any other connotations because I think it will be misleading to suggest that only people of color are corrupt and evil. So, the world will change drastically as new laws come into play and like I said death is the only reason why a person can be exempted from crimes committed since he or she was born. I will put new laws to remove all-time limits which deny victims justice. I think there is no way one can plead ignorance to certain crimes that are in international law and especially those that fall in the Jus Cogens category where any derogation is not permitted. Crimes of torture, genocide, killings of women and children regardless of which color are all common universal norms.

# CHAPTER FOURTEEN

ONE MAN FOR HIMSELF TWO FOR US ALL.

*Everyone should put an effort to make our journey achievable.

I think our approach is the only approach that will solve global issues. I know in the past they have put institutions like the UN to tackle global wars yet all that they did is watch and let happen. TWO has come in at the right time when issues are about to escalate in the wrong direction. To achieve what we want does not just depend on us, but everyone must put effort to make our journey as smooth as possible. In the above chapters, I have addressed global issues I think need urgent attention and clarified our position on a global scale whether we are for or against issues like sanctions, etc. Tomorrow's World Order has a big role to play leveling the playing field so that sometime in the future we can all gather together and address issues affecting us and issues we think we should tackle first as we go forward as a people. I think we need a comprehensive solution when it comes to the Middle East and Africa as recent wars can't be tolerated. I personally think everyone should take a turn for the good. Wars destroy innocent lives. Wars kill our future leaders. Wars are against what we stand for and in the New, World wars are banned. I think it's a pity to find sectoral fighting based on religious grounds, as these people worship the same God. Is religion the main cause of the issues we have in the Middle East and in Africa? If so, what can we do to solve these problems? But first I think we must look at why the developed countries like the USA are so worried about the Middle Eastern countries, especially Iran, and Syria in recent years.

## Threat of Nuclear Weapons.

Nuclear weapons are weapons that cause massive destruction because the bombs release huge amounts of energy in exponential volumes that the bomb will cause extensive damage. A small bomb can destroy masses of the population with devastating effects lasting for years and as such are referred to as Weapons of Mass Destruction [WMDs]. The law currently is selective with powerful countries allowed to make nuclear weapons and some countries banned to make these weapons. Some countries can have and test these weapons, and some are not. So, the current status of nuclear weapons depends on who is talking. Or put in other words, who is the boss.

All countries are banned to own, manufacture, test, produce, or process for the purpose of making weapons or for uses that might make it be used and used for weapons. New laws to ban everyone under the sun be it the USA, the UK, North Korea, China, Iran, South Africa, Mexico, etc. I mean everyone is banned to deal with nuclear for the purposes of making weapons. I will reiterate here that the time for ambiguity and selective advantage is over. Our stance on all weapons is to ban all and we stand firm about nuclear weapons. It is an offense to deal with nuclear weapons, regardless. There is no justification whatsoever in stockpiling these WMDs.

Total or absolute ban forever without any reverting to nuclear weapons.

No production of nuclear weapons and any WMDs.

No justification for making and using nuclear weapons or any WMDs.

No testing of nuclear weapons anywhere is permitted in oceans, land, air, etc.

**The nuclear weapons ban will be globally at a specific time.**

There is no country on earth that will make, use, keep, sell, produce, or test and be allowed to process uranium for the sake of making nuclear weapons this includes the USA, UK, France, Iran, Iraq, Syria, Israel, etc.

I think this is the priority of Tomorrow's World Order to make sure that the playing fields are leveled. We don't want the current situation where a few can be allowed through unfair laws not just to make but to go on and test these on humans. Something that must never happen in the New World. I emphasize that TWO will assess all past incidences and assess if the lives of women and children were killed due to undue care and what I can regard to as a lack of empathy if the same would happen in the country of the bomber and assess how they might react? I think it's fair that way. If they cry foul, then it's automatic that they are guilty. I think before going into more details I want to vehemently emphasis that we are in this situation because the current law depends on who is the boss who is talking, for someone or a country can break all current rules or override or replaces these rules with their own is a cause for concern. I think we must be responsible it's everyone's duty to make sure we all work together. There can never be a justification for using a nuclear arsenal for obvious reasons. Nuclear weapons are Weapons of Mass Destruction and they kill women and children. We have closed all loopholes that give leaders and those in power certain privileges and excuses say for using nuclear weapons to 'save going to war'. In the New World, this will never happen simply because it is killing women and children it doesn't matter if it is in another country of your enemies, for instance, etc. This is not a justification anymore and we will like I said bring new laws that bring criminal cages to leaders and commanders who choose to kill say 200,000 women and children as to avoid a war. The deaths of these people will come and haunt not just you but your immediate family too for we have a life for life approach. To love your own is to respect others' as well. I think we have worked around all the international laws and closed loopholes people are taking to make nuclear weapons and use these to intimidate and frightened others to destabilize peace and security. The crimes of aggression do not do justice enough here and we will go further and enforce other laws that ban acts that intimidate others leading them to want to make a nuclear weapon because the playing field is biased.

## Prohibition of Intimidating and provoking fear as a law against bullies.

It is a crime to intimidate and unsettle others provoking fear leading to them thinking and acting on their fears to get involved in nuclear weapons and WMDs. I know current laws punish only those who end up thinking about nuclear weapons as a realistic form of defense. I want to point out that global peace can only come if we really solve the real problems. Our stance is straightforward banning all weapons and ban all countries from processing nuclear for weapons reasons be it the USA or Iran etc. I think the problem of today is that the Allies or developed countries of today are grouping to an enormous scale with almost all of them part of NATO leaving the small countries feeling vulnerable, marginalized and fearful for their lives as they can't match the other side's threat no matter what. To make things worse through a strategy I believe or call the Colony Collapse Strategy the Allies and NATO members have been compiling lists for the past seventy years every twenty to twenty-five years with targets every President has to takeout as time goes on as a way of eliminating opponents leaving the society vulnerable to avoid losing if say a world war started. I explained above that war has no winners as they all lose soldiers and civilians in large amounts. After the effects of the First World War, the West or Allies or NATO members realized that attack is the best form of defense and so compiled a list of potential threats; people who might cause a war. The idea is not to ever go to war but to keep killing all opposing leaders. What this has created is a gross imbalance and unfairness with the small countries rich in oils fearing for their security. This is a natural survival instinct. These countries which are problem countries have resources in oil and are technically rich. This is more than the need to make nuclear weapons to show they have balls as well, no but a calculated plan that is modeled by the current situation. That situation is that we have a bully, a gangster or a mafia who if not matched will one day obliterate, the small countries for the resources in oil. These countries are not arming themselves because they can. It's a survival act. The odds are against you. Even though you will never see NATO standing side by side with the USA and threatening Iran or Iraq even though the USA has 100% backing of NATO. The USA is the representative of NATO the mouthpiece. So rich Persian Gulf countries resort to the production of nuclear weapons or think about doing so or are suspected to be making some simply because it is the natural way to deal with the situation.

Think about this imbalance or skewness. It can be argued that instead of thinking that the UK under Blair and the USA under

Bush were 100% sure that Iraq had nuclear weapons, it can also make sense that given the circumstance that almost the twenty-plus powerful countries were all after Iraq's oil and threatening to attack it can also be reasonable to suggest that instinctively it would be reasonable for Iraq as a survival tactic to think about making nuclear weapons. It can be argued so, to give them a chance of surviving an attack. So, the UK and USA did not mislead because it is a reasonable assumption that if faced with the kind of force, in NATO, USA, UK, France, Israel, etc. a reasonable man in Saddam would find ways to arm with bombs that have such devastating consequences to have better odds of standing an attack. But I think even if they threaten to start processing it's simply to act as a deterrent because the force in the cults of NATO is so formidable that you would better keep them at bay than pretending you can match them without the nukes.

## Double Standards.

The US got away for using nuclear weapons against Japan and not just once but twice within a week devastating lives for years and to their defense cited the need to deter war by their use. So, the Hiroshima and Nagasaki nuclear bombs prevented the war with Japan. So, let's look at the threat presented by Japan. Was Japan possessing nuclear weapons? Was Japan's army and capabilities greater than the USA's? What could have made Japan a real threat to justify the use of nuclear weapons, especially with the knowledge that nuclear weapons are WMDs? I think even in other areas of work the use of excessive force can be considered a criminal act. I personally think that there is no justification whatsoever for the USA to use two nuclear bombs on Japan just as a show of power whereas I think if Iran can be found in reality to possess nuclear weapons they can plead self-defense reasons to make such weapons and can "succeed" if we are to consider what is at stake and the threat they are facing. I want to make it clear that Tomorrow's World Order will try to close loopholes that can be exploited to abuse others and open lifelines where the odds are exponential against some. Once again, our first laws are about individual rights to life and to self-preserve. These laws go hand in hand with what means to have a right to life even your enemies have the rights to live too. You must observe if you don't want to be on the wrong side of the law. So, you cannot have a right to life unless if you can self-preserve yourself as well. In other words, you have a right to self-defense. This is an interesting area that is often neglected but one we will make paramount in order to solve global issues. Iran; just an assumptive argument is facing enormous odds stacked against it as in the threat of the USA, its cult; NATO, its Allies, the UK, France, Israel, etc. The Iraq war has taught everyone a lesson and we know once the USA decides to invade then the UK, France and in the future NATO will all group to attack whoever. But what the previous laws did not take into account are the facts that Iran as a nation with its citizens have a right not just to defend themselves but also to protect its oil resources against such attacks and where the odds of surviving an attack are stacked against them it can be reasonably argued that whatever stance they took it was in self -defense because the enemy is not just any enemy but a gang of oil-hungry countries, bullies , cults etc. that make any other decision not to arm themselves with nuclear as insane. This the only way they can self-preserve themselves by arming themselves with nuclear weapons. This does not stop there they can go further and argue that it's not like they have done something new out of the blue. They have just followed what the US has been doing for the past decades making nuclear weapons to bully oil-rich countries of which Iran itself is one and as such unjustified and flawed to let the US use the same weapons to intimidate and frighten them into not arming themselves. They might not succeed only if the US was not making nuclear weapons itself. The fact that the US is making the nukes themselves makes the steps taken by Iran as reasonably just. Any reasonable man would do the same because there are huge chances that the USA and its Allies might use nuclear on them refer to Hiroshima. So, self-defense might be justified. Still, they can add more grounds to justify the need for themselves to have nukes. This is something TWO will work to use to close loopholes and make the playing field fair to lay the right foundation for a world without nuclear weapons. So, they can say it can be argued that the intent of the USA and its Allies is to eliminate its opponents most of whom are people of color through a strategy TWO called Colony Collapse Strategy devised in 1654. All this talk about human rights is just bullshit. Look at Guantanamo Bay where is justice there and we have bullies in the Ghost and the Darkness and it is open to us and reasonably justified that we arm ourselves to protect us from this genocidal tendency and an unjust and wrong stance in broad daylight in the name of human rights or terrorism and the looting of our oil.

TWO will work very hard to ban worldwide all nuclear or uranium processing for the purposes of weapons. We will have a world without weapons completely and I think the current system is unjustified that all developed countries can and have nuclear weapons while in all developing countries weapons are banned. To correct this imbalance and level the playing fields TWO will vehemently argue for a lack of empathy laws to be used in mass killings and will fight for genocide charges against those developed countries who make and plan to use these nuclear weapons.

**The lack of empathy connotations in the use of weapons in order to ban all weapons globally.**

It is our duty and right to level the playing fields and remove evil privileges that make developed countries kill without due regard to human life especially the lives of women and kids. This shall be a thing of the past. The fact that after seventy-four years institutions like the UN are obsolete. The whole system crashed in 1914 and was supposed to have been replaced then but they thought they were clever and put things in place to stop future wars with the establishment of the league of Nations that proved to be not fit for purpose as the Second World War broke out. To make things worse, they just replaced the LN with the United Nations, which inherited most of the institutions established by this LN which they said was not fit for the purpose so what did you expect? Establishment of NATO, ICC turned a likely Third World War in the 1960s to a Cold war. So technically the UN was rendered useless during the 1960s as other killing machines reduced the chances of a Third World War but did not have the capabilities of stopping a war or of maintaining peace. How we are different from the UN is that the UN talks about maintain peace, but they never pushed to ban weapons that can only make us question the real reasons behind their establishment. The fact that they could not stop any wars, the Gulf wars, Kuwait, the Iraq wars and the last Iraq war where they had a chance to voice concerns and take action to save 500,000 women and children but they did nothing apart from saying it was illegal to them. I think it is wise to further explain the Colony Collapse Strategy here. A scientist called Christopher Wren in 1654 designed a transparent container made of glass which was a see-through one so he can easily see what is going inside the container with everyone observing. He tried to understand what would happen to the colony if the males were removed. Would the colony collapse. Years later we see the Allies, the West, etc. using the same strategy creating institutions like the UN just to observe and report in other words just to spy and report. This is true, look to what happened before the Iraq invasion. The USA and the UK accused Iraq of having Weapons of Mass Destruction. Iraq was sure that was a lie so allowed the UN Observers to come and check taking pictures etc. in fact the USA and the UK carrying out a Strengths, Weaknesses, Opportunities, and Threats [SWOT] analysis before an attack through the UN. The UN is used to prey on the targets who believe that the UN represents everyone but, in fact, they are used for cosmetics reasons so that the system looks to people most of whom are targets as fair as they appear unbiased. You will be shocked that the same system of the Colony Collapse Strategy was used to come up with the Guantanamo Bay cages. The idea of the wire cages is for transparency so that the world thinks it's okay and everything is right when it's the same thing done during slavery days. You will be shocked further to find out that the idea is to weaken the males, removing all potential people who can mount a war, confining them in cages for years so in the future that justifies implanting spying gadgets; lethal terminating devices that emits radiation with GPS properties in the name of health devices. The main idea behind this is based on a slavery law that says children of males in hands of the government mind you males in Guantanamo Bay cages under the government automatically fall in the hands of the government too. That way they have all generations under them; the total colony collapse as the breadwinners are held in cages forever without any chance of being released. It's a psychological mind-game people won't complain as they can observe the people and see no wrong, they appear happy that what matters. So back to Saddam. His trust in the UN observers meant his death as they entered Iraq. The USA and the UK were able to do a swot analysis analyzing the strength, weakness, opportunities, and threats through the UN observers. Sure, he was weak by allowing the UN Observers that made him be attacked to his doom even though he later refused them entry it was too late. So, the world as far as TWO is concerned is full of trickery and deception and evil people we all know that, but no one knows who the real evils ones are. So, we are going to level the playing field. Close all loopholes and give others our education so that they can make just decisions and give them lifelines to make the game fair. On one side we have the whole world, the USA, UK, France, Germany, Italy, Israel, Lebanon, NATO, UN, ICC and on the other side Iran clinging to its oil. It's a fact that TWO is not concerned about oil or how you rob each other if you don't kill women and children then we don't intervene. But we are not going this time to wait for you to do that. The world has trusted the UN with the lives of kids and women whom they let done by being perfect observers yet wolves in sheep's skins. We are no observers but educators who teach others tricks to level the playing field. All we can do is make you make the right decisions so as not to kill women and children.

**Proactive rather than reactive.**

We are not going to let any weapons, wars, evil incitements and the killing of people without due regard to life. We are from the word go going to ban weapons, wars and other things that lead to wars. We are going to put a stop on all activities that will make it easy to violate the first rules. The right to life, to self-preserve and to a good quality life. The current system is reactive they have no means of stopping any wars especially because they replaced earlier institutions like the LN with the UN but adopting the old system destining them to fail as well. I think the current methods are ineffective in solving global problems as they actual feds this vicious cycle and a good example is sanctions.

## Sanctions.

There are many kinds of sanctions but in this chapter, I want to look at sanctions that are 'claimed to be for disarmament'. I think there is a lot of controversy as to regard to the effects of sanctions as weapons for disarmament or deterrents, but one thing is for sure sanctions harm innocent women and kids the same reasons that these governments say about terrorists. Today's governments fight terrorists mainly because they use women and children as bargaining tools, yet they do the same with sanctions. I think it goes further than just to say that sanctions are used for bargaining and for forcing the sanctioned country to admit any accusations even if they are not true to save the lives of women and children. I am saying that the West know these countries don't have nuclear weapons but it's reasonable given the force that might attack them to resort to nukes but place sanctions that will create a situation where the leaders will admit or threaten to use or possess the nukes in order to save the lives of women and children or alleviate the suffering. I want you to understand that the West has a way to deal with people they regard as threats and a classic example are terrorists.

## Methods used in dealing with threats.

To understand the reasons behind sanctions, we need to see how government institutions like the FBI deal with say terrorists.

"The Bureau employs a variety of disciplines and works closely with a range of partners to neutralize terrorist cells and operatives here in the US, to help dismantle extremist networks worldwide, and cut off financing and other forms of support provided to foreign terrorist organizations by terrorist sympathizers."

FBI Website.

Most of the methods affect the target concerned and no women and children but sanctions dealing with deterrence affect the innocent. We cannot allow this on grounds that this does not give due regard to the lives of the people concerned. I think as I said earlier on it is a barbaric way of solving problems. Something we can't tolerate no matter what. I understand the USA are adamant that Iran has or is processing or enhancing uranium for the purposes of making nuclear weapons because they gave them the technology to do that in the first place as it is claimed that;

"Iran's nuclear program began as a result of the Cold War alliance between the United States and the shah of Iran, Mohammad Reza Pahlavi…"

Wikipedia.

**The danger of a huge loss of life as both own nukes.**

I want to make it clear that any country with nuclear weapons is a dangerous country and two countries both with nuclear weapons is a cause of concern. I think it's not only Iran who is a problem the fact that the US itself possesses these nukes are not just good for peace but a worldwide issue as these two might both use nukes on each other assuming the claims are true.

On Tuesday, Mr. Bolton appeared to simultaneously invite Iran into negotiations while demanding complete capitulation.

Accusing Iran of a "continued pursuit of deliverable nuclear weapons" despite the deal reached in 2015, Mr. Bolton said that Mr. Trump now sought "real negotiations to completely and verifiably eliminate Iran's nuclear weapons program, its pursuit of ballistic missile delivery systems, its support for international terrorism and its other malign behavior worldwide."

The New York Times 25 June 2019.

Tomorrow's World Order's stance is that the US is not doing anyone a favor by attacking Iran when it is them who introduced them to this technology and them having the nukes themselves will only make Iran be hostile or poses the nukes.

'US intelligence predicted in August 2005 that Iran could have the key ingredients for a nuclear weapon by 2015.[47] On 25 October 2007, the United States declared the Revolutionary Guards a 'proliferate of Weapons of Mass Destruction', and the Quds Force a supporter of terrorism. Iran responded that it is incongruent for a country [US] who itself is a producer of Weapons of Mass Destruction to take such a decision.'

Wikipedia.

Iran might in this case feel unfairly treated that they might in fear knowing that the US has nukes actually look for nukes but it could be just letting out the steam paving a way for negotiations with both leaders throwing the last punch before reconciliation with the Iran President ranting abuse at Whitehouse while the Whitehouse threatening to flatten Iran. If it's empty threats, then that's okay. But we are Tomorrow's World Order and we will never tolerate scenes like this where countries with nuclear heads come to this level, we can't leave things to chance. As such we think it will be the best option for all countries to disarm and never make nukes again, but we don't mind if nuclear projects are mainly for energy sources. Our stance is clear that developed countries are 'allowed' to have nukes while banning others lead for secret productions of nukes and as such we are standing for a global ban of any form of possession. The idea is for everyone to work together and we must destroy all the nukes we have right now and stop production globally at the same time.

# CHAPTER FIFTEEN

HEAVEN ON EARTH. HIGH SELF-ESTEEMED SOCIETY.

*One World One People.

I have dealt with this topic in detail above but mainly in reference to developed countries and globally in general and in this chapter, I would like to look mainly at the Middle East, Africa and other areas like Eastern Europe and globally as a whole. This is because we have issues that are less witnessed in other countries, mainly the developed countries. This is in relation to religion and suicide bombers or attacks. I argued that what the future holds is a stage when the earth will be so good to equal whatever people say is what heaven is like. My belief is that humanity must keep on developing and evolving changing the way you do things until you reach a certain level of understanding. I think religion must play a major part in alleviating the issues we have today.

## What impact does religion have on the New World? The idea of Self Worship.

Religion I think has a role to play if it evolves as well. Just like our current system that dates to centuries ago. What was effective and believed at that time can't still be the same twenty centuries later? Evolution in terms of adapting is a fundamental principle that keeps everything relevant and alive. I have argued in earlier chapters that what God or the creator whoever you believe in, wanted was not for humans to die and go to heaven and get-crash that is arrived uninvited in his kingdom. Godlike I said is the omnipotent, omnipresent and omniscience and as such does not need mankind to die and go to heaven and live ever after. I know this is my major difference with modern-day thinking in religious circles. Why on earth would God who only created man out of boredom and not as a necessity as religion want to portray it need men for? God has everything he wants and does not rely on men nor does he need men to worship him. I personally believe that God tasked himself to see if he can create mankind who will follow and evolve to become himself and as such to rule the earth just like he rules the heaven and the whole world. Something I have referred to as God's Dilemma. He kind of thought of creating mankind to take charge of the earth as a small god who will evolve to one day have a full understanding of how the world works and one day acquire such knowledge to know what is good and evil. Not just that but also to eat the fruits of the tree of life and live forever just like the gods. So God or Allah or whoever you want to call who created you created mankind and set up challenges to complete and puzzles to solve and if they do, they will evolve and understand the next stage so on until they are so full of knowledge and understanding that they will become 'small gods' and run earth as God runs the heaven and the whole world as in running a company that is managing. I used religion also to argue that the current understanding of the bible or the Quran is biased and flawed.

Genesis 3v22

22Then the LORD God said, "Behold, the man has become like one of us, knowing good and evil. And now, lest he reaches out his hand and take also from the tree of life, and eat, and live forever…"

I use religion to argue my point that mankind is one day expected to evolve and mature enough to understand that we have to think beyond the box to be able to think like creators and as such it's mandatory for us to evolve and know beyond what we know today about good and evil. So, to be able to live forever, it's not just a matter of knowing. Knowing alone is inadequate for we must reach out and go that extra mile researching about life and why people die and then find answers symbolized by eating once that is done then and then can we defeat death and live forever just like the gods. We must understand by investing in research and development and find all life answers asking questions about life and accept that we must overcome or solve something that stops us aging or dying early so one day we graduate and live forever like the gods.

So, I will put in point form what is expected of us.

1> God created earth first and put puzzles and obstacles and problems that work against mankind as a challenge to see if mankind will be like him one day.

2> God created mankind not because he needed mankind or rely on him or because he wanted to be worshiped. No point for all that simply because he owns the whole world and can easily make stones worship him if he needed it.

3> So why he created mankind? He is omnipotent, omnipresent and omniscience, meaning he is the almighty and powerful and does not need humans for his existence. He challenged himself to see if he can create a human being or people who will evolve one day to become him.; God's Dilemma just like we work hard to see if we can make robots as clever as us; Man's Dilemma. It's true also to point here that he created the world with a good side and a bad side and hoped that mankind will choose what they think is good for them and see if they chose the right direction to take. His idea is just to let mankind choose for themselves, so they gain an understanding of what is good or evil.

4> It's like a challenge there is a reward at the end. It's not just a challenge per se there are time limits as well. This is where I come in. My point is that we have lived very comfortably in this phase the defense stage as we are simply sacrificing other important events and even though our lives are perfect by human stands, it's because we are not evolving or advancing as we might be expected to but just wasting precious resources and time. Everyone when you say we are behind schedule looks at you and kind of suggesting that this is not the case. Okay, we have everything everyone seems happy. This is the best we can achieve they might argue and further, they can say we can't solve all the world problems and we can't make everyone happy. True that's correct but my point is we are comfortable because we are not sacrificing and evolving doing something we must be doing. This means we are technically stuck in the defensive stage which is a failure because we can do better. If we are to sacrifice, then we can see that we are not working at our optimal or moving up the ladder as we should. It's not just enough staying in one stage for centuries like what we are doing.

5> I looked at this as a challenging game that is timed. Okay, you might be in one stage, but time will run out and the game will be over. Just like that we are in the defensive stage and have been here as far as back as the early man's days. So, God challenged himself to see if he can create people who can be as smart as him but as far as the story goes it's not the situation. God is not happy with himself [my own opinion] because even though he is the greatest the omnipotent, omnipresence and omniscience he is not able to create a god or gods who live on earth. All he can do is create humans and as far as he knows humans lack the ability to think and solve puzzles like him and so far it's a daunting task that mankind no matter how he can do will never be as good as him to stand on his own two legs and run [as in a business or company] earth just like he does with the heaven.

The perfect example of God's issues with mankind.

6> I think a perfect example is the case of humans trying to make robots who are as clever as them. I know just like God humans are frustrated because no matter what they are doing they are unable to create robots that good that one day they will be as clever as humans and be wise and one day to understand life as we know it and as such to be able to run a part of earth as we run to earth as humans. We as humans just like God we wish that these robots will understand everything about humans so that one day we can give them a task and their own separate earth as we humans run to earth. Just like God, we have set up a task for the robots to evolve so that in the end they are just like humans thinking the same way and acting the same way so that they can run earth. Just the way God views humanity, we have been stuck in the defensive stages concerned with defending ourselves instead of developing and understanding other things. For the past two thousand years, we have been stuck in defense. The robots only know how to make weapons to protect themselves. Everything about them is to do with making guns and mobilizing the military. But we have removed all kinds of threats and proved that aliens don't exist and the dinosaurs which were threats are extinct so why are these robots so concerned with defense when they can be doing other things or even making other robots to teach as well or work for them? So, God even though removing some obstacles by making our threats extinct he realized mankind is slow or very fearful or the other reason lazy and evil-minded that he would kill to remain in this stage than to think about creating and moving to the next stage. This is true. Our mind when faced with a problem our first reaction is asking how we can kill to reduce numbers or solve the problems. The likely scenario.

7> We have too many people and the land in the future is not able to sustain the people what shall we do?

*Make viruses and kill some.

*Increase military budget make very destructive weapons.

*Starve some idea adopted by Hitler put them in concentration camps where no food leads to disease, the overcrowding to outbreaks, and because of outbreaks mass deaths and when that happens the population is reduced.

*Deliberately avoid providing basic needs like food always make these things scarce, so there are diseases that further kill people in the long run that reduces the population.

*Instead increase other budgets like the military and other areas that cause an imbalance that can trigger reactions and situations for conflicts that in the end we can go to war and reduce the number of people through weapons.

* Deliberately violate all human rights take your enemies and put them in Guantanamo if people don't comply then we have chances of going to a war that will result in population reduction.

* Make WMDs in the name of medical records and illegally tag every child at birth and put the whole country on death row. Take the bull by the horns don't leave anything to chance.

* Make the most destructive bomb and use it so that effects last forever and still have deaths for years.

I think you are familiar with all the points above but not with the following points that make our core focus.

Stop weapons manufacturing globally and reduce military budgets.

Channel all the money in critical areas like research and development even to provide food for most, etc.

Find ways of stopping people aging and dying

Increase infrastructure, etc.

Ban making of all viruses, bio, digital or cyber ones

Avoid overcrowding and improve facilities, etc.

Make it illegal to kill anyone's enemies or not life matters.

Priorities life and its self-preservation

Improve networking and communications and increase research and development budgets

So, the new approach the one in this book is that of doing everything differently altogether. It's like asking the military and soldiers how they can do the opposite of what they do? How can you create life instead of taking life? How can you close bullet wounds instead of killing? How can you build network infrastructure you normally destroy? etc. It's a new way of thinking now using the current system like the military to come up with solutions in a way making these institutions evolve to understand how to negotiate and get involved in dialogs etc. It's easy talking to a machine; a gun, a missile, a virus, a landmine, a watermark, a nuclear bomb, etc. but can you talk to people and how are your skills, etc. Anyone can talk to a gun asking it to kill etc. but can you negotiate and turn a sceptic into a lover, or you will simply increase the hatred. What are your people's skills? Do you have the brains yourself to understand humanity as a whole or just another idiot thinking within the box? Or you are good at just creating enemies and harden their hearts? Just like we humans create robots who must receive inputs all the time. The challenge is to create clever robots that can see life as we see it and change to move to the next stage.

**Can humans create robots that can be as good as we humans? God's dilemma; can he create humans that can be as clever as him?**

I ask you a question and would like an honest answer.

Do you think humans will ever create robots that can think and act like us humans? Honestly?

This is the same challenge God set aside to see if humans will ever be as smart as him and act just like him so that one-day mankind will run the earth just like he runs the heaven and the whole world? Just like us with robots God expected mankind to solve the life puzzles and evolve and be as smart as him so that we develop through the stages instead of spending $billions making things that makes sceptics keep doubting or stir others to be skeptical can you turn sceptics into lovers and make everyone love too. I mentioned above that the wars were like warning alarms e.g. fire alarms to indicate the best time to move to the next stage. What humans did instead was to disable the wars which acted as these alarms through the creation of NATO, the UN especially the ICC who are now acting to kill in advance people who might stir everyone to war. If wars were indicators of the best time to move to the next stage and if we 'disable' the alarms or warning in the wars how then are we going to move to the next stage if the wars or alarms where the triggers and catalyst that would make us move forward? So, disabling these vehicles of change we have made ourselves be stuck in one stage the defensive stages. We think everything is okay because we are comfortable, but the truth is, we are comfortable because we are sacrificing the most important things. We have chosen the easy way and we are lying to ourselves that everything is okay when we are working way below our optimal levels. My point throughout the book is that we as humans through cults like NATO, the UN and the ICC we have sat comfortably and we think we are great we can make the greatest weapons and start the greatest wars or the most modern concentration camps in Guantanamo Bay, etc. but if you were the current robots your owners the clever humans would be cursing calling you dumb fucks etc. just the same as God or the creator etc. is viewing humanity today as short-sighted only thinking about tomorrow and never about the time far ahead and our capabilities. We have the greatest potential to make sacrifices and evolve completely to live a better life globally not just one superpower.

So, going back to the issues at the beginning of the chapter about religion. So, what is the place and role of religion? I think religion distracts the true meanings in the bible or Quran, etc. I am seeping further into religion as it is linked to the issues in the Middle East and the fighting has religion as the underlying reason. My current understanding of what these holy books say about heaven, God or Allah and humanity. So, religion teaches humans that humanity will die and go to heaven. Life here on earth is part of the journey to go to heaven. The focus is on life in heaven. Our life's purpose is to prepare us to go to heaven. So, life on earth is a temporary feature but the main thing is in heaven. So, this kind of teaching or understanding makes other people want to skip this life to quickly go to heaven. If heaven is the best life can be with everything you want given to you why waste life here on earth, then? This is the main reason why some people would prefer to die through suicide bombing to avoid all the pains this life has to offer and enjoy a better life in heaven. In heaven as far as I understand it is a place so advanced that humans are happy ever after. In heaven, there are no worries like worries here on earth. In heaven, you can marry or be given as many virgins you want. In heaven, you don't worry about money and food which are abundant. In heaven, you don't get tortured, etc. or be forced to choose or fight others because everyone is a friend and in harmony with each other. There is peace in heaven as compared to life here on earth. So, you can see why people who are told about heaven would rather die to go to a better life than the current one. Religion states that God is loving and as such invites all to heaven after death. It's God's plan for us to die so that we go to heaven.

First, I ask you a question. What kind of self-esteem do people who commit suicide or kill themselves have? Just generalization I know no one might understand what people are feeling in that state but for argument's sake, I think very low self-esteemed people would fit this criterion. So, I can argue that self-esteem is linked and related to thoughts of suicide or dying or killing others, etc. or revenge. These situations are contradictory that it will be highly unlikely to find a person with high self-esteem who wants to commit suicide as well as high self-esteem contradicts or conflicts with feelings of suicide, etc.

## The situation in the Middle East, Africa, Eastern Europe, etc.

These areas fall under the poorest of the world with life so hard that people would wish to die to ease the pain and worries. Things you take for granted in some areas can be scarce to find things like food, etc. These countries are in constant fighting with no chance of peace. The whole world stirs the fighting without any solutions to stop this and you can ask why? The same areas are rich in oil and if these areas are peaceful, then the prices of oil will be very high than the current prices. So, wars are there as a means of getting these resources cheaper worldwide. So, the whole globe is happy if there is turmoil and fighting as peace can mean the destruction of economies globally. Imagine the world without oil as oil in the hands of a few countries can mean unaffordable prices globally. So, the more the Middle East is in misery the better the world around it. My question is; Is this fair when it involves children and women dying due to the war or military missile strikes as witnessed in Syria? The nations supporting these strikes argue too that globally if there are no oil resources women and children still die too from malnutrition as there is no oil to drive the cars to transport the resources. Their argument is that more children and women die than say those killed by military action, so their efforts are justified as they aim to provide oil globally cheaper.

## Little background to the problem.

Some years ago, the Persian Gulf countries realized that they can be very rich from the oil and can rule the world if they wanted as they could bring the rest of the world to a halt simply by forming cults to limit production to push the prices. Earlier on before this, the market was free uncontrolled, and people bargained and negotiated for oil through separate suppliers all with their specific yet different demands. Then after some time these oil-producing countries became greedy and decided to take things into their hands just like the Allies did earlier after the Second World War by grouping and forming NATO, the UN, the ICC, etc. So, these countries formed cults that controls supply and influence demand. To make things worse, these nations went on to nationalize oil reserves making it easy for the states to control supply linking politics and oil supply something that was taken in bad taste by the powerful countries as they woke up and found out that the only power they had was based on weapons. This is true of the long petrol queues that showed the world who was the real boss. I think this was the start of the real Middle East problems. I can argue that it could be a deliberate political strategy to destabilize and keep the Middle East in turmoil so that oil supply globally is stable and affordable.

**Global strategy to stir wars and turmoil as a strategic way of getting oil cheaper and to ensure a constant supply.**

So, the world realized that oil was one thing that can paralyze the globe, so the governments drew plans declaring war on all nations in the Middle East who had nationalized oil reserves. What is happening now is simply part of the twenty to twenty-five-year contingency plans drawn decades ago? Talking of peace in the Middle East will have to go a long way than just quarrels between the countries involved. First, let's look at the strategies to deal with the oil of the Middle East.

1> The first strategy was to supply weapons and destabilize the Middle East and destroy the control of the government thereby destabilizing the grip of the government.

This also involved the weakening approach that targeted governments who nationalized oils making them prone to being removed and create all kinds of problems so that the power of that government is reduced. The governments are less liked so that they can act to reduce their impact and policies regarding the amount of oil supply.

This led to the establishment of the so-called sanctions with the aim to weaken governments and reduce their power as to dealing with oil. Governments who had nationalized oil would and could use oil as a political agenda to bring the whole globe to a halt. Their power was so immense that they had become very powerful and only sanctions could destroy all that. Sanctions rally support and support-internal-turmoil to destabilize the government to be weak as regarding setting up oil prices and demand or production numbers. If a country is sanctioned, the idea is to rally locals to fight that government and make it easy to remove that government so that they can be weak as to regard to setting production limits and prices. Sanctions are a weapon as they will make it easy for these governments to increase production. Sanctions will make it easy for these governments to come to the negotiating table as sanctions affect the supply of basic goods killing the innocent and if the government can't do anything to avert such losses, then rebels uprise and destabilize the government weakening their stance. The government will be left with no option as they are made to not afford the basic and kids and women end up without food and medicines etc. while the governments are holding oil reserves. In the end, local instability will lead these governments to succumb to the demands of the West, etc. Sanctions go further to create instability on the basis that a hungry man is an angry man in the hope that the only way to remove governments from power is to use the locals to start a coup through civil unrest. The idea is to make the governments stay in power in short-term or facing instability all the time and not to be complacent to put real strict oil production limits etc. so to reduce global supply lowering prices.

2> The second strategy involves military action following the twenty-five-year-old contingency plans. One thing one must understand is that the military drafts contingency plans to deal with recurrent problems and given that lack of oil which everyone was depended on was a forever thing no wonder the military was drafted to be the solution. Lack of oil resources globally would only lead to one thing; wars. Picture the Persian Gulf wars of the 80s etc. these were no mere accidents but simply the fulfillment of contingency plans. That is true of 9/11 too as a trigger of the fulfillment to act on the contingency plans. I pointed throughout this book that a strategy centered around the Colony Collapse Strategy was adopted directly or indirectly and is used now and was used to compile a list of problematic countries especially those with oil. A list to be followed by each President or Prime Minister in power. They all in their four or eight years in office must tackle those on the list of the contingency plans. This involves every leader dealing with at least one of the so-called threats and eliminating that to minimize oil prices and ensure the future supply. I pointed out that the West and their cults have embarked on a contingency

322

plan or project to eliminate potential people who can influence events or lead to a war or bring the cult to a halt through restricting oil production. Each President must takeout enemies directly through military action or indirectly through the CIA, UN's ICC, etc. So, if the oil reserves are nationalized war is imminent and inevitable as a way of ensuring affordability and continuous supply. The idea behind nationalizing oil is to limit production and supply to push prices and gain global power as well. So, the strategy adopted is to eliminate the alpha dominant male to weaken the rest in order to conquer, move-in and change everything and put puppets who can abide by the production and supply of oil. In short, this Colony Collapse Strategy is the hacking literally to death of the leader and then moving in and just like a computer hacker to change, manipulate and modify with the aim to cause collapse one day. I mentioned Dwight Eisenhower during the 1956 Suez Canal arguing that only nationalizing oil reserves would make military action a must. Ever since the following Presidents and Prime Ministers have embarked on killing sprees to eliminate potential threats who would otherwise use oil to start a war.

3> We have seen the West invading in the name of human rights whenever things get better and when they leave, they leave sectoral violence rampant a strategy to keep the turmoil to ensure low prices and guarantee future supply.

4> Religion has been misinterpreted and used to drive instability agendas to keep these countries in constant wars. Some people have used religion to make life hard for the people and reduce self-esteem that further make the turmoil worse as people who face massive hardships despite the country owning oil worth $billions or more. In the end, they resort to violence with the promises of a better life in heaven where they can get whatever has been denied them here through several policies and other forms of interference referred to as protection.

5> Protection to keep people poorer and miserable to perpetuate the problems to ensure low fuel prices. Protectorate agreements with the Persian Gulf countries date back to the 1850s where all oil-rich countries signed the protection treaty where they gave up security and defense to a third-party in exchange of oil a formula that led to disaster after the treaties ended with the protectorates grantors always finding ways to influence activities still to help lower global oil and increase supply as an alternative to military action. The idea is that it is easy to supply things cheaply things like weapons that in turn lead to further instability as people kill each other in sectoral violence based on culture and religion. Protection also means 'tricking people to trap them' for example through deception to create situations where people do something after getting facts that tend up to be cooked up. A good example is the Iraq dossier where people went to war based on this report that tends to be a lie faked just to justify the war. So, people are trapped through a lie and in the end blackmailed and threatened and put 'on death row' whether they will be given a way-out usually through instant violence and death rather than be tortured for eternity. A look at Loose Change video will point to the more methods used where victims are tricked and lied to that they are carrying out a rehearsal or an act until that very moment they realize that they are caught up in some dodgy life or death situation. In the end, these people after being tricked and betrayed will aim to revenge as a way-out killing people in suicide attacks, etc.

6> The sixth strategy involves a global strategy that unfairly presses the Middle East down as a solution to global problems perpetrated at a global level through agencies like the UN imposing sanctions that only further increase the turmoil and instability. The argument being that depriving the globe of oil is a threat to peace and security itself and given the fact that the world's oil is in the hands of a few countries morally to these people, it is justified to interfere or take military action for the sake of all. These people usually the West argue that these countries in the Middle East with oil reserves have only been endorsed as the holders of oil on behalf of the whole world as oil is a commodity needed by everyone and it is simply a duty of these countries to ensure a good supply and nationalizing these oil reserves is not only a selfish act but a criminal one too to automatically invoke military action.

Dwight Eisenhower argued that;

Nationalizing the canal 'was not the same as nationalizing oil wells... [which] exhaust a nation's resources.'

Oil is too expensive to be left to market forces as it depletes the countries money as it increases the bill so that it will be cheaper instead of buying at such high prices to make weapons and go to war. The reason behind this is the fact that it is clever to look for cheaper ways of getting resources or doing business. The prices of oil have business strategic justifications that whenever the price goes high, it will be reasonable for a sound mind to make weapons cheaper and then use weapons to get the oil. It would be a waste of resources to spend all that money when you can kill and get the resources. This justified the adoption of the Colony Collapse Strategy in which the government of the developed countries with the backing of cults like NATO, the UN, ICC, etc. realized that it was cheaper to just kill the alpha male the dictator, Saddam, Gaddafi, etc. and see the collapse of the society as the alpha male is removed especially in traumatic ways to weaken anyone who might be thinking of launching revenge attacks etc. and to put their people or use locals who act as puppets and who obey the production targets to ensure affordable oil globally. This strategy is justified that the deaths if nothing is done are greater globally than the deaths resulting from military action. So say if nothing is done 3 million people for fuck's sake will die as no resources are transported globally or machines that use oil are not working due to lack of oil etc. and this can't be tolerated and it can be justified that 500 000 thousand people die through a military invasion that ensures supply and saves 3 million.

**Our laws and stance about all this.**

We stand for everyone and I have personally argued that we must change completely. We have been focused on trivial things which now are obsolete like wars and all the weapons, etc. Our laws will ban all these that in turn will free resources we are using for the military to buy oil at fair prices so that no one must die even a single child. Our laws will ban military action no matter what. Instead of finding wars as a cheaper way of getting oil at lower prices I am going to make these people think about other alternate energy sources like electricity and with time I will ban the use of fossil fuels for cars and other vehicles even if the oil is still there. The idea being that of forcing these people to invest in research and development and find other new fuels resources. There must never be any justification for killing even a single child. Our laws like I have argued throughout take a holistic approach to solving global issues. Everything will fit perfectly like a jigsaw puzzle. Prioritizing life and it's preserving will remove all the arguments for killing and stirring violence. Banning oil-dependent vehicles and machines will not just resolve a lot of issues in the Middle East but will make everyone think outside of the box. A true and sure way to bring peace to the Middle East. I can guarantee you that because I know for sure the past policies have failed to bring peace for the past seventy years.

**The globe stance and peace in the Middle East.**

Ever lusted for someone's girlfriend? Surely you would not make conditions for them to be in harmony with each other. You will do whatever you can do to make sure one day she might run to tell you how a freak the boyfriend is etc. and end up in your arms. You will play all the tricks so that they fight because you want her too. So, you have a vested interest and you can only weaken them if they fight. If they are solid and loving, you will wait forever. The same applies here. Everyone wants oil and oil to drive the economy to remember the long petrol queues? So, the global stance is to stir turmoil in the Middle East selling weapons behind back doors and selectively choosing certain countries to create resentment and at local level selecting one tribe or people over the other and labeling the other less superior just to stir sectoral violence and keep the region in turmoil. All this to weaken the powers of these governments who had nationalized oil reserves.

**Military action as a correlation of nationalization of oil serves.**

I think there is a strong link between military invasion and the nationalization of oil reserves globally if the country has oil reserves. The idea of nationalization of oil is to increase net present value and make the best profits out of oil for any government using political tools to influence prices through restricted supply. Producing less to increase global prices and above all to ban private international companies to control oil supply and oil prices. This makes these governments the sole decision-makers. So, the nationalization of oil makes these countries powerful as they can play with supply to bargain in other areas and show the world who is boss. So is there a link between military action or hostility towards a country and nationalization of oil resources.

*The Soviet Union nationalized oil in 1939

*Mexico 1969

*Iran 1951

*Iraq 1961

*Egypt 1962

*Argentina 1963

*Venezuela 1970s

* Libya 1970s

*Saudi Arabia 1070s

*Russia re-nationalized oil in the 2000s.

The strategy is to use sanctions or landmines to weaken the governments and stir a revolution that will result in the overthrow of the government to weaken the government stir unrest and then use that to justify invasion under human rights. All the countries that have nationalized oils are targeted and their leaders a task by each and every President or Prime Minister to solve through military action or the CIA with other African countries under the watchful eye of the ICC and the UN who are swift to impose sanctions. If not sanctions, then landmines do the same and produce the same results with fertile land rendered useless with the results that people will have less land to farm resulting in starvation that can lead to a revolution or simply justifies an invasion.

We have touched the background issues now I will look at sectoral violence.

This is not a recent thing and dates to the beginning of the bible times. Rifts exist and have ever existed and simply saying it's the West will be an under-representation of the facts. In the bible we have Abel and Cain fighting and trying to please God as the best and God choosing one over the other that leads to jealous. The Middle East is composed of people in the Quran and even then, the fighting existed, and the killings were there too for leadership and dominance with each group trying to be the best. In short, it's about the appointment to the throne as a leader. In life or religious circles, there are two ways in which people could be appointed depending on what you are talking about. There was and still is a belief that bloodline can determine who becomes a leader. Monarchies etc. follow this pattern. In religious circles, it's a different issue as God or Allah appoints people regardless of blood. It is up to God to choose who will be the leader and leadership unlike in kingship and monarchies cannot be guaranteed by blood. You must have a special standing with God or Allah than just by blood. So, the prophet died before deciding who would take over from him. Those in his bloodline assumed leadership roles while those who believed that leadership was not guaranteed by blood argued that the relatives or bloodline were not rightful leaders. That's the beginning of the split. The Sunnis followed the bloodline of the prophet and Shia's followed the spiritual successor. Another thing is religion as well.

In religion what was ever a prophet said even when just talking without any specific reference must be fulfilled. If I say I have to be a billionaire somehow in my life and everyone follows me that has to come true and all the followers will have to make it a reality otherwise there is no reason for wasting time praying or following that leader. Whatever is written must be fulfilled and so people do the wrong things to make the prophecy come true.

**Prophecy follows and the follower's thoughts.**

This is one of the reasons why solving the Middle East will go further away than just stopping the fighting. Religion is based on written things and everything written must be fulfilled. If it is written that there shall be a beast who will destroy another beast the followers and believers of these books must create the two beasts and make one kill the other. It is a kind of thinking that is troubling and one that acts like a Film Script. Everything that will happen on earth is already written and everyone must follow the film scripts and make sure that the prophecy is fulfilled. So, claims to solve the middle eastern problems without understanding all this might only fuel violence. The West's intentions might be genuine but the fact that they have no clue might make things worse. A perfect example is the making of Jerusalem as the capital of Israel as prophesied by the bible but something that increases tensions and fighting. So, if the people are only fulfilling what is already written what is the future of dialog and negotiations. You must also understand that the prophecies must be fulfilled, and the prophets prophesied that there shall be divisions and groups all who will claim to be the best and among all these only one will be pure the chosen one. So, everyone will try to be the best and even kill each other as a way of fulfilling all this as something to last a thousand years so until that has passed people will simply quarrel to fill this prophecy otherwise religion is nothing.

## Religion's Perspective of Heaven. Misconception.

Religion declares that mankind will live and let die before enjoying the best life has to offer. This life is just to prepare people for the good life. It's like saying I will torture you so that you enjoy tomorrow even better. Mind you there is no justification whatsoever for the torture you torture someone then be prepared to die. So, the pain and misery in this life are just to make the next life appreciated. Whatever you find hard to get in this life you will get easily in the next life. So, to be rewarded say with virgins in heaven you must recruit people as well. Yes, just like inviting your friends and getting a reward thing. Dying alone will not make you be rewarded but if you kill, you will have helped people avoid misery here on earth and to enjoy life faster in heaven and as such Allah will reward you. So, we have suicide bombers facing the hardest lives, or their kids being forced into being a martyr with their families promised to be looked after or rewarded in the event of death.

## Our Interpretation of Life.

Life is a development process an end and not a means to an end. I am referring to life on earth. So, we live to live forever, young, and happily forever. When people die, it's a shame because it only means that mankind has failed somehow. We see life as a puzzle to solve all obstacles so that we become like whoever created life. If we take the position of robots, robots are not there to die so that they enjoy life as other forms of robots somewhere. No one will create robots with the aim that they self-destruct and come back as say chickens or for them to live in space as spirits. Unless if we know that one day the robots will evolve so much, they will end up like humans thinking and acting like us. This is the main reason behind robot creation in artificial intelligence and not just for them to perform tasks or our wishful thinking that they will evolve to become something else. So, as humans just like we expect to create robots that can become like us and live like us God's plan is not for us to die and take another form and crowd his place in heaven. His idea was to create and make humans evolve to become like him so that they rule the earth just like he rules the heaven. God is creating a small god that will be him. This small god will be the god of earth while he is God of heaven. We create robots so they become 'small people' who will run some parts of earth relieving humans, so they do what we do while we chill and relax and still earn.

But life is not easy there are so many things we can do, and we must avoid, and as such we must think and solve puzzles to reach the next stages. Think of life as a game. To reach the next stage you must complete the first stage. Collect all rewards you can use like swords to strike the dinosaurs with and create some juju to heal the attacks by the dragon, etc. Once that is achieved then can you go to the next stage. [Maybe I should patent this idea?] Next stage we have killed the dinosaurs, so it is extinct, so we no longer need a sword or of that size, but we have new threats in the form of aliens. So, we work hard and get rewards with a different weapon that makes the aliens evaporate. We have realized that through luck we can make our bodies grow huge muscles around certain areas so we now know we don't need heavy metals etc. a metal jersey can save us from any attacks. So, armor changes too. We realize that some dangers that were there before are no longer there. We increase research and development. We find out that we have other planets. We start thinking about making vehicles to take us there. So, we now know we don't need swords and huge armor, etc. as there are no longer threats. So, we channel resources according. There is a thing to discover and make to help us progress to the next stage. There is no point getting stuck in stage one otherwise, we run out of time and the game will simply confirm a; game over status. So, we aim to collect rewards fast and move. So, likewise, life is about finding solutions abandoning other rewards and weapons we don't need so we progress further. God or the creator or Allah etc. puts puzzles we must solve. Life must mean living here on earth. All the misery we have are challenges that need quick and good thinking. Someone somehow must act and solve all this. It's a challenge but something that must be done. Life is not a vehicle-to-another life. Life is not a means to an end but an end in that we live to live life if possible and as happy as ever. Life as a journey to a better life and heaven is just a state of life where we have solved all the puzzles and realized that if tortoises can live up to two-hundred years can slowing everything down help? What can we do to avoid aging, etc.? We can't find these answers unless we invest and put resources and start working on finding answers. We must sacrifice other areas. This is the challenge. To progress, you can't do both as they are not complementary as they compete for resources. The military provides everyone with a smile but is it the best option or a trick to test who really has the big guns in brains i.e. a huge thinking power. So, if we are not able to progress then we are doing nothing at all in that direction. I argued that they disabled warnings or tips so that we can only be in this stage forever because in this stage they can be bullies, form cults and make weapons and take whatever they want at will. If the oil prices rise, simply invade and kill the leader then denationalize oil, simple. Or simply preach of another life and reduce the people's self-esteem and tarnish any hope of a better life. So, heaven to us is a stage we must strive to achieve here on earth. It's an advanced stage in the development process we must achieve through clever use of resources to abandon some even favorable ones to complete the challenge. So, heaven is life on earth that is so advanced that we all work together, avoiding wasting resources on things that are trivial like wars when we can use the power of speech to negotiate and make deals. Dying can make you get-crash God's residence. God to be honest he does not want humans in heaven above as heaven is for the spirit like him. His aim was to create mankind in flesh to live here on earth as equivalent to God's heaven. But if mankind can't solve the puzzle and end up dying and going to heaven as a spirit God as the omnipotent, omnipresence and the omniscient will always welcome mankind, but he would like all mankind to live forever on earth in flesh. It's mankind's duty and task to work out how to achieve that. Everyone should have high self-esteem and look forward to living life here on earth and never wish to die because according to God it's failing the test worse if one commits suicide. For now, death is the norm because we are not doing what we should do. We are spending $trillions e.g. $1,7 trillion in 2017 alone wasting on military when all that money can be used to solve improve life. We have legit governments making weapons digital or biological to kill people and reverse or speed up aging etc. and the whole world is just watching. I dwelt on this issue so you understand the laws and solutions we will implement.

Banning anything to do with wars and impose tight rules to make everyone comfortable and not worry about being attacked in surprise attacks. Research and development to understand and solve life's puzzles etc. Ban anything to do with oil as a fuel to make the world think about other cleaner energy sources. Protect the environment and reduce climatic change. Educate people and change people's beliefs about religion and why sometimes we need to adapt. Change people's perception of life and death. So, people throw in everything now to live forever happily rather than giving up becoming suicidal bombers. Make life better by following our first rules the right to life, etc. so that everything centers around humans and everything following which is not the case as now the military or for security and defense people can be killed conflicting with our first rule. That removes and deletes all war contingency plans and our laws will make the USA and Britain the two top assassinators of people of color think twice and drop their direct or indirect Colony Collapse Strategy and value the life of everyone and start looking for alternatives of fuels and stop using weapons as solutions for everything. That will stop or make cults like NATO evolve and maybe as a change spearhead the discovery of ways to create life instead of destroying it or finding alternative fuels.

### Future of religion. Own-Self worship.

In our New World, there is no room for religion as we know it. This is because the current religion is a way of pleading to enter the heavens rather than enjoying the life we have now. People worship as a way of praying to solve all of today's problems. Religion is there as a way of keeping people hopefully about the future. It is true people are more into religion when they are in trouble or need something. It is true also that religion arose as a way of giving people something to hang to when the odds are stacked against them when it's like fighting the goads. You can't solve today's problems so you tend to ask for answers from the creators but imagine when humans are so advanced that there are no wars, or oil to fight for, or no need to invade another country because we have learned to turn milk into butter rather than steal someone's else. Imagine a world where people have high self-esteem that no one wants to die. If life is so good who would want to die? That time humans can create virgins or restore virginity so that no one would wish to kill or be tricked with the hope of being offered wives in heaven. I will have launched a war with countries that provide evil protection tricking and blackmailing people holding them to slavery forever putting them on death row based on trickery and deception tagging people at birth. So, life will be so good that everyone will qualify to be the leader and only luck being used to differentiate between people. Governments who age their people faster will be a thing of the past. Everyone would appreciate life and want to live in flesh forever. People will have realized that going to heaven will be a failure as God created mankind wishing everyone to rule the earth forever. It would then be fitting to say heaven for God and earth for humanity. God ruling heaven and mankind ruling earth. God would have delegated and put man as a small god to run earth. Humans will have developed and gained enough knowledge to utilize all that we must to prolong life and life forever young.

To conclude a heaven is a form of advancement that will be achieved and to take place here on earth with people living like in paradise. Together without wars but communicating and working as a family for the betterment of the family unit. If I must design instruments that will act like family blood or DNA that connects us so be it. I think such a gadget would bring mankind together unlike today where technology is used to create divisions to select and differentiate people and to watermark some as to put them in a different category, etc. In the future, we will find a way of leveling the ground by making humanity all have something in common. The solution lies in something that acts like family blood and DNA nothing outward will ever be good enough. Education will play a great role.

# CHAPTER SIXTEEN

THE CRASH OF GLOBAL FINANCE AND THE NEED FOR A NEW SYSTEM.

*The role and place of cryptocurrency.

*Just like the onset of global wars as a trigger or indicator for a need for a system change

The global financial crash was a trigger or indicator of the need for a system change. When a system crashes, a new system is needed if the crash is to be avoided in the future. I explained in detail what led to the financial collapse. It was not a coincidence like they want you to believe but a carefully planned devious plan intended to steal money without being caught by those who are too clever and most of which were involved in the development of the current system somehow.

But first I want to introduce a new thought for a while so that you understand the problems we have and how we will solve these.

### What is the weight of the soul?

In 1907 one Duncan MacDougall did a controversial experiment in which he noted that a patient lost 21 grams of weight soon after death and as such therefore concluded that the weight of the soul was 21 grams. The issue of whether this is true or not is not the issue in this book. A human body to breathe and exist and live for an average of 70 to 100 years for argument purposes must have at least 21 grams or air. So, our bodies need air to function properly and blood too. What is air made up of? Air that is breathed is made up of atoms that are on the periodic table. In general, air is made up of nitrogen which accounts for 78%, oxygen which accounts for 21%, water vapor accounts for 4% and lastly, there is argon which accounts for 1%.

The other question I will need to pose is; How many liters of air are needed by an adult person per day? A human adult, according to science, inhales and exhales between 7 to 8 liters of air per minute. Per day, therefore, a human body will inhale and exhale at least 11,000 liters. Air that is inhaled is circulated and then exhaled. Of the 20%-21% inhaled, something like 15% is exhaled, which means 5 to 6 percent is consumed or used in the body or converted to other gaseous. What then affects amounts inhaled will depend on what the person is doing say if sprinting or jogging inhaled air is higher.

>A human body requires oxygen to live

>Oxygen [O2] inhaled is 21% of total air inhaled

>The weight of a soul is 21grams

>78% of inhaled air consists of nitrogen [$N_2$]

>What can kill a human body is ammonia [$NH_3$] which is dangerous and is a result of mixing nitrogen and 3 X hydrogen. It must be stored below 33.

>Water is needed by the body and consists of one atom of oxygen and two of hydrogens [$H_2O$]

>The body needs at least 60% as water intake is the 8x8 rule.

>It is a fact that the human body needs only twenty-five of the 118 elements in the world.

>Only oxygen is found in its pure form the rest as ions

>25 very vital to life

>4 make-up 96% of the body and these are carbon, oxygen, hydrogen, and nitrogen.

>Major elements 3.5% of the body is made up of seven elements; Calcium, phosphorous, potassium, sulfur, sodium, chlorine and magnesium

>Trace elements make of 0.5% and fourteen of these including Baron, Tin, Iron, etc.

>Glucose gives energy to the body and is $C_6H_{12}O_6$=Carbon x6, Hydrogen x12, and oxygen x6

>Overall too much or too little can result in problems

First, what is the periodic table?

"a table of the chemical elements arranged in order of atomic number, usually in rows, so that elements with similar atomic structure (and hence similar chemical properties) appear in vertical columns."

It is since elements are the building blocks of everything in the world. Temperature differentiates between solid, liquid and gasses. There are 118 elements of which around ninety-four occur naturally, leaving twenty-four as artificially induced. The elements are arranged in rows and columns. A Russian scientist invented the periodic table in 1869.

Let's look at the periodic table. The atomic number of oxygens which make-up 21% of breathed air is eight. Nitrogen's atomic number is seven. Argon which has a 1% proportion of breathed air has an atomic number of 18.

What is oxygen then? It is represented by the symbol O and the nucleus of oxygen has eight protons that have a positive charge. Surrounding the nucleus, the middle bit is what is called electrons and often has a negative charge. So, protons are attracted to electrons. The charge on the protons and electrons are the same but opposite. So is a proton having a 4+ the electron will have a -4. Neutrons have no charge so are neutral i.e. 0.

What defines an atom is the number of protons in the nucleus that is the atomic number represented by z.

The body needs blood to function properly and to sustain life. Without blood, there won't be life. Blood cannot be replaced or made, but it is essential for the transport of essential minerals like oxygen and nutrients to the body. There are four major components of blood, the red blood cells, the white blood cells, platelets, and the plasma. 40 to 45% of blood is made up of these red blood cells. The body produces 5 billion per hour of the red blood cells and they last 4 months 120 Days. Platelets control bleeding and blood loss. Plasma is responsible for the transport of water and nutrients. White blood cells make up only 1% of blood and are vital for defense. They travel through the bloodstream and move to tissue to protect the body.

So, what is the percentage of body weight accounted for by blood?

This is only 7% of body weight. A huge loss of blood can starve the brain of oxygen that is carried in the blood. A loss of blood greater than 2000ml is fatal, which is 40% of the blood volume.

A loss of the blood above 30% will not instantly kill you but will make one a higher heart rate above 120 per minute.

The breathing rate goes up and blood pressure decreases.

>After that, you can pass out.

>Experience shock

>Circulation failure

A loss of 50% can mean the body's inability to pump blood, resulting in the heart-stopping and other organs shutting down.

>And die

On the other hand, oxygen accounts for 65% of the mass of the body with nitrogen accounting for something around 3 to 4%.

65/100 a bodyweight = amount of oxygen in the body. In humans, oxygen binds to hydrogen to form water, which is 60% of the body. Too much is dangerous, as it causes cell oxidation that kills them.

Carbon 18% of body mass

It is vital as all elements in a human body contain carbon which has an atomic number 6.

10% of body weight is Hydrogen

Usually attached to oxygen to form water. Found in all other elements just like carbon.

3% of body weight is nitrogen.

Absorbed from food and transported to the lungs needed for protein synthesis. Atomic number 7.

Mass fraction of these elements;

Oxygen $6.5 \times 10^{-1}$

Carbon $1.8 \times 10^{-1}$

Hydrogen 1x10-1

Nitrogen 3x 10-2

I have laid out the basics about the human body and the vital elements needed to sustain life. The human body is a very complex system that really works and often misunderstood in that humans will never create for the foreseeable future another human being because the body is the perfect entity so complex that it's difficult to recreate. For argument's sake, I am going to argue that the human body is the miniature version or model of the big system be it company, an institution, a government, a nation or globe. My argument throughout this chapter is this; if you want a perfect system that really works you must design the system based on the functions of the body. This is a tried and tested way and it works if the elements and atoms, then protons, neutrons, and the electrodes are understood. For argument's sake, one can say the body is a model of a nation. All you need for the smooth operation is to use proportion and recreate the same system and everything is poised to work perfectly. This is true as the structure of the body and its functions are used to create a working model that is used to run a country. A few countries have two heads, but the other head is passive and doesn't get involved in the politics of the head as much but is often there. This system is associated with countries with monarchies. The monarchies are like overseers just to give advice and represent the system indirectly. Then there is a head who is active in decision making. Directing the way, the country goes. Some systems have two active heads all who make decisions but one of the heads has superior powers and often is a President with the other Prime Minister. All these two different systems have a central body symbolized by the heart that pumps the life of anybody in the form of blood which is represented by money in the real world. Other financial institutions are there to supply the body with certain elements vital like oxygen from the lungs. So, blood in the human body is represented by money in the real world. So, if blood is vital for any life of the body so as money is for the country. The system before was like a human being with blood and without anything else like oxygen yet it functioned but this meant central control and manipulation by the head through the central bank. In real life, we have seen that if it was a person he would not have lived, and this meant the government adopting a stringent plan that will create a ghost oxygen element to keep the system functioning. So, to start with our system is flawed in that the blood circulated has no oxygen in it and the government must create ways of making sure that the blood carries oxygen but supplied centrally. The system was suffocating and the blood alone was not enough as blood was mixed with oxygen centrally which is wrong as oxygen was to be channeled from the air into the system through the head's nostrils down to the lungs or financial institutions and carried by the blood to the central bank

## Rise of the Bitcoin as a solution

If a human body cannot live if starved of oxygen surely likewise, the system was bound to fail. The idea so far is that the monetary system on its own is bound to fail and we have seen the collapse of the financial institutions as a testament to this. It's just like blood in the body forcibly mixed with not enough oxygen in the heart centrally rather than being absorbed freely from prefect points like the nostrils. So, the notion here is one that highlights the need for oxygen not to replace blood but to supplement and augment the blood. In other words, digital currency is like oxygen it is part of and complementary to fiat money. The two together complete a perfect system. One must understand the proportions needed as one in excess will be toxic to the whole system. It's not a fact of Bitcoin as oxygen replacing the fiat money, no. It's a matter of the two to co-exist cushioning the effects of the financial markets with Bitcoin doing what the fiat money can't do.

First why Bitcoin is like oxygen in human anatomy. Cryptography;

It is defined as the art of solving codes, but this definition does not do justice. First, I think it's relevant to look at the properties of oxygen.

>It is invisible. Can you see the air? Can you touch the air? So, it is intangible but exists. You can contain air if you change its state say from a gaseous form to a solid or liquid. So, one can surely say that oxygen is hidden because we know air exist, but we can't see it and Bitcoin as oxygen is something derived from the idea that it is hidden too through encryption. Hence the term cryptocurrency meaning something hidden through codes because we can't see oxygen it is hidden but is there. So, bitcoins are not tangible. They don't exist intangible forms and as such can be said to be encrypted and so will require decoding of some sort.

Definition of cryptocurrency can support my arguments above;

"a digital currency in which encryption techniques are used to regulate the generation of units of currency and verify the transfer of funds, operating independently of a central bank."

Google Dictionary.

Encryption;

The central part of this idea is the fact that Bitcoin must go through a process called encryption transforming the messages so that only the intended people can read them.

>The other attribute is that oxygen is readily available globally and is everywhere and is not controlled like blood that must be pumped by the heart. Oxygen is in quadrillions in infinite form. It is not governed by the body as blood is. You can get oxygen from outside the system that is Bitcoin is decentralized, unlike fiat money or blood that must be contained in the body and pumped by the central agency or heart. It does not matter how much we can lose and can't be enforced or seized. But for blood, it's a different situation lose 2000 ml and you are in a deep problem that can see the collapse of the economy. Do you know the reasons behind these tough money laundering government schemes? They have roots in blood. Blood just like money can't be made somewhere else just like money it is made or printed by the central system only if some of this money or blood is missing or lost. A blood transfusion is behind the printing of new money into the

economy. There are certain levels that are needed for any country's finance system to function properly. I went a step further at the beginning of this chapter to explain the role and importance of proportions and quantities of a certain element in the body. Too much or too little will have disastrous effects. So, it's not just guessed work or luck but requires a great understanding no wonder why financial institutions have been collapsing now and then. Let's assume the body is like the national of a country. We know we need a certain percentage of weight as blood and oxygen for the body to function properly. So, I can say that the proportions of this element are directly related to the weight of the body and likewise we can create a formula in relation to the number of people in that country.

I can propose a theory in which I can say the amount of blood in a body is equivalent to 7% of the body or number of people in that country.

Money in circulation= 7/100 x the country has 4 million people.

$=7/100 x 4 000 000

For every 4million people, money in circulation must be around 280 000.

Like I said money should not be alone but must be complemented by oxygen as in Bitcoin which must be 65% of the number of the people.

Bitcoin in circulation= 65/100 x 4 000 000

B$=2.6 million for every 4 million people

But we have other elements as well but overall, I showed you at the beginning of the chapter that four elements make-up 96% of the mass of the body the rest are trace elements.

Mass fractions of these elements are

; Oxygen 6.5 x 10$^{-1}$

That is 65% of the mass of a body or total population.

Carbon 1.8 x10-1

That is 18% of the mass or population.

Hydrogen 1x10-1

That is 10% of the mass or population.

Nitrogen 3x 10

That is 3% of the mass or population

Carbon which is represented by another crypto current must be 18 percent of the population.

18/100x 4 000 000=720 000.

Hydrogen being =400 000

Nitrogen being 120 000 for any given 4 million people.

There are other smaller amounts of elements, but which are irrelevant at the time.

So, for a perfect system, if we are to use a human body, we would need the above amounts or percentage in circulation on top of fiat money that is centrally held and operated.

**Carefully manipulation and not centralized systems.**

I know you might be thinking that this is becoming a centralized system where everything is rationed. The idea being that for a perfect government system as argued above fiat money alone is insufficient to cushion the effects that lead to the collapse and financial problems but cryptocurrency is needed just like the body requires oxygen, carbon, hydrogen, and nitrogen with these big four accounting for 96% of the elements in the body. It is a matter of balancing these as proportions of the government system. I pointed out that excessive or inadequacy of one can be toxic to the economy. It is a matter of playing with the numbers to reduce or increase, respectively. There are other elements that can change their form by absorbing other elements or by losing some. Water is part of a body and as above, accounts for 60% of the body and we know water is made up of two hydrogen atoms and an oxygen and above all some elements are attracted to some who have a negative or positive balance and this information can be used to offset some colliding these to reduce their proportions. Such knowledge would be vital to maintain a perfect system. I have heard people asking if it comes to cryptocurrency which ones should you hold and in what percentages? I think this model I am proposing will answer that question. The cryptocurrency is to augment the fiat system by providing a cushion and new functions that the current system is lacking. To understand this, I think it is wise to know the problems with the current system the fiat. Just like blood alone there won't be enough oxygen in the blood to transport other minerals like iron and if the oxygen is limited, the brain might shut down followed by other organs and this is what is referred to as a system crash. Just like with the wars what mankind was doing all these decades was removing the fire alarms so that the warning part if removed and local people or organizations then used to fight local fires but remaining in the buildings. A big risk that the fires might be very huge to consume everyone something that already happened with the 2008 financial collapse. In a perfect system, fire alarms are there and when they sound warnings of fire people run out of the buildings all of them even the fire marshal who will go back to see if they can contain the fire. This is the perfect world. The current system ignores and conflicts with our rules the right to life and to self-preserve. The fact that when there is a fire the people are forced to remain in the building poses risks to life and contradicts self-preservation. Our system encourages running out as fast saving oneself and preserving oneself. The idea here is one of the people creating their own system that augments the current system so that the two can work hand in hand. I think you can recall from the earlier chapter that I argued that the purpose of life is that of us becoming so clever and intelligent and understanding that we know easily the things in life that we can solve our problems and even create our systems to match those of the central system. I argued that God or Allah out of bored and not because he needed mankind created humanity so that one day man will be very intelligent to know what is good and evil and can he be allowed to stretch his hand and eat the fruit of the tree of life and live forever.

Genesis 3v22

Then the LORD God said, "Look, the human beings have become like us, knowing both good and evil. What if they reach out, take fruit from the tree of life, and eat it? Then they will live forever!".

The gods are jealous that mankind now that he knows what is good and evil, what will happen if he can do the same as us and eat from the tree of life and live forever. This is a justification given for seizures by the state and all the money laundering schemes. The government can be rendered useless overnight if the people establish their own money just like with Bitcoin. So, we can see in countries like China governments clamping down on cryptocurrencies. My own belief is that in the end is to replace the government fiat scheme with not just cryptocurrencies but with something more advanced that combines cryptocurrency and something else. The current system although it is like the blood that is needed it has either to evolve greatly or be changed altogether. Fiat alone is unworkable and the arguments throughout this book are that all the current systems crashed years ago and the governments and everyone else are just hanging in there hoping for the best. But we know change is imminent and inevitable. So why do we have to wait? Our laws will clear all bottlenecks and problems with the current centralized system. I can say the current system has the following problems some of which are addressed by cryptocurrency nevertheless we need a perfect system without these issues.

### Problems of the current fiat system.

>The current system is based on faith and trust in the government. How many times have the governments deceived, manipulated and tricked their people? How many people honestly trust their governments. The current system relies on this idea that people will simply trust the governments no matter what with the results that they often deliberately abuse and use fiat money to justify their actions by manipulating their availability and controlling who gets it. A form of indirect blackmail. The current economic, social and financial climate has, so many problems induced or deliberately started and linked to the governments. This has led to the selective distribution of certain services to certain people while neglecting others especially those who don't trust the government with the resultant inequality. Trust in the government is the cause of huge inequalities as people put their trust in the government to deliver and often let down as they can be denied services. The current fiat therefore is biased and heavily influenced by the central parameters. The problems we have are a direct result of institutions and government influence. I gave my version of 9/11

as a trigger of the global collapse initiated by certain powers to gain from the crash. So, the government can do whatever they want to influence the outcome. I pointed out that 9/11 was part of a roll-back strategy designed to take money back from the people to the central governments taking even their savings and destroying all jobs leaving the people better off so that in the end the governments have so much power to bail banks out. So, in short, the current system is unpredictable it just depends on the mood of the President and government and financial institutions parameters. I as the leader of TWO am opposed to such ambiguity. We want a system that can be trusted and predictable and that is supported and augmented by-laws that close all loopholes and not just removes bottlenecks but also hold everyone accountable for their actions. The fact that the government can deliberately increase the money supply through printing some to devalue the money is a cause of concern as the value of money can easily be lost overnight. The government can implement policies that will affect everyone and give them a competitive advantage over its citizens. The fact that most governments are corrupt makes central control a dodgy aspect of the system.

>All the above only act to increase the risks of collapse as everything is systematized and the impact often great as a lot of institutions etc. will be affected in case of system collapse sending the whole thing down. The current system will only make things worse by increasing global debt that current is above $247 trillion. The governments are incapable of solving this let alone run their countries effectively. Our laws and approaches will not only eliminate these problems but provide a sound system that can be predicted and can't be abused or manipulated. Mind you we have outlawed all wars often used as covers for gross abuse and corruption. We will hold these people to account and no policies or strategies will be used to justify killing innocent children as they will comply with our laws which involves fiscal aspects. So, it's a comprehensive or holistic approach that will only see results.

>problems with centralization means most people will remain without bank accounts globally as they will not have government-approved IDs and the whole process treats everyone like terrorists and denying most of the people who really need such services. I

think it's a shame that some governments used terrorism to push as back into time. We were heading in the right direction with less fuss at airports, etc. Then after 9/11 everything become worse like in the previous decades. This is a common problem throughout history that mankind has a tendency of going back recreating previous problems to justify jobs. I pointed out that after the tremendous in medicine, living standards and knowledge and education humanity nearly eradicated diseases and all health problems. Then the leaders to fulfill their political agendas then started encouraging universities and private companies to make bio-engineered viruses. At the same time asking other companies to start working on the cures of these bio-engineered threats. After much controversy, the bioengineering stopped. Then now some countries have started making digital cyber threats and hoping that some people might start looking for ways to eradicate all these. The same issue here. People made traveling easy and fast and safe. Then come 9/11 everything went back again to the state things were like before. What we have been doing for the past century is to replace the same problem with an advanced one and then start all over again looking for solutions when we should be reducing and moving to other areas.

>The idea set out decades ago was to make everyone be part of the banking system and improve literacy rates yet still the system is so cumbersome and restrictive that not only people are denied services and facilities they are discouraged in knowing how things work as bureaucracy and central control and censorship make everything not appealing.

Our aim is to make sure everyone here on earth has a bank and access to bank accounts and it does not have to be so rigid. We will aim to provide a global space identity recognized worldwide that will simplify everything and make opening bank accounts as easy as getting a mobile phone. The basic accounts shall be for everyone with advanced accounts based on the ability to pay.

The role of cryptocurrency.

I think Bitcoin goes some way in dealing with the current fiat system, but it must be complemented by even huge projects. If money is blood and for argument's sake, I say the current system needs to be evolved but can still be part of the system mainly for larger issues and leaving Bitcoin and others dealing with the day-to-day of local issues. Then there must be another currency that combines the blood that is fiat money, Bitcoin that is oxygen and hydrogen to make water currency or equivalent as water accounts for 60% of the body and can solve shortfalls of both the Bitcoin and the fiat money system. Oxygen has a polarity in that it can be charged on one end whereas water is and can be charged on both ends. The stream of water tends to bend due to this polarity. A shared pair of hydrogen bonds the oxygen and hydrogen. Water's density has unevenly distributed electrons. There are other properties of water that includes having a high heat vaporization rate, huge surface tension, and acts as a solvent and has a high specific heat rate. Water presses non-polar molecules together. In other words, water can be ionized to release acids and attract bases where a pH of seven is neutral and between 1-6 the pH or acidity rate can be said to be acidity and above the neutral seven is said to be alkalinity usually between 8-14. So if water was a cryptocurrency it would be the ideal element in that it is needed as part of the whole system taking both the strength of the fiat and the Bitcoin combining these to come up with a solution that can be used and not be biased but easily controlled as we saw water being bent by static electricity. The fact that water is universally soluble if cryptocurrency will easily be used globally reaching billions still unbanked. The cryptocurrency must be easily absorbed and manipulated to convert other currencies or even join some currencies together. So, in short polarity of water makes it if cryptocurrency an ideal medium of exchange.

## Cohesion

It is the presence of hydrogen that holds water molecules together and creates surface tension that water can have a bigger surface tension than the area containing it before falling off. Imagine a cryptocurrency that can exceed the area it is to serve or a huge population before its collapse.

Adhesion which allows water molecules to the attached to another surface.

We have a detailed fiat and cryptocurrency plan. We have our own cryptocurrency the Futuregoldcoin and the Calycoin. I think it's best to illustrate the problems first before providing the solutions. Our comprehensive solutions are in later Chapters. You can read our Whitepaper that lays down our plan for the global system and the monetary policy. Check the appendix as well.

# CHAPTER SEVENTEEN

HUGE INVESTMENT IN RESEARCH AND DEVELOPMENT.

*We should aim to live longer up to 200 years for now and forever. What can be done?

*Imagine $1.7 trillion being poured into research and technological development?

*Imagine what things we can achieve that can help humanity? Imagine the kind of jobs that can be created? The possibilities are endless.

*Imagine companies' competition to come up with the best plans, software, technology, etc. all to improve human life?

Current military technology can be adapted or evolved to benefit humanity. We are tired of destructive technology we have seen enough. Can the same technology be used to enhance life? To create life. To help humanity solve today's problems. The military can adapt or evolve something I have been saying in earlier chapters. Above all, to help fulfill the first rule research and development into prolonging life, enhancing the quality of life, elimination of defects, diseases, and any genetic defects should be our priority. We are outsmarted by animals like tortoises that can live up to 200 years. It's not just about prolonging life it's about the quality of life as well. It is a grave offense to make technology that ages the population very fast as is the norm in some developed countries simply because the government wants to hold the bull by its horns and decide who dies and when. I think most governments are taking the easy route of failing to think and make bold decisions to change the current norm. I think it's not just irresponsible but very complacent for governments to make viruses that end life and load your own people with watermarks. Eugenic movements still exist although pushed underground and disguised as population or immigration controls. The same technology that is being used to reverse all life processes can be used to prolong life if perfected well and supported by new laws that punish anyone who reverses human body functions. The implanting of devices to all populations at birth poses a big risk and might threaten human existence. This is because since its artificial intelligence someone might hack the system and kill the whole country in their sleep. There are so many risks involved in replacing the natural nervous system with a remotely operated implanted medical device. This is what is happening especially in developed countries had nothing to do with the need to enhance or prolong life but everything to do with government population control. This is how it works.

### Artificial Intelligence to delay the aging process and or prolong life.

The technological advancement has meant devices being made to help governments control the population in these cases the aging population. The aging population is a big problem in developed countries as the strains on the government's balance sheet are huge with huge pensions and health bills. So, governments invested $ billions to find a way to kill the old after reducing their life span by speeding up the aging process and to raise money as well for those who can pay for aging to be slowed down, etc. At birth; all children through the works of the Pediatrician who implants a small device soon after birth on the baby's lumbar bone and an electrode needle fired into the left side of the back-leg area. The device is like a small propeller that rotates like the airplane engines but smaller with sucking and expelling properties and can rotate in either way with valves that can be opened or closed. The device has GPS properties and is operated like a drone remotely. The electrode is used for stimulation through electromagnetic nerve manipulation imitating the body functions through a sophisticated program. The device can be programmed so certain activities can happen at certain times. This device can be used to speed any processes like sperm production, puberty, growing fast and aging. The device acts like a mousetrap and can be used to blind people as it can pull the iris of the eye to the side or up to obstruct sight.

1. > Device is used to blind people as a weapon or a defensive weapon. Imagine walking and suddenly the device flips and turns the iris at a certain angle into the socket so the view is blocked, and you can't see. The device is used to immobilize people as well. Imagine you are an enemy and about to attack someone prominent and suddenly the iris rotates into the socket so that sight is lost, and you are automatically immobilized.

2. > The device is used as a warning and separation device in that imagine the enemy has the device as well and when you are in the vicinity, the device triggers a mechanism that warns you that someone usually an enemy is around. This is not a big issue since if you all have the same device then it means you are on the same issue above all both of you have to have GPS properties and there must be a third-party controlling the exchanges of transmitted signals acting as the receiver, the decoder, and the transmitter. This person will know as well if you are getting closer. The idea is derived from the airplane radar system with different planes on the radar and warning systems activating when a plane comes near the other.

3. >The device can be used as a weapon a Cyber high-tech gadget that emits electromagnetic signals that are harmful that can immobilize the enemy say by switching off the enemy's device putting him to sleep or blackout.

4. > The device can be used to store certain feelings and scenes in life. Let's say someone has the device and is hit by a lorry if someone is linked to that person through synchronizing the other person who is linked to the person who has just been hit by a lorry whom we can call the hacker can feel whatever the person who was hit felt. So, in other words, you can transfer the feeling of a person the moment that person died. That means you can use the device to torture other people or make them feel horrific feelings felt by a person just before he or she dies. This is one of the areas the device is being used as a weapon to traumatized people as they felt all the pain felt by say a stab victim. In worst cases, the device is used to kill as the device is used to imitate the same damage say suffered by the victim hit by the lorry.

5. > The device is a weapon in that it captures the damage done by

a bullet that hit another with a similar device. If the two are synchronized, then someone through amplifying the device can be used to cause the same damage to a person say thousands of miles away. So, the device is a killing machine too.

6. > The device can be used to stress a person to breaking point as it rotates continuously non-stop until a person commits suicide.

7. > The device is used to cause brain damage. Imagine a drone in your body rotating continuously shaking your brain until it's a mess. That can-do damage as all memories can be wiped out.

8. > The device is used to trick people as if they are testing how they can remember things or follow instructions. What happens is that a person is given instructions in his or her sleep and tested the next day if he or she can still remember the message in the dream. If he can remember the message in the dream, then the shaking to test what he can recall as brain porosity or the rate of retention of messages. What will then happen is that this becomes common that after being told a message in his dream his brain is shaken pretending to test the retention capability of his brain to easily remember things but what is actually happening is that the brain is being changed from a solid stuff to mash and liquid with time therefore causing brain damage?

9. > Linked to the point above is the fact that the teaching hospital pretends they are coaching secret tricks when whatever one does is told to through signs from other people or through digital messages that are sent to the device. What is happening is that there are creating a dependency situation where the person can't use his own decision waiting for input? If he disobeys, he is then tortured but if he listens, then he is rewarded. In the end, his brain is distorted as in the end they will remove input ending up hesitating fearing to be tortured he becomes undecided.

10. > A GPS on a human being is a breach of all international laws and above all, it conflicts with the first rule the right to life. GPS uses radiation and or harmful waves. The main reasons for these devices are to snoop and spy on everyone as a national security thing but nothing to do with security but a political strategy to control the people.

11. > The device is used to kill people at will simply by switching

off the device choking the victim or blocking other functions.

New strong laws are needed to make sure that the mentioned above will be a thing of the past. Only technology that enhances life should be invested into.

## Dangers of being hacked.

Implanting devices to the whole population might not be a clever plan if the system can be easily hacked and everyone blinded or put to sleep. This can mean cost in terms of security and new laws to punish hackers might be the answer.

## Cyber electromagnetic attacks.

There are dangers of attacks digitally through cyber electromagnetic waves.

Cyber electronic attack (cyber EA);

"Is the use of electromagnetic energy to attack an adversary's electronics or access to the electromagnetic spectrum with the intent of destroying an enemy's ability to use data via networked systems and associated physical infrastructures."

In the above chapter, this electromagnetic energy is used to attack the device of other people so that the device malfunctions or distorts the working of the device or completely erases the data causing the malfunction. Bear in mind that the device is a small computer running programmed software. This digital software can be tampered with and might malfunction. If an electromagnetic bomb is detonated all these devices might be affected and if everyone has this device, then it can bring humanity to extinction something referred to as Global Catastrophe and Existential risk.

## Benefits of such technology.

I explained in earlier chapters that a family is the micro perfect representative of a perfect world with everyone working together for the benefit of the family unit. No one in the family will waste precious resources to make weapons to kill other siblings it's just common knowledge. So, if the whole world is one big family why we waste precious resources on weapons, the military, and defense. The family unit is what it is because the head of the house makes stiff rules that must be followed for the betterment of the whole family. Likewise, Tomorrow's World Order will put laws to make sure there will never be wars as we know them. All weapons will be banned. Why make these old-fashioned weapons that are expensive and a waste of resources? A family is bound by blood and DNA with the father and mother there to cement bonds between siblings. So research will focus on finding ways to replicate the 'blood and DNA bonding' and if that means using advanced devices to link the whole world so that the device acts or replicates 'blood and same DNA' for the sake of peace and working together so be it. Now technology has let humanity down, but I can stand here and say that it is not the technology at fault, but you are the problems as humans. There is an old saying that guns don't kill people, but people kill people. There is a lot of truth in there. Now you have a visionary and as such I will do my best to make sure we put laws to deal with short-sighted leaders who go for short-term benefits and neglect long-term goals that really count. Technology shall be used to enhance life and not shorten it unless if you want yours shortened. So, devices can be used to connect everyone and bridge the gaps that cause you to fight each other.

## Other optional or likely situations. In-built guns.

I think if in the future we can't get rid of the need for guns what we can do as an option is to evolve these guns. We can have what I have always called an in-built gun. Only Tomorrow's World Order will have the license to operate these guns for security only as all security issues will be in the hands of us leaving the leaders concerned with running their countries and answerable to us only if they violate the rules. Like I said above the rules are universal and now is common knowledge but easily abused or overridden by other issues mainly defense is the bigger culprit. So, everyone knows that killing women and children is a bad thing so why on earth do we still do it? So, we have made these issues into the first laws. No one shall break these laws and these laws will detect what will follow. All other issues that conflict with these first laws are illegal and forbidden by law. So only TWO will have access to in-built guns we can use to terminate violators clean and fast in their sleep or in broad daylight. We are accountable and we are unbiased and therefore fair and the perfect body to run the globe and let the leaders run their countries. I mentioned the ineffective of the UN that they are like security guards with no guns or powers to arrest violators. We are different. We have powers to kill and impose immediate judgment and action. We are not a creation of any country and don't represent anyone. Only TWO will have the license to use these in-built guns to kill.

## The In-built Gun.

Guns of the future will simply be a thumbnail size device that will act as a linker of all humans and the device will have two sides like a coin and for most people, the device will be stuck on the good side enhancing life and keeping people young. We don't want people living forever wrinkly and old. So, the challenge is not just to prolong life but to reverse the harmful effects of aging. I will look at that later. The other side will happen when someone has violated our rules where we will use our powers to kill. Institutions like the UN are there to make sure the countries that formed them remain viable forever and as we have recently noticed these countries are the same countries, we are saying that they are causing worldwide problems by interfering without an understanding of local issues and with one aim to gain a competitive advantage whether of getting cheaper oil or other resources. We have noted recently that we have a bully or cult or gangster, so the system has crashed. Only a new system of running the globe can solve the problem. The rise of Tomorrow's World Order.

Huge investments in research and technological development will start from the basic to enhance and prolong life while reducing aging rates and reversing aging effects in everyone irrespective of ability to pay. The money we save from the military will do the job. In this age weapons made of metals, carbon fiber, etc. are and will be a thing of the past as I explained above if we still need guns for national security, we can develop thumbnail size devices that will be effective guns and or weapons of incapacitating enemies. But the goal is never to make weapons again wasting resources when everyone is becoming friends and a family. So, the reason behind banning guns, weapons and the military is to enhance life. Research and development should aim to understand why people age and the way they age. I know this could be going down, but I bet no one might have found the answers otherwise the richest people today would have paid $billions to have such a technology. We have billionaires aging very fast themselves unless it's a matter of choice. This is something we must not see in the New World because that will defeat the cries for longevity. No point living longer as a frail old man. So, more money into research and development. If the military somehow can help, then that's an evolving aspect of it. So why do we age as humans? Is this process reversible? Or can we delay the aging process? What can we eat and what must we not eat, etc.? I personally think there must be laws on what people can eat and can't eat and what people can apply on their skin and what can't they apply. I know this is a gray area that still needs a lot of research but TWO will ban eating of certain foods no matter what the general people think. The idea is for the betterment of humanity and the quality of life. What I have discovered is a growing trend that to be recognized as advanced you have to eat or use things that are developed with advanced technology. I think this is the only area I think technology will not work but stick to things we have known for some time. Although research is needed, I believe we age because of a natural process and because of the things we eat and apply to our bodies. Our bodies are made of flesh that is natural but recently we have been taking a lot of chemicals inside and on the skin. If a body is a natural flesh can chemicals of any type be a problem as the body lose their stamina? Are the chemicals dangerous over time despite taken in very small quantities? We apply a lot of skincare elements all of which have one or two components as artificial chemicals. Will these chemicals influence the functioning of the body? I know we have had stories of wonder chemicals etc. but we are aging fast and rough despite the advanced technology. So, my question is are we really doing great as in advancing or somehow technology does not work in this area. Would you not think it is wise to apply to your body or eat only things that your body can use? Surely a body will not use chemicals we see in lotions and other skincare so why do we feed our skin with dangerous chemicals. Would it not be wise to use the food we eat inside as care for the skin? You must know that the skin absorbs chemicals through pores on its surface. Imagine using light treated oil that has no chemicals that might be harmful to your skin. This natural oil will be absorbed and get rid of the body leaving the skin lubricated. Wrinkles are a result of face oil vanishing as we age and how we feel inside. So, a less stressful life can reduce the pronounced wrinkles so it's not just about cosmetics it's a comprehensive approach. Our laws of eliminating the stresses caused by weapons and other weapons and the competitions on resources can starve other areas. Our laws and policies will enhance life and help researchers find answers quickly.

## Traveling and technology.

There will be laws that encourage technology advancement into cheaper clean transport methods. Our dream is beyond the current system of boundaries. Our model of the future like I said of the family unit. Picture a family house with rooms up and down and a common lounge, etc. You know the easiness of going from one area to the other although your sister might shut the door to her room, but you can sneak in when she is not there. You don't need a license to go to your brother's room although he might kick you out. So, the globe is one huge family that must be linked somehow. So, transport will play a major role. The next stage we are pushing into is one of technological advances and advanced networking and cooperation. In this stage, we are so advanced and highly educated with high self-esteem that we are now mature we will have realized that we are all humans and as such, there is no need to kill each other. Imagine the days of slavery that really caused slavery was not the hatred as people think it was a need for cheap labor. A need to get things free and make a fortune. Now we have realized that instead of yearning for cheaper labor we have realized that we can sacrifice other areas like the military because there will be laws in place banning any kind of war. Laws that are enforceable and which TWO will carry with such effectiveness that violations will be a thing for the past. We will have developed rockets and spaceships that will not go to space or moon alone, but which will be used for global travel. Money should be used to make the globe one huge family without unnecessary boundaries. The idea is to have personal missile planes that will launch and travel to another part of the earth in minutes. If we can use the same technology to go to space and moon surely, we can use the technology to connect the globe. The idea is to choose cheaper energy that is clean. Eclectic cars or if we can use water as fuel then let us find that technology. Competition to find solutions and awarding huge contracts if a solution is found. We have a lot to do.

We have a website;

www. globalspaceidentity.com

that we will use to issue global identification that will in the long run replace your country identity or will complement your own identity. This will give everyone on earth license or passports to travel anywhere globally. Initial we might charge a small fee to get the identity that will act as a global passport. This will be easy to get and will be processed fast as well. Traveling should be easy and fast. Years before terrorism it was much faster than terrorism ruined everything and took us back to the years back. Our new laws dealing with terrorism will clear this bottleneck. I mentioned in an earlier chapter we must develop first-class infrastructure much better than now. Even if it means making houses in the skies, we shall do that so that traveling will be augmented by an excellent infrastructure with people easily booking hotels, etc. globally or others renting their houses when not in use for certain hours, etc. The idea behind this is that the world is like a family and as such, you can do anything you can do in your family house with easy. TWO will clear all the bottlenecks and unnecessary bureaucracy. Education.

Education should be responsible for education. I am surprised that some universities offer a course to find ways of making the deadliest strains of weapons biological, digital or electromagnetic. New laws must ban these courses or degrees I think it's irresponsible that encourages dodgy practices. If you find the strain, then what? It's not only banning these but giving severe punishment even death simply because making these strains conflicts with the first rule.

# CHAPTER EIGHTEEN

OUR JOURNEY SO FAR? WHAT IS THE YEAR? WHAT SHOULD
BE THE FUTURE LIKE?

I think the most important thing for the future is to change
drastically from the current practices. We should change from
making cars, trains, and busses made of metal and steel to more
environmentally friendly material tough but light as well. There
will be a law to ban all vehicles that rely on fossil fuel; petrol and
diesel vehicles. We can channel more money into research and
development to develop vehicles that use other sources of fuel like
electricity or even water. There must be laws to clean up the clutter
we have now on our roads and above all clean the atmosphere and
reduce carbon emissions. So, a law banning all today's cars by a
certain date. All cars made of metals and steel and use petrol and
diesel to be banned globally or phased out depending on region
but eventually with all these cars out of the roads. Heavy funding
into new materials preferably lighter cheaper or recyclable. This
will help fight climatic change in the long run. We can have
electric cars like now with the Tesla project spread globally with
cars being made cheaper but from other materials other than metal
and steel. This is the challenge. But we will not have issues as we
will have also changed the military and reduced the budget
channeling resources into things, we need rather than big boys'
toys. Mind you the laws to ban wars and any military interventions
will be in place. TWO will deal with all global issues. Most of the
buildings and infrastructure that are for a certain time or age must
be replaced with a more modern building, especially if they are
residential. The idea is to provide futuristic, modern-day buildings
that are energy efficient as we will pass new laws as well to replace
fossil fuel heating, etc. So, a new law as well as banning the use
of fossil fuels globally in residential buildings first but to include
other buildings as time passes. Heavy investment in solving basic

needs through the provision of modern-day energy-efficient infrastructure. There are other materials on a building that can be banned as well to improve the quality of life. Housing standards globally will be drafted and enforced. Each country will be forced to channel the military budget towards other areas so it's achievable as the money is there but being misused.

### Food security.

The final report of the 1996 World Food Summit states that food security "exists when all people, at all times, have physical and economic access to sufficient, safe and nutritious food to meet their dietary needs and food preferences for an active and healthy life"

Wikipedia.

Our new laws will make it easy for governments to priorities basic needs first simply because a lack of food has a direct impact on the first law the right to life. It will be illegal to satisfy other areas skipping the basic needs of which food is one. Imagine all countries globally stop making or buying anything to do with wars and using the money to improve the quality of life for everyone by making food easily available. The New World is a different world where it is a crime to jump sufficiently providing basic needs. Look at the basic needs pyramid and this is how most governments will operate in that decisions should be made to satisfy the bottom layer basic needs before moving to other level needs. So, it is common sense satisfies the base level before moving to a higher level. Then satisfy the next level before moving to a higher level. I know you might be thinking that it's impossible but if you look at all the laws, we will put in a place you will discover that all the laws all augment each other by freeing resources elsewhere as we ban unnecessary activities. We are going to be tough. It's not just about freeing up resources it is also about increasing food production.

### Democracy.

I think the main reason why we have the problems we have regarding democracy is a result of the by-product of our other policies. Defense as I have argued makes it easily to infringe on democracy as we prioritize other policies. But our laws will make it illegal to override the first laws the right to a life of everyone on earth, enemy or friend and the right for each person to preserve himself or herself. So, recognizing these first laws will make it easy to eliminate all the problems we have about democracy. We prioritize humans and the rest will follow. We will have removed the dependency on the military and defense to drive the economy. We will write more direct laws that will make it easy for everyone government to be as democratic as possible making sure that its citizens are involved through proper representations and making decisions that the government will take.

## Global Finance, Trade & Investments and Terrorism.

I personally think that the current financial system is flawed. I know it has been there for as long as mankind can remember but don't you think that it's time, we change everything? I think most of these financial institutions like big banks all have roots in slavery or were involved in one way or the other. Some were formed from proceeds from the sale of slaves that went on to be loaned. So, from the start, the financial institutions are tainted with blood. The theme throughout this book is that of starting again from start removing the current system because my argument is that the current system has crashed and therefore obsolete and only a new system will replace the current system. This is not replacing just for the sake of changing, no but this is coming up with an up-to-date system that will not crash. A system so robust that we won't experience the global financing crisis of 2008, again.

So, we will put new laws to target certain cults, governments or individuals who think they can steal global finances with some dirty tricks. Our research has uncovered some practices where certain cults are looting from all banks something I will discuss later. So, first things first, we need a new financial system. Since Tomorrow's World Order is responsible for the whole globe, we will make a single currency that will be used globally but can complement the countries local currency. Ours will be the main currency to cushion country-specific currencies to fight inflation and still make it possible for each country to be different and unique. I will reveal our financial plan later. This is different from say the euro in that this is not protected like the euro. The euro is not a free market, but a market restricted to its members. You must be a member to join and enjoy the benefits. Our currency will be the currency that can be used in all countries. New laws will secure the financial institutions from further collapse.

## The New World Order.

Here I want to divert a bit and mention something that you might confuse with Tomorrow's World Order called the New World Order. This is totally different from us in that these few, but powerful people are a group of people who believe they must play God to save humanity from things like overcrowding and starvation by killing people themselves. There is totally a different approach to ours in that these people are not concerned about changing the status quo no. They have ideas to let life go as it is but to take preventive actions that involve killing some people directly like what God would rather do through earthquakes, floods, famine, and diseases. These are not like us because these are the people advancing for the manufacturing of lethal viruses biological or digital with the aim to use these to kill some people in order to ease the pressure. Whereas our policies are to preserve all life but to change our priorities by ending some activities of which the military and weapons manufacturing is one. The New World Order advocates for the creation of vaccines that will act like time bombs and maybe explode after say 20 years killing everyone immunized as a way of controlling the population. Their main worries are that if the population is left unchecked human extinction might be the result as one day a world war might occur due to increased inequality and they can't leave things to chance. So, they must prepare and put things in place to reduce the population by killing some people. These people accuse others of having Weapons of Mass Destruction in order to attack nations and get resources like oil so that they make WMDs to use on the very people whom they stole resources from. These are the very people accusing others and then go on to make the same WMDs which they are killing others for then goes on to further kill these people. So, we are different. My vision is not to kill anyone but to enhance and prolong life through research and technology. I have put strict laws that forbid playing God. It is a criminal offense to play God by killing innocent women and children. In our New World women and children are the most valuable with most laws centered on them and the rest will follow from that. Our laws protect everyone including man, but I think all the problems we have are because we are not safeguarding the lives of these people as we should do. The New World Order is secretly advancing for a zero-carbon in Europe and other areas. This is not just the carbon as in carbon dioxide. This is a pseudo-name that refers to the reduction and completely the elimination of people of color from Europe by say 2025. This became an issue years before the world financial crises when coastal areas like Greece, Ireland, Portugal, Spain, and Cyprus did nothing to stop the influx of migrants. So, this crisis could have been a warning from the central powerful EU countries a strong message that says protect our borders or we are going to run out of money. These people are advancing the implanting of devices to all foreigners with GPS functions as a population control measure. I personally think that the financial crises were an induced event that was destined to cause the collapse of the financial institutions with the result that a few cults or some of the New World Order were to benefit heavily financially. How?

I will explain.

9/11 as a trigger of the financial collapse.

Although we share the same sentiments that if nothing is done, mankind will bring his own end as the world keep on increase making weapons and increase the military spending for example in 2017, we spent globally $1.7 trillion. But we have become one family and fewer countries want to be enemies of other countries. So why are we still making weapons? Okay, maybe who are we going to use the weapons on? Aliens? Dinosaurs? Or other people and who? North Korea ducked and all other countries want now to be friends opting for peaceful deals. Everyone fears that mankind will one day fight each other in a fast war where all weapons nuclear, digital, electromagnetic, etc. will be used as more and more resources are used war will be short resulting in the extinction of mankind. So, what the New World Order and other cults are doing is what all law enforcement agencies today would do. Remove and limit all financial access so that people won't make weapons and use the money to put things in place to make sure that people will never have a chance of forming groups or cults resulting in a war. So, all the looted money is then used to make highly sophisticated cyber high-tech gadgets that will kill all potential warlords. But still, this does not explain the financial crisis?

Okay, I will explain.

Financial crisis.

The New World Order is a group of highly educated people with degrees and all have been to a university and belonged to a university's club where ideas were debated, and suggestions made. More often where global problems were discussed, and solutions noted down. So, we are not playing with a layman with GCE O levels here. We are dealing with the cream of society here people who have learned secrets at universities and applied teachings to come up with solutions most of these solutions are used by say the FBI in tackling terrorism for example e.g.;

"cut off financing and other forms of support provided to."

FBI Website.

So, 9/11 was a calculated and coordinated way of causing the collapse of the economy. Thereby removing finance globally and accumulate this in order to make sophisticated high-tech Cyber Weapons of Mass Destruction. Through chipping everyone to control who dies and when as a population control to reduce pressures that will otherwise trigger an instant friction. Inequality rises as the government keeps making weapons at the expense of food etc. So, are you saying 9/11 was a prediction tool or trigger for the collapse of the global financial markets?

First, there is a scientist named Christopher Wren who in 1654 devised a clever way of predicting called the cycloid which can predict stock markets collapse.

Cyclone;

"A cycloid is the curve traced by a point on the rim of a circular wheel as the wheel rolls along a straight line without slipping." Wikipedia.

According to this Wren, a cycle can move in a straight line without falling over time and from there came up with an equation to predict precisely e.g. when the collapse or crash of say stock markets would occur.

A circle can be divided into twelve parts from 1 to 12. A line that is horizontal can then be drawn across the circle and marked in equal parts of twelve as well. The equation of a cycloid;

$x = r (\theta - \sin \theta)$

and $y = r (1 - \cos \theta)$.

The length of the hump of the arc length is 8a where a is a constant normally 9.99 rounded to 10.

The area $A = 3\pi A$

The cycloid in the stock market will show the highest point the price of a share will reach before the price starts falling. This is the highest point on the curve which is a cycloid that is half curves say as the circle spinning in a straight line. To find the period it takes for the share price to reach the highest level you will need to know some basics about a concept called the Time-ball. In short before the invention of personal watches time was determined by the fall of a Time-ball. A Time-ball is defined as an 'obsolete time-signaling device' used in the 1830s. The idea was that a ball called the Time-ball was placed high up the tower that was on top of a building before being dropped at a certain time say 1 pm to determine the exact time which is determined by the time it takes to drop to the roof of the building. So, the fall of this Time-ball was used to determine the exact time. Ship-owners and sailors as they had no clocks, or their clocks used to lose seconds would want to know the exact time. So, the local officials would ask for a small fee to tell the exact time. So, it was a way of raising money for the cash stricken local authorities.

So, the Time-ball was used to tell if a pocket clock was telling the correct time. Okay why this is important to 9/11? The twin tower's building 7 was built using the Time-ball principle. The way it falls was intentional as a Time-ball it is meant to fall the way it did in free-fall to determine the time it takes for the building to collapse an indicator of when the global financial markets would fall. So, to the educated sophisticated people or people aware of this they would easily note the time it takes to free-fall and uses the cycloid equation to calculate exactly in real-life that is in years and not seconds the time it will take for the financial markets to collapse. So, if you have this information you can invest by buying low and when the share or whatever you are trading reach their highest or if the time elapses, then sell high before fall and maybe buy low and sell high.

So, in the meantime, we go back to the equation to solve the equation now that we know that the World Trade Center building 7 free-falls at 6,6sec which is 6.6 years in real-life. If you look at the 9/11 attacks, you can see that the planes did hit the towers at angles. We need these angles to calculate when the markets would collapse remember we are in September 2001. So, a search on the internet for angles of impact. The North Tower was impacted at 45 degrees from the true north and the South Tower at 340 degrees. In mathematics, Y is the vertical axis of a graph and X is the horizontal axis.

R is the radius of the cycloid or curve we have drawn. [Read more about cycloid to understand this].

We know that $\pi$ is a mathematical value represented by 3.14159.

The value we get by calculating these coordinates on a graph will give us the Sell-point this is the highest price any share or graph will reach before starting to fall.

Radius from mathematics is the diameter divided by 2=d/2

Circumference is pi multiplied by the diameter $\pi$xd.

The cycloid is a split circle.

The length of the cycloid is 8a where a is a constant 9.9999 say 10.

C/2= $\pi$d/2

8a/2=3.14159xd/2

4a=2r x1,57

$4a=\pi r$

$4a=3.14159r$

$r=1.17a$

$\sin 45\circ=1\sqrt{2}$

$45\circ$ as a fraction $=45/360=0.125$ $x = r (45° - \sin 45)$

$x=1.17a(45°-\sin45)$

$x=1.17a (45°-0.707)$

$x=1.17a (0.125-0.707)$

$x=1.17a (-0.58\ 2)$

$x=0.68a$ A is a constant that is normally given a value of 9,9999999 or simply 10

Then x becomes $0.68x$ 10 $x=0.68x10$

$x=6.8$ that is 6 years eight months.

The year is 2001, 09 [September]

Plus 6,8 years

2007.89

So, the total collapse is in 2007 September. The exact time the global financial markets collapsed as well.

So, if you were in 2001 and know about all this the Time-ball and the cycloid you would know that by 2007 September the financial markets would have completely collapsed. So, you would have known that to gain you have to sell earlier or wait for the collapse in order to buy cheaper before selling higher just depending on what you are investing in. I will now explain the detailed points you must add to understand that okay terrorists destroyed the towers but were they part of the bigger plan? We know the Twin Towers contained financial records of investment banks and institutions and a lot of government departments with records if destroyed can cause major issues?

First, before all this, I will tell you a method used to recover if you like money from one sector to the other. In life, money move from central institutions to the periphery sectors. So, money moves from central governments in the form of salaries, wage bills, insurance, pensions, etc. and from banks in the form of loans and mortgages to the people in the form of salaries, wages, loans, mortgages, insurance payouts, pensions, etc. Normally there is a method that can be used to move money from normally the periphery back to the central institutions the central banks and the government which I call roll-back. This is a way of creating situations that you will be able to collect back money that has gone out and even more through a process of ball-rolling. Imagine a ball of money rolling from the hill the central institutions growing as it rolls squashing houses and taking all money. This money getting stuck on the ball that the ball keeps growing until it's big and somehow rolls along the hill to the other side of the houses where someone will pick it up and this person is part of the central institutions only working somewhere else who will keep the money because the ball can't roll up the hill. What you should know is that the method is used to reverse a former move to offset the negative effect of a previous transaction.

### Roll-back method.

So, to start with there must be a huge imbalance caused by the central institutions the banks and or the government. This creates a huge hole that needs to be closed or plugged. The decision-makers then create a situation that will trigger this process. So, the method cannot work without a form of trigger because the trigger will set a chain of events that will cause the roll-back process. One thing to note is that the method does not only offset the initial imbalance but cause the complete collapse of the periphery because the huge rolling ball will collect and destroy everything including the savings of the people that in the end, they will have nothing left even jobs as the huge rolling ball will empty all confer with a lot of the companies closing.

So, what starts the imbalance?

10 September 2001. The missing $2,3 trillion.

Just a day before the 9/11 attacks Donald Rumsfeld announce that;

"revealed that the Pentagon had lost a whopping $2.3 trillion (£1.72trillion) from its budget."

So, we have an imbalance that needs to be corrected. But first, how did this come about?

Wages can do real damage to the coffers of a government. Imagine soldiers, pensioners, and government contract especially military ones who just get paid while we keep the weapons without using them. This is like a waste because monthly you pay contracts for weapons deals weapons you are just going to shelf. This is a major problem that in the end governments might be compelled to start a war if criticized for wasting resources. Read again in an earlier chapter that we are creating a time-bomb still making and investing in the military when we don't have any enemies. A small friction can and will trigger a major world war that can result in the extinction of humanity. So, it can be inferred that criticism of wastage might have set a ball-rolling forcing people to trigger a situation that can justify a war. I am not saying this is exactly what happened but just a logical explanation. So, on 10 September we have Donald Rumsfeld criticizing the President that he lost $2,3 trillion and probably incapable of running the country. I explained why this is a problem; money spent on wages and salaries. So, war can get some of this get them killed and save some money. Or what the point of all these weapons deals and the military when we can't even go to war. What a total waste! Now wait for it; boom the trigger. The second is to do with oil purchases. Throughout this book, I have explained why nationalizing oil made oil prices to go up. I also mentioned Eisenhower's arguments that he can only go to war is the nationalized resource was oil simply because oil depletes the nation's money. Probably the real reason why $2,3 trillion was missing. It means had been used up through purchases of the oil. This coincides with the petrol queues of the last years. We can deduce that the two things doing damage to the government balance sheet are oil purchases and the military cost that includes the military wage and salary bill. So how can we solve these two issues?

## The trigger 9/11 attacks.

To set the ball-rolling there must be a trigger that will make the people make certain decisions to further trigger other events so that the ball will keep on rolling collecting all money as it goes in the process destroying homes. Picture a domino effect with pieces falling and hitting the next piece until all pieces are down. The trigger is not just any trigger but has to have certain characteristics otherwise the whole domino effect won't work.

Characteristics of the trigger.

>It must be a public event or things witnessed by all.

>It must be live and broadcast all over the globe

>It must be horrific to cause traumatic effect

>It must destroy instantly any sense of security and render everyone vulnerable

>Must shock and frighten to be the sole effect of the next move

>It must have a far-reaching impact that people will make decisions based on it

>Must remain in the minds of the people for at least two years

>Must destroy and cause death to cause the release of pensions and insurance.

First a little background on the idea behind the World Trade Center towers. In 1654 a British scientist called Christopher Wren designed a container for bees that had three levels that were made of glass that is a see-through container for keeping bees. His aim was to trap the bees inside the container so that they make honey inside. Also, to observe what would happen to the bees if the alpha males are taken and put in enclosures as in Colony Collapse Studies. Over time he observed that the bees no matter what avoided the third top layer when smoke from the fire is introduced in the container the bees would get stuck in the top layer but would try to fly out through the top layer instead of going down. In Wren's design, a single opening linked all three layers so that bees would fly up and down. In 1666 in London, a major fire that destroyed nearly all residential areas and the whole city of London broke out between 5 and 11 September 1666. Christopher Wren born 1632 now an architect saw an opportunity to solve all London's problems at the time and quickly drew a blueprint plan of London which he submitted to King Charles II while the fire was still on. The plan was the answer to all London's problems. London was experiencing the Great Plague of London that started from 1665 to 1666. This plague only ended as a result of this great fire. The plague was believed to have been spread by rats which were prevalent in the city of London due to poor building standards, overcrowding, and neglect by the city officials. It is believed;

"The earliest cases of the disease occurred in the spring of 1665 in a parish outside the city walls called St Giles-in-the-Fields. The death rate began to rise during the hot summer months and peaked in September when 7,165 Londoners died in one week. Rats carried the fleas that caused the plague. They were attracted by city streets filled with rubbish and waste, especially in the poorest areas." National Archives. The time the fire started the authorities had tried very hard to contain the plague, but carts of dead people made numerous journeys in and out of the city to the burying grounds. The Mayor was more like the undertaker organizing removal of dead bodies. The plague had killed nearly 70 000 recorded deaths just in London. The architects of which Christopher was one at the time had raised alarm bells that action needed to be taken. The problem was that he could not convince the people to sell their land and houses to be destroyed to pave a way for a new plan and city. The streets were narrow, and no one followed building standards and the authorities did not enforce either because apart from the plague England had just come out of the war with the Dutch. There was no money England was paying its navy soldiers with vouchers. So, the authorities knew it was pointless to enforce building standards as people had no money. Who set the fire is not important here because he did what was in the minds of most of the people? This Christopher Wren was overjoyed when he realized that someone had started the fire. He had advocated for a new building plan for London but faced still objection as the people demanded more money for their land and the king normally responsible for building houses at the time would not pay the requested money. He had no money his brother James was the commander of the navy ship. So, the overcrowding and poor standards and the narrow streets and the use of prohibited materials like grass for roofing and wood instead of mortar or brick were all common issues. The presence of rates had been attributed to the spread of the disease. After the Great Fire of London, insurance money was paid out for people to rebuild their houses. This was in 1666 and 80% of the city residents were made homeless. In 1667 A Fire Court heard the queries and claims submitted by the owners of the houses which were destroyed. So, the insurance payouts were for almost every house in the city.

Minoru Yamasaki designed the World Trade Center although not admitted he used Christopher Wren's ideas and designs of the bee's containers with transparent glass, three layers and a single lift that goes all the way to the top layer but with other local lifts. His plans for the World Trade Center were like Wren's designs in that the transparency was incorporated in through the use of the rib vaults and flying buttress. This Minoru Yamasaki had previously constructed the Reynolds Metals Company Building made from aluminum. This Christopher Wren discovered that if fire and smoke were introduced into the container the bees would not attempt to get down but would be stuck in the top-level or try to fly out through the top instead of flying to the bottom layers. I want to point out also that the design was a death trap and whoever was behind 9/11 knew this as the points of impact by the plans were the very critical points for any escape. The people had no chance of escape and the authorities knew this. That could explain why people were told to wait in there. [Listen to the tapes and calls for help-YouTube]. So, this was a death trap. The position where the planes impacted the towers were elevator accesses the only way-out. It can't be a coincident. The angles of impact which are crucial in the calculation of the cycloid used for prediction were the critical escape points. So, what the planes did was to block these points so that the people had no chance of escape. Their deaths were planned the very moment they entered the building and not when the plane hit the towers. The plans were just a means to an end. I mentioned above the characteristics of the trigger above. The trigger must traumatize the people and destroy any sense of security. Shock and frighten and show the authorities as powerless and must be in the open broadcast everywhere so that the impact is felt everywhere to induce a stage that will make them act on the next step. The idea here is for the trigger to be the sole cause of the next move. The 9/11 plane attacks were the perfect trigger as you will notice below. An event that would render everyone powerless and leave them fearful and traumatized. The event must be live and traumatizing to put everyone who witnessed it and watched it in temporary insanity due to traumatic events so that in the end, they will make decisions in that start. If the event had not occurred or if they haven't witnessed the event, then they would not be in a traumatic state and would not make the decisions they are supposed to. This event also would make say a bank that would not give mortgages or loans feel sympathetic to the people and not follow their rules or flex the rules out of sympathy if you understand. The event must make people use emotions rather than sound facts. Something we put into law called the Presence or Lack of Empathy. The event must make people change and not do what they would normally do. The authorities would feel sorry or be depressed that they won't care about say profits but helping people in times of sorrow. This is the reason why the planes hit the towers in those places to bloke entrance and create a death trap so that people die on your watch to put the whole nation in a traumatic state so that in the future they lax rules and regulations and start helping people out of emotions and not sound judgment. It's like a thief charming you in order to steal from you only that this is the opposite in that sorrow is used to make people vulnerable and above all to give authorities alibi for making wrong decisions, so they are not blamed or persecuted in the future. Temporarily insanity.

**9/11 characteristics as a trigger.**

>The event was live in broad daylight if you watch the videos some firemen were rehearsing for that event waiting under the towers with cameras. See the impact of the tower by the first plane what are the chances of an event like that being captured as it happens?

>9/11 trigger a traumatic state as people witnessed others dying helplessly.

>9/11 was broadcast on national television as it happened globally.

>Death traps as people jumped from the top level of the towers top their death as they had no escape routes.

> Desperate calls for help with the authorities not attending but suggesting people stay in there knowing that they were going to die.

>Death of the rescuers themselves in numbers further traumatizing the people.

So, before I proceed what do you think was the intended intention of such an event assuming it was deliberate? To answer this question, I will take you back to 1666 during the Great Fire of London. London experience a traumatic event like that with people shocked frightened and traumatized but unable to do anything. I can suggest that the fire was started deliberately. The fire was the only answer to all the problems of the day. You can imagine the feelings going through the architect or the Mayor for that matter. The Mayor of London was reduced to an undertaker instead of running the city he was now responsible for the removal of corpses. It is believed that 100 000 people died in less than 12 months most dying in their houses and the plague was contagious being spread by rats eating dead people or their excrement. Mind you London had no sewerage system people would collect stuff in buckets and a cart would go around emptying these. The streets were narrow and there was overcrowding. Building standards were not adhered to because people were broke. The authorities saw no need to enforce the building standards. The country had no money, and it was just after the war. So, it a war, then a plague and a fire in less than 2 years. The architect could not do anything people object to the plans of a new city. They refused to sell or give up their deeds. They asked for higher compensation rates for displacement. A fire was an answer to everyone including the king. The king's father Charles I was murdered by the people as he believed he was sent by God and 'only God can judge me' thing but the people refused that and said no one was above the law and got the king killed. So, at this time the kind was weak people often reminded him of his father, threatening to get him killed too. So, a fire was a blessing regardless of whether it was started deliberately or not. Come 2001, mind you, Newyork is an official twin sister of London of 1666 because this King Charles II's brother James of York whom the city was named after [New York James Duchess of York]. The blueprints design by the architect Christopher Wren above were used to build New York in the USA when they took the city from the Dutch through battle James of York has been a commander of the navy ship. We find the city authorities in the same predicament. The Twin Towers the time they were leased to Larry Silverstein they were nearly out of their life that is obsolete. The materials used to build were poor materials with asbestos etc. Removing asbestos would have cost them more than the value of the building. The heating and lighting were too expensive and occupancy rates were low. Larry just like Christopher Wren had shown much interest in rebuilding the buildings and was offered a lease.

## What is the catch then?

You must note the differences here between the Great Fire of London and the 2001 attacks.

>The Great Fire destroyed the whole city and more than 70% of residential accommodation. This means insurance payouts offered by the Fire Court in 1667 was for almost everyone who had a house so a huge influx of money from the central authorities to the periphery people. This money was plowed back into the market as deposits for more mortgages and loans. The money kick-started jobs as well in construction, etc. So here there was the multiplier effect that the whole economy benefited.

>The 9/11 attacks destroyed private buildings mainly for offices. Even if people died, people had houses already somewhere and the insurance payouts would not be plowed back into the economy.

> The effect of the 9/11 attacks was to make people feel vulnerable from tall buildings and choose houses and homes instead of security. Unlike the 1666 Great Fire of London, people did not get insurance money from destroyed houses, but people went on to

take houses and mortgages based on nothing. Before the 9/11 attacks people had no intention of getting a house or a mortgage simply, they were of sound mind and knew they could not afford it. Banks before 9/11 did not lend to a single-family etc. because they knew they could not afford these.

>9/11 changed everything and the government 'out of pity' relaxed mortgages laws and opened access to housing for everyone without the means to repay the loans or mortgages. See the difference with the 1666 incident. The people in 2001 could not afford the houses but mostly because of the easy access end up using their savings as deposits for the houses and relied on jobs to pay the mortgage. Before 9/11 they were sure they could not afford after 9/11 favorable conditions introduced by the government made it possible.

> Banks and mortgages lenders gave out loans and mortgages even when they knew they could not afford it. The people used their savings and wages to keep up with the repayments until a time when they could not pay. Two years after the event of 9/11 the trauma had started to be forgotten [psychological period for a traumatic event to last before people come to their senses. All a mind-game.] People realized that they could not afford and started missing out payments before default with repossessions following.

> People are now in a worse situation than before. Now they don't have their savings as they used all or some as deposits as owning a house was tempting. The market has no money. No influx of money from anywhere and the money has been collected by the banks. Companies start to feel the pinch and soon shut down as there is no money. In 1666 the influx of insurance payouts boosted the local economy above all the people had their savings and more jobs.

>Investments banks, banks, etc. now collect all these defaulted policies and bundles all and transfer or sell to another market say France, UK much cheaper than the market value. In the end, everything crashes as people lose their jobs and houses are

repossessed. A crash is then imminent as the bank makes losses by offloading these policies mainly abroad.

Recall I talked about the roll-back plan to take back the missing $2,3 trillion from the people back to the center? The effect of all this which I call a third type error which is to prescribe a wrong solution to a problem with the result that now the people will lose even their savings and jobs all the money now back to government as the government buys these defaulted securities and policies cheaply as well.

In that regard would you say 9/11 was a terrorist act or a sophisticated plan to make some people rich? So, guess who was the boss at the end bailing banks out and everyone else writing off debt? The governments. At first, the President was the man who lost $2,3 trillion, in the end, he was the main man bailing out banks.

## Coincident or a calculated murder plan?

I think you decide. In this light, I will make new laws that are enforced that will make our global finance secure. I will make laws that will close all loopholes and that will severely punish institutions, cults, government, and individuals who are too clever for all of us who would kill thousands for financial gains. This is not just about laws as well; I will put a dedicated team vested in all kinds of tricks that can be used by these crooks. It's about being proactive rather than the current system that is reactive. We need tough people who know how to keep our money. I will put recovery laws and punishment for those who think they can trick us and get away with it. We are not about change just for the sake of change we are about being smarter and training people to anticipate such actions. I think new laws should make it possible to go after some of these countries or cults or individuals even years after the incident. I will close certain institutions abroad and local that spread risks all over the whole hoping for a domino effect to roll-back the proceeds to them. When I am in power, this is a thing of the past. We want a world where everything is fair, and people are genuinely and deservedly rewarded. Tricks, short cuts, and abuse is a thing of the past it might cost you your life. I mentioned earlier that in the New World life is more precious than gold. Life is the sole existence of any government, institutions, cult and everyone else. The right to life is paramount and some actions regardless of what you are a President, Prime Minister, etc. can and will put you in deep trouble with TWO. Calls for a war to get people killed in order to reduce the balance sheet. Or acts that jeopardize the lives of firemen can't be tolerated. Under new laws, I pointed out that our boys and girls are the best we have so it is just logic that we protect them as well simply because you wouldn't want to lose your best. New laws will make it a criminal offense for the Commander-in-Chief etc. to give command that will result in the death of any soldier or any uniformed personnel including firefighters. These people and everyone else want to enjoy their pensions and all jobs that put lives in danger are to be carried out in accordance with the new laws. It's a thing of the past to make an order that caries risk to the lives of anyone. Our laws protect all Presidents and Prime Ministers and all kinds of leaders who would otherwise make a decision that would result in someone's death. Our laws if followed would see to it that no President or Prime Minister or anyone will ever be brought to a trial after their term in office has ended or lived in fear after that. I think it's morally wrong that President, Prime Minister and all other leaders would end up being given the so-called protection where there are used as guinea pigs being experimented on by the teaching hospitals doctors, etc. just to avoid being brought to justice. I know certain Presidents end up giving in to blackmail to avoid arrest warrants against their actions during office. Our laws make it easy for any leader to make the right decisions within the laws and celebrated for being a good President or Prime Minister. Weapons and wars are boys' toys that can get you. It is time the boys grow into responsible adults. I think countries that offer the so-called protection are the most abusers or influences of abuse of the global financial system simply because they let people do wrong so that they can show power by defending that person after the damage has already been done. I pointed out earlier that we must be proactive, and protection is based on a reactive stance. Look at the 9/11 hijackers.

"The 9/11 attacks were carried out by <u>19 men</u>—from Saudi Arabia

(15), the United Arab Emirates (2), Egypt (1), and Lebanon (1)."
Wikipedia.

If you know the history of the Persian Gulf, you will notice that
the source countries of these terrorists and protection which I think
is still implied and valid. There were nineteen men altogether. 15
of these were from Saudi Arabia. So, what happened in 1915 to
Saudi Arabia?

1915 Saudi Arabia. The treaty of Darin.

Saudi Arabia at the time during the treaty was known to be suicidal
fighters who would jump through windows to attack. In 1915 the
UK entered a protection treaty with the ruler of Najd who went on
to form Saudi Arabia promising him to protect him and as an ally
against the Ottoman Empire and against pirates and terrorists. So,
are pirates to Saudi Arabia? Was the USA considered as a pirate
just before 9/11? We can tell there were several incidents where
the US has been accused by the Saudi's as stealing oil and with
the USS Cole and the MJ Limburg incidents being the proof.

The Sultanate of Egypt in 1914.

In 1914 Britain declared war on the Ottoman Empire and later
signed a treaty making Egypt its Protectorate after having veiled
protection where it was just a de facto protection without formal
agreements.

United Arab Emirates as the Trucuial states in 1917.

The United Arab Emirates [UAE] had a Protectorate status from
1820 with the British to 1971. This was part of a lot of the Persian
Gulf states that included UAE.

Lebanon 1914.

In 1914 the British made a treaty with the Persian Gulf countries
of which Lebanon was part.

Between 1914 to 1956 Britain was the superpower giving

protection to Persian Gulf countries against oil piracy and terrorism. We see on the other hand the USA the Persian Gulf accused of being a pirate. So, can we say what happened on 9/11 was related to this? Even though these treaties ceased after 1956 there was a sense of Britain being a protector of the former Persian Gulf countries and we know the Persian Gulf always outsourced their protection. I think the effect of the Protectorate agreements offered by Britain is to give an exemption of any criminal acts by these countries even though they might have sent the terrorist. Recall I mentioned that they outsource their security through Protectorate agreements, and this exempts them as security is the responsibility of Britain.

This is the tricky part.

If Britain protects indirectly [implied] [see monarchical bonding between Britain and Saudi Arabia] all these countries where the terrorists come from, Saudi Arabia, Lebanon, Egypt, and UAE could that explain also why the USA never mentioned countries where terrorists come from? I would have thought the USA would have mentioned or threatened Saudi Arabia as well. This could also explain why Britain cooked the Iraq dossier to divert attention to Iraq without any implied agreements. It's a real challenge. To solve global finance and any impact of terrorism goes beyond all this but we are prepared to write a new chapter in history.

Terrorism.

I have looked at the issue of terrorism in earlier chapters, but I would like to point out that we are prepared to solve terrorism once and for all. I think it's a fact that terrorism is a horrible act and should be a thing for the past. Terrorists attack civilians to push their agenda and as such, there is no room for them in the New World simply because their acts conflict with the first rule. The right to life. I think it's not about putting people in Guantanamo Bay but to try to understand why they do what they do. This is not a recent thing the British have been dealing with terrorists since the 1820s the main reasons why they provided Protectorates status to all Persian Gulf countries. Back then it was understandable simply because the fighting was for oil with people grieved. Was 9/11 about oil? I mentioned above that 9/11 could be the culmination of grievances that started way back in the 1980s with the USS Cole and the MJ Limburg incidents among others. The Persian Gulf countries see the USA as a pirate crossing their waters to steal oil and waging wars that kill their women and children as they interfere favoring some countries like Israel at the expense of others. So surely Tomorrow's World Order would be in a better position to handle terrorist issues. The only promising fact is that all terrorist activities I have researched are associated with reactive motives. I can say these terrorists are revengers. They don't attack unless they are attacked first something that can give us something to work with. Most are reactive they kill as revenge for past events and their reasons [see Osama bin Laden's grievances] states that too. Banning weapons and wars is the first stance and making sure that no woman or child will die regardless of gender, genetic heritage or geographical locations. I mentioned earlier as well that we will look at cases to make sure that they don't have genetic heritage-related connotations where a person simply lacks empathy because he or she does not relate to the victims in other words he or she feels nothing to be bothered but this person is of good standing. Say a leader orders the waging of war knowing that even if civilians die, they would not be of his or her genetic heritage and as such is not bothered about what you can call collateral damage. Stiff punishment life for life here applies and in serious cases, his or her family should be included in the punishment as well. We want a world where our laws are effective and observed regardless of where one is. Gone are the days when these leaders give commands that kill more than the people they are trying to kill. Terrorism is banned under the law and we shall at the beginning address all issues globally as weapons and wars are banned. We shall start with a reconciliation method that addresses past issues. This will include bringing people to justice if are alive. New laws to change past laws that limit times when people who have committed grave crimes to face justice. I think this is a major problem, and this encourages people to commit crimes knowing that when the time to bring a case to court has elapsed, then they are free. New laws to make sure that the courts shall be funded heavily to deal with all cases. I mentioned from the beginning that if you are breathing, there will be no excuse not to be brought to justice for past acts. Only death can exempt anyone from facing justice and for some of the crime has a lack of empathy connotations or of grave concern even after death the courts will still pursue justice. We will make sure all the courts globally have no time limits. Look at the Crime of Aggression law. It's a good law in theory but what is with all the time limits? Are you telling me that people didn't know that killing women and children is wrong even before the inception of the law? I think this is a slap in the face of justice. We want a law that says it doesn't matter when you committed a crime if you are breathing TWO will fight for justice. Removing all-time limits is the only road to reconciliation and justice. The current system limits time simply because funding is inadequate but when we are in power, especially the first years the courts get the chunk out of the budget. They will operate 24/7 if need be. We shall rewrite new laws to support this. It's easy to see why this is easy. Imagine someone now enjoys life after killing 100 000 people and someone is dragged through the courts for killing a fraction of that? Time limits have no place in the New World. This will be the sole vehicle for reconciliation with everyone alive facing justice. The new generation will thank us for this as they will start with a clean slate. A real new start unlike if they are to mix with the evil they might be 'contaminated as well' surely something we don't want to see. A real problem passing of evil secrets from generation to generation. Imagine someone having known about the Great Fire of London and the current situation in 2001 and used the information to trigger the collapse of the global finance in the process kill 3000 people and after the war a further 500 000. I think the above argument will put an end to copycats' events or the use of past events to cause more problems for financial gains. New laws to deal with this in that if it's a crime, no one shall be exempted simply because he or she might pass the tricks to someone else hoping that he or she can make a score and get away with that as well. So, people who have committed crimes regardless of when should be brought to justice. For the sake of a new beginning.'

# CHAPTER NINETEEN

PUT THINGS IN PLACE SO THAT HUMANITY WILL NEVER REVERT TO OLD PRACTICES.

*Working at optimal capacity

*We have everything we need.

*No one should be sacrificed but aim to reduce aging rates.

Its criminal and therefore give severe punishment for those deliberately inducing aging of their population in the name of the so-called protection.

* Express-command to put an end to this through our laws and courts as a deterrent.

Putting things in place is something that will make sure that humanity will not be tempted to revert to old dodgy practices. I think this is an area where technology will play a big role. Use of open-source peer-to-peer and blockchain technology. I think it will be easy to develop software that will make it easy to report issues of abuse, torture, and violations of our new laws.

## Apocalyptic laws and reporting systems.

The peer-to-peer and the blockchain technology can be used to develop software that can record incidents as they happen and make then instantly report or log these onto the blockchain. This is useful in situations where abuse is perpetrated by those in power or in a position of trust. This will eliminate fears of being targeted or any further abuse, as the information can easily and instantly be stored on the blockchain and stays there. Countries where they violate rules the institutions are quick to cover up and further abuse the victims in order to silence them. I think this blockchain and peer-to-peer technology might be very handy as the culprits be it government officials can be pictured at the very moment the abuse is happening and the information can be sent instantly to a peer who then informs trusted bodies.

## Blockchain as a way of enforcing our laws.

Today's problems are augmented by the fact that most culprits in a position of trust get away with abuse and murder for lack of evidence. Countries violate international rules knowing that it will be hard if not impossible to be brought to justice and technology can become handy too as new gadgets that can be worn by all state parameters can be easily identified and by through apps in phones which send their details to the blockchain. So, all government officials are to carry gadgets that easily let the public identify them, their number, name, etc. The gadgets must be able to pick this information up if they are in the vicinity and be able to store this information on the permanent blockchain. This will deter any wrongdoing or stalking and make people accountable, so they earn respect and be respected and trusted too. I think this technology will come in handy as well when dealing with suspects and evil people. It shall be a law that everyone will carry or upload an app that will send information to the blockchain. The idea is that if you are not violating our laws, then you have nothing to fear. For the violators, you shall not hide or get away with murder. This technology will be used to track you and deliver justice. That alone will act as a deterrent too. Like I have said we shall swear by the assassin to deliver justice. It shall be one man for himself and TWO for us all.

## Technology in New Digital Identification.

I have proposed also in earlier chapters that the idea of the New World involves free or easy and fast global movements of people, goods, services, and money. The idea is to link everyone and connect everyone somehow and provide the means to do so. In the end, the world should relate to advanced and well-connected networks be it transport, communications, or monetary. This cryptocurrency is just the beginning. We need a form of digital identification that will avoid the current cumbersome bureaucratic system that is obsolete. It will be an easy task to create software and a system where people will have IDs or methods of identifying people that do not require physical passports, etc. The idea is to digitize everything and make it easy worldwide for people to travel from one country to another with speed. There could be a digital app that can verify a person's attributes to confirm it's him in seconds or minutes. An example would be the use of the peer-to-peer and blockchain that takes a person's fingerprints, records his or her voice, scans iris, and gets his digital signature that could be anything or a saliva sample and the information sent instantly to a checking and verifying service that response within minutes as information is sent swiftly. A scan code that acts as a digital passport can be released instantly which the person simply has to scan to pass the passport checking service. The idea is to provide the technology to everyone for a certain fee that can be paid in digital currency.

## New Global Currency. The Apocalypto Currency.

Read our Whitepaper for our detailed financial plan involving; The New Single Reserve Global Currency. This is a global currency for mainly global financial transactions but mainly to act as the new reserve global currency that will work side by side with local currency in line with our money-printing plan to fight hyperinflation. But here I shall only look at the other function that of global currency for all financial transactions as complementing and even replacing national currencies. I think the globe will need a new currency that I can call Apocalypto currency or Apocoins or Apomoney or simply Cryptocurrency or Calycoin and the FutureGoldCoin, in that this money is public money that is not hidden as opposed to the cryptocurrency that should be used for private transactions. Apocoins will be digital as well but used to pay for global services that are universal and involves governments and other institutions as well. The reason being that this currency will replace or work side by side with local countries' currency. Apocalypto currency is revealed or open money in that all the transactions will be available publicly and everyone will only need to make a request to see what the money was used for and when. This will show money spent on government services recorded as digital and easily accessible to the public. This will remove fraud and corruption as the money is digital and all transactions are recorded as well and can't be altered the only difference being that the recorded information is not encrypted or hidden but therefore for everyone to see. This will be government-to-government money, company to company with the idea of operation on a macro-level whereas the current cryptocurrency is mainly on a micro basis. The other difference being that digital currency privacy is important hence the encryption. The Apomoney is on a macro-scale and done between governments, institutions, and even country to country and there is a need for transparency so there is no need for encrypting the transactions. Apocalypto currency will be used globally as a digital currency to solve all the problems with fiat money. In short; Apocalypto currency or Calyptocurrency to replace fiat money based on a block in blockchains with bundled together transactions at a macro-level covering government-to-government bodies and globally. No encryption for transparency. Everything is revealed that is in the open. Used for government transactions and service. Used in conjunction with cryptocurrency where crypto for peer-to-peer at micro-level. This is at a macro-level with conversion to crypto for personal use and converting back for government use. Use advanced algorithms that use a block in blocks bundles systems.

Tomorrow's World Order patent for Apocalypto currency.

Patent Apocalypto currency, Apocoin, Apomoney

TO WHOM IT MAY CONCERN.

I David Gomadza has developed an idea today on 03 July 2019 and which I will patent as a new and useful process of the global financial system and the system is referred to as Apocalypto currency. [Read our Whitepaper as well in the appendix.]

This is a digital currency that is 'revealed' in the sense that the digital transactions are not encrypted but are left open so that anyone can see and verify them. This is based on 'macro or block within blockchain' where transactions are bundled and compressed before being recorded in a macro blockchain. There is no encryption as it is not necessary as we need transparency to fight fraud and corruption, etc. This is on a macro-scale but is based on the peer-to-peer notion but on a macro-scale [government-to-government or institution to institution] with a block or bundled together bundles within blockchains i.e. several bunches of entries bundled together which are compressed though. So, compression of the individual transaction will be involved and the individual files of say institutions or government bodies will be 'revealed' that is decompressed upon request. So, within macro-huge blockchains are bundles of related files e.g. transacted on the same day with details of the transaction, etc. The information is permanently kept. So, this system of government and global money will co-exist with cryptocurrency that is done on a micro-level peer-to-peer complementing this. Individuals are concerned with privacy so all transactions are hidden or encrypted whereas my method will be on a macro-level with transparency at the heart. Accountability will be guaranteed with such a system. This will remove issues of fraud and corruption associated with fiat money. The system will use macro blockchains with bundles instead of individuals transactions. The system can be used in line with another idea of global digitals IDs. This is a form of identification that records and gives access to people without the need for government-issued passports. Each person will apply online and submit digital attributes; fingerprints, an iris scan or even saliva, voice scans before given a digital identification like a scan code. The app will ask for face or iris, or saliva scan and the information sent digitally to a verifying organization or server who offer another pass as a scan code that will then be used to identify everyone making transactions. The idea is to link the person and the transaction digitally so there is traceability and accountability. All these transactions are recorded permanently and as the name says open or revealed to anyone if they can make an official request to access that information. This Apocalypto currency is not centralized in meaning that it is controlled by government no. It is centralized in that Tomorrow's World Order will be responsible or will nominate someone or agency or body or private company to run this. The government will have no part nor lot in influencing this currency's mining activities and will have no control in influencing it by say printing more as they do with fiat money this will keep inflation low and stabilize or even keep the currency at the above levels. How much digital Apocalypto currency will be mined or available depends on many factors, but the idea is to create a new system that settles today's global debt and provide a clean sheet at that time we will put current fiat out of use; obsolete. So global debt stands today at $300 trillion so the money should be maybe quadruple enough to settle the debt leaving the globe with more available.

## How apocalyptic currencies or money will work.

I think with digital currency it will be possible to have both at micro and macro-level in the economy, but I think a system must be in place that will see to it that crypto money will pay and be used for individual transactions and nothing to do with the government. If you want to pay for a government service, then you will need to convert the money to Apocalypto currency. So, Apocalyptic money will pay for government services and anything to do with institutions related to the government. A currency converter should be readily available the idea being that everything that uses Apocalypto money is related to the government or official global bodies and will be made transparent and every transaction regarding individuals and cryptocurrencies will be encrypted. Recording of transactions will be easy too as apocalyptic currencies will automatically be recorded on macro blockchains but after being bundled together. While cryptocurrency transactions are recorded on peer-to-peer micro blockchains. So, government officials will use apocalyptic money to pay for anything to do with the government and crypto for the private transaction and the transactions recorded separately even if carried out at the same time.

Sincerely

David Gomadza

Signed

03 July 2019

Technology can be used to create a system of networking that links people globally and where people can offer say accommodation to travelers. The idea is to facilitate movements and provide easy access to accommodation where people if say on vacation, can lend their houses for certain times or just for certain hours and everything is done through gadgets and apps that checks the identity of the person and pay in digital currency instead of booking hotels, etc. This is to work complementing the hotels and hostels of course. The idea is to apply smart contracts where individuals do everything themselves as a peer-to-peer and void the middlemen and paying high fees. The idea is to increase accessibility and networking globally with prices the only restriction if you like. The government and banks to have no links. Government should not be linked to banks or have contracts with banks where the bank might borrow someone money in bad faith knowing that the government will buy that debt and make the person 'a slave' as what was happening after the financial crisis with governments not bailing-out banks but buying slaves in broad daylight whom they later tag and abuse and put on death row blackmailing them claiming that they wrote off their debt so they have to do what the government wants. The idea here is to change the current money system replacing or complementing this fiat with the Apocalypto currency that is digital but can have some notes made and printed but ideally is to make sure that the whole world use this single currency but the government can have their own digital currency as long as it does not have the problems of the fiat money system or as long as they agree to follow our monetary policy. I have dealt with the global money system now I will look at the global law system.

## Apocalypto Laws.

I think it will be ideal to develop software that uses the blockchains and the peer-to-peer system and apply this to law. This will create another form of the law system where individuals can collect information and evidence and log this to the blockchain and then give addresses where the information has been stored before submitted this to decentralized judges and courts that will supplement the current system. Laws will be easily downloaded on apps and phones. No one will be able to plead ignorance as the laws will be easily downloaded on apps. Like I wrote above I will remove all-time limits to all cases globally. If someone lives if they had committed a crime, they must be made accountable to that. The court system will be 24 hours courts operating no stop with information sent to the blockchain easily accessed and downloaded and everything made fast. The laws are referred to as the Apocalyptolaws because they will be transparent without any encryption so that everyone can easily see them and read them. It will be easy to report officials who think they are above the law with individuals sending information or incident and pictures of the people involved straight away for safekeeping on these blockchains. The advantage is that that transaction or act will have several attributes like the time and date and location and possibly recorded conversations and images as well. The gadgets will have other properties like the ability to identify the blockchains being used in that vicinity as addresses where the information is stored. The person will later check the blockchain or app activity for that month that can be easily downloaded like a bank statement where he or she can cross-reference and check the details of the incident. The app will have the ability to identify say all apps IDs that can be traced to individuals.

The idea is to present an alternative with the aim of completely abandoning the current system so that humanity will never revert to ways of doing things we are saying are now obsolete and must be changed.

### Blockchain and the future.

I think blockchain has been a godsend and we haven't seen what can be achieved through the system and the distributed ledger that has made it easy to record transactions instantly and permanently cutting off a lot of waste and unnecessary bureaucracy. The idea is to use this system to change all current methods and replace all with faster methods that use this blockchain system. All current government services and systems can be replaced by ones that use this system.

### Digital ID system.

The identification system like I said in earlier chapters can be replaced by a system that is digital and one that uses the blockchain and distributed ledger so that IDs are easily obtained without the cumbersome time-wasting current system. I proposed the existence of an ID verifier who can be an agency or company contracted out or a smart server with results in minutes and a code given to confirm access. The scan code is then used to act as a pass-on top of the personal digital attributes used to ID a person. The system can be global something I am advocating and going to see-through. The idea is to sell the idea to those in power so that the private sector spearheads the change we need.

## Voting system

Blockchain and the distributed ledger and smart contract all present endless opportunities for improving or developing a new fast and fair voting system that reduces costs and mistakes and makes the whole thing transparency and faster. Linked to a person's digital ID people can vote in larger numbers than now.

## Patents and Trademarks

There is no doubt that the current system is slow and very costly. In fact, governments are providing these services simply to raise money than to provide a service. A lot can be done with blockchain and distributed ledger. The waiting times and the whole process after decades is not-fit for the purpose. The idea in the New World is to put more money in research and development that means the processes should be the best we have. There is no point in channeling $millions if not $billion when the system is slow taking longer and cumbersome and above all outdated. Blockchain and smart contract technologies can reduce waiting times and costs significantly. This is one of the critical areas that need a quick overhaul. Ideally, I would like a new system no matter what one that can be rated. This is the first step to modernize regardless if the current system is okay or not. If we are saying that all our problems are a direct result of the current outdated slow system, then the answer is to first put in a faster system so that the process of finding new technology and research is advanced. We must work hard on this area otherwise the whole project is a failure from the onset. This is a crucial area too as a major revenue for the governments concerned, they might push everyone else and chose to stick to what they know best then we are left with no choice but to put laws that will make sectors like this private. That is the offer to ambitious companies to handle these areas. I know this is controversial, but this is a critical area. Another issue is the fact that the government might ban aspiring companies or deny them licenses to do the same on the side and we are going to put international laws that make it a mandate that people have a choice and choose where they can register a patent or trademark. The idea is to give the company licenses too to do the same even cheaper and faster. Waiting for one to five years for a patent can't be tolerated. Other areas I don't mind this is a critical area and would prefer a 24-hour service for filling and all the needed checks and research. That also means super-fast search engines as there can be millions of items globally. I think developing technology is easy, the problems are to do with government bureaucracy.

## Technology development

Research and development are critical if we are to achieve our goals. The idea is to pass laws and remove all loopholes that make the process hard and offer an incentive. Governments usually discourage technological development indirectly through cumbersome laws and regulations. Laws should make the whole thing smoother.

## Financial systems

We have seen what the blockchain can do for the financial system with the rise of the Bitcoin and other cryptocurrencies. The good thing is that this will increase the number of people who can do financial transactions without the need to have a government given bank account. This means those denied a bank account can easily be involved in financial transactions. This, in turn, will improve connectivity and networking the most two aspects of the next stage of human development. This is mainly peer-to-peer private transactions where privacy is important. But what about the government sector? Don't they need a system similar? We know for sure the fiat money system is obsolete and not-fit purpose. Luckily, I have personally drafted a patent for an Apocalypto currency or simply FutureGoldCoin and or the Calycoin that is for government-to-government transactions. This is on a macro-level and since it's the government we are talking about building trust, we want a system that is transparent and that make people accountable. Combining all the crypto and the digital identity system will make the system fit for purpose again. We can talk about the New World but if the monetary system is not fit for the purpose, we will still have the same issues we have today. I personally declared the system obsolete and new laws and financial system is the way forward. I explained in earlier chapters why and if that is correct then we have been mending an obsolete system for seventeen years? I think it's time for a new way of doing things.

## Leadership.

You can invent the best methods of doing things or the best monetary system there can be but if you don't have the right leadership, I think it's a waste of time and precious resources because after some time they are simply going to ban everything. I think this has been the case for the past decades. I think this is not the first time we had cryptocurrencies or other ways to supplement or replace the fiat money system. The whole system is meant that the status quo is never changed. Not because these are perfect ways of doing things, it's hard to understand human nature. Some would rather waste resources to provide jobs for everyone than to improve services and become efficient and work fewer hours for more money. The idea in the New World is that time is very important. It will be a bad idea to trade time for money. In the future people will have other ways of making money easily. Time will be spent with loved ones and learning and inventing things. Digital currencies if understood will pave the way even if they last for a few years people will always find other better ways. So, the most important aspects now are creativity, innovation, and leadership. I think I will devote the next chapter to this topic; Leadership.

# CHAPTER TWENTY

LEADERSHIP, CREATIVITY, INNOVATION AND THE OBSTACLES AHEAD.

The business dictionary recognized that;

Leadership involves:

*Establishing a clear vision,

*Sharing that vision with others so that they will follow willingly;

*Providing the information, knowledge and methods to realize that vision, and coordinating and balancing the conflicting interests of all members and stakeholders.

*A leader steps up in times of crisis and can think and act creatively in difficult situations.

Read more: http://www.businessdictionary.com/definition/leadership.html

First, I differentiate between a terrorist and a New World visionary, a leader to lead the way by laying a clear path and vision to be followed. There is a great difference between a terrorist and the leaders of tomorrow of which I am. A terrorist is a vengeful person often according to him has been done wrong in the past and all that he is doing is revenging the past evil. Mostly they are not concerned about who dies. If people die these people will translate his feelings to whoever is the intended receipt of the message. So, terrorists use women and children and often target these killing as many as he can. He uses these as bargaining subjects with the aim that their cries will be his cries; their pain now was his pain in the past. In most cases, he has been through a lot directly and had lost a close one and this makes him kill without remorse. Most have what I can call local issues and their grievances are personal to them although they might use the religion to justify such acts. These people fight for the close ones and have a narrow focus in that their issues are localized. Visionaries or world leaders like myself are people who feel like humanity is not doing what they can potentially do and act upon that notion. These people see the waste and devious acts of the current leaders abusing everyone so that they remain in power. Their intent is not to fight the current leadership. They are not freedom fighters and don't feel oppressed. Leadership is not concerned with freeing oneself as they don't feel oppressed or abused. Their cries are for all humanity. They look at what humans could have achieved over time and why humans have the issues they have. This is the general view. These people have big dreams not just to change the world but to improve the life of all mankind. They invent new methods they strongly believe will work to change the current system. They always propose new systems better to current systems and, in most cases, establish a new system to prove it works in the hope that and strongly believe that humanity will come to their senses and abandon the wasteful, useless often obsolete current systems.

## My leadership.

I personally think humanity has missed several opportunities to advance the way we should have. I explained my views about life and humanity. I argued that life is not just life. Life is to be in stages of development and as such humanity has been stuck in one stage for centuries. Whose fault? I think there hasn't been a leader with courage, a clear vision, and the methodology to achieve that vision. Most of the leaders have been concerned with local issues central to them rather than humanity at large. We as humans have had several opportunities to move to the next stage of development the networking and cooperation stage where technological development will help connect everyone globally so that for the first time there is trust among different people globally. Trust is the most important thing. I can't blame humanity because a lot of things were working against trust. All surprise attacks, Pearl Harbor, Hiroshima, 9/11, etc. all have made it hard for anyone to talk about trust. Above all, this goes back to the beginning of the centuries with the two world wars. After the first war there was no leader to understand what was needed for humanity to move forward and as such what happened was talks about peace but without a clear vision of what world peace is and how we can achieve that. That was the first missed opportunity. What a visionary could have done was to oversee all the proceedings after the war. There lacked an unbiased person who would ban the war, draft new laws to ban the war there and then. Instead what happened is the creation of groups to cushion the effects of world wars rather than to stop the war completely. The LN was just there for cosmetics reasons just to make everything look good. It had no powers or have even attempted to ban wars and weapons production. That led to the Second World War. Even after the war what happened was another cushioning of the effects of war instead of stopping the war. A leader with a vision to pass laws there and then was not there. This time the West or Allies realized that wars were bad and never had a winner and as such changed their tactics from a defensive approach to an attack one. They then established the UN and the ICC to deal with the low-level threats mainly from Africa and NATO to back the USA and the UK who would be the leading countries in military attacks against any potential threats. We can see the problems developing already with all other people on a list drafted as part of a twenty to fifty-year war contingency plan. I explained in the other chapter that the West removed the fire alarms' in wars and decided to let everyone stay in a burning building by putting strong firefighters in place in NATO, the USA, the UK, and the UN through sanctions and ICC through the courts. So technically if these institutions are in existence and without them evolving, we are going to be stuck in the defensive stages for decades. Mind you it has been seventy years since these come into place and has the world become a better place? If they were humans, they would be pensioners now and as such hanging on by a thread. Here comes the need for great leadership skills.

**Need for a visionary leader of all leaders.**

The needed leader is one who is a visionary and is true to himself and believes he has a world to lead if that means banning wars, weapons manufacturing, changing the financial system, changing the courts, I mean everything so be it. My vision is to lead all and show the correct path we should have taken decades ago. We have a moral duty and obligations to all to make sure that we won't let a few people destroy all mankind. There are universal laws that give anyone a right to preserve humanity by showing the correct path especially when acts of some evil would result in the extinction of mankind. There are people who might take the law into their own hands and create mostly unknowingly a situation that will escalate and lead to human destruction. I think the current global leadership is tainted with the blood of innocent women and children and I personally think the line has been crossed unless a new system is put in place the world will always be the way it is with wars and all the killings and the wastage. If the world is beginning to trust each other is it not wise too to move away from the defensive economies which we are stuck in and save all these $trillion? Surely the world needs a new direction. The Iraq war was the final dagger into the system. The fact that even the UN acknowledged that the war was illegal makes it more mandatory to change the current system. It's time I put new laws banning wars globally so that no one shall die or be killed unlawfully. Laws that bring perpetrators to justice. Laws that will never be overridden resulting in deaths of women and children. Laws that demand evolution or the closing of most of today's institutions and practices. Laws that safeguards the life of every woman and child, regardless. Laws that put human life first where a command that unjustly results in the deaths of even a soldier can make the command giver be dragged to the courts. Laws that do not exempt or give immunity to acts of violence against women and children. Women and children are the voiceless people of any given society and a visionary would champion their cause and their safety. These are the people of tomorrow and if we let people kill these, then we are guilty too as this happened on our watch. All the above shall be the things of the past. The idea is not just to stop killings and unnecessary suffering but to improve the quality of life not just for women and children but for humanity alike. Our laws will remove all the obstacles to peace and the upholding of human rights. This is the big goal as all the problems we have today are due to people knowingly committing acts of violence directly or indirectly overriding common laws in favor of political and military strategies. There can never be such a thing ever again. Our laws will bring evil to justice for the next years. We need to start on a clean slate for the peace to take effect.

Technological advancement is paramount in the next stage and strong leadership is a must. Current laws are there to keep the status quo. The laws are drafted so that moving away from this tried and trusted stage is difficult if not impossible. The current leaders out of unfounded fear or experienced past evil acts will and might resist change. Strong leadership is needed to facilitate the development of technology. Only technology will see us through this stage. It's not just about technology as the current leaders will simply frustrate development by imposing restrictions or refusing to change. Change will only come when everyone understands and appreciates that the current system is obsolete, and change is imminent and inevitable. With good leadership, technology will make everything easy and fast. Technology will help the globe link and trust each other through fast communication and connections. Technology will make us realize that we don't need these obsolete forms of weapons and machinery that are heavy, relies on precious metals and fossil fuels, etc. We are in the digital age and we must move with the times. A strong leadership is needed and will negotiate on behalf of all technology-developers. To make it easy for their new systems to be appreciated and adopted if not by the mainstream then by an alternative system. I mentioned above the need for fast digital global identification systems. But the government might stifle progress by a cumbersome bureaucratic system and regulations, etc. A strong leadership will make it easy to establish a decentralized global system of governance as an alternative of the mainstream working side by side as a transitional phase until the government is able to improve its services as well. Good leadership will not just propose laws and regulations but will see to it that every government must follow these. This leadership must see to it that these laws are followed. My leadership is not about establishing another UN or NATO but about showing the injustice being down and let these institutions evolve. Evolve or cease operations simply because everything they stand for conflicts with the vision of the New World. There are so many areas that need changing and good leadership will come in handy hence the rise of TWO.

## What is the role of Tomorrow's World Order?

We are to lay down our vision of the world which humanity should know about and acknowledge and in the end be part of. This is for the good of everyone. We have a duty to make sure that a few people will not end up destroying everyone else. We have taken a leadership role because the situation has made us stand up. Instead of jumping out of the bus that is going to nosedive over a cliff thereby killing everyone, we have decided to stop the driver and let us drive the bus in the other direction. I think the world now is one-sided biased and getting more and more evil as they join cults and grow to enormous sizes. We saw the impact of such a situation during the Iraq war where there was no one to even try to stop the war with the resultant deaths of women and children. I think humanity is not performing as it should be. We are wasting a lot of resources on defense when we are forming networks globally and becoming friends with our once sworn enemies. So, there is no need for making weapons and keep investing in the military. All these decades it made sense to keep making weapons as there were sworn enemies but over the decades we have evolved as humans to realize that wars are a thing of the past. So, our concern is with the huge global weapons and military budget of over $1,7 trillion in 2017. Surely, it's a waste. All this money can be channeled elsewhere especially into technological development and modern infrastructure that does not use fossil fuels or materials that are not good to humans. Our duty is to facilitate good management and the wise use of resources globally. We shall be the leaders by ensuring that everything, laws, regulations, infrastructure, etc. support and favors technological advancement. Also, they are all modern; in line with current tastes. We shall facilitate research and development and provide a platform necessary for companies, individuals and governments to easily do what is better for all of mankind by finding new energy sources and new ways of doing things. We shall remove all obstacles and close loopholes exploited to frustrate progress. Imagine when one country can simply ban or block a useful technology simply because that technology will put them out of business. We will have global powers to offer licenses as well especially if it is a new technology. Our aim is to modernize the whole system by offering a new platform a global platform with universal appeal that if businesses are denied a license in certain countries, we will be able to provide such a license that will cover the rest of the world. Tomorrow's World Order will have powers over any President or Prime Minister. We shall have the last say if it comes to doing business globally. You can be denied a license in one country, but we will provide a global license, but the license might not include the country you were denied licenses. We will also respect individuals' country's sovereignty if they don't break our laws which are universal with universal jurisdiction. We are like a second chance to every businessmen and women. A good leader will lay out a vision and provide the information and methods to achieve that vision facilitating progress and removing all obstacles and making sure that that dream is realized. We are neutral we are not aligned to any country or religion or political party.

### The New Platform and a New Global Leader.

The trend at this time is the invention of a new system that will work alongside the current system. We have witnessed a new way of doing things and even the current leadership does not know what to do simply because it the new technology for a New World and this world is better than the current system. They are unsure of what to do. The current system biased because it benefits only those who put the system there. People are complaining and shouting for change because they are the ones who are feeling the pinch. Everyone who has worked hard to come up with a better alternative is somehow disadvantaged. They say necessity is the mother of invention. The inventors are the people who see the wrongs. Very often governments don't change the status quo because what is there is there for a reason. That delay in processing e.g.; a patent is there for a reason. That high cost is there for a reason. So, any request for change is a war starter with the current establishment simply because it's interfering with the way they run their government and if allowed to then you might hit them in the pocket. I explained in another chapter that intelligence is like beauty it is in the eyes of the beholder. You won't be shocked to find out that the way things are is the perfect way for the governments and their leaders. Chaos is the new way to do things.

If you have a perfect system, then how are you going to justify charging those high fees? If you have fast processing times, then what are all those employees going to do when there are no more customers? There is corruption and fraud so that the Mayor has something to talk about. We have people killing women and children so that we have courts to deal with them. So, everything you might be saying is a waste, some people see it as an opportunity. A way to fill a gap. A way to fulfill political agendas. A way to maintain huge employee numbers, etc. A fast system will mean doing the same job at a fraction that means to break even you would need a lot of people than say the current government's system that requires a few people but who pay high prices. The government benefits so all the talks about better this and better that conflict with the goals of the government's leaders. So is this the true picture. Money is not everything. Can this saying be relevant here? I highlighted that during the 1960s after people realized that it was a waste of spending money on wars that they started campaigning against the wars. The governments of the world then went on to create hoaxes about aliens etc. to keep everyone prioritizing defense. Conspiracy theorist thinks 9/11 was a government inside job to frighten people so that defense becomes our main concern as 9/11 left people vulnerable and fearful and so that they act on a 25-year-old contingency plan and invade Iraq. So, if this is the case that governments must go a long way to defend this how do we go about this? Is just good leadership enough? Leadership is not about bending to evil demands nor negotiating with evil. Leadership is about setting the right path and showing the people how to achieve that vision even if it means conflict with the governments. Our vision is for the betterment of all humanity. We have waited to see if these leaders will come to their senses and change. But over the past seventy years, nothing seems to be going to change. We have a vision to ban anything to do with the military and to destroy all stockpiles of weapons, etc. mainly because they are used to justify killing women and children. To aim to guide the current leaders by drafting and implementing laws that will make these leaders avoid persecution after leaving offices. The current laws and systems are cornering these leaders and trapping them by creating a situation where they act out of the heat of the moment ending up killing innocent women and children. Then after office-term, they are then blackmailed and chased by the courts or end up being given protection by the hospitals but used as guinea pigs. That shows that the current system is not fair but needs changing. We don't want honorable leaders to be treated like criminals later in life. We want a way of guaranteeing their safety and to remove any risk of going through the courts in retirement or having them held to ransom being asked to sign or agree to Protectorate agreements. We believe that this is a dark form of blackmail synonymous with slavery and something we must never tolerate. This gives us the power to do what is right. Our laws will make sure that no one President, Prime Minister or not will override these laws in favor of the military. We will have banned the wars, weapons manufacturing, making of digital agents or cyber gadgets used to electromagnetically attack ethnics, etc. Our leadership is the kind of leadership that will make the world a better place. We ask for our laws to be obeyed. We believe now that it's time we take a different route. The current situation where 'the leaders' actually make WMDs in the form of nuclear weapons and declare that these are for deterrence purposes only conflicts with our laws. Why? This is because they use the weapons to threaten wars to countries who might have nukes. This is irresponsible as they both might use the nukes if things get out of hand. This we believe can only lead to human extinction. This is because they both might poses nukes; they can use on each other with catastrophic consequences we don't want another Hiroshima or Nagasaki for that matter. We are neutral and have no WMDs and will never have. We don't rely only on negotiating and cooperation we know this is the way some governments make money or work. If no life is wasted needlessly, we shall try to negotiate and lead by example as well showing what is needed to be done. Our visions are huge, and we see a world without the main thing wars are fought for; oil. All fossil fuel usage shall be a thing of the past. We shall encourage other forms of energy. We aim to phase out all fossil fuel means of transport by a certain date globally. Our policies will remove everything that is creating all the issues we have today. These will have the 'multiplier effect' of spreading the benefits and because of that solving other issues. The perfect example is banning fossil fuels that in turn works towards reducing atmospheric gaseous hence reduces global warming and makes people invest in cheaper and cleaner technology that improves the quality of life. We don't want to talk about climate change and increase fossil fuel vehicles' production. We have adopted a holistic approach. Priorities life then the rest will follow. If you are a leader. You will not override this rule the right to life and to self-preserve if there are risks of killing innocent women and children. You would not send soldiers when there are chances, they will get killed easily say with roadside bombs. You might send snipers and not start a war. That way you are guaranteed your retirement in peace. We will do our best not to judge because of differences but we shall consider putting laws and enforcing these laws whenever we think the same differences might have influenced the decision and assessing if we can bring more charges on top. A perfect example is the fact that to kill Saddam they send the military, yet Saddam was not responsible for 9/11. To kill the 'real person behind the 9/11' masterminded they sent a sniper. So, we can check why Obama e.g. of the same religion and genetic heritage choose a sniper and not the military especially if Osama was the man behind 9/11. If it was another President, would he have sent a sniper too? Could the same method have been used and with what success and above all could the lives of women and children have been saved? We will look also if the victims were the same color as the command giver could he had given the same command knowing they would have been killed. We shall be very tough that all these leaders who are cocky today will obey our laws. The idea especially one that will make these leaders think twice is the fact that to protect your family depends on your actions too regarding the family of others. Some crimes will make it easy to jeopardize the life of your own as a deterrent as killing a certain number directly or indirectly can put them on the table as well. To protect life, one must fear killing others to protect his own life too. If you care for your own, then you would not kill someone else. Our laws will make it hard to be broken without shooting yourself in the head. That is the kind of leadership we have. We mean business. When we say we want peace we mean peace? The world will get. The way we drafted the laws is self-defending as those who think are above the law will mouse trap-themselves. It will be like fighting the goads. You won't win in the end our laws will prevail because everyone will swear that one man for himself and TWO for us all. Mind you we will be educating and promoting high self-esteem boosting techniques until people wish they can live forever. We will ban wars; a huge cause of misery. Ban making of bio-threats and digital ones and even the cyber ones. We will make life be enjoyed again by everyone. I know as I argued throughout the book the strategy of eliminating opposition adopted since the Second World War is the Colony Collapse Strategy and trust me it works see the list in one of the chapters. We shall be fair and use our laws too to target threats to peace. Threats to life for women and children and these shall be targeted individually. Even bodyguards won't die for anyone. No one shall plead that they don't know our laws for we shall use advanced technology and make all laws be easily read or downloaded on phones. This related to all countries on earth. I am only emphasizing this because I think if there is opposition it will come from the people who are doing all these things which we said are wrong. Planning to kill others in masses to play God and control the population.

A thing for the past. Leadership is about putting an effective system that is fair that can't be manipulated. Our system will make these leaders 'self-terminate' We are not asking anyone to be Jesus. We are only saying that we made the regulations and norms you already knew anywhere into laws. You cannot kill or make a command or decisions that can result in the death of someone else unless you are tired of living. Effective leadership is putting laws and methods to see your plans through and change current perception with little effort and make the world a better place. The new laws will be in all areas to facilitate and encourage good practices and respect for life. Some countries have no respect for the lives of others. This has slavery connotations and must not be encouraged. The stretching of work for financial gains will be outlawed maybe indirectly by reducing the number of hours people work and which days are worked. I think the current system is flawed. Our new system will make it easy for people to work for a few hours but make more money. It's not just about life but about the quality of life as well.

# CHAPTER TWENTY-ONE

## GLOBAL POLITICS AND OUR SHORT-TERM GOALS.

I think it's not an understatement if I say we have global problems that have been going on for the past seventy years. These issues have in the past decade become a cause of concern. Two or so decades ago these were not issues. People were very hopeful that the current institutions were going to solve the problems only for their hopes to be dented. I explained earlier that intelligence is like beauty it is in the eyes of the beholder. What I might today regard as problems could be other people's opportunities. The current system relies on chaos to function properly and justify its existence. A smooth operation will put it out of business. So, I ask the readers to trade carefully. Nevertheless, I think the world is a mess, and it's time for one man who will change everything and lay a new foundation for a new beginning. This is just the beginning of a new chapter. People might not see this, but when the time comes, it will make a lot of sense. Change is imminent and inevitable. There will come a time when everyone will opt for a new way of doing things. The days of these people who hang on obsolete practices for personal gains at the expense of everyone else are numbered. Change in the past was not fruitful simply because leadership was lacking. No one knew what was needed to push forward. No one was there to force new laws that safeguard the rights of everyone. Obviously, everyone benefiting from this system will oppose any new initiatives. It's human nature.

**The problem is real.**

I want to make it clear that the current system is obsolete and only a new system will solve all today's issues. There is no doubt that something must be done. We can't leave things to chance. So, there are two continuums of thought. Make no mistake, we all agree that there are problems that need human intervention. We both acknowledge that it's our duty and obligation as humans to get involved. Creativity, innovation, and leadership are things needed now to solve today's issues. We need more creativity and better methods of dealing with these issues. Research and development will play a big part in all this. We must go beyond our current status quo and think outside the box. Let's use technology to solve all global issues. I argued from the beginning that we are operating below our optimal capacity and all this waste can be avoided. I know we are advocates of a new way of solving global issues, and as such we are often regarded with contempt and suspicion. Nevertheless, only strong leadership can and will solve the issue. A strong leadership is not just a must but a requisite. What we are going to do has probably never been tried or done before for that matter. That said I believe that we all agree that the current system has failed and only worsened the problems. Any more time without changing the way we do things will only worsen the situation. The only difference is the ways we think we would be able to solve issues. There are three lines of thought.

### Three lines of thought.

The first is that the current situation being the way it is, is perfect for the current establishment. I argued that beauty like intelligence is in the eyes of the beholder. What we might advocate as great plans could be ways of putting the current establishment out of business. The idea is that the current system sees the system as perfect. It provides everything they need. This is a perfect script for them. There is a problem that persists and is always there. Here and there they put the head down and like a leading actor out of the blue solve the days issues before everyone goes home with a smile on their face. They argue that if it's a novel, this will be a bestseller. This is human nature. No one wants a perfect life where everything is perfect. After all, that perfect feature will only act to put them out of business. All the chaos can justify the huge fees and the delays keep everyone in the job. This is a government function and waste are expected and a must this is a characteristic of governments so why put a big fuss? These people argue that all these New World advocates are out of touch with their reality as they have no understanding of life in general, let alone at such an advanced level. The chaos justifies the presence of everyone from the huge budgets to those civil servants with jobs. A new system will only give vital jobs to robots and perfect systems like the blockchain putting everyone out of work. So, change is not needed as far as these people are concerned.

The second line of thought is embedded in the thinking of the New World Order. These people as I have already explained in the above chapters are very educated people with wealthy that makes everyone else look poor. These people have the brains and resources to play God and change the world. These people are the most feared as they have enough power to destroy the whole world. These are the people they call the New World Order. They have been to the universities and as such, they have debated in groups and cults at the universities and feel it's only up to them to decide the fate of billions around the world. They feel just like us that if the world if left to the current regimes without any interventions we are all going to perish. Mind you these people are the cream of any society. Very educated and philosophical in their dealings. They believe they are the only ones with the license to play God. They believe they have achieved such enlightenment that God on seeing this sat in his seat and sighed heavily saying; 'the day has come for man to act like [me] God managing the earth killing just like what I would do through nature; namely floods, earthquakes, etc.' God has seen his dreams come true. That one-day mankind would have such insight and foresight to be delegated the duties of God or Allah, etc. God has 'retired' and mankind has taken over his duties. Humanity must be controlled and protected from themselves. If left to run the world, they will end up destroying themselves. Thanks to these few people who have gained such insight God has nothing to worry about. So, in short, these people believe that God has granted them the authority to play him. So, these people believe they are doing mankind a favor. All their actions are for the good of making. It's a God-given right to kill and maintain the balance. The only problem they have is that they don't have the power to use nature to kill just like God or Allah etc. What do they do? Obviously, they have no option but to find ways of doing just like God or Allah killing thousands to serve humanity. These people don't feel any guilt or remorse simply because they have been delegated with a task which God would otherwise do. So, to them, there is no wrongdoing as they are doing humanity a favor. Their main arguments are that all superpowers pretending to maintain global peace have themselves developed and are stocking WMDs themselves but prohibiting everyone else. To make things worse, they are grouping into cults growing very fast that in the end it will be justified for the few minority countries, for the purpose of defense to make WMDs and or nukes to level the playing field. With the belief that if they don't, they are going to be obliterated. In fact, they don't have anything to lose and more often these nations are rich in oil reserves and would rather use nukes to protect themselves. The fears of the New World Order are that a nuclear war is a highly likely possibility. We have countries like Iran vowing to fight any form of aggression and threatening to throw everything they have. Who to blame them? They have a right to life and to self-defense. The fact that the whole world is unbiased with the West and its allies growing at alarming rates they are now threats to peace or perceived as such. So, the thinking among the New World Order [NWO] members are that something must be done. They must kill leaders and people who they think will cause a nuclear war. These people are not biased. They look at what is best for humanity. They don't see any wrong in making bio-engineered, digital, cyber viruses to kill people say a few years from now to twenty years ahead in the name of population control. Their arguments being that God would have done the same thing.

### The Role of Precedents.

These people believe that their actions are justified, and they are not doing any wrong simply because God or Allah, etc. has given them divine rights through precedents that nature must be maintained and controlled. They believe this is God's special plan that one-day mankind will be gods of the earth doing what he used to do. So these people would trigger the collapse of the world by collecting money to make WMDs so small yet powerful that they will use the same devices with the help of the satellite and GPS to hack everyone at birth and soon after put them on death row until the day they kill them. They would rather attack nations rich in resources like oil so that the money saved is used to create say vaccines that will wipe-out people after certain years. These NWO believes we have reached this far because God was killing people all the way and now that God has delegated to humanity to look after themselves, they have no option but to accept such a responsibility and start managing earth as if they are God. So, killings and mass extinctions are imminent and inevitable as this is God's plan. Their view is not to change the status quo but to intervene and mitigate by implementing measures to solve problems. You will never see these people trying to change the current system. To them, these are trivial issues that the governments must address themselves. In other words, they don't care about government failures, etc. so in fact they support the governments. They help governments do what they would not otherwise do. They are seen by the governments as providing a service not equaled anywhere. They rarely come into conflict with the governments. They have the knowledge to cause financial crises looting money as starving the system so that they don't make more nukes that will cause human extinction. They believe it's their duty to do whatever it takes to contain the risk of robbing banks for the good of humanity. They indirectly help the government by reducing the government salary balance sheet etc. Them and the government co-exist and this why the common men are against this NWO movement because they are the victims.

**Then us Tomorrow's World Order.**

We are against all kinds of killing. We will never encourage such evil acts and we are against such cheap ways of solving problems and as such we are not appreciated by the current systems. We all feel that mankind is his own enemy making weapons to use on themselves and others but when we are all becoming friends, that only leaves one question; who are you going to use the weapons on? Aliens? We believe just like the NWO that there is a problem and our differences lie in the methodology to be adopted. We strongly believe that there is no need to sacrifice people. We can adjust and priorities critical issues and needs. We believe that a critical path analysis is not just needed but mandatory. We believe that mankind is complacent and will always go for the easy and cheap method that requires no effort or thinking yet the most destructive. This is the reason why we are in this mess in the first place. Even though we believe that the current system is obsolete we also strongly believe that it's time we overhaul everything. We believe that as humans we can do better. We believe that no one must be sacrificed but we must sacrifice such luxuries like spending $1,7 trillion globally on things we don't need such as weapons and the military. If the human body has a defense and military that occupies only 1% of its total mass, why we as humans must have huge military budgets taking a chunk of the resources we have. We therefore argue that we need to reduce things we don't need and to manipulate technology for the benefit of mankind. Do you know that if needed we can make very powerful guns the size of a capsule that might use digital or electromagnetic waves so why we keep spending billions on the military? Our stance is to ban weapons production and reduce tremendously down the military budget and implement laws that ban all things leading to wars and abuse. We believe that we must work at optimal and realize all our potential. We therefore argue that there is no need for making bio-engineered viruses or digital ones to control the population. There is no need for dirty evil tricks like sanctions with the aim of killing thousands of women and children to reduce population pressure. There is no need to vaccinate say all Africans in the hope that twenty years from now they will all die as the vaccines become active from a dormant state. We believe we have enough resources to accommodate everyone we just need to work faster and provide a smooth environment that encourages research and development. We are against wasteful practices. We don't believe being wasteful just to keep people in jobs is right. We can improve the lives of these people by making them work a few hours but earning a lot. The money we serve from waste can be given to the people through increased wages and being paid when on vacation. Instead of aging people faster with the aim that they die faster as well is wrong and against our new laws. We aim to reduce and fight early aging. We will be tough with governments especially in the developed world who hack their population at birth with the aim to play catalysts and speed up the aging process to reduce the governments' wage and salary bills. These countries are illegally making and testing viruses. Now that I have explained our stance, we can now look at global issues. As a global movement we have three aims; to look at the political arena and find the problems and propose solutions and implement these. Secondly, we need to identify the social issues and solve these too. Thirdly, we look at the economics of the globe and solve the problems too. We argued from the beginning that our aim is to force if we have to humanity to move from defensive stages and to networking and cooperation which is globalization in short. Our short-term issues involve providing peace security and stopping wars and ending violence with the aim to give everyone the right to life and to self-preserve regardless of who they are and where they are. The current system promised peace for the last seventy years and we are still seeing wars and people being killed unlawfully. We think there is too much bureaucracy rather than solving the problems we have. We think it goes a long way. We must adopt a comprehensive approach that bans wars and all kinds of violence towards innocent people. Our laws will make today's leaders think twice about wars. Our approach is not just to ban wars but to go further to understand why wars occur in the first place then solve that. For instance, the main reasons for the last wars were to do with the nationalizing of oil fields. So, we are going to ban the use of fossil fuels that removes the dependence on oil and need to go to war. That also makes nations stop the military and invest in research and development. In the short-term is to level the playing field closing all loopholes so that people negotiate effectively. We will fight and advocate for disbarment so that we as the leaders of the globe will do our best to remove the threat to world peace. Any country with nukes is a threat to global peace be it the superpower or not.

So, our goals are to provide a platform for peace. We believe that there is mistrust in the current superpowers like the USA and the UK. They are biased acting on behalf of all the members of the NATO cult. Killing all threats one after the other while like a gangster using force to get what they want killing women and children in the process lacking empathy towards these innocent people. We are neutral and will represent everyone regardless of where they are or their social standing. The current institutions like the UN and its international laws court have been weakened even further. They are as good as dead. What is the point of making judgments that can easily be flashed? TWO will restore trust in the system. We will represent the whole globe and see to it that our laws that are universal are followed and observed. Our first aim will be to reconcile and level the playing field to stop the revenge attacks, etc. The fact that the USA the so-called superpower would be attacked in broad daylight with such destruction is a hint to the fact that the current system is obsolete. We will encourage the dialog and act as facilitators and or catalysts as a third-party encouraging dialog when two leaders disagree. Look at the current negotiating methodologies in all cases it's simply between the two leaders with no third-party to facilitate things. I think if a third-party gets involved the future is bright. Sometimes ego makes these meetings fruitless but if a facilitator or negotiator is there, the outcome might be different. This is true in hostage situations where an unbiased negotiator is brought in to act as a catalyst with the aim that negotiations will reach the required outcomes. If this method is effective and regarded as such why we don't employ it? We will change the way things are. We mean world peace and that is what we are going to get. We think it's a huge risk to let, say the US negotiates with Iran when both might end up using nukes what if they decide to use them both? It's the innocent who will suffer. So, doing nothing is no stance.

The same goes for terrorism sometimes its education and dialog that is needed. We must put tough terror laws that act as a deterrent but also, we will try to understand the reasons behind the attacks. The good thing is that most act in revenge. So, our first aim is to correct past wrongs. Ban sanctions in these areas and get international Non-Governmental Organization [NGO] etc. get involved in development projects that improve the lives of these people as a corrective stance. Reconciliation can only come when we start to heal past wounds and give these people something to look forward to. Education will and must play a great role. Self-esteem boosting projects will pave a way for a peaceful world where people value life and are afraid to die or kill others simply because life is good. I mentioned earlier on also that these people are held against their will indirectly secretly being blackmailed. Some forms of protection encourage dirty tricks to hold people to ransom and put them on death row where they are further threatened and abused. So, terrorism requires a comprehensive solution but putting people in Guantanamo is against our laws.

Everyone will have a right to life and fair treatment and to be presumed innocent until proven guilty. So, Guantanamo Bay is illegal and must not continue. It's an excuse to take people back to slavery where people are held against their will due to speculation. Reconciliation and healing the world will only start when we level the playing field and remove and revengeful feelings by being fair to all. Terrorist on the other hand must be punished but this must be done in the courts. We shall have a twenty-four-hour law system and with no time limits in that crimes will never expire and can be brought at any time in a person's life. Our laws will make terrorism a thing of the past.

## Government corruption.

As a global body, we will try not to interfere with the local country governments' system unless their acts come into conflict with our international laws. We aim not to force our ideas and rules but to remove the obstacles and the temptations that cause all the problems we have. I have advocated for a transparent system of governance where everything is transparent. The military gives people excuses to be involved in corruption etc. as the military indirectly threatens others and encourages people not to challenge the evil acts. So, the use of the military gives the leaders a right to abuse and get involved in corruption. Our laws and regulations will guide the leaders and make them make effective decisions and reduce waste while tackling corruption.

## Globalization and low unemployment levels.

The idea behind advocating for a globalized world is the need to encourage trade and increase jobs and make it easy for people to move around matching jobs and skills. There will be local initiatives to encourage jobs as markets open globally. We won't turn a blind eye also to the fact that some argue that globalization encourages inequalities as the big countries grow bigger at the expense of the developing ones. I think banning a lot of things to do with wars will free up resources that the developed countries will not use weapons to threaten the developing countries but will pay a fair price instead. I think this is true as most developing countries like Iran complain of bullying tactics where countries like the USA make nukes themselves then forbids the developing countries to make some as well. The idea being that if they did have the weapons, they would pay a fair price. I think this is true with the Iraq war where the use of war was a cheaper way of saving the nation by reducing oil bills. We will make all countries emphasis research and development creating new jobs and the other areas like the military being forced to evolve. Instead of killing to help create left and improve welfare.

## Outdated institutions as a problem giving people a false sense of security.

Some argue that the institutions we have are there so that they have jobs. In other words, problems are created so that the institutions will tackle these that they have created 'problems as a way of providing them with something to do'. A perfect example is regarding the use of landmines and 'use of bio-engineered' weapons. People create problems cheaply implanting landmines at $3 each then send people to remove these at $1000. The current laws are subjective and encourage evil practices where people are killed to reduce pressure on the land. The mines were planted to show that land will not accommodate too many people. We say these are evil practices and ways of doing business and as such we will ban and bring to justice people still practicing or doing nothing to correct their past mistakes. Doing nothing is something that will make you fall on the wrong side of the law. Some institutions exist to create problems to justify their existence. Or to worsen the situation. Our initial stance is to urge all to evolve and do good for a change or pay the consequences. I know people might be thinking that cults like NATO are so mighty to be touched let alone to be told what to do. So how come TWO are going to handle these? The easy thing and the reason they have grown so fast is that they are using 'tactics of attack' where they go after any potential threats and bring the person to court through the UN and the ICC or through military action. They rely on their courts, but first supply weapons then send the judges to trial these people. We are going to put universal laws that look at crime in detail and see if the same person would do the same say if people of the same background as he is involved. I think it's a fact it would be easy to just throw a bomb that kills Syrians than a bomb that kills say a member of NATO. Our laws will assess if we can put on the trial the command givers under biased undue regard to the lives of the people of other backgrounds. A law known as the lack of empathy towards the victims simply because they are remote. This is saying it's showing no care because he feels remote to the victims. It's human nature. We can't care for everyone that is the reason why we existed this far, but some crimes can't be left untouched otherwise the whole thing is a fake. To reconcile is to establish a common ground, and this means putting on trial individuals who recklessly kill women and children simply because they have no empathy for the victims because they are remote. Trust me once we started, we can't be stopped because no one can plead ignorance as an excuse because these laws existed for more than seventy years even before that. We must channel funds into the legal system make it a twenty-four-hour thing. No one is immune. Even Presidents and Prime Ministers will be brought to justice. In the end, there will never be a cult or group above the law. I have the feeling that even these cults would be willing to remove bad eggs as these spoils all. It's all down to TWO on how it will build a better world where all cults, institutions, etc. will understanding that the life of everyone matters. We have human rights abuses in countries with dictatorship and monarchies look at Saudi Arabia, North Korea, etc. even China. A lot must be done globally. If the problem is the government system, we will play a great role in educating them and making them evolve to remain viable and in power. Our aim is just initially to provide the means for governments to uphold the rule of law and minimize waste and govern fairly. We have important issues at hand. Our initial stance would not worry too much about things like climatic change and pollution directly like what is happening now. I think it's the wrong way to go about it. No point to talk about climatic change when we are increasing car production when cars emit huge pollution. The first stance is to increase funds for research development and encourage the development of other fuels sources like electricity. Then when solutions have been discovered then ban the use of fossil fuel in say cars and give a time period when all cars using say at first diesel will be banned and then phased out. In the end, it all fit together that climatic change and pollution will be reduced. It's the same with hunger. Our laws make human life a priority. We will ban wars and the money saved will be used for tackling global poverty. The idea throughout is to assess what I can call critical areas and satisfy these first. Linked with human rights you will find out that decision-makers will be forced to satisfy basic needs first before moving to the next stage say of buying fancy more destructive weapons.

### Third type of errors.

The current solutions can be described as third type errors. Yes, they are solutions there is no doubt about that, but they are wrong solutions to the problems at hand. The reader must understand that the problems could be an intended act to keep the current system going providing jobs and reasons to exist. That said still our job is to educate people that it's wrong to trade your life for money. Now people would rather be loaded with deadly watermarks in the form of viruses, so they are given help like help with buying cars, houses, etc. But have you ever asked yourself what would be the situation if these people didn't exist? Ever wondered what the problems are there as a direct result of their existence. In most cases, they are the ones using high-tech gadgets to spy on your activities so that they make your life hard so that they come to help but hold you or your family to ransom.

### Large scale global wars and religious conflicts.

Our stance is against any kind of conflict on reasons that they conflict with our major laws the right to life and self-preservation. Conflict resolution must and will be our strength. Where necessary our people will intervene to act as a catalyst or negotiator or simply a referee sort of making sure that meetings don't end fruitless. We will encourage following up on issues previously addressed and arrange meetings. We shall make sure we adopt a positive approach not just wish peace but act on it. Mediating and encouraging dialog. Religious conflicts might be difficult to solve an issue I address above. Education and solving local problems of inequality and poverty are important. Our laws will help governments to decide what is best by prioritizing people. Some issues regard the fact that developed world test misses making the rich developing countries afraid that they spend money on weapons at the expense of the local people who in turn use sectoral differences to engage in conflicts. Tackling poverty will help indirectly reduce religious conflicts. High self-esteem and better lives can make people understand that they come first, and religion might be something conflicting with that as it might enslave them wasting years worshiping someone, they never saw neglecting the immediate families. I think if God exists, he is so powerful that he does not need to make us slaves to him and as such does not require mankind to worship him for, he can easily command stones to worship him. Instead, he wants what is best for mankind. For them to become their own gods and spend all life waiting to die so that they go to him. I think a good person in the end will be the same as a bad person in the eyes of God if he existed in that once a person dies, he is forgiven because they say God is merciful and will forgive. This area is subjected to the idea is not to change people's faith but to ask everyone to priorities accordingly. Quality of life matters too. Spending time with loved ones might be important than worshiping. It should be understood also people tend to be very religious when they are persecuted air abused with no access to justice or hope that their problems will be solved. Care must be taken to assess the environment as well as these could be calls of help where people end up turning to God, Allah or religion. Assess mass abuse the people might have been illegally hacked as well with no way to prove it or out of fear as their families are put on the sacrificing table too.

# CHAPTER TWENTY-TWO

## NEW LAWS AND EVERYONE'S RIGHTS IN THE NEW WORLD.

I begin this chapter by asking you a question that will shed light on the themes to be discussed in this chapter. What was there first a chicken or an egg? I know it sounds tricky and there can't be a straight-out answer. If you suggest that the chicken was there first, then as we know the chicken can only come from an egg, so the egg was there first. Then again, some might suggest that the egg came from the chicken, so the chicken had to be there first for the egg to be laid. Clearly, you can see why the answer to this question is subjective. The answer simply depends on who is answering the question and their own beliefs. There is no clear-cut way of answering the questions. In that case, people tend to give an answer that supports their beliefs, and after that, they try to justify their answers based on that. In the New World, we are against such scenarios and laws or practices that will encourage an ambiguity and confusing scenario. Deceitful practices that automatically create conditions that will justify the outcome can't be tolerated. A closer look at the so-called protection.

### Protection

Definition: A sexy, modern-day, toned word that sounds funky so that it appeals to all people but, another word for modern-day slavery. This is as evil as slavery and something that can't be tolerated simply because it threatens the fabric of all fundamental human rights principles. It's something that justifies wrongdoing, so people have jobs and careers. The real problem is that this is a tool used to breach all human rights and cover a form of gross slavery that institutions and the whole fabric of society becomes deceitful and devious. This has encouraged dirty tricks at the national level so that people end up stuck under such evil schemes.

## Laws

Laws to safeguard human life and boost self-esteem needed to see us reach heaven on earth.

1. It is illegal to carry out acts or give commands that will result in the needless death of women and children no matter their ethnicity, background, genetic heritage or social status be it perceived or imaginary. Every life of women and children be it from the developed or developing world matters. It is a criminal act to carry out attacks or give commands that will endanger the lives of women and children. There is express universal expectation that all leaders and those in command will act in such a way to avoid killing women and children. In the New World, TWO shall make it a MUST that as humans we will have situations that will require enforcing our new laws and these will involve taking military action. In such cases, every tactical method to be considered shall OUTRIGHT eliminating or posing any danger to the lives of women and children. Our slogan shall be:

2. I swear by the assassin.

It's every leader's duty to choose and give the command to a method that will target only the "target." Recklessness or prioritizing political career at the expense of children and women is a criminal offense. We have seen over the century's leaders waging unnecessary wars wiping out thousands from the wage bills in a day and millions by the end of the war just to boost political careers. TWO has stiff laws that make everyone accountable and aware of the implications of their actions and what is expected of them and the punishment their actions carry. TWO shall adopt a life for life approach. The more you kill the more that threatens not just your own life but the life of your immediate family as well. TWO shall put laws that life shall be respected. Evil actions will not only threaten your life but the life of those you love too. We have put laws that make these leaders think twice. If you recklessly kill innocent women and children, the assassins shall eliminate you and your loved ones too. The life for life or soul for the soul approach shall deter evil doings. Most carry out evil acts knowing that the worst scenario is that they will claim immunity after their political career. TWO shall make it a criminal offense punishable by death. Express-command to put an end to this through our laws and courts as a deterrent. The life of women and children no matter their background and circumstances shall be respected and honored. TWO has placed laws that make it illegal not only to manufacture weapons but to use these especially if their use threatens the lives of women and children. Bombs and missiles all banned. Any weapon that possess risks to women and children are outright banned see under military actions and weapons manufacture.

3. Laws regarding the lives of military men and women.

It is everyone's right to have a career and reach old age. Every effort through laws is being and will be made to safeguard the lives of military personnel. It is not an implied right to die by joining the military. TWO has advocated for highly trained military assassins to solve the problems at hand. There won't be a reduction in the numbers straight away but more emphasis on turning these to be assassins. TWO's priority to force the world to move away from defensive economies that priorities the military in that our best boys and girls are sacrificed way too early so that the political career of these politicians goes smoothly. NO. The lives of these men and women matters. Taking oaths of enlistment does NOT mean giving up their lives easily. It does not mean making reckless decisions and commands to end their lives unjustly. It is a law that putting the lives of our boys and girls in danger is a criminal offense. It is every leader's or commander's duty to safeguard the lives of these men and women by making the right decisions. Methods to be used to achieve political objectives Shall consider this law. Where these men and women can be called upon to serve as they promised care has to be taken and detailed assessment carried out before sending them to be killed. Alternative methods and ways must be considered. I swear by the assassin shall be our motto. A tool to assess and eliminate the risk to the lives of military personnel. The military shall be like any other profession where everyone expects a pension and to die in the old age. Other laws that augment these laws are already in place for instance banning the manufacturing and use of weapons that put a risk to the lives of military personnel. TWO has advocated profusely for networking and cooperation. The idea is to move away from defensive economies. We are all one and we can all resolve our problems if not there is always an assassin, not missiles. It shall be every leader's duty to eliminate the risk of death in assessing military interventions. Any reckless commands shall carry the death penalty. Express-command to put an end to this through our laws and courts as a deterrent. The life-for-life soul for soul shall apply. Leaders will think twice before making commands that threaten their lives and those of the people they love. TWO shall make everyone highly self-esteemed that protecting life shall be everyone's priority.

4. Banning outright of digital-viral or biological weapons manufacture and use especially if they threaten the lives of women and children. It is a criminal offense to manufacture weapons of any kind be it biological, viral or the new so-called digital soldiers' weaponry. All plants and bases to close with immediate effect and any stockpiles destroyed safely. Owning, making, leasing or granting of such permission is a criminal offense punishable by death by the assassin. Where it can be proved that such acts are carried out. Express-command to put an end to this through our laws and courts as a deterrent. Any weapons that threaten human existence are outright banned. The lives of women and children regarding such weaponry. It is a criminal offense to make weaponry that will end up being used on women and children. Weaponry that can be secretly used on women and children must and are outright banned no matter whatever the perceived benefits might be. Anything that infringes on human rights. Anything that conflicts with the right to life no matter how good other benefits are banned. The manufacture and use of the digital weaponry to command the population as is currently in other developed world is banned and not just a criminal offense but an offense that has express-command of death by the assassins. Any laws and practices that conflict with the right to life are banned. Priority shall be given to the right to life. There are situations where there is a need to control and command people for the safety of e.g. the monarch or other important leaders in such situations it

is still a breach of human rights and the right to life and such practices are not just outdated but out of touch and they conflict with the right to life. The serialization of the population through the so-called medical records is not just illegal but conflicts with the first law; right to life. To carry out such surveillance and monitoring they have to use a digital computer-based system to give everyone in their population an identifying number e.g. national insurance that is then linked to a GPS and then medical records and such a system require implanting of chips at birth without the knowledge of the parents or individual concerned that most they don't know that these devices are being used on them and that they emit radiation and increases risks of cancers and other diseases are being used on them. The secret so-called commands are in fact based on viral-mutations. Any use of viral communications be it digital-remotely conflicts with the first rules the right to life. Any form of communication and control whatever the main use is, it threatens and conflicts with the right to life. It is a criminal offense punishable by death by the assassin to manufacture, authorize and use such communications and methods no matter what the intended use is whether to monitor or for behavioral-changing studies. The idea is to respect life. Such practices are prone to abuse and in most cases, such methods are used to unfairly abuse and enslave people against their wills. Such practices are done at the national level with the culprits doing this knowing that they are evil-doing never be caught as they can torture and abuse remotely through satellites and other local transmitters like devices placed on traffic lights or used in conjunction with the internet. The military can be used to track and trace. Express-command to put an end to this through our laws and courts as a deterrent as this is no better than slavery. People like these are Hostis Humani Generis and as such, there is a universal agreement that these people pose a real threat to humanity's survival. Mostly nations developing and carrying out such secret modern-day slavery acts are nations that have a dictatorship, tyrant or monarchy that gives everyone express immunity if the act is perceived as being carried out to protect the people.

5. The use of digital technology to harvest digital souls and carryout modern-day slavery is banned, and it is a criminal offense. In this digital age, some very devious nations have relied on secret slavery to extract money and resources everywhere through the use of manipulating methods. In the digital world, it is possible to have the whole population implanted with chips at birth that are later used to enslave or quicken the effects of aging in their population as the so-called protection. Devious and dirty tricks first to deliberately increase the rates of aging in their population using the remote control and commands. The system is based on rewards for taking part in society. In such instances, everyone is expected to contribute and take part. Secret commands are given remotely through the chips implanted at birth disguised as small computers for medical records something everyone must-have. Throughout life, people are commanded to take part and obey commands. The more commands you obey the more the remote commands are given but also the faster the rate of aging and deteriorating. Simply because first, the command is digital based on viral-mutations something that conflicts with the right to life. Over the years the more you are obedient the more the rate of wear and tear the more you age fast. In return the people behind this will offer rewards in the form of saved digital benefits like rejuvenation. In this case the subject's digital status is [subjugated] that is transferred to another person reducing your rate of wear and tear. In other words, the commands to you and the doses are reduced and channeled to someone else. Over the years you had been bombarded by remotely operated digital commands that have increased the rate of wear and tear. You have felt tired often being shaken and stressed quickly. In return for a price in the name of the so-called protection the doses suddenly reduce or stops. You suddenly feeling energized. The digital attacks have suddenly stopped, and your body starts working normally. This is not just unjust but a cheating crime that violates all fundamental principles and rights and as such these people are no better than the slave traders or the pirates. What happens now is that women and children often from poor countries are used to give you protection. To cover for you. To take the heat. To take the digital attacks on your behalf. The idea is that the chip and the attacks are

programmed and designed to reduce your life expectancy unless if you pay up or can afford to do so. Poor women and children are put in trances, enslaved and spending time sleeping or even killed so that you have a better life. In other words, your rights were violated in the first place as you chipped as a baby at birth. You are no better than a murderer on death row. Groomed to death unless if you can be of any benefit to these crooks. Your only way to escape such a horrendous act is to pay up, and a slave is then used to cover for you that is to transfer all your troubles from you to that slave. Hence the need for these people to wage wars to kill as many women and children pre-chipped who will make the plan of transferring 'digital status quo' possible. Pain and feelings are transferable from one individual to another digitally. Feelings of pain or even sexual arousal can jump from one person to another, regardless. In a world like this, these people are no better than murders out there. Such practices are no better than slavery. In fact, they are modern-day slavery disguised as secret commands and as such are criminal offenses punishable by death by the assassin simply because they are abusive as the people can carry out these remotely and disguised with their identities covered without chances of being caught or revealed. Such people ought to be dragged to court. Express-command to put an end to this through our laws and courts as a deterrent. People who can act like this have unwanted genes that are meant to abuse, and such people cannot change because it's part of who they are. Express-command to put an end to this through our laws and courts as a deterrent. Slavery and any form of slavery no matter how sophisticated it is. It is dead wrong, and they will find justifications to defend themselves simply because it's part of who they are they will never change. It's up to us TWO to send a clear message that if it means wiping out generations after generations of people like this; Hostis Humani Generis then we shall do that. A New World will never and must never tolerate people like this. Money and military resources shall be made available to tackle such a problem.

6. Express-command to put an end to this through our laws and courts as a deterrent to doctors who abuse people infringing on all

human rights based on immigration laws or the need to control and monitor. Evil breed evil applies here literally. A meat hungry lion can only give birth to a lion. A lion will never give birth to a grass-eating sheep. Likewise, evil can only give birth to evil. The right to life shall override all other laws and practices. The idea here is not just right to life but to a life that enhances the individual's self-esteem. Hacking and all other forms conflicts with these rights and there can never be freedom and the rights to the self-esteem of a hacked person or population. The military shall be educated and trained to be programmers and anti-hackers.

7. How do you feel when a person who is supposed to protect you is a digital attacker? A viral soldier? It is a criminal offense to arm people who are supposed to serve the public with or without their knowledge. Hospitals and doctors or governments or leaders are arming people who are supposed to protect the public with viruses. This is not just inhuman but a gross violation of fundamental rights. Anyone in a position of trust shall fight such practices and not be used in such a way. Who knows what the intentions of the programmer or manufacturer are? These people should be free from devious secret practices. No matter what anyone in a position of trust must and should be neutral. Heavy compensation schemes should be in place and stiff punishment to deter such practices. This can only lead to "monitoring and surveillance that leads to abuse and manipulation" in that these people will create situations themselves that gives them the end desired situation. Framing is a major problem in a situation like this simply because the person in a trusted position will always know he or she has a back-up plan: a viral soldier if accused he or she might use that undetected. Stiff penalties to deter and generous rewards in $millions to people who fight such evil practices. This in the end collapses institutions that practice such illegal practices. It is also beneficial to the people in the position of trust to fight these as these people are role models or regarded as such. You wouldn't follow a lunatic loaded with digital weapons. These weapons are also reducing his or her life span too simply because these weapons are based on viral-mutations and as such in conflicts with the right to life. If they can't fight and can be used like this at their expense too, then they

are no better than the burger in the street sleeping rough either way their right to life is not safeguarded. A New World is for the highly self-esteemed people. People who see themselves as their own gods and people who see themselves as their own Prime Ministers and President. They only acknowledge that the current President is only there simply because he or she was first in the queue. They acknowledge if it wasn't for that they could be in the leader's seat. It's not for people who die for another person simply because this conflicts with the first rule the right to life. It makes no sense to say I die for you that means you have overridden the right to your own life and therefore in breach and if in breach then something must be wrong with you. Maybe not wired properly and if so, then not in a position to be fully aware highly self-esteemed person to qualify in the New World. In short, such acts of allowing someone to load you with a digital soldier that interferes with the first rule the right to life is plain wrong and whoever does that is in breach and breaking the law. Punishment is death by the assassin. Make no mistake, we will need to reduce the population of evil people too and killing shall be our game too to punish and deter.

8.  You must understand that TWO is putting laws that can't be overridden to justify any prohibited acts. To achieve a highly self-esteemed society that will see humanity progress to the needed stages does not come easy or cheap. The first stages cannot be overridden or ignored. Everyone MUST acknowledge the rights to life. Any act that overrides this is not only in breach but also a criminal offense and an act punishable by death by the assassin. No men or women will deliberately carry out knowingly or unknowingly acts that conflict with the right to life. Being a soldier as explained above is not an act of giving up that right even though now it seems so. I have placed new laws that means being a soldier is recognizing the right to personal life. These men and women will and MUST put their lives and their colleagues first. They will have powers to refuse or override commands that interfere with the right to their own life especially if there is another way. Hence turning all of them into assassins. Highly trained soldiers that target and therefore eliminates the needlessly killing for the sack of killing. Mind you they are like leaders too

if they recklessly kill, they become liable to be dragged to court. They will have powers to challenge situations that result in the death of others needlessly. Express-command to put an end to this through our laws and courts as a deterrent.

9. To achieve our dreams and goals self-termination in any way is illegal and a criminal offense unless in severe medical cases where life will mean unnecessary suffering. Education and more research into suicides shall be given priority. Is there a link between hacking and suicides and if so, the hackers shall be dragged to court? Express-command to put an end to this through our laws and courts as a deterrent.

   An assassin will be given immunity by the courts as he or she is exercising the order and duties of our courts. If it can be proved that the killed person is directly or indirectly involved in hacking that resulted in someone taking his life. Remember life for life; soul for soul. Most people who self-terminate were abused and or illegal unknowing hacked at birth. The abusers and the hackers to face the assassin.

10. Banning of the so-called behavioral changes methods as these are the real problems to be tackled and above all simply because these interferes with the right to life. Monitoring and surveillance can only be achieved remotely and through radiation-emitting devices and as such conflicts with the right to life simply because a gadget that emits radiation conflict and interferes with the right to life. In short, the risks of death due to radiation effects outweighs any changes that scheme will ever achieve. Express-command to put an end to this through our laws and courts as a deterrent. No one shall command anyone else if doing so interferes with the other person's right to life. Who gives anyone powers that interferes with the right to life? In the New World no acts will be permitted that interferes with the right to life.

11. Banning of professions that encourage the breach of rights to life. Professions that rely on illegal hacking of the whole society and monitoring them using radiation emitting gadgets will be banned. The police, some doctors and nurses are at risk in this line of thinking. The first reason is simply because this is easily abused

in that they can frame people with the hope of monitoring them at a later stage through a remotely operated gadget under disguised and undetected. Such acts interfere with the person's right to life. Implanting a radiation-emitting gadget interferes with that person's right to life. Dirty tricks are prevalent in such cases because people can breach rights undetected and without being known who is behind such torture cases and attacks. Sexual abuse is done remotely in disguise. These people despite being in a position of trust most are no better than groomers and abusers out there. Any remotely carried out abuse carries an Express-command to put an end to this through our laws and courts as a deterrent. You can't expect such acts to be carried in a proper way when there is no accountability and the attacked don't even know who is doing that. This is remote slavery disguised and given a modern title but evil, nonetheless. Evil breed evil. Most often these people have been abused in silence and join forces to do something about it but in the end, start abusing as well in revenge in secrecy remotely and most for a personal reason simply because they too like whatever the person they are monitoring is doing. Imagine your children hacked at birth and end up being monitored by another person in a position of trust but also a victim. Hacked at birth as well now asked to ball-roll the abuse. Human nature in that in the end they are no better than the abusers. They are accessories as they know that the doctors illegally hacked everyone, and they go on to pretend to monitor that person. Would this be the same in real life? Or that the doctor must be brought to justice first no matter what. As he or she has committed a crime. No one shall take the law into their own hands. Whatever follows is void as we look at the bases or triggers. If illegally hacked start with the doctors first. Drag to court. It's like a child hacked illegally at birth who goes on to commit a crime only because he was tortured and forced to commit that crime. We would not punish that kid instead ball-roll to the hacker. Whatever the child did was because of the hacking that renders that person powerless and as such a hostage. See notes on hacking. A hostage has no rights and can only act in self-defense to preserve life as he has the right to life. Secondly, he was tortured that acts to void any crimes he might commit. You can't expect a torture victim to reasonably not commit a crime if that person is being tortured. Again, we revert to the hacker as the problem causer and therefore indirectly the violator of the crime. All what the child needs to prove is the fact that he is hacked beyond doubt and need not prove that he is tortured. This must be regarded as obvious no proof of torture is required. A hacker is a torturer since that is the main reason of hacking in the first place. To reiterate here torture is expressly proved as carried out once one can prove beyond doubt that he or she is hacked. The child is exonerated, and the hacker must pay. The line of thought is that if there was no hacking, then they wouldn't be any crime committed as there wouldn't be any torture. The child only committed the crime because he was tortured through hacking. This might not apply to people in positions of trust who are hacked as part of their job even if they are tortured but every case must be considered on its own merits. Nevertheless, here since the hacking is not illegal and part and parcel of the job, say a policeman is hacked as part of the job. On duties to control the crowds during riots then he is tortured to breaking point through the hacking and not verbal torture and then went on to ball-roll that anger to the crowd attacking a victim with maximum force to his death the policemen might be liable for using excessive force. Here he must prove somehow that his actions or stance he took was a direct response to torture. It does not suffice simply to admit that he is hacked. In this case, hacking does not amount to torture as hacking here is legal and part and parcel of the job. Even if he experienced the greatest torture there is no express torture clause. He must prove that he was tortured and, in most cases, cannot succeed because he might have sworn secrecy to hacking in the first place and might have consented. But because our aim is to fight torture and evil practices, he can sue on grounds that even though he consented he was tortured to sign that is tortured to consent.

The rationale behind this.

We are going to use the egg and chicken dilemma and argue that the fact that hacking is part and parcel of being say a cop or other government apparatus the person concerned was tortured by the fact that the job requires him to be hacked. Just that fact alone that hacking is a prerequisite to be a cop, 'tortured the person' so that when he consented and signed, he was in duress that is forced to sign as the requirement tortured the person. So, these can prove that they have been tortured by the requirement to be hacked as a prerequisite to the job and as such have been tortured since the day, they joined the force. Secrecy clauses are voided by the fact that torture was used. Here since hacking is a prerequisite, then so as torture and whatever the person went on to do be it kill a person in the course of duty was due to being tortured just by joining the force as such innocent and the hacker guilty. So a policeman can use extra force, kill someone as long as in the course of work and following command but the government to be held responsible and liable to compensate the victims' relatives and since our aim is to stop this then criminal charges to be brought against the head of the force concerned. Hacking is illegal, is a hostage situation, is synonymous with slavery and above all hacking people in positions of trust and loading them with digital or cyber weapons they use on anyone even children just because it can't be proved is illegal. Above all hacking conflicts with the first rules; the right to life. How can we allow role models to be loaded with weapons based on viral-mutations that reduces the quality of life? These must know better. The body is a holy temple. Fight the employers for better compensation claims in $millions. Torture voids secrecy clause. Again, there is express proof of torture but must be proved in a different yet complicated way. To hell with institutionalized hacking and torture. As these when people complain to them will simply do nothing but say 'we are being tortured too'. This makes them not act or take cases of torture seriously. They are also powerless victims. Ban all these evil acts. Compensation and criminal charges will collapse this system.

12. No matter how we might love and respect the monarchies of the world the fabric of their existence threatens the rights to life and as such must evolve as most are doing. Foremost, monarchies don't change simply because once they change then they cease to exist. They have been around for hundreds of years because they resisted change. True and for them to survive they must keep themselves as they are. Their laws and practices have been there

for generations after generations. That is what makes them as they are. Most overrides the rights of individuals to life simply because acknowledging this right will obsolete them. Clearly, there are conflicts with the rights to life. Countries with monarchies have the highest rights abuse cases. Monarchies of Japan, the United Arab Emirates, Russia, Britain, etc. murdered more than one hundred and fifty million people and still, it's okay simply because the monarchies guarantee them immunity. Idi Amin murdered 1 million people and he must die. A fact is that monarchies will never change. To exist they must practice laws formulated in medieval times. Just look at how many rights laws were breached by Japan, UAE, Soviet Union, the Ottoman Empire, Britain, etc.; surveillance and monitoring laws, human rights laws, hacking, secret slavery, forcibly grabbing of other people's land, use of viruses as watermarks and extensive use of landmines as watermarks to claim possession to once was not theirs surely you can see why in the New World monarchies must evolve. Simply because they interfere with every rights law. Abuse is at the national level those delegated, carry out abuse at enormous scales in broad daylight when someone complains they are further abused. In the New World, everyone has high self-esteem and they all fight for the top seat even though some are higher than the others they all must work to be the leader one day. If monarchies did the same, they would not have lasted this long. Fact. To thrive everyone must die for the monarchy. Everyone must have low self-esteem. The people must be controlled and tortured so as not to revolt. They all must be tagged and given serial numbers disguised as medical records to be monitored and subjected to torture to change their behavior all this conflict with rights to life and is against a highly self-esteemed society.

Fact:

TWO will offer monarchies maximum respect if they don't interfere with our first laws and are willing to evolve as not to conflict with these rules. Most countries with monarchies offer what is called protection but in fact another form of the 'death row' where people are loaded with all kinds of stuff to immobilize them fast in case, they pose a threat to the monarchies, etc. A breach of everyone's human rights. The locals are abused in silence, are made to age rapidly or are armored with lethal viruses (digital soldiers) and are falsely told that they will protect others as well as people who see them will be afraid. The lowest form of self-esteem to be used to protect someone else at your expense a form of slavery and abuse that will never see these people reach high self-esteem in order to progress to another stage. The lowest point in self-esteem as the people are tricked to help others making them be scared while deadly viruses are being used on them with unwanted effects all of which conflicts with the right to life. A highly self-esteemed society will rather get $million as compensation and see the evil-doers punished than be loaded with viruses to protect the leaders and or the monarchies in case of an attack. TWO shall advocate for compensation in $millions. We are not against monarchies. We offer to help preserve one of the wonders of the world. We believe most monarchies are excellent people, but most don't know their institutions are being used to justify a lot of evil going on. Most are encouraged to be dormant or not have an active role, yet all evil is attributed to them. With hospitals and doctors on behalf of or not of the politicians breaching all rights pretending it to be for the monarchies but in fact for their own benefits. Making and testing viruses and recreating situations at the time they were created to justify their relevance and existence and the huge budgets. These are the real problem causer and other institutions and not the monarchies.

**Laws pertaining to weapons.**

1. Express-command to put an end to this through our laws and courts as a deterrent. It is a criminal offense to make, authorize, give permission or command the manufacture and the use of any form of weaponry; missiles, bio-chemical, viral or even digital that threatens the rights to a life of others. Any breach has an express given command to assassinate [orders of our courts]. Life for life or soul for soul and evil breed evil applies here. Such acts in the New World are acts that cannot be justified humanely and are believed to be a result of such genetic deformities and as such committing these acts can only result in one thing. Death by an

assassin. Designing and patenting any weaponry is banned and prohibited whether you end up making the weapons or not. Thinking and encouraging the making of weapons if proved is a criminal offense. Every human being on earth should take care and responsibility to preserve and honor the right of life of his and others around him and such breach carries the death penalty.

2. All current stockpiles will be handed to TWO who will dispose of them correctly and in accordance with law. No arms dealing whatsoever. This also includes the manufacturing of vehicles or machines that can be easily used to pose a risk to life.

3. There shall never be rights to war and wars are a thing of the past although the last world war (World War Three) can be facilitated by TWO to get rid of all stocks of weapons in case some countries refuse to cooperate. TWO shall and have made it illegal and a criminal offense to provoke others with the aim to incite a war. TWO is advocating for a networking and cooperation development stage and wars are a thing of the past. Express-command to put an end to this through our laws and courts as a deterrent. TWO shall enforce these laws through the use of assassins who will only target the leaders. People will understand that no matter what. The right to their life is priority number one. TWO shall encourage internal coups where the risk of death of our boys and girls is high. TWO shall adopt a cooperate or die with a bullet in your chest and head. TWO has a plan to make the whole world cooperate in ending the dependence on wars to boost politicians' careers something that has worked magic in the past sadly at the expense of our best. Wars are viewed as immediate solutions to any government and politician even with the sad loss of life. Imagine crossing out 60 000 personnel's names in one day from your payroll. Imagine having a good justification for spending $billions on weapons and defense when the people are starving. Imagine the trickling down effects of the released life insurance paychecks. Image a boost of surplus income and cash injected from banks and insurance companies into the economy. Imagine the prospect of new arms contracts. Imagine the feeling of having thousands die for you a day and millions after the war. Imagine the loyalty and command you will get as the politician

who gets the job done. No matter what. War-politicians are remembered and often voted as the best because war-politicians give the people all kinds of reactions just like in a novel or movie. They are elected simply by giving promises. When in office they must carry out such promises? When there are calls for wars. We have all kinds of protesters for and against. The papers sell in millions, so business is big. Everyone has a part or say. When the war starts the weapons manufacturers immediately get a boost. The economy thrives at the idea of a new cash injection. The Chancellor of the Exchequer rejoices as now he can manage the budget. Thousands of names of wage or salary-earners are wiped off the budget's sheets. These people are active child bearers. A future population reduction. War-politicians have more power and say influencing every part of the economy. The ability to kill many and many dying for them easily makes everyone take them seriously and often faces minimum objections. In war times people don't care much about other things as the defense is the priority. These politicians cause humanity to not want to move away from defensive economies and as such hinder mankind's developments and as such, they are the problems to progress. In such light, TWO will make it a criminal offense to encourage, threaten or engage in acts that create a situation that will result in a war. Such an act shall carry a death sentence expressly given. TWO shall give every nation on earth options and rights to raise grievances with one another and if after a certain time that can't be settled peacefully then an option of a 'Mother Of All Wars' is expressly given and that after that no one shall raise the need for a war and forever remain in peace. TWO shall facilitate such wars with the aim to eliminate the world's weapons stockpiles before declaring wars as illegal forever. A two-year war period from 2020 to 2021 shall be given and in this period any disputes between countries will and shall be settled by war and after that, it will be a criminal offense to incite, urge or carrying out acts that will invoke or incite others to war. Simply because wars conflicts with everyone's right to life.

4.   Acts of sabotage or aggression that has a risk of endangering lives after 1 December 2021 shall be illegal and regarded as criminal

acts. No country shall sabotage another or occupy another sovereign country for the need to incite a war. Any acts of sabotage to provoke others to war are criminal offenses and the leaders concerned shall be a target regardless of how powerful their country is. No one shall be above the New World laws. TWO shall force humanity to move away from defensive economies for the betterment of humanity. We are behind in the development process. The current crimes of aggression laws do little to put things right in place. First, it must be enforced by institutions created and run by countries that we are saying are breaching these laws and other international laws. These countries after taking what they want to blind the world then propose laws to pretend to safeguard others from further attacks. The institutions in place are like scout leaders with no powers at all apart from singing the Scout Motto. TWO is independent and unique with powers through our internationally sourced assassins to remove immunity from anyone and deliver instant justice. Anyone who believes in a New World Order that will take humanity to the next level of development is a TWO and shall be recognized as such and shall carry out tasks justly and as have requested. TWO shall aim to use local assassins to solve local problems and reduce threats to rights to the life of our boys and girls.

**We are justified under international laws to act on behalf of humanity.**

Our laws are just and fair and for the sake of humanity as a whole and all commands to get rid of all violators and evil people who are against what is universally accepted are justified under international laws. This is within our rights as a global enforcer. We cannot be regarded as rebels. We are just introducing a better system that is for all humanity and we have a 'Responsibility to Act' and justified to intervene to save humanity from extinction potentially to be caused by the works of a few evil people. We can intervene on humanitarian grounds as well. The Jus Cogens norms gives us rights to call out for global justice where a certain people, country or cult breaches these rights automatically invoking international justice. Something we are now doing justified by international laws. The current system has crashed. We now have a dysfunctional system without recognizing the core aspects of international law, with bullies and cults growing and threatening the fabric of human rights where weapons are made cheaply. These then are used to collect expensive resources worldwide at gunpoint. So that more weapons are made and used to kill the same women and children who have been robbed now to silence them. There is no multiplier effect or trickling down of the benefits of such a system and is poised to crash. All resources are collected to make, sell, use and stockpile weapons while starving other areas. The reason being that if people are starved, they will always revolt. A guaranteed war, uprising or turmoil and therefore a market for the weapons. We have sanctions used deliberately to kill women and children to weaken governments' stance and trigger rebels uprising and destabilizing the country. With the government ball-rolling anger to the rebels using maximum force. That justifies invasions and wars that further kill innocent women and children. We have the UN, UNSEC, ICC, etc. giving women a false sense of security getting them killed as these institutions fail to stop the invasions. The innocent women and children are robbed of time to escape as they expect these institutions to buy-time by stalling invasions to allow them time to escape these wars. A crime on top of personating a war-stopper. Gross crimes that call for immediate closure and compensations to the victim's relatives. Making of bio-engineered, digital and cyber weapons and these being used on ethnics. Intentionally or not is not the point here. Use of watermarks; digital, bio-cyber, etc. on people. Making of prohibited viruses to be used on people. Genocide on a global scale with the Country or Global or Society Collapse Strategy. Above all lack of superior thinking of new ways of solving global problems with global debt at $244 trillion, and still spending $1,7 trillion on weapons and the military while poverty levels at an all-time high even in developed countries. Check UN 2019 reports. High levels of terrorism, political instability, the financial collapses and the current global crises all point to a need for a new system hence our presence. Collapse of the international justice system with courts issuing rulings that no one listens to. What is the purpose when no one listens to their judgments? Recent attacks on Syria by a gang of nations. We don't care who is attacked but we look at the methods and casualties. If an attack or a war does not kill women and children, I don't think we would be concerned much. Every war is justified in the pursuit of global peace. I ask you whose peace. What about the peace of the women and children dying? To us and all mankind. Global peace starts with these. We are going to send the message loud and clear and send shock waves until peace means peace for everyone, not just the rich and privileged. We are justified and no system can be a system without the enforcement part. We stand for global peace.

5. It is a common international knowledge that some acts that fall in the Jus Cogens category are not only illegal but have universal judgment in that any breach will mean a collective judgment. No man can rely on ignorance as an excuse simply because these are universal Jus Cogens that any derogation is not permitted and is regarded as a criminal offense. Having said that, the current crimes of aggression laws are based on dates when the laws were passed on. TWO shall argue that even though the laws came into effect on certain dates, the knowledge of such acts as being illegal existed even before the laws came into effect and as such the laws are there only to provide a legal framework to bring the perpetrators to justice and as such there is no time limit to any countries. The laws will and shall apply if that person who commits such acts is alive. Even after death liability might befall his or her immediate family. The notion of evil breeding evil and life for life shall apply here too. The main reason being that acts like these destroy the right to a life of many people needlessly and if not corrected, there is a direct effect on the survival of humanity. TWO's crimes of aggression will go back to the past simply because some knowledge existed even then but only that the people ignored it knowing that they will put laws to give them immunity. The idea here is to deter people from doing wrong things or neglecting their responsibilities today in the hope that they will make laws to evade justice or to cover their backs. It's like ignoring your duty today knowing that in the future you will still frame-up that person and can get away with it.

6. Any missile or other weaponry testing is banned simply because

it incites others to think about wars or to make illegal weapons in self-defense. No one shall be threatened, and it will be a criminal offense to threaten others (through missile testing, noises, sirens, etc.) hoping that they will buy your weapons or so-called protection for self-defense. These acts are not just criminal behavior but interfere with the right to peaceful life something I looked at above. It's not just a right to life but a right to a life free from interference, secret or direct threats, right to a life free from any unnecessary intimidation or psychological torture. Any institutions and people doing this are no better than muggers threatening with a weapon and therefore a criminal offense. Countries that act in such a way will cause uncertainty to the future of others and as such is a criminal offense. An intimidated and or threatened man or country can be a very dangerous man or country and causing such a state is a criminal offense punishable by death. These are dirty tricks to trick and corner others unjustly so that you have weapons to sell or a salary at the expense of others and rightfully a thing for the past. Cheap methods and shortcuts are and shall not be part of the New World. These people are greedy bastards trying to make a quick bark at the expense of others.

7. Banning of any use of any kind of weaponry to command others and get a response as a means of subduing others is illegal. Making and use of biochemical or digital weapons is illegal. There is no justification whatsoever simply because all these interfere with the right to life.

**Laws to encourage networking and cooperation.**

1. Work together to ignore the physical boundaries between regions and countries. The whole globe should work together to encourage connecting the world digitally and physical through highly connected networks and much emphasis on the small passenger plane like forms of transport that travail in air easily from one country to another just as cars take people from the city to the other. Private planes' investment should be encouraged. Tele transporting is a possibility should be encouraged. People flying like birds from one place to another should be looked at. All the money saved from weapons manufacturers should and MUST be

diverted into research and development. The globe; if not physically then virtually should be linked to encouraging networking.

2. Borders and walls should be a thing for the past. Security and defense should be the last thing to come to people's minds. Networking and cooperation should be the first. People should be able to leave their doors unlocked or share their houses with others for certain times when they are not home. The idea is to encourage traveling globally all the time with the need to just send a message stating the time and date you need to use their house or offices. It should be like I am in France tomorrow at 08.00 leave your house open or what is the password. There will be a system showing available houses or offices where you can simply make a booking to use the facilities even for a fee. The idea is to optimize the uses. When you are not home, let others use it at the time you are not home. People will be able to check the central database. Newyork city or Botswana has a house available at certain times. I am from Finland I need to be there say by 3 pm. You make a booking; make reservations etc. Forms of transport must be fast and efficient and occupants' rates at any time must be high. Rebates for houses, offices, and hotels, etc. occupied the most throughout the day or night. Everyone will have high self-esteem that will make them work very hard and smarter. We will have built the best infrastructure and futuristic houses that are energy efficient. People in this stage are not materialistic. They have advanced greatly; that money in the banks or private wallets will be important than say title deeds to a material house. Competition will be the word and that encourages development. Today's people would rather be loaded with all kinds of digital-viral-soldiers; to make then age faster, others to cause rashes and all that stuff, others to make their eyes reptile-like on the side. If everyone fights this so-called protection whereby people are deliberately being loaded with viruses be it digital or not the world will be a better place maybe not today but tomorrow. This encourages laziness and dependencies. I had this person saying if you had a mortgage you would understand. I am saying that to be smarter sue them so that they pay you $millions so you have a good life, a healthy life

in your hands. Why let other people take control of your life. To them, you are the investment. It does not work the other way. They choose you because you are an investment. You will make them $millions. This protection is to speed your aging and death so that they collect their $ millions faster in life insurance when you are gone. They have people everywhere. They say they offered you protection. Wrinkle you faster so that others don't suspect and promise to help you get a mortgage or a car or even a wife. What they are doing is putting things in place so that life for you becomes very hard than it is necessary. Why? So that they offer you $5 and pretend to help you when you can threaten them or the mortgage providers with legal action, so they treat you right and acknowledge your rights. These people rely on reverse engineering. You by yourself make the effort to go to the bank to arrange a mortgage. The mortgage lender then tells you to wait for his feed on preliminary finds if you are suitable. In most cases you are. But these crooks then listen to the conversation you had with the mortgage lender. They then intervene asking the mortgage lender to make your life hard or to refuse. They then step in and offer you protection and say they can help you get the mortgage something you could have done by yourself if they had not cheated and intervened. To keep you quiet and in some cases, they say to be given you must be loaded with these digital agents to show power. Behind your back, they have taken life insurance through their subsidiary branch in your name. Every command they give you or every call they make to you is a way of reducing your life span. This is through the 'wear and tear' that makes one age very fast so that they can collect their investment. You finally realize that you are aging faster than your peers. But by the time you realized that you were being groomed like a chicken you suddenly die of sugar. All people in the developed world are illegally tagged at birth and are all chipped. Most are implanted with spying gadgets without their consent or knowledge. Every bit in your life is recorded and every part of your life being tampered with. You don't wonder why the developed world has taken us back to the time of the early man? The time when there was no written language. The only way of communication was sign language. Now in 2019 we are still being encouraged to use sign language and other mirror-techniques of communication? Something must be wrong. Someone out there has breached your rights and is listening to everything you. All your secrets are being secretly recorded without your consent. You were a baby when a chip was implanted at birth and nobody dared to tell you that. You find out that all your secrets are in the open. Whatever you did last night is made public through sign and mirroring techniques. You blame your wife for letting out your secret but in fact the doctors, hospitals and a bunch of other institutions are busy playing God with your life. Welcome to the rise of the so-called compulsory medical records. A severe breach of the fabric of all human rights. A threat to national security itself. Hacking no matter what threatens the right to life. First the gadgets themselves pose a risk to life. Secondly, it's putting your life in someone's hands and conflicts with the right to life. If you are hacked, you don't have a right to life. \Your life depends on the mood of the beholder of the joystick remotely operated to choke you or pass electrical stimulus through your genitals today maybe strangle you tomorrow. Above it's a money-spinning business in that all these people sublet to groomers and all kinds of people who have fetishes of abusing others. These evil bastards get arousal as well as they must feel everything you are feeling as part of the monitoring or secret surveillance. Is this not trading one devil for another? No wonder why dictatorships, protectionist, monarchies, etc. are linked to rings of abusers. Because of monarchies everyone is digitized in that gadgets are used to control them so that they can be instantly immobilized or even terminated when they are a threat, and this is part of the requirement to live in a monarchical country. Monitoring is given to perverts who have fantasies of abusing others remotely that over the years these monitors become abusers themselves. Rejoicing when you are making love and, in some instances, organizing the women disguised as workers. Education and all kinds of help to drive self-esteem high should be prioritized. Express-command to put an end to this through our laws and courts as a deterrent.

3. Views on monarchies and the way forward.

In some cases, the government uses the monarchies to drive their political goals when in fact the monarchies have no idea of the real world. People get illegally tagged and tortured as a condition of being tested if you pose a risk to the monarchies and in some cases, the monarchies might not have ideas that this is happening. I personally think monarchies require a different kind of protection than they are given now. In the New World, there is a place for them on conditions that they must evolve too. Monarchies are everyone's dream growing up. The problems are the institutions that drive their personal agendas using their name. We have institutions like the public health system driving their goals of tagging and controlling the population in the name of the monarchy torturing people to test if they will pose a risk if allowed to stay violating all human rights. Doctors taking the law into their own hands with ambulances running around. Money grabbers to justify the huge budgets. We have genocides; people's lives, and brains being shaken so that the ethnic pause no risk to the current status quo. If they are all lunatics, no one will be able to challenge the current political system. We have all foreigners with potential ending up labeled unjustly as lunatics. The whole institutions are so corrupt that no one knows what is right and wrong or simply because no one gives a toss they all have express immunity from any crimes. Torture devices are known as the general's daughter mislead people who might be listening. People might think that someone has been given the general's daughter when in fact he was subjected to torture through a torture device known as the general's daughter. I think monarchies are good people but are powerless to challenge the status quo as they are tricked to be dormant and not participate. Often these evil acts are done to protect them and when they challenge this, they are threatened or even bad things happening to them or their loved ones. TWO shall offer protection to monarchies around the world unconditionally. First protection from these institutions in that most are the ones using foreign-made- sophisticated gadgets and foreign-trained doctors who in the end take things in their own hands and torture monarchies accusing them of hallucinating when in fact when they complained of someone listening to their conversations that were for real. When they complained of bulimia, it was for real someone was tampering with their system. Threatening and accusing them of being a snake indirectly making them keep everything for days when they threatened to go public. The monarchy does not benefit anything for accusing the doctors of using illegal digital agents on them, but the hospitals and doctors have every right and everything to lose. When they die unexpectedly would this be a surprise to all? No. In that case, the doctors and institutions through illegal hacking pose a real threat to the monarchy and often hide behind the monarchy that people end up steering their anger to the monarchy mainly for not doing anything to protect themselves and those loyal to them by not fighting these doctors and institutions. Most are blackmailed when they translate (through action) what is happening to them in the end they are forced to admit to hallucinating when in fact they are being tampered with. The whole institutions are controlled by the public health sector and doctors who threaten the first right. The right to life. Killing of monarchies through accidents and threats of them being attacked by car bombs etc. only make them quiet. TWO after years of observations and noting all kinds of shenanigans can safely safe there is a solution. These institutions have power because they threaten the first right. The right to life and control everyone's rights through gadgets they implanted without consent illegally most at birth. Remotely they can control these devices so that even some leaders show signs of being tampered with but for fear of being labeled as hallucinating and therefore crazy they don't challenge these. TWO have sourced a video that can prove beyond doubt that hacking does exist and is operated remotely, and it is true that these people tape and record the world's conversations. Carrying out reverse engineering listening to everyone's conversations illegally and then threatening the people involved with the death or to accept their protection. These people have become so corrupt that they have loaded all law enforcement with lethal digital agents that themselves have become subject to these doctors and institutions. TWO will protect everyone who what's to challenge these practices by providing proof in court that such gadgets that tampers with the person system do exist. Accusations of hallucinations in this case are unjustified and incorrect. These people ought to be dragged to court. Express-command to put an end to this through our laws and courts as a deterrent. Everything they are doing is a threat to humanity's survival. This is in direct conflict to the right to life. A gadget that can choke you, a gadget that can blind you in the middle of the road while driving at 70 miles an hour, a gadget that can incapacitate or immobilize you, a gadget that can shake you and leave you with a brain of a toddler is not only inhumane but threatens and conflicts with the first right the right to life. TWO will give express-command to put an end to this through our laws and courts as a deterrent. There is express universal knowledge that such acts fall in the prohibited category as they are threatening the fabric of human existence. To make things worse, that being done to monarchies is a grave cause of concern. Such acts make one regarded as Hostis Humani Generis because they can wipe-out the whole humanity. As such, there is an express universal command to put an end to this through our laws and courts as a deterrent. The New World will not tolerate such people simply because they use viral agents to subdue others and command them. Viral any form of bio, chemical and or digital threatens the first right. The right to life. These agents bring aging faster, encourages diseases using radiation and they are to weaken these people so that they die faster all is against what TWO stands for. We as the New World we aim to outlive the tortoise but at current normal speeds. If an animal can do that why not us humans. We should be living up to 200 years without much aging. It is a sad fact that some governments are spending $billions reversing previous achievements and efforts to fight disease and aging. They are recreating the medieval times when the black death and other bubonic plague were prevalent. They are using these as bargaining tools stealing resources and forcibly taking land everywhere living landmines and watermark; viral all of which are against what TWO stands for. Make no mistake these governments are not our friends we might cooperate or deal with them today as a way of closing loopholes but tomorrow TWO shall give express-command to put an end to this through our laws and courts as a deterrent. The Jus Cogens laws have given us express privileges to tackle people like these. TWO shall declare war to such practices once we have our people in place .These people shall fight too once they understand the first rights. Express-command to put an end to this through our laws and courts as a deterrent. People who think like this have something wrong in their genes that they will never see anything wrong with their actions. They will defend their actions at any cost even if we all know that this is wrong. I point you to the Nuremberg Doctors trials. Even until the end, the doctors were convinced that they had done nothing wrong. TWO recognizes that these people are bad to the bone the only way is to shock the system when destroying them and we shall. TWO shall recognize these people as suicidal maniacs and treat them the same way.

4. True! Monarchies are a rare phenomenon and as such TWO shall endeavor to offer a different personalized form of protection or an extra form. They can have their own protection as current, but some highly trained military personnel will be commanded and trained to jam any digital interference and to work for the monarchies. Reducing the need for war for soldiers will make it possible to have lifelong dedicated personnel to protect monarchies and leaders too. The main threat will be assassin threats as these will be legal globally. In the case of dirty tricks, some soldiers will always be there for the monarchies. The current system poses real threats from within. Politicians control the budget and therefore the public health system or hospitals worldwide, therefore, these institutions are likely to listen to the Presidents and Prime Ministers than monarchies and might go on to abuse monarchies in favor of politicians.

5. If monarchies will acknowledge that it's everyone's right to life and that no one shall die for them needlessly unless they are part of the trained military personal, then no one should be expected to die for them simply because they are a monarchy. TWO shall incorporate these rare institutions into the new system and offer unprecedented kinds of protection. No princess, king or queen shall die before their time and needlessly regardless of their country of residence. They MUST evolve and adapt to changing needs though. They can choose to remain as they are if they don't make demands that conflict with the right to life.

6. Funding the monarchies.

Conditional depends on merit we don't want to reward evil acts or promote abuse.

We appreciate the value brought to the world by monarchies and as such strongly believe that as they are one of the wonders of the world, they deserve funding by Tomorrow's World Order and all world countries contributing a percentage towards monarchies. Our system requires us to hold all nations' savings in the form of the freshly printed money as a strategy to fight hyperinflation. A percentage of GDP will be deducted from all nations as funds towards the Monarchical Global Fund. I think the current system that gives handouts to monarchies as if they are like the homeless beggars is the root of the problems and probably the bad acts associated with these monarchies. After careful considerations and with immediate effect of the date of implementation of the plan [to be announced] I would propose funding for all global monarchies. This is not handouts like the current system. If monarchies are the heads of any empire and nation and they don't have any source of income isn't that pathetic. Our system will allocate a percentage of printed money to the monarchies and a global fund for monarchies to be set up with all of those concerned countries contributing. This is and must be in $billions yearly. I personally think affordability is the cause of all our problems, not just national but also global and monarchical wise as well. As a new start. A percentage of fresh clean money in $billion or more must be for monarchies globally. We can afford it if its new money. Since all countries will be printing new money in our system, they must set a percentage of printing money towards a global monarchical fund run by TWO. I think if they have money all the bad things, we hear about them will be a thing of the past. My reasoning is that most have helped preserve ideas, technology, cultures, etc. the fact that they have carried over their laws for centuries although I am skeptical about some laws, I think that alone makes them the best preservers and transporters of everything good as well as bad. But we know today what is wrong and not wrong because they carried all the bad and good for us to decide and as such, we owe them. [Subjective according to acts in history as well]. Today I think we might not be able to know what is right and wrong or even push with our laws because we might have been in the dark. As appreciating their roles with immediate effect, we have created a Monarchical Global Fund with a percentage of the fresh new money in $billion or more annually regardless of their income. It's like overdue royalties for safekeeping everything we know today.

7. Succession.

We are neutral to the internal dealings of monarchies and governments. Our duty is to remove the things causing them to do what they are doing which is contrary to our laws. Our core thinking is that all is because of a lack of affordability the main theme of this book and the basis for our solutions. But we distance ourselves from internal affairs and would not want to change how they are run. Nevertheless, we think succession is none of our business they can continue globally like now maybe only death can change succession just like now.

8. Special Immunity.

Again, this is conditional on merits we don't want to reward evil or promote further abuse. Every case to be decided on its merits.

At first I thought these institutions did more harm and must be treated like every other tyrant or dictator out there but I think if you consider that they have no funding whatsoever relying on handouts from the government and the fact that we are saying affordability is the root of all evil I think looking as well to the contribution they have made. I think we are going to use the Offset rule for some but ball-roll to their governments who might be held accountable for their acts unless they can prove they had no direct or indirect effect upon crimes by these. Divine rights and absolute power to be assessed. Again, each case on its own merit. I know they did harm too but we owe them a great deal too. The fact that they revealed even their bad acts for us to see all counts towards them and weighing the bad and the good I think the offset rule will apply to bring everything to neutral therefore Immune to any crimes in the past.

9. The threat of the assassins. ONLY As orders of our courts.

TWO shall make it a mandate that all soldiers be trained to assassin levels and work separately or in groups and be trained not only to kill but to protect as bodyguards as well. Our slogan in this regard shall be one man for himself and TWO for us all meaning that individuals will be targeted and punished for their actions. The major threat will be the threat of an assassin. Some soldiers will have two roles to kill and to protect as well. Every member of the cabinet will be assigned one if at risk. TWO will make use of these soldiers and make them bodyguards as well and every member of parliament will have the right to these if need be.

## Laws regarding the monetary system.

I have argued throughout the book that the current system is now obsolete and must be replaced. I have proposed a new money system with our currency the Futuregoldcoin as the main global currency working side by side with local currency to boost economic growth while fighting hyperinflation. Read our Whitepaper in the appendix. We have a repetitive Five-Year Money Printing Cycle. The idea being that only new fresh money is the answer to all global issues we just need to tackle hyperinflation and all other issues regarding money. It's a win-win situation trust me on this.

# CHAPTER TWENTY-THREE

LIFE CAN NEVER BE THE SAME AGAIN.

*A look at the role of new methods like the blockchain and its role in the New World.

*Blockchains and other decentralized methods threats or opportunities for current and future governments?

Governments over the decades have remained as the sole holders of power and resources as they centralized everything making life for the ordinary man difficult. Centralization has concentrated power and wealth in a few people with most struggling. These are some issues raised by those who often are referred to as freedom fighters. They saw the centralization of everything as a problem and a perpetuation of inequalities with the results that the poor become even more marginalized with little power and resources going from the center to the periphery. Things are changing and a new phenomenon is developing where power is now going from the center to the periphery in a form of decentralization that has maybe never seen before. The decentralization you are familiar with is that of limited power and resources rationed by the center as a way of keeping those people quiet. This decade has seen power in the form of resources going from the central institutions to the average person in never seen before amounts. To understand this phenomenon is to understand that the two most world richest will never equal the power of a decentralized system based on the blockchain known as Bitcoin and others as of June 2019 it is estimated that cryptocurrencies have a value of nearly $100 billion. These funds would have either been kept by the central government or in banks, but a new wave is growing. Will power shift as well from the center of the decentralized periphery systems. Can this be equaled by power as well? What is the role of blockchains in the government fiat system?

Blockchains are;

"A blockchain is a type of decentralized database system based on linking together previous records in secure blocks of information."

Dictionary.com

Blockchains arose as a solution to the problems of the fiat system;

>Lack of trust in government

>government corruption and human error leading to hyperinflation and the collapse of the financial markets.

>The problems with centralization and bureaucracy

>Inequality caused by centralized parameters

>cumbersome and slow processes and government waste

>government stance of wall-building acting against globalization

>Global problems of identification and spying on their people.

The blockchain is a solution to all the above problems.

I dwelt a lot on issues with the fiat system above. In this chapter, I want to assess the impact of the blockchain and cryptocurrencies and their role and their future. My stance is that any change is not just necessary but inevitable and a must. We can do better as a people. We are wasting a lot of resources when others are dying of hunger, etc. Will the blockchain be the answer to all this? I think it's too early to say given that some countries like China have started banning systems linked to this but it's a fact that the blockchain system is the way forward. Governments at the time in the name of preventing another financial disaster have marginalized some even more with the results that most people have no access to banks or financial products. The blockchain will make the world have ways of transacting improving lives around the globe. The blockchain will transfer wealth from the center to the average man. Financial packages like Bitcoin will change and shift government power and scatter the wealth all over that would have been kept by the central institutions like government and banks. Will the government allow this new phenomenon? I think it might crack down on it but might face heavy opposition as well and the idea is to keep it in the system side by side with the fiat system.

## Role of cryptocurrencies a look at Futuregoldcoin and current impact of Bitcoin.

My thoughts about bitcoin. I think even though Bitcoin has started well having a combined value of more than $100 billion including other cryptocurrencies the fact that the leadership is anonymous has issues regarding its future as well as its global impact. Above all the fact that no system is behind it is a cause of concern something that can impact on its value over time. The fact that there is a limited supply of $21 million with some to be burned to increase value over time will only work to increase value but at a limited capacity. Above all its global impact is limited. What is $21 million when you are talking about 195 countries in the world? Therefore, you need a strong currency that can be skillfully produced in amounts above this and a system that will see continuous growth in value forever. Welcome to our Futuregoldcoin. The global currency used by all nations. TWO with a responsibility to collect local currencies and deposit this in our Global Reserve Bank and issuing our own currency in exchange to fight local country's hyperinflation means having an everlasting global impact in the long run. Imagine TWO holding all countries' savings and us issuing equivalents of the new fresh printed money. I can argue also that the value of our money can increase exponentially more than the current Bitcoin in that it is accompanied as well by the increase in local currencies through printing more money. The fact that countries will be able to do all transactions in our currency as well as theirs is vital in that on top of that they can hold our currency in their country's reserves. The idea being that to help boost growth each country will have to use its own currency locally for exports lowering directly their local currency. To make exports cheaper to boost local growth. At the same time to achieve this, they must not flood their economy with our money the FutureGoldCoin, but they must hold huge reserves of our money. So, they will be forced to hold more of our currency in their reserves making it scarce. This alone will increase the value of our currency as shortages in circulation locally, increase its value. If they don't do this their economy will stagnant. So, to boost growth they must collect more of our currency from TWO and others through trade deals but keep these in their reserves. That lowers the value of local currency but boosts exports. A very good example is what China is doing to the USA. We have now the USA complaining that China is not being fair. But in our system unlike now when the other country will feel the downward effects with stagnating economies and slow growth TWO is independent and we don't represent any country. We can tackle hyperinflation and slow growth unlike the USA now that must depend on exports as well to boost growth. We as a separate entity our money we print is the New Single Reserve Global Currency that is used by all nations. The US is feeling the effects because it has to do like China to lower its own currency to boost exports but it cannot because its reserve currency which is the same as the current currency is the one being used by every other country including China. It has no other currency it can use say to keep in its own reserves to increase the value of the local currency. I can say with great vigor that the USA is the country whose currency is used globally as a Single Reserve Global Currency is disadvantaged and will always complain as they will forever feel trickled etc. as long as China and other countries once they have understood the system. So, we are a lifeline to this great country. We can Make America Great Again. They can start doing what China is doing with our New Single Reserve Global Currency holding our FutureGoldCoin in their reserves limiting circulating supply at the same time even keeping the US$ where it is the same value without lowering like what China is doing but encouraging exports as well to increase growth. I think if you understand that China has grown fast in the last decade than what the USA and other developed nations have in past decades then you will understand the impact of our currency globally. Imagine all nations having access and platform to trade like this. Exports literally means growth. New fresh printed money and income from exports are all much needed not to mentions huge global markets. Mind you we will be printing money as a solution to all problems. And we all know that printing without exports and growth or increased production will only lead to hyperinflation. The main reason why China has grown is the fact that they are printing money. It has nothing to do with all the issues the USA is complaining about. All these are what I can call by-products or side effects. They are growing because they are printing new fresh money. To fight hyperinflation, they must lower the value of their currency that is a move in the opposite direction to correct inflation. Printing money will increase circulation and the value of goods. New money means increased purchasing power that increases prices. To correct this, you manually devalue the currency to boost exports. The main idea behind this is to increase production to match the new money.

I personally believe that FutureGoldCoin and fiat are complementary rather than exclusives. The fiat will need the Futuregoldcoin to help governments solve all the issues that have made them public number ones. People don't have to work long hours, and most will not rely on the government for jobs. Imagine if these civil servants have invested even a little funds in Bitcoin today, they would all be millionaires. They still have a chance and buy our FutureGoldCoin and Calycoin. A heavy load off the civil servant wage bill for the government

### Is Futuregoldcoin and other currencies like Bitcoin bad for the fiat money?

I personally think that in our system FutureGoldCoin is the king for all nations. The hinge-pin the cornerstone. The critical element for any survival of any nation. You can recall in earlier chapters I went to lengths to explain that the current system is like a human body with fiat the lifeblood of the system just like blood is central to a human body. I went further to show that Bitcoin is like the oxygen we breathe as such it is needed by the economy to complement the fiat. The two together make the perfect model. But in our system, things have changed.

### Our New System

The current system is at the national level with the fiat central to the success of any nation like I argued above with Bitcoin and other currencies complementing the fiat acting as how oxygen will in a human body. Since this is like looking at a nation and comparing the nation as a human being.

Points to note here.

Fiat will be the cornerstone or hinge-pin of the system because we are looking at the same fiat. It could be the US$, the GB £ or the Swiss Franc but all in all it's a look at the single currency. This is true as well to a human body. We have one person with a single blood group. It's either group A, B, AB, or O. It is also true that a country will probably have the same currency. But what about different individuals together and likewise different countries? How can we join all together? We can't mix different blood groups of different people. We can't find a way of making A, B, AB, O into one same as we can't use all currencies in one or all nations. But my point is that we must find common ground and a way of a single 'blood' that is compatible with all people. It's like those of blood group A, they can't take maybe another blood group without side effects. Just like we can't use say four currencies in a single country without problems. Why the current system is not working is that the US whose currency is used as a single currency will have to make bad deals in dealing with everyone. I think this is the greatest argument that made President Trump win the election. The truth is that not that the USA trade negotiators are incompetent, no. They have no choice. Their currency is used as the Single Reserve Global Currency and all the other countries doing deals with them can lower their currency for a competitive advantage whereas the USA can't. China can lower or devalue its currency and the US cannot because its currency is the same as well as their reserve currency. They can't reduce the circulating supply because they are using the same currency too. In our system we have one New Single Reserve Global Currency to connect all nations just like people with all different blood groups can be brought together with everyone with his own different blood group be it A, B, AB, O all working together all nations with different currencies, $. Swiss Franc, Zloty, etc. all joined together by our FutureGoldCoin, which is independent of any nations and we are representing the globe. Our system is to level the playing field. The current system sees the USA being screwed by everyone else because everyone can manipulate their own currency, devaluing it for a competitive advantage whereas only the USA cannot. Simply because for them the reserve currency is the same as their main currency. They can't do anything. Of all the countries the USA will benefit the most from our system. This eliminates the Beggar-thy-neighbor dilemmas as well as the Triffin Dilemma thereby removing all ill-feelings towards the USA makings global peace an achievable dream a real New World where the USA does not have to carry anyone anymore or be screwed by everyone or have to embark on military interventions at the expense of its economy and citizens. Now any country can pay another for any interventions or outsource to us, TWO. Forever nation will have enough money to deal with all issues. This is will make even the USA appreciate minding their own business. Now they have no obligation or feel that they must help everyone as everyone pretends to beg them while attacking them. Now peace will mean peace. This is not socialism like some have argued. Our system is based on equal footing and encourages competition. Whatever China can do the USA, the UK, Zimbabwe or Iran will be able to do the same thing to boost growth.

We are a blessing to the USA and the other countries as well.

Now we have given everyone the opportunities to play games and tricks and all shenanigans. We have leveled the playing field. Now even the USA that has seen all its leaders cry-foul-play in trade deals has the opportunity to do the same to any country and an increase in growth as well.

Our currency will be the currency to be used by all. With countries aiming to hold as much in their reserves and limiting the circulating volume to boost growth and make their currency favorable to boost economic growth. Now the USA has the chance to play clever rather than a complainer. The main idea here is that growth is only through printing new money. Like I said this has nothing to do with being clever for the sake of being clever. It is a survival strategy. If you don't do this hyperinflation is going to destroy you up. China does this to reduce and contain hyperinflation and nothing to do with trying to fuck-up the USA. They are scared to be destroyed by that animal called hyperinflation.

Our system will work wonders. This is the only new system that will work to eradicate all current problems. The only way to boost growth to levels never experienced before. The only way to increase wealth to levels only can be dreamed of today. I am ready!! Are you? I want all leaders, economist, financial planners, treasures, etc. to read my book and understand our system and without thoughts to subscribe and join. There is nothing to think about. I will judge your success by your first response and I still have faith in humanity, and I can lead all you to greatness. Don't think about being part of this. Just say yes to Tomorrow's World Order. Let's start a new journey together without suspicions and I normally judge people by their first response and hopefully, you will see the light and realize that we are entering a new era. An era where you don't ask why you simply say tell me more.

A look at the current crypto and bridging the gap with our FutureGoldCoin.

A human being is a small model of the whole global system. As such just like the oxygen, we need this Bitcoin or any cryptocurrency for breathing properly. There can never be life without oxygen, and this could explain the importance and sudden rise of Bitcoin. It's something the economy needs to survive and as such must exist side by side with the fiat money. To me the fiat money is like blood in the human body it can't be replaced or made and is needed for life as well. Without it, life is impossible. The world cannot exist without fiat. Now that we have Bitcoin or any cryptocurrency, we have two most important things in life. They co-exist as blood carry oxygen so fiat will need the cryptocurrency to do what it can't do. The advantages of Bitcoin and cryptocurrency are that it is readily available and is everywhere just like oxygen in the atmosphere. Air is not contained and can be in trillions whereas blood is limited and if you lose just a few can be lethal. High blood pressure can be viewed as inflation and if uncontrolled will result in the collapse of the economy. So, a great understanding of these things is needed and vital to a healthy economy. I think cryptocurrency will not replace fiat, but we can have a different cryptocurrency that act as fiat money. I have argued for a cryptocurrency known as Apocalypto or Calyptocurrency and this must not be confused with the end of the world. The idea is that the name is the opposite of cryptocurrency meaning open not hidden transparent. Crypto means hidden codes. The idea being that this is transactions between peer-to-peer where privacy matters. So, Calypto is ideal for governments where transparency is important. The government can be tempted to stop the operation of cryptocurrency because they might find it as a threat there to put them out of work. Most developed countries have tight money controls the European countries being good examples. The idea being that like human blood a loss of a few liters can be fatal. So, all government institutions and apparatus are given tasks to control the money keeping an eye on everyone that can mean an invasion of privacy, etc. They can justify such a breach on grounds of controlling money laundering, etc. In these countries, cryptocurrency redistributes money globally. I pointed above that the West has managed to grow the way it did because it was funded indirectly by developing countries supplying resources and skilled labor and taking money towards the center while printing most of the money and using the developing countries as markets to fight hyperinflation. So previous money has been flowing towards the center. Bitcoin and crypto reverse the process especially now. What is happening is that money is now going globally redistributing resources? The governments rely on limiting users and controlling boundaries, but Bitcoin removed all these boundaries and connected everyone globally. The idea that governments limit money etc. is also a survival strategy. Imagine when they abuse people and torture people and in the age of blockchain the word can travel globally fast and easily and the people have the resources or can easily raise the resources. Power is shifting now it's now like the power to the people. These cryptocurrencies raise money as people buy tokens in the hope that the token value will increase one day. To the owner a powerful way of raising money you would not otherwise raise. The government in this situation has no power to control who donates and how much he or she donates. So, a New World is booming. Blood like fiat as to be maintained to the same level. Lack of enough blood is lethal, and more blood can be lethal, so we have deflection and inflation. Okay too much oxygen is lethal too through oxidation, but oxygen can be manipulated by being converted or joined with other attributes to change the composition. I think this is true with Bitcoin too there are going to be FutureGoldCoin ours that will work well with Bitcoin before taking over as our currency's impact has far-reaching consequences. Making it a global phenomenon. Our currency apart from being a global currency for fast, easy and cheap ways to transact globally. It is also the New Single Reserve Global Currency. I refer you to the Whitepaper in the appendix for more details on how to solve all global problems. Bitcoin now is acting as money while FutureGoldCoin can and will work as a debt alleviation tool to fight global debt and as an insurance coin to cushion and boost the economy as well. Read our debt plan too in the Whitepaper. So, cryptocurrencies will have a great role to play. In the end I think just like the levels of oxygen needed will stabilize between 7 to 8 liters per day with the highest levels maybe around 11 000 liters per day intake can be influenced by activities etc. like running or jogging. So, inflation will be minimal as there is no control by the central authorities. The impact of Bitcoin will stabilize. I think our FutureGoldCoin can take over as it has global appeal.

There are benefits to the governments but it's a matter of weighing the pros and the cons. The current governments might not see the benefits of the new technology mainly because they will turn a blind eye and view any new technology as a threat but we as TWO will push harder and smarter to use technology to solve all problems and use the same technology to make us rich just imagine seating and earning even more than you would at work. It's not about trading time or life for money. Education and self-esteem will be boosted greatly. We will make technology work for us. I advocated for a better quality of life. Trading your life and time for money is wrong. The future is to digital governments as well with FutureGoldCoin and Calycoin not as alternatives but as the main digital currencies.

### The need for new laws.

I think new laws are a must. The FutureGoldCoin and Calycoin digital currencies are to be protected by our laws. I think it's everyone's right to have money only them can have access to. The current system makes it easy for the government to interfere and freeze your assets something I explained is used as a tactic referred to as the Colony Collapse Strategy where threats are targeted with lists drafted years in advance used and the assets of the so-called threats being frozen and taken by the governments. Governments might try to interfere with crypto and I think these accounts are out of reach they are personal properties and common goods sort off as they can easily be distributed globally and way-out of government control. We will protect people with crypto money as part of the freedom to possess and rights to wealth and riches. These governments have been in power for too long because they are playing unfairly taking all financial resources and using poverty as a weapon which is wrong. This conflicts with our laws. Above all money laundering will not apply to cryptocurrencies just like oxygen is everywhere and not contained in a body but can easily escape or be changed to carbon dioxide the same argument shall be used, and any people can easily convert the money to another currency. We as the global leader we will provide our own money the FutureGoldCoin and the Calycoin that can easily be converted to any currency mind you all 195 nations will print their new money and hand this new fresh printed money to us which we will deposit in their Global Reserve Bank account. We give them some money as our own Futuregoldcoin. The reason being that if they put their new fresh money into the economy, they will flood the economy and reduce the value of their currency. We take their new money and bank this in their savings account. We offer ours or equivalents to be offset or exchanged back when inflation has subsided. They use most of ours which is universal. Why it's a problem now is that the newly printed money has value only to that country only. The main reason why it's hard to get rich this way but we change that. But our plan works. We through Futuregoldcoin cushion the value of their currencies. Their new money can buy our money. As we exchange theirs with ours. They can trade globally using our money. Still can devalue theirs to boost exports. Above all, they have savings already with us. Our system forces nations to have savings that we pay interest on.

It does not stop there. We have a plan for global debt. All global debt contained and taken care of too never be a problem again. The only way to guarantee global wealth to levels never achieved before. Come ride with the best. We have the best answers. I AM Ready! Are you Ready?

# CHAPTER TWENTY-FOUR

## GET IN GET INVOLVED!

This chapter is for you the reader. I want you to be part of this change. I believe you must be part of this movement from the beginning. Your contributions, suggestions, and simply involvement means success for the project. We want you to be part of this movement. This is your chapter to write what you think so far. What we can change. How we can change that and how you feel about the whole issues discussed in this book. If you have any proposals, write them down in this chapter. I shall compile suggestions and all contributions to publish in the second edition. I want you to write down things close to your heart ones you think need attention. The way you are going to do it to help us priorities urgent issues is by prioritizing issues giving them points out often with the most urgent getting a ten and the least a one. We are a global movement and issues relevant to you in your area or region might be different from issues in other areas. This ranking method will help us tackle urgent issues first. We have new laws from Chapter Forty-One onwards that need adding on. We urge everyone to write what they think are to be classed as laws to tackle. Issues close to them etc. The whole process is open to discussions if hope now you understand what we stand for and what is needed of all mankind but what do you need? Our laws and systems are the framework for achieving our goals. This is the skeletal matter the foundation of who we are and what we stand for. We represent the wishes of you the people and as our slogan goes; Your Future Your Say. You will help shape your own future. We provide the platform for this to happen without you we would not be effective. We believe that we are here to be indebted to you the people. We exist to serve you the people, make you rich and take all humanity to levels never experienced before. We believe without you the reader our system will not be as effective as it would with you on board. So, the theme of this chapter is: Get in

Get Involved! Get in my seat and write this Chapter the way you want it. Tell us about issues you think need prioritizing and looking at. If you don't agree with some issues, I discussed above then state here why and what you think we should do instead. Rearrange our laws if you like and justify your decisions so we have a thorough evaluation of the best methods.

The idea is to involve everyone and be part of this. Although the idea is not to completely change the basic principles of this book because we believe the ranking of our laws and other issues is the best for solving global issues, but we can discuss all issues together. I will help you decide what is important to you, to us and to mankind.

### What do you think about banning wars globally and reducing and or evolving the military?

I think this is by far the most controversial part of our proposals. We are not surprised. In fact, we anticipated this. It's human nature to be skeptical and skeptical should you be. Life is unforgiving and unpredictable. We have the 'Element of Surprise Attacks' that have cost lives and trampled on all hopes we had on global peace and negotiations. People don't trust others and would rather be safe than sorry. The main issues are that after the wars there were talks of peace yet no effective laws to ban global wars were put in place. We believe that the current system is flawed it left loopholes that are easily taken advantage of. Above all, we believe that the current system is not designed to stop wars. Therefore. If you want to stop wars, you do like what we have done. Make laws and put these in place to stop the war. The UN declares peace, yet they have no powers at all to make laws and stop the wars. I have argued that to me and TWO the UN, it's Security Council, etc. are like impersonators who are giving women and kids all over the world hope and a false sense of security as these people believe that whatever threats of wars the UN or UNSEC will be there to stop these. So, what is happening is that people are given a false sense of security only to be killed through invasions and missiles attacks.

Our issues with the UN, UNSEC and all its subsidiaries are that they are trapping people to be killed. As they impersonate War Stoppers, they are making people not react. Instead of the women and kids running away from dangerous zones before the invasions or attacks they are made to take the risks of death lightly, so they stay. Our system identified and acknowledged these issues and proposed solutions. Banning wars and putting laws to do this globally is the only way forward. This eliminates fears of being attacked by others who might still possess' weapons. The second point is regarding national security. No one would wish to get rid of their national defenses. It's understandable and was justified a few years back but now people's perceptions and wants are changing. Most of the people in power or decision making are new generations with the hard-core warmongers gone or old who emphasized wars and defense. The new generations would rather stick to peace. A few years from now our system will be fully accepted globally with everyone getting rid of their fears and reducing defense budgets while evolving the military. If you know we spend $1.7 trillion on weapons and the military yearly, you will understand why we have all the problems we have.

Thirdly our system is to remove all fears and reliance on the military to boost the economy and fetch things we need cheaply. Our method ensures that everyone has enough money to buy at any price. If you can buy oil at any market price will there be a need for war? Those violating human rights is because they are choosing the wrong priorities. Instead of the people's welfare, they buy new missiles or defense systems, so people revolt or fight that injustice. But if they can afford to do both would there be uprisings? No. There won't be any. Think of any problems and the answer is new money and we have a perfect method just for that. Think of climate change. If there is enough money, we can invest in research and development into new energy sources. Everyone will be using electricity instead of oil, a fossil fuel. So, money is the answer. Countries that torture is because they don't have enough money and would try to silence the people who complain or report that way. If they had money people would not report because they would not feel compelled to push people away, in fact, they would need more people to stir growth so they would treat them right, etc.

The old generation of leaders are the problems, but as new blood gets into power, our ideas that are remote now will be the norm. People will start to see that we as a people can do better than we are doing. The current leadership's thinking is based on manipulation and the enslaving or abusing others for a living with the government apparatus at the forefront to justify jobs and huge budgets. But as the new generation emerges, people who want what's better for everyone, not just themselves then our system becomes the only true way to wealth and growth. So, it is fair to say that the current thinking is against demilitarization and cutting off military spending and channeling the resources elsewhere.

Your Opinion Matters.

## What do you think about Protection?

Some kind of government program where your father is killed unjustly after an accident where he is implanted with a chip or medical device that is said to help him with the injuries but only to be killed by this chip or medical device and then the government apparatus takes over the family pretending to teach and train but actually grooming everyone mostly for sexual favors to be used to further get other people chipped as well or implanted with medical devices. All this loss so that some idiot out there will have a job running around everyday thinking he or she is doing great providing for you throwing tips just for basic when you can drag them to court and get compensation or get them hanged. The scale at which this is happening is alarming and a cause of concern as everything is institutionalized and carried out by government apparatus. People in a position of trust.

Your Opinion Matters.

## We strongly believe that the current health system needs a strong revamp to keep it with the times.

We strongly believe that a lot needs to be done and imprint the ideas of saving lives again and not to play God and kill through the use of watermarks as ways to command people chipping of everyone as a health policy is against our laws. We strongly believe that the human body is pure and should be kept like that and some countries are deliberately changing their people as part of protection and a way of communication and identifying people through viral electromagnetic stimulation that is remotely operated by government apparatus. All this reduces quality of life and this chipping and implanting of devices is used as a business with people loaded with watermarks based on viral mutations and then asked to do worse things or pay high donations for the watermarks to be removed. Hell no. This must end one way or the other. It's the worst form of abuse and to make things worse it's done by people in a position of trust government apparatus; the hospitals, doctors police council, etc. This should never happen they are breaking all laws as the chipping is secretly done and after the time to take them to court usually 3- 6 months has expired, then you are abused at will. What is of great concern is that it is done by people in a position of power and speaking of grooming and abuse by people in a position of trust and the fact that they chip all kids would worry any human being? The whole system is based on rewards in the form of sexual arousal remotely through electromagnetic nerve stimulation where a diode and a chip are implanted or fired into the human body at birth and over years these kids are tortured and silenced by sexual arousal through the diodes and the chips. Over the years a pattern develops where they are abused and through the chips remotely aroused to breaking points as a reward. I think a lot, needs changing and doing. Express-command to put an end to this through our laws and courts as a deterrent. In some countries, the whole system is designed to age people faster. The chips and rotary devices implanted utilize radiation, and this is used to burn hair and make people look aged fast. We have conditions used as identifying marks and people are identified as under protection through these. What all they don't know is that the day they were born they were put on 'death row' and are genuine pigs with bioengineered, digital or cyber viruses being tested on them. Human testing as far as I know is banned yet it's widely practiced under the notion of the so-called protection. There are a lot of issues incompatible with our laws.

Your Opinion Matters.

## What do you think about sanctions?

We stand against sanctions as sanctions are used as a test of power; an evil and cruel way of aggravating others to act in order to justify attacking them. I think it's barbaric and evil. I don't care why they do it and what they are trying to achieve through sanctions I don't believe it's justified to kill women and children so that you justify an invasion. It evil beyond scope and in most cases it's people of one genetic heritage doing this on others and not on their own. So, we introduced empathy laws. If we are all humans and if one child dies in the west the whole world stands still and when 500 000 dies in Iraq it's acceptable and unavoidable collateral damage? Such thinking is against what we stand for and we have new laws to address this and trust me many will tumble to their deaths because of this. Do you know that terrorists use the same tactics as sanctions do? They both expose the intended target as weak and unable to protect his own women and children and can't fight back. This is followed by the local uprising against the target as they are angered as the target often does not react as he or she knows that the sanctions or terrorist act is to invoke them into attack mode to justify an invasion. What happens is that the target will channel his anger on the local rebels to revenge the death of women he will use the severe force, and this is what the people who imposed sanctions where after. A reason and justification for an invasion. Okay, this might have worked to justify invasion but make no mistake we have new laws that will sink all these evil trickery leaders who would rather play God and kill innocent women and children if they are not 'close to them'. Empathy laws will take the devil out of them.

Your Opinion Matters.

Every topic in this book is open for discussions and readers are encouraged to write down what they think, and use provided emails [info@tomorrowsworldorder.com] to give us feedback. Use space at the end of this book for notes, etc. Be part of this something new.

I need all your opinions to get involved. This is for you, your kids, and mankind. This is the perfect time odds are in favor of us. People at last have realized that there is more to life than being used as genuine pigs or lab rats with the governments making the illegal bioengineered or digital agents and testing these on their own people. Honestly, our laws will drag Presidents and Prime Ministers to court while still in office. Doing nothing when issues like this are raised is a crime punishable by death. Ignorance is not an excuse and doing nothing is the same as killing all these innocent people and we can't tolerate that. Topics to cover are endless. I have raised some challenging ideas and methods some wild enough but vital enough for steering change. This chapter is just for you to express how you feel about everything in this book.

Address the laws in Chapter Forty-One onwards.

Thank you for being part of Tomorrow's World Order.

Founder/President.

Signed.

# CHAPTER TWENTY-FIVE

## THE IMMEDIATE FUTURE.

A strong need to put things in place to kick-start the journey to a totally different New World. Some changes take time, but everything should be in place and people on standby to take certain strategic positions for a smooth implementation of our project. A clear and detailed plan is in place clearly stating our goals and what needs to be achieved with time frames. Our immediate plan is to establish units globally with people representing us occupying certain positions globally. I think first is to draft our laws and make these available globally where anyone can easily access and acknowledge reading and understanding these. Dates to be set when the laws will come into effect and what is needed from everyone that is to cooperate, acknowledge and confirm that they understand that a New World Order is taking over certain functions of the globe and there is nothing to panic about. We are just rewriting what everyone knows already and prioritizing certain laws over others and banning certain activities we believe are the root causes of issues we have today. When everything is in place, we make an official statement introducing ourselves and explaining what we stand for and how we have made new global laws that everyone must obey. These laws are not something new. Everyone is familiar with them. We are just arranging the current laws to remove any ambiguity and confusion. We will ban any wars from a certain date but for those power-hungry maniacs who would want one last chance to play with their toys there is a window say a one or two-year period to start a World War Three but after that, no wars shall be fought whatsoever. So initially is to lay the new laws that people can review and make suggestions and nothing more. We sat down and come up with these laws, and there is nothing that needs changing for the time being until we have passed the transitional stage. Everything in the place is for a purpose. After the implemented has been achieved, we might scale down some aspects and activities while augmenting others. Everyone must show commitment and work together with us for the benefit of all humanity. We will hold meetings to explain our initial stage and address any issues people might have. The initial phase is characterized by the implementation and publication and launching of our laws and platforms to achieve this. We will declare from day one fixed dates to ban wars.

>Wars banned after a year or two of the first announcement. Time period to destroy big boys' toys even if that means World War Three so be it.

>Weapons manufacturing for any reason is banned with immediate effect. These include guns, missiles, landmines, grenades, arsenal launchers, bombs, etc. Immediate ceasing of production. Closing or evolving of these facilities, etc. Fixed dates for everyone to comply with our new laws.

>Immediate ceasing of making Weapons of Mass Destruction for the few countries still with privileges to do so. Even though this is related to the above law I think this must be separate for everyone to understand the implications of continuing when we have ordered immediate ceasing of production. These include banning and immediate ceasing of production for nuclear weapons, especially by the developed countries. No country on earth will have any privileges to make nukes.

>Disarmament. Every country on earth should draft and implement a plan to disarm all its weaponry by a certain date. We don't want a situation where some have disarmed then we find some still having the weapons. Everyone shall disarm at the same time. This is to give everyone peace of mind and not fear surprise attacks when they had just disarmed.

>If there is not a World War Three, then all weapons must be handed to TWO or safely destroyed by approved methods which we will put in place.

>Our aim is to reduce too much bureaucracy and facilitate smooth operations encouraging networking and cooperation. We shall act as a catalyst to speed up negotiations and mutual understanding.

>It's our main duty to remove any fears of e.g. surprise attacks that

may arise after disarmament and stopping of making weapons in the belief that others might still be clinging to weapons. We shall make sure that everyone disarms at the same time as others in order to provide a platform where peaceful negotiations can begin.

>We are responsible for providing the platform and processes needed to achieve global peace.

>Our aim is not to tie down the people and leaders with too much paperwork to sign or read. We will advance technology that all our laws will be available on all gadgets and in public places for everyone to read and just confirm say on their phones. This information is recorded permanently if a blockchain is used. Follow-ups for those who did not acknowledge that they have read the laws. The initial acknowledgment is very important as everyone must read and understand our laws, so follow-ups and checkups are mandatory. Confirmations can be sent instantly from phones to decentralized systems for safekeeping and the computer or system will be able to confirm that that person has indeed read and confirmed the law.

>Governments are encouraged to draft or amend their own laws basing ours as the focal points. They can supplement but not alter ours.

>Everyone has a right to life, and no one shall be deprived of this right no matter what the circumstances. Your people and your enemies all have rights safeguarded by our new laws. It is a criminal offense to end life willingly or unknowingly through reckless behavior, ill judgment or indirectly. Our laws will protect everyone including the decision-makers by showing everyone which laws to priorities. No other laws whatsoever will override the first rule.

>The quality of life must be above reasonable standards meaning a person is entitled to a peaceful quality of life free from any kind of interference or tampering. Any tactics to reduce people's self-esteem conflict with this rule and therefore is illegal and can trigger proceedings to be brought against the person breaching these. There are so many things that tamper with the quality of life like unnecessary noise or intentionally created confusion scenes to distract and or frighten people. The provision of poor-quality

services can affect the quality of life as this might cause distress and anxiety in the affected people. Criminal charges can be brought against institutions that fall below standard intentionally or unintentional. We passed a stage when institutions and other government departments offer basic services. This stage if for these entities and bodies to provide above standard levels. Quality matters in this stage as simply providing a basic level can trigger a not-fit for -purpose clause. Accountability shall prevail and people will be answerable for their actions.

>Everyone has a right to self-preserve meaning people can use force to defend themselves and might get away with it. Unnecessary and unprovoked violence will not qualify for self-defense. A high self-esteemed society will understand the right to live if possible, maybe 200 years or forever and to achieve that in certain cases they must defend themselves may be using force. Unfair situations might trigger the right to self-defense clause. For instance, Iran might give a self-defense plea if say the US has imposed sanctions and wants to engage military action. Iran might argue that the system is unfair the USA, is not just the USA but is backed by other cult members of NATO who can rely on Article 5 that says an attack on one is an attack on all of them. It can go on to say not only does the USA part of a gang or bully but has unfairly chosen to make WMDs itself in the form of nukes which it is threatening to use on them. Such an unbalanced scenario can justifiably cause Iran to try to match the USA and its Allies' force and possession of nukes by making nukes themselves which they might argue that any reasonable man who is faced with such a threat who would not do the same is insane. Iran as a country rich in oil can be forced to take extra steps like making nukes too to give themselves a chance of survival in case they are attacked. The reasoning being that just like a businessman they are entitled to have a gun or a nuke license as the risks of being attacked due to their possessions or wealth are high. It might argue that the intention of the USA is to grab its oil resources rather than a case of human rights. In the New World, they might succeed that any reasonable man would do the same and as such, they are defending what is rightfully theirs from a formidable force in the USA and NATO with their nuke's arsenal.

You can witness that this is a total shift from the current situation and a real case of justice. This is what Saddam might have argued, and this is emphasized by the fact the Britain and the USA were adamant that Iraq possessed WMDs. To them given the formidable force, it was unreasonable of Saddam not to make nukes to leverage the playing field and give himself and his people better odds of survival. This can explain the fact that the two countries above thought Saddam had WMDs otherwise his actions would have been like fighting against the goads.

All this is not something that is new, but the current system gives everyone loopholes to take advantage of and kill innocent women and children. Never again. We as TWO we believe these people are the future of any country. It is not a surprise anywhere that the developed countries do not consider the lives of these people as it can be argued that they don't relate to situations like this. In their countries, the largest percentage of the population is made up of old people mainly pensioners. So, care must be taken when dealing with cases like this but nevertheless, that is not an excuse giving orders that conflict with our first rules. They know and it is part of the indirect international law that is often overridden by other laws that put weight on national security over rights of individuals. Too, a thing of the past. Tomorrow's World Order has removed all the justifications for overriding the first rules and end up killing innocent people. We worked hard and smart and we will continue to do so. Wars and military accounts for more than eighty percent of today's global problems.

Weapons manufacturing is used;

*to compete with other services like food provision, better education, better infrastructure and channeling of money into research and development or even health.

*weapons are used to instill fear with missile testing the main culprit causing anxiety and panic that smaller countries end up buying weapons sacrificing other social issues.

*weapons are used to boss others around and engaging in illegal wars for personal gains. Of course, everyone wants cheaper oil, but for mankind, it's easy-to-use weapons to get what we want than to pay a fair price. If no weapons, then we save all that money and plow it into oil and the oil-producing countries might plow the money back into oil and find cheaper ways of processing thus reducing the price thereby benefiting everyone.

*weapons are used to create a situation of dependence on fossil fuels that people are not plowing money into research and development for other alternate fuels.

*weapons are used to justify incompetence and wastage and just to fulfill political agendas and goals.

*weapons are used to perpetrate human rights abuses where warlords are given weapons to kill their citizens violating a lot of international laws.

I can go on and on, but you can agree with me that banning weapons production and forcing the military to evolve is a major step towards solving all our problems and achieving global peace. We must draft anticipatory laws that foresee future problems and put laws before the problem arise. This is true with digital weapons the so-called digital soldiers but to me WMDs. There are two sides of the same coin; one tail and the other a head. There are also equal chances that if a coin is tossed, the outcome can be a tail or a head. But what if the coin is a programmed digital coin no matter how you flip it the outcome will always be a head? What are the chances that when the other people, when they toss the coin the outcome for them is always a tail? What if the tail is a beneficial attribute like making one clever and the head side be a brain shaking device that rotates like a drone's propeller that is operated remotely through a satellite-programmed sequence with the aim of causing memory loss or brain damage? Mind you we are talking about the same coin here but with two different and opposite effects. Our duty of being the world leaders must be a duty to anticipate technology through research and development and plan and implement laws in advance. There are no universal digital laws and now we even have a new threat like a cyber electromagnetic attack. But the time people start understanding it and realizing that it's the same as the weapons which we have banned. The same weapons but only just with a fancy name that makes evil sounds sexy it might be too late by then. We cannot afford to be reactive and must be proactive. Being reactive costs lives.

Moving from the military and defense we can start implementing health laws too. The current health system is founded on war grounds and we haven't heard wars in years that can justify their huge budgets etc. and to make things worse they are still reacting like they are in war zones. The biggest threats to such a situation are the pressures to keep up that will force some to take dirty and dangerous roads of doing business. We end up with hospital evolving the wrong way and adopting extracurricular activities with disastrous consequences.

*Hospitals have moved from just hospitals to acquire other functions and becoming teaching hospitals. Universities work very hard promoting their universities to have enough students. Most of these students make free decisions and chose which universities to go to. But what about hospitals especially teaching hospitals? To remain operational and justify the budgets they must have enough 'students' to teach. Okay in some cases where it's natural it can be understandable that life can leave orphans and drugs can rack people's lives etc. but what if the hospitals have become assassins killing fathers around the globe so that they take over from these loving husbands and fathers and groom their kids to use as bait in prostitution, guinea pigs to test new drugs on, or bait to get the few lucky ones who are not chipped at birth be chipped? We all know the CIA used prostitutes in the 1980s to corner politicians and people they wanted. But where the whole institutions rely on tagging each one on security grounds, then it becomes an issue of international law. What if the hospitals now own poppy fields for growing heroin for prescription purposes? What if they have prostitution rings driving the whole system creating war zones like situations with prostitutes chased by ambulances etc.? What if these institutions with people in a position of trust are now the ones making digital and cyber weapons to recreate war zone situations, so they remain viable and having jobs? My point is to assess if this has gone too far to amount to poor-quality of life for those affected being deliberately being loaded with watermarks, digital and cyber agents. This is a new area that can't be easily proved but one we know is happening. What is enough to drive the institutions and what amounts to genocide tendencies and crimes against humanity? How do we strike a balance?

>The main issue is with the initial tagging at birth that is illegal and unjustified. So new laws banning secretive human chipping at birth without consent and waiting for court lifelines to expire so that they further abuse the victims.

>Banning of all-time limits regarding the law. New laws overriding all current practices especially regarding medical practices in developed countries where the problem has reached unacceptable levels.

>A new 24-hour system supplemented by the advanced smart contracts that execute cases without the need for judges etc. unless if the matter is serious enough or can't be solved.

>Stripping off immunity and using decentralized systems to encourage abused people to send information to the blockchain to be kept permanent and automatic linking to the smart contract system that starts the proceedings fast. The benefit that their parties mainly people in positions of power have themselves become so corrupt that they have lost the plot and what is expected of them. Removing these removes the situation of further abuse and intimidation with the result that the victims might be scared to come forward. The smart contract system allows people to do this secretly in the safety of their homes with information sent to other people within the block to validate before the smart contract executes.

>Banning of the making of any digital or cyber or any future digital or other technology that will conflict with the first rules.

? Any cases of death of the head of the house where the police and the doctors and nurses then went to take over must be fully investigated in most cases it's murder as the fathers had been in accidents where they are then illegally tagged and hacked which is often the cause of death as remotely gadgets are used to tamper with the body functions. This is hacking and a hacker just like a computer hacker has the following main aims and goals.

*To cause malfunction by altering the otherwise functioning system.

*A hacker's aim is to replace the system and reverse functions stopping some and doing all kinds of damage remotely through satellites, etc.

*Hacker's aim is to hold the person in ransom using the person's family or assets in the hard drive as ransom. In this case, threatening to take over the family who they groom and teach "how to live their way" matchmaking with people of interest to them or giving these as gifts to celebrities and other politicians for political gains like weakening the opposition by associating them with prostitutes or abuse that damages their political or social career.

*A hacker in the end expects drastic change that result in malfunction or death.

The fact that it is institutionalized with orders probably at the top is a cause for concern and as such we shall investigate suspicious cases where the implanted devices are the cause of death through hacking by people in power or their delegates. In some cases, they offer the victims to prominent people like celebrities in exchange for political donations, etc. Laws to ban such practices and stiff penalties in cases where it can be proved that the institutions encouraged abuse and waited until the person is dead to start condemning the problem.

Laws banning hospitals to own or get involved in drug production like heroin for medical purposes. Research and development into alternative medicines.

**Banning of heroin to be used as a prescription drug.**

Banning and stiff penalties for doctors implanting and chipping people secretly without them knowing.

Advanced research and technology that detect implanted devices by making them behave erratically that they can be recorded and the proof to be used in courts.

Laws to allow such evidence and use of phones and apps to provide such a technology to the world globe.

Again, uploading to the blockchain that can't be tampered with permanent transactions that can be revisited at a future date.

### Revoking doctor's licenses and starting court proceedings.

If the system is institutionalized in that the doctor's act was part of what can be regarded as 'initiation' then a change of accountability to include the order givers as well as the priority with both being punished severely. Change in law to summon the order givers as well as now it's just looking at the person who has committed a crime with the order givers walking away. Other laws can be used to bring the heads and order givers to justice too. One must prove that the issue is systematic that any one of the workers could have followed the order with the same disastrous consequences and as such then the order giver is answerable. You just need to prove that even if another person had followed the same command, the issue would have been created. Again, no immunity for anyone if there is the death of a person and a violation of the first rule. Some accidents if proved still might amount to killings through negligent acts or intentional. We will bring in other laws where we assess if this is done just to say indigenous people then we can check if it is through undue regard to lives simply because the person feels distance to them and show no remorse or empathy and if the same issue had been presented to those he relates himself with them could he have acted differently, then we will not hesitate to punish and get rid of such a person. We have a rule that complements that first rule we shall call this Article 1.

### Article 1

A killing of one shall be regarded as killing the whole. Abuse on one shall be treated as an abuse on all. The underlying principle behind this line of thinking is the fact that some crimes threaten the fabric on which society is founded on and all international laws. There are universal laws that fall under the Jus Cogens and as such any derogation from is not just prohibited but makes one regarded as an enemy of mankind. An enemy of mankind means a Hostis Humani Generis a person who threatens all humanity and as such acts of torture on one trigger Article 1 and such a crime is viewed as if the crime has been committed to all people on earth. It is everyone's duty to take things into their own hands as long as they can prove precedents before or prove that such an act was an attack on all humanity.

What actions will trigger Article 1

*Illegal hacking secretive or otherwise. Hacking conflicts with the first rules in that it reduces life and quality of life and anything that conflicts with the first two rules is punishable by death by the assassin.

*Hacking makes it easy to enslave people arising into secretive modern-day slavery with the hacked often with no rights at all with the hacker abusing for personal gains, sexual or other gratification of seeing someone suffering.

*Hacking violets all international laws as it restricts the right to family life, right to privacy. Right to life. Right to a free good quality life. The right to freedom of speech as the hacked is tortured not to speak or report the culprit. Hacking is used as a form of evil submission with the victim tortured until he or she obeys.

*The hacked is deprived of chances to bring the culprits to justice as he is often followed through GPS and people told lies about the victim to tarnish his or her name to destroy credibility and make him or her not trusted. And as such is not believed.

*Violets patents and trademark laws with the hacker stealing information which he or she can later show to the victim to intimidate or further abuse the person or maybe claim joint ownership of works they were never involved with in the first place.

*Most people who do this have evil blood. Their past point to a dark phase in history where they might have done something maybe outlawed today like slavery. They might have been at the forefront and then looked for advanced ways of doing the same thing but now hidden and out of sight without any chance of being caught. As such, they keep abusing. As such new laws to look at a period in history when the accused might have done something. These issues must be understood.

>All sanctions banned. I explained why they are a thing of the past. Sanctions are tactics that affect third parties and these people are used as bait to gain favorable stances in negotiations. Terrorists

use the same methods and they are against it but who then must allow them to do the same thing? Sanctions are targeted at women and children who leverage the power bargain in favor of the sanction grantor. If people declare terrorists as evil based on their tactics what makes them better if they use the same methods. Sanctions invokes Article 1. Sanctions have no negotiation aims but are there to weaken the opposition in most cases if used by developed on developing they are meant to kill women and children to justify military action. Our new laws prohibit the use of such tactics. Not even a single life shall be taken unfairly due to imposed sanctions which act indirectly limiting vital medical supplies and food with many dying of hunger and malnutrition. To show we mean business we are going to add other criteria to be considered too. If the person or nation that imposed the sanction is of different background, we shall assess if 'the fact that he or she doesn't relate to the victims' plays any role too. Again, I want to emphasize that this won't be a case of race but of the lack of empathy to people of different genetic heritage as you simply because you don't relate to them. This will be a case to show that some actions adopted are as a direct result of unfamiliarity with the victims that lacks empathy because he or she is not close or don't feel that closeness caused by different backgrounds. So, we shall say that 'he didn't give a fuck' pardon my French simply because he or she does not empathize with the victims.

"**Empathy** is the capacity to understand or feel what another person is experiencing from within their frame of reference, that is, the capacity to place oneself in another's position [1] Definitions of empathy encompass a broad range of <u>emotional</u> states. Types of empathy include cognitive empathy, emotional empathy, and somatic empathy."

Wikipedia

This could explain why if hundreds of people are killed by bombs etc. in the Middle East people in the West don't really empathize with them but if one dies in the West the whole world stands still. This is because the others are remote for one to care so much, human nature. Our aim is to put a strong sudden end of all this, and we shall be tough and use everything at our disposal to make sure that evil won't keep lurking. I am not declaring war on good people. I am not fighting law-abiding citizens; no. My aim is neither personal nor should this be taken lightly. We have a duty to do. We have laws to put an end to all these evil acts taking young lives. We don't care who you are rich, poor, educated or not. Our question is whether you respect everyone's life, or you are a cherry picker very selective choosing others for destruction and commanding others to be slaughtered. If yes, then why but still, there are no justifications. A life for life case can arise in these situations. There are a lot of other laws that can invoke Article 1 as you will find with time.

## Conflict resolution Platform.

I think after establishing all the laws and implemented these so that everyone on earth can read and understand these laws and know what is expected of them. Ignorance is not an excuse I know people can get away with it because laws are not clearly established and there is a lot of ambiguity and confusion with people taking the law into their own hands. In the New World, everyone is expected to know all the laws that relate to that person. Once the law issue is out of the way the next important phase is that of establishing a conflict resolution platform. This is not a physical place or area no but a way of dealing with issues that have global implications. Now it depends on the two leaders concerned where they communicate directly and arrange to say meetings and the outcome left to chance. I respect everyone's privacy and we will do our best that the initial communications will be between the leaders concerned until there is stalling in talks where they have to involve a third-party who will act as a catalyst just to facilitate and guide according to the New World laws. We can't allow situations where leaders meet and just abandon the meetings due to disagreements, etc. This is the time we come or other appointed leaders or bodies. The aim is to close deals. Any global issues can't be left hanging. This is a major problem currently. These leaders understand dialog is part of being a leader and they do their best and just ignore the rest. We have witnessed many meetings, but most ended up in a stalemate. The spirit is there but just needing the right person to act not as a judge or decision-maker but a facilitator and a catalyst who can keep removing obstacles and leveling the negotiating field. This is one of the main reasons why negotiations end without any results. It's not a matter of forcing but that of understanding and bargaining for both the parties involved asking both to sacrifice a bit until they can agree on something. Then we can follow on that to see that the plans are not abandoned after a first trial. Communication can be through a system like a blockchain or any faster system that enables instant messaging and linking between all global leaders where they can communicate and arrange meetings etc. Security will be provided, and privacy guaranteed as well. We need a system that easily connects all the leaders where they either choose to use the system or not, but it should be there. The idea is to reduce too much bureaucracy and not create another United Nations. No offense it has done great work in giving everyone a great job but without impact on the ground. They can't prevent any wars and we can't have a situation where we leave things to chance or where a few controls the lives of everyone especially if their policies are to keep making nukes and other WMDs. We have a duty to protect humanity and that can mean showing the right path and give genuine reasons that are universally accepted. There are a lot of areas that can be used to create jobs for everyone. We don't want the institution to be there just for the sake of it. We want genuine problem-solving institutions that in the end will have nothing to do so that they can evolve again. The idea is to create institutions that have no plans to be there forever but to solve problems and move on to other things. These are not companies so all government, independent bodies, and NGOs that are expecting to be in existence even after say 20 years from the date of inception to us are not serious about solving the problems at hand. We want to put a system where these bodies etc. have a limited lifespan where they can only extend based on what they have achieved. Our aim is to assess say an issue and draft detailed plans that show when we expect the problem to be solved and after that, we would not expect the bodies to be still there tackling the same issue but would expect them to move to the next issue.

**The idea of a short-term-relay approach to problem-solving.**

I think this is a fair method where institutions and government organizations etc. must tackle an issue for a limited number of years before they lose their license. The license can be extended based on merit. We expect these institutions to go in and solve the issues we identify. Once they have solved the problems, then they apply for another license for a different task. The idea is to incorporate evolving and make these institutions throw everything to solve the issue. The current system is the one making things worse where people look forward to their pension and thereby stretch the work to get as much as they can. Most of these people know there are real issues and choose to do nothing but wait for a fat check at the end of the month. Solving the problems would put them out of business and a loss of income. I understand but I say this is just to be comfortable. This is what is going on now but something we shall not encourage or tolerate. We are humans the best there can ever be. The idea is to keep evolving getting a better job after a better job. The ideas are to keep learning I don't mean going to the university again and again, but I mean everyone should keep challenging themselves to aim higher and higher. This is the only way you can boost your self-esteem as well. Imagine how you felt about your last job. You can only see the difference once you have got another job. Then you will realize the last job was probably the worst you have ever had. You ask yourself what was going on spending so many years in most cases getting peanuts or over-worked trading time and money. All this is poor thinking. We shall change even pensions schemes that you don't need to be with one company to receive pension the most important thing most people look forward to. You hear a twenty-something lad clinging to a dead-end job simply because of the pension. I think the pension should be like a personal savings account which you can carry all the time it doesn't matter which job you are doing. It's not employer-specific but employee one. There is a need for flexibility of some sort. So, all institutions will be registered and given plans or show their plans with time frames they expect to have tackled the issue. After that period, they cannot take the same task or issue but take a different one unless it is justified on merit that they did a great job and as such deserves an extension. Say after 5 or 10 Years one institution is tackling poverty after that they rotate and tackle a different issue say climatic change. In their place, another urgency comes in in their place with their own ideas and plans to deal with the issue until the issue is solved or reduced to manageable levels. So, we have a group of rotating institutions that are not tied to a certain issue all their existence but can only stay on that issue by merit. Our aim as a global leader is to tackle the issue that has been going on for the last seventy years. We can't afford to do nothing. It's time we tackled the basics and eliminate these first. There are real challenges ahead and it's worrying about a job sweeping dirt under the carpet, so you remain in your job. We will put laws that reward those who would prefer to work for short times on certain issues and change as the situation demands. We are humans and we are always learning and evolving. Those who change must be rewarded so they don't feel like losing out. In the end, we have advanced people who understand the whole life cycle the only way we will find real answers and invent new useful things. The current system makes people's hopes, passions and dreams die once they become civil servants, etc. That makes them age faster too and only look forward to pensions. This must not be tolerated. Our goals are to keep humanity ever-evolving and young. What makes people young or age faster also depends on what happens in life too. We need to keep everyone motivated and active. I am not saying this can be done say tomorrow we know people have obligations that make them tied to the boring energy-draining jobs. We will adopt a holistic approach where people are educated as well to reduce say the number of kids they can have. This is not a must like in China where the government takes the initiative, I know China's case is different but the whole globe can do the same willingly. We must provide incentives and things that make people put emphasize on themselves. A high self-esteemed society in the end would be willing to have a few kids in the hope that they would not afford to compete with their kids for financial resources. The current system is that once you have kids, you switch from working for yourself and family to working for the kids in the hope that they will look after you in old age. Imagine when you will be as young as them. You will need as much money as them. You will need that vacation too, etc. That new car too? A bigger house, etc. In the end, you will be forced to work smarter rather than harder as the current system encourages. The problem with the current system is that it rewards hard work better than smarter thinking that people must work like slaves all their lives without nothing to prove it. You must do overtime, work long hours, be stressed all the time to feel you are doing something and have a better salary as well. Our system is to make people work a few hours and not to rely just on their job for everything. We must come up with ways to make people make extra money on the side legally of course. If things like cryptocurrencies are understood and included in the system if the benefits outweigh the bad things, then people can use these for extra income. I think it would be a lack of good judgment to ban things that redistribute wealth. I justified my chance by explaining that cryptocurrency is like oxygen in the body and blood is like our fiat money system. We can't live without both; blood and oxygen, and other gasses but these are the two most important. If the world economy is like a human body suffering from high blood pressure when we have more of some elements and deflation when we miss some just like the economy too much money [blood] can give the economy a high blood pressure with inflation resulting. You can see the logic so banning cryptocurrency is like starving a body of oxygen with the resultant brain damage. We don't want that but likewise, too much of this oxygen can kill too through oxidation of the organs. The challenge is to strike the right balance.

**Against unnecessary government control and stifling of the economy.**

We shall pass laws that challenge certain government where we can prove that their policies are creating global problems or helping to worsen the situation. Gone are the days when some governments recklessly can choose policies that can do more harm than good. Mind you we are responsible for global prosperity too. The idea of doing nothing is a thing of the past we shall do all we can to achieve that dream. The immediate future is characterized by strong never heard before ambitious plans and laws that will change the scene we know today. Things will never be the same again. The first time in 'office' we shall draft laws that will ban a lot of things we think are creating the problems we are having. This includes banning reliance on fossil fuels. Anything that uses fossil fuels will be banned or mad to evolve or be redesigned. The idea is to push hard research and development into other energy sources. These fossil fuels are going to run out anywhere we might as well start now and not wait when all the oil reserves had gone dry. We shall spearhead competitive practices with the aim of finding technologies that rely on clean and cheaper energy sources mainly renewable ones. Cars that use fuels will be a thing of the past. Trains, lorries, machines, houses, etc. will all be banned and phased out globally. We shall force and distract the world's fears of killing each other by giving them challenges that will act as distractions that will make the world a better place for everyone. Nations will compete with each and reward the best. That is part of networking and cooperation.

## Networking and Cooperation.

The idea throughout this book is to bridge the whole globe literally and metaphorically. We shall do it cleverly without anyone noticing maybe until the end. We shall make sure we challenge all the governments concerned to see how best they can tackle certain issues in their countries., Give them time frames then see who is the most advanced and with better methods that can be adopted by others for a fee, etc. We are not against property rights or making the whole world socialist again, no. The idea is to network everyone sharing ideas through contracts where for a fee, other countries can use someone's technology too. This happens today although restricted. The idea is to open the whole globe that is what globalization is about. We shall let technology drive our policies as only technology advancement can help us achieve our goals.

## Institutions and their impact on our plans.

The immediate future will be characterized by conflicts with current institutions with us asking them to evolve or shutdown and them defending their roles and impact. No matter how sad and unfair it might sound the problems we have are a direct result of their existence. Most of these institutions were established just after or during the war mainly the Second World War. Their roles and aims then were different from the situation at hand today. After the wars, everyone was scared after witnessing the trauma caused by witnessing these wars. During wars, human rights laws are rarely observed or appreciated to such an extent. Seventy years on surely a lot has changed. These institutions were tasked with unique tasks and to be honest we still have the issues that were problems then. I am sure the UN for example was to maintain world peace. To stop wars etc. but we have wars even as recent of a few years back with strikes on Syria. The UN did nothing to stop the wars but actually acted as a catalyst for wars a good example being the Iraq wars where they went in Iraq to do a SWOT analysis for the West and their Allies to assess whether they can attack Iraq without suffering enormous casualties. All this talk about Weapons Inspectors is just a fancy phrase. In this case, they helped the West attack knowing having exposed the weakness of Saddam and his people. Now we are arguing that the UN can't be trusted to act neutral and as such, we can't afford to put the lives of innocent women and children at risk. We can't trust them to do what they promised to do. Their credibility is damaged beyond repair. We have 500 000 women and children who died when all they could do is say the Iraq war was illegal without any action to stop or intervene or even just to delay giving refugees to escape. In that case, they have blood on their hands too. These women and children put trust in them to stop the war and defend them and protect their lives, but they didn't. But who is to blame and what can they do when their hands are tied? That brings me to the main issue at hand. What else did you expect? Now we analyze what was expected of them anywhere in the first place.

>The UN simply took over from the LN which they all acknowledged was not-fit for the purpose. Just like this LN they had failed to stop the war that occurred on their watch. But to be honest, how can they stop the war without putting anything in place. This is where we differ from institutions like the UN. If you really want to stop the war, you ban the wars and put that into a law that everyone follows. Do they do that? A big no. So automatically from the word go they are not-fit for the purpose. If you want to stop the war, you must have the means to do so. The UN is a body of pen pusher who wouldn't kill a fly. A bunch of puppets put in place by the very same people we are saying they are breaking all international laws. They don't have the machinery or mechanism to enforce what they are set to do.

>The UN was established to be one of the attack mechanisms where they act proactively to list down threats who they bring to justice through the International Criminal Courts. I explained above how the Allies of the 1940s after witnessing the effects of the Second World War swore to never go to war like that before as wars have no winners. Before this war they adopted a defensive approach where they grow bigger and bigger to deter enemies and protect themselves but this did not work so after the 1945 war they embarked on an attack approach where they acted fast through a twenty-five to fifty-year war contingency plan where they made a list which is updated with problem countries if you like based on ability to start a war. Oil means easy money to develop and buy weapons, so we see the emphasis and merciless attacks of oil-rich nations especially those that have nationalized these resources. So, after the second war, the West adopted the Colony Collapse Strategy where they targeted the alpha threats and colonized the remaining society putting puppets. The Middle East is rich in oil and is an upper-level threat and for these, military action is a must for any President. You will see that Iran is the next on the list. The next President or Prime Minister will find a way to fulfill the war contingency plan and topple Iran then Syria or Saudi Arabia, etc. So back to the point in question the UN is there to monitor and inspect and provide feedback so that military action to be taken will cause fewer casualties among the West and its Allies and nothing to do global justice. These bodies were put in place by the West and are answerable to them. They are just an extending hand of the West even in the literal sense in that they are funded by the West through contributions with other countries donating generously to silence them. So, they are powerless to stop any wars. So how come they are responsible for stopping wars and maintaining peace. The last blow was just before the Iraq war or even the recent Syrian strikes where all they only could say was that the war was illegal without organizing rallies to protest, etc. We mean business and we shall use their laws to beat them at their own game. We shall be the voice of the voiceless. We shall defend those who need our defense. We shall stand for everyone even for the soldiers themselves. Our laws are not selective, and we see no boundaries, etc. We shall be very strict and when it starts to sink in these women-and-children-killers will wish they were never

born. The major crime one can commit is the crime being committed now against the defenseless.

## The Greatest Crime: Giving people a false sense of security.

I personally think this is the greatest crime one can commit. I think that this is not just a crime to give people a false sense of security and only for the worst to happen when you can't do anything. A very good example is the UN's approach of doing nothing to stop the Iraq war. Many people believed that they were going to stop the war. That could explain why a few people reacted or took to the streets than the numbers that could have been expected if the UN didn't exist. Most people saw the UN as bigger and powerful than the USA and Britain. Most did not react because they assumed the UN would spread its protecting wings and stop or at least delay the war. I am not going to talk about the benefits of the wars nor that am I happy that I am getting fuel cheaper, no. This is not the point. We as Tomorrow's World Order have a duty to prevent global wars and the needless deaths of innocent women and children. I think all those who died today would want the UN to explain to them why they let them down. People expected them to act as what they say they are there to do. Giving everyone a false sense of security leading to their deaths. I think it's one of the greatest crimes because the fact that they are there and say that they can act to stop wars prevents everyone else from acting. Most will simply do nothing just because a 'solution' is there. If the UN was not going on telling everyone that it's their job of protecting everyone some nations, bodies or leaders knowing that a huge number of women would die surely they were going to do something because it's everyone's duty to defend the innocent as stated by international laws. Killing these people is against what is called the Jus Cogens laws that stipulate that certain crimes have universal jurisdiction that committing them in one country or to certain people can make anyone face justice. Surely there were nations that could have talked-out these countries from invading. The UN establishment is the West's tactic to go around the Jus Cogens laws and make it easy for the West to attack. Have you ever watched rugby? I must say my ex played female rugby, and she was great while at Uni, so I know a few things. In rugby, there are strikers who must be protected. These are the targets of everyone and as such, every team must come up with decoys if you like. Or ones who obstruct or block the defenders of the other team so the striker can easily go and try that is scored by grounding the ball while touching it.

### Need for a [rugby] try.

What you witnessed with the events leading to the Iraq war was a perfect try. Yes, a rugby try. All these nations, NATO, the UN, the ICC, the ICJ, etc. are all rugby players in all parts of the West team. They all have important roles to play and the main aim is for the team to score as many tries as they can. When you hear about trials performed by the UN's subsidiary body the ICC the major players would also aim to score a try. Like I said all these are tactics to blind and deceive and make it easy for the team to score a perfect try what happens after is not important the goal of the team has to be realized as they can always sacrifice their own if the worst happens. You can see why I was talking about providing a false sense of security. This is a tactic so that the goal is achieved as people are surprised so much for the element of surprise. The UN as a rugby player distracted the opposition defenders pretending it has the ball in its possession so that everyone's focus is on them but in fact the striker behind is the one who had the ball and as such was unmarked left alone with everyone surrounding the UN the decoy. So unchallenged the striker went on to score a perfect try. The time the defenders realized that the UN the decoy had no ball it was too late the striker had already scored a perfect try. This has the effect that it further diminishes the after-math challenge that would otherwise arise if the defenders had not been tricked. The first reaction of the defenders in this case is a sense of guilt and blame themselves so actually shifting fault from the striker to themselves. This has the effect of psychologically attaching themselves and standing in the position of the striker. Whatever happened was partly for them to blame too. So immediately they soaked into feelings of guilt and not anger. The time it sinks in that there is nothing they could have done; they had been tricked by a clever devious manipulator the reaction time gap will have ceased. In life, there are things that can easily happen if something happens. People study these things and gauge people's responses to different situations. People with money would spend money studying these reactions and testing through drills with the aim of reducing casualties. Psychological test is carried out to check windows of opportunity where they can go in and do something that is wrong in the hope that they will use these tactics to make it look like nothing has happened. Imagine if the 9/11 attacks did not happen but the USA still went on to put people for years in cages as slaves do you think no one would have reacted? That is slavery; modernized and applied some cosmetics so that it looks pretty and modern but deep down it's the same thing. We can see all international laws being overridden that even if it was today, they would have been arrested. So, I am saying that the UN and its presence and involvement in global peace is a miscarriage of justice. It is giving a lot of people a false sense of security by preaching that they provide global peace when they cannot provide any form of security just puppets of the West and assassins to carry out the Colony Collapse Strategy.

**So, what is our stance on the UN?**

Throughout the book, our stance is straightforward justice for all. We must correct past mistakes and level the playing field, so everyone has the same rights as everyone else despite where they are. I think the UN them just being there is a gross let down for the people dying every time their creators invade and attack sovereign nations. I talked above about giving people a false sense of security as the greatest sin and that sums my stance. Criminal proceedings are a must. They let a lot of people down who counted on them by not stopping the war as they preached globally to be their sole existence. It does not stop there they let others who might have intervened unable to do so as they might have assumed that they had things under control. For me two counts of gross negligence and reckless behavior endangering the lives of 500 000 women and children blocking other sources of help. So, it's;

*giving a false sense of security to the victims and billions globally when they can't do anything.

*As good as a con artist manipulating and tricking people so involved in malicious acts pretending to be what they are not putting lives at risk. Their conduct lacked professionalism and they are deceitful in their dealings.

*Blocking other sources of help who would and might have intervened and stopped the war.

*Acting as conspirators to a crime going-in to help the USA and Britain unfairly get a competitive advantage as their inspection highlighted avenues that were easily manipulated by the USA and Britain to attack. They acted as informants putting the lives of women and children at risk.

*They weakened Saddam Hussein. If they had not entered Iraq, the West might not have invaded. They played on his trust and betrayed him as the photos they took were used for military strategic decision-making that gave the USA and Britain more confidence to engage in a war. They abated a war.

*They acted as catalyst speeding up a war that might not have occurred. I explained in one of the chapters above that Iraq or Iran can or could have used the self-defense argument to justify even possession of nukes. I think given the opponents who have literally grouped and ganged up so hugely that now they are like the bullies using weapons to get what they want to pay war debt killing women and children, regardless. That alone could have acted in favor of Iraq's. They could have argued that they have a right to protect themselves. All they needed to do was to explain that the attack is purely for personal gains.

Secondly, they have a right to defend their oil as an oil-rich country. We have business people given licenses for guns etc. based on such premises. So, Iraq could have relied on that fact too.

Thirdly, they could have argued that any reasonable man would make even more destructive weapons if faced with such a force, in the USA, Britain, and NATO [based on the assumption of Article 5 that can be invoked to defend the rest of the cult.]. I also explained that this could be the main reason why the USA and Britain were so adamant that Iraq had WMDs simply because it will be unreasonable not to if faced with such a force. Now back to our point on the UN.

Having the above point in mind the UN is part of the rugby team destroying and manipulating and tricking people so that their strikers can score a try. What it is doing is weakening the opponents so that the strikers can strike. Iraq might have agreed to possess as a form of a deterrent to protect itself so that it can't be attacked.

>Read between the lines here.

Iraq might have pretended or implied they have nukes to keep the USA at bay and stale attacks. Someone might have suggested that Iraq has nukes so that no one attacks them. So, they might have not denied that as a way of making the USA scared to attack it. This is Iraq's defense system. We see even recently as a few months ago Iran the next target on the war contingent plan adopting the same tactic of admitting processing but for energy sources. Leaving the possibility of making for weapons as well open to cushion the effects of sanctions imposed by the UN and to keep them safe from attack as they match the USA with their nukes. True, I always say wars have no winners and nukes have no winners as well as anything can happen say if they simultaneously deployed them. So, Iraq or Iran might have hinted on processing as a defense mechanism. I have seen these films where a person shouts that he has a gun when he doesn't have one just as a tactic to keep the other person away and not thinking of attacking.

>So, given the above facts and let's say the UN work for Iran for a change. The USA and the international community then ask Iran and the UN assuming the UN is part of Iran.

"Do you have Weapons of Mass Destruction?"

It is reasonable for Iran to hint that they might have so that the US fear them too and not simply attack. You would not expect the UN to shout that they don't have the nukes or the WMDs otherwise the US will invade. The reason why they were not attacking was the fear of casualties. During the first wars, they had underestimated the power of the insurgencies who previously used roadside bombs with a lot of US soldiers killed. But if the UN were on the USA's side, they would have raised their hands in the air and shouted.

"They don't have! They don't have! Come and attack."

I think you have seen hostage films with the hostage-takers hiding from the rescuers before the hostages somehow find the energy and courage to shout risking being killed calling for the rescuers in the direction the hostage-takers are. They might have screamed; "

"They are here! Over here!" waving their hands in the air before the hostage-taker knocks them down with a punch in the face.

So, I am saying that the UN's role involves knowledge that they were going-in to expose and weaken these leaders being targeted. They are just checking how easy and the number of casualties that might be suffered.

>Another issue is that the UN's Weapons Inspectors are used in a psychological game just to test the 'compliance of the enemy to gauge his stance before an attack. Let them in then he is weak and easy to attack. Kick the Weapons Inspectors then he is strong and might resist and put on a real fight so the USA and Britain stop attacking. This is true whenever the UN was allowed in war always followed with the demise of the target. It's a psychological game. Let them in then you are on the defensive mood. In this state, your aim is not to attack but to try to prove you are correct so weak and easily attacked. You tell everyone to go and 'screw their mothers' you are on the attack and you can put on a fight and that is true as well. Every inspection is followed by a ruthless attack.

So, what is the role of the UN?

Are there to weaken the targets? You can see why in our world we would drag the UN to court and put all in jail and ask them to pay the victims' relatives compensation until they have none for their own members and workers. The West is very clever, especially in the USA and Britain. They put the UN to shield themselves from any wrongdoing. The fact that they did nothing can be argued to be an indirect support of the war and you can see why even after the UN declared that the war was illegal and doing nothing about it did not stop the USA and Britain attacking. The USA and Britain if dragged to court would simply blame the UN as an overseer and a war stopper did nothing at all to stop them. They can say the UN indirectly supported the war by not stopping it.

>To make things worse for them the UN has personal gains from any invasion directly so stopping the war would be something unwise that any reasonable man would not do given the fact that they rely on donations from members of which the USA and Britain are. They rely on funding from these harvesting activities where these nations go to war in order to pay their debt. We saw that the day or so after the death of Saddam the UK announced that they can now repay the world war debt it owed the USA. So, one can argue that they both had personal reasons for going to war the UK through savings on oils, recall Dwight Eisenhower?

"nationalization of the Suez Canal was not like the nationalization of oil… that depletes resources."

So, removing Saddam increased production lowering prices down. It's not just a fact of saying that the UK gained directly from oil, but they saved a fortune as oil becomes cheaper. Mind you Saddam restricted production of oil so that oil went up recall the long queues in the USA?

The effect is like a trickling down effect or the multiplier effect where everyone down the chain benefits as benefits trickled down. The UN is poised to benefit so why would they stop the war if it means their end too? Any savings mean increased contributions from the USA and the UK etc. Stopping the war by the UN was like them slapping their own boss in the face with the resultant that funding would cease.

## Who funds the UN?

"The UN is funded in two ways—through mandatory payments and voluntary contributions. Each of the organization's 193 members is required to pay a percentage of both the UN's regular operating budget and the peacekeeping budget."

Wikipedia.

"The United States is the largest provider of financial contributions to the United Nations, providing **22 percent** of the entire UN budget in 2017 (in comparison the next biggest contributor is Japan with almost **10 percent**, while EU countries pay a total of above **30 percent**)."

Wikipedia.

Are you still asking our stance on the UN?

Really, I thought it's clear now. Okay, I will elaborate. Bring all to justice for giving all the victims a sense of security but getting all killed. The trials of all the top brass the Nuremberg style and even harsher. Nuremberg style court cases with everyone tried for all their crimes looking at the number of dead women and children that's above half a million they are all death sentences. Any wars they have let happen by doing nothing and the number of people dead for the past seventy years must be dug up and used to keep them all on trial. Tomorrow's World Order will have a Nuremberg like court system assessing every institution and their acts in relation to the number of those who died. If over a certain threshold then we give all death sentences. We believe in life for life. Strike the left cheek expect to offer your right cheek too. We shall be different from the Nuremberg courts in that we are not after revenge but justice and leveling the playing field by showing the world that no one is above the law. The fact that they receive huge donations from the USA the country that invaded that makes them biased and not fit for the purpose and as such compensation bills to the left behind relatives will and must put them out of business. The greatest crime is to pretend and trick people that they can protect them when they can't and as such they must be dissolved with immediate effect. Compensation is a must. Our approach is to provide any kind of correction that will help alleviate the situation and bring people to trusting terms again. A huge compensation bill for every woman and child killed in the Iraq war and the Syrian wars and the past seventy years if they did nothing. A figure will be set for each child and women and even soldiers who died in the war all ought to be compensated. Criminal proceedings can also be levied on the UN by the family of the dead soldiers and a hand in compensation claims with immediate effect. Our laws disregard all the good work you think you might be doing to billions if you get anyone killed. A lot of lives have been lost on their watch that they have blood stains that even trying to wash the stains is pointless. A new beginning can only start if a kind of compensation and forgiveness is achieved. A very good example is the $6,6 billion paid by Germany to the UK, France and the USA for damages done due to their initiation of war. I think the UN owe the people of Iraq and Syria a thousand lives each and the punishment is so gross that they must cease operating with immediate effect. I think calls for them to evolve don't apply because of the blood on their hands.

The UN is as good as gone!

Next!

NATO.

NATO adopts a passive role where it does not interfere in local disputes. That can be understood as they never declared to help anyone but their members but nevertheless, they have been involved in conflicts that resulted in the deaths of civilians in Serbia and Yugoslavia during Operation Allied Forces. Thanks to their honest spokesman;

"There is always a cost to defeat an evil," said NATO spokesman Jamie Shea,

"It never comes free, unfortunately. But the cost of a failure to defeat a great evil is far higher." He insisted NATO planes had bombed only "legitimate designated military targets," and if more civilians had died, it was because NATO had been forced into military action. He then defended this notion by stating, "NATO does not attack civilian targets, we attack exclusively military targets and take every precaution to avoid inflicting harm on civilians."

Wikipedia.

NATO's stance on collateral damage is that they always do their best to minimize that. I think to sum what is regarded as their stance I will quote;

'Statistically speaking, civilian casualties were lighter than any other conflict involving modern mass air-power.[5] From the beginning of Operation Allied Force, NATO pledged to minimize civilian casualties. Consideration of civilian casualties was incorporated into NATO's planning and targeting process. Targets were 'looked at in terms of their military significance in relation to the collateral damage or the unintended consequence that might be there,' General Shelton said on April 14: Then every precaution is made… so that collateral damage is avoided." According to Lt. Gen. Michael Short, 'collateral damage drove us to an extraordinary degree. General Clark committed hours of his day dealing with the Allies on issues of collateral damage.'

Wikipedia.

Okay even if the conflict yielded a few numbers of casualties a total of 458 Serbs and 528 Yugoslavs in the Allied Force Operation still that is a large number. Who says this is acceptable and more is prohibited? Our new laws give everyone rights to life and to self-preserve. No one shall deny that right. The fact that many human rights groups opposed these deaths of civilians means that any death can never be justified.

I think again it is helpful here to quote NATO's strategy about civilian casualties.

'from the very beginning of Operation Allied Force, minimizing civilian casualties was a major declared NATO concern. According to NATO, consideration of civilian casualties was fully incorporated into the planning and targeting process. All targets were 'looked at in terms of their military significance in relation to the collateral damage or the <u>unintended consequence</u> that might be there,' General Shelton said on April 14: 'Then every precaution is made… so that collateral damage is avoided.' According to Lt. Gen. <u>Michael Short</u>, 'collateral damage drove us to an extraordinary degree…[and] committed hours of [my] day dealing with the Allies on issues of collateral damage.'

Wikipedia.

First, I think it's beneficial to understand the aim and goals of the NATO treaty.

"The parties to this treaty reaffirm their faith in the purposes and principles of the Charter of the United Nations and their desire to live in peace with all peoples and all governments. They are determined to safeguard the freedom, common heritage and civilization of their peoples, founded on the principles of democracy, individual liberty and the rule of law. They seek to promote stability and well-being in the North Atlantic area…"

NATO 1949 treaty.

I think it's appropriate here first to define what a cult is and go from there.

A cult;

"A religious/non-religious group that follows a series of strict beliefs, may include worshiping a specific God/Deity or multiple Gods/**Deities** or following strict specific ideals. May involve some form of **brainwashing** that their knowledge is correct and that everyone else is wrong, will have a hierarchy and may be led by one of a small group of Charismatic leaders, and typically will **shun** those who are ex-members."

Urban Dictionary.

A cult from the above definition is a group of people with their belief that they preserve and as such will do whatever is necessary to preserve their ideology and protect their people. They are like a special elite club where membership is by special privileges. The emphasis here is that they are a group of people concerned with the welfare of that group and nothing else. That also does not follow that they are against other people nor are they bothered by them. NATO's aim is in line with the cult's thinking. It's for them by them although they have a "desire to live in peace with all peoples and all governments." NATO Articles Charter.

NATO does not represent the whole world or globe their impact is central and only for the benefit of its members. They don't try to take over global roles as their roles are specific to the needs of the members and Article 5 shows their main purpose for existence to gang up on anyone who attacks their member. Just like a cult at its inception, the agreement was to bind America to defend and protect the European countries from the Soviet Union's aggression. America's protection was the cornerstone of this alliance. It's correct therefore to say that NATO arose out of the Soviet threat as a coalition of nations to be able to withstand the threat and power of the Soviet Union in case it attacks. The Soviet Union was at the time aiming to be a global power spreading its communistic ideologies around the world. The USA as the superpower knew that the Soviet Union could be a threat and as such amalgamated all European nations into a cult that has little powers on a global scale due to membership requirements at the same time diminish the global impact of the European countries restricting their activities to Europe. NATO is a limited cult tied to Europe with a brief scale of operation and impact. Grouping all of Europe into a cult that is limited in scope itself meant limited scope and impact of all Europe on a global scale. It's true to say that NATO is for Europe and nothing more. Their aim is to protect their own people even though they aim to live peacefully with everyone else and every government. This could be the reason behind the threats by the USA of quitting the cult. Being a NATO member automatically makes any nation biased. You can't claim to be a global superpower like what the US is trying to do and then claim membership to a specialist elite club that is there to serve its people's interests.

## Conflicting Views.

This is what we think is one of the problems we have that the current superpower powers are biased from the word go and no wonder we have all the problems we have. The USA or Britain or France for that matter cannot carry a task that has a global impact and represent the whole globe while at the same time serving NATO's interest. NATO's Charter of Article states that there will not be any undertaking of other international laws or agreements that conflicts with NATO.

"Article 8. Each party declares that none of the international engagements now in force between it and any other of the parties or any third state conflicts with the provisions of this treaty and undertakes not to enter into any international engagement in conflict with this treaty."

We know the USA is a member of NATO and at the same time, the USA plays superpower bossing everyone around our view is that no matter what their actions will never be for the benefit of the whole globe but will have NATO's interest. So, the fact that the US is trying to play superpower is flawed in that it will ever be biased. That could explain also the Colony Collapse Strategy I argued that they base everything on. Its aims will ever be to protect a certain group of people defined by geographical attributes of the North Atlantic which includes North America and Europe. Whatever the USA does will be for the benefit of these areas.

Okay, let's go deeper.

## Communism, Socialism, the eugenics movements and the Rise of NATO.

Communism is;

"a theory or system of social organization in which all property is owned by the community and each person contributes and receives according to their ability and needs."

Wikipedia.

The Soviet Union grew since 1922 and was a threat by the West. Communist ideology was considered as a threat and had to be stopped and the only way the West was to stop the Soviet Union ideology spreading to Europe was to form a military alliance to fight the Soviet Union. We can look indirectly as to the main reasons why NATO was established by looking at what the Soviets stood for. Communism as the definition above states is a way to put everything in government control where there are no social classes and wealth is based on a need criterion. Communism was associated with overpopulation and over-breeding with all genetic issues. NATO was incepted at the time when the Soviet was associated with a kind of issues. At the time people realized that communism was a plague itself that needed to be controlled. Instead of power in one central country like Russia, the West realized that they can do the opposite and establish a common force responsible for military and security with all member nations represented. Instead of a group for all without any social class, NATO was established as an elite special group of the few with class in mind. OK back to the issue of this chapter. NATO's articles portray an organization willing to work with everyone globally and help maintain peace. But Article 5 declares that it will go to war with anyone who attacks its members.

"Article 5 The parties agree that an armed attack against one or more of them in Europe or North America shall be considered an attack against them all and consequently they agree that, if such an armed attack occurs, each of them, in exercise of the right of individual or collective self-defense recognized by Article 51 of the Charter of the United Nations, will assist the party or Parties so attacked by taking forthwith, individually and in concert with the other parties, such action as it deems necessary, including the use of armed force, to restore and maintain the security of the North Atlantic area."

So, no matter what they will engage in military action. It doesn't matter whether the member is the one who provoked the attack. I think it's a bit flawed. Okay from their point of view as a cult I think they are justified, but the world is not as simple as that and a lot of factors come into play.

## The role of 25 to 50-year war contingency plans.

A contingency plan is a plan that is drawn to reduce or avoid risk not known but with a high likelihood of happening. Things in this case are not left to chance, but the plan puts things in place in order to reduce or remove the risk altogether. This plan is a plan that changes the normal course of events by changing the direction of the otherwise normal event taking place. The idea is rooted in risk management. This is related to the issue I have been pointing out in this book that of the Colony Collapse Strategy. The West after the events of the Second World War decided to become proactive and instead of defense strategy of sitting and waiting, they realized that a war contingency plan to avoid major wars was needed. This included the establishment of the UN with its subsidiary the ICC etc. and a military wing in NATO. They adopted an offensive approach as a risk management strategy, and this included drafting war contingency plans that alter the course of events to avoid the risk of major wars.

"**Risk management** is the identification, evaluation, and prioritization of risks (defined in ISO 31,000 as the effect of uncertainty on objectives) followed by coordinated and economical application of resources to minimize, monitor, and control the probability or impact of unfortunate events [1] or to maximize the realization of opportunities."
Wikipedia.

The above definition is found in business thinking but the same applies to military settings. During the time after the First World War, the West did not expect another war, but the onset of the

Second World War meant the need to do something about this. The identification, evaluation, and prioritization involved identifying targets likely to cause wars or makes people fight and doing something about them. This involved or was part of what is normally regarded as a war contingency plan which has options to trigger an event as a risk management protocol. I say for example the Soviet Union was a threat of which it was before its collapse in 1991 then action was taken to dismantle it every means possible. I say for example certain leaders pose a threat of one day initiating a war, the CIA would send assassins, etc. If a nation can be a potential threat, then the plan provides beforehand of ways of reducing or removing the risk altogether. This involves taking action that can be morally or illegally wrong to remove the risk. A perfect example is the Cold War incident during Dwight Eisenhower. The US had a 25-year war contingency plan drafted during the late 1940s that anticipated that the Soviet Union might possess' Weapons of Mass Destruction or maybe planning to do so in the next decade or two. This plan was drafted years before the 1960 U2 incident. So, you can see there was a problem that needed it causes to be contained. The Soviet Union was a problem recall NATO was established as a response to the Soviet Union's aggression. So, NATO is part of the war contingency plan to quash the Soviet aggression and stop them from making WMDs. Every President or Prime Minister must fulfill the requirements of the contingency plan as a way of removing the risk and surprise attacks. So, President and or Prime Ministers can break the law and get people killed in the name of risk management required by a contingent plan and get away with it. The deaths are regarded as collateral damage. Something they can't avoid but one which they can reduce. This is the same thinking within NATO etc. check the first pages of this chapter.

1960 U2 incident.

The 25-year war contingency plan identified the Soviet as a threat and highlighted the need to act on it as risk management. President Dwight Eisenhower ordered the spying of the Soviet Union's possible nuclear developing facilities with the aim to start a war to fulfill the war contingency plan. The US President gave an illegal order breaking the law by sending spies into Russian's space with the resultant incident that the plane was shot down. The USA admitted that the plane was a missing "weather plane" but were later forced to swallow their words as the Soviet paraded the captured pilot with the plane with its equipment for aerial reconnaissance that is aerial spying. It later turned out that even the capture or shooting down was a deliberate move to start a war as fulfilling the war contingent plane drafted more than 9 years before. The US had suffered the Pearl Harbor attack years back and were not taking chances and this is at the height of the Cold War era. President Eisenhower asked for permission from the Pakistan government to establish a spying secret military camp which was to be used to launch the U2 spy plane into the Soviet Union's territory. Even though the intention was not to be causing acts of aggression that was the aim to start a war with the Soviet Union. The US President choose to send British pilots instead of the US ones in case one was shot down but what is the point when you are flying planes marked as USA property unless that is the main aim to start a war through acts of aggression of ordering spying into private territory. The idea here is to show that a war contingency plan which is a risk management strategy can cause leaders to make commands that will result in death which they can easily be regarded as collateral damage in order to remove the risk. Here we have a President breaking laws and admitting it because what is at stake is bigger than everything else and as such the death of civilians is regarded as collateral damage.

**Outsourcing of events or contracting out.**

In this incident you see the USA President contracting out services to the British to do their dirty work of spying;

"Using British pilots allowed Eisenhower to be able to use the U2 plane to see what the Soviet Union was hiding, while still being able to plausibly deny any affiliation if a mission became compromised."

Wikipedia.

Leaders therefore can get involved in risk management by ordering illegal tasks that they can deny vehemently. Having said that are you surprised then to realize that 9/11 might have been a risk management plan to reducing the bigger risk posed by terrorism? I dealt with 9/11 in detail at the beginning of this book but of interest here is the fact 9/11 was a risk management strategy to justify the need to go to war with Iraq as part of a war contingency plan to remove middle eastern threats of future wars considering that these nations have resources to be a threat in oil. That can explain all the previous Gulf wars that go back to the 1980s. 9/11 could be argued to be a trigger of the war. Over years people have turned against those insisting on wars as a solution and this has made leaders unpopular and terrorism would give the Presidents and Prime Ministers justifications for war. If it wasn't for 9/11 Iraq might not have been invaded. 9/11 gave everyone in power to rights to break all rules and international laws and ignore the advice of the UN etc. and embark on a revenge war. I explained in detail that whoever was behind 9/11 was very educated and skilled with inside knowledge not available to terrorists to make sure that the towers would act as death traps with everyone trapped inside with no way of escaping. I detailed in this book that the points the plane struck the towers were critical points the only points and exit points out of the towers. The people behind this the 'terrorist' knew that no one had the chance to escape. So, it can be said that the idea was to trap everyone not warned that day as it increases say maximum number of the people who would die. If many died helplessly that can easily justify going to war and even if people make-up dossiers can justify any action with little opposition. I explained also that $2.3 trillion was missing, and this message was announced just a day before the 9/11 attacks. Coincidence or not?

This could be a reference to President's Dwight Eisenhower remarks that he could only go to war if any nation had nationalized oil which exhausts the nation's resources. That could say fuel or oil bill and the salary or wage bill was making the money disappear. War can solve that easily. Simply use weapons to get the resources by force as oil production is increased and, in the West, companies running it that lowers the price. War can get numbers of soldiers reduced as well as they die unexpectedly through roadside bombs. Just like President Eisenhower the US government might have contracted out if this was part of the risk management required by the war contingency plan to the British again to do their dirty work. I explained in detail the origins of the terrorist attackers. The total number was nineteen with 15 from Saudi Arabia, two from UAE, one from Lebanon and one from Egypt. All these countries were Protectorates of the British and still with strong ties after getting independence. There are Protectorate treaties established in 1915 with Saudi Arabia, 1914 with Lebanon and Egypt. The origins of the Protectorate had to do with the threat of terrorism where the British watched the terrorist events without stopping them waiting after they had happened to sign treaties with the nations involved offering them protection. We can see the same situation arising after 9/11 with Britain offering to go to war side by side with the USA a form of Protectorate at friends' level as an ally. Do you know that the day the attacks happened the attacks were filmed by firefighters rehearsing how to fight if the towers were to be attacked? Do you know also that 7/7 attacks in the UK happened at the same time when a rehearsal of how the emergency services might cope in the event of such an attack? What are the chances of the same thing happening i.e. attacks happening when people are rehearsing for that attack, in London, and in Newyork? Do you also know that on 9/11 there was a military exercise through NORAD to rehearse how to fight and prevent such an attack? Exposing the weakness and inability to protect oneself to 'sell Protectorate' and force a country like the USA accept a treaty to go to war with the British.

I think it is justified and reasonable for anyone to conclude that given the facts above one will be left with no option but to suggest 9/11 was like what hackers do sometimes. Infiltrate to show the weakness of the system in order to offer ways to improve that system at a price. 9/11 was a way to show the USA that alone it was not the superpower but needed everyone's hand as we see NATO triggering Article 5 for the first time. The USA as not the superpower but any other nation requiring other's hands as well. Before 9/11 the USA was the superpower without doubt, and this takes over from the British who were the superpower was first witnessed during the Suez Canal incident. The British as the power of the day used force and invaded Egypt when it nationalized the canal. The British requested the USA's help but the USA once a colony of the British saw the invasion as a recolonization strategy by the British and as such denied that vehemently ordering the

British and France to withdraw their troops giving them deadlines. His arguments were that first recolonization was never to be visited again and above all what was the canal to the Americans? This was nothing to them they did not need to use the canal and as such this Suez incident was a trivial matter to them. The President had suggested he would only go to war if a nation had nationalized oil reserves. A lot of countries had, and these are the countries on the war contingency plan still pursued even today. The USA under this Dwight Eisenhower humiliated the British by ordering them out and ever since the British never gained their position again as the world leader. Instead, the US has pivoted above as the superpower.

*9/11 as the new Suez Canal incident.

*9/11 humiliated the USA and reduced it to a weaker nation that can be easily attacked in so many ways without itself defending itself with their people witnessing the worst incidents in history. How can a superpower be attacked that way with the cave people who have no technological advancement? At the beginning of this book, I explained that God or Allah, etc. is an omnipotent, omnipresent and omniscient entity that is the superpower the role the US tries to play as a superpower. If the US is the real superpower, how can it be attacked like that? It's like slapping God in the face when he is the superpower one must be very mad or something to do that. It's simply wrong because it's like jumping into the cage of a lion and slaps it before it devours you. This is what the terrorist did. But what if the attacks were a way of showing the USA that first, they were not a superpower anymore as it had blood on its hands and the feeling globally is that of hate and cries for revenge? A global leader ideally has no enemies to cause such destruction even though they might have grievances. Instead, the USA was a weak nation now requiring the help of who? Guess? Britain and NATO. I highlighted above that the formation of NATO reduced the whole European continent as nothing but continental powers not worth of the whole world. NATO made all European countries be short-sighted and only focus on Europe rather than be concerned with global issues and this left the USA as the only true leader giving all NATO protection against the Soviet Union. This could have been a psychological tactic to leave the USA as the only true superpower concerned with the welfare of everyone on earth and not just Europe. NATO's Article 8 conflict somehow with the idea of the US trying to be a member of NATO and being a global leader as well. 9/11 set this record straight by showing the USA that it needed NATO and not the other way around and to stick to NATO rather than try to please the whole world. This was evidenced by the invoking of Article 5 where NATO;

"enhance intelligence sharing; increase protection of key civil and military installations; back-fill US military assets; provide the United States with blanket overflight rights and access to ports and airfields; deploy NATO Airborne Early Warning aircraft to patrol US airspace, and deploy NATO naval forces to the eastern Mediterranean."

NATO.

This can also be interpreted as NATO's stance of telling the USA to work together and not to do things that jeopardize the safety of NATO. The USA's stance of being part of NATO and playing global superpower jeopardize NATO's existence as the USA might be creating problems for all by unnecessary interventions in the Middle East. Note that NATO is a regional operation. It has nothing to do with global issues even though they might have global interests.

### NATO's triggering of Article 5

I explained above that war contingency plans usually have a life span of 25 years drafted decades ago or replaced with new modern ones or just updated ones all pose a challenge to any President or Prime Minister. These plans are deep-rooted in risk management and are there to eliminate risk rather than wait for the natural course of events. There is an intervention element that is needed and since in a war plan, the logic is that war must be part and parcel of the plan. Risk elimination requires military action full stop. But with the human rights movement of the 1980s through to the 2000s starting a war or justifying reasons for one has become very hard. Human rights have meant the removal of all loopholes usually manipulated by the leaders and therefore made justification for wars very hard. Risk management must involve an element of collateral damage as the impact of the collateral damage is usually smaller as compared to the total damage that can be caused if the risk is not contained. I explained that Presidents and Prime Ministers can order illegal acts that can result in the death of people on security grounds. NATO triggered Article 5 just because the USA was attacked and is a member and this is a threat to democracy and the rule of the law. NATO is a regional entity and as such limited in scope and somehow a danger to world peace. Triggering Article 5 simply because a member is attacked threatens global peace especially after highlighting that some events can be argued to be inside jobs or contracted out events. If a government has no financial resources and in debt and owing $millions to other countries with debt going back as far as the 1940s and unable to pay that debt can use the easily available asset to them which are weapons and go on a robbing and killing spree making oil production increased as to lower the prices and putting puppets and international companies to export the oil and be able to pay war debts. Do you know Britain was having issues paying war debt and it announces that it will pay all the debt it owed the day or so after Saddam Hussein was killed? After his death, they could now afford to pay the debt. Guess who is the beneficiary? The USA. If two women who are in debt go on a robbing and killing spree in order to pay debt do you think the law will forgive them simply because they can do what they did as it was justified? NATO is an accessory to murder as it supports expressly without facts who had attacked the USA. 500 000 women and children died as a result of its support of the USA by triggering Article 5 on the fourth of October 2001 blocking any opposition and any kind of help to stop the war as whoever tried to stop the war was to be labeled as the enemy of all NATO members. Fear of being attacked by all NATO members might have weakened a lot of people and other countries who might have intervened to stop the war. Countries can manipulate Article 5 and contract out terrorism to be carried out at home just to trigger or make the whole NATO group attack a certain nation simply because it has oil and therefore can afford to buy technology or make nukes. After Iraq now we see the USA immediately jumping on Iran and criticizing them and accusing them of having nukes.

But what if Iran is on the USA's war contingency plan drafted in the 1960s or 70s when it nationalized oil reserves? Will NATO simply aid the USA on global security? But the USA and some NATO members have nukes themselves what makes them have the right to make but prohibit some? NATO's Article 5 makes nations in the future make WMDs as the cult or gang has grown to a disproportionate size and it will only be unwise not to especially is you have oil reserves as these countries have openly declared war on any who have nationalized. It is becoming like a gangster movie with weapons used to rob and kill without anyone challenging that. Article 5 gives immunity to all members regardless of whether they are the ones contracting out or outsourcing terrorist activities or not. Article 5 is a threat to world peace and human existence. This Article gives every member the right to do the wrong things and get away with it. This Article is a loophole that can be used to embark on a mass Colony Collapse Strategy where countries can provoke non-members knowing that they will get them attacked by all NATO.

Our stance is for NATO to evolve in the immediate future and amend Article 5 to be based on merit after assessments rather than just by membership otherwise it will clash with our laws because we will close the loopholes as well. In the end, we can prove that Article 5 can be used as an indirect biased Article that is used to carry out mass murder and a systematic and consistent attack and killing of all leaders of color through military action targeting the Middle East and the ICC targeting the Africans. It can be proved that terrorism is a way of destroying wealth among opponents as a way of confiscating funds to crash competition. The 9/11 'mastermind' Osama Bin Laden's father was worth $7 billion all from the demolition and construction industry and this money was inherited by Osama. We also know that the Twin Towers were obsolete, and the demolition costs were higher than keeping the buildings or leasing them out. We know in the end the Port Authority of New York leased the towers to a one Larry who had plans to demolition the buildings and rebuild these insuring the buildings before the attacks. Do you know also that the terrorists destroyed only prestigious buildings etc.? Al Qaeda can pass as a demolition company as they destroyed buildings globally targeting US embassies maybe with his father's construction business benefiting somehow say governments in Saudi Arabia awarding building constructs to USA firms who in turn provide other contracts abroad to Osama father's construction business. The fact that the whole 9/11 incident recreate the 1960 U2 incident is not just a coincidence. During the 1960 we saw the USA President asking the Prime Minister of Pakistan to break laws and help him establish a secret base to be used for spying and hiring the British to fly the planes in case if shot down the USA would deny any involvement. We saw Osama going to Pakistan and hiding there with Osama hiding with no one handing him over. There are so many issues to consider before just granting anyone immunity. NATO therefore like the UN is part of the rugby team to distract and encourage members to abuse others without any fear. I argue that the presence of NATO and its Article 5 is the major reason why we have global problems. All NATO members abuse the law. We have countries using torture in broad daylight. We have countries using landmines to hold on to what everyone is saying was stolen and therefore not there so they must return but this NATO and Article 5 gives these people rights to abuse and become above the law. Women and children are being killed recently in the Syrian attacks and through sanctions globally because they disregard everyone else and only their members. There is no rule of law or recognition of international laws NATO with its Article 5 removes the ability to perform justice. The UN declared the Iraq war as illegal, but the war still went on. Look at France, the UK and the USA ganging up on Syria simply because any condemnation is prevented by the presence of NATO. NATO acts to block and threaten otherwise objectors to illegal wars etc. Above all NATO was developed as a military cult to stop world wars but they keep growing and making weapons. Who are their threats?

Warsaw pact. The Soviet Union and other countries like Bulgaria etc. responded to NATO by forming the Warsaw pact but as soon as the Soviet Union collapsed the pact collapsed too. Recent we have heard the USA encouraging the Persian Gulf countries to form their answer to NATO. I think this is fair and should be welcome if it's a competition you need an equal and challenging competitor. You can't run a marathon by yourself. We are here to level the playing field redistribute the power and create situations where countries will not make secret WMDs to help them stand any chance of surviving in case NATO attacks them. This is dangerous in that WMD's war is a possibility. Nowadays you don't need nukes to have a WMD. There are some digital WMDs and some even went further to make cyber electromagnetic weapons that can wipe-out everything electric or using the electromagnetic field with everyone wearing in-built medical devices implanted at birth without their knowledge. In that regard, human extinction is a possibility. NATO was created as a military unit and once we ban weapons and military unless they can evolve, I don't see the future of NATO. NATO now obsolete. NATO just like the UN and other institutions created after the Second World War is now obsolete. When it was created the Soviet Union was a threat but has since ceased operation since 1991. Now everyone is like all these countries before the formation of NATO during the Soviet Union. It is them now who are a threat to global peace and justice, so it is not something new. The people feel the same way just before NATO's inception. The Soviet has since collapsed and likewise, the only true road for NATO is to follow the Soviet Union. So much of that saying that says what goes around comes around. Makes sense. Even though NATO talks about Russia as a threat and all that this is just a stance to justify their existence. You will be shocked that they have a joint operation with Russia to counteract terrorism.

NATO-Russia Council. This was established in 2002 as a joint plan to tackle terrorism. Russia and NATO are at equal footing and all this talk about NATO sending armies to Poland to train in case of a Russia attack are just grounds to justify their existence so that people won't criticize the huge budgets on weapons and military when the whole globe has become friendly. The joint venture is involved in not just terrorism but also narcotics in Afghanistan and Pakistan.

"Cooperation between NATO and Russia on counter-terrorism measures were launched in 2004 to improve overall coordination and strategic direction of cooperation in this area. An updated NATO-Russia Council Action Plan on Terrorism was agreed in Berlin in 2011. The action plan establishes the way by which NATO nations and Russia regularly exchange information and conduct consultations on various aspects of counter-terrorism policy."

NATO Publication.

## Can NATO change its membership criteria to become a global force?

So far as the name suggests it will remain a regional organization rather than a globe force unless it can change its name and criteria, etc. Nevertheless, it is spreading its wings as far as training African nations. Change alone will not solve the problems we have today.

To command respect globally NATO has to deal with Article 5 imagine if the law was like that as long as you a member even if you steal from others, you torture people or make digital or bio-engineered weapons and use these to kill other people you will still get the backing of the law then this world would be a mess. In international law, one can argue that NATO cannot stand. You should also understand that NATO was established when the British were in power. Ever since they have since ceased to be the superpower. What is the difference of NATO to a gangster offering protection to members and as collateral or insurance for secrecy are sent as initiation acts to commit crimes with express immunity guaranteed by Article 5? Please watch the 1980s or 1990s gangster movies first? Then assess NATO and the current climate where members don't even listen to their own courts the ones, they have established themselves. Where they don't listen to their own institutions like the UN that declared that the war as illegal. Where they start a war for personal gains killing thousands of women and children. Now watch a movie about the role and functioning of monarchies. You will see that the underlying basis is the same. To protect a few privileged with special privileges mainly through birth or geo-location. No matter what cost. Whether they have the merit of such protection or not. In that regard, there is no talking of global peace or global justice. It's the protection of a niche of people and their rights at the expense of everyone else. In the New World not trying to sound arrogant they don't fit. Okay, monarchies have evolved and taken passive roles letting the democratically elected leaders take center stage. What about NATO has it evolved and how? 500 000 dead and Syria getting ganged upon etc. Once again, I reiterate here that in the New World Tomorrow's World Order places the greatest weight on individual nation's sovereignty. No matter what no grounds justify attacking another sovereign nation. This is unjustified even on humanitarian grounds see below. Any country violating the right to a sovereign earned peaceful right is a gross breach of our laws. Any invasion will see the invaders as well as NATO facing criminal charges in our New World simply because they are the kingpin to us sending all these to do all kinds of robbing and killing. To us the blood of all women and children is on NATO's hands giving protection to illegal acts and backing the attackers. It does not stop there we are going to include the lack of empathy towards the victims trust me the law can break the mighty. We don't want another David and Goliath scene. We call for all humanity to evolve now any incidents will see you being dragged to court. We will close all loopholes, and in the end, it will be one man for himself and TWO for us all. Be warned.

## NATO ideology rooted in monarchical systems.

The Netherlands, Saudi Arabia, Japan, Britain, etc. are a monarchical country and the main reason why NATO acts like monarchies giving everyone protection regardless is the fact that Britain and the USA have links. Blanket protection is associated with monarchies and the first Headquarters of NATO was in England and the current one is in Brussels Belgium a monarchical country too. NATO's articles are based on the monarchical system to preserve what is theirs and protect its people. It is there to protect a special class of elites. If you recall, why NATO was established you will find out that the idea was to establish and protect the rights of a few elite groups. Monarchies do act like NATO and opposite to communist thinking where class does not existent and everything is for the benefit of the whole. But we know monarchies have been around for centuries and NATO is a new way of guaranteeing their existence. It can be argued that NATO is there to serve monarchical powers with THE Netherlands, Belgium, Britain as the leading monarchical countries. But what do we know about monarchies? Monarchies are the abusers of international laws or once were. The international laws arose to correct the impact of monarchies. Kings and queens were and have absolute powers and rarely observe human rights.

## Divine Powers and Appointment.

Monarchies believe that they are appointed by God and as such only God can judge me the phrase is their way of thinking. They believe that God has put them there on the throne so that they do what he would otherwise do if they were not appointed. This means correcting nature and eco-balance globally. They believe they have the right to kill and play God. Unlike God who uses natural disasters to correct the population levels, they must come up with ways of balancing this population. This is one of the reasons why you will find a lot of monarchies are accused of the mass murderer using bio-engineered weapons and that no one can bring them to justice. They make people believe that they are acting on behalf of God. You will also find out that they link themselves to the bible and are believed to having certain powers. They rob the whole world of resources to create new technologies of mass killings. You will notice too that they are advanced and usual y discover new ways of killing people like digital armies or weapons or cyber. They are always one step ahead as they use force or trickery to rob ideas through sophisticated gadgets that send everything through a video or sound sender. They deliberately 'put a nail' into the heads of ethnic to destroy chances of leadership challenges. They use implants chipped during birth to cause severe genetic disorders as an alibi for illegal tagging and hacking. Only monarchies are that evil. This is because as I stated above, they have been delegated tasks by God. As they can't create natural disasters, they must make Weapons of Mass Destruction. You will see that they can make and use weapons. Look at any list of countries that have murdered the highest number of people and broke all international laws and you will find out that the evilest ones are those with monarchies. NATO is a monarchical regime trying to adapt and evolve they don't recognize international laws because they and their members will simply disregard any court judgments. NATO's Article 5 is a direct opposite of the Hostis' Humani Generis law that states that certain breaches of the Jus Cogens makes the violator an enemy of mankind. International law placing emphasis on individual acts and judgments and declares that people who commit certain crimes will be judged individually based on merits. NATO contradicts that and gives every member express immunity and support regardless of the acts of the member concerned. International law says a person who commits certain crimes that fall in the Jus Cogens laws etc. like torture, genocide, mass killings can be regarded as a Hostis Humani Generis an enemy of all people. NATO ignores all that and gives express immunity. Look at the USA with the Guantanamo bays, look at the West's; torture record Britain's, the USA, France etc. and land grabbing, look at France just helping anyone siding with the British even if it means the death of children and women.

## Future of NATO.

The fact the monarchies who have a poor track record in terms of human rights have survived this far simply by not getting involved in politics and had evolved to have passive roles yet NATO insists on blanket protection shows the long way it has to go for the sake of global peace and justice. Evolve or cease to exist the Soviet Union ceased operations a very good precedence to follow. Something just meant not to last it is human nature.

# CHAPTER TWENTY-SIX

LAYING THE FOUNDATION.

*First a look at international law and military action.

*Current international law or treaty governing the use of force is defined by the UN Charter Article 2(4).

"All members shall refrain in their international relations from the threat or use of force against the territorial integrity or political independence of any state, or in any other manner inconsistent with the purposes of the <u>United Nations</u>."

First, to understand these laws, I must explain some laws that fall in the Jus Cogens category. These laws are laws that are peremptory in that there is no derogation that is permitted. These are laws that can never be overridden. These laws relate to international laws that are thought to be universal and understood by anyone. These laws prohibit things like slavery, torture, piracy which includes hacking, genocide and the crime against humanity, etc. Breaking of these laws can and will make one regarded as an enemy of mankind. Breaking these laws is like an attack on all humanity, and the punishment is a collective action. Only in this situation can military action or force be justified. So, the UN Security Council can authorize military force to maintain peace and uphold these peremptory laws. The problem with enforcing these calls for military action based on the breaking of these peremptory laws is that it is hard to prove that a country had broken these laws. Torture normally nowadays is done remotely and without leaving marks. Even if it is happening, proving that this is the truth has been an area of controversy. Therefore, what has been happening over the years was basing the use of military force on humanitarian grounds.

Humanitarian grounds.

"Humanitarian Intervention has been defined as a state's <u>use of</u>

516

<u>military force</u> against another state, with publicly stating its goal is to end <u>human rights violations</u> in that state."

Wikipedia.

The current ideal situation or consensus of initiating this humanitarian intervention is that it must be authorized by the UN Security Council. The main characteristic is that there is the use of military force against a nation that is a sovereign that has not committed any form of aggression. The whole thing is biased, and it depends on the strength of how powerful an invading country is. There is the crossing of sovereign borders into the country concerned even if it disputes the allegations of human rights abuses. The invading country simply must declare its grievances publicly and invade uninvited as a show of power to 'defend the defenseless'.

International law established that all nations are equal and sovereign in their own rights and as such can run their affairs and don't need outside interventions. So, this restricted any military action. The only situation is when a nation has broken the Jus Cogens laws. These laws have universal jurisdiction in that no matter where the crime has been committed any nation can punish the abuser. This is the basis now being used to invade other countries to stop the violations of human rights. The UN Charter of 1945 guarantees sovereign freedom of any nation to freely make decisions if they are effective only within their borders.

"7. Nothing contained in the present Charter shall authorize the United Nations to intervene in matters which are essentially within the domestic jurisdiction of any state or shall require the members to submit such matters to settlement under the present Charter; but this principle shall not prejudice the application of enforcement measures under Chapter VII."

1945 UN Charter.

The only situation when a country can lose sovereignty over domestic issues is when they break the Jus Cogens laws and these are;

*Breached anyone's rights to life by killing with genocide tendencies

*Breached a person's right to self-defend.

*Tortured people

*Practiced slavery

*Carried out crimes against humanity

*Hacked people and so becoming a piracy

*Use of military force between nations.

*Prevention of people's right to self-determination. To choose their own life, etc.

Maybe it's beneficial here to define these Jus Cogens.

"Jus Cogens (or is Cogens) is a Latin phrase that literally means "compelling law." It designates norms from which no derogation is permitted by way of agreements. It stems from the idea already known in Roman law that certain legal rules cannot be contracted out, given the fundamental values they uphold. Most states and authors agree that Jus Cogens exists in international law."

Oxfordbibiliographs.com

A country is entitled to its sovereign and must not be interfered with its decision if they are happening within their boundaries unless ... their laws, treaties or actions are in conflict and contradicting these Jus Cogen laws. In that case, any of the nation's laws are rendered void. Only the Jus Cogens laws have overriding effects if domestic laws, treaties or actions are in direct conflict with these and this is the main justification for military intervention linked to humanitarian grounds. Any nation has a right to intervene and punish the country breaking these Jus Cogens laws and all that it needs to do is to clarify what has been breached, how that happened and intervene to stop further breach. The country must declare publicly the intention to intervene and state the reasons. I will first raise the controversial issues of military intervention on humanitarian grounds. Who will intervene and on what grounds and what gives that person or nation that right to intervene and why? This is the million-dollar question. Ideally, it should and must be an organization like ours that has no personal interest and doesn't belong to any cult that is biased towards the Western nations. The nation or organization to intervention must have some global respect and standing to do so. The fact that the intervention is purely humanitarian there can't be motives of any financial or other personal or national gains. But who on earth would intervene unless if it's beneficial to them somehow? If there is a financial or other gain sought, then that can't be intervention on humanitarian grounds. Humanitarian interventions are often for charity or not for profit but generally for the welfare of humans. Any form of personal gain for argument's sake will make the intervention as an act of aggression against a sovereign state. I will show you that no western country can justify intervention on humanitarian grounds if the country to-be-invaded is not western and worse if the country invading belongs to a cult with specific interests like NATO without triggering acts of aggression and criminal charges. Little brief of humanitarian interventions. The main reason nations had used the excuse of humanitarian intervention was to prevent and punish genocides.

This is defined as;

The UN Convention on Prevention and Punishment of genocide declares that;

Article I The Contracting parties confirm that genocide, whether committed in time of peace or in time of war, is a crime under international law which they undertake to prevent and to punish. Article II In the present Convention, genocide means any of the following acts committed with intent to destroy, in whole or in part, a national, ethnical, racial or religious group, as such:

(a) Killing members of the group;

(b) Causing serious bodily or mental harm to members of the group;

(c) Deliberately inflicting on the group conditions of life calculated to bring about its physical destruction in whole or in part;

(d) Imposing measures intended to prevent births within the group;

(e) Forcibly transferring children of the group to another group.

Article III The following acts shall be punishable:

(a) Genocide;

(b) Conspiracy to commit genocide;

(c) Direct and public incitement to commit genocide;

(d) Attempt to commit genocide;

(e) Complicity in genocide.

This has been the major reason for intervention as nations use chemical, bio-engineered, digital or cyber weapons mainly in the name of population control or secret eugenics and recently as a form of protection in some countries. Watermarks in the form of viruses are used to reduce the lifespan of the people where they are made to age faster than usual as a form of protection. These people are loaded with watermarks that are loaded through chips implanted illegally at birth or on screening. These people are then tricked to believe these chips are needed as protection but in fact their life span is being lowered as remotely they are tricked to be guided and directed but what is happening is that the more they guide or direct the more they use radiation and harmful frequencies and waves and the more damage to the body. If it's foreigners or a certain ethnic group no matter what reasons the nations can be successfully be brought to justice for genocide tendencies. The chips that are remotely triggered can make the body vibrate as the rotary propellers just like those of the drone may be smaller are operated. This involves continuous vibrations that can cause brain damage and other effects. The fact that certain countries use these devices for the 'protection' of foreigners it can be successfully argued that their main intention is to cause brain damage to discredit the ethnics getting into politics. This is the main harmful waves that cause serious effects in later life. No matter their justifications a case can be successfully be brought against such an evil nation. This does not stop there. The nation can use watermarks in the form of bio-engineered ones or digital ones to restrict mixing of local with the foreigners or might spread rumors that foreigners would corrode their gene pool so discourage relationships and the foreigners are for example illegally tagged to prevent them mixing and that can cause the destruction of the group in the long run. This tagging can be used to control fertility like in China where women are implanted without consent or foreknowledge with electrodes that are operated remotely to kill all sperm or produce conditions not-fit for conception. This prevention of births can lead to the collapse of the group. Sometimes the implants at birth etc. are used to produce disabled babies in order to discourage breeding. The device through electromagnetic stimulation and nerve interference can be used to speed up or slow sperm or egg production that can result in immature sperms and eggs being fertilized with the resultant disabled offspring.

The children of the ethnic group can be taken into care as the parents through social workers are declared unfit to raise their own children. This if systematic and for a long period can be argued to constitute what is called genocide. The current situation encourages genocide and encourages the perpetrators to go underground where they are not easily detected using secret hidden devices to keep carry genocide. They know for any intervention to occur then all the above factors must be proved. Our laws will provide grounds for intervention at the earliest point possible and not wait until all the factors can be identified.

### Mass displacement as a reason for humanitarian intervention.

This is a recent phenomenon where people leave the country in masses due to conflict, etc. This triggered a crisis point that needs to be addressed and the military can go in to quell the fighting causing mass migration. This could partly explain the Syrian missile attacks by the West. A new recent issue is that of a nation's decisions to intervene on humanitarian grounds without any authorization from the UN Security Council. So, what would give any nation the right to invade a sovereign nation? Simply accusations of gross human violations even without proof have recently seen military interventions globally. Only two things can give rise to military intervention and these are;

Authorization by the UN's Security Council

Or if the nation is self-defending itself.

So, did NATO's actions during the Kosovo incident constitutes a breach of international law?

## Responsibility to Protect.

Can another nation intervene to protect another sovereign state's people if that state fails to protect its people? This is the basis for the Responsibility to Protect. This is rooted in the idea I explained at the beginning that advanced nations as a natural process understand that one day they will and must be global overseers who have a moral responsibility to make sure that everyone goes by the book. They view themselves as a superpower and would what the respect that goes with that. They believe that whatever they are doing is a task delegated directly from God or earned as they have become a superpower. They feel morally pushed to intervene and save people here and there and, in most cases, they see their actions above any international laws of crimes of aggression. They believe they are doing charity work where they don't expect anything in return and in some cases can provide funding for rebuilding. So, when people scream foul play and gross abuse they don't wait even if the cries are unsustainable, they simply invade and punish the accused. This is an ideal situation but is this what is really happening. We know throughout history we had two really superpowers in Britain and the USA for the past seventy years. The Suez Canal was a point of power shifting from Britain to the USA which has remained the superpower or trying to be one until 9/11. The idea of Responsibility to Protect is based on the principle that the nation acts on humanitarian grounds rather than for-profits or strategic gains. If we look at the Suez Canal case, we can see that everything done from the invasion of Egypt was for a gain of some kind. The Suez Canal was a strategic route to transport the Gulf oil and for letting the ship pass paying toll fees. The main reason for the intervention was to stop Nasser nationalizing the canal. The British asked for help from the Americans through Dwight Eisenhower denied on grounds that to the American people the canal was of no value. They had no ships that used that route or oils to transport but the only reason for them to go to war was if a nation nationalized its own oil reserve. The other reason why the US refused to let the recolonized by the British was the fact that themselves being a former colony of the British they saw this as a bad thing. So, any intervention would imitate or be like the colonization. Egypt was a sovereign nation after gaining independence and as such being the owners of the canal could do whatever they wanted with it. The invasion was a breach of international law and an act of aggression. The US has been intervening too here and there with condemnation throughout the Persian Gulf in the 1980s to 1990s where it was regarded for example by the Saudis as engaged in piracy with the resulting attacks of the USS COLE. Investigations revealed feelings of hostility against the USA and this might have triggered 9/11 as they were regarded as the same people responsible for the USS COLE attacks. If this is true, we can see that the Responsibility to Protect can be viewed with skepticism and mistrust with serious consequences. So, the US foreign policy can be said to be the trigger of terrorism. That could explain why the terrorists are going to America instead of just attacking American properties and infrastructure locally. I explained at the beginning of the book that the West or Allies initially adopted the defensive approach but that did not stop the Second World War and after the war, they adopted the attack approach. This is the same we are seeing now the terrorist doing. Instead of sitting and waiting they are now invading with disastrous consequences. The reason why I highlighted this issue is for you to recognize the shortfall of the Responsibility to Protect approach. No one has the right to intervene in sovereign nations. On what grounds? Whose superpower and who said you are a superpower?

The USA might have used the self-defense argument to intervene abroad on grounds that it's better to attack to prevent and deter further attacks. Whatever the reason to assess if it is justified or not, I think we need to go deeper.

First is to assess the superpower argument that gives the USA or Britain a Responsibility to Protect.

What is a superpower?

'a very powerful and influential nation (used especially with reference to the US and the former Soviet Union when these were perceived as the two most powerful nations in the world).'

'the threat to oil supplies brought the two superpowers closer together.'

Wikipedia.

The USA knocked Britain from a superpower position Britain was brought to its knees financially cutting off international projects and interventions leaving the US as the only superpower after the collapse of the Soviet Union. What are the real motives behind interventions and what are the associated links? The main reason why the USA was threatening leaving NATO is to do with the fact that being a NATO member can conflict with NATO's Article 8 where some acts can be regarded as in conflict with NATO's goals and aims and such acts can be said to destabilize and put NATO at risk. The main reason being that some 'Responsibility to Protect' or humanitarian efforts will further trigger attacks against not only the USA but NATO as all as it will be forced to act due to Article 5. Let's say that the US intervention in the Middle East is viewed as an invasion and an act of aggression all Middle East might group to defend that nation therefore putting NATO members at risk of being attacked. The fact that the USA is part of NATO a cult or organization with specific interest to the welfare of members and that being a regional body can mean that the USA's interest is not with the welfare of the victims in another country but rather strategic goals of NATO or the USA. There is no one who will intervene for the sake of intervening most have a hidden motive.

## Hidden Motives.

Throughout the book, I pointed out that the West to keep the status quo have adopted indirectly or secretly a Colony Collapse Strategy of dealing with the risk of wars. This strategy incorporates a war contingency plan over a long period where nations that have nationalized oil reserves are targeted by each President and Prime Minister. Wherever they intervene the goal is to eliminate the alpha male and replace this with a puppet who will perpetuate the unjust exploitation of resources through increased foreign investors who will benefit at the expense of the locals. In most cases, their policies would increase sectoral violence for the first years to justify keeping their forces in that country for a long time. What this says is another form of western colonization disguised as humanitarian interventions and human rights. The impact of the intervention is to leave a 'broken society' a collapsed society that makes it hard for any new leader to make laws and rules that will benefit the locals but instead due to the destruction caused by war the immediate needs are to rebuild but all the money would have been looted as the invasion was taking place that leaves a new leader now relying on the selling of oil to raise money for rebuilding. This means increased production and more investment contract to foreign investors at the time they start making money for their people sectoral violence would have further destabilized and weaken that new government that it will rely on the West for security and support instantly turning it into a colonized or dependent government. The NGOs, the UN, other institutions, etc. are all part of the 'rugby team' I mentioned above. Rugby team and what is its role?

The UN, NGOs, NATO, etc. are there just to:

>To give a false sense of security so people don't panic until the last minute but then it will be too late.

>They are there to block others who might complain and veto or stop the invasion until the last minute provide the invading country with clear access and less resistance.

>There are there to help the invading nation and its Allies carry out a strategic SWOT analysis as part of the risk management in order to reduce casualties and make the invasion short and fast. They are like spy planes (see U2 1960 spy plane incident.)

>They are corn artist tricking people when they have no powers at all even when they have not discovered any weapons, they can't act at all. They have courts but their judgments are useless no one listens. So, what is the point? They are a risk weakening the to-be-invaded leaders testing their ability to withstand an invasion playing psychological games putting lives at risk.

> Even after the war and deaths they can't arrange compensation schemes, etc.

>They help perpetuate the status quo of exploitation where the West uses weapons to go and take what they want when they run out of money to pay debt and justify that on humanitarian grounds. Altogether they kill more innocent women and children within a

short time than the dictator they are removing.

>They are the ones to impose sanctions that further or initially cause severe hardship and deaths.

>They are the same as terrorists in that they use women and children for bargain reasons through sanctions just like the terrorists who kill women and children.

>Even if they don't know it, they are part of the post-colonial movement to maintain colonial thinking where the alpha middle eastern males are targeted through military action by the superpowers while the UN through the ICC target the least threats in the African alpha males. To them, oil, means power, as it means money and opportunities for new technology.

>What is happening is that the West especially the superpowers sell the evil technology to the developed nations e.g. the US selling nuclear processing or enriching technology to Iran then later send the UN to investigate if the technology is used for nuclear weapons.

"In 1967, the Tehran Nuclear Research Center (TNRC) was established, run by the Atomic Energy Organization of Iran (AEOI). The TNRC was equipped with a US-supplied, 5-megawatt nuclear research reactor, which was fueled by highly enriched uranium."

Wikipedia.

Can it be said that the intervention by the superpowers is simply to help or it can be argued that, for example, that the US;

"Use pretexts to unacceptable geopolitical goals."

Wikipedia.

The UN Security Council and all UN bodies etc. must never have the right to call for military intervention as they are biased in addition to the above points. The whole system is to maintain the exploitative status quo and get all the potential warmongers assassinated or toppled through military force when the world continues to make weapons while becoming friendly. Increasing the risk of friction and the risk of a surprise war that can result in human extinction. I think interventions can be justified and to some extent, we must support it, but we differ in the methods and approaches adopted. To close the loopholes being exploited we saw it fitting to put new laws that recognize the right to a life of the local people and of the soldiers to be sent on the task. We are against the sacrificing of hundreds of thousand for humanitarian reasons. To us, this does not make sense if people die. We have put laws to ban wars. Military intervention is a war to us and therefore outlawed. Interventions we must accept involves a specialist assassin that will carry out the job with no civilian casualties. Even the life of the soldiers to be sent as part of the military intervention are protected by our laws. Care must be taken to find the least approach or tactic with death tolls. We support intervention and a collective response when our laws are broken, and these are the peremptory laws that must not be broken and includes but the list is not exhaustive;

>Right to life

>Right to self-preserve

>Freedom from torture

>Freedom from slavery

>Freedom from hacking and or piracy

>Freedom from any form of genocide

>Freedom from crimes against humanity

>Crimes of aggression

> Global banning or wars

>Global banning of all kinds of weapons bio-engineered, digital or cyber or any future technology with the same effect.

## False Flag.

The current system depends on just allegations of a breach of international laws without concrete evidence. Recently through the Iraq war and the Syria missile attacks, we have seen a growing trend of deception and trickery with the aim to get the leaders killed on false grounds and then apologies or claim that the place is better than it was. This is an issue discussed in detail above referred to as false flagship. We saw the British cooking the Iraq dossier just to give grounds of invasion. If they can invade a country and not kill any innocent people, then I think we might have compromised some tactics used. But when trickery and deception as in false flag results in deaths of innocent people then it is a whole different issue altogether. We must be swift to punish and take a corrective stance. Ideally in the New World setting the UN, NATO, etc. and all the superpowers have no right to engage in military intervention as any military intervention conflicts with the right to self-preserve. We have priorities in life and people over national security and other property or infrastructure laws. New laws will make it necessary and mandatory for some nations who might be attacked simply because they have oil reserves take some defensive stance and at times this might involve possession of certain weapons or attacking the invader on crimes of aggression stance. The nation will be forced to defend itself against even the UN inspectors who are just to further weaken the to-be-invaded nation. After all their interests are with the breadwinners who fund them and who created them. The fact that these institutions were created by the West who would like to 'intervene' makes them biased and unfit to represent the globe and be involved for global peace and security when they don't know what that means.

Tomorrow's World Order shall make the final decision if a military strategy is needed and beneficial and assess the use of other options through highly paid and highly trained assassins. Our new laws must state the only conditions for military action and be obeyed. The good news is that banning all forms of wars and evolving the military will make life simpler in the future. We shall ban reliance on fossil fuels and encourage the development of other alternatives that are clean and renewable. Oil use in cars machines or infrastructure to be phased out before the universal ban on its reliance. The idea being that it will be depleted one day we might as well start now. Imagine a world where every nation has developed its own method of producing energy without warmongers killing women and children for oil? We have a holistic approach to the problem, but everything shall fit perfectly and like a domino effect solve all the problems smoothly and efficiently.

# CHAPTER TWENTY-SEVEN

THE TRANSITIONAL STAGE AND OUR FINANCIAL PLAN.

*How do we intend to accomplish all this? A question of money?

This has been magnificently answered in our Whitepaper in the appendix of this book and in our book titled:

The New Single Reserve Global Currency by David Gomadza that can be bought in all shops all over the world. I think this is paramount to the whole project and setting this as a separate topic is not only vital but mandatory as you must understand and believe our plans that we mean business.

Find links below for the book about our detailed financial plan or read the Whitepaper in the appendix at the end of the book.

Google Playbooks;

Kobo;

https://www.kobo.com/dk/en/ebook/the-new-single-reserve-global-currency

In short, this is our financial plan:

Global Finance, Monetary System and Development.

1. Our goals are to boost global economic growth to levels never thought possible. We are going to change the current system completely. We have seen all kinds of instruments and apparatus in play, but all that they manage to do is keep the status quo. I personally think that humanity has lost the plot all they have done for the past 50-70s is worry about indicators rather than lifting the whole globe out of poverty. Countries deemed developing are still developing after seventy years. Even the developed countries haven't developed as one would expect as they are marred with

heavy problems as well.

2.    Global financial institutions put in place have only managed to stall development. In fact, this is the reason they were created to stabilize everything. All these years, the world has been obsessed with the stabilization of things. We as a people have failed to think of what is really needed. Are we just to stabilize things or what? How can we achieve new heights if we are concerned with stabilization? It's shocking to me to see that the creations of the financial systems that collapse more than three decades ago are still operating and expected to lead the globe out of poverty. We have the IMF and the World Bank still in existence. Would you be surprised to see that the world has the problems it had then? These institutions were created to stabilize everything. To avoid shock-waves, etc. To avoid crises etc. but do you know that stabilization conflicts with economic growth and development? This is true if you look at the strategies employed by the IMF which include austerity measures of cutting down everything and reducing expenditures to balance the books.

3.  Our goals are to boost economic development and increase national wealth which means global wealth too. To us, the IMF is the reason we have the problems we have.

First, I argued that these institutions only create global issues rather than solving any. The reasons are that;

*They don't have sovereign powers. They are not like nations with certain powers to solve national issues. They are institutions created by sovereign nations and rely on the sovereign nations who created them from funding and manpower, etc. Their aim is to represent the interest of the creators, full stop. They are just extensions of the sovereign nations who created them. They have no power to print money. This is the major issue with today's thinking.

*The only cheaper and natural way to increase money for everything is through printing new money free from loans and any repayments. You don't need a vetting criterion to print money. You don't need conditions imposed that will affect growth.

*Our arguments are that these institutions are no better than loan sharks. It will be absurd to suggest that loan sharks are concerned with global growth. These institutions are businesses to keep the status quo with the lender growing at alarming rates. This is a business model to take away money from everyone else and sink the other nations with loans and imposing conditions that will only keep these nations in poverty.

*IMF's loans are not interest-free loans. What I don't subscribe to is the fact that why sovereign nations with powers to print cheaper money would take loans from inferiors without any powers to print.

*These loans are burdens to do what the loan provider wants so that he remains in business. Don't tell me that a loan shark what you to grow and put him out of business. He wants you where he wants so that he remains in operation. This means in a position where your growth is a minimum and all you can do is make repayments only and feed your people and nothing else. There is no growth whatsoever during the IMF loan. Therefore.

>After a nation is given the IMF loan, certain conditions are put in place and these are to stifle development that in the end the loan is useless and keeps a nation the way it was at the beginning. The strategy they use is to keep the status quo by just shifting the focus. The idea behind the Bretton Wood system of which the IMF and the World Bank are a product is to stabilize everything by fixing exchange rates or other policies. The overall result is that the loans solve the specific issue but creates an equal and opposite problem. Money comes in through loan will just enable cuts in other areas as austerity measures part of the loan kicks in.

>Their aim is to fund the loan and create conditions that you will be able to make repayments but do nothing of beneficial else. Once the loan is handed, they call for cuts in other areas. Outright there won't be any development. It's just shifting focus.

>The provision of the loans depends on collateral and structural adjustments. This means no growth at all but maintaining the same status quo. Would you be surprised that the poor nations are still poor?

>After getting the loan they force balancing of budgets and cutting overspending.

>After loans they emphasize privatization that takes wealth from nations to foreign investors.

>Unlike printing own money that enhances the nation's people. IMF loans takes wealth out of the nations through foreign investors and privatization. As part of the conditions, they encourage relaxing laws to foreign investors. Automatically it's like secret looting as value is taken away and in exchange, you are burdened with the loans.

>We as a sovereign global leader we are here to ensure fair practices and inform and advise on best methods. We don't force our ideas on anyone, but we help you make informed decisions. Borrowing IMF loans is like getting chaff while behind your back they take all the grain.

>The loans, its conditions, and collateral only mean enhancing foreign rights at the expense of a country's laws. These conditions make it easy to make their repayments. This has nothing to do with the growth and development of that nation but with the ability to make repayments. For the period of the loan, the nation will only be making repayments and cutting down spending in areas critically needed. The initial problem will have been solved but another issue will have arisen through the austerity measures. Ever heard of the Economic Structural Adjustment Programs? These are the creations of the IMF. To worsen the situation so that a country is ever indebted to the IMF and the sovereign nations that created the IMF.

>Our laws advocate for a nation being forever indebted to its people alone. This shifts wealth to the local people. Anything that shifts this pattern conflicts with our laws as this takes wealth to external sources. From the beginning, we argued that for a nation to grow all government activities must have the focus of its people hence the need

to print own money. Every time it borrows money it shifts the wealth to external sources.

Impact of IMF loans on national sovereign and fiscal planning.

The IMF as I argued earlier on is an extension of the few global powers, especially the USA. Any country that takes loans loses its sovereign powers as it falls indirectly under the US. What effect this has is lining up the fiscal and monetary planning of the borrowing country to that of the US. In order words, through loans, the US markets are growing and what the structural adjustments are doing is making sure that the expanded economy benefits the US greatly as resources are extracted from the borrowing country to the US because the currency used for reserves is the US dollar.

## The Triffin Dilemma.

One reason why we are saying the problem will continue to exist if the reserves of another country is used as a global reserve for other nations. The US will have conflicting issues of maintaining national fiscal planning and reserve management while at the same time trying to satisfy global demands for reserves. That's when our currency comes in; the Futuregoldcoin and the Calycoin. We are a sovereign entity and we can print freely our money. We are not like the IMF who does not have printing rights and relies on the currency of the US for reserves.

>Our reserves will not affect other nations' fiscal planning. Countries adopting our currencies will not be influenced by our policies in that they can use our currency as theirs and come up with their own fiscal system whereas when using the US dollar for reserves they must follow whatever the US Fed set. They cannot plan anything that means fiscal manipulation is removed during the IMF loan. What this means is that they can't manipulate fiscal measures to easy others raising the problems. With our currency, they can adjust inflation by lowering or increasing interest rates or devalue the currency. In other words, taking the loan make that country loses control of its fiscal and monetary

system. That means it loses its sovereignty.

>If a country has no sovereignty whatever it does, there is a cost. Loans are not in their control. They can't spend at the same time. They must cut other areas so that they can afford repayments. That means no growth but economic hardship for the people. Everything is fixed.

## Our laws and stance regarding global finance.

An analysis of the effects of the IMF, World bank on living standards and poverty have pointed to one thing; they can't solve global problems but stabilize problems but perpetuate the status quo. For that matter we are officially ruling these as vehicles for development rather stalling tactics to development as such it's optional to get IMF loans. Our stance is that the IMF and the World Bank died with the Bretton Woods in 1971 who created them. Secondly, they don't fit in the new system and are therefore not fit for the purpose. As good as gone.

1. Note that what they do is take money from all the members and kept this money in reserves. This money could have been plowed back to spearhead development but no it's kept somewhere to milk more money through loans. We stand against institutions that take money from the economy and just keep it in reserves or account. In 2017 its fund has grown to US$667 billion.

2. Our system is to keep the money within the nation. In our system, the IMF does not exist. Loans like I said take wealth from the people to external forces. Loans conflicts with the right to self-defense. IMF demands collateral and imposes conditions that affect quality of life as the women and children suffer greatly during IMF loans, remember ESAP? So, I don't care about what they say are the benefits. The IMF loans are like sanctions. They punish the weakest of any society; women and children. Getting the loan means obeying the conditions and these means cuts and concerned with servicing the loan. Throughout the life of the loan, governments have no power to control their

destination their policies are detected by the IMF.

3. IMF loans mean you can't print and mint your own money to service the loans as the structural adjustment's conditions will play a part to further ruin the economy. We argued that real economic growth is only through printing money. IMF loans take value out and stale development. You can't stir economic growth.

4. No need for IMF loan when in financial difficulties. Master the art of printing money and fighting hyperinflation.

5. Printing money requires the exact opposite of IMF structural conditions. Instead of austerity, you need to spend and encourage economic growth to avoid hyperinflation. You need to increase the production of goods. You must match supply to demand which means heavy and systematic production methods. Industrialization is important as well to boost the economy and match the rise in new money. Corruption and government interference must be at the minimum, but the IMF encourages corruption and government interference all of which acts against growth.

6. Our laws and policies will discourage exporting of wealth that is financial resources outside the nation. IMF encourages giving foreign investors more privileges at the expense of the locals and what do they do? Take all wealth abroad without plowing any back into the economy.

7.
   Talking about growth is just plain out of touch with reality under IMF whereas with our laws and policies national growth is a fact as all aims are to keep the money circulating and growing in that economy alone.
   Institutions taking money out of the economy and holding it in accounts.
   What we have observed is the fact that a lot of institutions were created to take money out of the economy and holding it in reserve and use these to control the whole economy. Imagine if all this money in IMF accounts, the World Bank, the UN, etc. was

circulating in the system a lot of global issues would have been solved by now. These accounts hold a large sum that if plowed back where it originated would help lift the living standards greatly. The fact that too much bureaucratic issues and release of money are major issues makes no sense to us. If they plowed back the funds quickly and when needed, then we might have taken a different stance.

**Plowing the money back into the global system.**

8. Our stance is to boost growth within the next five years where nations will print money and fight hyperinflation. All this money in the World Bank and IMF accounts if it is plowed back would see our plans achieved faster.

9. We have laws to reduce the amount to be kept in these accounts. Laws that will allow only a small percentage to be kept for emergencies only.

10. Every 5 years the accounts or banks must be emptied, and the process starts again. If we are to keep the IMF and evolve their functions, then all funds collected must be used within five years. No point for these institutions holding huge amounts of money in $ trillions when the world needs this money.

11. We believe that all institutions created after World War II were created to act as banks for the founding nations for taking resources from the economy and be kept away from the economy with only the creators dictating where the money should go.

12. To adjust this, we believe ceasing operations of these institutions, the IMF and the World Bank or letting them empty the reserves every four to five years to stir global development and start again.

**Global laws regarding institutions.**

We have covered these laws above but to recap our laws will reduce the life span of these institutions on certain issues with rotation in mind. An institution operating for a limited period and only allowed to extend based on merits. Likewise, all institutions that hold reserves like IMF and World Bank to plow back the reserves or a huge portion at consecutive intervals to boost growth. No point holding $trillion for decades when the global situation is dire. So, every four to five years a huge portion of reserves is used among members, etc. Then the collection starts again.

## Using our currency as the reserve currency instead of the US Dollar.

We Tomorrow's World Order strongly believe that the world problems are because of the fact that all countries use the reserve of the US dollar. So, in short, US problems are also global problems. Look at the 2007 financial crises. This started in the US and because all countries use the US reserve, the problem spread globally. US problems are not global problems. The fact that everyone uses the US reserves also means its problems are dragging everyone down too. It is a different situation if you were all using our currencies. We are not tied to any country. This will solve the Triffin Dilemma as well. The main reason why the US is growing fast is the fact that everyone else relies on it. So, everyone at some point is under the sovereign of the US which expands its market globally and as such only the US will extract value from all other nations. The direction of the flow of resources and wealth is from the periphery [other nations] to the US. In this case, only the US will have the chance to grow faster at the expense of other nations. Globalization this way will only increase inequality as the US through institutions like the IMF, World Bank, UN all based in the state will keep collecting wealth from other countries. Remember what I said about the idea of being forever indebted to someone. Now the whole world is indebted not to their people that would have increased their people's wealth but to the US as they use the US reserves and all exchanges are in US dollars.

## Our system a problem solver.

Again, if a country prints or mints, its money and does not borrow it owes money to its people. Avoiding reliance on the US dollar and using our currency that is not linked to any nation but is a global currency easily adopted will change this pattern that has been going on for more than 70 years with marginal growth. We will start seeing nations not relying on expensive loans. You can't tell me that printing or minting money and getting loans are the same.

## The art of printing money and hyperinflation.

The reason why the US is forever growing is that they print money like no other country. Fact. So, to fight hyperinflation they need a huge market to cover shortages in demand and need a lot of countries to increase production. Everyone using US reserves or relying on the US dollar is part of the US market and this helps the US fight inflation. The increased supply of money is matched by the demand and supply of goods and services. Everyone globally using the US dollar stimulate growth and cushions the US economy from hyperinflation. I argued that the only way to grow fast and cheaply without paying back the money as with loans or paying interest is through printing. Are you surprised why the US is as huge as it is? It's not rocket science. Every nation can do it. Every nation has the ability and power to do it. This explains the IMF, the World Bank, etc. who act to remove surplus currency printed by the US. These institutions reflect how much extra money the US prints. What we are against is the fact that they hold $trillions all put together for decades when we have global debt in $trillions, poverty is rampant, unemployment and the financial crises all call for the need for a new system.

## Our currency.

Our currency will shift the focus from the US dollar to ours not tied to any country avoiding the Triffin Dilemma. Our policies and laws are aimed at helping everyone and not just the US. Ever learned about the bee colony?

The bee colony. The world today is like the bee colony with every nation on earth working hard for the bee queen. Only the bee queen can grow at the expense of everyone. To grow as well is for every nation to have its own bee queen so that all the bees work for that queen. Everyone else is borrowing from IMF, World Bank, etc. which are US-based. Our laws identify this problem and redistribute wealth. We stop sovereign nations from taking loans instead to create colonies large enough to produce to meet the demand created by new money. Our currency will provide a huge market and demand without taking wealth from individual countries. We are not against the US, but we believe the US has grown so big that it won't feel a thing if all nations establish their own colonies. In fact, the US will benefit from our method in that they will have the chance to do what China is doing to them even if it is not deliberately. China as a survival strategy to fight hyperinflation is devaluing its currency to make exports attractive so as to boost growth and increase production to match the new money. The US now sees this as a strategy but it's just a tool to tackle hyperinflation. Now with our currency, the US can use our currency as the reserve currency that is different from their currency. At the moment their reserve is the same as the day-to-day currency. Of all the 195 countries only, the US is a disadvantage this way as all countries can devalue their currency against the US for a better deal. Now thanks to us we have leveled the playing field. We believe the US has shown you the way and we are there to make it happened without you suppressing others. Our laws will create a perfect framework for growth by making the demand for good easily met. Our currency links the whole globe and foster economic development. It's achievable you just need to understand the basics. Our currency Future Gold Coin and Calycoin will become the single major global currency. This will solve a lot of current problems. Everyone will become sovereign in every meaning of the word. None relies on the US Fed's skills to manipulate money and if they get it wrong only the US will experience a crisis, not the whole globe. We can give you the sovereign rights to use our money as you wish with all fiscal rights unlike now with the US where what the US set as interest rates is what you will use too or line your according to the US's.

>This avoids the chain or domino effect where a mistake by the country of the major reserve country will take everyone down with them. What has been happening is that other countries create wealth and one wrong factor then destroys the whole wealth with everyone else feeling the effect and the US having the rest of the world as its shock absorbers?

## The Only Solution to Global Problems: Our Tomorrow's World Order Independent Global Currency.

I will for the first time advance further and explain why our methods will work to increase wealth to never seen before levels. I reiterate here that we are against loans, etc. We believe with loans you can never grow as you would when you print your own money.

### Our solution: Global printing.

Every nation is sovereign and has the right to print and mint money and not borrow. I explained the benefits of printing already above. We as the leader we want every nation on earth to experience massive growth turning developing nations into developed nations overnight. On the other hand, turning developed nations to advanced nations and with the time turn all nations to advanced ones.

### Our global currency and its role.

We have our own currency and as I said above; we are going to use this as the base reserve currency globally instead of the US$. The dollar is there to make the US great forever. Our currency is going to make not only the US but every other nation great forever. What is not to like there? Every nation on earth will use two currencies interchangeable. Their own currencies and our currency. Every nation will have sovereign rights to print and mint their money. So, they print their currency but not flood the market with their money instead will convert their money to ours. Meaning giving us their money in exchange for ours. So, they can use our which is globally available to boost their economy. We keep they're in our reserves until a time when demand has risen in line with supply, they can then withdraw their currency from our Global Reserve Bank.

### What is the effect?

The effect is not to flood the market with their own currency which is valueless to other nations. If they print extra money, it's only valued in their country unless agreements exist between countries.

So, the other effect is to remove their extra money from circulating in the economy without the matching supply. This will stop hyperinflation in its tracks. Tomorrow's World Order. We will be able to hold it in our Global Reserve Bank every country's money so that they can keep printing money and exchanging their currency for ours which they use. So, the money we hold for them will earn interest as well as an incentive to keep printing and depositing to us their cash. At the same time building what can amount to savings. They don't have to pay interest or any loan repayments. All money they print is solely for growth and their people. The more they print the more their reserves or savings grow the more savings grow as well so the more the wealthier they become. No more debt. No more global problems. Every nation will have surplus money in their own currency that can be redeemed for our global currency. Hyperinflation a thing of the past. Global debt a thing of the past. Furthermore, the savings can be used as collateral to increase the value of the inhabitants.

### Tomorrow's World Order's Role.

Tomorrow's World Order on the other hand can use the reserves to further develop the system and provide global infrastructure and services that a nation would not otherwise provide. So, what will happen is that we will grow in reserves of every nation as they keep printing and exchanging ours for theirs. We can use the reserves to boost supply globally so they can use the extra money to buy our goods to fight hyperinflation.

### Our Plans Behind the Printing of Money.

Throughout this book, we have presented ourselves as a powerful global leader that will solve all global problems. The printing of money will boost every nation's economy to increase at exponential levels as the wealth of these nations increases. We will provide our currencies to be exchanged with the printed money. Our currency is used globally the idea being to stop hyperinflation. The printed money is given to us or deposited in our reserves where the money earns interest in our currency where the nation can take the interest periodically. But the idea is that they will never take the money from us for some time as we will keep this money in our reserves. This will be their wealth or investment that is perpetual and never to sink in debt again. We at the beginning will decide with these nations to take a percentage of all printed money and plow it back in the economy. Initially, we might take as much as 70% of printed money and use it to further develop the nation concerned. We will use the money to increase supply as we produce more things and supply these to match the extra exchange money injected into the economy. Secondly, we will use the money to link the whole world say building global stations at borders with easy access and link all nations. The money is used to develop infrastructure as well as linking the globe. We will use the money to develop a global identity I mentioned at the beginning for easy access. We can use the money to attract foreign investment to remove hyperinflation. In fact, the money will be used to stimulate the economy to remove all the side effects of printing money.

>This will enable us to encourage overspending.

>Stimulate growth and development increasing production

>Create global markets to match increase money supply, etc.

After say the first 3 years to 5 years we can plow back the money if hyperinflation is under control until a time when we can just keep this money as savings of a nation or its investment.

>So, in short, global loans are banned. Why get a loan when you can print cheaply. You can see why I said IMF and World Bank have no place in our new system.

>In the end we have an independent global currency not linked to any nation but one that is used and converted to local currencies. If one nation falls, it will do that on, its own. The domino effect of the financial crisis is removed in a flash. One nation for itself and TWO for us all applies well here.

>In the end all nations will be equal and rich and skill and luck we determine the levels of wealth.

Even Worse Scenarios Are Under Control.

In case growth and supply did not match the supply of new money and demand for goods resulting in hyperinflation our currency will minimize the effect.

This is how a nation will tackle hyperinflation.

We understand at the beginning some nations will experience mild hyperinflation as the printing goes on. So, this is how they will fight this.

>The moment they realize this they must stop using their currencies. Take all currency out of the economy and leave our global currency. But keep printing but handing over the new money to us Tomorrow's World Order for holding in reserves and exchanging some of this for ours.

>Our money is a global currency better than the US in that it is not tied to a nation and nations can manipulate it in either way we can give license for that. Just like now nations when faced with inflation they will resort to the US. This limits their sovereign powers. They can't control anything, fiscal supply, instruments or use these to fight other side effects like rising interest rates. In this case, everything they do is according to the US's Fed system. Technically that kills their sovereignty. But with our currency, they have all fiscal instruments at hand. They use our currency as theirs simply printing more of their own and giving us that and we are giving them ours. Hyperinflation destroys the wealth of affected nations. Our system keeps the wealth as reserves with us until a time they can take back their currency. They won't suffer any lose. They will keep printing more. In most hyperinflation cases a nation at one-point stops printing at all and this results in the currency rendered useless. We have a solution for that.

>When using the US as the reserve currency a lot of other factors come into play. These can be political perception, reputation, and corruption all of which worsens hyperinflation. Some countries might not want to use the US dollar as they might not like the US's foreign policy, and this can influence the economy. As with us, we are a liked global leader unbiased and therefore the benefit of the whole globe. We want to see wealth, growth, development and never seen before living standards. This is the only way forward.

We have the whole world's currency in our hands and will use this to take development to new heights. We can be trusted, and our strength is not to be trusted just for the sake of trust but by actions. When we say we are going to do this, we will do just that. We shall have the resources at our disposal which we will keep on behave of all nations. The printing shall continue so as to the wealth of every nation that can print.

>This will enable us to drive the idea of sovereignty and all nations shall trust us as we will increase wealth exponentially. We shall treat sovereign nations as such and not like now where leaders are reduced or grounded to naughty kids with sanctions, etc. There shall not be a reason for fighting, sadness or quarreling. The only critical skills that will be challenging will be dealing with hyperinflation but like I said everyone has our backing.

# CHAPTER TWENTY-EIGHT

CHEMICAL WEAPONS AS WEAPONS OF MASS DESTRUCTION VIS-À-VIS INTERNATIONAL LAW AND RELATED INCIDENTS.

I know somehow chemical weapons are not regarded as lethal as other WMDs. I think we find cases of chemical weapon usage as something tolerated to some extent, and as such, maybe it's beneficial if we look at this separately. Our stance just as with all other weapons is that enough is enough it's time, we take a different road and let bygones be bygones. We strongly stand against the use of chemical weapons of any sort and this practice is banned in the New World. I think why we have so many cases or incidents is the fact that these are weapons easily concealed or easily used without being detected as the wind can easily disperse these leaving no trace of any kind. Nevertheless, any use is prohibited.

In short, a chemical weapon is;

"a substance, such as a poisonous gas rather than an explosive, that can be used to kill or injure people."

Their use results in death, blindness, and maiming. There are other chemicals that are used for riot control, and these are tear gas among others. The main stance is to ban all that can kill many people within a short period. There are laws governing their use but nevertheless, they are used despite these international laws.

Their use by Saddam was one of the reasons that brought his destruction. The international community is against any use of such weapons and would act swiftly, which is understandable. In recent years as recent as the beginning of this year, we have seen the USA condemning Syria's use of these weapons on its people committing what is regarded as unacceptable genocide with the resulting missile strikes by the big three USA, Britain and France. We stand with the international community against the use of these chemical weapons. Currently, the Chemical Weapons Convention is the treaty governing the use of these weapons and it prohibits;

Developing, producing, acquiring, stockpiling, or retaining chemical weapons.

The direct or indirect transfer of chemical weapons.

Chemical weapons use or military preparation for use.

Assisting, encouraging, or inducing other states to engage in CWC-prohibited activity.

The use of riot control agents "as a method of warfare."

**Arms Control Publication.**

Our question is that if there are treaties prohibiting this how come we have Syria swallowing missiles because of this? Maybe first let's look at what is a treaty.

'A **treaty** is an agreement under <u>international law</u> entered into by actors in international law, namely <u>sovereign states</u> and <u>international organizations</u>. A treaty may also be known as an **(international) agreement, protocol, covenant, convention, pact or exchange of letters**, among other terms. Regardless of terminology, all these forms of agreements are, under international law, equally considered treaties and the rules are the same'.

Treaties can be loosely compared to <u>contracts</u>: both are examples of willing parties assuming obligations among themselves, and any party that fails to live up to their obligations can be held liable under international law."

Wikipedia.

A treaty is something that can be entered by choice between parties that could explain why some countries like North Korea or Sudan never bothered signing such treaties. I think this is part of the problem. Although guided or rooted in international law treaties are like optional contracts where you can choose and see if it's beneficial to you and if it is then you must sign the treaty. I think this is the root of the problem. The Prohibition of Chemical Weapons Organization [OPCWO] is there just to inspect and monitor and prohibit. It seems from the onset it has a reactive role something we are against. We aim to be proactive. Our aim is not to provide 500 plus jobs, etc. Our aim is to stop the use and the killings using these weapons. We believe there are other areas we can create job areas that are geared to finding new ways of doing things not correcting people's mistakes. We aim not to have unnecessary wastage and mistakes.

### Our laws.

We must put laws that are recognized internationally by everyone this treaty thing leaves loopholes and we don't want an ambiguous system that is not predictable. Therefore, any use and possession of chemical weapons with intent to use to kill or main or blind is not allowed. Our goal is to use a fast system like the blockchain where everyone can read our laws at their own time and confirm electronically through the blockchain or other advanced systems that they have read and understood the laws. This confirmation will act as proof that they are aware of the laws and the consequences of breaking the law. I know the Organization for the Prohibition of Chemical Weapons [OPCW] emphasis on monitoring and submission of stockpile reports to be handed to them. Our aim is to remove unnecessary bureaucracy and all unnecessary time-consuming paperwork. We want to treat every country on earth as a responsible sovereign that understands what is required of them. We don't want to treat these nations like kindergartens who must be told and monitored. We give everyone the benefit of the doubt and let them be responsible for their actions. I think the issue is that there is too much monitoring that is making people do the opposite of what the monitoring is trying to achieve. But we will keep distance surveillance to make sure that no one breaks the law. Okay, we have looked at the basics now we want to look at the case of Syria the alleged use of chemical weapons and the missile strikes that followed.

### Douma Chemical attack.

In February 2018 the Syrian government is alleged to have embarked on an offensive attack to recapture the city of Ghouta in the hands of the rebels. It was here that seventy people were confirmed dead and the cause of death referred to as chlorine poisoning. It is allegedly by the West, the USA, Britain, and France that the Syrian government had dropped two cylinders that released chlorine and as high as 500 people were thought to have been affected as reported by the OPCW. The Syrian government denied such accusations and even invited the OPCW to inspect the possible use of chemical weapons. The accusations were that;

"The Jaysh al-Islam rebel group, which controlled Douma at the time,[19] along with several medical,[20] monitoring, and activist groups, including the pro-rebel White Helmets (Syria Civil Defense), all reported that two Syrian Air Force Mi-8helicopters had dropped barrel bombs.."

Wikipedia.

The three Allies USA, France, and Britain threatened the Syrian government while Russia and Iran deny that it was the Syrian government responsible for that. They declared this was a lie just another false flag. This resulted in joint military attacks by the three most powerful countries in the world.

"The strikes were carried out by the forces of the United States, the United Kingdom, and France [56] and were delivered by ship-launched, submarine-launched and airborne cruise missiles.[57] All the missiles launched by British and French forces were variants of the Storm Shadow missile, known as SCALP EG and Missile de Croisière Naval (MdCN for Naval Cruise Missile) in French service."

Wikipedia.

False flag.

"A false flag is a covert operation designed to deceive; the deception creates the appearance of a particular party, group or nation being responsible for some activity, disguising the actual source of responsibility."

This comes from the trick used by pirates of using another country ship's flag in disguised. Used by pirates who would then rob an unsuspecting ship approaching. The blame being labeled on the owners of the flag even though they are not the culprits. This is the oldest trick used for the past 40 years since after the U2 1960 incident. I explained above that the US President Eisenhower request permission from the Pakistan government to establish spying camps to fly a spy plane the U2 to Soviet airspace to carry out surveillance and aerial reconnaissance activities. This was vital to be a competitive advantage and assess the strengths, weaknesses, and opportunities. This task was carried out by the spy planes. But we can see that even during the 1960s this was an illegal act then as it amounts to crimes of aggression which is against international law. Years later the U2 plane has been replaced by various organizations of which the UN is one. Who can pretend to inspect to check but in fact carrying out spying activities just like the U2 plane but now under the disguise of the UN? This would clear the West or Allies of any wrongdoing because even the accused governments don't know that the UN's institutions like the Weapons Inspectors are like the bomb disposal unit just before an invasion. This is true because wherever they are allowed military invasion or strikes is almost guaranteed because they weaken the accused. Let them in then the whole crew will enter too. Deny them then the world might stand on your side. Syrian government to squash the accusations invited the OPCW to investigate.

"Syria is keen on cooperating with the OPCW to uncover the truth behind the allegations that some western sides have been advertising to justify their aggressive intentions," said Sana, quoting an official source in the Foreign Ministry.[46] Russia denied chemical weapons were used and on 13 April blamed Britain for staging the event in order to provoke US airstrikes."

Psychological mind-game. Invite or Allow Inspectors at your peril. A sign of weakness and can only led to military strikes. I have argued throughout this book that the West is very clever and uses psychological mind games. They employ a SWOT analysis through parts of its subsidiary branches like the UN or now the OPCW to assess the strength of the Syrian government. We have seen the same tactic used on Saddam that in efforts to clear his name he was signing his own death certificate by succumbing under pressure.

It is understood that this tactic of deception is used in military circles where an enemy is asked to come out with the false promise that it's a cease-fire but once he is out, then he is ambushed and killed. A term referred to as perfidy. International law makes perfidy illegal and people cannot be killed in such a way without the killer charged with war crimes.

The Geneva Convention;

Article 37. – Prohibition of perfidy.

1. It is prohibited to kill, injure or capture an adversary by resort to perfidy. Acts inviting the confidence of an adversary to lead him to believe that he is entitled to, or is obliged to accord, protection under the rules of international law applicable in armed conflict, with intent to betray that confidence, shall constitute perfidy. The following acts are examples of perfidy."

Wikipedia.

Okay, let's look at the main reasons why the West employs such a deceiving method that is clearly prohibited under international law. If they exploit any loopholes, then we want to know what loopholes and close these before introducing new laws that play fair.

How the West justifies false flags.

The method is accepted in warfare if at the last moment one attacker can show the true flag or identity just before an attack. So, it can deceive first but before opening fire to declare your identity.

Tactic mainly used a pretext for war.

Somehow it is permitted to fabricate an incident or apportion blame wrongly in order to engage or aim for a war. This is true as the war contingency plans must require such a move to eliminate risk and to change the direction events might take. Such actions are viewed as collateral nevertheless the risk outweighs these issues that it's justified in order to change the course of events and avert a catastrophe.

Precedent of False Flag.

World War Two.

"The Gleiwitz incident in 1939 involved Reinhard Heydrich fabricating evidence of a Polish attack against Germany to mobilize German public opinion for the war

550

and to justify the <u>war with Poland</u>. <u>Alfred Naujocks</u> was a key organizer of the operation under orders from Heydrich. It led to the deaths of <u>Nazi concentration camp</u> victims who were dressed as German soldiers and then shot by the <u>Gestapo</u> to make it seem that they had been shot by Polish soldiers. This, along with other false flag operations in <u>Operation Himmler</u>, would be used to mobilize support from the German population for the start of <u>World War II in Europe</u>."

Wikipedia.

The Germans used the same tactic to rally public support for a war with Poland that led to the invasion of Poland.

The Cuban Revolution: Operations Northwood.

The US government drafted a plan to fabricate incidents and killing which they would blame on the Cubans as a trigger or a pretext for an invasion of Cuba. The main aim; - to overthrow the communist regime of Fidel Castro. According to Wikipedia, this involved;

"scenarios such as fabricating the hijacking or shooting down of passenger and military planes, sinking a US ship in the vicinity of Cuba, burning crops, sinking a boat filled with Cuban refugees, attacks by alleged Cuban infiltrators inside the United States, and harassment of US aircraft and shipping and the destruction of aerial drones by aircraft disguised as Cuban MiG's.."

Operations Northwood did not go through as President J.F. Kennedy denied the plan. In the Middle East during the 1980s it is alleged that the Israel secret service planted car bombs that killed many Palestinians to trigger a retaliatory response that will see the Palestinian Liberation Organization use terrorism as revenge and give the Israelis reasons to invade Lebanon.

[Wikipedia]

**False Flag as a political tool to undermine opponents.**

This tactic can be used to undermine the leadership of a country and blame atrocities carried out on his people as his sole responsibility with the aim to get the leader to lose favor with the people and be toppled. False flagship is a psychological mind-game.

This can be used;

To create psychological support for a planned war

To pave the way for a transition to a less democratic form of government;

To consolidate a government when its power is dwindling

To defame an enemy by blaming an attack on them

Wikipedia.

Conspiracy theorists claim that the government might use the false flagship trick in order to extend its surveillance plan and or to justify military action against a nation or a certain group of people.

### What is the justification for such military attacks?

Evidence according to the OPCW report released a few months this year suggest fabrication of evidence or withholding of information of the alleged 'cylinders that were thought to have been dropped by the Syrian aircraft'. The report suggests the cylinders were never dropped from the planes but planted there. In that case once again just like the days before the Iraq war, we see the UN or other subsidiary bodies after the attacks had happened coming out and declare that the dossier of evidence used was incorrect. What does it matter now a year or so after the attacks? The USA argued that the missile attacks targeted strategy points mainly chemical making plants so that Syria won't have the ability to make more chemicals that they would use on their people. The Syrian government declared such missile attacks as attacks on his leader and the fact that the attacks did not last suggest acted in his favor that the attacks were not justified in the first place. Our analysis suggests he might be innocent but a bit naïve not to have learned from Saddam. We as Tomorrow's World Order don't want to see situations like this where leaders because of lack of skill, courage, and understanding of the world are taken advantage of. This is trickery and an attack on a sovereign nation. What gives the USA, France and Britain the right to invade and attack? So, are the accusations of death from chemical weapons real?

## Our Stance on deaths by chemical weapons.

We stand with the international community to strongly declare war on regimes that kill especially their own people through chemical weapons. Our laws are against any deaths whatever the situation. Everyone on earth including governments must recognize our first laws; the rights to life and to self-preserve. Any death by any means for us can bring the whole globe still. This is true as we believe that such an act can make a person regarded as an enemy of the people if they use chemical weapons that can kill many. Did the joint missile attacks result in the deaths of civilians? Luckily there were no reports of any civilian deaths as a result of the joint attacks something that is good even though we disagree with the invasion of a sovereign nation when your own track record is hanging by a thread. So why they did that? This can be best answered by President Trump's words according to a BBC report;

"The purpose of our actions tonight is to establish a strong deterrent against the production, spread and use of chemical weapons," he said. [BBC April 2018.]

## Our laws regarding the above incident and any related future ones.

>Implementation of laws vehemently prohibiting making, possession, and use of chemical weapons with the aim to kill others. We are not banning all chemical weapons only those used for killing, blinding or maiming others.

>Everyone must acknowledge reading and understanding our laws and confirming this at their own time within a given time frame. We shall have a ban that is universal. Any breach will have serious consequences. We shall expect every nation to act as responsible as they can and obey our laws.

>For the purpose of the right to self-preserve we shall protect all nations and give them rights to deny the UN and its subsidiaries' rights of entry into sovereign territory simply because for the past seventy-years their entry had been followed by military action.

They might be doing 'good' but overall, they jeopardize the lives of millions of women and children through sanctions that are aimed to weaken first and then through them encouraging wars.

>Banning of any form of inspectors on the grounds who are being used to carry out a Colony Collapse Strategy where nations are targeted according to the resources they have and not simply because of their human rights abuses. Saddam in 25 years is reported to have killed 250 000 and the Iraq war in 13 years or less claimed the lives of 500 000. Therefore, we argue and believe that the Weapons Inspectors only help the West carry out a SWOT analysis that will lead to an invasion. A strategic military assessment of the effects of an invasion. If they had not entered, the war could not have happened that is our belief.

> Honestly the UN and all its subsidiaries if they have no power to stop any wars are a risk to the lives of women and children as they are part of the rugby's tactical team blocking any kind of help from people who have the power to stop the war.

>It is a fact the UN is there just to create jobs and nothing to do with stopping wars. It never attempted to create laws that ban weapons. In this case; guns kill people without guns we have no gun deaths.

>We strongly condemn wars because just like terrorists the West is using women and children as bargaining tools and see them just as collateral damage using sanctions to cause severe sufferings simply because these people have no one to defend them. Now a thing of the past.

>No nations must group to attack a weak nation. The idea is to provoke a strong nation like Russia or China to try to defend the weaker nation in Syria and the Allies in Britain, France, and the USA then attack it. Such an attack can be disguised and used to attack the vital defense system of any country as this affect their right to self-preserve. Our new laws are a shift from the current ideology where military action can be carried simply because of the suspected use of chemical weapons. It's easy now because no one must prove that the weapons were used before attacking. They just attack and apologize later, look at Iraq the fraudulent dossier and now the OPCW's report is and was a scam that the Syria

planes dropped the chlorine cylinders. We can see a pattern developing.

>We must encourage the affected nations to take legal action against the UN, where the UN and all its bodies have entered on false beliefs and intentions of carrying out inspection that resulted in military attacks. Wherever the UN had entered and compiled a report that suggested that there were no WMDs but then went on to fail to stop the war and protect the innocent lives of women and children that it exposed naked. These nations must bring criminal intent war crime charges against the UN and its subsidiary bodies. This is fair because such entry gave the Allies a strategic advantage they would not have had. I will rely on the development of digital soldiers or gadgets that can be implanted or worn to pass information through satellite that can be used for military invasion purposes.

>Where ever there were deaths of innocent women and children the nation invaded by the UN and its subsidiary were allowed-in must claim compensation for every person who died as a result of direct military action and indirect as long as it can be proved that the war was responsible for the deaths. E.g. the bombing of a bridge that is used for medical supplies with the resultant deaths.

>The nation invaded after the UN had entered on false grounds to carry out inspection but resulted in the invasion must claim compensation for damages to infrastructure and other psychological trauma.

>There shall never be time frames or time limits and there shall never be limits of compensation.

>Any nation shall bring charges of spying and acts of aggression again the UN and all its subsidiaries as long as their entry resulted in an invasion in which as the so-called peacekeepers did nothing to stop the war even after declaring that there were no Weapons of Mass Destruction.

>Acts of aggression.

Forced entry in this cause cannot be limited to unauthorized entry by the UN to inspect but can and must include instances like the Iraq and the Syrian incidents where sanctions by the same UN bodies have weakened the government concerned to such an extent that he would invite them not just to clear his name but on humanitarian grounds to lessen the impact and severity of these barbaric tactics to save the lives of women and children. The fact that the UN and other subsidiary bodies are the ones imposing sanctions in the first place even if the leader invites them, we must recognize that he did invite them only to save lives. It's a barbaric way disguised as a cooperation tool. Our laws will make this a criminal case if there are deaths related to sanctions. The leader of the invaded country only had to prove that he invited them to save lives in other words to self-defend the lives of his people and as such justified and supported by the law.

>Acts of aggression shall not be limited to the obvious invasion but will include the use of sanctions as well. Such use is intended 'to force the way in' and use innocent people as bargaining tools. We see no difference in such tactics as those used by terrorists. The fact that one man's terrorist is another man's freedom fighter might apply here.

>Education in psychological thinking can benefit developing countries and laws shall make it mandatory that leaders through our teaching materials etc. must be equipped with all kinds of tricks which we will expose.

>False flagging is banned and must become a war crime if such an action resulted in the deaths of innocent people.

>If the West the USA, Britain and France's missiles had killed even one civilian new war crimes would have been brought against them. We are serious about global peace and our laws will take these cowboys. We are not in a position to bring reckless endangerment of life for personal gain and regardless of the lives of innocent women and children simply because they don't relate to the victims. Make no mistake this is a lack of empathy that amounts to gross human abuse simply because the West does not sympathize with the victims simply because of different backgrounds. I think this was proven after the 9/11 attack where Bush chooses military action that killed as many in retaliation or not while Obama who has a Muslim background decide to send assassins to do the dirty work. If it was a non-muslin non-person

of color President, he might have used military force to invade Pakistan to kill Osama. We want to assess the law from all angles and be as perfect as we can be.

>Personal gains of any military action.

We shall assess any personal gains resulting from military action. We shall assess the reasons forward as justifications for war. For instance, to topple a dictator and assess how many the dictator is alleged to have killed and how long that took and assess the military intervention and how many people they have killed and if there are personal gains, we assess these too. A good example is 9/11. Initially, the Whitehouse had $2,3 trillion missing. Assuming all this money was consumed through purchases of oil resources. Recall President Dwight Eisenhower arguments that oil depletes a nation's resources. We can say that the war was embarked to make oil production increased in volume thereby lowering the price of fuel and thereby saving the government money. We will need to assess the number who die as well say 500 000 and check if likely cost of such a loss by calculating compensation or life insurance policies. We can check the broader impact of such an act and use that to bring perpetrators to justice. On the other side we can check to see if just before the war the country concerned was in debt failing to pay debt and if they managed after the war if so then we can bring more war crimes that they killed such a number so that they can raise this money for such a debt and therefore evil and must be punished.

>The idea is not just to deter but to change the way these leaders view life. There is a new sheriff in town one might suggest.

>We are not against the West, but we believe as the titles reflect the West is a group of developed nations. Nations that ideally must lead by example and guide the developing nations. These nations don't pretend to know what they don't know and don't try to hide their intentions or tricks. They say we have this they mean it and if they say they don't have nukes for sure history has proved that to be the truth. They are like young sisters or brothers who look up to their brothers for all kinds of support and guidance. They are inexperienced and as such we try not to be strict with these only on that basis. We think they have a lot to learn just like how your

young brother or sister would come and ask you questions. Our goal is to guide and protect these from the manipulating, cheating, trickery sisters or brothers who are greedy and want to grow at the expense of their brothers. We are for everyone, but I think with great powers a lot is expected of them too. We have seen a pattern incident after incident of trickery, abuse and no respect of the law. We have a bully or gang situation where the bully is using all kinds of weapons to rob the young brother demanding the younger not to make weapons but himself making weapons and pointing these at the young brother and demanding monies. The West in the last decade has jumped out of sanity and are acting like a bunch of mad wolves with nails in the brain with no one to pull them out or contain this madness.

The West promised peace and prosperity everywhere for the past seventy- years but that has not materialized. Even the West now cannot afford to provide basic needs for their own populations recording high levels of poverty something not heard of in the developed world. So, we come in. There is a problem and doing nothing is not an option anymore. We are taking over the ship and changing direction for the betterment of everyone. Cooperate all humanity or you shall face our laws that close all loopholes which you have been manipulating for the past seventy years.

>Once again, we are neutral, but we seem to be strict with the West because the West is like an educated degreed person who has seen a lot and done a lot if this was our son we would advise and listen too. The developing world is like the daughter who had just finished A levels and about to start a university degree. These they need more guiding than say the elder degreed brother. So, if the elder makes a silly mistake you will be harsh with him or her because you would expect a lot from him or her as you view him or her as a role model to guide the younger daughter.

>It's not that we think the West is or not no, we know they are tricking and devious for self-gains and we know the reasons. The system has crashed and is obsolete so now they will never balance their budgets and will always have issues with debt, proper allocation, and global peace. We know why. They are wasting resources on obsolete functions that is why they are in this mess but don't worry we have the answers and the stamina to see our

plans through but if you resist, it might cost you your lives as we shall not leave any law stone unturned until you have succumbed on your knees if not six feet under.

The New World is not for the short-sighted leaders who want a perfect eight in office. This is for leaders who want twenty-five global contingency plans and we are the only ones who can do so. Throughout the book, I will show you how the current institutions have taken the easy and cheap road. Make WMDs and kill as many if they are not part of us why should we care? Reversing everything and because of the huge aging base that depletes the government's finances then make these people age faster than normal and use digital agents and chips to kill them faster. The reason being that if we don't, we will have an older population with stagnating economies a receipt for disaster.

>I personally think we need to dissolve all these institutions and bring new ones that have time limits on any one issue. Say human rights or climate agendas which they can only do for say five years with their progress checked and based on merit can extend or be forced to apply for a different license say eliminating poverty. etc.

>Countries like Syria must be forced to disarm maybe earlier as part of the global banning of weapons etc. and development packages offered to help with rebuilding with money raised from compensation claims, and the destruction caused by wars not prevented by the UN which they claim as their sole responsibility.

>I am not against the UN I explained why I am strict with them. They are misleading the world and blocking any form of help. They are like impersonators a crime even now which carries severe punishments. They jeopardize the lives of women and children by pretending to stop the war carrying out investigations in which they claim nor to have found Weapons of Mass Destruction but then be unable to stop the war. What is the point then? We are putting new laws saying their presence is not for the good of the accused nations but to give a strategic hand to the invaders. What is the point of investigating even after not finding the weapons you still can't do anything? If you can't stop the war, then don't inspect and weaken others. Our new laws give the invaded or targeted nations a chance to self-preserve through a

detailed analysis of the likely outcome and give them even grounds to arm themselves.

So why are we so strict when it comes to the killing of civilians mostly women and children?

The main justifications forwarded by all the governments breaking international laws are either national security or human rights abuses etc. or following certain treaties, etc. But to us, all these treaties are rendered void if they conflict with the peremptory norms of which the right to life and to self-preserve is the main one.

### Peremptory Norms that can't be violated.

"A treaty is null and void if it is in violation of a peremptory norm. These norms, unlike other principles of customary law, are recognized as permitting no violations and so cannot be altered through treaty obligations. These are limited to such universally accepted prohibitions as those against the aggressive use of force, genocide and other crimes against humanity, piracy, hostilities directed at the civilian population, genetic heritage discrimination, apartheid, slavery and torture,[15] meaning that no state can legally assume an obligation to commit or permit such acts."

Wikipedia.

### Sanctions.

I explained why sanctions are in contradiction and in violation of international peremptory law. Sanctions are an aggressive use of force in that they target women and children and are used to weaken the leaders into submission indirectly as countries under sanctions are reduced to worst states. The leaders concerned can succeed if they can prove that they bargained in order to save lives from such aggression. All they need to do is to establish that sanctions caused deaths and are used as an economic force that will result in deaths. Augmented by the first law it can be proved that they are a means of an aggressive force to weaken the government so that they help others force their way in.

## Civilian Deaths.

Any deaths of civilians are not permitted by law and there are no treaties or other laws that can override these. The first rule the right to life. Any breaking of these peremptory norms which we have turned into direct laws will cause one to be labeled Hostis Humani Generis. An enemy of the people and as such can be attacked by the whole world. The idea is that such a violation can threaten human existence so that a person is punished by anyone.

## Torture.

This is the worst crime as it has slavery connotations as slaves were tortured to perform certain duties and favors e.g. sexual where they are degraded and humiliated first to be abused later. Torture threatens the fabric of international law as we stand firm against torture for any reason. There is no use of corrective behavior etc. as in dog training on humans. Such practices can only get one be dragged to court.

We must be very harsh on nations and leaders who think they can develop sophisticated drone-like devices for torturing people secretly. Express-command to put an end to this through our laws and courts as a deterrent. It is true here that evil can only breed evil both literally and figurative. Very harsh sentences might be a ground to deter and stop such an evil practice so that the world understands how bad it is. Sometimes the seriousness of the act can also point to the importance and serious nature of the initial crime. Some people can only understand that way they are born like that and change does not come easily. If it means the obliteration of the entire nation for the sack of global peace that can be an option. We are tired and fed up. Talking is cheap. The notion of action speaks louder than words applies well here. The international laws through the Jus Cogens; the peremptory laws declare that torture can bring global justice and punishment to your door and yet you carry on torturing people what does that tell everyone. I reiterate here that all the Jus Cogens laws invokes Article 1 that requires a global collective punishment. Express-command to put an end to this through our laws and courts as a deterrent. No other laws can override these and any actions that conflict with these laws makes that agreement or action void.

**Piracy is the same as hacking in this case.**

Express-command to put an end to this through our laws and courts as a deterrent.

Some governments have invested $billions making chips to hack all its population at birth illegally. Implanting chips etc. reducing the quality and life span of its population as the metabolic processes are speeded up with the resulting aging of the population at a faster rate. Chipping and the use of remote-controlled radiation or electromagnetic frequencies can cause harmful effects to the body and therefore conflict with the first rule. The purpose of hacking is to change and cause modifications and at the end of death. Hackers are regarded as worst as pirates and as the slave traders before them and often regarded as Hostis Humani Generis as enemies of the people as they can destroy the gene pool and all humanity by playing God. Very strict punishment at the hands of the whole world. It applies here that an attack on one is an attack on the whole world and military action against such a country by all will and must be organized by Tomorrow's World Order as a deterrent and to set the record straight. We are tired of nations who think they are above the law. We shall swear by the assassin to do a great job. We don't want to take such roots, but some nations are begging to be annihilated. Change or we will change you apply here.

**Slavery**

You will be shocked to find out that some nations are still doing slavery in the name of disguised protection, and the people threatened secretly through the use of chips and satellite technology to command and torture and reduce someone to slavery levels. The devices being used to give the people watermarks that are irremovable lowering the lifespan and quality of life as a population control mechanism a eugenic tool or a genocide stance if you ask me.

>Laws to monitor activities of all satellites and checking and investigating slavery tendencies and any form of use of these to

secretly enslave people. We are not suggesting using the satellite to put as surveillance but to check the satellite usage to uncover it is used to enslave and monitor people through GPS locality etc. Slavery can result in the annihilation of a nation and governments are urged to think again and trade carefully.

>Need for advanced ways of detecting hidden uses of the satellite. Implanting GPS can make one an enemy of the people and such practices have no justification whatsoever as they conflict with the right to life and to self-preservation as well.

**Military action and international law.**

"The United Nations Charter requires a mandate from the United Nations Security Council for sovereign states to use force for the purpose of maintaining international security, but not for acting in self-defense or the protection of populations threatened by extermination at the hands of their own government. Since the UN Charter came into effect in 1945, military action in retaliation or reprisal to the act of another state has been prohibited; but a reprisal may be justified if its aim is to force the other states into compliance with its international obligations."

Wikipedia.

I think I need just a chapter on this topic.

# CHAPTER TWENTY-NINE

THE CURRENT SITUATION AND SLAVERY.

One day just after the 2008 financial collapse a person asked me what was the best business practice invented by men? Before I even answered, she said slavery. She said everything here centers around that every great idea today is based on this system now only developed and evolved but the basis is the same. I looked at the banking system and it struck me. The whole model is the same as those used with slaves. These people were loaned to other people as labors making money for the master. They were rewarded by the kings just for owning slaves and there was insurance for slaves in case he dies. Around 2010 the same person came to me and said she was happy the New World Order collapsed all the banks simply because they are still using slavery practices to get money from us through tricks like PPI and investing the money in Bitcoin and making $millions. She went further and said they are using the same principles as those used during slavery trick and again trick get what you want and invest the money. But also keep an eye on the people and even enslave them more by offering loans on top not to help but to keep them down and later use the offset rule. When you have made a kill, then admit the mistake fast and offer to refund a fraction of the profits but acknowledge the mistake and take the compensation money back to offset the loan. Do you know the main reason behind the PPI scandal was to gather as much money from the people as raising capital and invest in bitcoins? Do you think it's a coincidence that PPI is linked to the time Bitcoin came into play? Think again. If you had invested say $2000 in Bitcoin in 2010, you could have made $10 million. The banks are refunding the people peanuts as compared to the money they made with Bitcoin. What is the difference between this and slavery? So, this woman went on to say the New World Order caused the financial collapse to destroy banks for using slavery methods nevertheless refined? It hit me too I looked even at the blockchain. Are they using the same method but now to redistribute the wealthy from the banks who are stealing it and giving back to the people? If you look at the Merkle trees the idea resonates with ships, carrying slaves all chained together with a slave ledger with all the names of the slave for the master to see and for the record. That also makes sense. If this Sakamoto has gone underground without revealing his proper name could he be sending a message? Satoshi sounds like a 'satellite or ship'. Ships were used to carry and account for all slaves in chains carefully counted but hidden that could explain the encryption so does this mean they are doing the same thing but now using the satellite? Read again the first chapters. I argued that high sophisticated gadgets are used with GPS's functions to torture and spy on people. I argued also that everyone in developed countries if illegally hacked at birth without knowledge and if that is true; they are serialized that is given digital numbers just like the slaves with digits tattooed on them.

### Are the satellites the new slave ships?

Are some governments still practicing slavery using satellites? But hiding encrypted away from the rest of the world? Stealing money from everyone and blackmailing these. Who are the miners digging all the serials? I know the landowners i.e. the landlords kept slaves and were rewarded for these slaves who there were responsible for. Today who could be the slave owners? Teaching hospitals? What are these blocks? I know the formula or algorithm of the Bitcoin the idea is to reduce the number of numbers every 4 years until there are only 21 million left. It sounds like population control. It sounds like satellites are used to reduce life so as of people making them age faster, so they are killed faster too. All sounds like a population control goes bad that has become a genocide pandemic. If it's true who are still enslaving people secretly? All the articles I have discovered so far are attributing the satellite as having discovered slavery as the UN estimates that 40 million people are still in slavery as of June 2019. Wait, a minute. I think the satellite is the reason why we have slavery not because it is discovering slavery practices. Imagine GPS implants on all populations and all logged and tracked by a satellite.

Imagine the same satellite used to torture or abuse all victims through electromagnetic nerve stimulation? Does a tortured hacked person have rights? Are you sure you can trust the satellite? Or it's back to guns don't kill people but people kill people. Who owns the satellites and what are they using them for? Is it reasonable and plausible that the satellites can be used for modern-day slavery? A further analysis of the blockchain, the satellite, and its implications vis-à-vis slavery. Need for laws to deal with satellite, illegal hacking, and slavery. Come. Join in contribute what do you think?

# CHAPTER THIRTY

## REGULATING INSTITUTIONS AND NGOs

New laws to control institutions and their operations. I have stressed throughout this book that most of today's institutions are there solely for job creation and to act as killing weapons or vehicles for such actions and without goals to solve real problems. The existence of the institutions depends on several suffering at the bottom. It's like a pyramid. If there is a large problem base, then it can support huge numbers at the top levels, but if the bottom has fewer numbers, then the top will collapse in. So, these institutions might be creating problems just to justify their presence.

So, as such, we have new laws dictating their operations. First for all to understand our stance and reasoning we emphasize again that impersonating a problem solver when you are not, is a crime as it gives people a false sense of security making them misjudge danger as they might trust in you think you have the stamina to stop say a war or prevent a genocide when you don't. These people if you were not there, they might have run and escape or look for help somewhere else.

To make things worse, their presence might prevent real helpers from acting, meaning their presence blocks potential helpers in that their presence gives them a false sense of resolve. They might assume e.g. in the Iraq war that the UNSEC was to stop the war after finding no evidence of WMDs. Maybe reason they did not intervene. But if UNSEC was not there they might have voiced a concern or delayed the war giving people time to escape.

We have institutions waiting for a huge salary at the end of the month and doing nothing but perpetuating the issues delaying so that they make a kill.

Some of these institutions, NGOs, etc. have been associated with political affiliations that they are now biased. They increase inequality etc. as they help only those with the same political ideologies as them, etc.

Five years cycle for all institutions, charities and NGOs.

Our proposals are to create a time limit for their operation in one area of concern. So, if an institution or body deals with weapons disarmament. They can only do this for five years and can only extend license based on merit of achievement. If they don't meet a certain level, they simply must give another body or institution a chance and they simply move onto the next problem say poverty or globalization. So, every five years their roles and focus will change until issues reduce. So continuous existence is linked and based on achievements and progress rather than by special privileges given by those who formed these institutions. This is the case with the UN that represents the US, UK, France, Germany, Italy, etc. the nations who form them and above all contribute heavily to them. The main reason we think they did not stop the war. Fighting your breadwinner, you can only end up going hungry.

Separation of new institutions from cults like NATO, etc. and not linked directly to nations. Sources of funding should not be from the very people we are saying are needlessly killing women and children. Then you are not able to fight for the kids and children but will represent the views of the creators and funders.

Stopping all impersonating activities as they can get the innocent killed clearly assesses the ability to carry out the nation's task or goal. A classic example is for the UN to claim to stop any wars and enforce these when they are like a church security guard when invaded will call upon Jesus without doing nothing. You must understand that our value placed on life it does not matter whose life. What you can't create is holy and must be feared and respected. If you can't make life, then you can't kill life. If you can make life, then kill and create maybe we might understand but until then no killing. We are the voice of the voiceless and we shall punish killers of the innocent yet precious members of any society.

Cruel provoking tactics of targeting women just like what terrorists do we make you be treated like terrorists and be punished harshly?

Most current institutions when they finally understand our laws and what will happen to them will voluntarily change or cease operation altogether. We have drawn a line, and it's not time to worship people who rack lives.

If you say you are in the job of stirring development, then you must prove that and not do acts that conflict with your claims. A good example is when you use sanctions on everyone, yet you claim to fight for international peace. This is contradictory. This is what has been happening with the UNSEC. They provoke everyone and incite them to fight by killing their women and children and then talk about peace and removing threats to war when they are doing what they are saying to prevent. The minute they imposed sanctions is the minute they declare war on the sovereign nation they are dealing with. The very minute they breached international peace. To understand is one thing and to act justly is another thing.

Future institutions must find ways of funding themselves. We don't want a situation where they don't stop the war as the UNSEC in dealing with Iraq then accepts a huge contribution from the US or UK. If you know the issue the UK owed the US World War II debt and if you look at the whole picture, it's like going to rob to pay debt and not stopping the war and then receive a big reward is itself a threat to peace. UNSEC can be dragged to court under our laws for conspiracy to rob, take by force through weapons, endangering the lives of the victims, and murder using trickery and undue regard to human life on top of that lacking empathy towards the victim giving them a false sense of security. Above that getting women and children killed for personal gains as the invaders are also their breadwinners. It will be unreasonable for them to stop their funder as payment will be withheld. So had no option and intention to stop a war on personal grounds. New laws new interpretation of the laws and bringing the culprits to justice. Change is imminent and inevitable. Are you ready to change and prepare to deal with our no-nonsense laws? We are not against anyone, but we must make you understand our thinking and the new approach to dealing with what we have called global evil and injustice. Be on the good side. Treat every kid and woman as if they were your own.

We don't know what situations where the West goes in and kill thousand women and kids first through sanctions and when Assad the Syrian leader attacks rebels then the West uses humanitarian grounds to invade and attack a sovereign nation. This is a thing of the past. We don't see the logic of killing the innocent and defend the otherwise crooks and muggers of any society. We don't treat rebels the same as civilians who are unarmed and powerless who have no one to defend them and most of all who have a huge heart full of faith and trust that they put their lives for you only for you to let them down and choose muggers over them. Be careful you don't want to be on the wrong side of our laws for we will eliminate you and all your bloodline. Respect the innocent and future people of any nation or face the consequences.

Surely you will never find loopholes to exploit because we have closed all. What you can do is dig yourself a hole in the ground and hide for our wrath will scorch the earth like angry fires and consume everything to dust. Be warned.

# CHAPTER THIRTY-ONE

I SWEAR BY THE ASSASSIN.

First, I want to emphasize that this is not mere preaching of violence targeted at innocent children and women, etc. This is far from cries for crimes against others. It's not acts of terrorism or encouraging meaningless violence. This is far away from the scenes you have witnessed in the last decades. Those were acts of cowards and evil people who use and kill innocent women and children to push their agendas. We are different. We don't preach violence nor encourage violence. We don't encourage killings by assassins of innocent people. We condemn violence of any kind and ban all acts of violence against innocent people. We are a global order where some might see us as threats not because we are threats, no. It is within our rights through our justice system to use assassins who in our world will replace soldiers or soldiers evolving to these assassins. We see ourselves as opportunities that can help the globe realize its potential and this is through networking and connections; we think humanity can benefit from it. We have greater responsibilities for the law and order leveling the playing field and as such we might face resistance and even threats and we are ready to deal with them. Recall I advocated and emphasized that we have a right to life just like everyone else and above all this, we have a right to self-preserve. Yes, we have a right to protect ourselves and what we stand for and as such we are entitled to use assassins to achieve our goals. Our boys and girls will not initiate unprovoked attacks unless if it's an official command. We act as peacekeepers but bear in mind that an entity without an attacking force it's either non-functioning or useless. Look at the current UN without any powers is easily stampeded on. We are very different as we don't represent anyone. We are independent and rely on our highly paid and skilled man and women as a last resort when negotiations have failed. I have a motto that I swear by the assassin to carry out a brilliant job.

## Basis of our express commands.

Express-command to put an end to this through our laws and courts as a deterrent. Every judgment through our courts. Our commands in this book are not and should not be considered as incitements to violence or commands to encourage violence whatsoever. Our commands are what I call smart commands.

## Smart Commands.

These are coded programmed codes that check the decision based on the IF-THEN.

A line of action or decision must first hold water before a certain related action is reached. Even if it is reached, it must be confirmed and acknowledged first because a specific action can be taken or executed. This is not a direct express command to carry a task per se but depends on certain variables to be met first. A certain truth must be realized first, confirmed before triggering the related response. This is different from a command to go and kill for the sack of killing.

This is a command to ASSESS, EVALUATE, CONFIRM, THEN EXECUTE.

It's a sequence that can't be broken and depends on certain variables and truths to be met first before action is taken. So, in short, it's. If A breaches law 1and 2. Assess, if correct, Confirm, once confirmed Acknowledge, then Executes.

This is a situation where a decision is dependent on something to happen first before a related response is implemented. IF one breaks these rules THEN. Express-command to put an end to this through our laws and courts as a deterrent.

## Basis of judgmental criteria.

Legal Precedents and Justifications given by international laws regarding the Jus Cogens the Peremptory laws.

Throughout the book, I have declared that our laws are based on what today is referred to as the Jus Cogens the Peremptory laws where NO DEROGATION IS PERMITTED. There are no laws on earth that can override these guaranteed by international law. Breach of these will make whatever law that does that void.

Meaning no derogation is permitted.

Why? Rationale.

This is because these peremptory laws safeguard the fundamental principles of international laws and are the cornerstones of human existence and safeguards against human extinction hence the graveness. Breaching these laws can invoke the Hostis Humani Generis; an enemy of mankind.

This automatically invokes Article 1.

A breach of these laws which means a crime against anyone such as torture, hacking, genocides, crimes against humanity, war crimes, slavery, etc. are breaches against all humanity. There is universal jurisdiction in that any person can exercise judgment regardless of where the breach occurred. Anyone needs just to publicly announce that he has assessed and found a breach that is confirmed by the Law Smart Contract [LSC] all he will do now is acknowledge on the smart contract, confirms and Executes or acts.

Now it might not make sense but once the system is running, you will understand what is need. I argued in earlier chapters that we need a new system. We shall have the Law Smart Contract that uses instant messaging and permanent transactions. What happens is that a person after reading our laws must confirm as a prerequisite. This is logged on as a Timestamp with the date and place. Then through the Law Smart Contract Courts, any breach will be highlighted and linked to a person. The assassins will be working on these smart contracts and will get a report on violations. The need to check on the Law Smart Contract for the following.

☐ The timestamp first that the violator read our laws and confirmed that.

☐ The details of the violations and date etc.

☐ The assessment and who carried out the assessment if a smart contract he must check the identity of the smart contract and cross-check with the database to check for the second or third verification.

☐ He then after three verifications then Acknowledges taking over and dealing with the violators.

573

- ☐ He checks everything and Confirms first with the smart contract and then with the database.

- ☐ Then Execute once he has two confirmations.

People who end up here are serial violators who will end up labeling as the Hostis Humani Generis where the command applies. This is not a command to go on a random killing spree and then try to blame us. It will be impossible to prove. Our system is solid. The person must be on our Law Smart Contract. Secondly, you must be working for TWO and have logging details and you can assess the Law's Smart Contract; The Assassin division. You must have carried out the above procedure. Acknowledge the timestamp. Did an assessment. Assessed twice with the smart contract and then the Database. Verified three times. Confirmed twice with the LSC and the Database. Confirmed before Execution. All these functions cannot be confirmed at the same time maybe it takes one or two days.

The punishment is for anyone any human being to exercise judgment regardless of jurisdiction. These laws have universal jurisdiction in that anyone can assess one's breaches and pass judgment. Since there can never be allowed breach say in use of torture, hacking, slavery, piracy, genocide, etc. there is an express finding of guilty once one can prove that there has been a breach. What's different here is the fact that once the breach is established there is no need to take the person through the courts to be assessed etc. The judgment is obviously expressed. It's like Don't Do or Die. It's either you don't do, or you do once you do then expect to die. It does not say do and be tried and then die. This is the graveness of these laws. There is express the judgment. Breach and be punished. It's different from normal laws where you can breach and still you are presumed as innocent until proven guilty. This is way different. Hence the IF-THEN command. If there has been torture or hacking. Express-command to put an end to this through our laws and courts as a deterrent. Once our laws are into effect, it will make sense because people will know breaching carries an express command. To put an end to this through our laws and courts as a deterrent. These are the core laws where no breach of any kind is permitted. It's either you Don't Do or Do and Die.

This is how serious this is. I know with time this might change but the implementation phase is crucial to the success of the project and our laws MUST be respected and observed by all. So, people must know the consequences. We don't want like now where people kill 500 000 women and children and expect to be dragged to court and all that. Why because the law is ambiguous, they don't know or were not sure of the THEN part in IF-THEN. The new system will make it clear that everyone will understand every effect of breaking our laws as plain and direct as can be.

So, the express command is justified and supported by the Jus Cogen's norms. Legal precedents made us arrive at such a command and we are within the law. If a person breached our laws expect this to happen. Within the framework of our laws.

## Is this against the law?

We have rights just like rich people can get licenses to protect themselves we as the global leaders don't need licenses from anyone instead, we can grant ourselves any licenses we feel fit. We are not answerable to any present President or Prime Minister and all these leaders fall under us. The assassin is the executor of our final command when everything else has failed. This is a legal part of our organization. Assassins shall address a lot of the problems we have today. Our laws are and must be easily understood and observed.

## Aim Listing.

We shall target a list of organizations, governments, and nations we think are the root causes of the global issues we have. We shall use the law to aim these evil cults, institutions, organizations, governments, and individuals. We shall test-drive our laws by declaring war on all evil and no one is immune. One by one we shall test all our laws and bring people, institutions, and governments to the law system. This includes institutions benefiting from past evils or still using the same methods used during the dark ages. We shall be ruthless with those who think we are here to play. Those who think they can just develop new technology to do the same evil are totally on the wrong side of the law. In the process, we shall aim to establish that the current justice system is biased and therefore not fit for the purpose. We shall adopt the Nuremberg style system but without the revenge part but just to deliver justice before we declare our system the only just and fair global system and therefore the only one with the final say. We shall look at the current system like the ICC or the ICJ and prove that these are like the rugby players I explained above just to trick, distract and block any kind of help and maintain the status quo.

# CHAPTER THIRTY-TWO

THE EQUALIZER. WHAT GOES AROUND COMES AROUND.

One great scientist stated that for every force there is an equal and opposite reaction.

Newton's Third Law.

In simple terms for every action, there is an equal but opposite force that can be referred to as the reaction. Forces therefore occur in nature in pairs. But what if there is only one force achieved say the action and somehow the reaction is diverted or not established straight away enough to be regarded as exerted? In these instances, we will need an equalizer to exert the reaction so that the system is balanced. The forces as you know won't cancel each other as they have a different focus and therefore two different ones.

In football an equalizer;

"In sports such as football, an equalizer is a goal or a point that makes the scores of the two teams equal."

Collins Dictionary.

An equalizer can be a person, a thing or event that has an equalizing effect.

In audio recording;

"In sound recording and reproduction, equalization is the process commonly used to alter the frequency response of an audio system using linear filters ... Since equalizers "adjust the amplitude of audio signals at particular frequencies," they are, "in other words, frequency-specific volume knobs."

The process of equalizing in recording allows one to increase or boost the volume or reduce the volume to correct the problems created when recording. Life in general is unbalanced, but somehow things and forces tend to correct themselves over time. But sometimes the system grows rapidly very unbalanced that it will remain one-sided and offsetting the imbalance would be impossible because the other side grows very fast amalgamating fast and controlled that the free opposing forces are canceled out deliberately to create the imbalance.

Controlled systems.

Free forces always find a way of offsetting the imbalance and maintaining equilibrium.

Equilibrium;

1. The <u>condition</u> of a <u>system</u> in which <u>competing</u> <u>influences</u> are <u>balanced,</u> resulting in no <u>net</u> <u>change</u>.

2. The <u>state</u> of a <u>reaction</u> in which the <u>rates</u> of the <u>forward</u> and <u>reverse</u> reactions are the same.

3. (<u>physics</u>) The state of a <u>body</u> at <u>rest</u> or in <u>uniform</u> <u>motion</u> in which the <u>resultant</u> of all <u>forces</u> on it is <u>zero</u>.

-

**Offsetting the imbalance and Inequality: The role of an equal but opposite force that exerts pressure to reach equilibrium.**

Nature since the beginning of time always creates an offsetting effect to balance the system. I explained from the beginning of this book that the imbalance caused by the huge population, excessive weapons, inequalities in terms of opportunities, etc. would trigger an offset effect through wars. This triggered the wars in history and recently the First and Second World Wars. Depending on time say every twenty to twenty-five years the imbalance would be so pronounced that tension due to inequality and oppression would only result in a world war. After the wars, millions of people would have died including soldiers. Pressure on land would have been reduced, the government salary bill would have been reduced significantly with hundreds of thousands of soldiers being wiped out say the first weeks of the wars and the time the war ends many more millions of names would have been wiped off the balance sheet of the government. All weapons stockpile would have been reduced and some destroyed. All the major bombs would have their chance to be tested. The decision-makers now would be aiming for a position to either abandon the project or advance it further. All that budget money left would have been used up and the leaders would be willing to make new weapons contracts etc. Everything has a new start. Those who were oppressed and felt being treated badly would have had their say and revenged. Now after the wars, everyone is different and wants to start afresh. Periods after wars are the best periods for networking and negotiating. We have treaties and agreements drafted and signed soon after any major war. Everyone would be very optimistic about the future. Just two years from the day the war ended psychological effects kick in and the traumas of the war start fading off. People now tend to forget the horrors of yesteryear. They start again oppressing each other and spending more money on new weapons deals at the expense of other services like adequate infrastructure. The time it's 5 years since the war ended grudges and hostility among each other would be evident by now. Even here nature would always find a way of offsetting the inequalities. But after twenty years or more people would have grown up to put pressure on resources. Inequalities among men would be riff and more than 70% of resources would be in the hands of a few say 10% of the population. This creates situations where the few who control everything would start oppressing people as a self-defense mechanism hacking, torturing and even ordering the killing of those with big-mouths. The good thing is that the system if a free system governed by the forces of nature so either goes. This means for the few who hold most of the wealth there are equal forces who don't have the wealth but can exert the same power or force as to take over from them. In other words, there are people who can equally challenge the situation and declare war as a means of redistributing wealth and power.

This meant the Second World War.

As I always say the war has no winner. Both sides suffered huge losses in terms of the soldiers and civilians killed. The witnessing of the war leaves everyone traumatized that they realize that war is not the answer. Instead of banning war and signing treaties to end wars for good mankind decided to remove the things causing wars but continue to make weapons and increase the military budget. What he has done is remove all the alarms or safety features that say when the situation is at exploding levels wars would create an explosion that will deflate the problem. Instead of a huge nuclear war, normal world wars would be triggered to offset the imbalance. But after the Second World War mankind through the Colony Collapse Strategy tirelessly embarked on a killing spree removing all possible equally but opposite force. That means competition to such an extent that there was no opposition at all. The system is one-sided now and imbalanced. Recall Newton's third law that stipulates that for every force there is or must be an equal but opposing force acting in the opposite direction. The system is one-sided and growing fast. We have what can be described as a gang-or-bully situation. Now there are no balancing forces. The inequalities just keep growing. The poor keep on marginalized. We now have a situation where weapons are the language of the day. Dialog is out of the window. There are no other opposing forces now to challenge the status quo. We have a dictatorship where sovereign nations are sanctioned illegally before being stripped off any dignity before being invaded on false flagship. We have a situation where the system can't balance itself. The factors or forces that would have balanced the system have been jammed or disabled. This is an issue now that can result in human extinction as wars have been removed that normally offset the imbalance. Now the opposing forces might be thinking about real powerful weapons to use to have any impact. Hence resorting to nukes or other WMDs. In the end, both sides might use nukes. This can result in human extinction.

The West created the UN, NATO, UNSC, ICC, etc. to disable the balancing equal but opposing forces. These institutions are there to keep everything one-sided targeting enemies of the West and all those with the potential to oppose the status quo and start a war. The West or developed countries and their cults are growing fast. One day to such sizes that they would not see the need for the other weaker side who then they would see as parasites or leaches just there to suck on their resources. This a dangerous period. The few in power will start to feel like they are gods and unstoppable. They will start developing all kinds of WMDs and stockpiling these publicly and using these knowing that no one would stop them. They will start overruling all laws most of which they put in place themselves. They will feel above the law. They will start ignoring their own laws. The big problem is the natural equalizer or the equal but opposing force would have been disabled accentuated by the presence of the ICC, UN, UNSC, NATO, etc. Now, they can simply invade any country to rob resources one after the other eliminating the alpha male who might be a threat in the future thereby recolonizing these nations in the name of human rights but themselves killing even more. Their aim now as the new gods responsible for the whole earth they see themselves as having a duty to act by helping nature through killing the weaker forces left. What has happened is that they had disabled the natural equalizer and took over using highly sophisticated WMDs in the form of ether bio-engineered, digital or cyber etch would kill in masses planning everything as part of the contingency plan to play God? They won't see the need for the other weaker ones. So, they use WMDs on them to ease the pressure. They will keep on making WMDs and weapons until such levels when some within start questioning the whole thing. Then we have defects that would make equally powerful WMDs and simultaneously detonate these. Human extinction or near extinction but with severe exposure to toxins for decades until extinction.

Need for an artificial equalizer to balance and correct system.

I have explained above that the current global powers have disabled and removed the natural equalizers likewise we must enable and install artificial equalizers. The major ones have a corrective effect on addressing the root causes. Weaker laws that are outdated and not observed will be replaced by effective modern ones that close all loopholes and reverse the current processes. Tough laws that are fair to everyone and easily obeyed because they are for the good not just for the few top brasses but for everyone including the top brass. Don't get us wrong we have no revenge in mind even though some equalizing acts might seem as revengeful. The idea behind our approach is to create a sense of equilibrium where people throw in towels and choose to take a different road. Reconciliation as the first step towards networking and cooperation can only be achieved if the playing fields have been leveled.

In the end, the lost forces or the diverted forces that should have been exerted in Newton's third law would then be realized and exerted. What goes around comes around applies here. To achieve the equilibrium the reactive forces that had been lost or not exerted creating imbalances will somehow be realized and be applied. This can mean justice for some and punishment for some. Above all this can happen throughout without time frames or limits.

The good news is that in the end the system will correct itself and the process restarted. It is our duty as global leaders to make sure that humanity will never revert to these situations hence, we will put things in place. But as I pointed throughout this book, it's not a question of just dictating what needs to be done. We will take a holistic approach that looks at different issues including education and boosting the self-esteem of all humanity so that people will be able to fight. In the end, the equal and opposite forces will be permanently installed that will ensure a forever balance system always in equilibrium. A perfect system therefore will have a powerful force but that has an equal but opposite force to maintain the equilibrium.

Welcome to Tomorrow's World Order.

# CHAPTER THIRTY-THREE

THE BRIDGING.

Reading this book, you might think that the issues discussed here are years or decades away from now. I can't blame you for thinking so. It seems as if this is the final journey, but there is a lot to achieve and it starts now. I know the system can be easily changed if people are convinced that this is the right path. Of course, people need to believe, but that is the only way to solve all global issues and the only road to take. Above all, that this is everyone's problem and as such responsibility is on everyone to act now. It is hard to believe now as the dream seems decades away. I don't have to make you believe, but I must inform you, so you understand what is needed of you. Once you know what is needed, it will be instinctively for you to respond and act. It's like enlightenment you don't need to be convinced when it hits you, you will simply know. I think it's true they say education is the greatest equalizer. People need to be empowered through knowledge, knowing what is good and evil. This in turn can boost their self-esteem that all triggers other effects so that in the end we have people who are willing to push ahead removing obstacles like ignorance, poor self-esteem, procrastinating, etc. These tools are needed to bridge the immediate system and the future New World. Some things cannot be transformed or changed instantly or overnight and need time as such. Bridging is the phase between the current system and the New World. I advocated that the current system has collapsed and need to be replaced. New laws will make us achieve all our goals. We will have several bridging phases. We shall declare wars as illegal and ban them with the immediate effect of becoming responsible for the whole globe. We shall ban the use of fossil fuels among other things and this will involve phasing out in some parts until the date when the whole globe stops using fossil fuels like oil. This will trigger investment into other alternate energies. Bridging can be the phasing out phase and the actual stages when new fuels will start to be used.

Bridging here involves preparing to start the new system. This must not be confused with the transition period where the current system is forwarded to the new system sort of. The idea here is to see this as a completely new beginning. A new system and a new way of doing things but aspects and activities make it necessary to have a bridging phase even though the system replacing this one will be totally new. Something new planning ahead. Phasing out what we don't need in the new system but also putting new things for the new system. A lot must be done, and I personally think this chapter should be covered in volume II of the book. I think by now the reader understands and is very knowledgeable about what we stand for. Here is a chance for you to contribute and be part of this. We would like to know what you think. What you want prioritizing and how you think we should go about this. You must read our Whitepaper that has all the financial aspects of these projects. Money won't be an issue. Some things can be changed within a short period. Below is a list of things that will need replacing or changing all together and things you can start to think about.

## Global Leadership.

As you know we will take over as the overseers and rulers of the globe putting everything needed to see our plans through. I have covered a lot on this topic and need not reiterating. We are not going to change governments or interfere with current settings, but we urge them to evolve and recognize and incorporate our laws and adjust theirs using ours as the base reference. Current governments remain as they are.

## Global Finance.

A new financial system with our currency as the global currency as well as the only New Single Reserve Global Currency in preparation for the first Five-Year-Money Printing Plan. Once the system is there, we know we are ready to tackle all global issues and hyperinflation. All nations to cooperate as they must be ready to avoid inflation racking havoc.

Global Law System

A system without the law aspect is as good as nonexistent. The law system must be in place to deal with any resistance. Possibly the system must see a smooth transition. Every effort to make sure the system can function perfectly from the word go.

Lay Foundation and Platform to Launch the New System.

Even though we will be there we need to establish platforms to deal with local and global issues. Links, networking and cooperation with everyone concerned so all issues can be highlighted and dealt with quickly and efficiently.

New Fresh Thinking and Motivated Personnel.

No point taking the old personnel team to the new system. I know most from the old team will still be willing to be part of the new system but again the success of the new system depends on new personnel as well. People with new ideas and everything must feel fresh and to succeed you must understand that success depends on you. Your guts, your selection and believe that if it's a new system a completely new system but is run by all old personnel, then how new is the system. Be bold and not afraid to change. Usually, old personnel will bring things that have worked in the past to the new system but also remember that the current system crashed in the end. Avoid third type errors; good solutions to the wrong problem. It's now a new system can you mix the new wine and the old wine? Applies here.

Heavy Investment into Research and Development

Everything needed for the bridging phase depends on heavy investment in research and development. We need new alternative ways of doing things and only research and development can provide answers. We need to phase out fossil fuels and find alternate ones and how do we go about this? We have electric cars etc. How can we go about this? New contracts with Tesla? Or incentives to increase production or pay for a license to make electric cars as well. Can we buy the technology to expand? Who and how do we fund this to meet deadlines before even thinking about phasing out the fossil fuels? We need a plan to make sure that production will meet demand and know when we can realistically start the phasing-out-stages. Everything depends on how bold we are. We don't want to leave things to chance. This is a critical phase and must be done but how much is this going to cost us? The current car manufactures can start producing electrical too and incentivized to recall the fossil fuel-powered ones and replace these with electrical ones or other alternate fuel-powered cars. How are we as the leaders going to see that the first years are as smooth as possible? Mind you most countries will afford hence the Five-Year-Money- Printing-Phase. A task team to be set up to oversee this project.

This is done for all things that needed phasing out.


Building Projects.

We believe that the current infrastructure is not futuristic we need new infrastructure and up-to-date buildings that use clean energy sources. Some infrastructure is critical to the success of the project and everything must be modernized. New building standards that are futuristic. Much research and development as well. Fast ways and cheaper but don't compromise quality. The idea is to create projects that we match the new money to and boost growth so everything must be done fast again without compromising quality. Strategic planning targeting certain areas capitals first and so on. Don't be afraid to change. Start building another city from starch to make sure all is futuristic which can be easy than say improve the current capital system. Always have in mind that this is a new system. Don't be afraid to be bold. Start a city in a desert, in the fields and be ambitious. In the long run, we will change laws regarding shifting of capitals and loosen up heritage laws, etc. that make other buildings untouchable despite them posing risks to people. I think overall is to think about starting from scratch. New fresh site new plans rather than improving the old systems. Again, can you mix the new wine and the old wine applies here? This is a completely new system. Can we start from scratch? A new beginning? Should be the first thing that comes to mind. It would cost less to start from the beginning than improve existing.

The reader this is your chance to be part and parcel of this great project so contribute tell us what you think can be done and what needs improving. Feel free to rank all your suggestions prioritizing these. We want to know what you think. What do you want to see changing and how? You can always email us

Email: info@tomorrowsworldorder.com

# CHAPTER THIRTY-FOUR

HOSTIS HUMANI GENERIS.

I think it won't be okay not to keep a chapter for this title; - the enemy of the people.

"Hostis Humani Generis (Latin for "enemy of mankind") is a legal term of art that originates in admiralty law. Before the adoption of public international law, [when?] pirates and slaves were already held to be beyond legal protection and so could be dealt with by any nation, even one that had not been directly attacked."

Wikipedia.

In short, in international law, a person who breaks our laws and the current Jus Cogens laws is Hostis Humani Generis. An enemy of the people in that anyone breaching these laws is committing a crime against everyone. An attack on one through torture or hacking or slavery is an attack on all humans. [Article 1 of Tomorrow's World Order]

"The torturer has become – like the pirate and slave trader before him -Hostis Humani Generis, an enemy of all mankind," wrote the court.

Filártiga v. Peña-Irala,

You would think that terrorism would be classed as such but the fact that the West uses the same tactics as the terrorist make them avoid labeled as such. The West through sanctions use the same tactics to kill and use women and children as bargaining tools.

Article 1

There are crimes in international law that can never be broken there is no derogation that is permitted. These norms now our laws are peremptory laws that have international jurisdiction that all humanity is guided by these. In other words, they don't have

588

jurisdiction in that any human being can exercise judgment by taking the violator and passing judgment as if the crime was committed in his country or jurisdiction. The violator is considered having committed a crime against all mankind. This is because certain crimes are so grave that they threaten the fabric of human existence that breaching these can and might result in human extinction if not corrected. These crimes threaten the fabric of human existence. Genocide, torture, slavery, hacking under piracy, crimes of aggression, war crimes, etc. We as humanity we are obliged to act to prevent and put a stop to that crime and punish the violator. There is express punishment in that the violator is a threat to humanity. Someone who commits these crimes is not just ignorant but is evil to the bone he can't be changed. This is because these laws must never be broken. Express-command to put an end to this through our laws and courts as a deterrent. They are peremptory norms but when someone violets these it shows that person is beyond control. He is a threat to the existence of humanity hence the phrase the Hostis Humani Generis. If not stopped that person can bring humanity's destruction because he doesn't know what he is doing. He has no clue about the implications of his actions and to be honest the fact that he has committed these crimes is pure evidence that if left alone he is one day going to get all humanity destroyed. International law therefore puts 'Responsibility to Protect' humanity as a whole and a 'Responsibility to Act' as a mitigation measure to stop and remove the risk as in risk management. Therefore, all human beings have an obligation not to let someone get you all killed. You must act to save not just yourselves but humanity at large. This applies to nations and people who build nuclear weapons, viral, digital or cyber WMDs. It doesn't matter who in that such actions puts the whole humanity at risk. There are no privileges that some might have skills of containing the WMDs and that they might use them wisely. It's like the USA using the bombs on Japan not just one but two with the results that even today the effects are still being felt. Such a move requires and cries for global disarmament and destruction of all nukes whatsoever. In our world presence and ownership of nukes by anyone; the USA, UK, France, Germany, etc. is prohibited as this will invoke Article 1.

Such acts are an attack on all of humanity. In the future, it will be possible to label other countries as the enemy of mankind once our laws are in force. It will not be a problem as one man for himself and TWO for us all will apply here in that we will persuade everyone to deal with violators on an individual basis. In the end our laws will prevail as we will invoke the lack of empathy laws to stop this evil behavior. Peace means peace and to us peace starts with these innocent women and children who are often victims being tricked by everyone else. We stand and are the voice of the voiceless and champions of the weak and defenseless. A new world a new beginning surely by now you must know and understand we mean business. It is in your best interest to change and be part of something great.

I declare today that it is a win-win situation.

JOIN US TODAY!!

I can't express enough how you all ought to be part of this great movement. We ought to move away from the current thinking of visualizing power as embedded in possession of weapons etc. and where being evil is the 'new cool'. This is exactly what the early man had in mind some 2000 years ago, but I stand by the early man just because the dinosaurs racked havoc and were a menace. But all this has since gone extinct. This is a new era of enlightenment. We have come up with a new system of doing things. We have proved that it is inferior thinking to invest in weapons and use the weapons to get all the expensive resources which we can't afford. We believe the root cause is affordability.

So, we have a plan that will work. Our method is the only way that can see wealth never thought of. The only method to see true global wealth and a move from defensive stages to better stages as nature intended. We are stuck in the defensive stages and has been for the past 2000 years, but we are ready to lead and take you there. Are you ready? Our plan works. Printing money is the only way out of this mess but to do that we must change. We must abandon some of our best practices. We must drop our fears today. We must start somewhere. I can't guarantee you that someone tomorrow might refuse to stop making weapons or try to use these to steal expensive resources. But I equally rest your fears that we have a new legal system that will instantly immobilize any threats and eliminate these with no harm to all of you. We shall deal swiftly with unnecessary resistance just there to stall progress and the inevitable. We shall be ruthless as well so there is nothing to fear. Change is knocking at your door today. But I can also guarantee you wealth never dreamed of before. I can guarantee you peace and global justice. I can guarantee you a system that works one fit for purpose. A system that brings back trust again. A system that is trusted by everyone. A system that everyone believes in and one all are bound by.

Ladies and gentlemen, we have a journey to embark on. Be part of something special even if it takes us longer to get there what is not to like here? Imagine a world without;

*Wars

*Weapons

*Deaths of innocent women and children

*No bullies or gangsters

*Corrupt institutions there to save their skins

* Corrupt and obsolete systems that witness a crash after a crash with all your wealth saved over the years destroyed in a flash.

*Peace

 *Rights to life and these always overridden in favor of something else.

 *Polluting fossil fuels that are often fought for. A new world with clean energy sources that are cheap and renewable.

 *Above without threats etc.

A world you contributed towards and not imposed on you. Something new that is relevant not just to you but to your children as well. Who better to start planning for yours and your kid's future? Your grandmother or grandfather? I don't think so. A new era. It is hard and challenging and I understand most are afraid of change but even failure is a stepping stone to success. Nevertheless, our plans are ambitious to match our ego and guts above all we believe that if not for us but for future generations. We must start somewhere. I say today is the perfect day to start.

Are you ready? I am ready.

Imagine a world where all your savings and wealth will ever grow.

A world where peace means peace.

A world full of hope and enlightenment.

A world where we strive to bring the best out in people.

A world where we don't trade time for money.

A world where living standards are above current levels where we will penalize below standards provisions of services etc.

A world where everything is futuristic, and the people are put first. Which means good quality life with nothing against humanity's quality of life.

A world where we work a few hours but also make even more.

A world where global travel is like traveling from one city to the other without boundaries etc.

A world where society's self-esteem is at the highest

A world where we are no longer concerned with material things where we have placed importance on networking and cooperation and building relations and learning from each other.

All this is achievable here on earth we don't have to die first in order to experience all this like the current thinking.

All this will happen here on earth as a stage of human development but to reach there we must start somewhere.

Tomorrow's World Order.

# CHAPTER THIRTY-FIVE

TORTURE.

I think this is one of the challenging issues to overcome probably the more troublesome as the people advance; They develop advanced secret easily concealed weapons of torture. Hard to detect and operated remotely with the victims with no recourse to justice. When they complain they are further abused and the system, is such that they protect the culprits at the expense of the victims because torture is institutionalized and part and parcel of the whole system. The torture I am talking about is not verbal abuse and all that stuff. This is extreme pain achieved by modern easily hidden devices and chips implanted at birth without consent. To recap;

Torture is; "the action or practice of inflicting severe pain on someone as a punishment or in order to force them to do or say something."

Google Dictionary.

Torture is banned by all international laws on earth, yet it is widespread globally. The Human Rights Watch website declares that:

"The prohibition against torture is a bedrock principle of international law. Torture, as well as cruel, inhuman or degrading treatment, is always banned in all places, including in times of war. No national emergency, however dire, ever justifies its use."

Yet we have cases of torture worldwide daily. What is really the issue? The laws are not defined enough, or people simply choose to ignore these laws?

**Torture and technology.**

I have dwelt with this issue briefly in earlier chapters and here I would like to explain how torture can still be a big problem but with little ways to be proven unless we match technology with technology. Nowadays there are a lot of devices the size of rice grains that can be chipped or implanted and operated remotely like a drone to torture the victim with him or her without a way to prove it. Some countries illegal chip everyone at birth and then torture the people as they grow initially disguised and concealed from the public. The fact that it is widespread and rarely people are successfully brought to justice speaks volumes to why globally we have several countries that have been accused of torture. The definition of torture includes infliction of mental as well physical but how to do measure that or notice that? When today's torture devices are well concealed and most living no physical marks, unlike the torture acts of past decades that left people with bruising, etc. Why if the laws states that torture is banned, and evil do some people still practice torture? I think the first is to look at the punishment for those found guilty of torture.

If found guilty of torture, you can be put in prison for less than 20 years and if death results because of torture, then a death sentence can be given as well. The truth is that cases rarely pass the preliminary stages, and most are thrown out for lack of evidence, etc. Technology has been slow in helping to find ways to identify and record such torture so that there are more convictions. Most of all torture is institutionalized 'and carried out by state operatives' who are given immunity as it is carried out for 'national security reasons' or to protect dictators or monarchies, etc. There are more than sixty countries where torture is believed to have occurred in one form or the other. It is widespread and most are used to:

*extract information.

*but more important to weaken the victims and damage their credibility and personality.

*if used for political reasons it is used to oppress the people unfairly.

The fact that remains is that even the government carrying out torture would vehemently deny such accusation as pointed out by Wikipedia that;

"While many states use torture, few wishes to be described as doing so, either to their own citizens or to international bodies. So a variety of strategies are used to circumvent their legal and humanitarian duties, including plausible deniability, secret police, "need to know", a denial that certain activities constitute torture, appeal to various laws (national or international), use of a jurisdictional argument, the claim of "overriding need", the use of torture by proxy, and so on.[3] Almost all regimes and governments engaging in torture (and other crimes against humanity) consistently deny engaging in it, in spite of overwhelming hearsay and physical evidence from the citizens they tortured."

[Wikipedia].

So, it is a fact that everyone even those practicing torture knows that it is illegal, yet they still carry on doing it. The main reasons are that there are other pressing issues to be bothered about torture. Recent terrorist activities have seen an increase in state-sponsored torture in broad daylight as in Iraq and Guantanamo Bay cages. Other issues call for the need to override abstinence from torture, etc. But why all the laws state that it is absolute that no other reasons override that? Is there something that can be done to put an end to all this? I know where there is a lack of evidence people can and might get away with torture even though everyone knows that torture is happening. Our stance is that it's a must to have laws that stop torture. The current laws seem ambiguous and out of touch with reality. In that, anyone can carry out torture in broad daylight and simply give national security reasons and get away with it. What if that is the root cause of say terrorist acts? The system is unjust with people being tortured without any chance for the evil culprits to ever get caught and be punished. We have laws in place prohibiting torture as it is one of the fundamental principles of international law and falls under the peremptory norms that must never be broken. Putting just laws is not enough especially considering the number of countries that are said to be still at it. Some countries have no rule of law, are a dictatorship, have a monarchy, and most importantly torture is linked to past roles in slavery. Countries that were the drivers of slavery at the beginning have high torture cases. These countries have in the past obtained information cheaply through torture, have punished their enemies through torture, and have used torture as a command to make people obey commands which means it is institutionalized. Every time cases are brought the more the torture is hidden through devices that are used to replace the traditional torture methods like the five techniques of torture. We have sophisticated gadgets now used to do the same as the past methods. Take hooding for example. In the past, a hood was placed on the head of the victim so that he can't see, and fearful with panic attacks kicking in that set a chain of anxiety and disorientation, etc. Nowadays a small chip or device can easily be chipped in or implanted without consent and that is hidden and operated remotely that hides the iris of the eye so that vision is lost and the nerve manipulation through electromagnetic nerve stimulation can induce panic, anxiety, fear, etc. How can such a person prove that he is abused in front of everyone by people in a position of trust? We need a technology that can detect or increase the speed for a short time of these devices so that the effects are evident to the visible eye that they can be recorded, and the evidence used in courts. Imagine a rotating propeller as part of the device shaking the person and mashing his or her brain as they use the leg muscles to achieve the shaking effect. What happens is that a small device with rotary blades can be implanted and left to rotate continuously with GPS positioning pinpointing where the effect would occur. Sometimes the effects can be very pronounced that if recorded can be viewed. Our aim is to create a Blockchain of Evidence where any such evidence can be instantly sent to a blockchain system or smart contract and kept there permanently so everyone can see. We must start somewhere simply putting laws is not enough. Only technology can alleviate the issues. If they know that the effects of the devices can be recorded that will reduce or even stop prevalent cases that are occurring in broad daylight. We have seen pure violence in response to such evil, but we are not for violence against innocent people and we condemn such acts. We are for peace or lawfully stopping of evil acts even if that means putting all our trust in the assassin so be it. I think this is one area that harshest laws can play a part and might prove to be very helpful. Sometimes traumatic events e.g. live execution of the violators. The only way for evil to be understood and for this to change behavior. Our laws in extreme cases where torture has been systematic and institutionalized can trigger Article 1 where collective action and punishment are the only effective punishment to stop and change behavior.

We must put laws to monitor satellite and GPS activities and make sure that such a technology is not used to enslave and torture people against their will. These people must understand that someone's will must be respected and come first. I think it's evil for governments to try to dictate the lives of their people. Everyone is free to choose and do whatever he pleases if this is not in conflict with our laws. I think there are countries that try to hide abuse in the name of the so-called protection where torture is disguised as a way "to afford what they would not otherwise afford." In this case, people are first tortured and then compensated. This is barbaric and is associated with slavery where slaves were tortured, and latter given certain rights and favors because they were deemed as not worthy of any help and were not considered as humans enough. This is a way of thinking acceptable in former slave owners' countries. Countries that never had slaves or were vehemently against slavery would easily notice the implications of such a setting. The world should not be reminded of the evil period in history and the fact that this is still happening disguised as protection is a cause of great concern. Why I personally am against this is the fact that in these countries the governments deliberately make life tough. Life that would normally be easily so that they give people this protection. If they were not there, people's lives would be easy. All the problems are there simply because they are there. Removing this evil will see life becoming easy for the ordinary people who end up being loaded with watermarks to 'drive' institutions like the hospitals, etc. This is evil. This is more than torture as people are degraded to zombies with digital nails embedded in their brains and all kinds of abuse going on. These are scenes from a zombie movie and surely international justice is the only answer. Look what happened to Hitler. If some governments do the same should they not walk the same road as Hitler? Our laws are against anything that conflicts with the right to life, quality of life and the right to self-defend. The fact that this is used as a command tool with people abused for food handouts is a gross injustice. I know you can't mention torture without degrading treatment and other abuse. Most of these countries still are practicing torture and dirty tricks of treating people like pigs which is a tactic to hide the real evil going on; that they are making bio-engineered, digital and cyber viruses and testing them on their people. A breach of international law.

Our laws prohibit the making of all these so-called weapons in fact WMDs and still getting away with it. We have banned all these, but I think banning alone is not enough. We shall delegate to the assassin and hope he or she is a sharpshooter and takeout evil. Most countries get away with murder simply because they can't be caught. They are way ahead and technology is trailing way behind to be effective. Therefore, we shall invest in technology to find ways of jamming or stopping such attacks before punishing the culprits severely. This is another area where a crime trickles down to the family of that person too. This is the area where fight fire with a fire applies here. We shall aim to make matching torture devices and hack just like them before frying them dead too. We know they are torturing people even though we can't prove it we can only make the same gadgets and use them too. We shall use GPS technology as well to find and locate these. New laws to make accessibility easy. A dedicated team shall search and find those remotely torturing others and reduce them to dripping fat. Express-command to put an end to this through our laws and courts as a deterrent. Once again there is no justification for torture where a person has been abusing then is tortured against his or her will disguised as training or whatever. This is a crime and must not be permitted on any grounds. Some countries trick people in order to hold them in slavery and abuse them forever through torture.

No research or other testing to be allowed that involves torture. The world must be free from all tortures. Recall above I cited a court judgment where it is acknowledged that the torturer has become like the piracy or hacker before him and the slave trader and as such Hostis Humani Generis. An enemy of humanity who can be collectively attacked or punished. This is the worst a human being can be. A torturer is an enemy of the people; as he threatens humanity by torturing people against all international laws. This is the strongest condemnation you will find anywhere yet people are still enslaving and torturing people. If an activity is associated with a dark past and you start doing the same would that not take people to the past era? I think we passed the period of negotiating and educating people. This is evil embedded in the bones and part of the whole-body system and you can't separate that from the whole-body the only way is to destroy such evil. For some, this is part of their genetic make-up and to them, this is normal because they can do worse. Watch the Nuremberg trials and see how confident the evil-doctors were believing that they did not do anything wrong. But we're not most of them hanged? People who do this have a history of abusing others even worse. Checks should be carried out to assess if they had a dark period in history. If yes this must work against them. Can a leopard change its spots apply here? They were slave traders at one-point and to them that could be the worse so if you say torture, they might be laughing at you saying; you aren't seen anything. There is too much arrogance you just can't believe that such people exist. Our laws prohibit any violence to anyone especially the innocent women and children and we shall not encourage it. All we can do is educate and advise before we send the assassin if there is no change. Everyone wants a world free from torture or any abuse. We shall target leaders who give the command to abuse and torture we don't care for what reason. Express-command to put an end to this through our laws and courts as a deterrent. Our stance is anti-torture because of what torture really stands for; a part and parcel of slavery and abuse.

# CHAPTER THIRTY-SIX

THE LIST.

Our aim is to make the world the best it can be. Life is a right and quality of life should be everyone's privilege simply because you are a human being. Every government on earth exists to serve its people and not the other way around. We have banned a lot of things triggering any forms of abusing. We surely hope that everyone will come to their senses and realize that we can do great. But we also believe that some people will never be satisfied and will always want to get cheaper things and therefore might use easily made weapons to torture others so that they get what they can. This might include sexual factors or trickery of some sort where a person is tortured first before being further abused as a 'compensation' aspect. No matter how many laws we put down, there are other people who will never see things our way and will always want to abuse. Systematic and institutionalized torture, we hope will be a thing of the past. But some people will always have their own excuses and ideas, and if they break our rules, they might end up on the list. The list is the final way of dealing with these rights' abusers. Once you are on the list, collective assault from all the corners of the earth must be the right punishment. Some governments are champions of rights abuse, but we can't bring them to justice simply because they are clever, and manipulative all we can do is add them to the list. Our aim is to do away with evil and be very strict;

*Short-sighted governments making all kinds of watermarks and weapons in the hope of using these for getting things cheaper and easier.

*Governments taking the law into their own hands reversing previous achievements of improving humanity by degrading humanity. This applies where they tamper with the quality of life in the name of protection, for example.

*Playing god is the duty and role of no one we are better to decide on that because we are universal and represent humanity and not some cult or skewed view.

*Governments doing this will only see their leaders be dragged to court.

*Torturers must be number one on the list. Torture has slavery connotations and its evil torturing people with an aim to compensate them later and this can only get you to be dragged to court. Once again, it's our privilege to fight all forms of evil even if that means getting evil people to be punished. We will never target innocent people. Every governing body must have some form of punishment and governance according to international laws. We have a right to recruit assassins and use them according to our laws. Our men and women are of the highest caliber. Men of honor. Men who would never do wrong but rather fight the oppressive and obsolete system where the few fat cows grow at the expense of everyone else and on top of that abuse everyone. A thing of the past.

*Any governments inciting and encouraging degrading treatment as a way of compensating the people. It's evil. Your presence makes life hard and therefore you are to blame.

*Hackers who can be referred to as pirates as well who take, and abuse others are as evil as torturers both enemies of mankind. Collective punishment applies. If such evil is carried on one person, it is like a crime against all mankind. This triggers Article 1 where an attack on one is a breach of international law and an attack of humanity at large.

*Institutions that are modern but use tricks associated with dark periods in history. More often these are founded on evil practices. These institutions were initiated with capital obtained in an evil way. This is true you will find out yourself. Some things never change. We are the only answers to fight such institutions until they are a thing of the past. No one is immune.

*Any country or leader or government that does something that can lead to war. Acts of aggression without time limits can be visited here. Countries must never do anything that jeopardizes global peace.

*Some crimes have a lack of empathy connotations. Their acts lack understanding, and, in most cases, these people have been masters of slavery, they can't tell the difference between right and wrong and must be told. I think we don't have time to waste. For some people, it's in their genes and they will never stop. It's our duty to clean the human gene pool of evil.

*Unambitious people who would prefer stealing other's ideas and technology when everyone knows they are incapable of such brain-power might be on the list. This is because such people will cause all the problems we are trying to solve. They can provoke others to start a war or feel revengeful.

*I have noticed that people who hang onto outdated ideas tend to prefer methods in the dark ages in history. They hang to old laws and practices so that they keep abusing people using these obsolete laws. People who are not interested to change can and might be a problem. Some dictatorship, cults or monarchies for example benefit when their people's self-esteem is at their lowest so that they easily submit and 'worship' them pledging to die for them. If that is what the people like, then that's okay but if they are forced or food used as a commanding tool, etc. then we might look at it as if our laws are coming into conflict with this. You cannot declare to die for someone and have the highest self-esteem needed in this stage of life. Highest self-esteem will make one prioritize himself or herself rather than dying for someone else. Not diminishing the importance of these people but just saying that the stage we are talking about it will be rare to see this happening. Dirty tactics to 'weaken' the people often associated with dictatorship, cults or monarchies and kings and a kind of compensation is also associated with this, etc. Whereby people are reduced to animals by the local authorities for the dictator, cult leader, or king to come and 'lift' them up as to boost the king's ratings, etc. is not just gross decadence but a crime that see one on the list. It's not just life but the quality of life which must be of the highest for everyone. This normal life of today will be banned. It will be a crime to provide a poor quality of life.

\*It will be a crime to provide mediocre standards of living. Anything that reduces quality of life like intimidation by those in a position of trust will result in people being dragged to court. We take abuse by those in positions of power very seriously. If these can't behave properly what else do you expect of the others? This is not a circus, like in some countries where professions are so stained with dirt that you can't tell a crook from those in a position of trust. Barbaric ways of thinking a thing of the past.

\*Some governments; former slave masters themselves teach institutions like banks on how to rip off people using tricks they once used. To be tricking and manipulating people to make as much money they can at the expense of the hard-working men and women. We shall target both simply because they are spreading evil themselves making deals with these banks to hold people into slavery through unjust methods of tricking and deceiving people with aim to sink them then hold them at ransom before putting them on death row or offer them protection where they further abuse them when they were innocent in the first place. In the end have viruses tested on them. We shall dedicate a team on this issue and make sure that old tricks from the dark times are not 'pimped' and deployed in our times.

\*We also believe in the chain of command where the people at the bottom will simply follow the commands of those at the top and as such blame can be apportioned accordingly especially targeting the root causes. Our aim is to eliminate the problem. We are neutral and judge people according to their acts and evil. We believe that the West as the developed countries and leaders must also lead by example showing the developing countries the way and how to do it. We therefore hold the West accountable when they fall below standards. They are very clever and well educated and we expect a lot from them. In most cases, they are the ones who wrote the laws they are cherry-picking and neglecting now. We hold the developing to account as well when they fall below standards, but our first stance is that of advising on the best way unless if the acts committed to conflict with our laws.

# CHAPTER THIRTY-SEVEN

THE PLAN.

~~Top Secret Classified.~~

## Goals and Objectives.

To take humanity to the next level of development where there are no wars or global conflicts but networking and cooperation. A phase where we achieve the most and enjoy global peace and a new era of technological advancement making life the sweetest any human being can wish for. To achieve that, we are going to priorities human life, knowing that everything will follow. We as a people we are working below the optimal level. We are under-performing if we were a company we would be out of business. We can achieve better much better than the current levels. Therefore, we need to re-prioritize some laws, put new ones and remove things hindering or conflicting with our goals. We want to improve human life through improvement in living standards. The current standard is below the minimum. It will be an illegal act and breaking the law to provide living standards and conditions below a certain standard. Ban all activities with a negative impact on human rights. End torture globally and put new laws to punish the lawbreakers in this area. End all kinds of secret slavery and if it means choosing collective judgment against the worst countries doing this so be it. Ban all kinds of hacking. We shall ban wars and weapons manufacturing the biggest drainers of resources and channel these resources towards human life, improved infrastructure, and living conditions, better transport and encourage global networking. We shall ban reliance on fossil fuels in order to encourage the discovery of other cleaner renewable energies that in turn would reduce pollution and climate change. This will improve the quality of life, too. We shall aim to improve the health of everyone to the highest levels possible by putting new laws that will automatically ban a lot of things and practices that are acting in conflict with our laws. There shall be minimal standards to be accepted as provided by health institutions. Those who make back-door bio-engineered or digital viruses to recreate the conditions when their institutions were formed in order to keep these viable are on the wrong side of the law. We shall be the toughest with the health sector, as our aims are greatly affected by the quality and professionalism of this sector. Still punishment for the evil-doctors and those who want to play God. Banning of making and of creating all kinds of harmful weaponry be it bio-engineered, digital or cyber and stiff penalties that amount to death by the assassin. Need for institutions to evolve or face the shutdown. New laws to deal with global and country-specific financial laws and regulations. Need to encourage technological advancement and increase global jobs etc. New laws to encourage and facilitate and act as a catalyst rather than delaying progress. Removal of all bottlenecks and cumbersome bureaucratic process. Encourage good networking and cooperation globally. Increase education and end poverty.

## Objectives and Methodology.

## Life

The first laws that can never be broken are in relation to life. Recognizing the importance of life should be the sole existence of everyone and every government and institutions. There must never be anything that can override this first rule. Everyone no matter what social standing or background has a right to life that must never be traded for anything else. It is a crime to end a life deliberately or indirectly. Even the lives of your worst enemies are now protected by our laws. No one shall kill and ever do something that leads to the death of another person globally and this might extend to other planets as well. Life for life applies. Ending a life recklessly can put your family and loved words in front of the firing assassins. If you negligently or without any empathy do something ends in someone's death you will be putting your own life and those of people close to you too at risk. No laws will and must never override this first law. No national security laws must override this law.

## Quality of life.

It is everyone's duty to provide the best life can offer and achieve the best quality of life. We must ban anything that affects the quality of life. Our aim is to boost everyone's self-esteem to the highest levels through education and showing how it's done by removing everything lower quality of life. Noise, air and land pollution all to be dealt with. Living standards to be improved greatly. Laws banning satisfying higher needs without achieving a certain level of basic needs. A crime for local authorities and other bodies to provide below standard services and infrastructure. Removal of any toxics to life in buildings etc. Banning of fossil fuels by a certain date to improve the air quality and removal of toxins from fumes. Hospitals and doctors to be of the highest quality and no mistakes or dirty tricks. Believe in quality rather than quantity. Highest paid best value. Very strict rules and anything that conflicts with the right to life and quality of life to be banned. No chipping with radiation or other dangerous waves emitting devices. More search and technological advancement to improve standards and quality. Less working hours but high pay or alternative income sources. More time enjoying life and networking or socialization. Better education and better practices in food consumption avoid anything that quickly induces aging and diseases. Better research and methods to prolong life and keep everyone young. Express-command to put an end to this through our laws and courts as a deterrent. Strict laws to kill [as orders of the court] on the spot those who violate these laws by deliberately induced aging and using hidden devices implanted in people's bodies to cause wrinkles and all kinds of unwanted. Ban protection still practiced in other countries that deliberately 'give' people viral watermarks as ways of identifying people under this protection e.g. pulled iris or some genetic mark etc. These people are making viruses and then test them on the population under the disguise of protection. All this lowers quality of life. Everything is viral-based and will only act to reduce lifespan and quality. It's broad light murder better murder them first through the courts. No place for barbaric evil ways. Very tough on these. Drag to court if you can prove that they are tampering with your system and are loading you with watermarks that will result in death and or conflict with the first rule. Countries doing this as institutionalized and systematic probably with orders from the top we must act. Express-command to put an end to this through our laws and courts as a deterrent. Collective punishment by the whole world for nations who think are above the law. No one is above the law you all must obey our laws or if found guilty through the courts die at the hands of the assassin.

### Right to Self-Defense.

This is part of the first rule; the right to life. Everyone shall have the right to self-defend themselves. No one shall trick others or manipulate them to deprive them of the right to self-defense. No one shall and must not do something that will sink others in situations where they are deprived of the right to self-defend. This could be creating a situation where one will be enslaved to someone unfairly, so they are helped as 'slaves' with no rights to defend themselves. A good example is when a government makes deals with the banks or other bodies to trap people in debt with the aim of holding them as ransom when they fail to settle say mortgages or loans. Where the government will buy the debt cheaply from the bank of all defaulters but also put all those who defaulted on 'death row' or under its wings or given evil protection where viruses are tested on them or where radiation is applied on them as they ended up chipped and as government property. A lot of factors will come into play. In some cases, it can be argued successfully if a nation made Weapons of Mass Destruction [WMDs] to defend itself or to deter invasion and this depends on the following factors as well that will be considered;

1} The level of threat and if they too have WMDs. Imagine if the USA, Britain, France, Italy, NATO, UN, ICC, etc. are all ganging up on Iran simply because they have oil and have nationalized this oil and nothing to do with human rights and to make things worse these nations which I will call the cult have nukes themselves. In this case, it would be a lack of good judgment for Iran not to take any precautionary measures to self-defend itself. In this case, it would be reasonable for it to have some form of weaponry that will give them any chances of survival. They might justifiably admit that they have WMDs to deter invasion and attack as a self-defense mechanism. It would be illegal for any of the cult members to attack Iran when they also possess the WMDs themselves. It will be illegal to invade as they will be in the same place as Iran; possessing WMDs for whatever reason they might give.

2}If Iran can prove that the reason for the invasion is to steal resources then they would be defending what is rightfully theirs and the method used is in relation to the threat at hand. It's not like one country has a right and 'Responsibility to Protect' no. All they need to prove is the right to defend what is rightfully theirs matching the threat to the weapons. They can easily point to Article 5 of NATO and use that to show that it's all the cult attacking, and the invading country or countries are just the 'front-line of the army' with the backups at standby mood.

3} They can use precedents in their favor and point say to Iraq and prove that the cult did more harm than the Saddam they toppled and their main motive was to loot the oil and pay the debt and to cause sectoral and insurgents to destabilize the country so that there is no stable government that will in turn mean reduced oil prices. They killed more women and children than Saddam since the invasion and insurgency or sectoral violence has increased ever since.

4} Iran or any country that meets the criteria can effectively argue that these cults and the so-called world leaders are not able to have everyone's interest. They are selfish and the fact that they are NATO members indicates that whatever they decide is never for the benefit of anyone other than themselves. They can point to NATO's Article 8 that states that all the members activities must be for the benefit of NATO and no country will carry out activities that will conflict with the aims and goals of NATO and as such NATO is a regional organization called 'The North Atlantic Organization' and as such anyone outside that zone is not their interest. In such a line the USA or any other country has its own or NATO's interest and nothing to do with helping them.

5} Can ban the UN and refuse its judgment as they have no jurisdiction on anyone as they are biased and serve the interests of their creators and investors the cult. Even more, they act only to act as spying planes [U2 Incident] for the cult trading information for money. Mind you they are funded by the very cult members who founded them who are declaring war on oil-rich nations who are their breadwinners. They can't have anyone's interest.

6} They can go on further to argue that the UN, UNSC, etc. all are biased and have no remorse or feel empathy with the local women and children if they are the ones imposing sanctions that are killing women and children then surely, they have no interest in helping anyone. If they can kill women and children with sanctions after sanctions why would they be concerned or care for adult males being tortured by the government? This shows that they are just there to weaken Iran and other oil-rich nations on the condition that if they are allowed in, then invasion follows. Look at Iraq. Saddam let them in and the USA and the British using psychological mind games followed and caused the death of 500 000 women and children.

7} If they can't show empathy towards women and children through non-use of sanctions there is nothing of use, they can do to help. Claiming invasion on humanitarian grounds of rebels cannot stand and is highly flawed. A miscarriage of justice an act of aggression. Why show no remorse to innocent women and children who are killed by your sanctions in the first place. What they do regarding these innocent people is the litmus test. Show kindness to these then we know you mean business. Neglect and kill these then whatever you claim to represent is void.

8}Instead the UN, UNSC, etc. should be brought to justice for false Pretenses that they can stop wars and bring peace. They must be severely punished for tricking people and giving women and children a sense of false hope that they were dedicated to stopping the war when they can't. Most wars have happened even if they had been invited and found no WMDs. They failed to act to stop the war look at the Iraq war all they could say was that the war was illegal but did nothing even to delay the war to give women and children time to escape the invasion to neighboring countries. Their existence and their declaration that they can stop the war when they can't and the fact that they have no powers is a miscarriage of justice and have led to the deaths of innocent people for the past seventy years. They must be dragged to the courts and face punishment and every family member of anyone who died when they did nothing be compensated until they are out of business. It is the greatest crime to give people a false sense of security when you can't do anything. This is because they block 'potential help' as people then assume that they are going to stop the war only to find out last minute that they are part of the rugby team to deceive and trick the defenders of the opposition so that their striker can score easily a try.

9}Our laws will put an instant end to all UN, UNSC, etc. We believe their presence perpetuates global problems. They are there just for cosmetics purposes just like mannequins in a shop window and to create jobs where people do nothing but expect a check at the end of the month.

10}Individuals can use self-defense laws as well. In cases where governments or people in positions of trust betray them by violating their right to life and to an excellent quality of life say by being loaded with harmful watermarks in the name of protection, they can use this defense to evade death, etc.

## Our Methodology

*Provide laws in all formats and as part of the modern and fast blockchain where laws can be accessed on mobile devices and anywhere where everyone must read and understand and confirm that they have done so where a transaction or recording can be visited at a later date to confirm that and if a person breaks these laws, we can easily access the date the laws were read. A fast way that removes bureaucracy etc. where laws can be read in a person's spare time and where they can confirm that electronically.

*Twenty-four-hour justice system and a fast modern blockchain-based system that operates 24 hours that is automated and is used for fast processing. This is to complement the current system that must be evolved to be faster.

*Removal of any time limits with minimum time limits lasting 25 years. This is because the current system relies on time limits to oppress the people with government bodies withholding correspondence or the victims further abused or forced to move from place to place as institutions use all kinds of watermarks and viruses to drive the victims away so that these institutions make deals with banks and other financial institutions and get a commission or donations. Or even sell the victims as slaves to the government if they are sunk into debt by dirty tricks and ending up on 'death row' or slavery as governments claim possession of these individuals ending up testing viruses on them.

*Tough laws giving everyone the right to life, excellent quality and self-defense, etc.

*Making it illegal to do anything that conflicts with these first laws.

*Reduce military budgets and functions no wars so these must evolve and adopt other legal functions no point adopting evil functions to worsen the problem.

*Prohibit practices that conflict with these laws e.g. evil hacking that reduces the quality of life and interferes with the right to life.

*Educate every leader on earth let everyone make an informed opinion and act to mediate conflicts and act when a few take the law into their own hands.

*Remind everyone on earth that there is no justification whatsoever for killing even one person.

*Mediate and act as negotiators in conflicts bringing the concerned to the table for talks making sure that they must agree on something facilitating and speeding up the process.

*Clearly define the laws and position of everyone act as advisers based on our laws.

*Take proactive action through the banning of wars globally.

*Ban all weapons manufacturing, weapons possession, trading, and distribution.

*Put a date and time frame for the globe to cease weapons-making, trading, and possession.

*Arrange ways to destroy stockpiles

*Unless World War Three is triggered first put a date and time frame when wars will be banned globally. If WW3 breaks out first, then after the war put a date and time frame to declare a ban on anything to do with wars, weapons, etc.

*If dialog fails then to facilitate a Third World War where 'boys will have the last time to play with their weapons' but after that never have wars again. Put laws to ban wars after the last major war. A way of getting rid of weapons and evil people too. Some will never give up or surrender.

*Ban the manufacturing of WMDs.

*Disarm those members of the cult or West who have WMDs in the form of nukes. Our aim is to level the playing field. We are never going to let a few have the right to make and keep WMDs while forbidding everyone else. We have established that their interest is rooted in the interest of NATO with articles that prohibit any member of self-interest or anything that conflicts with their aims and goals. You can't be part of a regional secretive organization where members must meet certain conditions and at the same time purporting to have global interest. Only Tomorrow's World Order has the global interest as we are not biased and don't belong to any cult etc. that can restrict our scope.

*Ban all institutions to do with wars unless if they can evolve and take a different road.

*Ban tactics that will cause others to resort to violence. Ban anything that cause fear and anxiety in others. Mind you we will have banned wars and weapons possession globally so the people will have nothing to fear. We anticipate others might start using digital or cyber weapons to intimidate and threaten others so;

*Ban all future weaponry even if the technology to do so is not yet developed. Anything that does the same as weapons and wars no matter how sophisticated it is if it is used to create the same situations as those banned is banned as well.

*Become proactive and monitor activities and future technology and its impact on global peace.

*Educate everyone and boost people's self-esteem. Put incentives for people to look forward to life.

*Ban sanctions globally and dissolve the UN, UNSC, etc. and drag these to court and make them pay compensation for every women and children died on their watch. If you can't prevent wars don't give people false hope and block people or countries who might offer actual help. Impersonating greatest sin. Stiff punishment even death charges apply here. Life for life applies very well here.

*Create a world free from weapons and wars through continual monitoring and implementations.

*NATO is regional and if they can evolve to do something else apart from intimidating people through missile testing or unlawfully invasions or killings as in Kosovo. Then they are fine but if they are warmongers, then we will bring charges against them for unlawful killing in every operation they undertook that resulted in deaths. They must evolve.

*There is no justification whatsoever of killing a few and it's not enough to declare that collateral damage is unavoidable, and we are doing our best to minimize deaths. I understand they were bragging that they only killed 428 and something Serbs and 538 Yugoslavs. Even one death with our new laws will see them dragged to courts.

*Provide a framework and guidance that protect leaders from future persecution. All our laws if followed will mean a happy free life after office-term.

*Ban situations where leaders and other people are misguided in decision making and are encouraged or tricked to kill. When they are out of office, then they are offered evil 'protection' where they sell not just their souls but the souls of their families as well to the devil where watermarks or viruses are tested on them or forced to drive a campaign that will help the protection givers e.g. hospitals. Who aims and targets prominent people to fight for them to drive their agendas to raise money for drugs etc. or use these to lobby for lax drug laws or licenses?

*The satellite has been used illegal especially this decade where people have been illegally hacked with the satellite used to track them and provide the GPS coordinates. In serious cases where it was used with some form of weaponry to pass harmful radiation and kill people or where it is used to spy on sovereign nations breaking privacy laws and acts of aggression.

*Acts of aggression to be banned. The current laws don't do enough to stop and provide justice. No point to carry out crime with the hope to introduce a law after you have gained unfavorably from invasion etc. above all killing innocent people then use new laws to cover your back. I will remove all-time limits. My argument is that it was common knowledge and international law that any killing of innocent women and children was and is illegal. There is no excuse. The Jus Cogens norms now most of our laws that prohibit all these were there since the 1940s and so there is no justification, and no one can be given immunity now just because the laws were passed recently. Drag all these to court and get them punished.

The E-Laws. The empathy laws.

*Introduce new empathy laws. Take a new direction in law and start looking at the E-laws too; the empathy laws. These laws will help assess if the warmongers gave reasonable regard to the value of life of other people of different backgrounds. Usually, people would sympathize with people who have the same common ground. It can be justified that those who cry for war at the expense of innocent women and children do so because they don't empathize with the victims in other words they give undue regards to the lives of 'remote' people but if one child dies in their country one they relate to they might end up killing the whole group of people who killed that child. This is not human nature we are saying look both ways level the playing field. It's the fact that we are declaring that we are going to be all equal one day as such so we should assess if the leaders can give the same command if the to-be-victims were ones they empathize with. The classic example, although other factors come into play, is the tactics employed in going after 9/11 plotters. Obama went for the shotgun approach as a Muslim or person of Muslim background he might have chosen this method because he empathizes with the Muslims in Pakistan and aimed for zero casualties while Gorge went for the rifle approach simply because he did not relate to Muslims. Just an example that might point light to our new laws. In the-heat-of-the moment will be considered as well. The bottom point is that we will not leave any stones unturned until we put an end to all this.

*New laws to protect servicemen and women. It is now a law that military work shall be like any other profession where they expect to enjoy their pensions as well. Unnecessary military commands that put the lives of soldiers at risk will be illegal. Unlawful killing charges will be swiftly brought against leaders who negligently put the lives of people who took an oak to protect them. The idea here being that it's not just giving away their lives by taking an oath to die for leader and country but a hidden mutual belief that if I can die for you then you must be prepared to protect me as well and not throw me to be slaughtered by insurgents or underestimated enemies. The burden is placed on leaders to do whatever in their power to avoid the loss of life. If a sniper can do the same job, then there is no need to get our best be slaughtered like dogs. So, making an oath is as good as a bargaining stance for the leaders to do their best to safeguard the lives of these men and women. To add to this is sending people to war without proper gear or understanding of; local issues and the enemy-threat-level. Judgment in the-heat-of-the-moment can get you killed as a leader through the courts. Life for life applies in this case. To be the President or Prime Minister comes with greater responsibility and an oath is not a sacrifice but a direct command to do your best to save that life that offers to die for you.

*It is expected of any President or Prime Minister to command a method that avoids the deaths of these men and women.

*To add to the above is the due care that is needed even after these men and women have left the military. It is a President's duty to make sure that they are safe and somehow provided for when military services have ended especially if wars have impacted them psychologically.

*Greatest crime to use devices originally meant to help them [In-built exercises devices etc. supposed that the soldier was a Royal Navy or Navy Seal and would spend 6 months in a submarine at sea, Surely some form of body aid would be needed for breathing and exercising as they are below sea and gravitation forces can cause health issues.] When the service is over these soldiers are mistaken for the retarded and all evil of society. Mind you these men took an oath not to reveal such secrets even to be labeled as such in the name of national security and protection of the President or Prime Minister or the dictator or Monarchy for that matter, but they did not agree for the same device to be used to damage them through hacking. To be used to torture them or make them narcotic through continues shaking and rotating. These men and women end up in local neighborhoods where the local councils have no clue what means to take an oath to protect and honor. In military circles, your word is as strong as a bond yet the leaders to push political agendas to let local councils abuse these men of honor. Therefore, we shall put new tough laws against local institutions like the councils, hospitals, and police who take over or hack these men and women and to justify their jobs further abuse these people. These people gave their lives to this country and why let uneducated government instruments who are failures themselves abuse them. These people would fight even burgers to have a salary at the end of the month. So very tough laws to tackle evil local councils who are hacking all military men and women and use them as bait to attract more investments or justify housing issues. There must be trading places or sacking of these government instruments who are abusing our best boys and girls. Life imprisonment or even death. Hacking military men is a gross crime that conflicts with rights to life and quality of life. Hospitals and councils to be held to account and severe punishment. Reduction of areas where issues are a problem as it only shows an unbalanced pyramid with more government personnel on top of few base people; drug users, homeless and muggers, etc. They end up using soldiers in return for food handouts and safe houses. Mind you these are the people who gave their lives to die for the leader and country and you let these people abuse them.

*The burden is on the President because the oath declared to protect him and the country after the service, he then has a burden to protect these men and women. So, our laws will link these men directly to the President not necessarily the one who they made an oath to but any current or future President. This is one way to tackle this problem. If that means a special fund for the President or Prime Minister's office for such uses, then so be it. Instead of weapons and the military, these leaders have a burden of care of duty to these men and must allocate a certain percentage from the military budget to former soldiers and servicemen especially if the wars had an impact on them the more the funding should be. It is a President or Prime Minister's duty as well to raise money through donations for the servicemen who have left the war when still in office to this fund for ex-soldiers. Money is out there; people need to be reminded and be asked to donate.

*In the long run when all wars are a thing of the past the problem will subsidize.

*The government must compensate these men and women in the case where there is a breach of contractual terms and where the information is withheld from them of what will happen to them as regarding to this extra 'protection' especially when they end up being hacked by local hospitals and councils and used to drive local agendas. They were not told so when they enrolled and must be compensated, and the culprits brought to justice. There has been an abuse of power and trust. You should understand that in military circles a word or oath or contract is the greatest bond one can give and as such these men and women expect that bond to be respected and never be broken. If it's in local settings, it's a different matter how many times politicians have lied and retracted their comments. It's of little issue to them. To a soldier, this can be a thin line between life and death. So, these people must understand and where the breach can be proved to be severely punished. This is a law that applies directly to the President Office or Prime Minister's office because these men did not make an oath to protect abusive local councilors who don't even know what a war is. The oath was a bond between the soldiers etc. and the President that makes the issue one of the President's offices and should never be delegated to the local councils. Death penalty applies here it's a breach of trust that can result in the death of the soldier and as such the President or Prime Minister having a direct responsibility towards the welfare of these soldiers etc. must show that he or she does not allow abuse of the best men and women who not only gave their lives but are betrayed on his or her watch.

*In countries where they are monarchies soldiers are abused in the name of monarchies as they are tricked whatever is done to them is for the sake of the monarchy. These are lies as the monarchy encourage all citizens to report abuse even if they are not citizens. The monarchical rules or regulations advocate that everyone is equal be it a homeless soldier or not and should not be violated but to bring perpetrators to justice. Stiff punishment for those who would want to tarnish the monarch's name with lies pretending that they are torturing people to protect the monarchy.

*Encouraging of all service personnel to log grievances through blockchain or other faster permanent ways that can save files permanently to be used. The reason being that most are abused being prescribed methods that damage their brain as therapy to forget the war-traumas but the therapy causing severe mental problems. Very strict sentences that include the death penalty as this breach the oath of enlistment.

## Human rights violations.

We also have huge plans with human rights issues and how we can totally stop all the abuses that are going on right now. This is in part linked to the above issues. We want a world where there is peace, respect for human rights and the upholding of the rule of law. All our laws remove the triggers of abuse. Wars; - where leaders override rights to life and give orders to kill and then regret after office. We are and believe in pro-activeness and would not want unnecessarily killings or regrets, so we have banned wars and military interventions, etc.

## Military Interventions.

We have watched over the past decades and have concluded that military interventions only benefit the invaders who often benefit at the expense of innocent women and children and as such we have banned any military intervention for any reason whatsoever. Our challenge is for anyone to show us an intervention that did not result in the deaths of women and children? Mind you our laws put people first. We don't care if you provide the whole world with cheaper oil the questions did you get some innocent kids and women die so that you can provide that cheaper oil. There is a cost. A human cost and the fact that you can't provide back the lives of these people make any gains useless because our laws will haunt you till death. Express-command to put an end to this through our laws and courts as a deterrent. We have devised a criterion to assess whether any military intervention is beneficial or not.

*Any intervention that results in deaths of innocent women and children is illegal and can get the command issuer be punished. Express-command to put an end to this through our laws and courts as a deterrent. The reason being that we might not be able to bring this leader to justice as we might see an invasion resulting in civilian deaths but nevertheless, we might send our best assassin. Through education, it will be easy because we will empower everyone to have a very high self-esteem that they will put themselves first and ban and close all loopholes taken advantage of that encourage bribery and make some people kill for money, etc. We shall raise living standards and make one man stand for himself and only Tomorrow's World Order for everyone. Bodyguards and soldiers will not defend a rotten President or Prime Minister and might do us a favor and terminate that leader and use the right to a life of the innocent dead as the defense it does no matter that the dead are their enemies' kids and women. They are all protected by our laws which are global as we are a global leader not specific to any one country. So rotten evil leaders will be dragged to court. Our laws must be respected and above all life be given the importance they deserve. Express-command to put an end to this through our laws and courts as a deterrent.

*Everyone shall have the Responsibility to Protect the defenseless in the women and kids globally. It is irresponsible and arrogant to invade a country by claiming Responsibility to Protect those say chemically gassed and end up killing more women and kids. In most cases, the same countries that invade are the same countries for years that had brought the invaded country to its knees through sanctions that killed many women and children. To rely on humanitarian grounds will not suffice if you had weakened the people through sanctions. It's like the USA or UK fighting for sanctions against Syria and stopping any foreign aid that resulted in the deaths of women and children over the years then when the leader in self-defense gassed the insurgency with chemicals the USA or UK would then try to use humanitarian grounds or

Responsibility to Protect the insurgency as excuses to invade. Such claims will only result in the USA or UK dragged to court for acts of aggression;

>for invading a sovereign country

>undue regard to the lives of the women and children who died first through sanctions and secondly through the invasion with bombs spread everywhere, regardless.

> Third charges of lack of empathy [E-laws] with the victims can be brought on top of that as one can prove that the sanctions and the invasions were imposed and carried out without due regard to the lives of the victims because the USA or UK lacked empathy towards the victims.

>In relation to the above it can be argued that the USA or the UK has no right to intervene as their sole interest is personal for financial, strategic advantage or resources gains only in that everything they are doing is for personal interest other than the welfare of the Syria people. They failed the litmus test regarding the welfare of the women and children whom they killed through sanctions over the years. Even if the sanctions were imposed by the UN all that is needed is to prove the fact that they created the UN and that the UN is funded by them through contributions and as such the UN is doing things on their behalf.

They can never succeed on humanitarian grounds and Responsibility to act if at one point they advocated for sanctions that killed or even created hardships for women and children. It starts with these. It can never suffice to use humanitarian grounds to invade when you were harsh and lacked empathy towards women and children. How on earth would anyone believe you when you used sanctions to kill or affected the quality of life of these people how on earth can you sympathize with gassed rebels when you neglected women and children? Flawed is the word. Crocodile tears. In such cases drag to court and use the E-laws to bring to justice for past sanctions imposed by these. Our laws make it easy to assess motives. You can't kill women and children and vow to defend a rebel?

>Charges of looting indirectly or paving a way for multinationals to come in and take over after toppling of the leader result in

misuse and looting that will disadvantage the local people and increase suffering and insurgents as disgruntling can be a problem.

>Charges of breaking the peace and interferences with a sovereign nation's affairs can be added on top of that. Recall in our world all nations are sovereign and nothing at all tampers with that. This is the critical point to us as all our methods depend on all nations being sovereign. Global emancipation of every nation on earth.

>On top of that impersonating and a false sense of security charges can be mounted onto that as well. Here all Syria would need to prove is that the US and UK are tricking people into believing they are for peace and defend the defenseless when it's their foreign policy and evil sanctions that have caused the suffering and deaths of innocent women and children. As such they are tricking people preaching peace when they are racking lives. Above all, they are impersonating true global leaders and as such might be blocking potential people or nations who would otherwise if they were not there or impersonated the global leader would have taken steps to defend the women and children even if it means stopping or delaying the war giving the women a chance to escape the invasion. Look at the Iraq invasion it took only 48 years to invade and everyone including myself had beliefs that the UN would stop the invasion especially when they declared that there were no Weapons of Mass Destruction. Impersonating a global leader is one of the greatest crimes of the century and every death of a woman and child and all civilian people must be blamed on these. If they had not pretended to 'act in humanitarian grounds' some nations might have intervened. China and Russia condemned the invasion but put trust in the UN and the fact that these nations were responsible world leaders but what happened was far from that. We saw the deaths of women and children. Torturing of prisoners and other abuses violating all international laws and even the Jus Cogens laws that are never to be broken. What we saw was yes, a show of power but nothing than a bully and gangster without any empathy or remorse towards innocent women and children. One who would use a bazooka to kill a fly and destroy the whole ecosystem in the process. It's like justifying the Hiroshima bombs and Nagasaki on self-defense or to deter surprise attacks. Okay at the time it might make sense everyone was a barbarian but what

about now when we know better what is right and what is wrong. The fact that severe defects are still an issue rules out the USA as the global superpower. Too much blood on their hands to justify such a 'responsible office'. The 9/11 attacks put a dent into the superpower theory. Such coordinated attacks can only be carried out with people with very deep-seated grievances. That itself rules out the USA as a responsible superpower with everyone's interests. A superpower as I argued at the beginning of the book is the next thing to a God who looks after everyone. When the ignorant, uneducated cavemen carry out such attacks successfully, it only points that something is wrong unless it was sabotage so that they lose their title. This shows that their foreign policies lack understanding of foreign nations and what is needed of them and as such cannot trick people that they are for global peace. Even if their intentions were good, they lacked understanding and foresight of local differences and religious or cultural ideas. That rules them out of the game. Together with the UK they can't claim to have global issues and everyone's interest at heart. Simply because they belong to a regional cult with strict rules [NATO's Article 8] declares 'personal interests as against the core values of NATO' as I have argued above NATO is regional and only concerned with protecting members in that region. Any global interventions are to squash potential threats other than anything else. Look at NATO's intervention in Kosovo. One can argue that it was just to give NATO credibility as a regional player other than maintaining global peace.

>We don't care what the past Soviets or the now Russians would do they can be as communist as they can we don't care about its individual sovereignty a case of personal preferences. We would not group to stop democracy.

>What about the UK as a superpower? I have dealt with the USA. The UK failed a long time evidenced by the collapse of the empire. They grew at the expense of others abusing people and breaching all international laws. It is understood that to grow bigger you must be bolder and ruthless but if that happens currently, I think is not just a cause of concern but a global problem. I understand that they often rely on humanitarian grounds as they declare they have a 'Responsibility to Act' but is that true? We have still countries

under 'colonial' rule and under the British. Maybe it's by choice but still, this has colonial implications. The Chagos case tore any hope of them becoming a global leader, a bully yes and part of the NATO gang yes sure why not? The fact that they don't listen to the courts they established themselves in the ICC etc. means they are self-centered and any claims they make might be taken with suspicion. Ever since they are self-centric and humanitarian grounds don't suffice. They are in most cases at the forefront of sanctions and withholding aid. Promising to fund and then failing to do so at the time of need. Does that ring a bell? Nasser during the Suez Canal. They gave Nasser a false sense of security by promising funding for building the bridge. France etc. withdrew their funding as the British had promised to fund until the very last minute when they refused to release the funds causing Nasser to nationalize the canal. You can see the issue I am against is evident even as far back as the 1950s. The issue of giving a false sense of security as an act to cancel any other help and in the end withdrew at the last minute resulting in imminent damage or catastrophe. France was willing to sponsor Nasser but did not want to do it at the same time as the British. A perfect reason to invade and so they just did that and invaded an independent foreign nation with sovereignty powers taking it back into recolonization. They cooked up the Iraq dossiers so that the US would be side by side [picture the Ghost and the Darkness movie] and went in for personal gains rather than emancipating Iraq's. Half a million dead. The war-debt that had brought them to their knees solved. Foreign multinationals took charge and drilled oil until the price was very low. The day or after the death of Saddam Hussein they publicly announced that they were now able to pay the debt they owed the USA since World War II. It's like two robbers who can't pay a normal price going to rob a bank with guns. Killing as they like and getting away with loot which one pays the other a larger share to cover past debt. The day the owner of the bank died they declared settlement of the debt. Is it justified? In real life what are the consequences of such a move?

We don't care about the past that much for the meantime unless if we face problems of cooperation then we will go back in time and use our laws to take their leaders to court not for revenge but for the sake of peace and justice. You must understand the reasons they embark on wars as put right by Dwight Eisenhower simply because; nationalizing of oil wells was the only reason that justified to go to war. Since oil is the most expensive expenditure of any government that depletes a country's resources. These nations are like gangsters who use cheaper guns to go and get what they want. Guns are cheaper to make than pay high oil prices. We have shed light on what we believe are real problems. In response, we are banning all military interventions as they are not justified on any grounds than personal gains and the need to act like gangsters to use weapons to rob. Stiff charges against violators of our laws. No nation shall falsely use humanitarian grounds or otherwise to invade a sovereign nation. No national shall use military force to force a nation to denationalize its resources; oils or canals for that matter. Criminal charges for possession weapons and using these to rob another foreign nation. Stiff punishment in terms of the instant death penalty through the courts for leaders of countries tricking people and taking people back to colonial times. Any invasion with colonial connotations to be punished severely. Collective punishment applies here we don't want a second Hitler. We can't wait for people to die first and act as with Hitler. By 1939 all Allies that is the West knew Hitler was carrying out mass assassinations of the Jews but turned a blind eye as they had made deals with Hitler. After they got what they wanted technology etc. they then went after Hitler. No recreating colonial times as this can result in the whole country being invaded. Analysis of the invader's past link to colonization and other oppressive tactic to get cheaper resources etc. will be assessed. Can't allow a former slave-master and colonial addict falsely claim to act on humanitarian grounds but getting innocent women and children dead. This should be assessed to see if there is a link between the country's financial status and whether this has a bearing on the invasion. Any personal gain motives will be treated as war crimes; crimes of aggression, intimidating others with the aim to incite wars that destabilize global peace. Invasion of sovereign nations. Killing innocent lives, trading money or oil for the lives of these people. It's like killing to get cheaper oil or be able to pay the debt. What about the lives of the kids who died? What is the value of the deaths of women and children? Is cheaper global oil worth the lives of the kids?

No humanitarian grounds or otherwise shall suffice. We shall use the litmus test. A test of using the duty of care as an indicator of the likely motive of humanitarian grounds. We look at specific past relations as regards sanctions the most commonly used weapon to weaken governments and damage the credibility of leaders. To destabilize the government by making it unpopular and above all our main concerns for this test. The duty of care to women and children or in other words the 'Responsibility to Protect' these women and children. It is a fact that sanctions kill women and children and most people who dispute this remark are the very people imposing sanctions. What we all don't like about terrorists is the fact that they target women and children and kill these to push agendas and to bargain for better deals and simply as revenge. The West and all its Allies do the same through sanctions punishing women and children needlessly. This vulnerable group suffers for nothing and die avoidable deaths. Any country that has imposed sanctions or advocated for imposing sanctions on a country which they are now claiming to invade on humanitarian grounds is in breach of breaking international laws. You can't kill the innocent future of any country in thousands through sanctions and then claim to invade on humanitarian grounds to rescue otherwise terrorists or rebels. That can't stand. Our new laws will bring heavy penalties that include death or collective attack by the whole world. Gone are the days when your reckless evil leaders take the lives of women and children as a show of power. To us, these are unforgivable evil acts that make us bring any nations to court as a Hostis Humani Generis notion and deliver punishment even if it has not been affected directly. Above all attacking, any sovereign nation has colonial implications and can never suffice. Any attack on a sovereign nation to be considered as acts of aggression and a country is justified to defend itself by any means necessary. Attacking a sovereign nation will trigger the right for that nation to self-defend itself and its people. If it has precious resources like oil, then it has a license to act to protect those resources by any means necessary just as a businessman will be given a license to own a gun just because he has a special resource; his business. The same must apply here. Nations should find ways of becoming rich and buy at market prices. We have a method that works be part of us. Together we can start anew. A new chapter. I think as time goes on we will put more weight on evil empires or countries that make a change for the better and probably work with these in the future than those who stick to what we are saying is NOW wrong according to our new laws.

Such evil acts will trigger Article 1 that states that the person or nation is to be regarded as Hostis Humani Generis that is an evil and enemy of mankind. Breaching of the Jus Cogens rules and our rules which declare that killing of innocent women and children is a crime against all and an attack of all mankind and as such will trigger collective punishment that can lead to an invasion, just like what happened to Hitler. This era is no time for evil acts as they might cost you and everyone else their lives. As a responsible global leader, Tomorrow's World Order has recognized that oil; these bloody fossil fuels are the root of most of the major issues we have today. People for lack of thinking power instead of investing in research and development are making cheaper weapons to use to rob those rich in resources. We are against inferior poor thinking ways. We are against fast but cheap methods. This is like an armed robber I understand the law relating to this is tough so why can't we exercise the same judgment and as such we have first banned reliance on fossil fuels for everything. We believe it's a privilege and luck that some countries have oil and not a common good as declared by the West who see nationalizing oil as a war-trigger. We believe in individual sovereignty and the rule of the law. Invading a sovereign country is the worst that can happen. Therefore, fossil fuel, vehicle, infrastructure, and other uses are banned with immediate effect, but a grace period shall be considered for a few years before global cessation of its use as a fuel in cars, busses, lorries, boats, planes, machines, homes, etc. We are serious about stopping future wars. This is the first step. Today's nations are lazy opting to wage wars and still make weapons instead of research and development into alternative fuels. Electricity has proved a success in cars, etc. This is the new way, and a given date will be set when everyone will be forced to start using electric cars. All current cars to be phased out from the roads in phases and this applies globally. Building etc. that uses oil etc. to be replaced with modern and efficient ones that use renewables which are cheaper and cleaner. Critical time frames to be used to give dates when it is likely that phasing out might start with the earliest possible dates and the latest given to everyone globally. Military budget to be drastically reduced and any savings to be diverted to the research and development of alternative fuels. Fossil fuels are not meant forever and will run out one day so why not start now to look for better alternatives? It will be unjustified to invade a nation for the sake of lowering global oil prices. Stiff punishment to deter further breach and abuse. It might sound that our laws are to stop the West, but we think all the problems we have are induced and caused by the West and that could explain our stance to deal with the issue for the sake of global peace and human development. I am not saying that the West is the only culprits we have other countries in the Persian Gulf and elsewhere e.g. Russia invading other states and for most, it's for a sectoral, religious or political reason rather than for resources.

I have in mind the invasion of Kuwait by Iraq.

Israel's invasion of Lebanon or Egypt etc. or the fighting with Palestine, etc. The reasons are totally different.

**Political and religious instability.**

The Middle East and the Persian Gulf are the worst culprits in this regard. Unnecessary killings and fighting of different sectors for religious grounds etc. must stop. We understand the fighting goes back to the AD era and to be honest we think education and change of beliefs and attitudes and self-empowerment will play a crucial role than just laws. There is a need also to look deeper into the root causes. Unsettling issues remain that make the whole thing a hard task nevertheless we are for global peace and that is what we are going to achieve. I think understanding and coming together to work together and compromise some aspects for the sake of peace will be pivotal. The fact that they rely on books written centuries ago in the Quran and bible etc. is a challenge to be viewed and solved with great caution. I understand one of the issues is regarding prophecy.

## Prophecy.

I understand whatever is written must be fulfilled if it hasn't been. That creates a problem. Whatever decisions you can make today have little bearing as at the end of the day prophecies will play a bigger role. I understand they follow two sets of leaders one for the Shia and the other's Sunnis, etc. That could be the root of the rift and an everlasting one in that they have to fulfill the prophecies of these leaders who predicted that these two sets of people will fight each other for a thousand years before only one of them is chosen at the end of the day. So, in that case, sometimes the people fight and refuse to compromise as to fulfill these prophecies. I also understand that whatever is in the books must come true, so they do what was written centuries ago even if it is not irrelevant now? Could this explain why wars and sectoral violence is never-ending? Now you can understand why I explained our stance as to religion the main reasons why I used the bible and Quran to explain world issues as well. I think religion is a sensitive issue that needs understanding from all perspectives to find common ground for peace's sake. Nevertheless, that is not a justification for wars and as such our laws apply globally and we may be very strict with nations from these regions. We don't discourage religion but if that is the reason for wars then we need to change people's perceptions and understandings. I argued that the heavenly life in the bible and Quran is a state we must achieve here on earth one day. People need to believe that too and work towards achieving that. What I like about our laws they are universal. There is no one who doesn't want peace and the best life has to offer. I think you need to compromise and lose some beliefs and gain some too. If Allah and God are for peace, they would not want to see sectoral violence. We have all we need and shall sacrifice other aspects like investing in wars and weapons, etc. This money shall be used to uplift the lives of everyone. Some living standards and services shall be declared below standard and institutions, governments, organizations, etc. providing these be held to account and be forced to provide better ones. Once education [not academic] but spiritual and psychological has been delivered, we expect people to change and have high self-esteem to believe that life is worth it and no one shall be a suicide bomber, etc. Need to provide here on earth everything people they wish to get in heaven. Beautiful wives, virgins, loads of wealth and simply peace of mind. There was in the past so much violence with bombs going on non-stop. This is a criminal offense as it impacts heavily on quality of life. First, encourage development. Military money to be used for the betterment of humanity. Life must come first. No foreign nations to manipulate oil resources at the expense of the locals.

**Better living standards and the elimination of poverty, etc.**

Religious leaders to play crucial roles in educating people spiritually to give everyone hope. Stiff penalties for stirrers of violence to destabilize these countries. We have banned arms, so no arms deal, etc. a first step to keeping and maintaining peace. Development programs aimed to alleviate poverty and increase literacy skills and above all provision of best infrastructure. Dubai led the way instead of using oil revenue on weapons they should improve the quality of life of their people. The West has been a very bad role model and if these changes in the future the developing countries can learn one thing or two from them. The idea here is to facilitate global networking and cooperation. Education in warfare tactics and general life should be taught as most fall in the West's psychological traps of trusting people who have been evil to them as far as they can remember. If they can kill women and children through sanctions, then they are no good to you. The Persian Gulf leaders [PGL] must understand the West. If they use force and group together into cults, then they are no good to you as well. You can tell the PGL will not even defend their own people. These leaders must face our laws. Apart from being the victims of barbaric abuse, they do nothing for their people. If a businessman can defend what is rightfully his by owning a gun license, why let others invade and rob you killing your women and children too. I personally think the equal and opposite force is lacking and if left like this will only result in human extinction. If you can't change then better group. An Asian equivalent of NATO is welcome even though we will be banning wars and weapons they can evolve. They can lead to finding a better alternative to fuels, even better, they can invest in cyber and digital defense, etc. There are so many areas to get involved in.

We can ban all wars and weapons but still it does not mean the end of the military. My main idea is that these people are success-driven and determine to find what they set to do. We need them but not killing people but being the leaders if you like development. We can use their technology for human development. Fighter Jets can become for private use. All the advanced gear and gadgets can be used for human development, so the military is still viable, but they must evolve and whatever they do being for the benefit of humanity. What is even better is the increased salaries? Why channel money to huge weapons etc. when you are out of pocket. We change people's perceptions. More money for you. Meaning incentivizing people and ask them to create solutions and lead the way. It will work. I have faith in them.

## Responsibility to Protect their people.

They have a greater responsibility towards their people, yet they just go by the floor and get millions of innocent women and children killed needlessly. We shall also drag them to court for impersonating a true regime that will protect their people. It's not just a matter of sitting and waiting to be the next in the line. They don't even challenge illegal invasions or call others for help. We have others who can help those who have a Responsibility to Protect their people if the invasion is for personal gains. We think they are neglecting their duties to their own people. To protect them at any cost and defend them. The fact that they do nothing puts everyone at risk. We are against recolonization and we will use our powers to avoid some governments enslave the world again. So, there is help all they need to do is ask. We are saying we can bring the same charges as we do to the invaders. They have given their inhabitants a false sense of security. They might hope they would trade oil for support and help, etc. Our laws give everyone the right to defend themselves and their people and resources through force as well if invaded. Foreign invasion is banned by all laws and there is no justification whatsoever without consequences. Look at 9/11 it can be argued that this is a direct response to the USA's crooked foreign policy.

Lack of the duty of care to the women and children where they did nothing to prevent deaths of women and children when sanctioned instead just seated and waited until sanctions had killed many. Education is vital in military strategies. The West is a formidable force to be reckoned with simply because they have grouped into a cult in NATO. Why not do the same for the sake of your people? Value your life and start thinking as if you are on earth to stay forever. Change the mindset that kills people's hopes and giving them fear and hard life that they wish they killed some to go to a place where there is peace. Self-defense is your right. Especially considered what you are up against. It is a reasonable excuse to arm yourselves and group as well with real nuclear weapons. The world is unfair anyway. If the USA can use some nukes on Japan and get away with it, why can't you use some to defend yourselves in the worst-case scenario? [NB we are going to ban use of all anyway WMDs, anyway. Just an eye-opener.] It's illegal to use WMDs. It is irresponsible for a government to let others kill their own children and women without international calls for help. Iran should and must not be another Iraq. We don't stand for anyone but for all hence one man for himself TWO for us all. The fact that the aftermaths of wars are worse than before invasions make us take a different stance. We have realized that affordability is the root cause and our method will change global politics as we know this today.

We shall lobby globe response to armed robbery and unfair killings of women and children. No women and children shall die at our watch and without severe consequences. Our laws will clarify international laws and remove any ambiguity or loopholes being exploited e.g. humanitarian grounds. These will never stand with our laws especially if the invaders have a shabby past and have no empathy for women and children of different backgrounds. We believe an attack of innocent women and children is an attack of all mankind that triggers Article 1.

### Terrorism.

Very strict with these. Tough sentences as well. The main reasons are that they kill innocent women and children as well. They use these as bargaining bags as well. That makes us not even have sympathy with them. All these people are protected by our laws and an act on civilians is an attack on all humanity and can lead to global collective punishment. Death penalties as well for anyone who kills women and children. I don't care for what reason. They might have been wrong okay, but two wrongs don't make a right in that way we must treat these as enemies of the people too. Ban all terrorist activities there is no justification whatever. Be strict with governments that support or incite others to terrorism. This means banning acts of provocation where the innocent are killed or oil looted so that they revenge the attack. In such situations, if the other side can prove that you deliberately provoked them to use terrorist acts to revenge then you are like someone running and attacking a lion and getting mauled you can't blame anyone but yourselves. These would be treated as self-inflicting wounds. All the other party needs to prove is the fact that there is a cause-and-effect relationship. The initial act is the main trigger for the terrorist act. Had they not killed or looted in the first place none of this would have happened? My main base for this stance is in line with the psychological games of the West. Mind games to deliberately create situations that justify military action. It's like killing with a missile the innocent women and children say in Afghanistan and when the Jihad retaliates and carries out terrorist activities, then you are to be blamed. Even though they are dragged to court and using our laws to punish them you too are dragged to court for self-inflicting wounds. For aggressive acts that put the lives of your own people at risk. More charges of endangering the lives of your own people and putting them at risk will be leveled against you. We will further go on and claim undue regard to life for personal gains. You are in the same position as the people who attack themselves just to make excuses to attack others. To us you are a threat to global peace and as such must be severely punished and labeled unfit to rule and run any country. No other national security laws can override these laws and we will have banned all other justifications for not putting the lives of everyone including your enemies first. Severe punishment for leaders doing this attacking oneself is not just a disease but gross evil that can threaten human existence in that these people have no fear and one day might use nuclear weapons that will kill even their own people for personal or selfish gains. The greater the risks of using nukes and WMDs as they are not afraid to sacrifice their own too. Death penalties apply here. Evil with evil applies here as evil can only breed evil. Severe punishment for false flagging. This is a common practice to get others attacked on false accounts. It's not just evil but irresponsible too and puts innocent lives at risk. Dirty tricks can cost lives.

Tough laws outlawing any direct or implied false flagging as to unfairly attack normally powerless people in order to rob or impose inhuman degrading treatment or revert to colonial times. This applies globally, not just to the West we have Persian Gulf countries doing the same. Clearly, state our laws and provide these through advanced ways e.g. blockchain system that is fast, or a centralized version that can easily be used for everyone to read and acknowledged the knowledge of the laws. There will never be an ignorance plea as an excuse after the laws are published. It is everyone's responsibility to make sure they are familiar with these laws and have read and understood them.

We do our best to link everyone globally and provide a platform for interaction, cooperation, and negotiations. Global peace is our must and everyone's responsibility and a breach of law to incite others or cause instability very strict punishment to deter. Laws to ban situations where some dodgy leaders would try to sacrifice their soldiers to reduce the military salary bill or sending troops in war zones without proper gear from that specific zone. Slaughtering charges can be brought against such leaders. Every family of soldiers who died this way to receive compensation with a need to prove that. Burden is on the government and the President or Prime Minister to ensure the welfare of the soldiers. The duty of care or Responsibility to Protect is derived from the oath which is a request to do the same as they offer to die protecting these leaders and country. The leaders and country in turn must reciprocate and swear to do anything in their powers to show gratitude toward these men and women. In this case, compensation would not be enough. To discourage taking advantage of the situation first; use them for political propaganda or to drive local budget campaigns by local councils and then compensate them after abusing them very strict laws that include the death penalty. These soldiers were prepared to die for the leader and the country who ever abuse them must be willing to die for them and the country. Like for like to apply here. These men as we saw fit shall be the responsibility of the President's Office and not some local councils who don't know what the military stands for. A word and promise in army circles are every soldier's assets something to put your life on and breaking or betraying this trust carries severe punishment. Local authorities to be trained to understand this as the only way to a solution. Providing housing and food handouts is not the answer probably a third type error. Solving the problem but with the wrong solution as good as not solved.

## Africans Leaders.

The same issues apply globally but Africa has its own continental problems and I will look at it here. African leaders as low-level threats concerned about self-governance rather than international inclines. Africa leaders and other countries are regarded as low-level threats with little or no potential for global military attacks as what the Middle East rich in oil is perceived as. As such the UN's judiciary system in the ICC is left to eliminate these low-level threats in the Colony Collapse Strategy, which I advanced at the beginning. Most countries in Africa are poor by global standards with most are regarded as developing nations. No wonder their problems are specific to Africa with dictatorship, corruption, genocide tendencies, tribalism, poverty, and instability the main issues. These nations need foreign assistance to topple the dictator and this gift is the same to be used to topple them and get them dragged to courts by the ICC on weapons charges or use of force or genocide and war crimes after being given weapons by the West.

>All our laws will apply globally without cherry-picking. Banning of wars and weapons purchasing here applies.

>New laws to deal with dictatorship and the need to solve the real issues.

>New ways of recording and safekeeping of war crimes. Use of the blockchain as well where necessary to collect and process or keep evidence to be retrieved later. Our laws to life and self-preservation applies here too with stiff punishment for breaches,

etc.

>Finding ways to tackle corruption, poverty, illiteracy, etc.

> Encourage development packages and aid to boost progress and networking.

>Money saved on military and weapons to be used for research and development poor industrialization of farming whatever improves life and later education to be used to boost self-esteem etc. Religion and other political and tribalism are major causes of wars and we have ways to deal with these. As basic needs are met, the less people tend to fight. Most of the fighting is for basic needs when others are spending huge sums on weaponry, etc. They say a hungry man is an angry man, and this applies here.

>Strict laws on genocide and its prevention. With stiff punishment for culprits, etc.

>Empowerment of governments against the West who might choose to test their man-made viruses on them in exchange for food handouts or weapons. Poverty can influence the decisions to take and the national policy too. Development packages would be beneficial.

>All sanctions to be banned and never to be used for any reason. Countries that offer conditions that mimic sanctions will face international laws and any unfair practices with colonial connotations or slavery to be dealt with swiftly.

>We don't like to witness situations mimicking say slavery or colonialism no.

>Military training in warfare tactics can be beneficial although the locals are used to destroy their own leaders through food bargains etc. with some people in Africa will go to lengths for handouts selling their own people for advantageous situations and benefits, etc.

>Crimes of humanity and aggression the two main trappers of most African leaders committing these through fighting to remove the dictator and themselves be taken to courts etc. Very strict laws to prohibit the acceptance of any military favors in terms of weapons etc. mainly from the West as these will be used to trap them and get them killed.

## Human rights.

Nevertheless, just like any other country human rights abuses are prevalent with leaders forced to opt for other issues overriding the rights to life, etc. Another major issue is the lack of democratic situations that allow people to freely choose their own political inclination.

>Laws to encourage freedom and rights to choose freely, etc.

>Lack of the rule of law

No upholding of the rule of law and the need for new laws and support toward achieving that with extra funding for the provision of basic needs. More accountability to be demanded and laws put in place to deter this. Training can benefit some while some are unredeemable.

## Tribalism.

This is specific to Africa with violence and unfair civil wars resulting in the deaths of women and children. Our rules apply here too and reckless and undue regard to innocent lives can get the leaders to be dragged to court.

>Aim to eliminate factors causing all these tribal conflicts. If education both academic and tradition might be beneficial and encourage everyone to some form of compromise and sacrifice for the betterment of others. Any causes of divisions to be addressed and a lasting solution be found to stop this fighting.

## Torture.

Torture is a problem in Africa with the good part being that the methods of torture are still primitive that leaves marks etc. and can be easily proved unlike in developed countries where it is hard if not impossible to show evil hacking as the source of all issues. With the right technology that is still a possibility. So, African torture cases are easily collected and for such reasons, people have easily seen scars that can be used to push for justice. But this presence of evidence in form of scars has made African leaders refrain from torture because they might be taken to the court that has meant high genocide rates where people are killed with bodies hidden away from the view of people. We have advocated that even though the African leaders are still corrupt and favor dictatorship, we think the ICC is not-fit for purpose due to the bias and targeting of African's and since 1945 bring only African's to trial and letting others get away with murder. So, ICC is biased and represents the views and goals of the West who created and funds it. Whatever they do so is in the interest of their investors the West and the very people we are saying that they are breaking international laws by targeting ethnic and carrying out ethnic cleansing of killing potential threats who might one-day group and form wars. Drag the ICC to court for ethnic cleansing and being biased with aims to eliminate future leaders to reduce the likelihood of wars. Charge them with bias and targeting attacks against the Africans and putting lives at risk as they drag them to court to be further abused. Reluctance and powerless of these institutions to solve global issues compounded with lack of a military wing all acts against them. Look at the source of weapons in most cases they are a gift from the West and bring charges to the country involved for supplying weapons that are used to kill women and children and therefore the source as such apportion blame. Add the E-laws as well to prove that they lacked empathy even though they knew that weapons were to be used on women and children. They must have anticipated or foreseen this coming therefore aware but acted negligently and lacked empathy towards the victims. If personal gains through sales of guns if not given as gifts, then advance on E-laws that they preferred profits over the lives of these people simply because they are remote to them. You would not sell or give guns to someone who might use them on your own women and kids, would you? Our laws will punish everyone involved and especially the real culprits the weapons supplier. If there were no guns easily available women and children might not have died in such numbers. Change all laws relating to this. Add a lack of empathy with the victims by the West who offload weapons cheaply or unjustly knowing that they will be used to kill these. An accessory to murder.

# CHAPTER THIRTY-EIGHT

THE IMPLEMENTATION AND THE EXECUTION.

Our model focuses on people rather than governments as the current thinking in that the governments are trusted to act in favor of the people. At first instance, it might seem to be the case that governments are in a better position to be the focus that trickles down benefits to the whole society. But this is the root of all the problems we have. The current system demands the people put their faith and trust in the government and leave them to do everything for their benefit. This hypothesis assumes that overall governments are there to serve the people so trust in the government will result in it acting for the enhancement and well-being of the people. But is this true? We disagree as this will lead to the government to take the trust and faith and take advantage of that situation to abuse the people it is supposed to look after or be responsible for. This is true and as you will discover is the root of all the problems we have today. Governments can't be trusted.

### Our Thinking; People-centric rather than trust in governments.

Our thinking is to be people-centric in everything we do and let everything else follow. If you put the people as a priority, then everything is supposed to follow suit. This idea of putting trust in the government is associated with inferior societies and thinking. No one should trust the government in the sense that people should be the ones responsible for their day-to-day and all future planning. Governments should owe, people and not like the current situation where the government tries to hold everyone in ransom through debt, etc. In our New World people are so advanced and have high self-esteem that they truly believe the government is there to serve them and not the other way around. Governments must do whatever they can to increase the value of the people and not sink them with debt etc. like the current situation where they make deals with banks to hold everyone down or enslave them.

## The government must owe its people money wealthy, etc.

This is true and the current setting is wrong where banks take sides with governments to sink all the people through debt. The government ended up bailing banks out instead of "bailing the people" out. The idea being that governments must do whatever it takes to make sure no matter what it should always have the people in mind and as it's reason for its sole existence. What happened during the financial system is the opposite of what the government should have done. Misconception and wrong thinking of governments bailing-out banks. The sole existence of governments is to serve the people. The financial crisis 'ripped off the people' taking money from them and giving this to the government and banks. What governments should have done and what is going to happen in the future in the New World is for governments to be proactive and stand for the people.

## The Do-Nothing Approach.

During the financial crisis, governments did nothing but encourage the impact on the people. What they should have done was to do whatever it can to stop the effects of the financial crisis on people. They should have intervened and printed more money or supplied more money to 'bail-out' people and not wait until it was too late for the people only to jump to help when the same effects were now happening to banks. My point is that governments are elected by the people and their sole existence is to serve the people and not bloody banks. In our world government must and will do whatever it can to serve and cushion its people first. The current system values banks more than people. This is totally different from our approach. What should have happened? When the credit crunch's impact was first felt governments should have acted fast to provide loans to the people and if this meant printing more money so be it. After all the money government prints is money borrowed from the people. All government debt is a debt to the taxpayers the people and not to banks or external forces. Our aims and goals are to increase the value of the people and not to rob them or let the banks rob them. When governments borrow money by printing more money, it is getting indebted to the people. The more it prints money the more it owes its people and the more the value and wealth of the people increase and therefore the living standards as well. This is true and the only way to beat the poverty trap and all the problems we have today.

## The No Can't Do Approach.

There is a global misconception and exaggerated fears about government printing money which it can easily do and at will and owe its people money at the same time boosting the wealth of its people. Most people think this is a dangerous road and can only lead to the financial collapse and poverty of the people concerned but this is a misconception. Globally we have seen countries acting their best to keep money growth through government borrowing that is printing more money at minimum levels for fear that this will only mean high inflation rates and future financial problems. We have institutions like the International Monetary Fund encouraging 'living within your means' as a strategy that will improve global wealth and avoid financial catastrophes etc. but this is the very same reason why we have the problems we have. High unemployment, slow globalization in terms of industrialization, etc. High inflation and stagnation of economies. We have had the current thinking and institutions preaching this for the past seventy years and still, we have the same problems globally.

## A new broader and bolder approach.

To solve all the current problems that we have today and emancipate the world by raising living standards to unprecedented levels we must take a broader, bolder approach. Fears of financial disasters etc. should and must not stop the big brain from acting. We must see this as collateral damage that is unavoidable in that even with the strict monetary discipline, we had we will still have global financial collapses. Our model is to look at the big picture.

## Empower every nation on earth.

How can we do this? The only way is to do what is right for the people. We are people-centric in that people come first. We believe governments exist to serve the people. So how can we empower the people? How can we improve and boost living standards to never seen before levels? The government is the answer. Only the government can do that, and this is through owing the people. If the government owes its people, then everyone's wealth and value increase. Look at a company. A company owes its shareholders interest and dividends on top of their capital they have invested. The sole existence of a company is to serve the shareholders who are its investors. It's not there to make a profit. It's there to make a profit so that it pays interest on capital and shareholders after these are paid then it will have profits which it can keep for growth and development. Likewise, governments are there to increase the value of their people.

### How does a government increase the value of its people?

Simply through owing them money and paying them here and there. So how does a government owe its people? Simply through printing more money. To increase the wealth of your people and country is simply to print more money. This is the only source that guarantees enormous wealth for the people and growth at enormous levels that will increase living standards. Can you recall our goals? To boost the self-esteem of everyone on earth and increase living standards to improve quality of life. I proposed that it will and must be illegal for the government to do anything that affects the quality of life.

**Printing more money and owing your people is the sole reason for the existence of governments.**

There is no other way that can benefit the people than for governments to deliberately print more money and ignore inflation fears. There is nothing rewarding to your people than increasing their value by owing them if you are a leader or government. So, our goal is to encourage all governments to abandon all planning that restricts monetary printing. This is the only source that benefits your own people. The other methods will only benefit external sources. If we are to borrow or trade to owe other nations, it's them who benefits greatly as the country will owe that country that can imply less favorable conditions for your own people. Borrowing other nations involves sovereign risk. The borrowing nation might pose a threat to the well-being of a country as they might wage a war or use sanctions in case you default.

**Fears about excessive borrowing through fiat printing are clearly unfounded.**

Our thinking is that there is nowhere any nation can improve the living standards or its wealth to levels, we want by restricting printing at will. We have had an economist for the past seventy years and since then we had numerous financial crises, the worst being the 2008 one. If the governments had intervened and bailed out all people by giving them extra loans through fiat printing the crises would have been avoided. The people will have money to pay for the repayments. They would not have had the houses repossessed their wealth would have increased and, in the end, they would have owed the government for a certain period until the debt is written off. It is the duty of the government to act and react and not to wait and bail the culprits like what is happening now.

**Bank robbers.**

The banks sat down through this Payment Protection Insurance and devised a devious plan to put all people out-of-pocket by stealing from us in small quantities but over years enough to have triggered a big financial crises where money moved in small-but spread all over the years to be huge enough to put a dent in the people and on top of that the banks used a rule called the offset to make sure that after robbing from us for years when we finally notice that the banks would not pay us back our money or any compound interest. Daylight robbery and who are the master minders? Some governments exchanging slavery tricks for our freedoms in order to hold us into slavery forever monitoring and putting on surveillance breaking all international laws. I explained in detail in an earlier chapter the triggers of the financial meltdown. It was a calculated plan to roll all the money from you the people to the government who would bail-out the banks and exchange your debt for your freedom with government buying and writing off the debt and holding the defaulters at ransom.

## Government fault.

The government in the New World must prioritize the people. All our laws help everyone understand this. The government exists to serve the people and not the banks. They should have penalized the banks heavily and take back the money they stole from all of you and gave it back to you. Where is Robinhood? Instead, your leaders dine and wine with these trickery-clever manipulating bankers who would not stop at anything. A devious and dodgy way to raise capital to further loan-out. Banks have for a decade or two been cheating people collecting PPI insurance maliciously with the aim to gather funds to invest in the new cryptocurrency the time it was launched in 2009. The banks had anticipated this or forehand set to collect enough capital either to have a chance of competing with the cryptocurrency Bitcoin or enough to surge enough competition. The PPI was no coincident like they want you to believe. They used the oldest trick in the book used during the slavery days of 1835. The slave traders to avoid being captured by the British ships that hunted slave traders at that time organized and loaded small faster ships with more slaves and transported these at the same time sending large cargo ships to the coastline as 'diverts' to offset the hunt as the hunters of slave traders would follow these large ships and only to find no slave in them and assume everything is okay when the smaller faster ships were still on it trading in slavery and in this case representing the small premiums they took every month and cover these with loans so as to sink the people even further in debt. This is because people will have lost the insurance premiums. The banks would not give these backs. So technically this is money lost. When, for example, the people have lost their jobs they would expect the insurance to pay for the repayments but only to be told that the PPI was useless and could not cover but still the people now in deep debt have the repayments to payback plus repayments of the loan. Double impact sink even faster in debt. Imagine roughly $30 billion in PPI mis-selling has been claimed back so far with another $10 billion set aside. The banks made even more money for them to offer to return this money. Mind you the time in question coincide with the launch of Bitcoin in 2009 up to a few years ago when the scandal surfaced. The average PPI a person is getting is around $3000. If the banks had invested this money in Bitcoin, they would have made a profit of over $2m per person. Now imagine if they took from the people $40 billion that is the amount to be given back that means assuming they invested all the money in Bitcoin they had made a huge fortune. Even if they had just invested this elsewhere through loans, they would have made a fortune still. To cut the story short, we shall be strict with banks. They have taken you for granted and assumed they will be there forever but guess what? Not anymore. To emancipate the people and improve living standards to levels they have never been before requiring a total change. In this book, the idea is to present the current system all of it as unworkable and obsolete having crashed so many times. Every time we had a credit crunch or a recession or a financial crisis etc. was the crash of the system and calls for a new one. I also pointed out how we used wires instead of fuses to keep it going for longer. But we are saying that that is irresponsible and dangerous and can't be tolerated anymore. The system must be replaced. So here we are. First the banks if they are not prepared to clean up and give-back all the PPI insurance and lower fees etc. then we need new systems like the blockchain. The idea is to put humans first. The idea is to prioritize the people and their needs first and this means wealthy of the people and excellent never achieved before quality of life. If we are saying that the banks are growing at our expense and if we still let the banks exist, then how are we going to improve people's wealthy and their quality of life. If removing the middlemen, the banks, etc. is the answer then keeping banks there in the system is a third type error; prescribing a wrong solution to a problem that means okay' tackling the problem but not solving it. The same reason why even after all these institutions to boost wealth and living standards we still have the same problems.

### Government attitude towards its people to change.

Globally governments must change their focus and start doing everything for the people. Fear is the hindrance to progress. The government must not fear to print money if it is for the benefit of its people and be used to boost its people. This is not the same where governments print extra money that is then sent abroad to benefit projects abroad. This is the root of future and current problems because the value is giving to foreigners at the expense of the local people. This is only possible in cases where the lender is that developed and very wealth that its people will not feel any effect of such a move. But as far as I am concerned there is no country that has reached that stage yet. I am not saying it is impossible. This is your dream, but it takes a lot to achieve. Look at the USA it has claimed to be the superpower because it can print money at will to benefit its people and globally too. If you look at the US, it is the richest country on earth but also the one with the greatest debt globally.

High printing related to the developed nations means high debt.

The most developed nations are also the ones with the heavy debt and the highest and most frequent printers of money without fears of the collapse of any kind. This is true and the current thinking and practice of using the International Monetary Fund [IMF] to dictate to other nations what to do in terms of their fiscal and monetary policies are biased towards the already developed nations. These nations preach of austerity measures etc. and encourage better fiscal policies yet the top five countries with the highest debt are also the richest countries. The US is the top country with the greatest debt as of 2019, followed by the UK and France in third position and Germany in the five places. It is a matter of fact that the rich are rich simply because they are not afraid to print and all this talk about good fiscal management and restrictions globally is misleading others to keep the poor poorer and the rich richer. The nations which I have called the West in an earlier chapter created the IMF to keep them in that status quo as a political and a psychological brain manipulating technique. The idea to keep these in the superpower position. If we are to grade countries by how much they are good at financial planning, surely these countries will be at the bottom as they have a huge debt amount as much as 45 to 80% of Gross Domestic Product.

**The only way to develop at an enormous scale is to print money.**

Printing is the only method that is guaranteed at lower rates. It's not like borrowing money where you must pay interest rates or be sanctioned as part of the loan or be threatened with an attack if you fail to repay the loan. This is the only method that increases the value of the people. Governments owe their people money simply by printing more money. Automatically the people become more valuable as the governments print money. The money printed increases the wealth of the nation. Forget about what they say about inflation, etc. More money in the economy means more loans, more mortgage, more credit for new cars, education, research and development, more capital for businesses, more loans for banks, etc. Everything increases in value in one way or the other. More jobs are created as well. More disposable income, etc. More people and relatives will have money. There are also many cushions, and this means the people hold on to their savings, etc. Everything had a multiplier effect in that value is increased with every transaction that even if the country is in more debt, the living standards can never be equaled. The greatest advantage and one that has kept the developed countries growing while the developing countries stay the same as the fact that printing money makes the government owe the people and this will be very helpful when something happens to put people in difficulties say a sudden crunch or financial crises because they will use a trick called the offset rule.

**Offset Rule.**

Initially, the government's tactic of printing money instead of austerity measures shifted the debt of the people to the government. Printing money makes the government owe the taxpayers who are the people because they are printing from nowhere which means they can only owe the people. Now that they have used all the money to increase loans, provide easy capital, improve living stands and infrastructure, etc. if say a credit crunch hits a nation as more money means more inflation, etc. the effect will be minimal or even offset if they use the offset rule. During a credit crunch since the government owes the people the day, they printed extra cash now the people will owe the government when they fail to pay. In this case the debt the government owed the people will be set off with the people's failure to pay and the debt will cancel each other with no one losing as the government can further print even more money to inject into the economy so the cycle is started again but the value of the people keep increasing. Their savings are intact. When they defaulted the government used the offset rule to write off the debt [as the debt cancels each other] and now that they are at equal with no one owing anyone they can start again. The government then goes on to print more money that is injected again into the economy. Say if people bought cars, houses, and other household goods the second wave of loans or injection of money into the economy will be used for something else. As the years go by the people keep advancing accumulating wealth, the correct way from the government. The only reason why the top five countries are developed countries and the same reasons, they are the worst in debt.

Our Policy. I will deal with the effects of hyperinflation at the bottom towards the end of the chapter and provide solutions.

**Printing and printing and more printing as the only way out of poverty and not debt.**

The saying that forever indebted to you applies here very well. The idea of a government is for it to be indebted to its people. There are there to serve and increase the value of the people. Printing money rounds after rounds injecting the money into the economy to boost all kinds of development. Printing will only increase development and growth. It is a fact that the only growth just like in a human body is through huge food intakes. If you want to grow, you don't limit food intake. You keep growing and taking nothing out and keep eating common sense. All today's policies by the IMF etc. are only to keep the poor poorer. Every nation on earth has the potential and ability to become a developed country or to grow even further simply by printing more money or eating more food.

**Global empowerment and emancipation.**

Our policies, regulations, and laws are there to make every country here on earth take the bull by its horns and be responsible for their own growth. All nations on earth have this ability and can grow all that they need if education and balls to do it despite all fears and discouragement. This is the reason why most countries have their own currency apart from the Euro nations and that can explain the stagnating growth and the recent recessions and all the problems with the Euro something I will look at below.

Our aim is to educate and empower all nations. Our goal is to increase living standards and draw a line at which no one shall fall below in terms of the standards provided. It's all in your hands and don't look to anyone else and don't be tricked by handouts and don't be oppressed by sanctions as we have banned all these dirty tricks to keep a few controlling everyone. Sanctions are banned globally, and people should not be oppressed by a few countries. We stand against all this.

### Drastic change of government attitudes and fiscal policies globally.

Our approach is to change and emancipate and encourage a new way of thinking even if our methods are not perfect in the short run at least we know what they have been preaching for the past seventy years and that that does not work. Their ideas are now stale and old and to be honest obsolete. A new way of thinking. What are you to lose? If the time was a person, he or she would be a pensioner on state benefits sidelined. No offense to anyone. We need to change globally that means new thinking.

### Never Fear Debt.

Debt should be part and parcel and your major attribute if it's internal debt one you can manage. We are against any form of external debt in that it has a high chance of sovereign risk. Borrowing abroad will only put you at risk of being attacked if you default and that conflicts with our first rules; the right to life and to self -preserve. The idea behind this is that countries or nations that are prepared to lend to anyone have more power and are a threat to you. This is the reason why they lend to you in the first place. Mind you externally very few laws relate to international debt. If it is to lend nationally, then take the person to court if he defaults. If it is a foreign nation that borrowers and defaults, then you have no courts to deal with that. What can the lender do? Very few courts to deal with these issues. Countries that lend like the USA and the UK only borrow because they can use military force on those who they are lending to in case they refuse to payback. They are more a threat with nukes which they use to guarantee the return of the loans. The US is the largest lender use this notion to its advantage and can easily lend knowing that any default they can sanction or attack the defaulter. We are against such practice because this gives the US the right to make nukes and use these nukes to guarantee the return of the loans. Hell no. We are talking about potential human extinction and using nukes to force countries to pay back loans is not just irresponsible but a threat to humanity, global peace, and justice.

## Our policy and aims.

We are going to ban all international borrowing. Why borrow and pay heavy interests and unfavorable conditions when you have a God-given right simply to print and at the same time boost the value of your people. Every time you borrow globally you are lowering the value of your people and making them owe you instead of you owing them to protect them against future defaulting and hedging them to protect them. Again, borrowing abroad is increasing the other's position in the global world but weaken yourself. So, banning all global loans, etc.

## International laws regarding international credit and debt.

We must establish new courts that deal with global debt in the transitional phases before ultimately outlawing international borrowing. Institutions like the IMF are acting only to perpetuate the imbalances and inequalities and they are dead to us. We need solutions and honesty it's not working. They are like loan sharks even though they don't demand the money back their subsidiaries might impose sanctions and other unfavorable economic attributes slowing growth and development. I will look at the IMF below.

## National sovereign must mean just that.

What I think is a current problem is the lack of education in most developing leaders about money management and the best way out of this vicious circle. They say knowledge is power. My stance is to view everyone as your enemy, and you can never gain anything from them as they are your competitors so how can they have your interest at heart. The best way is to tackle all your problems yourself. Why if you are a sovereign nation rely on another country to tell you how to run your sovereign country? Why borrow from them when you can simply print and boost your people in the process.

**Selfish of governments.**

The idea lies behind the fact that most governments think it's being reduced in value if they are there to serve the people and be indebted to them forever. But this must be the sole existence of any government because without the people the government wouldn't exist. Who will they serve? So why not do whatever it takes to increase the value of your own? Why borrow and increase risks of attack in case you default when you can exercise your rights and simply print. Fear not about the debt. This is the way things are intended to be as the debt as I explained above will simply be written off to cancel out the indebtedness between you and the government. This is the natural way. The only way to grow. All other methods I can tell you that they are just fantasies to keep a few jobs for nothing. You are sovereign why not print?

Eurozone.

That brings me to the issue of the euro. The Euro centers around a common good where everyone is equal and work together to tackle problems, etc. The idea is still the same every nation within the EU can print their own money except Portugal and Luxembourg who buy their own currencies. The difference in economic wealth is regarding the idea of not afraid to be in debt. Look at Germany, the UK, and France the heavy printers and the two most heavily in debt countries they are not afraid of. They know it's better to be in debt but distribute wealth to their people. Most governments around the globe try to do what is right economically at the expense of the people they are trying to serve.

Solution to global government problems.

Education in understanding global notions is very critical in solving global issues. All the problems in the world if really understood can and must be solved.

## Role of our laws in global empowerment and economic development.

Our laws and policies are drafted in such a way that if you give the people the focus, they need everything will follow. Go out of your way. Think outside the box and do whatever it takes to make your people happy. You can please the whole people globally but if you ignore the local people, you won't last in power. Look at the Middle East and Africa. These nations ignore the simple common rules. You are indebted to the people and everything else follows. Our laws set the record straight. Most adopt austerity measures to boost the economy but how can cuts solve problems. It's like a bodybuilder starving himself when he what's growing big. Supply is the only answer relying on the fact that the multiplier effect or trickling down effect will provide a cushion to any crunches or crisis. Governments can simply write off the debt. They can simply say money is missing with no effect whatsoever apart from the only fact that the balance sheet won't balance which can be balanced by ghost figures and still the President or Prime Minister remains in power. But it's a different situation when the people are hungry, out of jobs, with cuts everywhere with other nations calling for your head.

The secret to why the developed nations never faces internal uprising a lesson for developing countries.

The developed countries will never experience revolutions in developing countries and the reason is that they understand why and how they become to be in office. They were elected by the people and put there by the people. Their sole existence is to serve the people. That is exactly what they do. They please these people first at the expense of the balance sheets and never the other way around. A lesson for the developed countries whereas the developing countries fight to reduce national debt. What happens is that one term of a President or Prime Minister is completed making cuts and the term of the next President or Prime Minister spent boosting spending and printing, etc. It is a vicious circle that has kept the developing nations as developing.

## A case of China.

China has learned this aspect and ever since the leaders have ignored global condemnation and printed money increase the nation's debt to the highest levels ever and what was the result. China in terms of exports and economic development can be said to be a global power that has understood what is needed to get out of poverty and empower its people. Japan is another country as well as doing the same boosting economic growth even though it is slightly different in Japan with more foreign debt than the domestic one. The US is heavily indebted to China and Japan and this is weakening the US's global stance as the superpower. We can see problems back home in the US with high unemployment even though rates have fallen since the new President took over. Still a lot to be done. The more you borrow abroad the more you export wealth at the expense of your own people.

## Misuse and wasted.

A major factor I want to clarify is the fact that printing money does not always equal increased wealth. There are a lot of factors that must be considered too. Wastages and corruption can have a negative impact on the idea above. Care must be taken to read the context in which this is achievable. Corruption can reverse the benefits as in most cases the people don't feel the effects of increased wealth through printing as the money is siphoned or is held within a few percentages while the majority suffers.

## Need for a holistic approach that addresses all the issues.

Transparent structures that have people at heart are important and a must. You can print as much as you can but if it does not reach the intended recipient, then this is a waste that increases the problems with stagnating economies lack money, credit, jobs, mortgages, etc. despite huge monies that are misused. Corruption to be eliminated. Increase human rights awareness and government accountability will go a long way to solving all these problems. Our laws will center around all the issues and the emphasis on people will see a change in the long run. Initial implementation is other issues that are not fully addressed can create pseudo-scenarios where problems exasperate before becoming stable again. A new court system is needed to deal with bottlenecks, etc.

## Support and advise.

Our role must be supervisory and guiding in a way of educating the globe on the best ways to deal with global issues. To grow is not to be afraid to be in debt.

## Methods to deal with debt.

Debt is and must be part of any government. I will explain this using bodybuilding training. If you are bulking or intending to grow, it's unwise to be afraid of pain. Pain makes you grow. Pain is growth. If you are training and you don't feel pain your percentage change in muscle volume and strength will be very minimal. Muscle grows in response to pain. The first stages of training are the most difficult and painful as your body is not used to the pain. But this is the time too with the greatest increase in percentage changes as the body grows to cushion the weight and therefore the pain. No pain no gain. This applies here too. Debt is a pain not to be avoided as it is needed for growth so that tomorrow you are in better shape. You can't grow without pain and you can't grow without debt. Austerity and all that stuff are just ways of stalling growth delaying tactics. If you are serious about growth, then debt should be a must but be very cautious you need proper channels in place for the generated funds to be used effectively otherwise it's a huge costly waste.

It's easy to say print money and equally easy to waste that money through corruption, mismanagement, lack of understanding of what is needed. We are there to guide and provide a framework and platform to be used as the base platform in that people can use our laws as reference points. People can use our laws as guidance to see if they are on the right path. We are not proposing a blanket policy or framework for everyone. Like I have been arguing throughout the book we believe in the sovereignty of every nation. We are saying global reliance on others is the root of all these issues we have today. Just as the name means sovereign must mean sovereign. We don't like situations of dependencies. Crying for loans abroad when you can simply print more money. To achieve a level of standard we are going to set, nations must act as sovereign nations and start tackling issues in their countries rather than waiting to be rescued.

## More Money Printing: Link between huge debt, wealth and living standards.

The four biggest developed nations are the ones with huge debt. Huge debt means money spent among its people boosting the local people's wealth and status. The standard we will set to be achieved by every nation on earth is a standard never achieved before and this will be a universal standard anything below will be illegal. To achieve this the only way is for the government to print more money and never look at the balance sheet for a certain period that we will allocate. The idea is to boost every nation on earth without further putting it in more debt. Imagine if already in debt and then borrow abroad with a different currency than the one you can print. Paying or expected to pay huge fees in return. The result will be disastrous, and we have a real-life case study in Greece. Our proposals work only if the currency to be printed is own money they can print locally.

Countries should not be afraid to be in debt and countries like Poland, Spain, Holland, etc. must not worry too much about balancing books but their goal must be to empower their people. If Poland is to do like the big four US, UK, France, Germany, etc. they have a greater chance of heavily boosting their people's wealth that can increase the value of the zloty greatly to Euro levels. They must quit emphasizing debt-free measures. These tactics will keep their countries with little wealth than they can potentially have. The reason is that most countries gained wealth during the credit crunch as the financial crises occurred. When a crisis occurs as in 2008 one there are winners and losers. Some people benefit as they can purchase houses and completely pay for these increasing their value as they end up with assets. Companies can make huge housing developments that will later be owned by the people. Spending is the answer and doing nothing in terms of spending with the aim not to have a crisis is absurd and can constitute a lack of empathy with the local people who put you in power as you are concerned about balancing figures and not with the wealth and welfare of your people. New laws around this area too. It will be illegal in our New World to balance books and have no debt while living standards of your people are pathetically low. Criminal charges to be brought to these leaders. If 194 countries are defaulting and only you do not. Does that mean you might be right? In most cases not it's because you are not seeing the global picture. The idea is to lose to be in debt but improve the wealth of everyone. More loans, credit for better housing, increase the value of your currency to its potential levels. In the first five years, it will be acceptable for countries to be in debt and not balance their books as long as the people's wealth has increased through loans, etc. which they might not pay back but to be written off by the governments. The reasons which I will explain below. Fight corruption if it is the problem and above all don't be afraid to print because first you are sovereign and secondly you can use the offset rule to write off the debt and thirdly you can create a risk or contingent fund that cushions the defaults. This acts more like a depreciation account where companies set aside money at the beginning to account for the fall of the value of their assets.

Debt Risk management and planning.

Another very important aspect of our proposal is the fact that we can set aside a separate account and funds in it that will cushion the debt defaults. So, debt in this case is part of being a government. Without debt written on your forehead means you are not a government with the interest for the people and our laws can make you be dragged to court for negligence and showing no care for the welfare and quality of life of your own people for personal political agendas. The E-laws will haunt you to death. You are in government to be indebted to your people forever. If you don't understand this our laws will teach you a lesson. So, don't fear debt but put things in place to cushion that.

**Print more but don't expect all to be paid back but a certain percentage.**

The idea here is that you don't stop lending because of fear that people will default and lose everything. Secretly at the beginning apportion a certain percentage of that debt as 'lost or irrecoverable' just like a depreciation account would work. If you bought a car for say $10 000. Every year after you write off say $1000 the first year so that its value will be $9000 the next year. Say after five years the value of the car would be $5 000. So, after 5 years you would expect to get back only half the amount you paid for it say if you sell the car. Similarly, as you are a government, you are not a loan shark like the banks there to make a kill taking every penny, they can lay their hands on. After all, you printed this money and owe the people this money. The more of the money they keep the more they reduce your debt to them. In the end, if they default, they will still have savings, jobs, and loans as well and you must be prepared to intervene and bail-out people, not bloody banks. The idea is not to make people lose whatever they have accumulated. Remember our goal is to increase the people's wealth globally. If they fail to repay offer cheaper more loans with the view as to write off a percentage of the debt or use the offset rule to achieve a zero balance.

**Sanctions of the IMF and the UN act against Sovereignty and wrong to us.**

Banning of sanctions globally and banning of institutions like the IMF who are there just to increase global inequalities etc. Empower everyone to be sovereign as the name means and print your own money to boost never seen before development. Don't rely on institutions created just after the war to help those who created them with little ways of real impact. My idea is based around the idea of every nation being sovereign. If you are sovereign, why rely on institutions that are not sovereign themselves for handouts. Why drink from the cup when you can drink from the well applies here. I am not against post-war institutions per se, but I am arguing that for the past seventy years they have not solved the global problems. The system has crashed and only a new system is needed. This is the new system. I am not going to look at the problems of the IMF or the UN for the matter my point is if the US the most developed nation can simply print more money for all its problems and write off debt in a flash what is stopping you from doing the same? Are you sovereign and how sovereign?

Once that's understood I think all our laws will connect and provide a way forward to take the people out of today's problems.

### Our stance.

We believe we as Tomorrow's World Order a global leader and the overseer with impartial views and everyone's needs at heart, we think more is needed to tackle global financial issues, including debt. We shall have our own currencies that are provided globally and can supplement or work side by side with local currencies. These are digital but transparent to cushion the effects and early shock-waves and provide an alternate cushion. Our money FutureGoldCoin or simply FutureGold will be used to act as a cushion against debt defaults etc. giving all nations a cushion and peace of mind. Our money will be used globally as well with transparency.

### Futuregoldcoin. Answer to Hyperinflation.

This is not a cryptocurrency but an Apocalypto currency in that it is the opposite of the cryptocurrency that is for peer-to-peer transactions that needs hidden messages as they are private between friends, etc. Our money will be Calypto short for Apocalypto but must not be confused with the end of the day's messages of doom, etc. The name comes from the Greek or Latin name meaning revealed in that the currency transactions are not hidden. There is a need for transparency when dealing with governments in government transactions. The transactions can still be done on a blockchain style but will resemble block within blocks bundled together and or compressed and to be unzipped when needed. The transactions can be in billions hence the need to group like transaction according to the source of function, etc. This system can replace the IMF with its bureaucratic and inefficient nature and above all with its being politicized and inability to solve other social factors with the resultant global inequalities and problems. This will be open to everyone and at short notice with issues solved instantly and all transactions for all to see to increase transparency, etc. This is not involving any human bias etc. as the money can be accessed easily with little or no cost as it reduces the middlemen the IMF, UN, etc. This is like a cushion and last resort as all nations are encouraged and empowered to print and just provide cushions. My argument is that recession and financial crisis can be cushioned if happening during the early stages. Heavy developed nations even if their debt is high the wealth is enough to cushion most from any crises. These people will have huge savings, capital tied in assets in $millions, a lot of assets more cars per household, etc. When the worst hits they can sell some and still be better off than say a nation where people have little income, savings and few properties.

## Dealing with hyperinflation

The most known issue is that printing more money can lead to hyperinflation, but we have a solution to that. The idea throughout this book is not just to print without the supporting infrastructure and policies to help boost production, industrialization, and development of new goods, etc. A holistic approach is needed to avoid hyperinflation as printing money can easily increase prices if there is no correspondence increased in the production of goods, etc. Printed money is to be used initially to boost development creating more jobs and encouraging more industries, more goods manufacturing, etc. The first wave is plowed back to increase production that will in turn increase demand and consumption.

Our currency will be used as a cushion where nations facing hyperinflation can temporarily abandon their currency until they have established a huge industrial base or developmental base to accompany extra money supply with huge developments and production of goods. Our currency will be global and can be adopted anytime if needed with even better results that it will be available globally and not specific to one country say the US that tends to restrict other nations' growth in industrial production etc. as they end up importing rather than making their own in line with their local currency. Above all, we will have agreements with all governments for our money to be used globally as to cushion hyperinflation of local currencies and be trusted as well. All nations to use two currencies; their own currency to steer growth and autonomy and ours as the backup. Normally governments having hyperinflation are mistrusted governments due to corruption, misuse, the mismanagement that in turn dampen the people spirits and destroys the confidence that most people would not create the needed jobs and production to cushion against hyperinflation. We will restore trust as our money is revealed in that transparency is embedded in the idea with records and transactions permanently recorded and available on request with business and the foreigners to invest in this country choosing to use our currency as the situation improves then reverts to local currencies. We can't tolerate a situation where fears of hyperinflation will keep everyone below the poverty level. We shall never have countries that are referred to as the developing countries. One standard.

**Global standardization.**

One criterion one standard throughout the world. One currency Futuregoldcoin that can be supplemented with other peer-to-peer currencies like Calycoin for personal use with all official government transaction processes only in Future Gold Coin and recorded in separate ledgers or blocks separating government and private spending. Everything in FutureGoldCoin ledgers or blockchain for government and official use and everything in Calycoin as personal all these to be side by side with country-specific currency. You are sovereign so you must use your own currency together with ours for growth and wealth and to fight hyperinflation.

The advantages of adopting Future Gold Coin is that we will make agreements with you still to use this currency as your own with every monetary and fiscal policy with the ability to even create more and set inflation levels things you can't do if you are to adopt say the US dollar. Most countries facing hyperinflation will resort to fully adopting the US dollar but with no rights to any monetary policies in the end can mean temporary loss of sovereignty as a country can be viewed as under another country. Our money will remove all these, and we can guarantee you using our currency as if it was your own.

Using the US dollar to fight hyperinflation can further damage that countries trust bestowed on them by the people. The people will believe it will be difficult if not impossible for the government to have local influences that are suited to their needs. The US Federal Bureau can influence local policies through the dollar which can act against local needs. Above all, it is a disadvantage to the US since they can't use the devaluation of their currency as a strategy to fight hyperinflation. But thanks to us they can now if they adopt our currency the FutureGoldCoin as the only New Single Reserve Global Currency.

Dollarization can mean the inability of any nation to use fiscal measures to help boost their economies through devaluing to increase export to gain more foreign currency and boost growth, etc.

Adoption of our currency Future Gold Coin and or Calycoin during hyperinflation must be part of the solution. Governments in these situations must stop being involved in anything that requires the export of money abroad without tangible effects e.g. supporting wars as this can increase periods of hyperinflation, etc. You can see the reason why we banned wars in the first place here. If you are printing money, you can't spend that money abroad without feeling the effects of hyperinflation. You must not export your printed money abroad during the printing years. All new money to be used locally within the country. In this case, the US might get our FutureGoldCoin and use this for international obligations. No nation facing hyperinflation must be subjected to other punishment e.g. sanctions, etc. As global leaders, we will also provide stability to any country through temporary inflation to stabilize the government and instill trust as well so that recovery is fast and a country can continue to use our currency as theirs with all controls without any loss in control, etc. Our two currency can and will deal with any inflation with the Calycoin used for use in spending and the FutureGoldCoin for development projects to increase supply of goods on top of their own currency. Mind you I spoke of our Global Saving Reserve Bank? [GSRB]. This is to hold the newly printed money of every nation on earth to avoid flooding the economy but instead to deposit this new money in our

GSRB as collateral where we will issue ours which they take and use in the economy depending on hyperinflation levels. The idea within the first years is to encourage printing and depositing as savings. The problem of hyperinflation arises when the government prints money for spending. New money is for boosting the economy and not to service debts and deficits initially. These governments can adopt our currencies for spending and their own or our FutureGoldCoin for further development. Printing of this money is not just printing for the sake of it but a guided process that visualizes new money as blood in the body with too much or too little causing problems of high blood pressure or low blood pressure that is inflation and deflation. A clever technique can be used to print a certain amount in relation to the money already available. We will guide nations on the right amounts to print at a time to ensure a smooth transition until one's money is back on track. They can even choose to adopt ours for good. Our money will not be like the Euro in that it is not regulated or does not depend on prices being subsided. The effects of hyperinflation are to encourage people to buy now cheaper to avoid higher prices tomorrow, so demand becomes high due to scarcity without support production and in the end, the goods run out sending prices even higher. Other measures can be put in place to ensure production and increased supply while maintaining lower prices. A lot of factors play a part that a holistic approach is the best. Never mind the initial hyperinflation but aim to tackle the issue fast and permanently. I know I dealt much on this topic as it is central to the success or failure of any initiative. Sort out the money first, rebuild buffers to offset future risks, etc. and everything else follows if you obey our laws, regulations, and policies.

### Gross Domestic Product [GDP] and growth.

Once the above is tackled everything else is easy. GDP will grow as well in response to the level of debt as debt is not always a bad thing as people want you to believe, Debt can mean new jobs, more capital, more production, more disposable income, etc. all which tend to influence GDP. Again, the world's countries with the highest GDP s are the same countries with huge debt who are not afraid to print who don't care about national debt but with the welfare of their people. The US again tops this list. So, don't be misled by the IMF encouraging everyone to live within their means, etc. but to put buffers to cushion bad debt, etc.

## Cleaning the Corrupt System.

Ever wonder why digital currency has been on the rise lately? The fiat system is corrupt, and every monetary transaction has been laced with viral watermarks? Yes, every transaction of fiat you make is accompanied by a corresponding watermark that is a viral-digital mark tracked using satellites. The whole world is now flooded with these digital-viral-watermarks that it's rare to find 'normal people' nowadays. Some countries have gone way too far protecting money. Going to lengths to chip all their people and assign digital watermarks that accompany every transaction you make. I know from their point of view they might see this as an effective way of controlling and protecting the money. They view national fiat money the same as blood that must be maintained at the same levels to avoid inflation or deflation as in high blood pressure and low blood pressure, respectively. These few evil countries have gone to lengths to track everyone's purchase and transactions that they even know how much you have in your bank account and telling everyone is you are loaded or not as a way of keeping an eye on the money but a gross violation of everything we stand for. Invasion of privacy. Breaking of rights to life laws. Torture and freedom from hacking and all degrading treatments. These governments have crossed the line and broken every international rule on earth. They have used protecting money as an excuse, but the truth is these are worse than Hitler. That is what Hitler did physically with the Jews who kept money under the bed and not in the banks. Nowadays through hacking the same is till occurring with watermarks and satellites used but the same way that everything is hidden, secretly with torture chips out of sight and operated remotely. The whole population has been loaded with these watermarks that even those who devised these now don't know what to do. But there is hope we know exactly what to do with such evil. They are breaking all our laws. Everyone here has a right to life. Everyone has a right to defend himself or herself. There is no excuse for evil whatsoever. Do you think protecting money is more important than human life? Do you think your jobs are more important than human life? Do you think we can tolerate evil this period in time? The world has been tainted. All their people are corrupted loaded with watermarks. Look around you. Can you tell the difference between what is natural and what is man-made? If people, make digital agents that erode the quality of all humanity in the name of protecting money can they not be classed as the enemy of mankind? What is important to you? Money or human life? First, in order to understand our solutions, you must first understand the problem at hand. Everyone somehow has been chipped and assigned a number like your driving license or for those who understand the blockchain and cryptocurrency it's like the public key. Every transaction you make is accompanied by a watermark one that's specific to you. Everyone you send money also receives an unwanted gift which is your watermark or your other digital identity. You pay for everything for this government to track every move and account for the money in the economy they also send that watermark. The recipient of the money to lose that watermark he or she must forward the same amount ideally but how many of you receive with the right hand and forward the payment with the left hand? It's just not practical. So, in the end people have no option they must keep the money. No one wants to work for someone else, so they are left with no option to keep the money and the watermark. Overtime the world society starts to look like zombies you can tell something artificial is going on. The whole system now relies on everyone having to be loaded with watermarks that will end up killing them. Do they have an option if this is systematized and institutionalized?

The whole world now is corrupted. The fiat money system itself is not the problem but has now been associated with all kinds of government dirty tricks and manipulation of their people. Going around parading your financial status to everyone to gain the trust of the people they are telling. This is a government in the twenty-first century doing this to its own people. Loading everyone with all kinds of watermarks to protect the money, etc. The chips that are being used to track through GPS and digital software are all illegal in the first place with people hacked at birth without their knowledge that this seemed to be the norm. Is it? Or the fact that it is systemic and done by the government especially with everything to do with money leaves people with no option. We don't care about the money. A wise brain will know that you can simply print the money all you need is time and investment in counter hyperinflation techniques. Our main concerns are the right to life. The quality of life and the right to defend one's self. All these tricks to shield money are against what we stand for. They might run around every day chasing the money but it's against everything in the law books. A nation that does not respect its own people the same people who put them in power is an evil government. Shall we let old barbaric practices flourish at the expense of what we stand for? Or it's time we put an end to all this. The traumatic effect can and might give rise to a response and an awakening that this is wrong. In the New World, such acts can only get one dragged to court. That is evil thinking a corroded brain that will never change. Money is nothing and these good-boys and good-girls who go to extremes to please those in power should be dealt with accordingly. Even if the leader breaks our rules to us, he will be the same as the laymen facing the same punishment. There is no immunity for people who are still medieval times when we all have moved.

## The Cleaning Operation.

Now a new system that captures all these watermarks and sends them back to the sender is in place. What goes around comes around applies here. The world has listened. Life is more important than money. It's only unwise to run around chasing money when your leaders can easily print more. It's inferior thinking and a gross miscarriage of justice for some people to think that they can load everyone with watermarks to safeguard the circulating money. This is a lack of understanding of what is important in life. It's not ignorance but evil that drives these people. So first we have the task of minimizing the effects of the watermark. We need to identify the source and deal with it as per our laws. These people doing this are dead to us. The watermarks no matter what reduce the life expectancy of their people and contamination can be a problem. We have started to a 'cleaning processes' that will enable people to 'trap' the watermarks and collect these. The blockchain is a one-way of doing this. Since fiat money is the one linked to these watermarks for some time, we shall shift to the digital blockchain system that will always capture and keep these watermarks for the team to have enough to work on. We shall identify and return these to the rightful owners and see how they will like that. We say it's evil deliberately killing your people nevertheless others globally just because of money. The collection will involve decrypting and identifying transactions. The blockchain makes it easy for these people to increase their activities in the hope to put people off this new system but at the same time will enable us enough watermarks to identify these and the source. The idea is that every transaction is permanently written in the blocks for visiting in the future collecting any digital watermarks as well for analysis. The second phase is associated with severe punishments for these culprits. Life must be of the highest level and all this action against our dreams. Stop or we will stop you. Any act that breaks the first rule can only make one be identified as the enemy of mankind and the idea of collective punishment applies here.

### Our Stance on those Harboring Evil.

The axis of evil applies here too. Some nations have done everything they can to break all international rules on earth to provoke others into acting and above all simply because they have the backing of the most powerful cults, etc. Some cults like NATO 'harbor evil nations' that are still doing everything banned by international laws, torture, hacking, breach of human rights, tampering with life, mass murder, making of digital or cyber weapons and using these on foreigners in the name of protection. Making otherwise simple life difficult in order to justify protection and create jobs for their apparatus. This is evil and anyone who harbors these nations by articles like Article 5 is an enemy of mankind. We are not against any cults if they obey international laws and our laws but if they defend evil when everyone knows that they are no angles it is a cause for concern something that we can't tolerate. These nations have devised tricks to provoke others knowing that any attempt to defend oneself can trigger Article 5, a blanket immunity whether they are right or wrong. NATO being NATO a regional cult to protect a specialized group of nations who qualify by certain rights attributed by geographical position and us being a global power we think if NATO does not evolve surely there can never be a place of cults like that, 'Our enemy is a radical network of evil and every governments that supports them…'

[Wikipedia].

If NATO had not given everyone express immunity but insisted on nations being judged on merit, then we would not have the problems we have today. Anyone who supports the mass murder of children and women is not just our enemy but also an enemy of mankind.

## What is wrong with the current system?

The system has become a government apparatus for abuse and a way of controlling the people rather than anything else. The governments have broken all the rules, from chipping everyone to hacking and illegal surveillance. They go around robbing and killing people around the globe put their trust in NATO for protection and what does NATO do? Ignore and pretend nothing is happening. 500 000 women and children dead. The world now loaded with watermarks and people are starting to look like zombies. We are saying that the whole system needs a total overhaul. Changing the way people think and act if not then changing them is the only option for we shall never tolerate evil anymore. The world has changed than it was decades ago. An approach or strategy for global issues has and must go beyond solving the methodology but the way people think and perceive the issues at hand. A comprehensive approach is needed that focuses on education as well so that everyone understands the real root of the global issues.

# CHAPTER THIRTY-NINE

VICTORY!

We won already the day we came up with our plan where every step is a win and the winning never stops even after we have achieved all that we planned to do and achieve.

We won the day we put a law to protect the weak, innocent but highly valued leaders of tomorrow in women and children.

We won when I said no woman or child shall die at the hands of evil ignorant and arrogant leaders.

We won when I said no soldier shall be made to sacrifice his life to protect your leaders. Being a soldier is a profession, and just like any other, why should they sacrifice old age too? Commands and reckless missions to get our best boys and girls be slaughtered as to reduce the military wage bill is not just evil but a crime punishable by death. Life for life applies here.

We won when we declared war on governments reversing everything and killing their own by reducing life span through hacking causing early onset of graying and wrinkles to kill them faster as a population control measure.

We won when we declared war on governments making bio-engineered, digital and cyber viruses and test these on others out of unconfirmed fears of global population catastrophes.

We won when we declared war as illegal and banned globally. I said a lot about the trauma wars create.

We won when we banned the production, use, selling, keeping, or acquiring weapons of any form.

We won when we challenged the military to evolve and do the opposite of everything they do; they can kill can they create life too? They destroy and can they build? They weaken, can they strengthen? They make wounds and can they heal wounds? They can make weapons can they destroy weapons. Can they take on the challenge of the day and lead in the technology that helps humanity?

We won when we advocated for a better quality of life for everyone. The current normal standards will be banned in that providing the life we have today will be illegal. Minimum standards to be raised with anything in conflict with quality of life eliminated. Poor buildings with banned materials etc. all to be banned. A lot of money from printing and the military budget to be used for development and technological advancement to boost humanity.

We won when we stepped in and banned institutions and organizations that are causing the current problems and giving people a false sense of security helping the West to slaughter women and children in thousands.

We won when we banned all sanctions. It is illegal to impose sanctions of any kind on other sovereign nations. Sanctions are evil tactics that hold women and children in ransom and use them as baits before slaughtering them. We have a Responsibility to Act and be the voice of the voiceless. The protector of the weak.

We won when we declared an end of the defense stage and moving now into networking and cooperation. We are never going to waste resources making things we don't need in the weapon, etc.

We won when we challenged the whole world to think outside the box and change for the better. We have so much potential and not operating where we should be. Opportunity cost is a crime too and we are not here to procrastinate and disadvantage future generations.

We won when we banned the use of fossil fuels like oil by a certain date globally. That means challenging everyone to think and come up with better alternatives to fuel forms. Oil is going to be extinct anywhere why not start looking for new solutions now and become proactive? We might even find better renewable fuels and save the planet too by reducing gasses in the atmosphere and reducing climate change. Improving the quality of life in the process.

We won when we banned all vehicles by a certain date; they use fossil fuels. We have electric cars now even though they are still expensive but at least that is the start.

We won when we declared war with useless institutions that create problems so that they have a salary pretending to solve global problems. Pretense carries a maximum punishment in that it blocks others who might have helped. It's stalling and frustrating to progress a crime that can cost lives and as such severely punishable. The only way to understand this is to dismantle the organization concerned until it ceases operations and existence.

We won when we made the legal system that is laws etc. open 24 hours with the law blockchain supplementing the traditional courts who will evolve too.

We won when we declared the removal of time limits on any case. We have courts open 24 hours why have time limits on when a case will be brought up. We shall have permanent records of evidence on the blockchain with everyone educated to send evidence to the blockchain and judiciary system linked to the blockchain. The evolved courts dealing with complex cases, etc.

We won when we removed protection and all kinds of immunity and removing the age when a person can stand trial. If the person is alive, he can stand trial for a crime he or she committed.

We won when we introduced global identities linked to the blockchain or another fast method similar to where everything is simplified and easy above all accessible for everyone. We shall give everyone universal global identities that enable smooth flows between countries.

We won when we stood as the global advisers to the leaders and President and Prime Ministers in making sound decisions based on facts and not the-heat-of-the moment thing that can come back and hunt them in the future. We must have a dedicated team to advise everyone if needed.

We won when we banned landmines etc. and forced the owners to remove these at their cost.

We won when we educated everyone about our role here on earth.

# CHAPTER FORTY

## DOCUMENTS: FUTUREGOLDCOIN, PATENTS, AND LAWS.

### Background and Purpose

This will be a government monetary system to work side by side or in the end replace the fiat monetary system where corruption, fraud, bureaucracy and tampering all creates issues with unaccounted-for money and the people's mistrust as governments simply prints more money with the resultant inflation. Too many links between governments and banks ending up with situations that banks enslave everyone with loans and high fees knowing the government will bail-them-out buying all those who can't afford repayments as slaves automatically put on death row with illegal tagging and blackmailing. This is the answer to a block in block bundled transaction system at macro-level covering departments. This uses advanced algorithms that use multiple blockchains with blocks inside blocks. This provides transparency as the information in blocks is not encrypted but bundled or compressed together to be unbundled or uncompressed on request. This is a macro-level digital currency that works side by side with cryptocurrency but ideally for government transactions or buying of government services.

### Essential Function

This is a digital currency at the macro-level that uses bundled transactions placed in blocks that are then placed in blockchains. The transaction is not encrypted for transparency and can easily be accessed upon request and unbundled or uncompressed. The idea is to make the whole system transparent and permanent without alterations. This will be used with a digital identification service where the person can digitally prove his or her identity digitally and the id then linked to the transactions as they are entered in the blocks before being bundled. So, you can identify the user and the transaction which is not the same with the fiat system where money can't link to a specific person and transaction can be entered without identifying oneself. This different from cryptocurrency in that cryptocurrency is for micro-level peer-to-peer and privacy is important hence the encryption. Here, transparency is important for accountability and an efficient system where every transaction can be traced back to a specific identity. This uses advanced algorithms with blocks of bundled transactions placed in blockchains. Currency to be used globally Ideally, the money should be converted from say cryptocurrency to cryptocurrency depending on use. All government transactions or payment of government services to be in Apocalypto currency [CalyptoCurrency our FutureGoldCoin] because the idea is that recording of every transaction will be separated depending on whether it's for personal or government services and goods, etc. Government transactions will have to be bundled before being placed in blocks, whereas peer-to-peer transactions can be entered straight into a blockchain.

## Result

This removes issues of mistrust in the current fiat monetary system. This solves issues of corruption and fraud, as all transactions are recorded permanently without encryption for all to see upon request. It solves issues of government tampering where they can simply print more money with the resultant inflation. It increases accountability if used with the digital identity technology which I will patent as well that links the person and every transaction. There is no secrecy or privacy to be incorporated into the system. This is the opposite of the cryptocurrency in that cryptocurrency is a private thing with encryption and remaining anonymous at the heart of the invention whereas this is at the macro-level and where transparency and accountability are paramount. Instead of just blockchains with transactions, we have bundled together transactions in blockchains that are placed in main blockchains. This removes cumbersome bureaucracy and costs as well, solving a lot of problems due to human error and corruption. This builds trust in

the government and makes everyone accountable as each
transaction can be traced back to a person.

# CHAPTER FORTY-ONE

FUNDAMENTAL LAWS.

## Global Leader, National Sovereignty and National Leadership.

1. Declaration that the globe is a single entity and or should be such. Whatever laws and principles all affect the whole globe nevertheless each individual state will have its own laws and rules but also these must be complementary to the global laws and not in conflict. To achieve networking and cooperation, the globe must act as one limiting difference but maintain state autonomy.

2. Tomorrow's World Order is the global leader but has an overseer role where it is a mandate for it to establish and provide a working platform for all other nations to network and cooperate for the advancement of mankind. Its initial primary role is to act as a catalyst to speed up the shift from defensive economies to networking and cooperative. It must write laws and implement these. Laws that will spearhead the move away from the defensive economies. A framework to put things in place so that mankind won't revert to the 'tried and trusted'. A framework for proactive decision making and adjustments as we enter a new era and a new road with so many unpredictable.

   *A framework to find the best course of action and to guide everyone.

   * A framework to act as the facilitator.

   * A framework to act as the negotiator.

   * A framework that will help to impose effective laws that are fundamental to the advancement of humanity to the next stage of development.

   A framework that will see our laws be obeyed and respected globally and where there are violations to assess the punishment and implement it.

*We are to represent everyone as we are not biased and can treat everyone fairly.

3. Sovereignty of all nations.

Our principle laws state that each nation is sovereign in the fundamental sense that it's up to each nation to control its destiny. We are against the current thinking that some sovereign nations must be under another sovereign nation or established bodies like the UN, etc. who have no sovereign powers.

A sovereign nation;

"Sovereignty. ... Sovereignty is the power of a state to do everything necessary to govern itself, such as making, executing, and applying laws; imposing and collecting taxes; making self-defense decisions and peace, and forming treaties or engaging in commerce with the foreign nation."

[Legal dictionary].

We believe the only way to empower every country is to empower it to be self-sufficient enough in every sense of the word and be as sovereign as can be. We believe in empowerment to a level never achieved before and this can only happen if each state recognizes this and affirms its stance and believes that this is the only way to riches and solving global problems. We are against hands outs to sovereign nations. We are against imposing sanctions to control and manipulate others, etc. We believe each sovereign nation can control its destiny. All they need is the belief and self-conviction that they can do it and do it. Gone are the days where nations look to other nations for handouts. Look to the IMF for loans, etc. You are sovereign and we have empowered everyone never to take any loans. Never to ask for handouts and never to be sanctioned. We banned all these. If you are sovereign all this is within your power. You have the power to print and mint your own money. It's a right we will give everyone. Exercise that right. Sovereign means sovereign and we mean that. We will ban institutions that sink other nations into debt through biased loans that are just there to manipulate and control others. The IMF doesn't have rights or powers to print or mint money so why rely on them? Master the art of printing money and fighting hyperinflation. Our currency will help you with that.

Our fundamental principle is the sheer acknowledgment that each nation has the power to control their destiny and defined how rich they can be and as such must never look for outside help but to be self-sufficient and as sovereign, as can be.

Leaders, Prime Ministers, Presidents, etc. have powers to rule and control the administrative and external affairs of their nations if their actions don't conflict with our laws. This also means that we have stripped the right to declare wars or make weapons or kill women and children etc. Otherwise, these leaders still have the same powers to rule effectively and make sound decisions to boost economic growth and development. They have sole prerogatives if they don't breach our laws, and everything must be complementary. We will empower them to have powers to make peace treaties and work well with others. We are not banning differences for we shall never be equal per see but we shall strive to be equal for some years to come until we have found common ground. We are not banning fighting for competitiveness aims no. They can fight each other if no one dies and without using weapons if that means doing it the old cowboy way so be it.

4.  Linked to the above point is the need to see national and global debt as part and parcel of the advancement and development of any nation and global. National debt is an inevitable part of development and economic growth and must not be feared.

Our aim is to increase the national wealth of every nation on earth and make all nations developed. It's achievable, and this is the only way to grow and increase the wealth of a nation. We have seen all kinds of fiscal and economic planning for the past seventy years and it's not working. Our strategy is to give every nation on earth a five-year grace period where debt is not to be feared or even talked about.

5.  Five-year printing plan.

We strongly believe that to grow and develop is only through the printing of money. There are no other plans or tactics that can induce growth other than increasing gradually the supply of new money. Only new money can increase growth. We are against borrowing from other nations or institutions like the IMF. The fundamental law of state sovereignty is the only vehicle for development. For a five-year continuous growth plan; every state must gradually and systematically increase the supply of their new money without fears for hyperinflation or national debt. At the same time, no external loans or funds must be accepted unless it's interest-free or your own. No international interventions that use local currencies with time frames.

i]    Fundamental principle here is to cut off paying any interest rates by borrowing. Printing your own is free and instantly increase supply in a flash and the only people the state or government will owe, are its own people.

ii]   Printing money means the government concerned owes its people money and when this happens the value of its people increases rapidly. What's best to print money easy and fast with interest-free, boosting the economy and above all increasing the value of your citizens exponentially?

iii]  Like I said the national debt is part and parcel of growth and must not be feared or give people sleepless nights. We have everything under control.

6.  It is a compulsory global plan for every sovereign nation that has and must have powers to print and mint their own money. Our plan is that for five years every nation prints money and increases the value of its economy and people, regardless. It is a must. I will explain later how to deal with hyperinflation, but no one should be worried about this if you do it systematically and periodically as advised by our team hyperinflation will not be a problem.

7.  How to deal with debt. The current debt is difficult to solve

because it might belong to external sources. We shall negotiate with everyone concerned and see if global debt can all be written off mutually before we start afresh. We have methods to deal with this debt.

i]     Treat global debt as a depreciating attribute of a nation rather than as an asset that increases in value. Our aim is to be realistic. We don't want situations like today where global debt has risen to $244 trillion and still growing when we know there is no way we are going to resolve this and pay it. So, we shall use the principle of depreciation to deal with national and global debt. Each debt must depreciate with time. We shall nominate depreciation percentages for the whole globe. Say for example debt shall depreciate by 30% the first year, then 20% the second year and then by 15%, 10% and the fifth year by 5%. Meaning if you have a national debt of $100 million the next year the debt will have fallen by 30% to $70 million and so on.

ii]    We are acknowledging that debt is part of the system and it will always be there no matter what we do. To grow and develop a nation to borrow money through printing new money only which is a cheap and freeway. The current system of borrowing from others is increasing global problems.

### Dealing with Debt.

iii]   How to deal with the five-year printing plan vis-à-vis debt. Offset rule. The idea here is that when governments print new money, it owes its citizens the debt. When it spends on the people and economy it boosts growth. What it must do is to encourage lending ideally directly somehow or through banks. We will work on that later. It can do that through banks in the meantime. Increase loans and mortgages. If the people defaults which must be seen as well as part and parcel of the system as a side effect of increased money the government must act and not leave its citizens the ones whom they have increased value when they printed the money lose this value.

iv]    So what does it do. It's a government's mandate and

obligation or duty of care to its citizens to bail-out them. Government bailing-out citizens and not banks. We are against governments bailing-out banks. Why banks? When you have printed new money, you increase the value of your citizens. When they are failing to pay you step in and bail-them-out through new loans and or mortgages.

Offset rule. Initially, the government owed its citizens and now the government will sort of have paid the debt by bailing-out citizens. So, this offset the previous 'I owe you' clause now they will be on an equal footing. So, any debt is to be written off by the government without victimizing its citizens. This is the true role and reason for the existence of any government to be indebted to its citizens forever.

8. After five years of printing money, all the national debt and global debt must be written off. We have seen this method of dealing with debt for the past seventy years since all these monetary institutions were created and honestly, it's not working, $244 trillion is a large number not to act. Our methods have intelligent thinking and a sure-fire way of solving this issue.

9. Debt Relief Orders.

   A very vital tool to clear the ever-growing national and global debt. We acknowledged that debt is inevitable and part and parcel of the need to grow. Without debt, no nation will experience growth because you need new money which you can only print and therefore, we are saying it's better to owe your citizens than externals. So, the current debt must be dealt with a Debt Relief Order. It is absurd to think that we can grow and service the debt or even pay it off. So, we want real growth and be realistic. In the five-year printing plan, we cannot increase external debt. The only increase will come from interest on debt. But we also agreed to treat debt as depreciation. So, on top of writing it off yearly globally, that is if your debt is external as the case with many. We must negotiate debt relief orders globally. We are here to be very realistic. $244 trillion can never be paid off. A new system is to organize debt relief orders globally. See who owes who and negotiate to write it off and start again. After we have written off this debt, no nation shall owe others any debt. The only debt acceptable will be internal debt owed to citizens the only debt that will increase their value.

10. Dangers of external debt.

There is the idea of sovereign risk discussed above. External debt makes people indebted to others and increases the likelihood of being attacked by the lender. In most cases, the lender has more power than the recipient and that is the reason why the nation lends out in the first place. If you default, they can impose sanctions or hold the whole nation to ransom. Recall our laws gives everyone rights to life, to a good quality life and to self-defense. External debt conflicts with all these. The more you borrow the more you increase the chances of being attacked. If sanctions imposed this affects the quality of life as more women and children die for lack of basics. You can't self-preserve or defend yourself and above all, you lose your sovereignty. You can end up a puppet who can't print own money and therefore are not guaranteed rights to become wealth the easy and cheap way through printing new money.

11. Laws relating to people.

The current international laws apply but we have given these priorities and the highest rank in importance and all can't be overruled by any laws including national security laws. We have banned wars and weapons and leaders will have powers to laws for self-defense. It will be a crime to wage a war or provoke others aggressively or incite wars. We are not banning unarmed conflicts I think for the initial stages that should be part and parcel of the whole process until a time when we will say that's it. Our laws focus on people and believe that everything should follow from there.

*Emphasis of protection from unlawful killings. Even your enemies' civilians are protected by our laws. Any activities or rules that conflict with freedom to movement, speech, participate in the society, rights to freedom from torture, human degrading treatment, rights to privacy, family life, freedom of association, etc. are not to be breached or interfered with. At this stage we take these rights to be part of the basics even if we don't mention it here, we assume you already know this. People come first; the rest will follow is our guiding principle.

i]   We emphasize rights to private property. This is a fundamental right that is paramount and a cornerstone to the success of our aims and goals. We are for the emancipation and empowerment of everyone. We believe rights to wealth must be a basic right. Everyone must own property and wealth. It is the duty of a government to make sure that it increases the wealth of its people through printing money.

ii]   Related to this point is the fact that It is the government's obligation and duty of care to preserve the wealth the citizens have acquired by offering loans and mortgages during the five-year printing plan. It is the government's responsibility to bail-out its citizens and not banks.

12. It is illegal for governments to favor monetary gains as opposed to the welfare of its people. It is a criminal offense to emphasize the balance sheet and not the welfare of your people. There is no point in a perfect balance sheet when living standards are mediocre or below the global standard. Our laws change the mindset of everyone. Start thinking about people. You re in power because of the people. Print money and boost wealth and use the offset rule to write off the debt after all you owe these people your citizens. Have a crooked unbalancing balance sheet and a happy wealthy nation.

13. It is illegal to have standards below what we deem as minimal globally. So, our plan is to increase the wealth of every nation in five years drastically to levels never achieved before. After the five years we shall write off all debt and the current debt will have been written off or depreciated. A new start and a new equal or almost equal level for everyone. We shall declare what standards are minimum. After that falling below that standard will see your leaders punished.

14. We shall have tough laws for negligence and a lack of the

duty of care to the people who put you in power. The E-laws will haunt you. The aims of every government are to increase the nation's wealth and improve living standards. Austerity measures shall get you punished under our laws for willful negligent, lack of the duty of care and above all for lack of empathy towards your own citizens who are suffering. It is your duty as the one empowered to print money to make sure that minimum living standards are met.

15. Rights to Wealthy.

This is linked to the rights to the property above but wealth here is broader to include other than property, e.g. shares, stocks, and bonds. It is the government's duty of care to protect the wealth of its citizens by laws safeguarding them. It must be the mandate of the government to bail-out its citizens first and not wait for repossessions first before they can act. Any loans by the government to its citizens are to be treated as having a depreciation effect in that they reduce or lose value with time rather than gain with interests. Banks can do this but not the government. We shall establish a way where the government will lend in addition to banks and government to be not for profit but to provide a service.

I]    The governments must not confiscate or seize their citizen's wealth unless obtained illegally. When the citizens are in debt, the government will negotiate to have the debt written off rather than have the wealth already accumulated seized. Again, debt must be treated as having a depreciation value. Laws to be changed or new ones to come into effect protecting the citizens. A certain percentage can be seized as not to encourage bad behavior on the part of the citizens and any unlawful dealing can make them punishable by our laws but care and priority to be given in wealth preservation than destroying it.

Ii]   The government to view its role as to build its citizen's wealth and provide perpetual loans and mortgages where citizens when vetted met a certain criterion.

16. Citizens' eligibility criteria.

As not to encourage bad behavior a criterion must be met

by the citizens in all aspects mentioned above. To get a loan a certain criterion must be considered. Our aim is to change the current situation to increase wealth to new never witnessed before levels and we can only do this if we change attitude and thinking. So sometimes even if people can't meet the criteria but are of a certain age and are willing to earn more money to service and pay the loans, they might be eligible. The government will then depreciate the loan over the years to help these people say, new homeowners, etc. That is why we are going to print free money for the next five years of the plan. In the end, write off all the debt at the same time boosting living standards to new high levels.

17. The government when printing money will print some that 'will act as depreciation' in that a certain percentage is regarded as irrecoverable and a certain account put aside to compensate for this loss. If out of $100 million printed say $20 million might not be recovered the government can or might print $120 million and set aside the $20 million in a default account to act as depreciation and the loans over the years will lose value with depreciation being deducted yearly helping the people be debt-free and be able to pay back the reminder with time.

18. You must understand that our aim is for growth and development and improving living standards to new levels and not with a perfect balance sheet as what has been happening for the past seventy years.

19. Governments and institutions.

I believe some government within the Euro and globally might not have rights to print money. I think that is a lost opportunity and one that must be corrected. So, all governments like Portugal or Luxemburg must have printing powers to print their own currency we don't want people relying on others.

i]   Buying or using other people's money is expensive and will mean you being in debt forever. We are against this. If you are sovereign, then take control of your destiny and print!

ii]   Any institutions with the sovereignty rights or powers to print money but rely on other countries like the US are to be banned. No offense or underestimate the hard work they have done. But they rely on debt and interest and to be honest they are run like businesses and to me loan sharks. Whatever they do is to make a kill and run or sink the people in debt to justify their existence. Or they will stifle progress and development to keep their jobs. Why if you are sovereign with powers to print money then go and get loans from institutions below you? Empowerment and education must play a crucial role here. Never take your privileges for granted use them.

iii]    I think it will be doing everyone justice to institutions like IMF that are political in nature and do little to alleviate poverty, etc.

My view is that they give nations a false sense of security that they can always get a loan. Loans are expensive and will sink you in debt if they are external and loans remove the value from your own citizens if they are external. The best way that is cheap and free and readily available without interest worries is by printing. It's like if you want to grow you eat more food that will make you grow all you have to do is increase intake.

20.    To establish a framework that makes everything transparent and fair. Corruption is a real problem, especially when printing money. No point to print money to be stolen by a few people because the wealth of the whole citizens will not go up. It's not just a case of printing money. Establish transparency by using methods that can be checked by everyone. New technology like the blockchain needed to make sure that an audit can be done to make sure that citizens are receiving the loans and the distribution is national without having increased inequality as well. It's not a simple thing to do. A comprehensive approach is needed. To remove corrupt people and a system to remove government bureaucracy and waste. If these are not controlled, surely it will be pointless to print. This will worsen the issue. As the money can be siphoned abroad to swiss accounts etc. and not increasing the local wealth. Hyperinflation can rack havoc in such cases.

# CHAPTER FORTY-TWO

FUNDAMENTAL LAWS II

**Oil drilling, fossil fuels, and alternative energy.**

1. Oil will never last forever even though it might be enough for our lifetime, but we must make sure that we lay the foundation and a way to come up with alternative energy sources by being proactive and not wait until it has run out.

2. If applicants meet our permit requirements, I think the drilling part is not an issue. Our laws in this area are to do with the side effects of drilling to the environment vis-à-vis the quality of life. Gas drilling can increase harmful gasses in the air and therefore laws must be in place to make sure that any drilling is safe and follows our laws and guidelines. Oil drilling and spillages can be detrimental to ocean life and wildlife and can destroy the ecosystem. Tough laws to deal with negligence, etc.

3. Drilling also means transportation by pipelines. We will need to check if the pipelines are away from densely populated areas and risks of exploding and fires are under control. Laws can deal with all these issues at local levels and national levels where they apply. Safety is the key here.

4. To reiterate our stance on fossil fuels is to ban these at a certain date in the future for use as the main source of fuel. Electricity will replace these even if we still have reserves. Vehicles, including cars powered by fossil fuels, will be a thing of the past.

5. Honestly recent wars had oil as the trigger. Banning these fossils will mean a peaceful world. No pollution and very good quality of air. It will be illegal to use fossil fuels in

buildings, vehicles, and machinery because the pollution will be way too much for the time in question. This will decrease the quality of life. Driving inside fossil powered cars will reduce quality of life, too breathing all that smoke and burned oil is no good. Life will be high, and a certain minimum standard must be met to rule out fuel fossils.

6. Huge investments in alternative energies as a proactive measure and a better way of life. Renewable energies are cheaper and cleaner. All vehicles must have a renewable energy fuel source. All current cars that use fossils will be a thing of the past. Adoption of electric cars etc. or even better ones. Some materials will be banned from being used in vehicle manufacture, etc.

7. Incentives search for alternative energies. Loans and capital made easily available provided by governments possibly through banks and these should be like depreciation that depletes in value with time to enable people to keep working on finding better alternatives.

# CHAPTER FORTY-THREE

## FUNDAMENTAL LAWS III

**Globalization, Employment Creation and Job Opportunities.**

1.  It is a fundamental aspect of our printing money strategy that governments must go out of their way to make sure that they create and sustain new jobs and development otherwise hyperinflation will tear them down. Printing money without correspondent investment and development of industries and production can be disastrous. It is a law that the government creates and puts a framework that is easy for job creation and facilitates rather than stale development.

2.  The government of all global nations must remove complex bureaucracy and must ensure a simple process from company incorporation to operation to facilitate and promote huge production and development that is needed to avoid hyperinflation. This is a critical area and must be identified as such. Measures to provide state-of-the-art technology that is easy, fast, and transparent.

3.  Employment creation must be prioritized with every opportunity tried to increase jobs available and the actual taking of these and maintaining people into work by providing fast infrastructure and services like fast trains. It will be illegal to provide services like transport below a certain standard.

4.  It is our duty to make sure that we reduce global inequality associated with globalization. Our strategy of printing money will take living standards to a new level globally. We shall provide a framework and system to encourage networking and free movement of resources and labor, etc.

5.  We shall devise a system that is comprehensive enough to stop and eliminate hyperinflation a problem with printing money. We have our own currency to beat that that is

globally available, and we can give the nations affected by hyperinflation rights to use as they wish until they can use their local currency again.

6. It is our duty to fight hyperinflation and provide a system that works for every nation.

# CHAPTER FORTY-FOUR

FUNDAMENTAL LAWS IV

## Sanctions.

1. Never to be heard of again. Banned. This is a cruel form, whether applied to individuals or nations. It's a cruel form of treatment that targets the innocent; women and children and kills these too. Individual's sanctions by state are banned and punishable under our laws. Sanctions are cruel and are used to make the targeted leaders, individuals and nations lose credibility and succumb weakening them as to get a favorable stance when bargaining. We stand against such barbaric, cruel, outdated ways of dealing with other human beings. We can bring new empathy charges to make sure that those who breach our laws will succumb to our laws. Trust me no one will ever get immunity when it comes to empathy. It's everyone's duty of care to every human being and imposing sanctions will conflict with the right to empathize with the innocent mostly women and children. We have laws punishable by death that emphatically prohibit reckless killings of women and children of any background. We will assess if you can do the same to those 'close to you' from the same background as you. If not, surely you will go down.

I have argued throughout this book that the United Nations Security Council is the vehicle to implement the Colony Collapse Strategy. Since 1966;

"The Security Council has established thirty sanctions regimes, in Southern Rhodesia, South Africa, the former Yugoslavia (2), Haiti,

Iraq (2), Angola, Rwanda, Sierra Leone, Somalia and Eritrea, Eritrea and Ethiopia, Liberia (3), DRC, Côte d'Ivoire, Sudan, Lebanon, DPRK, Iran, Libya (2), Guinea-Bissau, CAR, Yemen, South Sudan and Mali, as well as against ISIL (Daesh) and Al-Qaida and the Taliban."

[UNSEC].

For the past fifty-three years, sanctions have been the choice strategy to induce discipline, and still, we still have the same issues since then. The poor developing countries are still power if not worse. All sanctions have helped do is to kill the innocent and increase sectoral violence like in Iraq. The suffering of the people due to sanctions can be argued to be the trigger of the rise of terrorism in recent years. All that they are doing is provoke-to act the otherwise harmless nations causing all kinds of instability to justify future military action. The UNSEC through sanctions has been treating sovereign nations like school kids who deserve to be punished.

Our laws put emphasizes on state sovereignty and we argue that the UNSEC has no right to interfere with the actions of a sovereign nation. In our system, the UNSEC is under any sovereign nation in that the UNSEC was established by a few sovereign nations the big four whose goals and objectives they help to serve. The UNSEC has no peace in all its decisions and actions. For us as the global leader's international peace starts with sheer recognition that women and children must be respected and protected. Sanctions target these vulnerable people and use them as bargaining baits. Where is the need for global peace when you abuse the very vulnerable of any nation? We argue that this is a way of provoking the targeted nation to act in turn so that the UNSEC has jobs as now they would send peacekeepers, peace monitors, sanction valuators or implementors and above all inspectors who if the truth has to be said spies for the West Allis. This is a job creation strategy that lacks empathy towards the victims. But our E-laws to sink you down where you belong in the mud.

What is good if sanctions target deliveries with food and medicine for kids and women? What is good if sanctions block any aid and

690

assistance towards a nation viewed as violating international laws? What is good when sanctions restrict financial, trade and commodities to a nation?

Sanctions to be honest are there to block any development. When a nation is about to lift itself out of poverty, they start talking about human rights in order to suppress that nation with sanctions. Sanctions block sources of finance, trade, commodities, etc. so that development is suppressed. A very hinge-pin theme of the Colony Collapse Strategy. It's a fact that sanctions are used against developing countries the very nations that need guidance and assistance. We stand against such an outdated way of thinking. Our goals are to empower sovereign nations to be sovereign as the name means and help them move out of poverty. All these interventions etc. are stalling tactics so that they have jobs. The fact that sanctions kill innocent powerless people of any nation triggers Article 1. An attack of these weak powerless people for any reason let alone economic or political for that matter can alone call for collective punishment. We need to change the mindset and way of doing things. They talk about international peace as if they can do something about that. All they have done is give these women and children a false sense of security only to be killed on their watch. They initiate the attack through sanctions. We are saying that sanctions are the first line of attack paving way and justifying whatever follows. Look what happened wherever initiated the attack through these sanctions. The sanctions killed the innocent and weakened the leaders as they are proved to be powerless that a foreign nation or body would deliberately kill their women and kids without them doing anything. A sign of weakness and see what follows. They are then sent in to inspect but to spy and further weaken the local leaders. What follows this is an imminent attack killing even more people. This has been going on for the past 53 years. Today we say no never again. Our rules shift the focus from evil sanctions aimed to maintain the status quo in the name of peace. What peace? Whose peace? If you want peace, you do what we are doing. Ban wars. Make this a law. Ban weapons globally target those leaders as well who think are above the law. **Express-command to put an end to this through our**

## laws and courts as a deterrent.

What gives them the right to kill other's families? If that does not work use empathy laws and drag them to court. If that does not work bring in the Colony Collapse Strategy argument. They are biased. Look at all their victims of these sanctions. The very nations who need guidance and help. Look they are sanctioning Iran on perceived nuclear proliferation, but the US has nukes, the UK has nukes, Germany, France, etc. and were these ever sanctioned for possession. What gives them the right to make and stock? Is this the main reason they are the ones destabilizing the globe through wars? Look at all the wars for the past 50 years. They are the ones at the forefront. We don't care for what reason. Has the US been sanctioned or punished for the Hiroshima bombs? So, based on this we think sanctions are a bullying tactic and as such these nations have rights under self-defense laws bearing in mind the threat they are facing in the US, UK, France and their backing power in NATO. It will be unwise for any of these nations not to think about getting enough power to counteract any attack. Under our laws these nations are doing everything reasonable given the circumstances. We believe and stand firm with the idea of sovereignty of all nations and their right to self-preserve. The UN etc. have no sovereign powers and they can't stop any wars and talking about peace is an insult. A false sense of security as a deceiving tactic to block any help. Imagine if Russia or China wanted to help during the Iraq war. The presence of the UNSEC blocked any form of intervention to help. They might have assumed that this UNSEC was going to stop the war only to wake up hearing that women and kids were attacked in their homes. Where is justice? We are saying the UNSEC is the problem. Removing these and empower all these nations is the only way forward. Imagine years under sanctions and this means stalled development. These nations if the UNSEC is there will never become developed nations and will remain as developing. We don't want this. To stop this, we argued throughout the book that our laws will break even the mightiest nation or cult if we wanted.

Our goal is to get every nation to become very rich the only easy and cheap way. If we are to start printing money, we will not need any stalling tactic as we need full speed and firing on all cylinders to avoid hyperinflation. If we let a country be a target for sanctions that will mean the collapse of that economy. For printing to work, there must never be interference or too much government interference, let alone the UNSEC's. Above all, we will never tolerate the death even of one child or woman needlessly. It's best to drag these to court.

*causing death by recklessness and lack of a duty of care.

*Impersonating a body that can stop wars.

*causing grievous bodily harm and unnecessary deaths due to sanctions. Murder and manslaughter charges.

*targeting the weak and powerless and using these as bait and bargaining tools to weaken the leadership.

*Colony Collapse Strategy as an act of genocide targeting a special ethnic group to wipe them as they see them as threats to their existence instead of peace.

*acts of aggression provoking a reaction to justify military action through sanctions. The idea here is that it is an evil way to anger someone by killing his women and children. These nations are forced to react as this is seen as a sign of weakness. It's the implied reaction we are concerned with here. This act of targeting someone's vulnerable and kill them at will.

*enticing others to anger and war.

*inciting and triggering acts of terrorism. Under our laws, they can be punished for terrorist acts that happened to their people. We will extend punishment to include willful provocation in anticipation of such a response. In this case, we will treat them as themselves who have ordered the terrorist attacks and above all treat them as the ones who carried out the attack. Our basis here would be to assess the contributory factor here. If their acts trigger the terrorist act, we can treat them as the terrorist themselves in that the terrorist simply wore their shoes and did what they would have done anywhere so they are in the same position with the terrorist.

*lack of empathy. Gone are the days when we turn a blind eye to acts that can be assessed under empathy. This is the only way to put an end to all this. I reiterate here that our laws see no differences even though we are different, but this difference is the reason why some things are happening the way they are. If we don't address these, then we will not solve the issues.

*charges of stalling development and keeping the developing nations as poor as they are can be punished under our laws. We will use the quality of life argument. We are saying globally some standards if below a certain level will be categorized as criminally negligent and a lack of a duty of care on the part of the provider. So stalling development that affects quality of life can result in punishment as well.

*Their inspecting acts can and must be viewed as weakening tactics exposing the leader and his people to the attacks of the West. Spying charges as they are no better than the U2 Spying Plane [U2 1960 Incident] Picture what happened during the Iraq saga. They weakened Saddam the moment he agreed on them to inspect. Their inspection which is spying meant that their findings were used to assess the strengths and opportunities for an attack.

*Even not finding any WMDs they did not stop the invasion, so what was the point of the inspection. It can be argued that they should have done everything to stop the war. They did not even try to delay the invasion. Charges of unlawful killing in that they gave a false sense of security secondly they did not delay the invasion did not even rally support as such did not give the victims chances and time to escape worse because they entered Iraq and found no WMDs so people expected no invasion. But failed to stop the war. Now we are saying they meant deaths of these victims surely what was the point of inspecting unless it was a SWOT analysis?

*inciting the making of nuclear weapons or the need to possess some of the initiation of nuclear proliferation. Here we are saying that the sanctions created a 'need to act'. If it wasn't for the sanctions and hardship it brought, then there would not be a need for what follows. Our thinking here is that the targeted nation was not even thinking about say nuclear proliferation. But sanctions induced the need to do that on two bases.

i] As a defensive mechanism. The targeted nation was left with no option but to self-preserve, as it will be unwise of it not to start the proliferation as a self-defense mechanism or ii] as a deterrent even if they were not actually going to start the nuclear proliferation. The idea here is that the admitting of carrying out the proliferation is a way of keeping the threat at bay and away from the perimeter. It's like a scared person shouting that he has a weapon when he does not have any but to keep away danger from approaching. So, the nation is justified to do all this in order to protect its people. So, it is in no wrong, but the sanctions are. The triggers.

We are not saying sanctions don't work at all for the better, but we are saying the effects are more severe than the good they bring. Sanctions conflicts with all our laws. We don't and must not tolerate even the death of a single soul. Show us sanctions that don't take any 21 grams and we will show you a way to use them.

* Sanctions make the UNSEC treat sovereign nations like kids who must be punished and told when to eat or sleep. This is a gross abuse and a lack of judgment and an act of aggression in that we consider this as slapping a lion in the face only to be attacked. That means you put yourself in danger and might treat you as suicidal or deranged of some sort. We can put charges of lack of judgment and self-harm. So, the UNSEC can be said to be putting itself in danger and if it wasn't of the presence of the 'other' in the West and NATO one of these nations might have done them harm. Again, we can say they are provoking others knowing that they have the backing of NATO, etc. Acts of aggression. Worse who on earth would deliberately impose something that kills the vulnerable unless it is to provoke or weaken?

*Another big issue is that of forced entry through the use of sanctions. Okay even though the leader invites them it is forced entry in that the leader does it on humanitarian grounds to save the lives of women and children dying.

The time he invites them damage will have been done. His stance is a mitigation stance where he acts to reduce further deaths. It's not because he invited them willingly. He does that to save lives. So, the UNSEC forced their entry just like a burglar and I understand a burglar can be shot dead and the owner of the burgled house walk? Again, UNSEC's self-harm risk is evident. Lack of judgment to the risk involved. But because they are part of the gang the bully or cult, we can assume that it's an act of aggression inciting others to war. Acts of provocation.

*Lastly but not list unprovoked gang attacks by the UNSEC who acts as the front line of the attacking gang going in to do a SWOT analysis checking the strength, weaknesses, opportunities, and threats. Collecting information and acting as spy planes before giving the go-ahead to proceed with the attack. Even if this was not their intention one can reasonably conclude that to be true. The thinking here is that UNSEC attacks the leader concerned through inspection weakening him even if they did not find the WMDs they will have left him for dead so that the others can attack him. They remove his defenses and highlight his weakness making sure that invasion is imminent.

### Zero casualty tolerance.

*Too much power as a threat to peace. Belonging to a gang and the unbalanced threat in that all nations US, UK, France, etc. and NATO are ganging up on Syria, Iran or Iraq, etc. are like gangs that need to be broken down for the sake of peace. Their presence and membership to NATO is the main threat to peace and not the individual states they are going after.

I know most argued that collateral damage can be minimized and never avoided. NATO used this defense in the Kosovo war and justified their stance on killing only 400 something Sebs and 500 something Yugoslavs. Their stance is that a lot more would have died. We say enough is enough you spoil a gram of soul and we will spoil your gram too. If we are to go to war with sanctions surely now and day, we will. So, banned!

# CHAPTER FORTY-FIVE

FUNDAMENTAL LAWS V.

**Global Population.**

1. Our aims are to make people as healthy as possible. We stand firm against those who believe in the divine right or divine appointment that is they believe to have been chosen by God himself to act on his behalf. We are not against this just for the sake of it but only when the people involved start playing God. We believe God or the creator gave humans everything they need to search for solutions and find answers. We believe playing God in killing people to maintain the population to reasonable levels is plain wrong. It's the cheapest way to go about it.

2. Imagine God giving humanity all the brains so that he can kill? I always say you can close your eyes and easily kill someone, but you can't open them wide enough and create a human being. The easy things to do are always cheap and the wrong ones. They don't need anything. You can leave your brain at home and still do a great job. Surely this is not what God wanted assuming he is there. Imagine him creating you and everything only so that you easily kill? Does that make sense? Or he created you so that you become a God-like him too and create your own people who will work for you and make money for you or worship you just like we do. That is a challenge. It makes perfect sense. This is the idea behind artificial intelligence. Listen to the name; artificial intelligence. What does that sound like? If you are talking about this, then maybe I agree with the divine right of appointment. So, I agree God appointed some men to act just like him and one day find ways of creating their own people to work for them. Have you ever

698

seen how some people spend their life worshiping a God they never saw? Don't you want someone who will trust you that much to dedicate all their life just for your sake? I think this is nearness to God. But I am not for 'trust' in that way. I think to some extent it comes down to slavery. I don't think God wants us to be his slaves. I think mankind has failed and just wants excuses. But I am not judging.

3. So, our duty is not to kill.

*We are against government who make lethal bio-engineered, digital or cyber viruses to play God and wipeout people as during the bubonic plague, no.

* We stand against governments making vaccines that will 'explode' say in twenty years killing 99% of the population for fears of population growth.

* We stand against governments chipping everyone illegally at birth as a medical record thing or for national security as a disguised plan to be able to kill at will, especially in the developed nations where most are old sucking all the resources without economic benefits.

*We stand against governments making lethal mass murder weapons and testing these on others before granting them protection or donating or sending help.

*We stand against governments provoking wars to get the soldiers killed as to reduce the balance sheet bill and control the population.

*We stand against governments False flagging in order to provoke wars or incite terrorist activities to justify wars in order to control the population. We are not against family planning and birth control if it's voluntary, but we believe also that the area is open to discussions as some nations can benefit from forced birth control methods if no one dies. Restricting pregnancy etc. can be subjective and open to debate.

4. Our strategy is to match development to population growth. Instead of the easy way-out of killing, I think population growth should be a challenge. How can you provide for everyone without sacrificing quality? That's a challenge. Our goal as you know is to take living standards to never experienced levels before. Our five-year printing plan will

help us achieve that. But to avoid problems with hyperinflation and stagnating development and unemployment etc. growth must be equal too. We must use new money to boost development. This can't be simply killing. We must create new ways of doing things and new services and infrastructure. We must grow and keep on growing to experience a huge shift from developing to developed or from developed to the very advanced. Growth should also be unseen before levels. We must find ways to expand and spend new money by providing new things. We must match population growth with corresponding service and infrastructure provision. This should consider quality too. So, we have endless opportunities that we are our only drawbacks. What level achievement we make depends solely on our inputted levels of thinking, dedication and manpower or technology.

5. The biggest problem is prioritizing here and knowing what is important or not. We can print $trillions but if we don't manage the money properly, we will still have problems and in the end, resort to easy and cheap ways of killing people. I think the fact that most are resorting to cheap killing ways is the fact that mankind has failed to think and priorities over the decades. Look now even with the huge population growth we are still spending huge budgets on military; okay this trick has worked in the past in that the weapons and military will eventually cause deaths of the people and reduce the population numbers through wars but now wars are a thing of the past. Look North Korea etc. are aiming for peace. We have banned wars and weapons, yet the military budget is high. Our argument is that we are wasting resources and mismanaging these. The only war that will result will be a nuclear war a big one as everyone in the end will see the need to kill each other as you might have grown to un-tolerated levels. But in this war, everyone might use nukes hoping to kill as many as can be as we will have gone maybe for centuries without global wars. This war will cause the end of humanity as everyone will throw everything in.

6. So, if we make use of the critical needs first then the plan

will work as we will stop wars. Weapons making and evolve the military in creating rather than destroying, etc. All other resources channeled to match population growth to resources and services, etc.

7. Global population shifting can play a big role here too. We believe the problems with population are related to geographical areas as some areas are rarely populated while others are densely populated. If we provide opportunities everywhere people will be willing to relocate to these new areas. Globalization in terms of resources and people can play a pivotal role too. Encourage networking and cooperation to evenly disperse the population.

8. Improve the quality of life, prolong life and reduce aging rates and punish governments deliberately aging their people to kill all early. Huge funds plowed into research and development to find cures, ways of stopping aging, prolonging life in youthful stages, etc.

9. Punish anything contrary.

# CHAPTER FORTY-SIX

## FUNDAMENTAL LAWS VI.

NGOs, Institutions and other bodies.

1.  New laws to control institutions and their operations. I have stressed throughout this book that most of today's institutions are there solely for job creation and to act as killing weapons or vehicles for such actions and without goals to solve real problems. The existence of the institutions depends on several suffering at the bottom. It's like a pyramid. If there is a large problem base, then it can support huge numbers at the top levels, but if the bottom has fewer numbers, then the top will collapse in. So, these institutions might be creating problems just to justify their presence.

2.  So, as such, we have new laws dictating their operations. First for all to understand our stance and reasoning we emphasize again that impersonating a problem solver when you are not, is a crime as it gives people a false sense of security making them misjudge danger as they might trust in you think you have the stamina to stop say a war or prevent a genocide when you don't. These people if you were not there, they might have run and escape or look for help somewhere else.

3.  To make things worse, their presence might prevent real helpers from acting, meaning their presence blocks potential helpers in that their presence gives them a false sense of resolve. They might assume e.g. in the Iraq war that the UNSEC was to stop the war after finding no evidence of WMDs. Maybe reason they did not intervene. But if UNSEC was not there they might have voiced a concern or delayed the war giving people time to escape.

4.  We have institutions waiting for a huge salary at the end

of the month and doing nothing but perpetuating the issues delaying so that they make a kill.

5.  Some of these institutions, NGOs, etc. have been associated with political affiliations that they are now biased. They increase inequality etc. as they help only those with the same political ideologies as them, etc.

6.  Our proposals are to create a time limit for their operation in one area of concern. So, if an institution or body deals with weapons disarmament. They can only do this for five years and can only extend license based on merit of achievement. If they don't meet a certain level, they simply must give another body or institution a chance and they simply move onto the next problem say poverty or globalization. So, every five years their roles and focus will change until issues reduce. So continuous existence is linked and based on achievements and progress rather than by special privileges given by those who formed these institutions. This is the case with the UN that represents the US, UK, France, Germany, Italy, etc. the nations who form them and above all contribute heavily to them. The main reason we think they did not stop the war. Fighting your breadwinner, you can only end up going hungry.

7.  Separation of new institutions from cults like NATO, etc. and not linked directly to nations. Sources of funding should not be from the very people we are saying are needlessly killing women and children. Then you are not able to fight for the kids and children but will represent the views of the creators and funders.

8.  Stopping all impersonating activities as they can get the innocent killed clearly assesses the ability to carry out the nation's task or goal. A classic example is for the UN to claim to stop any wars and enforce these when they are like a church security guard when invaded will call upon Jesus without doing nothing. You must understand that our value placed on life it does not matter whose life. What you can't create is holy and must be feared and respected. If you can't make life, then you can't kill life. If you can make life, then kill and create maybe we might

understand but until then no killing. We are the voice of the voiceless and we shall punish killers of the innocent yet precious members of any society.

9.  Cruel provoking tactics of targeting women just like what terrorists do we make you be treated like terrorists and be punished harshly?

10. Most current institutions when they finally understand our laws and what will happen to them will voluntarily change or cease operation altogether. We have drawn a line, and it's not time to worship people who rack lives.

11. If you say you are in the job of stirring development, then you must prove that and not do acts that conflict with your claims. A good example is when you use sanctions on everyone, yet you claim to fight for international peace. This is contradictory. This is what has been happening with the UNSEC. They provoke everyone and incite them to fight by killing their women and children and then talk about peace and removing threats to war when they are doing what they are saying to prevent. The minute they imposed sanctions is the minute they declare war on the sovereign nation they are dealing with. The very minute they breached international peace. To understand is one thing and to act justly is another thing.

12. Future institutions must find ways of funding themselves. We don't want a situation where they don't stop the war as the UNSEC in dealing with Iraq then accepts a huge contribution from the US or UK. If you know the issue the UK owed the US World War II debt and if you look at the whole picture, it's like going to rob to pay debt and not stopping the war and then receive a big reward is itself a threat to peace. UNSEC can be dragged to court under our laws for conspiracy to rob, take by force through weapons, endangering the lives of the victims, and murder using trickery and undue regard to human life on top of that lacking empathy towards the victim giving them a false sense of security. Above that getting women and children killed for personal gains as the invaders are also their breadwinners. It will be

unreasonable for them to stop their funder as payment will be withheld. So had no option and intention to stop a war on personal grounds. New laws new interpretation of the laws and bringing the culprits to justice. Change is imminent and inevitable. Are you ready to change and prepare to deal with our no-nonsense laws? We are not against anyone, but we must make you understand our thinking and the new approach to dealing with what we have called global evil and injustice. Be on the good side. Treat every kid and woman as if they were your own.

13. We don't know what situations where the West goes in and kill thousand women and kids first through sanctions and when Assad the Syrian leader attacks rebels then the West uses humanitarian grounds to invade and attack a sovereign nation. This is a thing of the past. We don't see the logic of killing the innocent and defend the otherwise crooks and muggers of any society. We don't treat rebels the same as civilians who are unarmed and powerless who have no one to defend them and most of all who have a huge heart full of faith and trust that they put their lives for you only for you to let them down and choose muggers over them. Be careful you don't want to be on the wrong side of our laws for we will eliminate you and all your bloodline. Respect the innocent and future people of any nation or face the consequences.

14. Surely you will never find loopholes to exploit because we have closed all. What you can do is dig yourself a hole in the ground and hide for our wrath will scorch the earth like angry fires and consume everything to dust. Be warned.

# CHAPTER FORTY-SEVEN

FUNDAMENTAL LAWS VI.

## War on Terror.

    1. Express-command to put an end to this through our laws and courts as a deterrent.

> We are against all terrorists and are very harsh with these mainly because their tactics are barbaric and attack the very innocent people of any society. Terrorists are viewed and must be treated harshly as they threaten the fabric of our laws. Their acts of using women and children to push their agendas conflict with the right to life and self-defense. We are harsh with those who target those who can't defend themselves. Our first laws state that one has the right to self-defense. If you attack those who can't defend themselves, then you are the worst thing on earth, and we shall treat you as such. Here, the express command applies. I feel the same way with sanctions for the same reason because it's challenging us and what we stand for when you attack those; we are saying they can't defend themselves, yet our laws clearly state that they have the right to defend themselves. That shifts the burden of care and to acts onto us. To be the ones to defend them. So, we see this attack as a direct attack on us. An act of aggression to see how bad we can be. To us, terrorists and sanctions are the same as they use the innocent as bargaining aspects to be manipulated and abused. So, an attack on the innocent by terrorists will invoke Article 1 that says that an attack

2. But we believe some have genuine concerns as false flagging might have been used to provoke them but still killing women and children overshadows that we don't sympathize with them. Two wrongs don't make a right.

3. Nevertheless, we shall provide a framework for addressing the real issues and misunderstanding of local needs, etc. This is one of the reasons why we stepped up. Some country's foreign policy has become a self-inflicting wound in that they have brought terror to themselves just for misunderstanding local needs and impersonating a global leader when you have your interest at heart. Probably the reason for the 9/11 attacks. I argued that a global leader must not be biased to avoid being regarded as an aggressor or an oppressor. This is true and we see the problems arising from this. You can't try to fulfill your own personal global policy and at the same time declare to have everyone needs at heart. It is just impossible hence the rise and worsening of the terrorist acts in the last decade. We must intervene and provide a framework for understanding, rebuilding, forgiving and simply cooperation. We always have the view and stance that global issues are too complicated to be easily solved by the current methods and institutions. We have come up with a different approach. That is assessing all sides. There is a problem, and that is a fact. To address the issues and act as the new global leaders is the only way forward. All impersonators are biased. They belong to cults like NATO with strict rules and articles that hinder pleasing everyone at the expense of the members see Article 8 of NATO. So, in that case, talking of global leadership is like slapping a lion in the face he will only attack you. A self-inflicted wound and putting yourself at risk and unable to judge scenarios collect therefore unfit to be the global leader and a peace monger for that matter.

4. Ban forms of protection in some countries confused or linked to terrorism in that this protect gives everyone express immunity no matter what the people can easily kill and are tortured as a way-out after being held for ransom and cornered to kill themselves and other. This is a medieval practice and we believe we should die with medieval times.

5. Harsh punishment for government false flagging and

outsourcing terror to pursue military goals laid out in long-term contingency plans. Use harsh punishment for leaders killing their people to justify wars this is not collateral damage but murder and if applicable a new form of genocides tendencies. Very harsh punishment.

6. Our aims are to look at all angles and draw up comprehensive plans to deal with this so that we can start building again.

7. Education in the form of affirmative information provision should be our goal. We are there to supply information and advice on the best courses of action to guide and lead as to avoid abuse and manipulation of these leaders after leaving office. Our laws will support and help people make sound judgments and prevent facing punishment in the future.

8. It must be stated that some terrorist acts can trigger Article 1 that request collective punishment as attacks on the defenseless is an attack of all humanity.

# CHAPTER FORTY-EIGHT

FUNDAMENTAL LAWS VII.

**Research and development.**

1. It is a law requirement that countries set aside a certain amount of their GDP as a percentage as funds towards research and development. Our aim and goal are to take humanity to another level never achieved before and only through research and development shall we be able to achieve that. This is one of the critical areas that need funds. We are going to ban a lot of things like reliance on fossil fuels and we shall need new alternative sources and only through research and development can we be able to do that.

2. Doing nothing is a crime. Plans and evaluations of progress to be part of the system with monitoring and evaluation compulsory.

3. Government to help provide a framework that makes everything smooth from obtaining patents and establishing companies, research, and development, etc. Laws that make the process simpler.

4. Encouraging investment in this area through incentives, reduced taxes, and provision of state-of-the-art facilities, etc.

5. We shall provide a framework as a catalyst, a facilitator, a negotiator and implementer of things necessary to see this go smoothly.

6. A global fund towards global research and development as well with a comprehensive plan that is linked to all levels. A global plan that recognizes national, regional plans, etc.

# CHAPTER FORTY-NINE

FUNDAMENTAL LAWS VIII.

**Potential for World War III.**

1.   Our concern is not just with the likelihood of a WWIII but with issues that this can be a nuclear weapons war were WMDs might be used from both sides to match the uneven threats with the West ever-growing in NATO and the Middle East resorting to nuclear for self-defense. That war can and might result in human extinction as the weaker outnumbered nations will have nothing to lose but to take as many as they can as they see their chances of self-defending themselves and their people reduced to nothing as NATO, the US, UK, France, Germany all group together to form a war conglomerate.

2.   We shall aim to avoid any wars in the initial implementation of our laws, but we also acknowledge that some countries might want to throw in the towel after the last one for the road. In that case, we leave all doors open but for the sake of children and women will do everything in our power for peaceful endings. But the possibility of any resistance can lead to WWIII. But after that our laws will come into effect banning all global future wars and provocations or invasions.

3.   If there is a WWIII our role is to make it as balanced as possible in case this initial one is unstoppable.

FUNDAMENTAL LAWS IX.

**Potential for World War III.**

1.   Our concern is not just with the likelihood of a WWIII but with issues that this can be a nuclear weapons war were

WMDs might be used from both sides to match the uneven threats with the West ever-growing in NATO and the Middle East resorting to nuclear for self-defense. That war can and might result in human extinction as the weaker outnumbered nations will have nothing to lose but to take as many as they can as they see their chances of self-defending themselves and their people reduced to nothing as NATO, the US, UK, France, Germany all group together to form a war conglomerate.

2.   We shall aim to avoid any wars in the initial implementation of our laws, but we also acknowledge that some countries might want to throw in the towel after the last one for the road. In that case, we leave all doors open but for the sake of children and women will do everything in our power for peaceful endings. But the possibility of any resistance can lead to WWIII. But after that our laws will come into effect banning all global future wars and provocations or invasions.

3.   If there is a WWIII our role is to make it as balanced as possible in case this initial one is unstoppable.

## FUNDAMENTAL LAWS X.

### International laws.

1.   Effective dealings with;
     *need for global peace.
     *justice
     *interest and finally
     *trade.

2. Effective ways to deal with war crimes of past

   *disarmament

   * enforcing our new laws

   *banning of global wars

\*new laws to deal with terrorism and their financing

\*dealing with crimes by state and corporates.

\*New laws to deal with laws of the sea, etc.

## TOMORROW'S WOLRD ORDER: MEET OUR TEAM

What's not to like?
No Wars.
No Weapons.
No Deaths of Women and Children Needlessly.
No Sanctions.
Above all a Great Investment.
WOW!! JOIN US POSITIONS OPEN!

MEET OUR GLOBAL MEMBERS

Honorable Founder / Overseer and President of TWO:

Hon. Mr. David Gomadza

...................................

...................................

APPENDIX

# Whitepaper

The executive summary for those who want to know about us fast.
Everything we stand for in a short summary. Straight to the point.
Our Roadmap.
FEEL FREE to
Download from:
www.tomorrowsworldorder.com

or buy from all bookshops: The New Single Reserve Global
Currency .................Get the Whitepaper.